DATE DUE

SOMETHING ABOUT THE AUTHOR®

Something about
the Author *was named
an "Outstanding
Reference Source,"
the highest honor given
by the American
Library Association
Reference and User
Services Association.*

ISSN 0276-816X

SOMETHING ABOUT THE AUTHOR®

Facts and Pictures about Authors
and Illustrators of Books for Young People

EDITED BY
ALAN HEDBLAD

VOLUME 109

GALE GROUP

Detroit
San Francisco
London
Boston
Woodbridge, CT

STAFF

Editor: Alan Hedblad
Associate Editor: Melissa Hill
Features Coordinator: Motoko Fujishiro Huthwaite

Contributing Editors: Sara L. Constantakis, Catherine Goldstein, Arlene M. Johnson
Assistant Editors: Maria Job, Tom Schoenberg, Mark Springer, Erin E. White

Managing Editor: Joyce Nakamura
Publisher: Hal May

Research Manager: Victoria B. Cariappa
Project Coordinator: Corrine A. Boland
Research Associates: Patricia Tsune Ballard, Tamara C. Nott,
Wendy K. Festerling, Tracie A. Richardson
Research Assistants: Phyllis J. Blackman, Tim Lehnerer, Patricia L. Love

Permissions Manager: Maria L. Franklin
Permissions Associates: Edna Hedblad, Sarah Tomasek

Composition Manager: Mary Beth Trimper
Manufacturing Manager: Dorothy Maki
Buyer: Cindy Range

Graphic Artist: Gary Leach
Image Database Supervisor: Randy Bassett
Imaging Specialists: Robert Duncan, Michael Logusz
Imaging Coordinator: Pamela A. Reed

Library of Congress Catalog Card Number 72-27107

ISBN 0-7876-3218-X
ISSN 0276-816X

Printed in the United States of America

10 9 8 7 6 5 4 3 2 1

Contents

Authors in Forthcoming Volumes

Below are some of the authors and illustrators that will be featured in upcoming volumes of *SATA*. These include new entries on the swiftly rising stars of the field, as well as completely revised and updated entries (indicated with *) on some of the most notable and best-loved creators of books for children.

Joan Abelove: Abelove spent two years in the Amazon jungle of Peru researching her young-adult novel *Go and Come Back*, which is narrated by a fifteen-year-old girl from a fictional South-American tribe.

*Eve Bunting: Praised as a master storyteller of exceptional range and depth, Bunting has published almost two hundred books for children and young adults, and has contributed to nearly every genre of juvenile literature. Some of her recent picture-book efforts include *Train to Somewhere, So Far from the Sea*, and the autobiographical *Once Upon a Time*.

Judith Ortiz Cofer: Drawing on her own experiences growing up in two cultures, noted Puerto-Rican poet and author Cofer published *An Island Like You: Stories of the Barrio*, a series of short stories with young adults as central characters living in a multicultural world.

*Gillian Cross: In works such as *The Dark Behind the Curtain, Chartbreaker*, and the Carnegie Medal-winning *Wolf*, English writer Cross has blended suspense, history, adventure, and social concerns to concoct a heady brew of young-adult novels. One of her latest efforts, *The Great Elephant Chase*, won England's prestigious Whitbread Children's Novel Award.

*Paul Fleischman: Fleischman's recent works—including *A Fate Totally Worse Than Death*, a humorous parody of teen-horror novels, and *Whirligig*, a novel examining suicide, death, and the psyche—demonstrate the range of styles and themes that have made the Newbery Award-winning author such a versatile writer.

Kristine O'Connell George: George's playful, engaging language brings a fresh new voice to children's poetry, as demonstrated in her award-winning collections of verse for young people, including *The Great Frog Race and Other Poems* and *Old Elm Speaks: Tree Poems*.

*Shirley Hughes: Winner of the Kate Greenaway Medal for her 1977 work *Dogger*, English author and illustrator Hughes is lauded for her ability to describe a full range of childhood experiences with honesty, warmth, and humor. Hughes's recent efforts include *The Lion and the Unicorn*, which was highly commended for the Greenaway Medal in 1998.

David Rish: In novels for older elementary-school students, including *Sophie's Island* and *Detective Paste*, Australian resident Rish often combines elements of mystery with character studies that lend his simple plots an intriguing depth.

*Allen Say: Say is the celebrated author and illustrator of books that explore the lives of young Asian-Americans and contain such universal themes as the search for identity, the multicultural experience, and respect for the environment. His recent picture book *Grandfather's Journey* won the 1994 Caldecott Medal.

Joan Steiner: Mixed-media artist Steiner made a successful debut into publishing with the popular *Look-Alikes*, her collection of visual puzzles made from everyday objects.

Connie Willis: Willis has delved into the many facets of science fiction to earn a dozen Hugo and Nebula Awards—more than any other writer in the genre. Her latest works include *Bellwether* and *To Say Nothing of the Dog*.

Introduction

Something about the Author (*SATA*) is an ongoing reference series that examines the lives and works of authors and illustrators of books for children. *SATA* includes not only well-known writers and artists but also less prominent individuals whose works are just coming to be recognized. This series is often the only readily available information source on emerging authors and illustrators. You'll find *SATA* informative and entertaining, whether you are a student, a librarian, an English teacher, a parent, or simply an adult who enjoys children's literature.

What's Inside SATA

SATA provides detailed information about authors and illustrators who span the full time range of children's literature, from early figures like John Newbery and L. Frank Baum to contemporary figures like Judy Blume and Richard Peck. Authors in the series represent primarily English-speaking countries, particularly the United States, Canada, and the United Kingdom. Also included, however, are authors from around the world whose works are available in English translation. The writings represented in *SATA* include those created intentionally for children and young adults as well as those written for a general audience and known to interest younger readers. These writings cover the entire spectrum of children's literature, including picture books, humor, folk and fairy tales, animal stories, mystery and adventure, science fiction and fantasy, historical fiction, poetry and nonsense verse, drama, biography, and nonfiction.

Obituaries are also included in *SATA* and are intended not only as death notices but also as concise overviews of people's lives and work. Additionally, each edition features newly revised and updated entries for a selection of *SATA* listees who remain of interest to today's readers and who have been active enough to require extensive revisions of their earlier biographies.

New Autobiography Feature

Beginning with Volume 103, *SATA* features three or more specially commissioned autobiographical essays in each volume. These unique essays, averaging about ten thousand words in length and illustrated with an abundance of personal photos, present an entertaining and informative first-person perspective on the lives and careers of prominent authors and illustrators profiled in *SATA*.

Two Convenient Indexes

In response to suggestions from librarians, *SATA* indexes no longer appear in every volume but are included in alternate (odd-numbered) volumes of the series, beginning with Volume 57.

SATA continues to include two indexes that cumulate with each alternate volume: the Illustrations Index, arranged by the name of the illustrator, gives the number of the volume and page where the illustrator's work appears in the current volume as well as all preceding volumes in the series; the Author Index gives the number of the volume in which a person's biographical sketch, autobiographical essay, or obituary appears in the current volume as well as all preceding volumes in the series.

These indexes also include references to authors and illustrators who appear in Gale's *Yesterday's Authors of Books for Children, Children's Literature Review,* and *Something about the Author Autobiography Series.*

Easy-to-Use Entry Format

Whether you're already familiar with the *SATA* series or just getting acquainted, you will want to be aware of the kind of information that an entry provides. In every *SATA* entry the editors attempt to give as complete a picture of the person's life and work as possible. A typical entry in *SATA* includes the following clearly labeled information sections:

- *PERSONAL:* date and place of birth and death, parents' names and occupations, name of spouse, date of marriage, names of children, educational institutions attended, degrees received, religious and political affiliations, hobbies and other interests.

- *ADDRESSES:* complete home, office, electronic mail, and agent addresses, whenever available.

- *CAREER:* name of employer, position, and dates for each career post; art exhibitions; military service; memberships and offices held in professional and civic organizations.

- *AWARDS, HONORS:* literary and professional awards received.

- *WRITINGS:* title-by-title chronological bibliography of books written and/or illustrated, listed by genre when known; lists of other notable publications, such as plays, screenplays, and periodical contributions.

- *ADAPTATIONS:* a list of films, television programs, plays, CD-ROMs, recordings, and other media presentations that have been adapted from the author's work.

- *WORK IN PROGRESS:* description of projects in progress.

- *SIDELIGHTS:* a biographical portrait of the author or illustrator's development, either directly from the biographee—and often written specifically for the *SATA* entry—or gathered from diaries, letters, interviews, or other published sources.

- *FOR MORE INFORMATION SEE:* references for further reading.

- *EXTENSIVE ILLUSTRATIONS:* photographs, movie stills, book illustrations, and other interesting visual materials supplement the text.

How a SATA Entry Is Compiled

A *SATA* entry progresses through a series of steps. If the biographee is living, the *SATA* editors try to secure information directly from him or her through a questionnaire. From the information that the biographee supplies, the editors prepare an entry, filling in any essential missing details with research and/or telephone interviews. If possible, the author or illustrator is sent a copy of the entry to check for accuracy and completeness.

If the biographee is deceased or cannot be reached by questionnaire, the *SATA* editors examine a wide variety of published sources to gather information for an entry. Biographical and bibliographic sources are consulted, as are book reviews, feature articles, published interviews, and material sometimes obtained from the biographee's family, publishers, agent, or other associates.

Entries that have not been verified by the biographees or their representatives are marked with an asterisk (*).

Contact the Editor

We encourage our readers to examine the entire *SATA* series. Please write and tell us if we can make *SATA* even more helpful to you. Give your comments and suggestions to the editor:

BY MAIL: Editor, *Something about the Author,* The Gale Group, 27500 Drake Rd., Farmington Hills, MI 48331-3535.

BY TELEPHONE: (800) 877-GALE

BY FAX: (248) 699-8054

Acknowledgments

Grateful acknowledgment is made to the following publishers, authors, and artists whose works appear in this volume.

AIKEN, JOAN. Aiken, Joan (seated), photograph by Rod Delroy. Reproduced by permission. / Mermaid Street, Rye, from a painting by A. R. Quinton. Reproduced by permission. / Aiken, Conrad (peering into mailbox), photograph. Reproduced by permission. / McDonald, Jessie (wearing a white dress, dark belt), photograph. Reproduced by permission. / Aiken, Joan, with sister, Jane (seated in the sitting room, Jeake's house), 1935, photograph. Reproduced by permission. / Farrs, childhood home of Joan Aiken (side view), Sussex, England, 1935, photograph. Reproduced by permission. / Aiken, Joan (seated on steps in garden), with family, 1935, photograph. Reproduced by permission. / Armstrong, Jessie, son David (middle, holding cat) and Martin, 1941, photograph. Reproduced by permission. / Aiken, Joan (seated on arm of chair) with Ron Brown, 1945, photograph. Reproduced by permission. / Aiken, Joan, standing with family (outside their home), Milltown, 1954, photograph. Reproduced by permission. / Aiken, Joan (serving dinner to family in their home), 1952, photograph. Reproduced by permission. / White Hart Inn, as a pub, about 1930, photograph. Reproduced by permission. / Brown, Elizabeth Delano and John Sebastian Brown (seated outdoors), The Hermitage, 1977, photograph. Reproduced by permission. / Goldstein, Julius (standing on city street), about age 30, photograph. Reproduced by permission. / Aiken, Joan (standing outdoors), 1972, photograph by Barbara Sproul. Reproduced by permission.

ANTHONY, PATRICIA. Anthony, Patricia, photograph by Milton Hinnant. Reproduced by permission.

APPLEGATE, KATHERINE. Mattingly, David B., illustrator. From a cover of *Animorphs #13: The Change* by Katherine Applegate. Apple Paperbacks, 1997. Illustration copyright © 1997 by Scholastic Inc. Apple Paperbacks and Animorphs are registered trademarks of Scholastic Inc. Reproduced by permission. / From a cover of *Zoey Fools Around* by Katherine Applegate. An Avon Flare Book, 1994. Copyright © 1994 by Daniel Weiss Associates and Katherine Applegate. Reproduced by permission of Avon Books, Inc.

BLOS, JOAN. Lambert, Stephen, illustrator. From an illustration in *Bedtime!* by Joan Blos. Simon & Schuster Books for Young Readers, 1998. Illustrations copyright © 1998 by Stephen Lambert. Reproduced by permission of Simon & Schuster Books for Young Readers, an imprint of Simon & Schuster Children's Publishing Division. / Birling, Paul, illustrator. From a cover of *Brooklyn Doesn't Rhyme* by Joan W. Blos. Atheneum Books for Young Readers, 1994. Jacket illustration copyright © 1994 by Paul Birling. Reproduced by permission of Atheneum Books for Young Readers, an imprint of Simon & Schuster Children's Publishing Division. / Schutzer, Dena, illustrator. From a cover of *The Hungry Little Boy* by Joan W. Blos. Simon & Schuster Books for Young Readers, 1995. Jacket illustrations © 1995 by Dena Schutzer. Reproduced by permission of Simon & Schuster Books for Young Readers, an imprint of Simon & Schuster Children's Publishing Division.

BRAUN, LILIAN JACKSON. From a cover of *The Cat Who Ate Danish Modern* by Lilian Jackson Braun. Jove Books, 1967. Copyright © 1967 by Lilian Jackson Braun. Used by permission of Putnam Berkley, a division of Penguin Putnam Inc.

BRIDGERS, SUE ELLEN. Bridgers, Sue Ellen (holding open book, posing), photograph. Reproduced by permission. / Bridgers, Sue Ellen (with mother and sister), 2 years old, 1944, photograph. Reproduced by permission. / Hunsucker, Wayland with son, Abbott, 1949, photograph. Reproduced by permission. / Four generations of women, 1942, photograph. Reproduced by permission. / Bridgers, Sue Ellen, 5 years old, photograph. Reproduced by permission. / Bridgers, Sue Ellen and Ben (seated in back seat), on their wedding day, March 17, 1963, photograph. Reproduced by permission. / Bridgers family portrait, 1980, painting by Shirley Grant. Reproduced by permission. / Bridgers, Sue Ellen (marching in Sylva Christmas parade, carrying sign), 1975, photograph. Reproduced by permission. / Bridgers, Sue Ellen with Sue Hager and Judy Budd, before graduation from Western Carolina University, 1976, photograph. Reproduced by permission. / Bridger and Hunsucker family Christmas, photograph. Reproduced by permission. / Bridgers, Sue Ellen and daughter, Elizabeth (before church service), 1976, photograph. Reproduced by permission. / Bridgers, Sue Ellen with husband, Ben, and children, photograph. Reproduced by permission. / Bridgers, Sue Ellen's children and grandchildren (seated on couch), photograph. Reproduced by permission. / Bridgers, Sue Ellen with husband, Ben, and their four grandchildren, photograph. Reproduced by permission.

BROUWER, SIGMUND. Brouwer, Sigmund, photograph. Reproduced by permission. / From a cover of *Thunderbird*

MINOR, WENDELL. Minor, Wendell G., photograph. Photo credit © 1995 Judith Petrovich. Reproduced by permission. / Minor, Wendell, illustrator. From a cover of *Red Fox Running* by Eve Bunting. Clarion, 1993. Reproduced by permission of Houghton Mifflin Company. / From a cover of *Grand Canyon: Exploring a Natural Wonder* words and pictures by Wendell Minor. The Blue Sky Press, 1998. Copyright © 1998 by Wendell Minor. Reproduced by permission of The Blue Sky Press, an imprint of Scholastic Inc.

MIRANDA, ANNE. Miranda, Anne with boys, photograph by Saturnino L. Miranda. Reproduced by permission. / Stevens, Janet, illustrator. From an illustration in *To Market, To Market* by Anne Miranda. Harcourt Brace & Company, 1997. Text copyright © 1997 by Anne Miranda. Illustrations copyright © 1997 by Janet Stevens. Reproduced by permission of Harcourt, Inc.

MOWRY, JESS. Mowry, Jess (seated), photograph. Reproduced by permission of Jess Mowry. / Dinyer, Eric, illustrator. From a jacket of *Babylon Boyz* by Jess Mowry. Simon & Schuster Books for Young Readers, 1997. Jacket illustration © 1997 by Eric Dinyer. Reproduced by permission of the illustrator. / Mundahl, Kurt, photographer. From a cover of *Six Out Seven* by Jess Mowry. Anchor Books, 1994. Reproduced by permission of Doubleday, a division of Random House, Inc. / Cover of *Way Past Cool* by Jess Mowry. HarperPerennial, 1993. Reproduced by permission of HarperCollins Publishers. / Jeffery, photographer. From a cover of *Children of the Night* by Jess Mowry. Holloway House Publishing Company, 1991. Reproduced by permission.

MYERS, WALTER DEAN. Myers, Walter Dean, photograph by David Godlis. Reproduced by permission of Walter Dean Myers. / Bacha, Andy, illustrator. From a cover of *Scorpions* by Walter Dean Myers. HarperTrophy, 1996. Cover art © 1996 by Andy Bacha. Cover © 1996 by HarperCollins Publishers. Reproduced by permission of HarperCollins Publishers, Inc. / From a cover of *Now Is Your Time!: The African-American Struggle for Freedom* by Walter Dean Myers. HarperTrophy, A Division of HarperCollins, 1991. Cover © 1991 by HarperCollins Publishers. Reproduced by permission of HarperCollins Publishers. / Dietz, Jim, illustrator. From a cover of *Fallen Angels* by Walter Dean Myers. Scholastic Inc., 1988. Jacket illustration copyright © 1988 by Walter Dean Myers. Reproduced by permission of Scholastic Inc. / French, Fiona, illustrator. From a cover of *The Dragon Takes a Wife* by Walter Dean Myers. Scholastic, Inc., 1995. Jacket art © 1995 by Fiona French. Reproduced by permission.

NOLAN, HAN. Nolan, Han, photograph by Brian Nolan. Reproduced by permission. / Kahl, David, illustrator. From the cover of *If I Should Die Before I Wake* by Han Nolan. Harcourt Brace & Company, 1994. Cover illustration copyright © 1994 by David Kahl. Reproduced by permission of David Kahl. / Lee, Paul, illustrator. From a jacket of *Dancing on the Edge* by Han Nolan. Harcourt Brace & Company, 1997. Jacket illustration copyright © 1997 by Paul Lee. Reproduced by permission of Paul Lee.

ROBINSON, KIM STANLEY. Robinson, Kim Stanley, photograph by Gloria Robinson. / Dixon, Don, illustrator. From a cover of *Red Mars* by Kim Stanley Robinson. Bantam Books, 1993. Cover art © 1993 by Don Dixon. Reproduced by permission of Bantam Books, a division of Bantam Doubleday Dell Publishing Group, Inc. / Roberts, Tony, artist. From a cover of *The Wild Shore* by Kim Stanley Robinson. A Tom Doherty Associates Book, 1984. Copyright © 1984 by Kim Stanley Robinson. Reproduced by permission.

ROWLING, J. K. GrandPre, Mary, illustrator. From a jacket of *Harry Potter and the Sorcerer's Stone* by J. K. Rowling. Arthur A. Levine Books, 1998. Jacket illustration © 1998 by Mary GrandPre. All rights reserved. Reproduced by permission of Arthur A. Levine Books, an imprint of Scholastic Press, a division of Scholastic Inc.

SANDERS, SCOTT R. Sanders, Scott R., photograph by Eva Sanders. Reproduced by permission. / Cogancherry, Helen, illustrator. From a cover of *The Floating House* by Scott Russell Sanders. Atheneum Books for Young Readers, 1995. Jacket illustration copyright © 1995 by Helen Cogancherry. Reproduced by permission of Atheneum Books for Young Readers, an imprint of Simon & Schuster Children's Publishing Division.

SANDERSON, RUTH. Sanderson, Ruth, photograph by Ken Robinson. Reproduced by permission of Ruth Sanderson. / From an illustration in *The Twelve Dancing Princesses* by Ruth Sanderson. Little, Brown and Company, 1991. Copyright © 1991 by Ruth Sanderson. Reproduced by permission of the author. / From a cover of *Papa Gatto: An Italian Fairy Tale* by Ruth Sanderson. Little, Brown and Company, 1995. Copyright © 1995 by Ruth Sanderson. Reproduced by permission of the author. / From an illustration in *Papa Gatto: An Italian Fairy Tale* by Ruth Sanderson. Little, Brown and Company, 1995. Copyright © 1995 by Ruth Sanderson. / From an illustration in *The Enchanted Wood: An Original Fairy Tale* by Ruth Sanderson. Little, Brown and Company, 1991. Copyright © 1991 by Ruth Sanderson. Reproduced by permission of Warner Books.

SCOTT, MELISSA. Scott, Melissa, photograph by Ryan Mercer. Reproduced by permission. / Johnson, Kevin Eugene.

something ABOUT the AUthoR

AIKEN, Clarissa Lorenz 1899-1992

OBITUARY NOTICE—See index for *SATA* sketch: Born January 28, 1899, in Milwaukee, WI; died May 16, 1992, at the Goddard House, in Jamaica Plain, MA. Writer and music teacher. Married poet and critic Conrad Aiken, February 27, 1930 (divorced, 1938). Aiken moved to Boston to study at the New England Conservatory of Music in 1920. Although she taught music in public schools and piano at the Brookline Music School, Brookline, MA from 1960 to 1973, she is best remembered as the freelance writer who produced a series of profiles for the *Boston Evening Transcript,* as well as numerous other articles that appeared in the *Boston Globe, Christian Science Monitor, Atlantic Monthly, Redbook, Harpers' Bazaar,* and the *New Yorker* over her sixty-year career. Her first book, *Junket to Japan,* was aimed at teenagers and appeared in 1960. Illustrated with photographs by Peter Bell, the book evolved from the letters and journal entries of Bell, a Massachusetts youth who spent a summer in Tokyo. "From his observations and impressions," Aiken once told *SATA,* "I distilled the excitement of his experiences, the warm friendly contacts he made with the Japanese, the exuberance of his comradeship with other teenagers." Late in life Aiken penned a memoir, *Lorelei Two: My Life with Conrad Aiken,* which outlined her brief marriage in the 1930s to the renowned poet and critic.

OBITUARIES AND OTHER SOURCES:

PERIODICALS

Boston Globe, May 20, 1992, p. 33.

—Robert Reginald and Mary A. Burgess

Autobiography Feature

Joan Aiken

1924-

A happy childhood is supposed to lead to neurosis in middle age. By which criterion I should be a hundred percent neurotic, for my childhood was, in most ways, extremely happy.

Another maxim from the experts has it that childhood almost entirely shapes one's outlook later; that we can never escape from our early conditioning. Chagall, to his ninety-seventh year, painted the village where he grew up. I go along with this theory. I have total sympathy with Chagall's cows and cottages. I know them too. When I start to lay out a setting for a story—unless it is unmistakably located in Battersea, or Nantucket, or the Pyrenees—I too inevitably begin by thinking of a village—a village of forty houses. That is why a large part of this memoir is concerned with childhood. The adult years are just like anyone else's. Whereas the village—

But I anticipate.

My childhood was divided into two parts, and the first part, until I was five, took place in a town, the medieval town of Rye, Sussex, England. Rye has a population of 4,000 now, probably less in the 1920s, consists of cobbled streets and red-brick houses jostled tightly together on a high little hill rising out of the flat green plain of Romney Marsh. Two miles distant lies the English Channel. Some of Rye's walls and fortified gates still remain. Jeake's House, where I was born, stands halfway up steep, cobbled Mermaid Street, at the top of which Henry James had a house and died in 1918, six years before my birth. Jeake's House, built in 1689 as a granary or storehouse, had belonged to several members of the Jeake family. One, Samuel Jeake, was an astrologer and mathematician; a huge leather-bound book by him was at one time in the Aiken family possession. I was too young to understand it then, and doubt if I should make much more of it now. One of Jeake's concepts was about particles of infinite smallness called zenzicubes; I can remember my father telling me about that. Then there were even smaller things called zenzizenzizenzizenzizendykes. The book got lost; I think it vanished in World War II. Samuel Jeake also invented a flying machine, and, trying it out, boldly leapt off the high wall of the town. It didn't work, and he crashed into the tidal mud of the river Rother, which partly encircles Rye.

My family had not always lived in Rye; they moved there just before my birth, because there would not have been room for me in the tiny house, Look-Out Cottage, in Winchelsea, two miles away, where they had spent the previous three years. But they had come from America.

My father, the American poet Conrad Aiken, had a family tragedy in his own childhood. His father, my grandfather William Aiken, a doctor from a New England family but practicing in Savannah, Georgia, had, in 1901, suffered from a brainstorm and shot first his wife, then himself. Conrad, aged twelve, heard the shots and found the bodies. His sister and two brothers were adopted by relatives. Conrad, the eldest, refused to change his name to Taylor, the condition of adoption, and so grew up parted from his siblings. He had a lonely and unhappy adolescence, haunted by the fear that he might end up as mentally unbalanced as his father, who, towards the end, had suffered from paranoid suspicions and beat Conrad savagely. Nonetheless William had been a brilliantly intelligent and original man and, as a child, Conrad had worshipped him.

When he was at Harvard, Conrad met my mother, Jessie McDonald, doing her Master's degree at Radcliffe after taking a B.A. at McGill; she was a Canadian from Montreal. She had black hair and green eyes and was, judging from photographs, stunningly pretty; she also had an acute intelligence. More important, from Conrad's viewpoint, she was a peasant: that is, she came of plain sound Scots ancestry on both sides. Her father was a first-generation emigrant from Tain, in Scotland, and ran a successful accountancy firm which he handed on to his two sons. His wife, Jean Cross, was of Scottish and Huguenot descent. Conrad met the family—two brothers, six sisters—during summer visits at Cap-a-l'Aigle on the St. Lawrence. His own parents had been first cousins; he felt that Jessie would supply the solid down-to-earth sense and ballast so notably lacking in his own family. (Other members of it besides his father had suffered from instability; he talks a good deal about the family *petit mal* in his autobiographical book *Ushant*. In fact, even fortified by the prosaic McDonald strain, his own children had precious little chance of growing up well-balanced and sane, he declared in his gloomier moments; I can remember his confidently predicting that my offspring would certainly go mad when they grew up.)

At all events, whether their union was based on romantic love or practical common sense, Conrad and Jessie were married in 1912, a year after they met, travelled in Europe for a year, lived for a little in Cambridge, Massachusetts, then moved into Boston, where my elder brother and sister were born in 1913 and 1917 respectively. After a spell at South Yarmouth, on Cape Cod, the family then migrated to England, partly for the benefit of the children's education, partly because, after reading *Tom Brown's Schooldays* as a child, Conrad had always had intensely romantic feelings about the Isle of Albion.

Mermaid Street, Rye, from a painting by A. R. Quinton. Jeake's House is third on left with protruding gable.

Settling in Rye, with all its literary associations, was a natural step. He did not, however, stay very long in Rye at that time. After my birth in 1924 he became ill with a rectal abscess which required several operations. Convalescent from these, he went for a two-month trip to Spain. His travelling companion and long-standing friend, the English writer Martin Armstrong (referred to as Chapman in *Ushant*), was later to play an important part in Aiken family affairs. In 1926, when I was two, Conrad, restless again and desperately worried by shortage of money, returned alone to Boston, hoping to find reviewing or teaching jobs.

So my early recollections of my father, before the age of seven, are minimal. Is there a vague image of him sitting in an armchair in the shadowy drawing room, of my tiptoeing behind to gaze at the back of his head? Perhaps. A family friend, Beatrice Taussig, told of calling at Jeake's House, finding that Jessie was out shopping, Conrad typing in his study, while I yelled my head off in my cot; Beatrice advised Conrad that I needed changing, but he said he didn't know how, so she did it. I don't remember that. Conrad later recalled that when he returned to Jeake's House in 1928 to arrange for a divorce (he had, meanwhile, in Boston, met and fallen bang in love with Clarissa Lorenz), I greeted him with a suspicious scowl, demanding, "Who's that man?"

Much of my childhood was haunted, not unpleasantly, by nostalgia for previous places, previous modes of existence, not necessarily my own. Conrad himself wrote a poem on this theme:

But alas, alas, being everything you are nothing
The history of all my life is in your face;
And all I can grasp is an earlier, more haunted moment,
And a happier place.

("At a Concert of Music,"
John Deth and Other Poems)

I suppose nostalgia is an infection almost inevitably picked up in the course of such a migratory career as that of our family. During my early years I used to hear John and Jane, my brother and sister, talking wistfully about the joys of South Yarmouth and Winchelsea; then later, Rye, in its turn, became for me imbued with the same haunting charm, the magic of a lost paradise.

Even before it was lost, the life in Rye, in Jeake's House, had immense charm. A letter of Conrad's describes the house as it was when he bought it in 1924, vast, tall, "roped with webs, littered with bones and stinking of ghosts," holes in its floors and beetles in its woodwork. My mother, and later Conrad's second and third wives, had a hideous time coping with its inconveniences, cavernous coldness, barbarously steep stairs, precipitous ledges from which children could and did fall, archaic plumbing, antediluvian heating, lack of light, lack of a back door. Just the same it was a house to love. I can instantly, at any time, summon up the individual smell of Jeake's House—a delicious blend of aged black timbers, escaping gas, damp plaster, and mildew; I can remember the exact feel of the brass front-door knob turning gently in one's hand, the shape of the square black banister post, the look of the leaded windows with their small panes (which let in little light and must have been hell to clean). The flight of stairs leading to the third floor was so steep that it had no rail, only a knotted ship's rope; and the flight above *that,* leading to the two little attics where slept my brother John and the maid Alice, was, unabashedly, a ladder like that leading to a yacht's cabin. Conrad's study, a big double room, had a huge, south-facing dormer window that looked out across the marsh to Winchelsea. Between the ages of eight and twelve I spent hours stretched out on the bone-hard couch in that window, reading. From a gully between the two peaked roofs, which could be reached from John's attic window, one could climb on to the roof of the next-door house and, if one had courage, on down the street. John and Jane, and a friend of theirs, Juliet, had a Secret Society called the JJJ Club. Among its conditions of entry was the performance of this and other fearsome roof-climbs. I was too small to belong to the club and admired its proceedings from a distant and humble standpoint.

The activities of my elders were for me imbued with magic. They had a rich fantasy life and lived in a world of imagination, surrounded by invented characters—Robin Hood and all his men, a group called The Playlanders whose leader was called Gold Kingy, not to mention the ghost of Samuel Jeake who was said to haunt the house, quite benevolently.... Part of this richness came from Conrad, who told them a wonderful serial story called *The Jewel Seed*, in which S. Jeake was the hero, and the villain was a Chinese magician. John wrote it all down, as related, in tiny notebooks. Forty years later I discovered these, cached away in Conrad's house at Brewster on Cape Cod, and typed out the whole saga—but Conrad thought poorly of it when I showed it to him, and said it was best relegated

to oblivion. I dare say it is now in the Huntington Library, with the rest of his papers.

As I have said, Conrad played no part in my own early memories, and I imagine that my mother's life at that time was sad enough. She had to cope with existence in a foreign land, on her own, with three children and very little money. Though, apparently, the news of Conrad's various infidelities came as a fearful shock when he broke it to her, she must, by degrees, during his two years' absence, have come to the conclusion that their sixteen-year marriage was at an end, that she had to make a decision about what she would do next. Go back to Canada? She never showed the least inclination to do that. Stay in England? But how? Take a teaching job?

Meanwhile, with characteristic stoicism and reserve, she buried pain and anxiety at the back of her mind and created a cheerful family life: picnics to the beach or to bluebell woods (John and Jane walked; I rode with the food on the back of Jessie's bicycle), birthday and Christmas festivities. The height of the downstairs hall allowed an enormous Christmas tree; John and Jane went out with baskets into the nearest woods and picked enough holly leaves to make an immense rustling chain that wound from top to bottom of the high house.

I remember no conversation from this period, only literature and happenings. The literature was read aloud to me, in the bedroom that I shared with Jane, and it comes back with intensely dramatic emphasis: first *Peter Rabbit* and the *Just-So Stories,* fairly milk-and-honey stuff; then *Pinocchio,* rustling with assassins, evil plots, death, moonlight, and irony; then *Uncle Remus,* told in mysterious dialect, full of lethal intentions, wicked Brer Fox, and ominous characters called Patter-Rollers; then, most dramatic of all, *The Cloister and the Hearth,* in fact read aloud to my elders but soaked up by me with passion. Two scenes were stamped on my mind for all time: the comic one with the ill-intentioned doctor who gets knocked into his own basket of hot coals; and the horrendous siege by brigands including a corpse decorated with luminous paint. For lighter relief came *Peacock Pie*—"Grill me some bones, said the Cobbler"—and the folk tales of Jean de Bosschere—one particularly riveting about a forester treed by wolves who climb on one another's backs to get at him; that was the one which upset Freud's patient, the Wolf Man, but all it did to me was increase my passion for the written word. All the scenes from these books take place, for me, in Jeake's House—"Ann, Ann, come quick as you can, There's a fish that talks in the frying-pan!" is in the dark Jeake's House kitchen, and the story of the "Butterfly that Stamped" out in the little snaily garden.

Notable happenings at that time included my contracting diphtheria picked up while visiting the maid Alice's family in the slummy lower town. (Her family were extremely nice to me; I remember eating pickled cabbage in their kitchen and still have a stool, tossed together from the offcuts of toilet seats, which her father, a carpenter, made for me.) The diphtheria imbued me with a hatred of doctors—no doubt why the scene from *The Cloister and the Hearth* struck such a chord. I was segregated behind disinfected sheets, had to have my own small Christmas tree, and my books were burned when I recovered, but *Peacock Pie* and the *Just-So Stories* were instantly replaced.

Father, Conrad Aiken, 1960.

At this time I discovered that I could make it rain by emptying a glass of water out of the window. Although much impressed by finding this power in myself, I have not found the need to use it much; in fact, never since that time.

The garden of Jeake's House consisted of two little paved courtyards, one about five feet higher in level than the other, approached by a flight of stone steps. I fell down these steps, of course, and my sister Jane fell out of the swing in the lower court and cut her head on the paving stones and needed stitches; I can remember that drama, but not my falling into the river Rother and being rescued by my mother's sister Barbara who dived in fully clothed. Used to swimming in the St. Lawrence, no doubt she found the Rother child's play. I can remember a day when, for some reason, John and Jane took pairs of saucepan lids and, joyfully banging them together like cymbals, went processing round the house; but I can't remember the painful occasion when Conrad returned, in December 1928, to ask Jessie to reconsider the divorce on which she had finally decided. She refused even to talk to him, jumped on her bicycle, and went off to the house of a friend. He took my sister for a walk round the town, then returned miserably to London. Soon after, the divorce went through. Conrad married Clarissa; then, next year, my mother married Conrad's English friend Martin Armstrong and went, with us three children, to live with Martin in his small house Farrs at the other end of Sussex. Conrad was outraged by this and felt that he had been betrayed by both parties. They never met again.

I had heard talk of Farrs before. Martin had often come to visit at Jeake's House—he was actually staying in the house on the night of my birth. My brother John had been to stay with Martin and came back with descriptions of the beautiful aged cottage, close to a line of grassy hills, the South Downs, with a huge garden and fields all around. John was a passionate naturalist and had a collection of pressed wild flowers, seashells, and snail shells.

I can still recall my original mental image of Farrs—just—and the way in which, as always, this differed from the reality when I finally got there.

The move from Rye really meant the end of childhood for John and Jane, aged sixteen and twelve; for Jane, a painfully premature and abrupt end. Trying to grapple with unhappy and complicated circumstances, my mother acted with uncharacteristic haste and bad judgment. Farrs was situated in a remote village where there were no educational facilities for my elders, so Jane was despatched to a boarding school recommended by an acquaintance. It was a snobbish place where Jane was laughed at for her American accent and homemade clothes; she was miserably unhappy there and used to cry for days, on and off, before the start of each term. John was sent to London to board with friends of friends and attend University College School, from which in due course he graduated to University College. This was a better choice as he was scientifically minded and later took a first-class degree at U.C., but he was not very happy with the family in whose house he was quartered and missed Rye Grammar School which he had loved. In the school and college holidays John and Jane came to Farrs. Farrs was a tiny house and Martin, born in 1882, had been a bachelor up to the age of forty-seven

Mother, Jessie McDonald, age sixteen.

when he married Jessie, not at all used to living with children; no doubt she was anxious to keep wear and tear on all parties to a minimum. I missed my siblings sorely when they went and looked forward passionately to their return in the holidays. I can't help wondering if their life would not have been easier if Jessie had remained in Rye and tried to get a teaching job which, with her M.A. degree, should not have been impossible.

Still, her marriage to Martin was a happy one; they remained married until her death, forty years later. "Shine after storm," she said once, comparing it to life with Conrad. They made Farrs into an unquestionably happy home, a solid base for us three Aikens and our half brother, David Armstrong. I think of the house always in sunshine; as one came in the glass-paned front door there would be warmth, a smell of apples and wood smoke, the contented sound of a house where quiet, busy activities are proceeding, the sound of a typewriter or sewing machine, cooking noises, Scarlatti from the piano, the rustle of a log fire.

I can remember a few moments of my arrival at Farrs. Martin had fetched me from the friends in London who had me to stay during the wedding and honeymoon. It was dark when I arrived and I was put to bed in the room which later became my half brother's. I was impressed by the fact that the bath was low and small enough for me to climb into myself—the bath at Jeake's House had been of Victorian

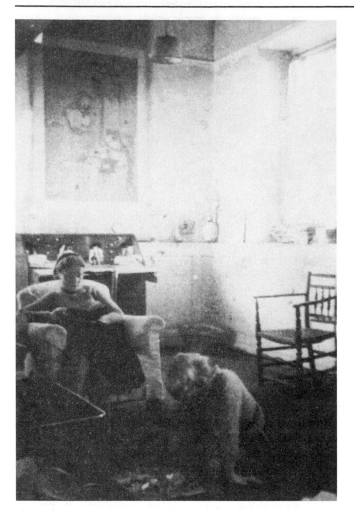

Joan Aiken, right, with sister Jane in the sitting room at Jeake's House, 1935.

vastness, to match the towering brass gas geyser which sometimes exploded, formidably. Everything in Farrs, I discovered, was of small, manageable size; the stairs had only thirteen steps, ceilings downstairs were low, and upstairs they sloped, so the furniture had to be low-slung.

To my amazement I discovered next day that the street in Sutton, a village of forty houses, was not called a street but a road; there were no pavements (sidewalks, my mother called them), only grass banks with little scuffed paths along the top where children made tracks of their own. Sutton had one shop, which sold everything. Halfway to the shop, four minutes' walk, was a forge, where the blacksmith, Mr. Budd, worked at his roaring bellows or clanged shoes onto the great fringed feet of farm horses. There was one pub in the village, the White Horse, just down the road from our house. Martin went there to drink beer and chat with the village elders. You could walk to the shop and return by a footpath across the fields, for the village swung round in a curve, along the edge of a plateau in a loop of the South Downs. A gate from the fields led into the back of our garden.

This garden was my sudden emancipation from the grown-up world. Half an acre in size, it had been created by an elderly lady, Miss Alice Cohen, from whom, at first, Martin rented the cottage. (Later he bought it from her for

£800.) Her standards in gardens were high; Martin had a job keeping up with them. The Farrs garden was a paradise for any child. For a start, there were great expanses of lawn. Grass! Accustomed to the unkind paving stones of the Rye garden, I could hardly believe that I was free to walk, crawl, and roll as much as I pleased. Then, there were any number of trees, most of them climbable. The best was a walnut tree, from which hung the swing. You could climb up the rope, and so into the heights of the tree. There were secret places behind lilacs, a summer house that rotated on a circular base, a wild area up at the top of the garden, a wild, steep cliff at the front, leading down to the road, and all kinds of flowers, masses of them—roses, peonies, lilies, irises, oriental poppies, phlox, anemones, and in spring, masses and masses of daffodils, narcissi, hyacinths, snowdrops.... There were no flowers, of course, when I first arrived in January, the best month of the year, when everything is starting. For a country child, January is full of promise: drainage runnels by the roads are full of water pouring over white, hollowed chalk beds where one can wade in one's rubber boots; the banks, far higher than my five-year-old head, were neatly trimmed and the hedges clipped, so that one could climb them and explore and see the bones of the landscape.

From this point on, I can remember conversation. With John and Jane away at school, I suppose more remarks were addressed to me.

Martin, though civil and civilised, made it perfectly plain that he was not prepared to be a father to us Aikens; after all, we had a perfectly good father of our own. While my mother was settling in, Martin kindly took me for one or two walks and explained the difference between a pub and a club (I knew about clubs, for there had been one next door to Jeake's House). But our conversation was stilted, and remained so for the next fifty years; Martin was not at ease with small children until his own son was born, and by that time his and my relationship had set into its mould; I was rather nervous of him and he, probably rightly, found most of my remarks silly. Still, at meals, in the company of the whole family, he was immensely entertaining, both witty and erudite. Life at Farrs was graceful, in spite of poverty. Martin, like Conrad, depended for his living on what he wrote—novels, short stories, and poetry; my mother had a small income, but this had been invested ill-advisedly by her brothers and she lost most of it in the slump. Her relationship with her brothers had never been good: her father died when she was twelve and the brothers, in their twenties, had been left to deal with most of the family affairs, which probably made them rather bossy. To the end of her life my mother, though gentle, courteous, and accessible to reason in general, had a tendency to bristle into fight if any male tried to lay down the law or get didactic with her. Undoubtedly this was a legacy from her feelings about her brothers.

So at Farrs there was no money to throw about. My mother's depleted income went mostly on educating Jane and John. Conrad paid her a little rent for Jeake's House. I remained at home and she taught me herself until I was twelve, which she was well qualified to do. I learned French, Latin, English, history, arithmetic, geography, a little Spanish and German.

The house had four bedrooms and one bathroom; Martin's study was upstairs; downstairs there was a dining room into which the front door opened, a sitting room, kitchen, pantry, and scullery (in which the cooking was actually done, on a kerosene stove). We had no radio, car, main water, or refrigerator—no electricity at all; water came from a well, pumped by hand; at night we lit oil lamps and candles. One of our daily tasks was refilling all the lamps and the metal tank of the cooker, rubbing down the charred wicks with a twist of newspaper, cleaning the smoke stains off the fragile glass chimneys with more newspaper and a bit of rag. I can still remember the gentle squeaking of the paper against the glass. If you rubbed too hard the glass broke and my mother wrote down "two small lamp chimneys" in the weekly-order book for the shop. The floors downstairs were of brick and icy cold at all times. Our food was sumptuous—fruit and vegetables from the garden grown by Martin; magnificent eggs, cream, and milk from one of the village farms; home baked bread from the village shop, local meat. Martin was a decided gourmet and my mother a terrific cook. For the first seven years of life at Farrs we had a maid; a local girl would come daily to sweep, dust, scrub, and wash dishes; she was paid about fifty pence a week. The first girl, Lily, came when she was fourteen, having just left the village school. One of the first things she did was to drop a whole trayload of wedding-present Wedgewood china onto the brick floor and smash the lot. She was terribly upset and cried floods, but my mother comforted her.

Lily was fourteen, I was six; she had much more knowledge of the world than I, because she was the youngest of a family of six. Her mother was a widow. Thinking about it now, I realize what a number of widows there were in the village: Mrs. Standen at the shop; Mrs. Leggatt, who had been Martin's housekeeper and still came up for spring-cleaning; Mrs. Clare, her mother; Mrs. Harwood next door, who sold us eggs and milk, did our heavy laundry, and whose son Frank drove the village taxi; and several others. World War I had taken a heavy toll of the village.

Lily had been to school for seven years and loved reading stories; she lent me *The Golden Key* by George MacDonald, a marvellous tale. I learned to read at once after arrival at Farrs (I expect my mother saw to this); so I was happy to share with Lily the fruits of my reading the Pink, Crimson, and Green Fairy Books, Hans Andersen, and Grimm. For her part, she had been to the movies, and could tell me about them.

Our nearest movie house was a five-mile walk, in a small corrugated-iron shed outside Petworth (where I now live); this was also where our nearest chemist, butcher, draper, ironmonger, fishmonger, and doctor were located. Lily went to the cinema once a week, Saturdays, on her bike. She tried to describe to me what the films were like. "It's like a picture, but it moves, and sometimes you hear the voices too." I simply could not conceive how it worked, and only half believed her; but still she did tell me those amazing stories which I knew she could not have made up. My imagination rose to the challenge time after time, like a horse to an impossible jump, and sank back defeated. But I curled on the striped cushion in the old wicker armchair in the kitchen every teatime, eating fresh crusty bread (often without butter because it was so good on its own), drinking ice-cold well-water, while Lily told me the plots of films she had seen, till they lay embedded in my mind like

fossils. Many were war films—*Tell England, The Dawn Patrol, Journey's End.* They were terribly sad. On a lighter note was Tarzan, also Felix the Cat, Charlie Chaplin, and Buster Keaton. The two last I despised, being a little snob. I know better now. We preferred films of heroic action and self-sacrificing friendship. Lily took me for walks in the afternoons; I expect my mother was glad to get us both out of the cottage, whose ancient floors were very thin; one could hear conversation clear through ceilings. Going up to the top of the garden among the brussels sprouts was the only way to have any private conference; I can remember various fraught interviews with my mother in that region.

Lily and I used to climb the nearer slopes of the Downs, half a mile away, or pick cowslips and kingcups in the marshy meadow behind Lily's mother's cottage (shared with another family), or walk two miles in hot summer to a shallow pond where one could bathe, after a fashion. On these walks we developed our private mythology, woven across the framework of the films Lily had seen, the books I had read. I was in love with Kipling; I had read the *Jungle Book* over and over, and knew whole pages of *Stalky* by heart. In our private world Lily was Tarzan and I was Mowgli; we spent a lot of time tree-climbing and swinging on the ropes of wild clematis that hung from beech trees on the Downs. Lily, born in the village, knew all the local names: Sutton 'Ollow, the deep-banked road that climbed to our village, haunted by a ghost who sat on a leaning tree; Crouch Cave, an underground brick vault in a wood, really an old icehouse; The Decoy, another haunted path (by the ghost of a shot gamekeeper); The Slipes (possibly an Anglo-Saxon version of slopes?), where we picked young beech sprays to decorate the May Queen's Throne; the Birket, where birches grew; New Barn, several centuries old; the Cuckoo Tree, "where a cuckoo built its nest"; best of all, Burton waterfall, a twenty-foot artificial cascade, underneath which a damp and drippy tunnel ran clean through from one side to the other. Later I used many of these locations in my own books.

The only film I actually saw myself was *The Count of Monte Cristo.* Jane and I and a school friend of hers did the walk there and back, taking a supper picnic and returning after midnight. It was a terrific occasion.

Of course the village had its own festivities: an occasional cartoon or magic-lantern show would take place in the Women's Institute hall; or there would be an evening of song. I can remember a teenage boy, someone's visiting talented nephew, plaintively rendering "Sing to me, Gipsy," which I found inexpressibly moving, and then we all sang "Flow gently, Sweet Afton," as the words were thrown on a screen. In August there was the flower show, when everyone exhibited fruit, vegetables, flower arrangements, cakes, and jam, and the children made wild-flower collections. Once I won a third prize for one of these—two shillings—but my mother would not let me accept the money, for, she said, it should properly go to a village child. I am sure she gave me the two shillings herself, but still her veto filled me with a deep sense of injustice.

The best event of the year, for me, was May Day. This had been revived by the Rector, a morris-dance enthusiast. The festivities opened with a morris procession—the young males of the village, prancing, white-trousered, straw-hatted, cross-gartered, accompanied by bells, fiddle, and accordion; also by the scoffing comments of their relatives lined along the grassy banks of the village street. Then came the best part, crowning of the May Queen on the grass plot behind the Women's Institute. Of course my personal ambition was to be May Queen myself, but even then I probably knew this was out of the question, since to qualify one must attend the village school. (My mother had quite correctly estimated that I would learn a great deal more from her, without taking into consideration how much this would cut me off from the communal life of the village children. They used to shout "Gin-*ger!*" after me in the street, and I was scared and shy of them.)

The May Queen wore white, and a wreath of primroses and pink campion; while she sat enthroned the schoolchildren did their elaborate dances with ribbons round the white maypole. The music of the maypole dances, the intricate turnings and spiderweb patterns made by the ribbons filled me with supreme ecstacy.

I was writing a lot of poetry at this time in a notebook I had bought for two shillings at the shop on my fifth birthday. From that age I knew I was going to be a writer, like Conrad, like Martin, whose books were to be seen around the house. I knew that writers didn't make much money. Martin used to give me his old royalty reports and typed sheets for drawing paper. I planned to be a novelist and tried to write stories as well as poems, but seldom finished them. An exception was one based on a dream: *Her Husband Was a Demon; or, Eight Tormented Years.* I just managed to get through that one by cramming the action—a fault I have succumbed to ever since.

Lily began writing poetry too, and showed it to Martin, asking how she could get it published. He must know, after all. He found this a trial and complained, also, that whenever he went into the kitchen, there was Lily moonily gazing at herself in the glass instead of getting on with what had to be done; so, shortly after, she left us, which was a shock and great grief to me.

I had planned to tell her about a visit I had paid to some cousins in the north of England who owned a monkey—her dismissal had been tactfully arranged while I

Farrs, 1935.

was away—and when I encountered her in the street, arranged to meet her next day in Sutton 'Ollow for a long talk. My mother looked doubtful when she learned of this assignation but did not try to deter me from going. I arrived early, waited and waited—but Lily never showed up. At last I went home, dissolved in tears.

"I was afraid that might happen," my mother told me, with her usual mixture of sympathy and realism. Characteristically she had let me go because she thought I might as well learn that people are unreliable. Some years later I heard that Lily had, in fact, suffered from a mild mental breakdown. The mixture of Tarzan and housework had been too indigestible for her, poor girl. But she recovered and married happily.

This episode illustrates a rather drastic side of my mother's apparently mild and gentle nature. Similarly I can remember her, the first time I made pastry, silently watching me as I rolled and re-rolled it. When, later, Martin made some tart comment on its leathery inedibility, my mother said tranquilly, "I thought it would probably turn out very tough if you rolled it so much. But I thought that, once you knew that, you would never make tough pastry again."

My mother had an immense notion of people's right to learn their own lessons, make their own mistakes. Her tact was exquisite; when teaching one some operation which she had done a thousand times, she would say, diffidently, "I *think* you might find it easier if you did it *this* way . . . ." When I had a spell as a Little Helpful at the age of ten and, without being requested, filled hot-water bottles and stuck them in beds, she remarked mildly, "I think you might find a hot-water-bottle makes a more *comfortable* companion if you bend it so as to let out the air before putting in the stopper . . . ."

The winters in brick-floored Farrs were arctic. Heat consisted of an iron stove called an Ideal Boiler, which burned anthracite and heated a tank of water; I used to huddle against the tank and wrap my chilblained fingers round the hot pipes. I suffered from excruciating chilblains on fingers and toes every winter until I went to boarding school. There were other coal-burning stoves in the dining room and Martin's study, but they were seldom lit; lack of money I suppose. Towards teatime the sitting room fire, in an open brick hearth, would be laid and lit by Martin. The Persian tabby cat, whose real name was Teglees, but who was addressed by everybody as Pussy, used to spend the mornings crouching on this brick hearth, absorbing the residual warmth from yesterday's fire. I wrote a poem about this habit.

In winter I did lessons with my mother as close to the Ideal Boiler as we could huddle. She used to go out and warm herself by chopping wood. She would come in with a bruised face from flying kindling. On her bike she took corners with such carefree abandon that she often came back with cuts and abrasions. Her nature combined reckless energy with meticulous care and delicacy in such arts as embroidery, knitting, tatting, dressmaking. She was continuously creative and always had some project in hand; she gave lectures, made preserves, sketched, made clothes, worked in the garden (when Martin would let her; he said she was too rash and hasty to be let loose among his more cherished plants); the only thing she didn't do was write books. "I could, if I wanted; there's nothing to it," she asserted. But after her death, my sister and I found the beginning of a novel, written in her thirties, about life in South Yarmouth, which, regretfully, we agreed, would not have succeeded; she had not grasped the mechanics of storytelling. I am sure she would have done so if she had applied herself; but she had other, more pressing concerns. Her criticisms of other people's work were extremely shrewd, and more temperate than those of Martin, who could be witheringly dry.

My stepfather's opinions occupied a very distinct place in my early life; I was conscious all the time of living by a double standard, his and mine. I knew that he thought some of my favourite reading—the poetry of Walter de la Mare, Alfred Noyes, Kipling—sentimental, crude, or vulgar. Martin would sometimes walk through a room where my mother and I were reading aloud, and let fall some light, totally blighting comment:

"'And when I crumble, who will remember
That lady of the West Country?'
Crumble! What an extraordinarily silly word to choose!"

Other, perhaps more deserving targets—*Peter Pan, Winnie the Pooh, When We Were Very Young,* a book of John Drinkwater's poems for the young called *All about Me*—also came in for his broadsides. A lot of the books I adored, the Katy books, *Little Women, A Girl of the Limberlost,* he had luckily never opened; full well can I imagine the kind of things he would say about them. I myself lived in a dream world, peopled with characters out of my favorite books; I would never have mentioned it to anybody and was vaguely aware of the huge gulf between it and Martin's realities. Even now in my mind's ear I can hear his voice as I enjoy some best-seller—"Surely this must have been written by an extraordinarily silly young woman?" Silly was his most condemnatory adjective and the term young woman, as used by him and my mother, had a decidedly pejorative ring.

When I was seven or eight my own father came back into my life again. Like my elder siblings, I began to go and visit him and Clarissa in Jeake's House, for a week or so, two or three times a year. I loved these trips back into the nostalgic past but found it hard getting onto conversational terms with Conrad; we had been parted too long, all my life really. It was easier when John and Jane were there. But I developed a great romantic devotion to Conrad and used to invent tales of how he and Jessie made up their differences and came together again. Conrad encouraged my poetry writing and gave me books to read—Vachel Lindsay, Fitz-James O'Brien—and books by infant prodigies like Daisy Ashford.

It had been decided that I should go to boarding school at age twelve, when Jane would be at university. Determined that I should not suffer as she had, Jane looked about and chose a school for me in Oxford where, as she was at Somerville College, she would be able to visit me and see that I was all right. Then Conrad suggested that, so as to mitigate the shock of being plunged into boarding school after hardly having had the chance to meet any other children, I should come to Rye for a summer, live with him

Jane, Jessie, Joan, John, and David in the garden at Farrs, 1935.

and Clarissa, and go to a small day school round the corner. This was agreed and I went.

If Conrad's idea had also been that he and I should get to know one another better, it did not work out; he was on the brink of divorce from Clarissa, they had frequent savage quarrels, and a lot of the time he was not even in Rye. Where was he? I don't know. Meanwhile I was moderately happy at the cranky little school where there were only ten pupils, only one of them my age, a boy called Christopher, the rest much younger. With Christopher I roamed about Rye and flew windup airplanes. Clarissa, despite her rather miserable situation, was very nice to me. In August Conrad went off to America where he met and fell in love with Mary Hoover, who became his third wife; in September I went to boarding school in Oxford. My mother had invited the headmistress, Margaret Lee, to stay beforehand, and also came up and spent a couple of nights at Miss Lee's house in Oxford to "settle me in." I am not sure whether her presence on the fringe of school life for those two days helped, or made the agony more severe. I can remember her taking me for a walk down into Christ Church quad and telling me that she had always considered me her special child. Even then I understood this to mean, not that she loved me more than the others—she was always scrupulously fair—but that, since I had had so little attention from Conrad, she was resolved to perform the part of father and mother both. Thinking this over later I concluded that Conrad had neither intended nor been

Jessie with son David and husband Martin Armstrong, 1941.

pleased at my birth, which so soon preceded the breakup of their marriage. My rather cursory christening to match the other two—as if we were a batch of factory products—reinforced this view. But when I was in my forties and he in his seventies, Conrad and I became very close.

Back to my initiation at school. Severe the agony certainly was. The contrast between our small, orderly, quiet house, filled with ancient, beautiful objects and civilised practices—and this noisy, bare, crowded, ugly barrack, and its bleak, trampled garden, both filled with girls in uniform, came as an inconceivable shock. Bells clanged, buzzers roared, one was perpetually being hustled, in a clattering throng, up and down steep flights of lino-covered stairs, along dark passages, heaven only knew where. On my arrival at Wychwood School at age twelve I was one of the tallest in my class, but I stopped growing at that point and never increased another centimeter. School uniform, too, was an intolerable constraint. After the freedom and comfort of home clothes—socks, shirts, skirts, shorts, sweaters—suddenly one had to plod about in layers and layers of thick woollen garments: things called combinations, plus two pairs of woollen knickers, plus vest, plus wool blouse, woollen stockings, suspender belt, a cripplingly heavy garment of serge called a gym tunic, all pleats, and over that a school blazer. Still I did stop having chilblains. There was a velour hat for weekday wear, and a felt hat for Sundays; there were Panama hats for summer, lacrosse boots, tennis shoes, netball shoes, indoor shoes, outdoor shoes, dancing shoes, galoshes, and endless sports equipment. All that must have cost my mother a pretty

penny; she begged me to be economical at school, and for years I never dared have a bun at breaktime.

Just the change from country to town made my spirit wither inside me. At Farrs nobody questioned one's movements; since the age of six I had roamed for miles, unescorted, all over the grassy landscape. Here we were not allowed outside the school gate. Not that I wanted to go: the roaring Banbury Road, outside, seemed to me hideous, the Oxford parks, where we were taken for walks, two and two, in crocodile, were bare, muddy deserts, utterly unlike the country they were supposed to imitate. Oxford, for the first two years I lived there, confirmed my lifelong hatred of cities. It was a long time before I began to appreciate its beauty.

As for school . . . after a couple of terms I began to realize what it had to offer. I always, always hated and dreaded having to go back at the start of each term; always longed for home, where I now felt no more than a visitor, always pined for its peace, beauty, and civilization. But school stirred up a strong competitive spirit (inherited straight from my mother, who was a tremendous passer of exams); in no time I was devoting all my energy to getting the highest marks in class, getting parts in school plays, getting poems into the school magazine, being elected Form Representative, and so on. Wychwood was a self-governing school to some degree (not where health, manners, or curriculum were concerned); we held a lot of meetings and did a lot of voting, which has given me a profound dislike of the committee system ever since.

Looking back I can see that Wychwood was, as my sister had judged, a very kindly school. The classes were small, the teaching pretty good, particularly that of English, the staff were intelligent and friendly; but I came there too late. I had had those seven years of living on my own, with adults, in a gracious environment; I could never be reconciled to the world of school. My reports said that I was self-centered, went my own way, was antisocial; as I got higher up the school they began to be critical of my friendships. I had a friend called Evelyn, two years older, two forms higher; she was witty, intelligent, entertaining; I liked her because she reminded me of home. Authority disapproved of this friendship because of the age gap, because we used to break rules and go off to wander about the Oxford colleges, whose beauty we had just noticed. At Wychwood there was a tradition of "pashes," younger girls having raves on older ones, or on the staff; there was nothing of this in my relations with Evelyn, we simply enjoyed each other's conversation and liked walking about Oxford. Our particular enemy was the games mistress (neither of us showed the least aptitude for any form of athletics); later there was a lesbian scandal and that same games mistress left abruptly; it is to be presumed that she had viewed our friendship from her own angle. Evelyn, being older, left two years before I did, and I missed her badly. Then World War II threw the school into disruption; half the staff left, the numbers dwindled, presently the school went bankrupt and had to amalgamate with a bigger school, the Oxford High School. I had just taken the School Certificate examination (what would now be called O-Levels) in eight subjects and done well, getting five distinctions (over 80 percent) and three credits (over 60 percent); but the sudden amalgamation with a larger school completely threw me; I developed a swollen gland in my neck which would not respond to treatment, spent a term in bed, had two operations, and my schoolwork went to pieces. Refusing to attend classes at the larger school, I worked at Wychwood, mostly on my own, tried for Oxford Entrance, failed (shaming my brother and sister who had sailed through and won scholarships), and declared that I wanted to leave school and become a Land Girl. I was now seventeen.

School was glad for me to leave, as I had become a dissident element, but my father, now back in America (Rye, only two miles from the coast, had been declared a restricted area where foreigners were not allowed, even if they owned houses there), wrote expressing his extreme disapproval of such a nonintellectual career. So did Jane, now doing a Master's at Radcliffe. So instead I applied for a job in the British Broadcasting Corporation, having a vague inflated notion that there I might find some interesting niche putting poetry magazines together or becoming a studio manager.

What I really wanted was to marry a rich man who would support me in the country while I wrote books.

The BBC were impressed by my school certificate marks and took me on. But the job they gave me was a letdown. By now it was 1941, the middle of the blitz. Their filing system had been evacuated from London to a mansion in the Thames valley near Reading. Here dwelt thirty women, all ages and classes, sleeping in bunks, filing and indexing the corporation's written matter, scripts and letters, which arrived daily in sacks. My first duties were to

Joan Aiken and Ron Brown, 1945.

open the mail, cycle to the post office four miles distant for more stamps, and (because of the national paper shortage) rule lines on the back of used index cards, so that they could be used again. Life at this hostel (it was called Great Oaks and had been built by the millionaire manufacturer of H. P. Sauce) was almost as rude a shock as the initial arrival at Wychwood. I learned a bit of Spanish and Portuguese, in order to file letters in those languages, but, after nine months, saw that this job would lead nowhere. So I enrolled in a secretarial school and did a course of typing and Pitman shorthand. The course had some fancy touches too: bookkeeping and journalism. None of that, except the typing, has been the least use to me, whereas in the BBC, I had at least learned how to cross-reference. The principal of my secretarial school was a Christian Scientist; when I had appendicitis she sat by my bedside and told me that if I thought hard enough, the condition would go away. I can't have, because it didn't; I had to have the appendix removed.

The secretarial college found me a job in the Ministry of Information. It would have been quite an interesting job, but I found that I would be working as assistant to the mother of one of my school friends. This lady was a very formidable character with a vitriolic tongue; I had seen her in devastating action on excursions from school and did not look forward to working for her; so I politely declined the

Living in the bus, 1952: from left, Joan, Liz, John, and Ron.

job and got myself in trouble with my secretarial college, who washed their hands of me despite my 130 wpm shorthand. But a friend was working in the newly formed United Nations Information Office (U.N.I.O.), an offshoot of the Ministry of Information, and she told me of a job going there, in the library. It was extremely well paid, by the standards of those days—£4.10 a week! A female official at the Labor Exchange, where I had to register myself and my employment, was scandalized that a girl of nineteen should be so lavishly paid. I shared a flat in Earls Court with two friends and began paid employment, in a bomb-damaged house on the corner of Russell Square. The house got damaged some more during the next three years; the main London blitz was now over, but there were stray raids, and the V-1s and V-2s, which made a lot of noise, interrupted work, and did a fair amount of damage. A V-1 fell in Russell Square, blowing all the leaves off the trees, breaking the office windows, and messing up my filing system.

Of course I hated living in a city, hated London—yet, looking back, how pleasant it was! The streets were almost bare of traffic. No high-rise buildings had gone up—the trend was the other way; they were toppling down. The blitz spirit was still in being, citizens were friendly to one another. I was working in a group of about fifteen intelligent and interesting people, all nationalities. My two immediate seniors were Irish and Czech. There was a democratic and friendly spirit in the office, and we had a lot of jokes about the United Nations. The Press Officer, Ron Brown, made up a theme song for us:

For news of the Thirty-five Nations
Inter-allied of course,
And Russo-Polish relations,
Inter-allied of course....

It went to a jingly French tune, "ça, c'est bien entendu," from one of the French films that used to find their way to London, and we used to sing it when there was particular friction between the Russian and Polish members of our governing committee. For London, then, was the dwelling place of half the exiled governments of Europe, and some were *ancien régime* while others were *nouveau;* it could at times be awkward. Two lots of Greeks, two lots of Poles, two lots of French....

What about my writing, all this time? Well, I had bought a typewriter from a bookseller, Bob Chris, whose tiny shop off the Charing Cross Road, into which I wandered one day, was the most amazing salon; at different times I met there Professor Joad, the philosopher; Dannie Abse, the poet; David Piper, who later became head of the Victoria and Albert Museum; Ruthven Todd; Pamela Hansford Johnson; not to mention my brother John. Half literary London were Bob's friends, if not customers; he seldom seemed to sell a book.

Bob encouraged me to keep writing. I had sold some children's stories to the BBC "Children's Hour," a radio programme, inspired by the example of my stepfather. Martin, a serious adult writer, had been invited to do something for "Children's Hour," and produced a family saga, *Said the Cat to the Dog,* which was immensely successful, repeated over and over, and earned him far more than any of his novels. Impressed by this, I too sent the BBC some stories, a couple of which they took. I had also had a couple of poems accepted, two years before, while still at school, by a prestigious little magazine, *Abinger Chronicle,* run by E. M. Forster, Sylvia Sprigge, and Max Beerbohm. They printed my poems but never paid me, which gave me the idea that poetry was not a remunerative occupation. However I did keep sending them to the *New Statesman,* who took one but never used it.

While working at U.N.I.O., I fell in love with its Press Officer, the aforementioned Ron Brown, and married him in 1945 at Russell Square registrar's office. He was fourteen years older, had been married before and divorced, had had various jobs in journalism, was at Reuter before he came to U.N.I.O. He was handsome, six-foot tall, a Marxist, full of charm and cheer, a tremendous arguer, and could be a trial in an office, as he was convinced that he knew the best way to do everything. To be fair: he often did know the best way to do jobs, and his two children have taken after him in this respect. All three are, or were, models of capability around the house or garden; shelves go up, curtains are made and hung, everything works. But nonetheless, Ron was continually at odds with his superiors, and, soon after we were married he shook the dust of U.N.I.O off his feet and went, first to *The Times,* then to Associated Press, where he stayed for seven years, engaged in constant bloody battles with the head of his department. Nonetheless he had dozens of good friends and was a lot of fun, one of those husbands who can take care of everything.

"Don't you worry about me," he used to say. "Nothing ever happens to me." He was a very heavy smoker: fifty a day.

Meanwhile I had a miscarriage, quite a bad one, malnutrition from World War II, and was told: no children for at least four years. I was promoted, by a reshuffle at the U.N. office, to Librarian, wrote a number of short stories, not very good ones, and we moved out of London to Lewes in Sussex (midway between Rye and Sutton; Martin and Jessie used to meet there for lunch before they were married). Ron thought country air would do me good. Lewes is quite a large town, bigger than Rye, but country is easily accessible from it. It is a handsome town, too, on a hill with a castle, just across the road from our flat in the High Street, a racecourse, a jail, grassy Downs all round, and the sea only eight miles off down a valley viewed from our windows. It was a fine place to live; our only problem was that we seldom met, as both of us were still working in London, Ron often on night shifts at his news agency, so our life consisted of leaping on and off trains and leaving notes for each other—Feed cat, fish on shelf. The first winter we were there, 1947, was exceptionally severe; trains kept getting derailed or stuck in snowdrifts and taking five hours on circuitous routes to do the trip to London which should have taken one hour and a bit.

I loved Lewes. It started me off writing, and the town formed the scene for a number of my short stories, *The People in the Castle, More Than You Bargained For, Belle of the Ball, The Ghostly Governess,* and a novel, *Foul Matter.*

By now, though still determined to write serious adult novels, I had fallen into the habit of producing quite a few children's stories, mostly fantastic. These are a tremendous pleasure to write—perhaps the most exhilarating among all the forms of fiction that I practice. They must be written in one session, with one idea, mood, voice; the process is fairly close to poetry. As well as these I wrote a nasty satirical story called *The Dreamers,* about a man who boiled up his wife in a pressure cooker, which was accepted by *The New Statesman.* This was very exciting; the first piece of work I had sold to a serious periodical. The *N.S.* didn't print the story for about three years, which taught me some of the patience and resignation so necessary to a writer. When they did print it, a firm of literary agents, Pearn Pollinger and Higham, got in touch with me and offered to take me on. Jean LeRoy handled their serial market; Paul Scott (author of *The Jewel in the Crown*) handled novels.

Ron's hours at the news agency worsened, and the trains to and from Lewes proved inadequate to his needs. So, sadly, after the birth of our son John Sebastian, we moved to the village of Chipstead in Kent, closer to London.

It had always been Ron's ambition to live beside a stream, or river, and in Kent he found a large wild piece of land, part of a park which had been divided, with an indubitable brook at its far end. But would we be allowed to build a house on it? The land was scheduled as Green Belt around London, not for building development. Ron acquired a lawyer who thought he could find a loophole in the local application of this, and managed to battle successfully against the interdiction. Meanwhile, having bought the land, we squatted on it in an old single-decker bus which we converted into a cosy dwelling. It had three rooms, kitchen, nursery, and living room. Water and electricity were laid on, and the loo was in the driver's cab. Ron won his case against the Town and Country Planning Act, and we built our house. Now, if I ever revisit Chipstead, which I do as seldom as possible, I feel drowned in guilt, because our house was the opening end of the wedge. What used to present, in 1950, at least the

appearance of a rural community is now a mass of houses, cheek by jowl, intersected by motorways. The inhabitants really had cause to hate us.

I was never happy at Chipstead, though the house we built was pleasant enough. The bit of land, two acres, was too wild for me to manage, and had had its topsoil removed, not once but twice, by the shark who sold it to us; nothing would grow on it but thistles. There was no real country round about; one could not walk for the land all belonged to Government departments guarded by barbed wire. My second child, Elizabeth Delano, was born while we were still in the bus; but the affronted local authorities insisted on my going into hospital for the birth. A bus was not considered hygienic. I wrote an article about our life in it for the magazine *Housewife.*

Now our life began to deteriorate. Ron had really exhausted himself, racing about on his bike, appealing at local courts, interviewing builders, lawyers, architects. His temper worsened, he became morose. We had spent a lot of money and found it hard to keep abreast of bills; all my thoughts were concentrated on how to earn money by writing. I sent stories to women's magazines, but they all came back. I had, however, amassed enough children's stories to offer as a collection. I tried them first on Faber, who refused but made encouraging noises; then I tried Jonathan Cape, who took them. That was my first book, *All You've Ever Wanted,* published in 1953. (I had written a full-length book, *The Kingdom and the Cave,* when I was seventeen, reading it aloud in daily instalments to my younger brother David. It was heavily influenced by John Masefield's *The Midnight Folk.* I typed out one copy and sent it to a literary competition. I assumed it didn't win, as I never heard any more, and never had my copy back. That taught me always to keep a carbon copy.)

Encouraged by the publication of *AYEW,* I thought I would write a children's novel. I had an idea for one, a kind of spoof melodrama. I bought a kitchen table and typed two chapters in a corner of our bedroom as I had no study. I

Ron and Joan with John and Liz, Milltown, 1954.

thought I would call the book *Bonnie Green.* I was full of excitement about it.

Now Ron's chest pains and bad temper were found to have a physical cause: tuberculosis. His office gave him six weeks' sick leave, a small amount of severance pay, and the sack. There we were, fairly destitute, with children aged two and six months. My Aunt Grace in Suffolk, my mother's youngest sister, who had married an Englishman, Oswald Sitwell, suggested that I come and housekeep for Oswald while she returned to Canada to superintend the birth of a grandchild. We could rent our house and get some income for it. Ron, who was prescribed six months' bed rest, could take it just as easily in my uncle's roomy Suffolk farmhouse. So that is what we did.

While living in Suffolk I wrote enough stories for another collection. "I bet you can't write a story every day for a week," said Ron, who was enthusiastic and proud of my writing. He lost his bet. Also I fished out *The Kingdom and the Cave* and laboriously revised and retyped it. Cape turned it down, but accepted my second batch of stories, *More Than You Bargained For.*

Winter in Suffolk seemed to do Ron good; he recovered and it was decided that we should move to the West Country, run a guest house, which I could do while writing, and Ron would raise pigs. He had been conducting a long and bitter correspondence with his office, arbitrated by the National Union of Journalists, who managed, in the end, to wring a larger amount of severance pay from A.P. With that, and the proceeds from selling the house in Kent, we had enough to buy a property in Cornwall where the climate was benign and tourists plentiful.

Ron went ahead, stayed with friends of mine, scouted around, and found a dream place. This time it really was a dream place: Milltown, a Georgian farmhouse, white with slate roof, a mill building, barns, pigsties, two orchards full of daffodils, four meadows, a row of cypresses and three ruined cottages—all for so small a sum that it makes me wring my hands when I think of it now. There was a palm tree in the garden, white azaleas that smelt of honey, and

Liz and John at the Hermitage, 1977.

not one but three brooks. It would be perfect for the children, secluded in its own deep little valley. We were given a breeding sow by a Hungarian friend, Oswald gave me fifty hens, and I built a yard for them.

Some improvements were necessary before we could run Milltown as a guest house; Ron, throwing off all signs of illness, raced about, organizing. We put in an efficient cooker, hot water system, brought down our furniture, and started having guests, which was simple: we advertised in *The New Statesman* and they came flocking. The summer passed in a flash.

Two people we knew had, unexpectedly, moved down to Cornwall when we did. We had not known them long. One was a journalist, Elsie Bourke, who had edited a magazine called *Woman and Home*; the other, her elderly friend Muriel Tuck, a retired headmistress. They had been our neighbors in Kent, while Elsie was editing her magazine; then, for some mysterious reason, she threw up her job, went to Australia, came back again, and when we moved west we found them already settled in Cornwall about five miles from us. Elsie was in her forties, Muriel in her sixties. They bought a smallholding, cows, hens, ducks, and were learning, very efficiently, considering their former urban existence, how to tackle this new life. Often they came over to help me with my garden, and, as well as gardening advice, Elsie gave me a lot of practical counsel on writing female fiction. It was no use in the world, she said, my trying to write sentimental women's- magazine stories; I would never bring one off in a million years; I should rather aim at suspense or mystery fiction. With her encouragement I began a prototype gothic called *House of Shadows.* This was before the spate of gothics hit the market in the '50s and '60s; my story had the basic *Jane Eyre* plot: young governess arrives at a mansion to care for little girl who has a Rochester-type father and mad mother. I also, with Elsie's encouragement, wrote some semi-fantastic stories, satirical, inspired by our Cornish neighbours who were upper-crust eccentrics of a particularly picturesque and wild variety. Jean LeRoy, my new agent, sold some of these to the short story magazine *Argosy,* which belonged to the same group, Amalgamated Press, who owned Elsie's *Woman and Home.* This turned out to be lucky for me since, after a year in Cornwall, Ron's health deteriorated abruptly. The guest house and pig breeding were now established, nothing challenged him, and he needed a challenge to keep going. A Londoner born, he grew miserably bored with country life, and all his ailments assaulted him at once. He was found to have lung cancer and a condition of muscular dystrophy, probably latent from childhood, aggravated by the huge doses of streptomycin taken for the TB. He went into a London hospital and died in 1955.

I had to leave Cornwall and find some way of supporting myself and the two children aged three and five. Elsie Bourke wrote me a letter of introduction to the director of Amalgamated Press; I went for an interview and was offered a trial period on *Argosy.* They took me on, and I soon settled into a small but congenial office where everybody did a bit of everything. Work was the only consolation in that bad time.

White Hart as a pub, about 1930.

Reading was one of our main tasks. Bales of manuscripts arrived daily, unsolicited ones besides those sent from agents and publishers. We read dozens a day. Jean Malcolm, the formidably efficient Chief Sub, gave me a thorough editorial training, teaching me far more than I'd learned at school about the niceties of grammar, punctuation, spelling, and style. The salary was low, but one could augment it by contributions to the magazine: poems, quizzes, small anthology features, and in my case stories—I sold them about twenty-five while I was on the staff, having worked out the necessary combination of elements—exotic background, touch of sex, twist ending, touch of humour if possible—that would make a story acceptable. I was also set to write an editorial column and allowed to interview contributors to the magazine such as H. E. Bates, Geoffrey Household, Ray Bradbury, Paul Gallico, which gave me new insights into the different ways that writers worked.

I was living in a one-room flat in Wimbledon and my children were living with an ex-sister-in-law who ran a small school in south London for children with parents abroad; I had them at weekends. This was a miserable situation for all of us and I was resolved to change it as soon as I could scrape up enough money to buy a dwelling—Ron had left me with nothing but debts. So I worked like a beaver, selling stories to *John Bull, Housewife, Vogue,* any magazine that would take fiction other than the woman's sob-type. Jean LeRoy encouraged me to write more and more stories. But I began to feel this was an uneconomic use of time; I wanted to write longer pieces of fiction that would sell for larger sums, and did

manage to sell a couple of 30,000-word suspense stories to a monthly, *Everywoman,* which used them serially. These I later expanded into mystery novels, *The Silence of Herondale* and *Died on a Rainy Sunday.*

The work on *Argosy* was of infinite value to me, and I shall always be grateful to the editor-in-chief, D. M. Sutherland, whose shrewd editorial sense taught me a terrific amount about how to improve my work, as well as other people's. One of the more eccentric tasks I was given consisted of writing stories to accompany left-over glossy illustrations bought by our sister magazine *Woman's Journal* from American periodicals such as *Redbook* or *Saturday Evening Post* and then, for one reason or another, not used. One of these illustrations—two people on a beach, a cat, an oil painting stimulated me to a 30,000-word effort which W. J. turned down, but I later enlarged it into my little mystery *Night Fall,* which won a Mystery Writers of America Edgar for a teenage mystery in 1971.

After four years on *Argosy* I was offered free accommodation for myself and children in Sussex in the beautiful farmhouse of Martin's brother Basil Armstrong, in return for a bit of driving. The children could go to the village school and we'd be together, and I would risk free-lancing. My bosses at *Argosy* told me I was mad, and gave me the chance of commuting up and down for a three-day week at the same pay I was getting. I began doing this, cramming a week's work into the three days and doing my own writing at home. But the sharing plan with Basil and his wife didn't work out; his health deteriorated, they decided they must move to a smaller house in a town. I had to look, fast, for accommodation for me and the kids, found a house in Petworth unbelievably cheap at £1800—it had been empty for six years and was semi-derelict—borrowed £300 from my mother for the deposit, got a huge mortgage from Barclays Bank, and moved in, with £50 worth of junk furniture from auction sales. That was a happy day: the children rushed about hammering in nails to hang their clothes on, and I for the first time actually had a study, a room to be devoted to nothing but writing. White Hart House, a Tudor ex-pub, was like a rabbit warren inside, with rooms leading out of other rooms, panelled downstairs, sloping ceilings and low doorways above; it was a happy, eccentric dwelling, Jeake's House in miniature, a wonderful house for writing; we stayed in it twenty years and I must have written nearly forty books there. My mother and Martin, still at Farrs, were only five miles off; lacking a father, the children would at least have grandparents close at hand.

One of the first things I did at White Hart was to fish out those two chapters of *Bonnie Green* which I had begun in Chipstead seven years before, and finish the book. It almost wrote itself, I picked up the mood and voice again so speedily.

While in London I had revised, yet again, the book I had written at seventeen, *The Kingdom and the Cave,* and it had been published by Abelard-Schuman. My agents sent them the new one; they accepted it, but were doubtful about it: too frightening, they thought. Would I make it milder, take out some of the wolves? No, I wouldn't. Terrified, wondering if I was mad, I asked David Bolt, who now handled novels at Pearn Pollinger and Higham, to withdraw it and send it somewhere else. He said he would. A year went by. I finally plucked up courage to ask what had happened to my book? Apologetically he confessed that he had forgotten all about it. It was on his office windowsill under a lot of stuff. He would send it to a publisher at once; whom did I suggest? I suggested Cape, who had published my two collections of stories. Within two weeks I had a lovely letter from Michael Howard at Cape. They saw that the book was meant to be funny; they wanted to publish it. But the title—could I think of something more exciting? So *The Wolves of Willoughby Chase* was retitled. It did moderately well in England, then much better in America, where a wonderful review in *Time* magazine helped sales.

Two years after the move to White Hart I left *Argosy*—though continuing to read and edit for them at home—and worked for a year as a copywriter at J. Walter Thompson's London office. The work there was fun and well paid, but it meant leaving home at 7:30 A.M. and not returning till 8:30 P.M.; I hardly saw the children, and my daughter, aged eight or nine, was showing signs of deprivation. For the second time I decided to leave office work and write full time, and this time I brought it off. The first thing I wrote was a sequel to *The Wolves—Black Hearts in Battersea.* That, too, was wonderful fun to write. I wanted it to be like *The Wolves* only more so—more wolves, a kidnapping, a long-lost heir, underworld nineteenth-century London, a bomb plot, a tragic death—all the ingredients I hadn't managed to cram into the previous book. Instead of taking seven years, it took seven months— I wrote it all in one happy whizz. It and *The Wolves* were set in an imaginary historical period, the reign of James III of England, which I have used intermittently ever since. I did use, however, a lot of real historical detail, and after I

had accumulated quite an amount of research material I began writing adult historical fiction of a more serious kind.

After *Black Hearts* I followed a more or less instinctive pattern of alternating juvenile and adult books—with a kind of cementing mix of short stories in between and all around; these ultimately result in short-story collections when enough of a particular kind have accrued to form a book.

My adult books were thrillers at first. Isabelle Taylor, the mystery editor at Doubleday (who had published *Wolves* and *Black Hearts*), wrote asking if I had any adult material; I showed her my *Everywoman* stories, and it was her help and advice that encouraged me to expand them into books.

Jean LeRoy, my first agent, was immensely helpful to me when I was getting started, in persuading me to write short stories and finding markets for them; at that time I had neither the time nor the confidence to produce anything longer, though I did begin a novel which later turned into *The Ribs of Death* (in the U.S. *The Crystal Crow*). Jean, a forceful and dominating character, told me sternly, over and over again, that I had no talent at all for the novel form, that I would never produce one, but that I could write a classic short story and should stick to that genre. *The Wolves of Willoughby* she dismissed as clever pastiche, not likely to lead anywhere. Instinctively I began to rebel against this didactic attitude and to wish for a different mentor. In 1962 I went to the U.S. for the first time, with the children, to visit Conrad, who now had a house on Cape Cod. He paid our fares for a six-week visit. *Wolves* was about to come out there, and we went to New York to meet the Doubleday children's editor, lovely Peggy Lesser. Since Pearn Pollinger and Higham's connecting agency in New York, Harold Ober, had done nothing for me, Conrad had suggested that I should switch to his agents, Brandt and Brandt; so I met Charles Schlessiger at Brandt, and thus began a lifelong friendship. Charles is so enthusiastic, participatory, helpful, untiring, that I can't imagine a writing life without him. No one could possibly ask for a more concerned and caring agent. In England, therefore, I switched to Brandt's connecting agency, A. M. Heath.

On the whole, in my working life as writer, I have not had the intense creative relationship with any editor that some writers achieve. During twenty-five-odd years I have now passed through the hands of numerous editors at my four main publishers, Cape, Gollancz, Doubleday, and Delacorte Press; most of these have been kind, helpful, reasonable; many—Larry Ashmead, George Nicholson, Olga Litowinsky, Carolyn Blakemore—have turned into long-standing friends; but, by and large, they have confined themselves to working on what I produce, and not pointing out further possibilities. Perhaps I am resistant to that. Though I did miss Isabelle and Larry when they left Doubleday. Lately I have had some juvenile books published by Charlotte Zolotow, for Harper, and am impressed by Charlotte's perceptive and highly creative attitude—not surprising since she is a fine author in her own right. I look forward with excitement to this relationship.

Meanwhile my children (to whom at first I read books as they were written) grew up and left home. I moved to a house, still in Petworth, with fewer, larger rooms and a larger garden: The Hermitage. It is slightly haunted but I have not seen the ghost. I have written a trilogy of books about it—*The Smile of the Stranger, The Weeping Ash, The Girl from Paris.*

In the mid '70s I married an American, Julius Goldstein, a painter, and now spend a portion of the year in his hometown, Manhattan. This has inevitably affected my writing life, made me more aware of the American literary scene, though not to the point of feeling confident enough, yet, to lay any fictional work in America. Manhattan itself I love—its bookstores, coffee shops, movie houses—in many ways I feel more at home there than in London, which is invested with too many sad associations.

Every writer needs a sounding-board reader. My sister and I perform this function for each other. We read each other's books in manuscript, first draft, and vigorously criticize. I find this an essential stage of the process: comment by a detached critic, assessment by a fresh eye. One may become so involved in writing that obvious faults or needless complications pass unnoticed. Having this built-in sisterly critic is why, I suppose, I have not felt the need for a highly creative editor. Of course when my mother and Martin and Conrad were still alive, first copies of Jane's and my books went automatically to them and we relished their comments. In the case of Martin and Conrad these were often acutely critical—though Conrad could be heart-warmingly enthusiastic too. Our mother was critical, too, shrewdly so, but subjective; she inevitably saw herself as any villainess depicted. But her pride in having two novelist daughters was a great and touching pleasure.

With over sixty books listed on the British Public Lending Right register, I feel I have achieved my ambition to be a professional writer. I know that my books vary. Some I am proud of; some are mere jobs of work, money-earners; a couple now fill me with slight embarrassment. Which do I love best? A pair of books with Spanish settings—*Go Saddle the Sea* and *Bridle the Wind.* Sometimes when you write a book you can feel it take off and lift away from you into unexplored regions—I felt those two did that. With short stories this experience is much more frequent; so, if I am remembered in future times, I think it more likely that it may be for some of those, "Crusader's Toby," or "The Man Who Pinched God's Letter," or "More Than You Bargained For."

More than I bargain for, really.

(c) Joan Aiken Enterprises Ltd., 1985

Postscript

What has happened to me since I wrote the last lines above?

Well, principally, books.

I added a third part to the pair *Go Saddle the Sea* and *Bridle the Wind,* and turned them into a trilogy with *The Teeth of the Gale*—to acquire background for which Julius and I spent an entertaining period with an English painting colony in a wonderful little Spanish town, Berdun, in Aragon on the south slopes of the Pyrenees.

Then I fell into writing Jane Austen follow-ups. To beguile the languish waiting periods, while I was writing a series of small historical TV plays for the British Broadcasting Corporation Schools programmes, about British emigration to Virginia in the sixteenth to eighteenth centuries—each of my pieces had to be okayed by a committee and the process was a mighty slow one—I had diverted myself by lightheartedly producing a Jane Austen fantasia, a sequel to *Mansfield Park.* It was called *Mansfield Revisted.* After it had come out I was interviewed by a south of England television programme, in Chawton Cottage, and actually allowed to sit in Jane Austen's chair, at her desk, which was an unforgettable experience. On that visit to the cottage I discovered that Austen's great-niece, Mrs. Frances Brown, had already done sequels to all the books; her Mansfield plot was remarkably similar to mine. My book did moderately well and I loved the challenge—more like an elegant game, really—of writing a story exactly to Austen's specification, with strict rules governing location, number of characters, and plot. I worship Austen's novels and continually re-read them, so it has been a delight to have this excuse for reentering her world. Since *Mansfield Revisited* I have written five more Austen spinoffs: *Jane Fairfax,* following the Emma story from a parallel point; *Eliza's Daughter,* following the fortunes of Willoughby's illegitimate daughter, briefly alluded to in *Sense and Sensibility; Emma Watson,* taking up the thread of Austen's own unfinished novel, *The Watsons; The Youngest Miss Ward,* inventing an imaginary fourth sister for the trio of ladies in Mansfield Park who become Lady Bertram, Mrs. Norris and Mrs.

Julius Goldstein, about age thirty.

Price; and my latest (at the time of writing), *Lady Catherine's Necklace,* a frivolous follow-up to *Pride and Prejudice.* Critics have scolded me for trespassing on the hallowed Austen territory, but I do not believe that Jane herself would disapprove; she was broad-minded and generous; and it is such a terrible deprivation, to her and the world, that she died after having produced only six books, that any attempt to set foot in her territory seems to me forgivable. (I am currently thinking about the family of slightly lower-class connections of the Musgroves, the Hayters, mentioned once or twice in *Persuasion;* I believe there might be an interesting story attached to them).

My brother John died in 1990. That was an unassuageable grief, for he was wonderful company— always—and a most appreciative and critical reader of my work. It was his persuasion that started me on a sequel to *Go Saddle the Sea;* without John's urging I would have left Felix, the hero, forever on his journey back to Spain. In memory of John I wrote a three-part ghost story, *The Haunting of Lamb House,* set in Rye, England, where I was born, and where John lived the last years of his life. My story was about the house where Henry James lived, just up the hill from Jeake's House, where I was born, and where the Old Master was succeeded by other writers, E. F. Benson, who wrote the Lucia books, and Rumer Godden, both of whom had mysterious ghostly experiences there. (Lamb House now belongs to the National Trust and is open to the public; Jeake's House, which has a plaque commemorating my father, is also open to the public for it has become a B & B.)

The years 1991-93 were enlivened for me by dealings with the British Broadcasting Corporation's children's television. Twenty years earlier I had written a series for a BBC children's TV programme, "Jackanory." This consisted of stories designed to be read aloud daily for a week by an actor, while drawings were shown on a screen. The pictures in my case were done by wonderful Quentin Blake, who has been appointed the first junior laureate of Britain. Now the BBC approached me and said they would like to use my story characters for a live television series in twelve episodes. The main characters were Arabel and Mortimer, personifications of the Ego and the Id, Arabel the sensible, virtuous little girl, and Mortimer, her utterly unbridled and unpredictable raven. The BBC asked me if I would be prepared to write a new twelve-episode script about them, suitable either for live actors or, possibly, puppets. I said that really I had not time for this massive task (I was in the middle of a full-length adult novel, *Morningquest,* at the time) so they suggested that I should outline a plot and they would find a scriptwriter to do the spadework. I suggested my daughter Liz for the job, since she had done work on television with a Theatre-in-Education group. This was agreed, and Liz and I had a most enjoyable couple of years, tossing plots and bits of dialogue and bizarre situations back and forth between us; the first Arabel and Mortimer stories had been written when she was in her late teens, so she was well-acquainted with the characters. The BBC decided on puppets, which were constructed to be faithful presentations of Quentin Blake's crazy illustrations, which exactly portrayed my characters. Liz and I were allowed to be present at rehearsals, so that the script could be altered if necessary. These took place in a huge deserted West London bus depot converted to TV studios. In the end the

series was prolonged to twenty-four episodes and five paperback books, and was hilarious fun all the way.

Another television excitement was the BBC production of *Black Hearts in Battersea* as a serial using live actors. This time I was not involved with the script, and, although it was beautifully done, with lavish period detail, castles, tunnels, shipwrecks and Dickensian London streets, I thought a mistake had been made in over complicating an already involved plot. Still, it was ripsnortingly enjoyable, and the little girl who took the part of Dido Twite was absolutely perfect.

Dido Twite is a character who has pushed herself into a firm place in my life. At the conclusion of *Black Hearts in Battersea* she was intended to come to a tragic end. But this was prevented by a child who wrote to me from America after *Black Hearts* first came out over there. "Dido should *not* have drowned," she wrote to me, "it was *wrong* that she should die, for she was a *good* character." I could not reply to this touching letter for the American publishers, who forwarded the letter, had omitted to include the envelope which had the address on it. What could I do to make amends? I wrote *Night Birds on Nantucket,* in which Dido was rescued from the sea. (It also gave me an excuse to take a trip to Nantucket while visiting my father on Cape Cod.) Since then, Dido has roamed the world in more books, *The Stolen Lake, The Cuckoo Tree, Dido and Pa.* At one point I decided that she was growing too old to figure

Joan Aiken in America, 1972, taken by friend Barbara Sproul.

in such helter-skelter stories (after Simon had proposed to her and she had turned him down) so I introduced her younger sister, Is, who had a couple of books on her own, *Is Underground* and *Cold Shoulder Road* (which won the Lindbergh Award). But Dido proved impossible to suppress. Her latest adventure, *Dangerous Games* (*Limbo Lodge* in England), came out in 1999. In this story I shunted her back in time to a point where she is still voyaging around the world, hoping to get home to London. I invented a Pacific island, and to enrich it, borrowed some names from the young Brontës' Angrian chronicles. (No reviewer has so far picked this up, nor Dido's own Dickensian parentage.) I have an idea that Dido is due for another slotted-in adventure before she finally makes her landfall in England to connect up with *Dido and Pa*. Dido has a real-life existence too: back in the days when British women were protesting against the American air base at Greenham Common in Berkshire, I was startled one day to see a picture in an evening paper of "Dido Twite and friends" sitting round their camp fire beside the barbed wire. By now that Dido must be quite grown up.

Since I had a knee replacement operation five years ago, I am not able to pay such long visits to New York as I used to. But I did get over for a week last Christmas to see a performance of *The Wolves of Willoughby Chase*, which the Berkeley Carroll school in Brooklyn puts on every winter. It was wonderful fun. I still love Manhattan and miss its bookshops and art galleries, but Julius's apartment, although it is rent-controlled and commands a wonderful view of the Empire State Building, is at the top of seventy-three stairs. Climbing up these more than twice a day is not to be thought of, and climbing down is, if anything, worse. Julius has now retired from teaching at C.U.N.Y. and is happy to put in longer periods in England.

In spring 1988 I was, for a couple of months, writer in residence at Lynchburg College in Virginia. I had expected a balmy southern climate, magnolias and azaleas, but in fact I arrived to deep snow and, as the furnace in my little writer's house kept going out, I nearly perished of cold during the first two or three weeks and wore all the clothes I had brought, by day and by night. I taught a lively class in creative writing (is there any kind of writing that is not creative, I sometimes wonder) and had a good time, after the snow melted, roaming around the very pretty campus and local groves and lakes. Being at Lynchburg also gave me a chance to fly over and spend a weekend with my stepmother, Mary Aiken, still living at that time in Savannah. While at Lynchburg I wrote a mystery, *Blackground,* which came out in 1989. But my time there convinced me that teaching is not my vocation. This has recently been confirmed by a week spent teaching short-story writing on a Greek island, Skyros, where there is an English-speaking center dedicated to self-enhancement and various different types of communication. This was an interesting and richly varied experience, but it buttressed my basic conviction that people such as myself turn into writers because they are of a naturally reclusive and hermit-like disposition. They tend to find mixing with other people, especially other people in groups, very tiring and stressful. I would far rather live alone in a dusty house and weedy garden than be obliged to put in conversation with a cleaner or gardener and feel the presence of another personality close at hand, while my thinking processes are

Joan Aiken

compulsively involved with synonyms and syntax and plot. My friends know that I would rather not be phoned before six P.M.

Julius loves ships, so we have taken to exploring Europe by river—the Danube, Rhine, Rhone, Elbe, Moselle, Douro. This is a most restful and agreeable form of travel, since the ship keeps gliding along, offering new landscapes all the time, one can step ashore in riverside towns, see what is to be seen, and then return to one's home-like cabin without having to heft luggage on and off buses or planes or trains. And I had the excitement, last year in Nuremburg, of finding in a bookstore a whole row of my books in German translation. Sometimes my sister Jane accompanies us. Jane and I both used our Douro trip to supply Portuguese background for novels: hers, *Whispering,* mine *Eliza's Daughter,* both set in the Peninsular War period. Last year drifting through Germany, Jane and Julius got back from an after-dinner stroll along the bank at Nuremburg to find the ship in the process of casting-off from the shore, and only just managed to scramble on board before she steamed away down the river. They would have been in a fine predicament with no cash or identification on them, and I would have been startled indeed to discover no sister or husband on board.

Where else have I been in the last twenty years? To Canada (the first visit since, at age three, I was taken to stay with my Canadian grandmother McDonald in Montreal) to talk about writing at London, Ontario; to Alsace, Tel Aviv, Munster, Barcelona, Madrid, Albi, various Greek islands; sometimes for literary conferences, sometimes just for diversion. Yet the luggage a writer carries round is unchanging. I remember sitting on the floor in a hotel room in Stockton, California, suddenly taken with the first chapter of my novel *Foul Matter;* I remember sitting in a clump of heather below the acropolis wall in Lindos, Rhodes, with my portable Olivetti on my lap, wishing I had something to keep the paper in the typewriter from flapping about in the wind, looking down and seeing a red clothespeg at my feet, kindly dropped there by the goddess

Athene; I remember walking about the city of Prague and seeing the end of my novel *Morningquest* take shape.

Writing is a mixture of two impulses: the urge to describe our surroundings so clearly, so precisely, that future readers, future generations, will know exactly what it was like here—now—at this moment. Why do we do this? We hardly know. It seems to be an instinctive process, as spiders spin their webs, as bower-birds build their bowers. The second impulse is to tell a story—to keep the audience snared and helpless while they listen. Why do I tell you a story? To assert my power over you. Or, it may be, to soothe and calm and heal. Stories are magical, both for the reader and the writer. From time to time I have a night-time dream, that I am engaged in writing some wonderful new book—and I wake from it with the remains of intense happiness, which turns to frustration and grief as I realize that the dream-story has escaped from me, that I will never be able to catch it again.

Sometimes I am astonished when I remember that I have written over a hundred books. Where have they all come from? How lucky I have been! And I am truly proud and happy to have been awarded the British honor, the Member of the [Order of the] British Empire (M.B.E.), for services to children's literature. In fact, I feel, it is the other way round, literature has served me, and I shall be always in its debt.

(c) Joan Aiken Enterprises Ltd 1999

Writings

FOR YOUNG PEOPLE

All You've Ever Wanted, and Other Stories, illustrated from drawings by Pat Marriott, J. Cape (London), 1953.

More Than You Bargained For, and Other Stories, illustrated from drawings by P. Marriott, J. Cape, 1955, Abelard (New York), 1957.

The Kingdom and the Cave, illustrated by Dick Hart, Abelard-Schuman (London), 1960, illustrated by Victor Ambrus, Doubleday (Garden City, NY), 1974.

The Wolves of Willoughby Chase, illustrated from drawings by P. Marriott, J. Cape, 1962, Doubleday, 1963.

Black Hearts in Battersea, illustrated by Robin Jacques, Doubleday, 1964, illustrated from drawings by P. Marriott, J. Cape, 1965.

Nightbirds on Nantucket, illustrated from drawings by P. Marriott, J. Cape, 1966, illustrated by Robin Jacques, Doubleday, 1966.

A Necklace of Raindrops, and Other Stories, illustrated by Jan Pienkowski, J. Cape, 1968, Doubleday, 1969.

The Whispering Mountain, J. Cape, 1968, illustrated by Frank Bozzo, Doubleday, 1969.

A Small Pinch of Weather, and Other Stories, illustrated by P. Marriott, J. Cape, 1969.

Night Fall, Macmillan (London), 1969, Holt (New York), 1970.

Armitage, Armitage, Fly Away Home, illustrated by Betty Fraser, Doubleday, 1970.

Smoke from Cromwell's Time, and Other Stories, Doubleday, 1970.

All and More (contains All You've Ever Wanted, and Other Stories and *More Than You Bargained For, and Other Stories),* J. Cape, 1971.

The Cuckoo Tree, illustrated from drawings by P. Marriott, J. Cape, 1971, illustrated by Susan Obrant, Doubleday, 1971.

The Kingdom under the Sea, and Other Stories, illustrated by J. Pienkowski, J. Cape, 1971.

The Green Flash, and Other Tales of Horror, Suspense, and Fantasy (includes Belle of the Ball and *The Dreamers),* Holt, 1971.

A Harp of Fishbones, and Other Stories, illustrated by P. Marriott), J. Cape, 1972, Hodder, 1999.

The Escaped Black Mamba (as told in "Jackanory" by Bernard Cribbins), illustrated by Quentin Blake, British Broadcasting Corp., 1973, published as *Arabel and the Escaped Black Mamba,* Knight (London), 1984.

Tales of Arabel's Raven (as told in "Jackanory" by Roy Kinnear), illustrated by Q. Blake, J. Cape, 1974, published as *Arabel's Raven,* Doubleday, 1974.

The Bread Bin (as told in "Jackanory" by B. Cribbins), illustrated by Q. Blake, British Broadcasting Corp., 1974.

Midnight Is a Place, illustrated from drawings by P. Marriott, J. Cape, 1974, Viking, 1974.

Not What You Expected (includes *The People in the Castle),* Doubleday, 1974.

A Bundle of Nerves: Stories of Horror, Suspense, and Fantasy, Gollancz (London), 1976.

Mortimer's Tie (as told in "Jackanory" by B. Cribbins), illustrated by Q. Blake, British Broadcasting Corp., 1976.

The Skin Spinners: Poems, illustrated by Ken Rinciari, Viking, 1976.

The Faithless Lollybird, and Other Stories (includes *Crusader's Toby* and *The Man Who Pinched God's Letter),* illustrated by P. Marriott, J. Cape, 1977, illustrated by Eros Keith, Doubleday, 1978.

The Far Forests: Tales of Romance, Fantasy, and Suspense, Viking, 1977.

Go Saddle the Sea, illustrated by P. Marriott, Doubleday, 1977, J. Cape, 1978.

Mice and Mendelson (stories), illustrated by Babette Cole, music by John Sebastian Brown, J. Cape, 1978.

Tale of a One-way Street, and Other Stories, illustrated by J. Pienkowski, J. Cape, 1978, Doubleday, 1980.

Mortimer and the Sword Excalibur (as told in "Jackanory" by B. Cribbins) illustrated by Q. Blake, British Broadcasting Corp., 1979.

The Spiral Stair (as told in "Jackanory" by B. Cribbins), illustrated by Q. Blake, British Broadcasting Corp., 1979.

Arabel and Mortimer, illustrated by Q. Blake, British Broadcasting Corp., J. Cape, 1979, Doubleday, 1981.

The Shadow Guests, J. Cape, 1980, Delacorte, 1980.

The Stolen Lake, illustrated by P. Marriott, J. Cape, 1981, Delacorte, 1981.

Mortimer's Portrait on Glass (as told in "Jackanory") illustrated by Q. Blake, British Broadcasting Corp., 1982.

The Mystery of Mr. Jones's Disappearing Taxi (as told in "Jackanory"), illustrated by Q. Blake, British Broadcasting Corp., 1982.

Bridle the Wind (sequel to *Go Saddle the Sea*), J. Cape, 1983, Delacorte, 1983.

Mortimer's Cross (includes *The Mystery of Mr. Jones's Disappearing Taxi* and *Mortimer's Portrait on Glass*), illustrated by Q. Blake, British Broadcasting Corp., 1983, Harper, 1984.

The Kitchen Warriors, illustrated by Jo Worth, British Broadcasting Corp./Knight Books, 1984.

Fog Hounds, Wind Cat, Sea Mice, Macmillan (London and New York), 1984.

Up the Chimney Down, and Other Stories, illustrated by P. Marriott, J. Cape, 1984, Harper 1985.

The Last Slice of Rainbow, illustrated by Margaret Walty, J. Cape, 1985, Harper, 1988.

Past Eight O'Clock (stories), J. Cape, 1986, Viking, 1987.

Dido and Pa, J. Cape, 1986, Delacorte, 1987.

The Moon's Revenge, J. Cape, 1987, Knopf, 1987.

A Goose on Your Grave (horror stories), Gollancz, 1987.

The Teeth of the Gale, J. Cape, 1988, Harper, 1988.

The Erl King's Daughter, Heinemann, 1988.

Voices, Hippo, 1988, published as *Return to Harken House,* Delacorte, 1988.

Give Yourself a Fright (horror stories), Delacorte, 1989.

A Foot in the Grave (ghost stories), J. Cape, Viking, 1989.

A Fit of Shivers (ghost stories), Gollancz, 1990.

Is, J. Cape, 1992, published as *Is Underground,* Doubleday, 1992.

The Winter Sleepwalker, J. Cape, 1994.

(With Lizza Aiken) *Mortimer's Mine,* BBC paperback, 1994.

(With Lizza Aiken) *Mortimer's Pocket,* BBC paperback, 1994.

Mayhem in Rumbury (two Mortimer stories), BBC paperback, 1995.

Cold Shoulder Road, J. Cape, 1995, Delacorte, 1995.

A Handful of Gold (stories), J. Cape, 1995.

The Cockatrice Boys, Gollancz, 1996, Tom Doherty Associates/Tor, 1995-96.

The Jewel Seed, Hodder Headline, 1997.

Moon Cake, Hodder, 1998.

Limbo Lodge, J. Cape, 1999, published as *Dangerous Games,* Delacorte, 1999. *In Thunder's Pocket,* Cape, 2000.

PLAYS:

Winterthing, illustrated by Arvis Stewart, music by J. S. Brown, Holt, 1972.

Winterthing [and] *The Mooncusser's Daughter,* music by J. S. Brown, J. Cape, 1973.

The Mooncusser's Daughter, illustrated by A. Stewart, music by J. S. Brown, Viking, 1974.

Street, illustrated by A. Stewart, music by J. S. Brown, Viking, 1978.

Moon Mill, first produced at Unicorn Theatre, London, 1982.

FOR ADULTS

The Silence of Herondale, Doubleday (Garden City, N.Y.), 1964, Gollancz (London), 1965.

The Fortune Hunters, Doubleday, 1965.

Trouble with Product X, Gollancz, 1966, published as *Beware of the Bouquet,* Doubleday, 1966.

Hate Begins at Home, Gollancz, 1967, published as *Dark Interval,* Doubleday, 1967.

The Ribs of Death, Gollancz, 1967, published as *The Crystal Crow,* Doubleday, 1968.

The Windscreen Weepers, Gollancz, 1969.

The Embroidered Sunset, Gollancz, 1970, Doubleday, 1970.

The Butterfly Picnic, Gollancz, 1972, published as *A Cluster of Separate Sparks,* Doubleday, 1972.

Died on a Rainy Sunday, Gollancz, 1972, Holt, 1972.

Voices in an Empty House, Gollancz, 1975, Doubleday, 1975.

Castle Barebane, Gollancz, 1976, Viking, 1976.

The Five-Minute Marriage, Gollancz, 1977, Doubleday, 1978.

Last Movement, Gollancz, 1977, Doubleday, 1977.

The Smile of the Stranger, Gollancz, 1978, Doubleday, 1978.

A Touch of Chill, Gollancz, 1979, Delacorte, 1980.

The Weeping Ash, Doubleday, 1980.

The Lightning Tree, Gollancz, 1980.

A Whisper in the Night, Gollancz, 1982, Delacorte, 1984.

The Young Lady from Paris, Gollancz, 1982, published as *The Girl from Paris,* Doubleday, 1982.

Foul Matter, Gollancz, 1983, Doubleday, 1983.

Mansfield Revisited, Gollancz, 1984, Doubleday, 1985.

Deception, Gollancz, 1987, published as *If I Were You,* Doubleday, 1987.

Blackground, Gollancz, 1989, Doubleday, 1989.

Jane Fairfax, Gollancz, 1990, St. Martin's Press, 1990.

The Haunting of Lamb House, J. Cape, 1991.

Morningquest, Gollancz, 1992, St. Martin's Press, 1992.

Eliza's Daughter, Gollancz, 1994, St. Martin's Press, 1994.

Emma Watson, Gollancz, 1996, St. Martin's Press, 1996.

The Youngest Miss Ward, Gollancz, 1998, St. Martin's Press, 1998.

Lady Catherine's Necklace, Gollancz, 2000.

NONFICTION

The Way to Write for Children, Elm Tree (London), 1982, St. Martin's (New York), 1982.

TRANSLATOR; FROM THE FRENCH

The Angel Inn, by Sophie De Segur, illustrated by P. Marriott, J. Cape (London), 1976, Stemmer House (Owings Mills, Md.), 1978.

SOUND RECORDINGS

The Wolves of Willoughby Chase, Caedmon, 1978.

A Necklace of Raindrops, Caedmon, 1978.

ANTHONY, Patricia 1947-

Personal

Born March 29, 1947, in San Antonio, TX; daughter of Ray and Evelyn Anthony; married Dennis Hunt, April, 1968 (divorced); children: Lisa Isaacs, Chris Hunt. _Education:_ University of Texas at Austin, B.A. (English literature); graduate coursework at University of Santa Catarina, Brazil. _Politics:_ Democrat. _Religion:_ Zen Buddhist philosophy, metaphysical practice. _Hobbies and other interests:_ Mentoring new writers.

Addresses

Home and office—9712 Amberton Pkwy, Dallas, TX 75243. _Agent_—Donald Maass, 157 West 57th St., No. 703, New York, NY 10017. _E-mail_—panthony@ FastLane.net.

Career

Novelist, 1987—. Professor of English, University of Libson, Lisbon, Portugal, 1969-70, and University of Santa Catarina, Brazil, 1970-75; worked in sales, 1976-78 and 1980-95; Southern Methodist University, Dallas, TX, instructor in creative writing, 1996—. _Member:_ Author's Guild.

Awards, Honors

Locus award for best first novel, 1993, for _Cold Allies;_ Recommended Book, American Library Association, 1999, and Books for the Teen Age, New York Public Library, both for _Flanders._

Writings

Cold Allies, Harcourt, 1993.
Brother Termite, Harcourt, 1993.
Conscience of the Beagle, First Books (Woburn, MA), 1993.
Happy Policeman, Harcourt, 1994.
Cradle of Splendor, Ace, 1996.
Eating Memories (short stories), First Books, 1997.
God's Fires, Ace, 1997.
Flanders, Ace, 1998.

Work in Progress

Mercy's Children and _In His Place,_ both mainstream novels; research for _The Choirmaster,_ a mainstream novel set during the Great Lisbon Earthquake of 1755.

Sidelights

Patricia Anthony appeared on the literary horizon in 1993 with her first novel, _Cold Allies._ Taking place on a future Earth that has suffered climatic collapse due to the ill effects of greenhouse gasses, _Cold Allies_ earned its author the Locus award for best first novel, and was described by _Washington Post Book World_ contributor Robert K. J. Killheffer as a "very promising debut by an exciting new voice." Continuing her exploration of futuristic themes, Anthony has produced several more popular works of fiction, including the novels _Cradle of Splendor_ and _God's Fires,_ and the 1997 short-story collection _Eating Memories._ Commenting on her 1993 novel _Brother Termite, Booklist_ contributor Carl Hays called Anthony "a skilled stylist ... whose work ... puts her in the front rank of contemporary [science-fiction] writers." While her novels contain sophisticated themes and elements of violence, teens will find much in her fiction to enjoy and ponder.

Born in San Antonio, Texas, in 1947, Anthony attended the University of Texas at Austin, where she graduated with a degree in English literature and a minor in art. Continuing to make her home in the Lone Star State, she worked in sales and as a teacher of English in both Brazil and Portugal prior to the publishing success that allowed her to devote her time to writing fiction. In fact, _Cold Allies_ sold only after what Anthony described to _SATA_ as "eight failed novels and 12 years of dogged persistence."

Anthony quickly followed _Cold Allies_ with _Brother Termite_ and _Conscience of the Beagle._ The quirky titles she bestows upon her books belie the seriousness of her science-fiction themes, although her tendency toward satire has been noted by more than one critic. In _Brother Termite,_ insect-like humanoids called "Cousins" have come out into the open after secretly pulling the strings of government since the Cold War, and become accepted members of society. However, the Cousins, who now occupy several key government posts, have encountered certain problems, the most pressing of which is their inability to produce intellectually sound offspring. Realizing that this puts them at a disadvantage, a group of Cousins decides that ridding the Earth of its human population would prevent the Cousins' otherwise inevitable removal from power. Praising Anthony's style and poetic prose in his _New York Times Book Review_ piece, Newgate Callendar called _Brother Termite_ a mix of science fiction and political thriller that results in "a dark, moody, scary, imaginative, sensitively written novel." A _Kirkus Reviews_ contributor declared the book "chilling, memorable work, with splendid characters and utterly convincing aliens, set forth with unstoppable narrative momentum."

In Anthony's third novel, _Conscience of the Beagle,_ Major Dyle Holloway and his team of experts are sent to the planet Tennyson, a colony of Earth, to investigate the terrorist bombings taking place there. Holloway's efforts are hampered by his guilt over his failure to solve his own wife's murder, and the knowledge that one of his team is a spy. A critic for _Kirkus Reviews_ praised the "creamy-smooth first-person prose" in this "altogether satisfyingly complex" book, adding that "Anthony's meteoric rise to the novelistic front ranks is thoroughly deserved." Carl Hays of *Booklist* had similar words of praise: "combining quick, deft characterization with sharp, suspenseful first-person narration . . . , Anthony's third and shortest novel is easily her best."

Other novels continue Anthony's forward-looking view of Earth. 1996's *Cradle of Splendor* finds the people of Brazil benefitting from the competent economic stewardship of the country's new president, Ana Maria Bonfim. The attention of the world is focused on Bonfim's progress, however, when Brazil develops the first antigravity machine and begins preparations for sending a rocket into space. Suspecting that Bonfim may have help from an alien source, the CIA and NASA are quick to get involved, in a novel that a *Kirkus Reviews* critic praised as "mesmerizing, full of terrible insights, deeply disturbing, and quite unforgettable." A contributor to *Publishers Weekly* declared: "Anthony adds to her reputation through a briskly involving narrative that offers disturbing glimpses into the black holes of the human heart."

While alien intervention in Earthly affairs is the thread running through most of Anthony's fiction, sometimes her story carries the reader back, rather than forward, in time. In *God's Fires,* the main character is Father Manoel Pessoa, a Jesuit priest attempting to survive the Spanish Inquisition of the seventeenth century by using more reasonable standards to determine who is a heretic and who is not. During his rounds, Pessoa discovers a small group of aliens, whose spacecraft, crashing near the small Portuguese village of Quintas, has sparked a host of otherworldly visions among the locals. Joe Mayhew of *Washington Post Book World* called Anthony's characters "keenly drawn and complex" and her prose "vivid and careful." With *God's Fires,* "Anthony has created a beautifully written speculative historical full of complex characters and difficult moral dilemmas," according to a reviewer for *Publishers Weekly.*

Even more of a departure from science fiction is Anthony's 1998 work, *Flanders,* in which the reader learns that alien worlds can sometimes be the worlds of the inner mind. In what *Booklist* contributor John Mort called "a haunting, sometimes almost hallucinatory, yet surprising war novel," Anthony introduces Travis Stanhope, a young Texan fighting in France alongside the British during World War I. Although a growing friendship with a fellow officer, Captain Miller, takes some of the sting out of war, Stanhope's experiences in the trenches first disillusion, then desensitize him, and bring on bizarre dreams of death and the afterlife. Constructed as a series of letters from Stanhope to his brother at home in Texas, *Flanders* is "mesmerizing stuff, highly textured and brimming with insight," according to a *Kirkus Reviews* contributor. A critic for *Library Journal* enthused: "Anthony's . . . subtle and innovative storytelling reaches a new plane."

During the writing process, Anthony joins her future readers in wondering "What will happen next?" "When I began *Flanders,*" she told *SATA,* "I created the character of Captain Miller, basing him on two compassionate Jewish employers of mine. I knew going in that my character Miller was gay, that he would face anti-Semitism, and that the British Army would eventually execute him. I had no idea why. The novel was two-thirds complete before I realized what was inevitable from the beginning: Captain Miller's own moral courage would cause him to end up before the firing squad."

Anthony learned to write through trial and error, without the formal instruction that would have taught her the disciplined process of outlining her stories. Despite what she calls "the blind, gibbering fear [that] I won't know what happens next," she has trained her fertile imagination to let the story take her where it will. "It's a glorious way to write——I call it my 'voyage of discovery'——but it's risky," she admitted, weighing the pros and cons of her approach to fiction writing. "In relying on my subconscious mind, my novels not only entertain me as they unfold, but they teach me about myself. For example, my character Travis Lee Stanhope in *Flanders* taught me a difficult lesson about forgiveness. The final paragraph of the penultimate chapter of *God's Fires* taught me a truth about faith so personally powerful that it sent me out of my chair and away from the computer screen."

With two decades of writing experience behind her, Anthony's technique is simple: Create characters who are convincing and real, confront them with an initial conflict, pebble their path with minor crises, and those characters will shoulder the storyline and carry the novel or short story to an appropriate and meaningful conclusion. "I often tell people that I jump off cliffs for a living," Anthony noted. "Indeed, that is how my subconscious puts things together: using one small crisis at a time to build toward the overall climax."

Patricia Anthony

While Anthony enjoys the suspense of not knowing where her fictional creations will lead her, she has contrary advice for writers-to-be: "If you are an aspiring writer, I urge you to read books about writing. I suggest that you outline, outline, outline."

Works Cited

Review of *Brother Termite, Kirkus Reviews,* July 15, 1993, pp. 896-97.
Callendar, Newgate, review of *Brother Termite, New York Times Book Review,* October 31, 1993, p. 27.
Review of *Conscience of the Beagle, Kirkus Reviews,* September 1, 1993, p. 1105.
Review of *Cradle of Splendor, Kirkus Reviews,* February 1, 1996, p. 180.
Review of *Cradle of Splendor, Publishers Weekly,* March 4, 1996, pp. 58-59.
Review of *Flanders, Kirkus Reviews,* April 15, 1998, p. 536.
Review of *Flanders, Library Journal,* May 15, 1998, p. 118.
Review of *God's Fires, Publishers Weekly,* March 24, 1997, p. 63.
Hays, Carl, review of *Brother Termite, Booklist,* September 15, 1993, p. 132.
Hays, review of *Conscience of the Beagle, Booklist,* October 15, 1993, p. 422.
Killheffer, Robert K. J., review of *Cold Allies, Washington Post Book World,* May 2, 1993, p. 8.
Mayhew, Joe, review of *God's Fires, Washington Post Book World,* May 25, 1997, p. 8.
Mort, John, review of *Flanders, Booklist,* May 15, 1998, p. 1593.

For More Information See

PERIODICALS

Booklist, August, 1994, p. 2029; March 15, 1996, p. 1245.
Dallas Observer, June 11, 1998.
Kirkus Reviews, December 1, 1992, p. 1470; July 1, 1994, p. 891.
Publishers Weekly, January 11, 1993, p. 56; August 29, 1994, p. 65.
Voice of Youth Advocates, October, 1997, p. 239.

ON-LINE

Author's web site at http://www.patricia-anthony.com.

*   *   *

APPLEGATE, K. A.
See APPLEGATE, Katherine (Alice)

APPLEGATE, Katherine (Alice) 1956-
(K. A. Applegate)

Personal

Born in 1956, in Michigan. *Hobbies and other interests:* Playing the cello, traveling, reading, gardening, her pet cats.

Addresses

Home—Illinois. *Agent*—c/o Scholastic Inc., 555 Broadway, New York, NY 10012. *E-mail*—kaapplegate@scholastic.com.

Career

Freelance writer.

Writings

"ANIMORPHS" SERIES; FOR JUVENILES; UNDER NAME K. A. APPLEGATE

The Invasion, Scholastic, 1996.
The Visitor, Scholastic, 1996.
The Encounter, Demco Media, 1996.
The Predator, Apple, 1996.
The Message, Scholastic, 1996.
The Andalite Chronicles, Scholastic, 1997.
The Capture, Scholastic, 1997.
The Stranger, Scholastic, 1997.
The Alien, Scholastic, 1997.
The Secret, Scholastic, 1997.
The Android, Scholastic, 1997.
The Forgotten, Scholastic, 1997.
The Reaction, Scholastic, 1997.
The Change, Scholastic, 1997.
The Hork-Bajir Chronicles, Scholastic, 1998.
The Unknown, Scholastic, 1998.
The Escape, Scholastic, 1998.
The Warning, Scholastic, 1998.
The Underground, Scholastic, 1998.
The Decision, Scholastic, 1998.
The Departure, Scholastic, 1998.
The Discovery, Scholastic, 1998.
The Threat, Demco Media, 1998.
The Solution, Demco Media, 1999.
The Pretender, Demco Media, 1999.
The Suspicion, Demco Media, 1999.
The Extreme, Little Apple, 1999.
The Attack, Apple, 1999.
The Exposed, Scholastic, 1999.
The Experiment, Scholastic, 1999.
The Sickness, Scholastic, 1999.
The Reunion, Apple, 1999.
The Conspiracy, Apple, 1999.
The Illusion, Apple, 1999.

ANIMORPHS "MEGAMORPHS" SERIES

The Andalite's Gift, Scholastic, 1997.
Animorphs: In the Time of the Dinosaurs, Scholastic, 1998.
Elfangor's Secret, Apple, 1999.

ANIMORPHS "ALTERNAMORPHS" SERIES

The First Journey, Scholastic, 1999.

"EVERWORLD" SERIES

Search for Senna, Scholastic, 1999.
Land of Loss, Scholastic, 1999.
Enter the Enchanted, Scholastic, 1999.

OTHER

The Story of Two American Generals: Benjamin O. Davis, Jr., and Colin L. Powell (nonfiction), Dell, 1992.
Disney's The Little Mermaid: The Haunted Palace, illustrated by Philo Barnhart, Disney Press, 1993.
Disney's The Little Mermaid: King Triton, Beware!, illustrated by Philo Barnhart, Disney Press, 1993.
Disney's Christmas with All the Trimmings: Original Stories and Crafts from Mickey Mouse and Friends, illustrated by Phil Wilson, Disney Press, 1994.
The Boyfriend Mix-up, illustrated by Philo Barnhart, Disney Press, 1994.
Sharing Sam (novel), Bantam, c. 1995.
Disney's Tales from Agrabah: Seven Original Stories of Aladdin and Jasmine, illustrated by Fred Marvin and Jose Cardona, Disney Press, 1995.
(With Nicholas Stephens) *Disney's Climb Aboard if You Dare!: Stories from the Pirates of the Caribbean,* illustrated by Roberta Collier-Morales, Disney Press, 1996.
Listen to My Heart ("Love Stories Super" series), Bantam, 1996.
Jack Rabbit and the Beanstalk (picture book), illustrated by Holly Hannon, Inchworm Press, 1997.
Escape (picture book; "Magic School Bus" series), Scholastic, 1998.

"BOYFRIENDS AND GIRLFRIENDS" SERIES: REISSUED AS "MAKING OUT" SERIES

Zoey Fools Around, Harper, 1994, Flare, 1998.
Jake Finds Out, Flare, 1998.
Nina Won't Tell, Flare, 1998.
Ben's in Love, Flare, 1998.
What Zoey Saw, Flare, 1998.
Claire Gets Caught, Flare, 1998.
Lucas Gets Hurt, Flare, 1998.
Aisha Goes Wild, Avon, 1999.
Zoey Plays Games, Avon, 1999.
Nina Shapes Up, Camelot, 1999.
Ben Takes a Chance, Avon, 1999.
Claire Can't Lose, Flare, 1999.
Don't Tell Zoey, Flare, 1999.
Aaron Lets Go, Flare, 1999.
Who Loves Kate, Flare, 1999.
Lara Gets Even, Flare, 1999.
Two-Timing Aisha, Flare, 1999.

"SUMMER" SERIES

June Dreams, Archway, 1995.
July's Promise, Archway, 1995.
August Magic, Archway, 1995.
Beaches, Boys, and Betrayal, Archway, 1996.
Sand, Surf, and Secrets, Archway, 1996.
Rays, Romance, and Rivalry, Archway, 1996.
Christmas Special Edition, Archway, 1996.

In this installment in Katherine Applegate's Animorphs series, Tobias, a young boy who has previously morphed into a red-tailed hawk, is given the power to transform into other kinds of animals. (Cover illustration by David B. Mattingly.)

Spring Break Reunion, Archway, 1996.

BY L. E. BLAIR; TEXT BY KATHERINE APPLEGATE

Horse Fever ("Girl Talk" series), Western Publishing (Racine, WI), 1991.
Family Rules ("Girl Talk" series), Western Publishing, 1991.
Randy's Big Dream, Western Publishing, 1992.
Randy and the Great Canoe Race, Western Publishing, 1992.
Randy and the Perfect Boy, Western Publishing, 1992.
Randy's Big Chance, Western Publishing, 1992.

Also the author of many other juvenile novels, including installments in the "Sweet Valley Twin" series, the "Ocean City" series, the "Changes Romance" series, and Harlequin romances for adults.

Adaptations

The "Animorphs" books have been adapted as a television series for Nickelodeon.

Work in Progress

Further novels in the "Animorphs" and "Everworld" series.

Sidelights

Katherine Applegate, who also writes as K. A. Applegate, has authored more than one hundred books. While her publications include romances for the Harlequin line, she has aimed most of her writing at middle-grade readers, penning some titles for the popular "Sweet Valley Twins" series and authoring several books featuring Disney characters. Applegate's most successful venture in juvenile fiction, however, has been her creation of the "Animorphs" series. These books, about young adolescents given the power by aliens to "morph" themselves into various animals, have rivaled R. L. Stine's "Goosebumps" series in popularity. Applegate has completed many titles either in the "Animorphs" series or related to it, such as the "Megamorphs" series wherein the characters take turns narrating chapters, and the "choose-your-own-adventure" "Alternamorphs" series. Writing in *Horn Book,* Christine Heppermann attributed the series' success to this: "Readers can take what they want from it—the animal info or the aliens or the realistic adolescent dilemmas of crushes and problem parents. They can skim over the rest." According to Sally Lodge in *Publishers Weekly,* by the late 1990s, the series "reside[d] at the top" of that publication's "children's paperback series bestseller list, where booksellers predict it [would] roost for the foreseeable future."

During an interview in *Publishers Weekly,* Applegate told Lodge where her idea for the "Animorphs" books came from. "I grew up loving animals and lived with the usual suburban menagerie of dogs, cats and gerbils," she confided. "I really wanted to find a way to get kids into the heads of various species and decided that a science-fiction premise was the way to do this." She worked up a plan for an entire series—which she initially called "The Changelings"—and submitted it, with rough drafts of chapters for several different novels, to Scholastic. Picked up by the publisher, Applegate's "Animorphs" series received heavy promotion from Scholastic, and the firm gave the books eye-catching, die-cut covers. But Jean Feiwel, a vice president at Scholastic, credited Applegate's skill in bringing to life the series' main concept with the success of "Animorphs." Feiwel explained to *Publishers Weekly* that the concept "is absolutely unbelievable but utterly possible. The notion of kids' morphing is also close to adolescent body changes in some ways. It is out of their control," the Scholastic staffer continued, "but becomes something quite fabulous—which is what you like to think happens in the process of growing up." Feiwel also noted that while the protagonists of "Animorphs" "may go off to defend the earth against aliens, at the end of the day they still have math homework to do."

One of the earliest novels in the "Animorphs" series, *The Message,* features a young woman named Cassie

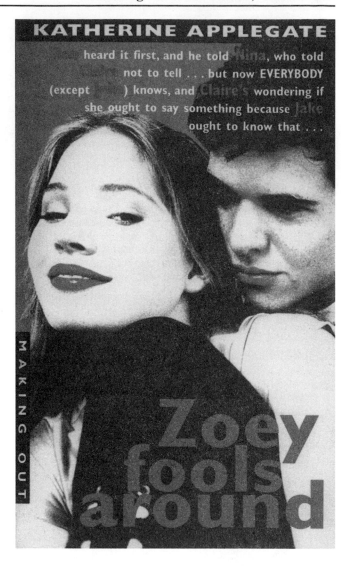

New couples are formed and friendships are tested when teenage Zoey chooses between her long-time boyfriend Jake and the enigmatic Lucas in the first book in Applegate's "Making Out" series.

who is disturbed by strange messages in her dreams. Cassie eventually realizes that she is receiving a distress signal from the Andalites, the aliens that gave her and her friends morphic powers. She persuades her friends that they should change into dolphins in order to rescue their allies from an invading race of aliens, the Yeerks. Linda Bindner, reviewing *The Message* for *School Library Journal,* praised Cassie's portrayal, stating: "... her struggles to come to terms with her decision are realistic and engaging." Bindner also judged that "the descriptions of becoming and living as dolphins and other animals are impressive."

Before embarking on the "Animorphs," Applegate authored a nonfiction work aimed at young people interested in the achievements of African Americans. *The Story of Two American Generals: Benjamin O. Davis, Jr., and Colin L. Powell* examines two African Americans who became pioneers in the United States Armed Forces. Sheilamae O'Hara, who critiqued the volume for *Booklist,* found it to provide basic facts about its two subjects, and suggested that "libraries needing additional material on living black men of achievement may find it useful."

Applegate was also selected to write the first novel in Harper's "Boyfriends and Girlfriends" series, later reissued as the "Making Out" series. This book, *Zoey Fools Around,* is composed of both a normal third-person narrative, and what a *Publishers Weekly* contributor described as "autobiographical fragments" from Zoey herself. Zoey, a senior in high school, has a long-time boyfriend named Jake; they live on a small island off the coast of Maine, where they are awaiting their graduation. The balance of the relationships between Zoey, Jake, and their circle of friends is upset when Lucas Cabral returns to their high school after spending two years in a juvenile facility because of his part in an alcohol-related accident that caused the death of Jake's older brother.

Zoey Fools Around also contains a subplot revolving around an African-American girl named Aisha, who is frightened of having a relationship with a boy who might prove to be her romantic destiny. Complicating matters further is Claire, who, in the words of a *Publishers Weekly* reviewer, "is more unhappy and confused than evil." The reviewer cited "better-than-average character development" in predicting that *Zoey Fools Around* would be "likely to hook its intended audience." The same cast of characters returns for more adventures in several additional titles in the series.

Another of Applegate's young adult efforts is *Sharing Sam.* In this novel, Alison is just starting to get to know Sam, the new guy who rides his own Harley Davidson motorcycle to their school in Florida, when she learns that her long-time best friend Izzy has developed brain cancer and has only a few months to live. When Izzy begins expressing interest in Sam, Alison decides to put her own desires on hold in favor of making her friend's last days as happy as possible. Alison manages to talk Sam into dating Izzy; meanwhile, Sam is dealing with the aging process in his much-loved grandfather and trying to face their inevitable parting. A contributor to *Publishers Weekly* praised *Sharing Sam* for the "thoughtful characterizations and the logical, not entirely strife-free way in which the premise is developed." Frances Bradburn, writing in *Booklist,* stated: "While adults will find the premise uncomfortable, teenage girls will be fascinated."

Applegate discussed with Lodge her feelings about writing for middle graders, calling her audience "the best readers on the planet. They are open-minded, imaginative and willing to embrace ideas." She also revealed that she enjoys the challenges presented to her by "Animorphs," because "a series writer has to develop plotting and pacing that become a well-oiled machine. You don't have the luxury of spending a year on a book and absolutely cannot indulge in writer's block. Yet I knew," Applegate continued, "I had to write in perfect language and choose just the right images, to make sure

that my middle readers fell in love with the characters and returned again and again."

Applegate's most recent venture is the "Everworld" series. It mixes the fantasy of an alternative world where gods and wizards and all manner of mythical creatures abide, with the trials and tribulations of five present-day high schoolers. When the universe created by Earth's ancient immortals is invaded by creatures of myth that are not part of human tradition, the Norse god Loki recruits Senna Wales and her four friends from the real world. Discussing her new series on the Scholastic website, Applegate stated: "I felt it was time to come up with a follow-on, or companion series for 'Animorphs.' I knew I didn't want to do straight science fiction. I felt I should try my hand at fantasy, but I wanted contemporary characters. In other words, I didn't want the characters to belong in the fantasy environment, I wanted them to be from our own world. And I wanted them to continue to be part of the real world. So from there I just had to come up with a device to allow me to do that."

Works Cited

Applegate, Katherine, comments from Scholastic's Animorphs website at: http://scholastic.com/everworld/evqa.htm.

Bindner, Linda, review of *The Message, School Library Journal,* June, 1997, p. 114.

Bradburn, Frances, review of *Sharing Sam, Booklist,* March 15, 1995, p. 132.

Heppermann, Christine, "Invasion of the Animorphs," *Horn Book,* May, 1997, pp. 54-56.

Lodge, Sally, "Scholastic's Animorphs Series Has Legs," *Publishers Weekly,* November 3, 1997, p. 36.

O'Hara, Sheilamae, review of *The Story of Two American Generals: Benjamin O. Davis, Jr., and Colin L. Powell, Booklist,* April 15, 1992, p. 1532.

Review of *Search for Senna, Publishers Weekly,* June 21, 1999, pp. 69-70.

Review of *Sharing Sam, Publishers Weekly,* December 19, 1994, p. 55.

Review of *Zoey Fools Around, Publishers Weekly,* February 28, 1994, p. 89.

For More Information See

PERIODICALS

Booklist, January 1, 1996, p. 813.

Kliatt, March, 1995, p. 8; November, 1995, p. 21. *School Librarian,* August, 1997, p. 157.

Publishers Weekly, July 10, 1995, p. 59; February 16, 1998, pp. 178-88.

Voice of Youth Advocates, February, 1996, p. 368; April, 1996, p. 21; April, 1997, p. 21.

ON-LINE

Scholastic.com—K. A. Applegate, http://www.scholastic.com/Animorphs/kaa.htm (June 24, 1999).*

ARUEGO, Ariane
  See DEWEY, Ariane

B

BLOS, Joan W. 1928-

Personal

Full name is Joan Winsor Blos; surname rhymes with "dosc"; born December 9, 1928, in New York, NY; daughter of Max (a psychiatrist) and Charlotte (a teacher; maiden name, Biber) Winsor; married Peter Blos, Jr. (a psychoanalyst), in 1953; children: Stephen (deceased), Sarah. *Education:* Vassar College, B.A., 1949; City College (now of the City University of New York), M.A., 1956.

Addresses

Agent—Curtis Brown Ltd., 10 Astor Place, New York, NY 10003.

Career

Jewish Board of Guardians, New York City, research assistant, 1949-50; City College (now of the City University of New York), New York City, assistant teacher of psychology, 1950-51; Child Study Center, Yale University, New Haven, CT, research assistant, 1951-53; Bank Street College of Education, New York City, associate editor in publications division, 1959-66, instructor in teacher-education division, 1960-70; University of Michigan, Ann Arbor, MI, research assistant and specialist in children's literature for the Department of Psychiatry, 1970-73, lecturer for School of Education, 1973-80; writer and lecturer, 1980—. Connecticut Association of Mental Health, volunteer reviewer of children's books and chairperson of children's book committee, 1954-56.

Awards, Honors

John Newbery Medal, American Library Association, and American Book Award for children's hardcover fiction, both 1980, Best Books, *School Library Journal,* and Ambassador Book, English-Speaking Union, all for *A Gathering of Days: A New England Girl's Journal,* *1830-32;* Ann Arbor "Anny" award, and award from the Midland Society of Authors, both for *The Heroine of the Titanic: A Tale Both True and Otherwise of the Life of Molly Brown; Boston Globe-Horn Book* Honor Book, for *Old Henry;* Best Books, Bank Street College of Education, 1998, for *Hello, Shoes!*

Writings

PICTURE BOOKS

(With Betty Miles) *Joe Finds a Way,* illustrated by Lee Ames, L. W. Singer, 1967.
"It's Spring," She Said, illustrated by Julie Maas, Knopf, 1968.
(With Betty Miles) *Just Think!,* illustrated by Pat Grant Porter, Knopf, 1971.
Martin's Hats, illustrated by Marc Simont, Morrow, 1984.
Old Henry, illustrated by Stephen Gammell, Morrow, 1987.
The Grandpa Days, illustrated by Emily Arnold McCully, Simon & Schuster, 1989.
Lottie's Circus, illustrated by Irene Trivas, Morrow, 1989.
One Very Best Valentine's Day, illustrated by Emily Arnold McCully, Simon & Schuster, 1990.
A Seed, a Flower, a Minute, an Hour: A First Book of Transformations, illustrated by Hans Poppel, Simon & Schuster, 1992.
The Hungry Little Boy, illustrated by Dena Shutzer, Simon & Schuster, 1995.
Nelly Bly's Monkey: His Remarkable Story in His Own Words, illustrated by Catherine Stock, Morrow, 1996.
Bedtime!, illustrated by Stephen Lambert, Simon & Schuster, 1998.
Hello, Shoes!, illustrated by Ann Boyajian, Simon & Schuster, 1998.

FOR CHILDREN; FICTION

A Gathering of Days: A New England Girl's Journal, 1830-32 (historical fiction), Scribner, 1979.
Brothers of the Heart: A Story of the Old Northwest, 1837-1838 (historical fiction), Scribner, 1985.
The Heroine of the Titanic: A Tale Both True and Otherwise of the Life of Molly Brown, illustrated by Tennessee Dixon, Morrow, 1991.

Brooklyn Doesn't Rhyme (short stories), illustrated by Paul Birling, Scribner, 1994.

OTHER

In the City (reader), illustrated by Dan Dickas, Macmillan, 1964.

(With Betty Miles) *People Read* (reader), illustrated by Dickas, Macmillan, 1964.

(Adaptor) Margaret Wise Brown, *The Days before Now: An Autobiographical Note,* illustrated by Thomas B. Allen, Simon & Schuster, 1994.

Contributor of articles and reviews to periodicals, including *School Library Journal, New Outlook,* and *Merrill-Palmer Quarterly. Children's Literature in Education,* London, member of editorial board, 1973-77, U.S. editor, 1976-81.

Brothers of the Heart has been translated into Swedish and *Old Henry* into German, Dutch, and French.

Adaptations

Brothers of the Heart was adapted for the stage by the author and first performed in Ann Arbor, MI, 1999. *Old Henry* was adapted for audiocassette, National Library Service for the Blind and Physically Handicapped, 1987; *A Gathering of Days: A New England Girl's Journal, 1830-32* was adapted for audiocassette, Random House and Recorded Books; *Brooklyn Doesn't Rhyme* was adapted for audiocassete, Recorded Books.

Sidelights

While Joan W. Blos is an award-winning author of historical fiction for young people and has several popular picture books to her credit, she has earned the most recognition for *A Gathering of Days: A New England Girl's Journal, 1830-32,* about a young female growing up in nineteenth-century New Hampshire. Blos's interest in writing for children evolved after conducting graduate study in psychology, working in child development, and teaching children's literature. She also served as a volunteer reviewer of children's books beginning in 1954, and "from that time on," Blos explained to Betty Miles in *Horn Book,* "I never thought of other work, and I doubt that I ever will."

Born in 1928 in New York City, Blos was the only child of Max Winsor, a psychiatrist who worked with troubled young people who had experienced their first brush with the law, and Charlotte Winsor, a highly esteemed teacher of education. As a child, Blos was encouraged to read by both her parents. "My parents were both idealistic believers in the power of education and the educative process," the author related in an essay for *Something about the Author Autobiography Series (SAAS).* "We went to the library often ... and both of my parents, as I recall, read aloud to me.... We read my favorites over and over again—some of them so often that I still know them nearly by heart." In addition to being an avid reader, Blos began writing at an early age. "By the time I was three or four years old," she

A school writing assignment is the vehicle by which eleven-year-old Rosie details her experiences growing up in a Jewish immigrant family in Brooklyn at the turn of the century. (Cover illustration by Paul Birling.)

once told *SATA,* "my parents were writing down my 'poems,' of which only one has survived."

At about the age of seven, Blos enrolled in an experimental school at which her mother taught. Uniquely structured, the school not only strongly emphasized academics, but stressed that children engage in all types of activities. Girls, for example, would work in carpentry, while boys were encouraged to take part in cooking classes. "My school experience was so different from that of my friends and contemporaries," Blos declared in *SAAS,* "that now ... it is almost hard to believe that we were going to school at the same time and in the same country.... My friends speak of punitive teachers. We respected ours ... and we mostly called them by nicknames.... Friends recall how they would contrive to miss a day of school. For us, the worst possible punishment was to be sent home from school."

During World War II Blos attended high school, where she nurtured her writing skills. One of her short stories earned publication in a national magazine, and she had a hand in writing her school's musical. Despite her penchant for English literature, Blos, upon enrolling at Vassar College, studied science and eventually became a physiology major. "If my newfound interest in physiology exerted a pull toward science, disappointment with courses in the English department seemed to push me away," Blos related in *SAAS*. "It was hard to respect myself, the faculty, or my fellow students when I regularly received A's with but little preparation.... It came down to the fact that I was doing too well too easily in English and I didn't like knowing I was getting away with it. Besides, doesn't every doctor's daughter want, at one time or another, to be a doctor too?"

After graduating from Vassar in 1949, Blos got a job working as an assistant in a special school for emotionally disturbed children. Developing an interest in psychoanalytic theory, she enrolled in the master's program in psychology at New York's City College, but soon left the program to become a doctoral candidate at Yale University in New Haven, Connecticut, where she worked as a research assistant in the school's Child Study Center. While at Yale she met Peter Blos Jr., a medical student whom she married shortly thereafter.

"By the time we left New Haven three years later, it had become clear that academic psychology and I were not a good match," Blos explained in *SAAS*. Having worked with child patients and having taught student nurses in Yale's School of Nursing, Blos began to develop an affinity towards children's literature. "Suddenly," the author continued in *SAAS*, "there was a place where all I had learned about child development, all my interest in language, and all my love of books could at last come together."

The Bloses moved to New York City, where the author once again resumed graduate study and her husband completed his medical training. After the birth of their second child, Blos began working at the Street College of Education, an institution dedicated to progressive education. There she taught language arts and children's literature and, as a member of the Publications Division, prepared numerous articles and book reviews and began to write for children. Her first two publications, written in collaboration with Betty Miles, were the primers *In the City* and *People Read,* both published in 1964. A few years later, Blos realized the publication of three more children's books, *"It's Spring," She Said, Just Think!,* and *Joe Finds a Way,* the last two also in collaboration with Miles.

Also around this time, Blos became fascinated with the history of an old farmhouse in New Hampshire that her husband's parents had owned for several decades. After researching the building in local libraries, she discovered that the house had been built in 1827. Uncovering several interesting facts about the house's former owners, Blos was intrigued enough to keep digging, and her quest took her to New York City libraries. "Wonder-

ful things, such as a collection of New Hampshire legends compiled in the mid-nineteenth century ... were to be found," Blos recalled in *SAAS*. "Memoirs and reminiscences, biographies and autobiographies became interesting for what they told of childhood in nineteenth-century New England. Novels and magazine stories gave further hints as to the sorts of things people cared about."

While her fascination with New England's history began as a hobby, it soon became much more. "I went on and on, filling notebooks...," Blos continued in *SAAS*. "It was quite a while before I began to think that I might have a book on my hands. Then it took me several more years before I was able to settle on the journal form." Before she could complete the book that would become *A Gathering of Days: A New England Girl's Journal, 1830-32,* she and her family relocated to Ann Arbor, Michigan. Throughout the 1970s, Blos worked at the University of Michigan, first as part of the school's Child Development Project and then at the School of Education, where she taught classes and seminars in children's literature with an emphasis on materials for the pre-reading child. Even though removed from New England by several hundred miles, she was able to continue her research on New Hampshire history at several Michigan libraries, and finally, in 1979, *A Gathering of Days* was published.

The story of fourteen-year-old Catherine Hall and her childhood in the early 1800s, *A Gathering of Days* relates Catherine's innermost thoughts as she grows up. The experiences she records in her journal include offering assistance to a person of another race, dealing with an intrusive stepparent, and coping with the death of a close friend. Praised for its striking realism as well as its accurate representation of a specific time in history, *A Gathering of Days* earned Blos a Newbery Medal, the highest honor in children's literature.

"It is an awesome thing to be told that you have made a distinguished contribution to children's literature," Blos reflected in her acceptance speech for the award, excerpted in *Top of the News*. "I learned that I had won the Newbery Medal late in January [of 1980]. The actual moment of notification ... was an event of transformative proportions, having all the trapping of magic, and not to be believed." As a result of her earning the prize, Blos was catapulted into international stature and found herself in demand as a speaker. "Because I was a Newbery winner, what I had to say about children's literature was more interesting to more people!," Blos exclaimed in *SAAS*.

Since writing *A Gathering of Days,* the author has penned several works of historical fiction. Her *Brothers of the Heart: A Story of the Old Northwest, 1837-1838* focuses on a young boy coming of age in nineteenth-century Michigan. Calling the work "a first-rate, powerful novel," Alice F. Stern went on to note in her *Voice of Youth Advocates* review that the story, though moving due to the plight of its crippled narrator, Shem, "never sinks to sentimentality." Other books by Blos include

Blos's picture book depicts the loving relationship between a small boy and his grandmother as she prepares lunch for him. (Cover illustration by Dena Schutzer.)

The Heroine of the Titanic: A Tale Both True and Otherwise of the Life of Molly Brown, about the woman who survived the sinking of the world-famous luxury liner dubbed "unsinkable;" and *Brooklyn Doesn't Rhyme,* a short-story collection that focuses on a family of Polish Jews who immigrate to the United States in the early part of the twentieth century. Narrated by eleven-year-old Edwina "Rosey" Sachs, the book is imbued with her enthusiasm and curiosity about her new homeland, and her stories detail the day-to-day adventures of her close-knit family as they attempt to assimilate into a new culture. Also integral to the story are social issues such as women's suffrage, the advent of the telephone, and the needs and rights of workers. Describing individual stories as "touching," "affectionate," and full of "wit and verve," *Booklist*'s Hazel Rochman commented that the "family folklore" aspect of *Brooklyn Doesn't Rhyme* should "encourage kids to find their own family stories."

In addition to her novel-length works, Blos has also written several successful picture books. *Old Henry,* published in 1987, tells of an eccentric man who antagonizes his neighbors by refusing to renovate his dilapidated house. *The Hungry Little Boy* shows a doting grandmother adding her own special touches to her young grandson's peanut-butter sandwich, finishing the feast off with a carrot, an apple, cookies, and a cold glass of fresh milk. "The pleasures of ordinary days ... are captured here" for the picture-book set, in the opinion of

a contributor to the *Bulletin of the Center for Children's Books,* while a *Publishers Weekly* reviewer called *The Hungry Little Boy* a "soothing text" that "creat[es] a true sense of one family's camaraderie." *Bedtime!,* which Blos produced in 1998, finds grandmother and grandson together again, this time at the close of day. Noting that the book "beautifully captures a child's reluctance to leave activities of the day behind," *Booklist*'s Stephanie Zvirin praised Blos's portrayal of a sensitive and experienced grandmother who "knows just how to cope": the patient granny puts the boy's stuffed animals to bed one by one, until the young lad decides to join them under the covers. *Hello, Shoes!,* Blos's most recent picture-book offering, follows a boy and his grandfather on a search for the boy's favorite red sandals. Along the way, they encounter many other interesting items in a book that a *Publishers Weekly* critic noted "clearly speak[s] to a child's everyday experience."

Blos has dedicated the greater portion of her adulthood to the field of children's literature, and continues to write books for children and preteens. "Writing begins with concern for the world, the events and the people therein," she was once quoted in *Twentieth-Century Young-Adult Writers* as saying. "I believe that this world of ours matters and that our small lives count." While creating fiction has never been easy for Blos, she remains dedicated to her craft as a way of contributing to the lives of today's young people. "In her pursuit of truth in her writing, Blos demonstrates her respect for young readers and for the power of their imagination," maintained a contributor to *Children's Books and Their Creators.* "What do books tell [children] about their world?" is a question Blos has often pondered, and she discussed its answer in *SATA:* "What might I wish to say? 'Don't be scared and don't hang back,' my protagonist writes in *A Gathering of Days* as she ... reflects on her own long life. That pretty much sums it up."

Works Cited

Apseloff, Marilyn F., essay on Blos in *Twentieth-Century Young-Adult Writers,* St. James Press, 1995, pp. 58-60.

Blos, Joan W., "1980 Newbery Acceptance Speech," *Top of the News,* summer, 1980, pp. 393-96.

Blos, Joan W., essay in *Something about the Author Autobiography Series,* Volume 11, Gale, 1991, pp. 51-68.

Essay on Blos in *Children's Books and Their Creators,* edited by Anita Silvey, Houghton, 1995, p. 65.

Review of *Hello, Shoes!, Publishers Weekly,* May 31, 1999, p. 91.

Review of *The Hungry Little Boy, Bulletin of the Center for Children's Books,* June, 1995, p. 338.

Review of *The Hungry Little Boy, Publishers Weekly,* May 1, 1995, p. 56.

Miles, Betty, "Joan W. Blos," *Horn Book,* August, 1980, pp. 374-77.

Rochman, Hazel, review of *Brooklyn Doesn't Rhyme, Booklist,* September 15, 1994, p. 135.

A wise grandmother eases her grandson's transition from day to night by tucking his stuffed animals into bed and reading to them until the child is ready to join his furry friends. (From Bedtime!, written by Blos and illustrated by Stephen Lambert.)

Stern, Alice F., review of *Brothers of the Heart: A Story of the Old Northwest, 1837-1838, Voice of Youth Advocates,* April, 1986, p. 28.
Zvirin, Stephanie, review of *Bedtime!, Booklist,* May 15, 1998, p. 1629.

For More Information See

BOOKS

Children's Literature Review, Volume 18, Gale, 1989, pp. 14-19.

PERIODICALS

Booklist, February 1, 1994, p. 1019; December 15, 1994, p. 755; February 15, 1996, p. 1024.
Horn Book, September-October, 1994, p. 585.
Kirkus Reviews, April 1, 1995, p. 464; February 1, 1998, p. 192.
Publishers Weekly, November 7, 1994, p. 78; May 11, 1998, p. 66.
School Library Journal, June, 1995, p. 77; April, 1996, p. 99; December, 1996, p. 44; July, 1998, p. 64; July, 1999, p. 61.

*   *   *

BRAUN, Lilian Jackson 1916(?)-

Personal

Born c. 1916, in Massachusetts; married, c. 1943 (first husband, an accountant, died 1967); married Earl Bettinger (an actor), 1979.

Addresses

Agent—Blanche C. Gregory, Inc., 2 Tudor Place, New York, NY 10017.

Career

Mystery writer. Crowley Knower Company, Detroit, MI, freelance advertising copywriter, 1929-1930; Ernst Kern Department Store, Detroit, began as advertising copywriter, became public relations director, 1930-1948; *Detroit Free Press,* Detroit, editor, 1948-78.

Awards, Honors

Edgar Award nomination, Mystery Writers of America, 1986, for *The Cat Who Saw Red.*

Writings

"THE CAT WHO . . . " MYSTERY SERIES

The Cat Who Could Read Backwards, Dutton, 1966.
The Cat Who Ate Danish Modern, Dutton, 1967.
The Cat Who Turned On and Off, Dutton, 1968.
The Cat Who Saw Red, Jove, 1986.
The Cat Who Played Brahms, Jove, 1987.
The Cat Who Played Post Office, Jove, 1987.
The Cat Who Knew Shakespeare, Jove, 1988.
The Cat Who Had Fourteen Tales (short stories), Jove, 1988.
The Cat Who Sniffed Glue, Putnam, 1988.
The Cat Who Went Underground, Putnam, 1989.
The Cat Who Talked to Ghosts, Putnam, 1990.
The Cat Who Lived High, Putnam, 1990.
The Cat Who Knew a Cardinal, Putnam, 1991.
The Cat Who Wasn't There, Putnam, 1992.
The Cat Who Moved a Mountain, Putnam, 1992.
The Cat Who Went into the Closet, Putnam, 1993.
The Cat Who Came to Breakfast, Putnam, 1994.
Lilian Braun: Three Complete Novels (contains *The Cat Who Knew Shakespeare, The Cat Who Sniffed Glue,* and *The Cat Who Went Underground*), Putnam, 1994.
The Cat Who Blew the Whistle, Putnam, 1995.
The Cat Who Said Cheese, Putnam, 1996.
Three Complete Novels (contains *The Cat Who Wasn't There, The Cat Who Went into the Closet,* and *The Cat Who Came to Breakfast*), Putnam, 1996.
The Cat Who Sang for the Birds, Putnam, 1998.
The Cat Who Tailed a Thief, Jove, 1998.

OTHER

Work represented in anthologies, including *Mystery Cats: Feline Felonies by Modern Masters of Mystery,* Dutton, 1991, and *More Mystery Cats,* Dutton, 1993. Regular columnist, *Lilian Jackson Braun Newsletter;* contributor to *Ellery Queen's Mystery Magazine.*

Sidelights

Former advertising copywriter and newspaper editor-turned-novelist Lillian Jackson Braun has made a name for herself and won a large and loyal audience with her carefully crafted, witty, and highly entertaining "The Cat

Who . . ." mystery series. Since her debut, *The Cat Who Could Read Backwards*, the author has completed more than twenty novels in the popular series. While that in itself is impressive, what is even more striking is the fact that the prolific Braun is a spry octogenarian who wrote her first three books in the mid-1960s only to abandon her literary career until 1986—a hiatus of eighteen years. Since then, she has made up for lost time, turning out a number of novels and giving no indications that she is ready to slow down. Reviewing Braun's novel, *The Cat Who Came to Breakfast*, a critic for *Kirkus Reviews* commented: "Like Agatha Christie resolutely keeping up British standards in the face of a shrinking Empire, Braun maintains the forms of the American cozy [mystery story]." When Catherine Nelson of *Armchair Detective* asked Braun in a 1991 interview how long she intended to keep writing her trademark series, the author responded with characteristic verve. "Psychologically I'm 39, and physically I'm about 50. I don't think about it," she said.

Braun was born around 1916 in Massachusetts, where she spent her early years. Her family moved to Detroit in the late 1920s, when she was in her early teens. The eldest of three children, Braun came from a creative family; both her parents were imaginative, resourceful people who encouraged their children to think for themselves. Braun's father was an inventor, her mother a born raconteur. The latter, in particular, sparked her daughter's passion for storytelling at an early age. Braun recalled in her 1991 interview with Nelson how, each day at the family dinner table, her mother would recount the events of her day and then ask her two daughters and their younger brother to exercise their own imaginations to do the same thing. "I really think I learned how to describe situations, events, people, and scenery through that early custom in our family," Braun explained to Nelson.

Braun was precocious, and she was just three years old when her mother taught her to write so that she could correspond with her grandmother. This early interest in words stayed with Braun. She was fifteen when she began selling "poems" about baseball—written in prose and under a pen name—to the *Detroit News* and other publications. Surprisingly, Braun did not dream of becoming a writer, but rather a school teacher. She might well have done so, had the Great Depression not hit Detroit hard, ending Braun's plans to attend college. Instead, she began writing baseball poems for the *News* on a daily basis, earning $12 per week for doing so. When the baseball season ended she went knocking on the doors of Detroit retail stores, trying to sell them advertising poems. She was eventually hired by the Crowley Knower Company in 1929 to work as an advertising copywriter for a local department store. Braun did so well that a year later she was offered a better job by the Ernst Kern Company, which ran one of the other stores in town. There she settled in for the next eighteen years, working her way up to become public relations director at Ernst Kern. In 1948 Braun decided it was time for a career change. She took an editing job at

the *Detroit Free Press,* remaining with the newspaper until she retired in 1978.

Throughout her early life Braun had written short stories as a hobby, although few were ever published. An incident that occurred in the early 1950s prompted her to begin writing about cats; it would also change the course of her life. Braun adored a porcelain figurine of a Siamese cat that someone had given her, and so her husband gave her a real flesh-and-blood feline as a fortieth birthday gift. She adored the animal, which she named Koko after a character in the well-known Gilbert and Sullivan operetta *The Mikado*. Unfortunately, Koko fell from the balcony of Braun's tenth floor apartment and died; neighbors speculated that the cat had been pushed. Braun, feeling angry and sad, began having nightmares about the incident. As a kind of self-help therapy, she wrote a short story called "The Sin of Madama Phloi." "It was not a re-enactment of the incident, but it was inspired by what happened," Braun explained to Nelson. "In it, [a] murdered cat was avenged—which seemed to help me cope with [Koko's senseless death]."

Braun's literary agent sent the story to *Ellery Queen's Mystery Magazine,* where it was published. When the editor asked for another, Braun responded by penning "Phut Phat Concentrates." When that story also proved successful, Braun began sending the magazine one cat mystery story per year for each of the next five years. After two of the stories were included in an anthology published by E. P. Dutton, an editor at the Manhattan-based publishing house asked Braun to write a mystery novel with a cat in it. Although she was busy with her job and married life, Braun felt "one doesn't turn down a request from a publisher," as she later told Nelson.

The Cat Who Could Read Backwards, Braun's first novel, was published in 1966. That book featured a Siamese tom cat named K'o-Kung (Koko, for short) and his amateur detective owner Jim Qwilleran ("Qwill" to his friends), a middle-aged, former big city crime reporter. Qwilleran has just gone through a messy divorce and is drinking too much, so he tries to start over in a small Midwestern town, where he lands a job on a newspaper called the *Daily Fluxion*. Qwilleran is hired by an old friend who edits the paper, and is assigned to the local art beat, although he knows little about the subject. Once on the job, Qwilleran soon discovers the petty jealousies and rivalries among the characters in the local art community, which also involve the *Fluxion*'s own critic, George Bonifield Mountclemens III. When an artist is murdered, Qwilleran's crime reporter background and his own innate curiosity inevitably draw him and Koko into the mystery.

Braun's debut novel sold well enough that Dutton asked for two sequels. Braun responded by writing *The Cat Who Ate Danish Modern* and *The Cat Who Turned On and Off,* both of which featured Koko, Qwilleran, and a young female Siamese cat named Yum-Yum, who have become the three most prominent recurring characters in Braun's "The Cat Who . . ." mysteries. *The Cat Who Ate*

Danish Modern takes Qwilleran and his feline friends into the world of interior decorating; *The Cat Who Turned On and Off* involves antique dealers. Reviews for both books were varied. "A ton of cat drool to only a peck of proper murder mystery," a British reviewer quipped about *The Cat Who Ate Danish Modern* in the *Times Literary Supplement.* However, a *Publishers Weekly* critic praised *The Cat Who Turned On and Off* as a "witty treatment of a curious animal whose curiosity helps to catch a killer."

By now, Braun was beginning to enjoy writing her cat mystery novels. She had already completed a fourth book, *The Cat Who Ordered Caviar,* when Dutton informed her that the company was no longer interested in publishing her work. Around this same time, in 1967, Braun's husband of twenty-four years died. Although Braun continued to create short stories, she abandoned novels and concentrated, until her 1978 retirement, on her job at the *Detroit Free Press.* The following year she married her second husband, actor Earl Bettinger.

One day Bettinger read *The Cat Who Ordered Caviar,* and he encouraged his wife to clean it up and resubmit it to publishers under a new title: *The Cat Who Saw Red.* To Braun's surprise, Berkley bought it and the book appeared in 1986, eighteen years after the publication of her previous novel. The reappearance of Qwilleran—now a restaurant critic in a small town called Mooseville—Koko, and Yum-Yum after so many years did not attract a lot of media attention, but those critics who did review the book reacted favorably; for example, a *Publishers Weekly* reviewer commented that "Although Braun ... occasionally verges on the cutesy, she offers here a delightful tale." Even more important to Braun than any reviews was the fact that *The Cat Who Saw Red* sold strongly and was nominated for an Edgar, an award given annually by the Mystery Writers of America. As a result, Berkley offered Braun a contract to write ten more mystery novels.

In the years since, Braun has written many more "The Cat Who ..." mysteries and a book of cat stories, the latter being the only book she has done outside the series. Braun generally starts each new book by coming up with a catchy title; from there, she invents a good mystery to go with it. Oddly enough, Braun commented, the series title, "The Cat Who ..." just came to her "out of the blue" one day. Each of the works involves Qwilleran, Koko, Yum Yum, and a variety of other characters who turn up from time to time, in intriguing mysteries that play out against different backdrops. "Being a Gemini, I like variety," Braun admitted to Nelson.

Braun offers a great deal of variety in her works by means of her plotting. *The Cat Who Talked to Ghosts,* for example, deals with strange goings-on at a historical museum in Qwilleran's hometown; *The Cat Who Knew a Cardinal,* with the theater; *The Cat Who Came to Breakfast,* with a redevelopment scheme at a resort hotel; and *The Cat Who Blew the Whistle,* with railroading. Murder just seems to follow Qwilleran and

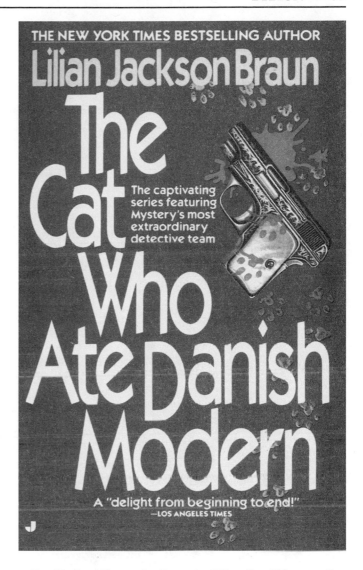

In this installment in Braun's "The Cat Who . . ." series, reporter Jim Qwilleran, with the help of cats Koko and Yum-Yum, solve the murder of a woman whose exclusive home was featured in Qwilleran's magazine.

his cats wherever they go. "The most difficult part of any of my books is figuring out what a cat can do to alert Qwilleran to solve the mystery," Braun told Nelson. "That's the crux of the whole thing. When I know that, I'm all set."

Braun, her husband, and their four Siamese cats—Koko III, Yum-Yum, Pitti-Sing, and Pooh-Bah—spend summers in Michigan and winters at their home in the foothills of the Blue Ridge Mountains in western North Carolina. Braun's husband tends to the house and does the cooking, leaving Braun free to concentrate on writing, when she feels like it. "I'm very casual about the whole thing," Braun admitted to Nelson. Writing can "be a very selfish and demanding occupation. Particularly if you have a deadline to meet." Now in her eighties, Braun is "officially retired" and has had cataract surgery to correct eyesight problems, yet she continues to meet those deadlines, and to write mysteries that satisfy her legions of loyal readers. "Braun's plots are always original. The murder victims are the rich and famous as well as the poor," Carol Barry noted in *Twentieth-Century Crime and Mystery Writers*. "The murders are both surprising and shocking, but the dialogue, the local color, and the characters make up more of the story than the act of murder itself."

Works Cited

Barry, Carol, "Lilian Braun," *Twentieth-Century Crime and Mystery Writers*, St. James Press, 1991.
Review of *The Cat Who Ate Danish Modern, Times Literary Supplement*, June 6, 1968, p. 603.
Review of *The Cat Who Came to Breakfast, Kirkus Reviews*, January 1, 1994, p. 18.
Review of *The Cat Who Saw Red, Publishers Weekly*, March 28, 1986, p. 55.
Review of *The Cat Who Turned On and Off, Publishers Weekly*, September 30, 1968, pp. 60-61.
Nelson, Catherine, "The Lady Who . . . ," *Armchair Detective*, fall, 1991, pp. 388-98.

For More Information See

BOOKS

St. James Guide to Crime and Mystery Writers, St. James Press, 1996.

PERIODICALS

Armchair Detective, spring, 1996, p. 233.
Booklist, August, 1992, p. 1997; February 15, 1993, p. 1038; May 15, 1993, p. 1716; December 1, 1994, p. 635.
Cat Fancy, November, 1994, pp. 40-43; December 1, 1994, p. 635.
Globe & Mail (Toronto), December 17, 1988.
Library Journal, May 1, 1966, p. 2368; May 1, 1991, p. 123; November 15, 1992, p. 120; March 1, 1993, p. 112; May 1, 1993, p. 130; December, 1994, p. 138.
New York Times Book Review, March 6, 1966, p. 38; June 18, 1967, p. 37; January 12, 1969, p. 43; April 2, 1989, p. 33; May 19, 1991, p. 45.
Observer, July 16, 1967, p. 21; March 16, 1968, p. 29; March 24, 1968, p. 29; July 27, 1969, p. 25.
Publishers Weekly, July 8, 1988, p. 29; March 22, 1991, p. 73; October 11, 1991, p. 52; January 25, 1993, p. 80; January 17, 1994, p. 412; January 16, 1995, p. 40.
School Library Journal, August, 1988, p. 196.
Times Literary Supplement, September 21, 1967, p. 844; September 18, 1969, p. 1018.
Tribune Books (Chicago), October 19, 1986, p. 5; January 7, 1990, p. 6.*

Autobiography Feature

Sue Ellen Bridgers

1942-

I have always loved the One Hundred Thirty-ninth Psalm in which the psalmist sings that his whole life is written in God's book. These words appeal to me not only because of the implication that I am known to God in a special way, but also because of the image of a book, the actual writing of a history of which my life is a part.

I can't remember a time when I wasn't interested in my connection to other people. "How is this person kin to me?" was one of my favorite questions and one my grandmother Abbott loved to answer. She, too, felt keenly the blood attachments of her family, and drawing from the rich store of her memory, she wove a continuous, dramatic tale of powerful relationships, of connections to the land and the homeplace, of survival. Through her, my heritage was laid out on a map of family memories, and there it has remained.

If there is a book with my life written in it, I'm sure that my conscious memories are only tiny, sporadic visions of all the experiences, thoughts, and dreams recorded there. My earliest memory is of my great-grandmother McGlohon. For most of my life I believed I had dreamed of being with her, of seeing her at a distance and then closer and closer until I was looking up at her. This face looking down into mine is crystal clear to me, as if it is a photographic image locked in my brain. Only recently did I discover that this vision of her was not a dream at all but a recurrent event. Almost every day when I was a baby, my mother carried me down the hall to the room where my great-grandmother was bedridden. I would lie on the bed next to her, and she would talk and play with me. I was only eighteen months old when she died.

What is memory that all these years later I am filled with a tearful kind of joy, with such a powerful remnant of love that I am still warmed by it? Memory comes to us floating on smells; it pierces our bustling days with incongruous sounds, makes us pause at a name, an address, a postcard, a photograph, a baby bonnet, a china plate. A melody, a phrase of speech, the walk of someone approaching us on the street, the feel of a certain kind of cloth, makes us remember. Sometimes we can't even discern the stimulus; suddenly we are captured by a memory, locked into another time, and for just a moment, we are someone we used to be.

I was born afraid of water. I don't think I almost drowned; no one maliciously tossed me off a pier or dropped me into a wave. I was afraid of water in the dishpan, in the bathtub, in an overflowing street gutter. Getting my hair washed was an ordeal that announced my plight to the entire neighborhood. I screamed myself into a frenzy whether a drop of water splashed into my eyes or not. I sat on the sand with my back to the ocean. I dreaded the swimming pool, hated the dank chlorine smell of the dressing room, the slick footbath we stepped into, the slippery cement, the other children sailing happily over my head as I clung to the side in two feet of greenish water. When I finally learned to swim, it was with a thrashing, anxious motion that exhausted me but by which I eventually reached the other side of the pool without drowning.

When I was twelve years old, I was baptized in the baptismal pool behind the pulpit in the Winterville (North Carolina) Missionary Baptist Church. In line with my girlfriends, all of us wearing white dresses, barefooted, prepared to share this experience as we had so many in our childhoods (it was as much a club initiation as anything else), I lay the burden I alone carried (all my friends were good swimmers) in the hands of God and Edward G. Cole, our minister who fished with my father as faithfully as he did everything else. I had seen those tanned fingers dig into a pail of shrimp bait, tie a fly, catch a glistening, flapping trout in midair, tighten a winch. I trusted those hands and they didn't fail me. I survived baptism.

I have always loved my sister, but I doubt she can say the same about me. In fact, she has admitted that during our childhood she hated me occasionally but intensely. And no wonder. I came screaming into her life ten days before her second birthday. At first colicky, then a miserable teether, I generated a certain amount of confusion, frustration, and hostility in the small, one-bedroom apartment where she had so recently reigned as queen. I used to bite her, but I don't remember what she did to me to precipitate my going for her leg. Surely I didn't bite without cause, knowing that some punishment would follow her screaming charge to Mother.

Mother was not an especially strict disciplinarian. Her spankings "hurt her more than they did us," a probable truth since she had a notoriously weak wrist. Neither Sandra nor I wanted to be first in line since the second culprit always received a lighter punishment. One of Mother's frequent disciplinary measures (and one we could hardly object to) was to make us sit in our small rockers until she saw some sign of contrition. Every time she left the room, we moved our chairs around, holding them tight to our behinds so we would always be sitting. Our worst punishment was simply her disapproval, a quivering sigh of disappointment that we were less than good.

Every afternoon while we napped, she polished our white hightop shoes and washed the laces. Because of the war, rubber was scarce, and there were no rubber pants, no teething rings, few nipples for the sterilized baby bottles. Mother once drove ninety miles to Raleigh to get a teething ring which turned out to be plastic, wearing precious tires in the process. While my sister liked to be fed, washed, and generally cared for, I rebelled. I thought I could do everything for myself and always tried.

In July before I entered first grade, our brother, Abbott, was born. Sandra and I were hoping for a boy, and our aunt Sue drove us all over town in "Blue Heaven," her 1936 Dodge sedan, going slowly so we could hang out the windows grinning ear to ear and shouting to everyone we passed, "We've got a baby brother!" The whole town smiled back at us, except for Thomas McLawhorn, who stuck out his tongue and said with all the vehemence a six-year-old could muster, "I reckon you think you're something now because you've got a brother." His mother had brought home a baby sister a few weeks before.

We lived between two houses. At the turn of the century, Pa—my father's father, Richard Hunsucker—had begun the haphazard building of one of those houses. Pa built the first three rooms before he married. He was a conservative man of German descent who had come to eastern North Carolina to ply his skill as a carriage builder. Hunsucker buggies and surreys were popular modes of transportation in the area for many years. Four years after his arrival in Winterville, he married Rosa Cox, the oldest daughter of the town's founder, "leaning on the arm of his best man," according to the newspaper account. As their family grew, so did the house. Eventually it sprawled across the lawn, a collection of gables and oddly shaped rooms with a porch that zigzagged across the front like a piece of rickrack trim.

Pa died soon after I was born. Ma lived until I was fourteen. We saw her frequently but our formal family visit was on Sunday nights. The grown-ups (there was always one or more of Daddy's six siblings in attendance) visited with Ma in her sitting room while the children were relegated to the parlor accompanied by Alice, our aunt who lived at home with Ma. Alice's task was to keep us entertained while the adults talked. She read to us (we especially liked the Peter Painter stories which appeared in a regional magazine), played Parcheesi, Bible Lotto, or held a Quaker meeting, the only rule of which was complete silence. We acted out our conversation, which inevitably resulted in gales of uncontrollable laughter. In desperation, Alice would march us to the kitchen where she made fudge, popped corn, or served the crisp lemony tea cookies she always kept in a tin for Ma's afternoon entertaining. As we got older, we joined the conversation in Ma's room, although we were careful to be seen more than heard. At Ma's, we were expected to be "good." Although I remember many happy times there, the "feel" of the house was nonetheless one of strict discipline, of self-control, of judgments passed down with sighs and frowns.

Then there was the Abbott house, where my mother had grown up. It was symmetrical, open, deep. If a child stood in the front door in the summertime, she could see the sun at the back, see patches of light in the open doorways

Sue Ellen Bridgers

along her path, view books, paintings, china and silver, camellias floating in glass bowls, gilded mirrors that reflected each other. But in the winter, when the doors were shut and no light or heat pervaded the hallway until night when the bedroom fires were lit, the hall was like a dungeon, a walk in a horror house where floorboards and shutters creaked, shadows took on monstrous proportions, and bloody hands were waiting to pull children into secret passages where they'd never be seen or heard of again.

This was a house for the imagination. In the window seat in the living room I was Jo, reading and scribbling as in *Little Women.* On a chaise lounge in the front bedroom I died many deaths. Before a dresser mirror I preached sermons that began with biblical texts and wandered into fairy tales, liberally strewn with bits of poetry and nursery rhymes. On my knees at Grandmother's mahogany and brass tea table, I was an English lady. On cold evenings, with the smell of cedar and winter fruit permeating the warm air of the closed-in back porch and firelight licking the glass pane of Grandmother's stove, I was a pioneer girl. In summer, my sister and I created a world of our own on blankets spread in the pale shade of a weeping willow in the side yard. At night we listened to the frogs that lived near the fish pool, creaking the porch glider between "ribbits." Here I learned to play "Sally in Her Petticoat" on the piano, listened to Grandmother quote poetry and read Granny Fox stories. (When she became a great-grandmother, it seemed natural that my children call her Granny Annie, which was her family name for eighteen years, until she died at the age of ninety-five.) Here I heard the stories of her childhood, of growing up among the McGlohon clan a few miles away at Renston. Here I learned what dying meant, for she could not speak of her dead sisters or her

small son without a hard shuddering in her chest that told me she was still bereft and would forever be.

In this house, emotions ran high. There was constant company and more work than could ever be finished. The emotional demands of her extended family left Grandmother exhausted. Exhaustion made her irritable and demanding. Everybody loved her, and she, wearied with protecting her family against the odds of human failure, had little energy to love anyone. The home she created collapsed around her periodically, brought down by her frustration that domestic help was shiftless, that her favorite child had died as the result of a freak accident, that her husband lacked the social aptitude and interests she treasured, that her daughter had missed the family beauty by being black-haired, dark-eyed, a foreign child. She was plagued by terrible headaches and palpitations of the heart. The emotional support she needed she found in her daughter, heaping on her the same expectations and obligations and limitations she felt herself.

Here family life was exposed. Here I was afraid and yet loved. Here I was valued and accepted, but I felt responsibilities, too. On Saturdays I set the Sunday table for Grandmother, cherishing each piece of china, each stem of crystal, each dull silver spoon. I pinched off bits of dough from the dough board to make funny peaked biscuits. I stirred the peach preserves for her to keep them from scorching. I held the casing to the sausage stuffer on hog-killing days. I tried to sew at her pedal machine and made disastrous attempts at embroidery. I delighted in turning the crank handle of the huge Victrola, sending whiny, recorded hymns into the gloomy hallway.

I took courage approaching her back steps, which were always covered with cats that wouldn't give foot space unless nudged. I didn't like cats. Once when Grandmother was laid up with a broken arm, she sent me out into the backyard to rescue a baby kitten that had been abandoned in a rainstorm. I was terrified at the prospect of touching the limp, mewing little body, but I was more afraid of Grandmother's ire. The kitten died, but at least it didn't drown, and I did not disappoint Grandmother.

The house my parents built, and into which we moved when I was six, was beside Grandmother's. Ma's house was perhaps a half-mile away, on the other end of Winterville, an easy walk. One block over from us lived Ma's sister, my great-aunt Dora, in the house their father had built in 1880. Out in the country three miles from Winterville was Renston, where Grandmother had grown up. Although the McGlohon homeplace was deserted, the mill and store owned by her parents were still in operation, run by my uncle. We were surrounded by kin. The lessons of such an upbringing are both difficult and joyful. There were perhaps too many eyes focused on us, and yet there was an abundance of concern and well-intentioned affection. We learned to be proud of our heritage; we knew the unyielding, powerful hold of family; we recognized our dependence on the land, on the weather, on the changing seasons, on daily physical labor. It was the love of land that shaped our lives. Both my grandfathers, in addition to being businessmen, were farmers. Their wives had brought to their marriages large tracts of fertile tobacco and cotton land, packhorse, tenant houses, curing barns, dense woods. Our family's tenacity was itself a product of the earth, for the land was truly priceless then. Its connective powers

Sue Ellen (right) with her mother, Bett Abbott Hunsucker, and sister, Sandra, 1944.

bonded as much misery as joy, as much history as prospects for the future. It gave us boundaries but also space. This is where I come from, I could always say, holding a dark clump of soil in my hand. And then, opening my fingers, I could watch it fall.

My parents grew up together. Wayland was two years ahead of Bett in school, a good student, popular with his peers and in the community, industrious and interested in getting ahead in the world. Mother thought she was too big, although in all her photographs she is tall, slender, and pretty. She played basketball and starred in the school drama productions. She went to college. Daddy wanted to, but because of the Depression his father asked him to help out the family financially, so he began farming instead. He always regretted not having a college education.

He and Mother were married in 1937 when he was twenty-four and she was twenty-three. They visited his sister in St. Petersburg, Florida, on their honeymoon and came home to the apartment his father had fashioned out of half of a two-story dwelling he owned. Daddy's brother and his wife eventually moved into the other side of the house. Daddy had been elected mayor of Winterville when he was twenty-one years old, and he served the town for thirteen years. During his administration the water and sewer system and the first telephone lines were installed. We had the first residential telephone, which was the envy of all our school friends, even though there was no one for us to call.

We were more excited when phones were installed in our friends' houses because finally we had someone to talk to.

Mother and Daddy's first child, a daughter named Susan Elizabeth, died the day she was born. Sandra Elizabeth was born the next year. Two years later I arrived on my aunt Sue's birthday, September 20, 1942. Aunt Sue asked if she could name me Sue Ellen, and Mother approved. When I was three I became ill, the main symptom being a continuous low-grade fever. Because I already had an enlarged heart and a murmur, my case was diagnosed as rheumatic fever, and I led a sort of semi-invalid life for several years. I don't remember this as much of a hardship on me, but I'm sure Mother found it difficult to keep me quiet. Rest was the only recommended therapy other than a terrible-tasting liquid, occasional penicillin shots, and treatments in the doctor's office that are best left undescribed.

The pediatrician was in Greenville, eight miles away. Usually Mother drove, but sometimes we went on the bus. We always went up to the doctor's office in a freight elevator enclosed in a black metal grid, the door of which unfolded to shut us in, in the most sinister fashion. After being seen by the doctor, we always went to the drugstore and sat on the spinning stools to have a fountain Coke mixed by the waitress and "nabs." If anything appeased my bad disposition more than a trip to the drugstore with its black-and-white tile floor, its heavy medicinal smells mingling with cosmetics and cola syrup, it was getting a new coloring book from a rack in the dime store next door. My favorites were those which purported to depict the daily lives of popular movie stars. Even better than that was going to the movies.

Mother took Sandra and me as often as she could. Those were the days of musicals, when Jane Powell or Doris Day could break into song at any given moment, when Fred Astaire danced everywhere, even on the ceiling (we went home and tried to figure out how), and Judy Garland and Van Johnson fell in love over and over again. We loved them all. Equally inspiring were the biographical films—*The Great Caruso, With a Song in My Heart, Look for the Silver Lining*. When we were small, we went on Sunday afternoons when the Technicolor movies played. As we grew older, we finagled rides to the Saturday afternoon matinees as well and took in our share of B westerns, adventure serials, and gangster films. We even went to the drive-in, all of us piled into Daddy's Chrysler, the staticky speaker attached to the window, trying to stay awake to see Jackie Robinson being cheered around the bases at Ebbets Field. My weekend of movies and church filled me with such dramatic fervor that I wanted to be both a movie star and a missionary.

I remember the strangeness of my first night in our new house. I was in a twin bed rather than sharing with my sister as we always had, and although she was in the same room, I felt a separateness. The house felt so big after the cramped space of a one-bedroom apartment occupied by the five of us. The living room looked like a palatial hall, the kitchen big enough to throw a party in (and we did), the paneled den wonderfully cozy.

Soon we had a television, and I was immediately addicted to the dramatic shows, all of them live, where I first saw many stage actors picking up extra work in that exciting new medium. It was acting in the raw, experimental direction, strange plays written more for psychological impact than anything I had ever encountered. Then there was Ed Sullivan bringing New York to me every Sunday night. Before that snowy screen I heard arias for the first time, watched the Dying Swan and the *Pas de deux* from *The Sleeping Beauty,* saw Mary Martin washing that man right out of her hair in a portable shower stall, heard Pearl Bailey sing and talk her jive. With Edward R. Murrow, I went into the living rooms of the famous; from John Cameron Swayze, I heard what was happening in the world. From a news bulletin flashing across the screen, I learned that the Korean War was over and that there was no reason to fearfully watch the sky and race inside at the droning approach of every airplane. Now television is too much with us; it has become invasive in our lives. But then, in the early fifties, it was a miraculous link to an expanding world.

There was a world close at hand for me to study as well. In a small town, children see people who affect their lives, and yet those people themselves may remain strangers. One such person was Henry, a deaf-mute who also had a debilitating illness that caused him to suffer tremors. Henry rode in a cart pulled by a mule, and every day when he passed our house, he would seem to be nodding a greeting to us and struggling to make a lopsided smile. He was, we believed, a madman among us, and we lived in fear that one day he would spring off the cart and take us screaming through the streets while the town looked on, unable or unwilling to save us. I was a teenager before I went close enough to Henry to see that he had only one leg, the other a stump at the knee, and even then I felt not sympathy, but wariness. Even then I did not see a human being when I cast hurried, sideways glances at Henry, for over the years he had come to represent the menace of abnormality. On him I focused my early, unspeakable fears, my first inklings that all was not safe, that there was suffering that could not be soothed. And if my town, even my parents, harbored such sickness, what other horrors lay beyond the boundaries of my narrow world?

Then there was Uncle Mose, a black man who lived in a tiny house on the edge of Daddy's farm. He was an old man even then, doing odd jobs rather than a full day's work. He planted his garden in spring, kept the curing fires going in summer, picked up pecans and raked leaves in the fall, dug potatoes in winter. He would come to our house with something from his garden or with nuts in a soft, ragged paper sack or with cups of vanilla ice cream he'd bought for a nickel apiece at the store, and he'd thrust his gift at Mother and then stand there on the steps and fuss at her, while she stood in the doorway holding the sack, head bent, not really looking at him. Was she ashamed to look? What did the fussing mean?

As a child, I recognized bitterness in his voice, such discontentment at his lot in life, and yet I knew he could speak to her as he did only because he sensed in her a common ground, a core of likeness that went straight to the heart. And she, so free with the black women with whom she cleaned house, made pickles, and rendered lard, lowered her head as if she were taking a deserved tongue-lashing. What strange kinship was between them? Why didn't she talk back, spitting out her own tightly locked frustration at what life had dealt her? I don't know. Perhaps he was just a crazy old man whom the family indulged, but

"My father, Wayland Hunsucker, with my brother, Abbott."

I remember him because, together, he and my mother showed me that no race, no condition of living, no degree of ignorance or intelligence, is without its own rage and its own kind of affection.

When I was eleven, my father suffered his first debilitating bout with mental depression. The treatment of mental illness was too modern a science for our rural area, and Mother's desperation to find him help led her to a psychiatrist in Raleigh. She drove Daddy to Raleigh twice a week, and finally he was hospitalized there. Periodically over the next fifteen years he was hospitalized, treated with medication and shock treatments until he was able to function, then sent home for a period of time during which he farmed and carried on some semblance of normality before slipping back into a catatonic, depressed state that once again required hospitalization. The effects of his illness on each of us children were individual and private. On the surface, we continued our lives, went to school, had friends over, participated in all the activities of church, school, and community life. It is to Mother's credit that she, frequently ill herself and living under tremendous emotional stress, gave us a supportive environment in which to grow, constantly reminding us of our capabilities, demonstrating every day her unflagging love and commitment to us and her intention that we use our talents both to

Four generations, 1942: Mother, Bett Abbott Hunsucker; grandmother, Annie McGlohon Abbott; great-grandmother, Elizabeth Kittrell McGlohon holding Sandra. "Mother was expecting me at the time."

make our way in the world and in service to the community.

I have always wanted to be a writer. The first sign was, I suppose, that I loved to be read to. Mother bought us books before we had our own resources, and they were my most treasured belongings, respected but well used until the pages were soft, the bindings worn, the covers frayed. No present delighted me more than a package just so in shape and weight that it could only be a book.

I wish I could remember the first story I ever heard. I'm sure it was either a Bible story or a fairy tale. Mother read to us daily with good humor and patience because she enjoyed those moments of escape as much as we did. Never mind that our escape route became familiar, even memorized territory. There was such pleasure in knowing the next phrase. There was comfort in the shapes of the letters from which she drew those memorable visual images.

My favorite Bible stories were Old Testament ones—the stories of David, his friendship with Jonathan, how he danced before the Ark, the tragedy of Absalom. Then the story of Abraham, of the brothers Jacob and Esau and the stolen birthright, of Ruth, of Joseph and his brothers—all stories of family and separation. I was both fascinated and

terrified by the theme of separation. Those stories defined a child's anxieties, and yet they comforted me as well. At least they confirmed my fears rather than ignored them. They also expressed my need for some power beyond human existence.

Of all the secular stories told me, there were two I didn't want to hear and still don't like: *The Three Little Pigs* and Carolyn Bailey's *The Little Rabbit Who Wanted Red Wings*. They are both separation stories but there is no divine hand hovering over them. Mother says she used to start reading *The Three Little Pigs* with bets among family members on how far she'd get before I broke into sobs. It was always about the third line, when the little pigs decided to leave their mother and go out into the big world alone. I was even more afraid of the little rabbit's tale, so terrified that I was struck dumb with fear at the first words and never cried at all. I would listen breathlessly to the horrible circumstances that surrounded not being recognized by one's own mother. It was too horrendous a fear to ever admit, but for many years I didn't make a wish, trying to avoid the foolish vanity that got the little rabbit into such terrible trouble.

What I did love were the adventures of Winnie-the-Pooh and his friends, the accompanying Milne volumes of poetry, *A Child's Garden of Verses*, the Uncle Remus stories, a host of children's books from *The Poky Little Puppy* to *The Little Engine That Could*, and many more which I learned by heart.

The revelation of my life was probably the moment when, in the first grade, I connected the printed curves and angles in the books at home with the alphabet I was learning to write myself. Now I had the tools! Now I could write a poem! So I did.

I wanted to write as much as I wanted to read, maybe more so. There was a thrill about it that I still can't describe, a sort of letting go that is, at the same time, extremely focused so that in the process actual words appear on the page. I still revel in it. Even now, knowing many of the pitfalls, the difficulties, the struggles of writing, I expect and sometimes receive that burst of spontaneous creative energy I felt as a child. I am always grateful for it.

My early career as a poet was sporadic, even seasonal, since most of our creative writing assignments in grammar school were associated with holidays. I covered all the angles of Halloween, Thanksgiving, Christmas, Valentine's Day, Easter, and then went on to Arbor Day, Columbus Day, any celebration I could find. By the time I was in high school I was writing personal poems, my subject matter drawn from real life. Quick and frenetic, born out of that moment of ecstasy when words would spring into my head, I wrote about a bird outside my window, the first snow of the season, the mingled smells of a kitchen on a wintry night, about being in and out of love. I sent several of these poems to a newspaper that published a daily poem and was therefore in constant need. Every one I submitted appeared in print. There was no pay, but the sight of a thirteen-year-old's words on the page was heady enough. I was proving myself, at least to myself.

I was also writing short stories. I saved enough money to buy a used typewriter and gave up writing in longhand permanently. During this time I frequently felt as if I were living two lives. At school I was involved in all the typical activities—band, chorus, clubs, cheerleading, piano practice, enjoying a social life; but in my private life, in my room, I was a writer. It is hard to sustain a writer's energy, especially when one has no understanding of it. I didn't know how to tap into it, only felt the necessity of using it when it appeared. I banged the typewriter frantically as my fingers learned how to keep up with my head. I didn't know anything about planning. Wonderful beginnings met defeat on the second page because I hadn't learned about the subconscious thinking that the work required or the conscious period of discovery and thought before any successful writing could be done. I hadn't found my method, but like most people compelled to use their creative energy, I tried everything I could think of: borrowed ideas, themes, even characters; invented plots about which I knew absolutely nothing, followed by rebellion against the research the idea required. With all these failures, I kept on writing.

All this time, my mother supported me in her quiet, noninterfering way. She never asked to read what I was writing but took it upon herself to tell friends I was busy if they phoned or came by when the typewriter was clicking. Such an attitude from someone whose opinion you treasure is a validation of yourself; it is the beginning of dreams turned into reality.

I remember being in the car with Mother driving when I was twelve or thirteen. I remember the intersection at which we stopped for the light to change. The sensations of that moment—the lights from the service station on the corner, the other cars, the hum of our engine—are still with me. I was talking about the future the way young people do, wanting one minute to be a teacher, the next an engineer. I thought perhaps I would be a nurse. "Oh, Sue Ellen," she said almost sternly, as if to make finally clear what she had always known, "you are going to be a writer." And so I am.

The road took turns I didn't expect. I entered college in the fall of 1960. The trip took twenty minutes on the narrow "tar road" to East Carolina College in Greenville. I knew the campus. It was where Mother had taken me to concerts and plays, where as high school students, my friends and I had cruised to get a look at the college scene. But now it was different. Now it was where I lived. My roommate was my best friend. Elizabeth Carroll and I had known each other all our lives. We were in the same classroom from the first through the eighth grades and then shared most of our high school classes. We had studied together, learned dance steps together, were cheerleaders together, ate, talked, and commiserated together. We rode together on the activity bus on band trips and to ball games. She taught me to skate. We shared vacations, church pews, giggling fits, sang alto side by side in the school chorus and the church choir. She was the epitome of a good friend, for in the twenty years we shared, she was never cruel, rarely irritable, and always supportive. When we were eighteen, she was the only person I knew who could and would live with me. What I offered her, I couldn't say, unless it was the security of the familiar. She knew me well.

These events colored my college life: John Glenn orbited the earth, John Kennedy visited our campus and subsequently became president, James Meredith was en-

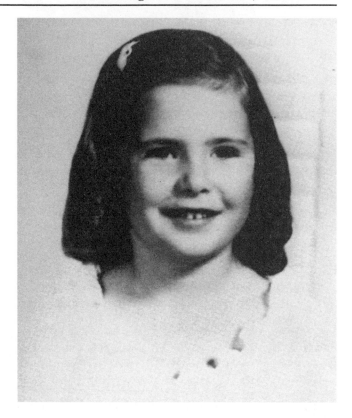

Sue Ellen at five years of age.

rolled as the first black student at Ole Miss. We were optimistic, expectant for the future, reveling in being young, and our music—the black bebop singers, Paul Anka, Dick Clark, and especially Elvis Presley—made being young a position of power. Yet we spent a sleepless night during a hurricane, another during the Cuban Missile Crisis.

The first week of college I climbed the worn steps to the third floor of Austin Building and entered, without knocking, a small windowless world of literary ostracism. What can compare to a college literary magazine for snobbery, ego-tripping, and scorched coffee? It was a community completely foreign to a girl from a small-town high school, but for all its intellectual snobbery, its closed-circuited, heated relationships, it was where I wanted to be. I volunteered as a typist. Intellectuals back then didn't bother to learn to type, and so I found myself indispensable typing correspondence, copy, even drafts of would-be writers' manuscripts. I made no mention of my own ambitions, and no one asked.

Meanwhile, I was reading the submitted poems, essays, stories. I was figuring out where I could fit in. I was also discovering that my work, as unpolished as it was, was better than most of theirs. In the winter, I slipped a couple of poems into the submissions box, and they appeared in the spring issue. I became the book review editor. The next fall I submitted a short story. The editor read it; the associate editor read it; Ovid Pierce, writer-in-residence who also served as the magazine's advisor, read it. The pronouncement came down as if from on high. It was good. I became the associate editor.

In the fall of my junior year, Mac Hyman came to campus as visiting writer-in-residence. His office, like that of most of the English faculty, was on the third floor of Austin along with the campus radio station and the local literary society. We were all stuck under the eaves with the pigeons, and it made for a congenial mix of students and faculty who took phone messages for each other, shared tables at lunch, and socialized in general. Mac, who had written *No Time for Sergeants* and was working on another book while teaching American literature, introduced me to Ben Bridgers, his office mate who was twenty-three but looked even younger, had curly black hair, blue eyes, and a soft, Southwesternly way of speaking. Ben and I shared many academic interests, although his knowledge of contemporary literature went far beyond the Southern genre I was steeped in. I could imagine us in a big, old white house surrounded by books, he writing scholarly essays in one room while I produced poems and fiction in another.

We were married in March 1963, during the break between winter and spring quarters. My professors let me take my exams early. Ben graded the last of his exams on our wedding night, turned in the grades the next morning, and we were off to Washington, D.C., to troop through the National Art Gallery. Books, art, music—we had those things in common. The next year we had a baby as well.

By the time Elizabeth Abbott was born, my life was on its way to being so strange and complicated I can barely straighten it out even now. At the end of the spring quarter,

Ben had resigned from his teaching job at East Carolina, suffering from academic burnout. He wanted and needed a break before tackling a doctoral program. He wasn't even sure he wanted to teach at all. With Mac's encouragement, he joined the air force, which would provide a living while he mulled over the future. I dropped out of college and went with him to Mississippi for a year. The next year we moved to Rapid City, South Dakota, where Ben was stationed at the SAC base. There, in 1966, Jane Bennett was born. Meanwhile, Ben had decided to go to law school, and a chance trip to Chapel Hill during a Christmas holiday convinced him that he wanted to attend the University of North Carolina. A year and a half later, we were back in Chapel Hill, with Ben enrolled in law school and me in an apartment across town with two small daughters and a baby on the way. Sean MacKenzie was born in March 1968, and our family was complete.

When Sean was in the first grade, I finally went back to college. We had moved to Sylva, a small town in the mountains of western North Carolina which met our basic requirements: a job for Ben, a college for me, and an Episcopal church for all of us. I graduated from Western Carolina University in 1976, the same year my first novel, *Home before Dark,* was published. I was finally, after so many years, a college graduate and a professional writer.

Sue Ellen and Ben Bridgers on their wedding day, March 17, 1963.

Marching in the Sylva Christmas Parade, 1975. Sue Ellen is under the sign "Make Policy, not Coffee."

With one book to my credit and a recommendation from *Redbook* magazine, I was awarded a fellowship to the Bread Loaf Writers' Conference in Vermont that summer. The next summer Ben and I took the children to England for a month, visiting many of the places already familiar from our studies. Elizabeth spent her trip with an exchange family in Lincolnshire, so we were able to take Ben's teenage sister with us. Returning home, I set about writing a second book, concerned, as all writers must be, that the success of the first had been a fluke.

When I was growing up, reading had been a way of avoiding housework. Our other deterrents to developing any domestic skills were homework assignments and piano practice. Sandra and I have never been more than mediocre pianists, but we became voracious readers. Mother considered reading a serious endeavor, and she tried not to interrupt us whether we were reading *Doctor Zhivago* or the *Saturday Evening Post*. She understood that the reader must enter a book, and she hesitated to call us out of an invented world into our more mundane one.

Paperback books were affordable then, most of them costing less than a dollar. We discovered writers, exchanged books, read straight through Hemingway, Fitzgerald, Steinbeck, Porter, Wolfe, waded into Faulkner. "Aren't you finished yet?" we would ask, although we were never anxious to finish a book ourselves. School assignments introduced us to Thomas Hardy, the Brontë sisters, Jane Austen, George Eliot, Dickens. We read popular novels, too, those by Leon Uris, Allen Drury, Daphne du Maurier. On Grandmother's shelves we discovered a first edition of *Gone with the Wind,* old copies of women's novels she'd kept, collections of poetry, the works of Sir Walter Scott.

My writing style changed with my reading. While absorbed in the poetic flow of Thomas Wolfe, I flowed a little myself. Escaping into *Tom Jones*'s country, I ad-dressed my reader at every opportunity. When reading Hemingway, my style became spare, sentences chopped, meanings understated. Mother counted five repetitions of the word "fine" in one meager postcard I sent her from the beach.

Sandra and I read in the bathtub, in bed, sprawled on the wicker porch furniture, on the beach. She tanned easily to a beautiful dark brown. I burned while getting in one more chapter before gathering up armloads of beach paraphernalia to find a bit of shade.

Because there was no entertainment in Winterville, much of our drama came from religion. Except for a rare three-truck, one-ring circus that pitched its ragged, musty tent on the edge of town for one night, tent poles being hoisted in a vacant lot meant an itinerant preacher was on the loose and frothing at the mouth to bring us word of damnation, salvation, and healing. How he wanted to make us whole!

My friends and I lay in a dry ditch in the dark and peered over the bank to watch the pianist make rippling flourishes on an old upright piano as she played "Jesus Is Calling" and "Throw out the Lifeline," songs of tender mercy, of saving embraces, of Jesus lifting us up in gentle arms. But then the preacher started, casting away our tinny hope, trampling it as he stomped across the rickety platform, pounding the Bible in his hand as if to destroy it. Flinging his arms wide, fingers flapping like a twenties' dancer while he roared out our doom, he exposed our unwashed souls to a God of wrath who wielded a bloody swift sword ready to cut us down if we so much as raised our sinful heads. And then he prayed. Sweat dripped off his nose, ran down his neck into his collar; splotches appeared under his arms, down the seam of his coat. He strained and sobbed and shouted. The way to salvation was made known to me: through this man to Jesus to God. Thus was the straight and narrow path to redemption.

The congregation poured forward to touch him, to reach God through this outstretched hand with its diamond ring, its manicured nails, its soft palm. We lay in the ditch, terrified of exposure, of being the last, the worst sinners, because we had come to spy not to pray, to giggle not to sing. Although watching this spectacle was irresistible, I always felt remorseful afterwards because part of me did believe. Somewhere deep inside, I harbored that black spot the preacher ranted about. I was in need of healing.

I used to put my hand on the radio. Before I saw a faith healer in action and recognized the psychological sham, saw the frenzy of it and knew what a momentary burst of adrenaline could do, I heard these messengers of renewable health on the radio. They were smooth talkers begging for donations for their ministry—"love gifts" they were called—then preaching fire and brimstone and ending with a plea for the listeners to pray with them. Without my particular prayer and my small hand touching the warm surface of the Philco, no healing could take place. I believed it! It was consistent with my belief that I was responsible for the world, that whatever action I took affected the course of all human events. My failure with the last forkful of string beans meant some child in Africa would starve. (What a terrible philosophical approach! Because millions of children heard and discarded that feeble didacticism, we did not believe until it was too late that the Third World was starving.)

In addition to being a believer, I was people-oriented. The natural world didn't interest me nearly as much as the people who inhabited our town, whom I read about, or who came alive in our family stories. I believed in the Easter Bunny, imagining a stand-up rabbit much like the one in the advertisements for *Harvey.* I believed that Jack Frost curled the leaves in fall. No matter that an actual rabbit couldn't possibly carry Easter baskets or that frost appeared with a burst of cold air from the north. For generations, our family had planted seeds in spring, tended corn, beans, cotton, tobacco through the summer, harvested the crops in the fall. I saw no miracle there, only hard work, the labor of humans set against the fickleness of the weather.

I was also gullible. My mother once told me that if I picked up an elephant the day it was born and continued to lift it daily, I would be able to pick up a grown elephant. It made sense to me. Grandmother told of having seen Santa Claus, and her renditions of this story caused me to hold my breath, seeing in my mind's eye the flickering firelight of the bedroom and a bright red arm with its furry cuff extending across the orange glow to put a china doll in her stocking. In the bed where she lay as quiet as a mouse, she watched the shadow of the figure until it simply vanished. Then she closed her eyes, afraid to believe what she had seen but more afraid to doubt. When she opened her eyes to the gloomy, cold dawn of her room, the fire was ashes, the magical play of light and shadow forever gone, but the doll was there. It was real and she held it gently, carefully, as she would a bird's nest of blue-speckled eggs or a newborn kitten. Her belief in the mystery and magic of what could happen on Christmas Eve made it more true to me than if I had seen Santa myself. I believe in him still.

I have always believed in visions. While I've had no mystical experiences myself, I pay attention to claims of them because in my work I have seen one level of that kind of attunement. Periodically, there occurs in my mind a time of heightened awareness, of sensitivity to everything seen or heard, to every internal sensation, that makes creative energy churn until it boils to the surface, bringing actual words with it—visions made concrete, tangible, formed into these curlicues that represent our thoughts in language. My early books were begun because of a visionary moment, a scene that came to me spontaneously with images so potent I couldn't shake free of them.

Home before Dark began with a family whom I visualized in the car with my own family when we were on our way to Winterville for a weekend visit. *All Together Now* began with Hazard Whitaker doing a soft-shoe dance on the front porch, a scene my friend Judy Budd once described from her own childhood. The first sentence of *Notes for Another Life* was written on the edge of a pocket calendar because I was driving the car at the time. I heard a girl and her grandmother singing old popular songs, and I

The Bridgers Family Portrait: (clockwise from bottom left) Sue Ellen, Elizabeth, Bennett, Ben, and Sean, 1980. Painting by Shirley Grant.

Sue Ellen (left) with Sue Hager and Judy Budd before graduation from Western Carolina University, 1976.

knew where they were going and why. I began writing *Sara Will* when, in my mind's eye, I saw Sara coming down the road in the twilight. I recognized her as someone I knew.

The later books, *Permanent Connections, Keeping Christina,* and *All We Know of Heaven,* came from a combination of vision and story. Our son, Sean, experienced a moment of kinship with his grandfather that gave me the impetus for *Permanent Connections:* when Sean was a boy, he and his grandfather hiked into a national park in the Ozarks to find the foundation stones of the cabin where his grandfather had been born and reared. Resting there, his grandfather told him stories of the deprivation and isolation of that life. Recounting the adventure to me, ten-year-old Sean ended with "So now I know Grandpa"— the value of story made crystal clear.

Christina in *Keeping Christina* was in some ways like a woman I have known in my adult life, but I knew that young women dealt with the same issues of trust that Annie does when she befriends Christina. Christina ingratiates herself to Annie's family, making it even more difficult for Annie to be attentive to her own intuition about Christina's motives. In addition to being a story about friendship, *Keeping Christina* delves into the tension between a mother and a teenage daughter, that painful pushing and pulling we've long believed denotes new birth—daughters becoming women. Perhaps that time of angry outbursts and fierce combat we thought necessary for girls to become women isn't necessary at all. Mothers in solidarity with their daughters is strengthening for both of them.

Another issue dear to my heart in *Keeping Christina* is the Shakespeare authorship question. Years ago, my

husband and I became interested in the possibility that Edward de Vere, the seventeenth earl of Oxford, was the author of the plays and poems attributed to one William Shaksper of Stratford. We gradually began accumulating research on the subject and found ourselves leaning more and more toward the Oxfordian argument. Our children, always excited by a mystery, became interested in the question as well, so I knew it could be intriguing even to students without a literary bent. Since the school setting is prevalent in *Keeping Christina,* I decided to use the question to create an intellectual freedom issue in a public school. The students want to have a debate about authorship, and eventually they do, giving the reader a chance to learn some of the arguments made by both the Stratfordian and the Oxfordian contingencies. This sub-plot also affects Annie's relationship with her mother, who is an avid Oxfordian.

I was privileged to speak to the Oxford Shakespeare Society in 1994. I recalled for them sitting in a college classroom in 1962 while a gale outside brought torrents of rain through the tall opened windows as Miss Mary Green leaned against her desk reading *King Lear.* None of us moved. At the end of the hour, Miss Green looked out at her drenched students and said with a tremulous sigh, "How perfect for Lear!" I don't know what Miss Green thought about the authorship controversy. I'd never heard of it at the time. Perhaps neither had she. But she knew the plays, and her enthusiasm for them kept us still through a thunderstorm. She loved the characters, the insights, the words. Her delight reminds me that we needn't answer the authorship question to love the work, but I do want students to have a chance to know this controversy exists. It makes studying the plays more interesting and gives them a new forum for thinking about creativity—where it springs from and how to nurture it.

The central event in *All We Know of Heaven*, published in 1996, occurred in my family when my mother was a child. The story tells of her young cousin's marriage, which ended in tragedy. It is a story I had always wanted to tell—my first attempt was as a college student when I wrote a couple of scenes from Bethany's childhood, but I wasn't ready to tell her story yet. Years later, in the nineties, I made another attempt and, several revisions later, had compressed the story into a small book that I hoped captured the essence of Bethany's story, a life lived with courage and compassion and with much to forgive. Many of the actual events were lost to me. My mother had been a child when her cousin had married and could not recall many details. My grandmother, who told me the story when I was a child, censored it heavily for my ears although I heard the sadness in her voice. I envisioned the world she described and held that memory until I thought perhaps I knew enough myself of courage and compassion to write it down.

After the visionary moments with each story, the hard part begins: months of writing and revising, periods of doubt, moments of rapidly flowing words too intense to sustain, days of mental aridness. But with all that, I know that my writing history sounds too easy. I sent *Home before Dark* to Anne Mollegen Smith at *Redbook* asking for suggestions for placing it. *Redbook* bought the manuscript, and Anne suggested I send it to Pat Ross, senior editor and later vice president in the juvenile department at Alfred A. Knopf. Pat called within a few days to introduce herself and to say that she was enthusiastic about publishing the book. I knew absolutely nothing about young-adult fiction, but I was delighted to learn Pat believed the story would find an audience among young people.

Home before Dark appeared in *Redbook* in July 1976, and the hardback edition with Knopf came out in the fall. I received the first copy in New York on my way to Bread Loaf. It was beautifully produced, and browsing through it, I wasn't embarrassed by it as I'd feared I might be. Instead, I felt quite detached from it. I was a little disappointed with myself because I wanted to get really excited about this tangible evidence of my success. After all, my name on the title page of a Borzoi book had been one of my lifelong dreams.

I don't think I showed the book to anyone at Bread Loaf except Toni Morrison, who carefully turned it over in her hands as if testing the feel of it before saying, "A book is a good thing." That was what I needed to hear—not that I was wonderful to have written it or that it was an extraordinary accomplishment, but simply that with it, I had joined the ranks of those with an opportunity for doing a good thing. It is, beyond all else, what we are striving for.

When we moved to Chapel Hill in 1967, I went from one isolated environment to another. The air force (and South Dakota) had provided a kind of immunization against the struggles and tragedies of those years. The world came to us via television, and although we grieved over the Tonkin Resolution, the murders of civil rights workers in Mississippi, and the burning of Watts, I was too involved with babies and managing a household to be more than a social-gathering activist, always ready to expound the liberal Democratic principles I was raised on.

In Chapel Hill, with three small children and a law-student husband holding down two part-time jobs on the side, I found myself trapped again, although most of the time I was too harried to notice. I wasn't doing what I'd intended with my life, but I was achieving what seemed necessary at the moment: keeping children safe and clean, putting meals on the table, and being as thrifty as our limited income demanded. I didn't write at all. The typewriter, which I sometimes bumped against while getting the vacuum cleaner out of the closet, seemed like an enemy, a hidden menace that would, I prayed, keep silent as long as it was left undisturbed.

But where was *I* all this time? Hidden too, I suppose. I never talked about writing. (I have not changed much in that. Writing still seems something better accomplished than talked about.) Now and then, what seemed like my secret demon raised her head to question what I was doing, chained to either the kitchen sink or the clotheslines. My response was simple and truthful: I loved the people in my care. I had responsibilities to them. There were only so many hours in the day and just having done what seemed essential, I always fell into bed exhausted. There was no time, no place for myself. I hesitate to say that I was a little mad and yet, looking back, I think I was. I was like a prisoner incarcerated in the room. The room was nice, and I was busy and productive in it, and yet I knew there were other rooms I couldn't go into. The locked door was maddening, holding tight my doubts about my abilities beyond keeping house. In 1970, I gave the door a tentative push. One of the first stories I wrote was about a young woman who wanted her true self acknowledged by someone, even a stranger, for just a moment. I didn't connect the story with my own life at the time, but I see the connection now.

Sue Ellen and daughter Elizabeth before church service, 1976.

Christmas in Winterville, 1984. (Front row from left) Lynn Hunsucker, Bennett, Sean, Elizabeth; (back row) Sue Ellen, Abbott holding Matthew, Bett holding Caitlin, Ben holding Megan, Sandra.

Ben was supportive of my fluttering attempts at writing professionally, but there was little he could do to eliminate or help with the roles I fulfilled in our family. His own taxing lifestyle as student, financial supporter, and parent took all his energy. I'm pleased that the children don't remember the grind of our daily lives during those years. They remember that Daddy was home with them in the evenings from dinnertime until they went to bed. They didn't know that his only studying time was after they were asleep, which prevented our having more than occasional private moments and little social life.

I sold my first stories. I wonder if I would have given up had not these small successes come so quickly. It's a question I'll never be able to answer. Wanting desperately to succeed as a writer and believing some minor success was possible, I began searching for ways to make my two lives coexist. Having opened another room, I needed to make sure it fitted with the rest of the house. I began reading the work of women writers with a conscious goal of discovering how they wrote and how they managed their lives. I attended a few feminist meetings in the Chapel Hill area that year, but they involved kinds of activism I didn't have time for. Although I supported the goals of these groups, I felt my professional life was too new and needed too much nurturing for me to dissipate my meager store of creative energy on anything but my own work.

However, when we moved to Sylva in 1971, I began to look for other women who were struggling to achieve autonomy. I joined the League of Women Voters and there found a group of young women whose interests in political and social issues came directly from their personal needs for equality, places in the job market, recognition of their value as wives and mothers, but also validation of their decisions to fulfill themselves in other ways. Out of that core of women and joined by others, we formed a consciousness-raising group which met weekly for several years, forming bonds of support and friendship that time and distance can never obliterate. Three of us—Judy Budd, Sue Hager, and I— went back to college in 1975, and Judy and I graduated together. Veronica Nicholas ran for public office and served as a county commissioner before entering a graduate program in public policy. All of us joined the work force.

Although I was involved with the issues crystalized by the feminist movement, I set my second novel, *All Together Now,* in 1951. One of the main characters, a retarded man named Dwayne Pickens, was based on a person Ben had known in Fort Smith, Arkansas, in the fifties, and I wanted to set the story in the same period. *Notes for Another Life* takes place in the present, and although I didn't think consciously about dealing with a feminist issue, I know that the choices the mother Karen makes reflect a growing urgency on the part of women to refuse entrapment. *Sara Will,* published in 1985 by Harper and Row, is about a woman learning contentment in relationships, but it is a struggle for her. She is working her way out of isolation into a fuller life, and that is also a feminist theme. The chance to be one's authentic self is one of the goals of all worthwhile social movements, but the commitments involved must be personal choices. Those decisions come from the individual heart and mind, not from a platform or agenda.

Such is the case with Ginny Collier, the mother in *Permanent Connections.* She has left an unhappy marriage and brought her teenage daughter, Ellery, to a little mountain community where she intends to have a fuller, freer life as a weaver than she'd had as a corporate wife. The friction between Ginny and Ellery is palpable—Ellery longs for her former life and resents her mother and the provincial atmosphere she's forced to inhabit. Ginny knows she must wait out her daughter's defiance; meanwhile, she initiates friendship with an agoraphobic neighbor and eventually helps the woman enter the world again. In *Keeping Christina,* Annie treats her new friend Christina with the care and affection she's been taught to offer, so when she begins to distrust Christina, she also begins to doubt herself. Young women as caretakers are vulnerable, willing to avoid acknowledging and exposing a fraud. Because *All We Know of Heaven* was written from an actual event, I knew some of the strengths and weaknesses of the major characters, especially Charlotte, who is based, in part, on the character of my grandmother Abbott. The older I am, the more I recognize my grandmother in my own actions. In fact, when I was working on the earlier version of the book, a third-person narrative but with the sensibility of Charlotte at its core, one of our sons-in-law read the manuscript and complained about Charlotte's "voice", which he felt colored the story in a negative way. "But that's my voice," I responded. "I know," he said. So much for our family dynamics! But now it is obvious that one of the strengths of the published version is the multiple voices, only one of which is Charlotte's.

Virginia Woolf said, "We think back through our mothers." I sense in all my books, and most especially in *All We Know of Heaven,* the connection I have to the women of my past, many of whom I never met but whose stories deepened in the living and are constantly recounted in words and actions. Although quite different in looks and personality, I see my mother taking on some of my grandmother's attributes. She is our storyteller now, our keeper of memory. Having laid down many of the burdens she carried as a younger woman, she approaches her eighty-fifth birthday alive to the simple joys of arranging a bouquet of flowers, reading to a great-grandchild, reveling in a sunset, going on her first sail.

At fifty-six, I am more aware than ever before of my opportunities to make choices. My family heritage both burdened and blessed me with an accumulation of maxims and dictated certain behavior, a life view which is finally my choice to accept as my own or to reject, like uncomfortable clothing or a shoe that doesn't fit.

My cousin Mary Virginia, an artist living in Washington, D.C., and I shared many experiences growing up in Winterville, and when we are together now, we frequently compare the steps we've taken since then, each in her own place and time, to find ourselves once again on the same path like the comrades we were as children.

Mary Virginia's great-grandmother and mine were sisters-in-law, and in the eighties, I frequently spoke at conferences and in classrooms about their fierce commitment to land and family and the courage with which they survived the conditions of their difficult lives at the turn of the century. Their legacy is one their great-granddaughters share, holding close those memories of another time, and yet we want more for ourselves, more visions made reality, more choices, more boundless leaps toward creativity in our individual work, of which I can only believe the women of our past would be proud. For that reason I dedicated *All We Know of Heaven* to Mary Virginia as well as in memory of the women of Renston who have gone before us.

My life has been touched by so many people, some of them mentioned here, many of them not. My sister remains an important part of my life. Over the past ten years, we have traveled together, both in the States and abroad. I've visited England with her on three occasions, gone twice to France, visited Ireland, Italy, Spain. One of my favorite traveling memories is visiting Monet's home at Giverny with her, but I also have special memories of the Great Vigil at Westminster, an Easter sunrise service in the burned-out shell of Coventry Cathedral, a morning in Thomas and Jane Carlyle's house in Chelsea. Sandra is a fine traveling companion, and we have especially enjoyed including Mother in our stateside adventures. Since her retirement from teaching high school English, Sandra and Mother have come to the mountains more often than ever before, and we love having them here for all our special occasions: the weddings, birthdays, and baptisms which seem to be frequent occurrences in our expanding family.

In 1972, my brother married Lynn Webster. Their children, Matthew, Megan, Caitlin, and Melissa are growing up quickly and continue to bring excitement to our family gatherings. Ben's sister, Leah, married in 1988, and she and her husband, Steve Baker, have two adopted Mexican children, Jonathan and Marcy, who finally have brought brown eyes as well as beautiful smiles into the family.

On June 27, 1992, our daughter Elizabeth, who had graduated from Oglethorpe University in Atlanta and was working in public relations there, married Joel Chambers in our little Episcopal Church in Sylva. After more years working in Atlanta where their daughter, Carly Jane, was born on April 17, 1997, they left city life for an old farmhouse in West Jefferson, North Carolina, where they continue to live and work but at a less hectic pace. Joel keeps bees that produce delicious locust honey; they garden, do restoration work on their house, hike, and enjoy two-year-old Carly.

Our second daughter, Bennett, graduated from Hampshire College in Massachusetts and from the Writers Workshop at the University of Iowa before entering Tulane's School of Social Work. Married on August 14, 1993, to Mitchell Moss, whom she'd met in Iowa at the workshop, she worked as a social worker in New Orleans for several years while Mitchell attended Tulane Law School. Their son, Quentin Alvin, was born on January 12,

On the set of Paradise Falls, 1996: (from left) Elizabeth, Ben, Sue Ellen ("We are all extras in a scene"), and Sean.

1996, and their daughter, Vanessa Ellen, on April 11, 1998. After clerking in Federal Court for a year, Mitchell joined a law firm in Asheville, North Carolina, an hour's drive from Sylva. They will be leaving Asheville in the fall of 1999 to accept an appointment with the Foreign Service. We expect to do a lot of traveling in the next few years!

Sean, our son, graduated from Western Carolina University and attended graduate school in theater at Louisiana State University before embarking on a film career. He has appeared in many television movies and some theatrical releases, most notably the Jodie Foster film *Nell*. In 1996, he and I wrote a script titled *Paradise Falls* that he and his associates produced and filmed here in Jackson County. The story tells of Henry Bancroft, a young man in western North Carolina during the Depression. Sean played the leading role. Now being readied for theatrical release in the southeast, the film has won many film festivals, including Charleston Worldfest, Houston World-fest, the Atlanta Film Festival, and the Hollywood Film Festival for a drama with a budget of less than a million dollars.

The basic story for the film was Sean's idea. He was thinking about how much he loves the mountain area where he grew up and, as one idea expands into another for a writer, he ended up with a character who also loved our mountains dearly but who inadvertently set on a path that

caused him to lose all that was dear to him. Our collaboration created a script we felt celebrated a way of life lost to Henry Bancroft, but also lost to the rest of us with the progress and changes of the second half of the century. It was wonderful having an actor in the room because Sean could try out our dialogue on the spot. I stayed at the word processor, and he paced. Although our working styles are quite different, the finished product has found a responsive audience wherever it has been shown.

On June 27, 1998, Elizabeth and Joel's sixth anniversary, Sean married Rachel York, a Canadian with Jackson County connections who had come here to attend graduate school at Western Carolina. Their son, Jackson Finn, was born in Richmond, Virginia, while Sean was working on the television series *Legacy*. Now back in California, Sean is auditioning and enjoying his free time with baby Jackson. We are pleased that all three children chose to be married in Jackson County, and all our grandchildren have been baptized at St. John's Church. Being grandparents has added a new and unexpected dimension to our lives. We are "Nina" and "Da" now, even to each other! And we come close to espousing the sentiments of a local bumper sticker: "If we'd known grandchildren were this much fun, we would have had them first!"

Ben and I continue to travel. A few years ago, we spent time in the Lake District in England and, as usual, visited as many literary sites as possible. I remember especially a rain-blown day at the abbey at Whitby where Saint Hilda gave sanctuary to Caedmon, our time spent on the Holy Isle of Lindisfarne between tides (although I had not yet read Frederick Buechner's wonderful *Godric,* which is set there), and immersing myself in Dorothy Wordsworth's diary in the evenings after days hiking around the lakes. This fall Ben will celebrate his sixtieth birthday by swimming the Hellespont in Turkey, a section of the Dardanelles made famous in the myth of Hero and Leander and by Lord Byron's swim in 1810. Our treasured friend and priest, Claude Stewart, who performed two of our family weddings and one baptism, will be traveling with us in Turkey and then around the Greek Islands. I continue to travel professionally, speaking and teaching about the writing process as well as about my books. Most of our free time these days is spent in a little cottage on Santeetlah, a lake an hour away, where we swim, sail, canoe, hike in a virgin forest, and entertain friends and family.

I have been fortunate that my work has had expert care and nurturing from professionals who saw a place for my characters in the publishing world. Pat Ross at Alfred A. Knopf smoothed the path between Appalachia and New York City. She remains a dear friend. After being published at Knopf, Bantam, and HarperCollins, I brought my

professional life closer to home by joining forces with Ellyn Bache, a well-respected novelist who has a small publishing house, Banks Channel Books, in Wilmington, North Carolina. Ellyn's mission is to publish North Carolina writers, and she began her venture publishing out-of-print books in paperback. Since then, she has published original work as well, and I am so pleased to be associated with her in the publication of *All We Know of Heaven,* both in hardback and paperback editions, and a new updated edition of *Permanent Connections.* I admire tremendously the work she is doing and her commitment to quality books that otherwise may not find a niche in the marketplace.

Others who have supported my career as a writer include Ted Hipple at the University of North Carolina, who wrote the Twayne Series volume *Presenting Sue Ellen Bridgers* in 1990; Virginia Monseau and Gary Salvner, who have invited me twice to the Youngstown State University English Festival and allowed me to contribute to their text *Reading Their World*; Sissi Carroll, now at Florida State, who did the first graduate thesis on my work while at Auburn; Charlie Reed, who as a professor of education, editor of the *Alan Review,* and officer in Adolescent Literature of the National Council of Teachers of English (ALAN), gave me good advice and a lasting friendship. There are so many others, especially the membership of the

(Front row, from left) Mitchell Moss with Quentin, Joel Chambers, son Sean with Jackson. (Back row) Daughter Bennett Moss with Vanessa, daughter Elizabeth Chambers with Carly, Rachel Bridgers.

Ben and Sue Ellen with their grandchildren Vanessa, Quentin, Carly, and Jackson in 1998.

Assembly on Adolescent Literature of the National Council of Teachers of English who in 1985 granted me the ALAN Award for outstanding contribution to young-adult literature. Later, I served on the ALAN board for a term and saw the dedication these teachers have to inspiring reading and writing skills in their students. Other awards of which I am especially proud include the Ragan-Rubin Award given by North Carolina English teachers in 1992, the Distinguished Service Award from Western Carolina University in 1991, and a North Carolina Arts Council Artist Fellowship in 1994-95.

Over the past twenty-three years I've spoken to many teachers and librarians across the country. I am always encouraged by their concern for their students and impressed with the inventiveness and enthusiasm with which they do their work. I have spoken to quite a few students as well, challenging encounters with eager minds that have forced me to think about both the subject matter and method of my work. The mail brings treasures of its own. A girl writes that reading *Notes for Another Life* helped her understand her troubled boyfriend. A sixth grader informs me that *All Together Now* is the first book he's ever read all the way through and now he thinks he'll read another one. An eighty-year-old man writes, in the florid script of another era, a vivid description of a funeral he once attended, the memory evoked by a scene in *Home before*

Dark. An elderly woman writes after reading *All We Know of Heaven,* "I have been living in the thirties for several days now. Thanks for bringing so many memories back to me." Boys in a local remedial reading class have the first literary discussion of their lives while reading *Permanent Connections* because, as one of them says, "these are people we know."

And so my world conjures up other worlds, brings into focus the reader's own experience, forms a magical link between writer and reader. As you have read, my personal life is an ordinary one, confined for the most part to small-town living, and yet I have gone many places that only mood and memory can take me, and I expect many more such travels. A book, especially a novel, provides a journey into another heart and mind. It urges us to discover and explore. "I sha'n't be gone long.—You come too," Robert Frost wrote in his poem "The Pasture." Every book is such an invitation. Come and share a life, accept its special reality, be one with it for a little while. After all, we are fellow travelers, and our finest journeys, our most challenging explorations, are those of the spirit.

Writings

FICTION

Home before Dark, Knopf, 1976.
All Together Now, Knopf, 1979.

Notes for Another Life, Knopf, 1981.
Sara Will, Harper & Row, 1985.
Permanent Connections, Harper & Row, 1987.
Keeping Christina, HarperCollins, 1993.
All We Know of Heaven, Banks Channel Books, 1996.

BROUWER, S. W.
See BROUWER, Sigmund

* * *

BROUWER, Sigmund 1959-
(S. W. Brouwer)

Personal

Born in 1959, in Canada; married Cindy Morgan (a Christian recording artist). *Education:* Calvin College, degree in commerce; Carleton College, degree in journalism. *Religion:* Christian. *Hobbies and other interests:* Biking, racquetball, hockey, golf.

Addresses

Home—Red Deer, Alberta, Canada; Nashville, TN. *Agent*—c/o Chariot Victor Publishing, 4050 Lee Vance View, Colorado Springs, CO 80918.

E-mail—feedback@sigmundbrouwer.com.

Career

Briefly played semi-pro hockey. Freelance writer. *National Racquetball Magazine,* editor; co-founder, lecturer, The Young Writer's Institute, 1993—.

Awards, Honors

Twice received the Alberta Film and Literary Arts Writing Grant.

Writings

"ACCIDENTAL DETECTIVE" SERIES; JUVENILE CHRISTIAN NOVELS

Indians in the Deep Woods: A Ricky and Joel Adventure, BT Pub. (Grand Rapids, MI), 1988.
Lost beneath Manhattan, Victor (Wheaton, IL), 1990.
The Mystery Tribe of Camp Blackeagle, Victor, 1990.
Phantom Outlaw at Wolf Creek, Victor, 1990.
The Disappearing Jewel of Madagascar, Victor, 1990.
The Missing Map of Pirate's Haven, Victor, 1991.
Creature of the Mists, Victor, 1991.

Race for the Park Street Treasure, Victor, 1991.
The Downtown Desperadoes, Victor, 1991.
Madness at Moonshiner's Bay, Victor, 1992.
Sunrise at the Mayan Temple, Victor, 1992.
Short Cuts, Victor, 1993.
Terror on Kamikaze Run, Victor, 1994.
Tyrant of the Badlands, Victor, 1995.

"DR. DRABBLE" SERIES; JUVENILE CHRISTIAN NOVELS; WITH WAYNE DAVIDSON

Dr. Drabble's Astounding Musical Mesmerizer, illustrated by Bill Bell, Victor, 1991.
Dr. Drabble's Incredible Identical Robot Innovation, illustrated by Bell, Victor, 1991.
Dr. Drabble's Phenomenal Antigravity Dust Machine, illustrated by Bell, Victor, 1991.
Dr. Drabble's Remarkable Underwater Breathing Pills, illustrated by Bell, Victor, 1991, revised edition, Word (Dallas, TX), 1994.
Dr. Drabble's Spectacular Shrinker-Enlarger, illustrated by Bell, Word, 1994.
Dr. Drabble and the Dynamic Duplicator, illustrated by Bell, Word, 1994.

"WINDS OF LIGHT" SERIES; JUVENILE CHRISTIAN NOVELS

Wings of an Angel, Victor, 1992.
Barbarians from the Isle, Victor, 1992.
Legend of Burning Water, Victor, 1992.
The Forsaken Crusade, Victor, 1992.
A City of Dreams, Victor, 1993.
Merlin's Destiny, Victor, 1993.
The Jester's Quest, Victor, 1994.
Dance of Darkness, Chariot Victor (Colorado Springs, CO), 1997.

"LIGHTNING ON ICE" SERIES; JUVENILE CHRISTIAN NOVELS

Rebel Glory, Word, 1995.
All-Star Pride, Word, 1995.
Thunderbird Spirit, Word, 1996.
Winter Hawk Star, Word, 1996.
Blazer Drive, Word, 1996.
Chief Honor, Word, 1997.

"SHORT CUTS" SERIES

Rippin': Snowboarding to the Extreme, Word, 1996.
Cliff Dive: Mountain Biking to the Extreme, Word, 1996.
'Chute Roll: Sky Diving to the Extreme, Word, 1997.
Off the Wall: Scuba Diving to the Extreme, Word, 1997.

Sigmund Brouwer

"CYBER QUEST" SERIES

Pharaoh's Tomb, T. Nelson (Nashville, TN), 1997.
Knights Honor, T. Nelson, 1997.
Pirate's Cross, T. Nelson, 1997.
Outlaw's Gold, T. Nelson, 1997.
Soldier's Aim, T. Nelson, 1997.
Galilee Man, T. Nelson, 1997.

"SPORTS MYSTERY" SERIES

Maverick Mania, T. Nelson, 1997.
Tiger Heat, T. Nelson, 1998.
Cobra Threat, T. Nelson, 1998.
Titan Clash, T. Nelson, 1998.
Scarlet Thunder, T. Nelson, 1998.
Hurricane Power, T. Nelson, 1998.

NOVELS FOR ADULTS

Double Helix, Word, 1995.
Magnus, Victor, 1995.
Blood Ties, Word, 1996.
The Weeping Chamber, Word, 1998.

*"THE GHOST RIDER" SERIES: AS S. W. BROUWER; FOR
    ADULTS*

Morning Star, Victor, 1994.
Moon Basket, Victor, 1994.
Sun Dance, Victor, 1995.
Thunder Voice, Victor, 1995.

OTHER

*The Carpenter's Cloth: Christ's Journey to the Cross and
    Beyond,* Word, 1998.
Into His Arms: Seeing Jesus Through Children's Eyes, J.
    Countryman Books (Nashville, TN), 1999.

Sidelights

Canadian author Sigmund Brouwer has been reaching both children and adult audiences in the field of Christian fiction. He has created juvenile series such as the "Winds of Light," the "Cyber Quest" books, and, with Wayne Davidson, the "Dr. Drabble" adventures. His youth series such as "Short Cuts" and "Lightning on Ice" draw on his love of sports, including mountain biking and hockey, to engage reluctant readers. Crediting his affection for The Hardy Boys Mysteries, Brouwer also writes mystery series such as "The Accidental Detective" series and the "Sports Mystery" series for ten-to-fourteen-year-old readers, and "The Ghost Rider" mystery series for adults. Brouwer's better-known titles for adults include the novels *Double Helix* and *Blood Ties*— suspense thrillers that also tackle redemption and morality issues.

Brouwer's first series for young readers, the "Accidental Detective" books focus on the adventures of Ricky Kidd, his younger brother, Joel, and their friends. Whether the detectives are on an archeological dig in Mexico, trapped on a boat in the wilds of Canada, or lost in the streets of Manhattan, they always manage to uncover a mystery. Fred Boer, reviewing *The Missing Map of Pirate's Haven* in *Quill & Quire,* compared the series as a whole to those featuring fictional adolescent detectives, Nancy Drew and the Hardy Boys.

The "Dr. Drabble" set of adventures soon followed, co-written with Wayne Davidson. In this series, "genius inventor" Dr. Drabble devises lots of wacky machines such as the "shrinker-enlarger" and the "dynamic duplicator," and young pranksters Chelsea and P. J. try them out, often with interesting results. In addition to Dr. Drabble, Brouwer created more fantasy adventures to tempt reluctant readers. The "Wings of Light" series is a historical fantasy series, beginning in 1312 A.D. with a young orphan setting out to reconquer an oppressed earldom. Future adventures take the reader through periods of history such as the Crusades and the time of the Black Death. The "Cyber Quest" series is a set of virtual reality adventures with titles such as *Pharaoh's Tomb, Outlaw's Gold,* and *The Galilee Man* wherein Mok travels to ancient Egypt, the wild West of the 1870s, and Old Newyork, three thousand years in the future. In *The Galilee Man* not only does Mok travel to a futuristic Big Apple, but he also finds himself in ancient Jerusalem during the crucifixion of Christ.

The "Lightening on Ice" "Short Cuts," and "Sports Mystery" series all use sports to entice youngsters who aren't particularly interested in reading. *Quill & Quire* reviewer Fred Boer discussed *Thunderbird Spirit,* a title in the "Lightning on Ice" series, saying it is "smoothly told, well paced, and has interesting characters." *Thun-*

derbird Spirit* involves characters who play hockey, and has a theme of adolescents overcoming racism. Boer rated *Thunderbird Spirit* as "readable and entertaining."

In the "Ghost Rider" series for adults, Brouwer blends mystery and morality into old-fashioned westerns. Set in Laramie, Wyoming, in 1874, *Moon Basket* is part of the series that features Brouwer's protagonist Samuel Keaton. Keaton has just been named marshal and must investigate several related murders. According to John Mort, reviewing the novel in *Booklist,* the "whodunit is engaging." He added that the "real charm is to be found in [Brouwer's] laconic, self-effacing narrator."

Double Helix concerns a laboratory where fetal tissue research has gone horrifyingly awry. Mort, in another *Booklist* critique, noted that in *Double Helix* Brouwer handles controversial issues "with impressive control and no preachiness." The reviewer concluded that the author "has written a scary, maniacal novel."

Blood Ties explores the Federal Bureau of Investigation's pursuit of a serial killer whose crimes began in 1973. They think they have solved the case, but after many years, murders with similar circumstances begin occurring again. Though the crimes are gruesome, and the tale, according to Mort, is "harrowing," the novel also includes conversations between characters about "how one can believe in God in the face of relentless evil." *Blood Ties* prompted Mort to proclaim Brouwer "one of Christian fiction's most interesting talents."

Brouwer's 1998 title, *The Weeping Chamber,* juxtaposes the life of Simeon of Cyrene with that of Jesus of Nazareth. When a fire devastates his family, Simeon decides to journey to Nazareth to take care of some business and then take his own life. He continually crosses the path of Jesus, witnesses miracles, and is present at the crucifixion. Simeon is transformed by the experience and returns home to his ravaged family a changed man. Melissa Hudak, writing in *Library Journal,* called the characterizations "intense and dynamic" and stated: "While biblical fiction is common in this genre, it is rarely as powerful as this work by Brouwer."

Brouwer attributes the underpinnings of morality and redemption that appear in his novels to the influences of writer C. S. Lewis. Commenting on the Cool Reading website, Brouwer said: "C. S. Lewis is definitely one of the writers I admire most. He wrote as well as possible, knowing that the Truth would speak for itself. He always tried to be logical, and true, and never tried to inject things for the sake of putting them in there. He's the one who said, 'There's no Christian way to write, just as there is no Christian way to boil an egg.'"

Brouwer added: "I continue to spend a certain part of my year speaking to kids, and writing books that grab reluctant readers. From what I've seen, there aren't a lot of books out there designed for eighty-five percent of the kids who are not avid readers. Most books are written for the fifteen percent who love to read. I have a real concern about that. So, I will keep writing one novel a

Winning the league title in hockey becomes secondary to new player Mike Keats and his friend Dakota, who find themselves trapped in a web of racially motivated deceit and violence.

year—that takes six-to-seven months—and spend the rest of the year writing for reluctant readers and developing the Young Writers' Institute."

Works Cited

Boer, Fred, review of *Thunderbird Spirit, Quill & Quire,* May, 1996, p. 34.

Brouwer, Sigmund, commenting on the Cool Reading website: http://www.coolreading.com/cgi-bin/alda.cgi/ sigmund/sigmund/meet, 1999.

Hudak, Melissa, review of *The Weeping Chamber, Library Journal,* April 1, 1998, p. 74.

Mort, John, review of *Blood Ties, Booklist,* September 1, 1996, p. 65.

Mort, John, review of *Double Helix, Booklist,* June 1 & 15, 1995, p. 1682.

Mort, John, review of *Moon Basket, Booklist,* October 15, 1994, p. 401.

For More Information See

PERIODICALS

Booklist, May 1, 1998, p. 1503.

Library Journal, June 1, 1995, p. 96.

Quill & Quire, October, 1991, p. 38.

ON-LINE

http://www.sigmundbrouwer.com, 1999.*

C

CHENG, Shan
See JIANG, Cheng An

* * *

CLAPP, John 1968-

Personal

Born August 20, 1968, in Santa Clara, CA; son of Daniel John (a real estate broker) and Lois Joyce (a teacher and gourmet cook; maiden name, Gruchow) Clapp. *Education:* Art Center College of Design, B.F.A. in Illustration, 1992; Syracuse University, M.A. in Illustration, 1999. *Hobbies and other interests:* Tennis, reading, music.

Addresses

Home—Pleasanton, CA. *Agent*—Steven Malk, Writer's House, 21 W. 26th St., New York, NY 10010. *Electronic mail*—john@johnclapp.com.

Career

Freelance Illustrator, 1992—; Academy of Art College, San Francisco, CA, Instructor, 1993-1998; San Jose State University, San Jose, CA, Lecturer, 1994—; California College of Arts and Crafts, San Francisco, Adjunct Professor, 1999.

Awards, Honors

Several pieces selected for the Society of Illustrators Annual Show since 1995.

Illustrator

Robin McKinley, *The Stone Fey,* Harcourt Brace, 1998.
Sharon Hart Addy, *Right Here on This Spot,* Houghton Mifflin, 1999.
Liz Rosenberg, *On Christmas Eve,* DK Ink, in press.

Clapp has also illustrated numerous book jackets for young adult novels.

Work in Progress

Illustrating *The Prince of Butterflies* by Bruce Coville for Harcourt Brace.

Sidelights

John Clapp told *SATA:* "I was born in Santa Clara, California, on August 20, 1968. I grew up near the San Francisco Bay and still live in the area. According to my parents, I began drawing while still in a high chair. In

John Clapp

Clapp's watercolor illustrations beautifully complement Robin McKinley's novel The Stone Fey, *a passionate and haunting story about a young woman who falls in love with an elusive mountain creature.*

nursery school, I became the first four year old to draw the correct number of fingers on my people and draw them with articulated thumbs. Apparently, this caused quite a commotion. I was also the one who didn't want to go around to all the different 'activity stations' and do anything else; I just wanted to stay at the easels and draw. This caused a less positive commotion.

"Growing up, I was drawing all the time. My dad worked in real estate in the 1970s and used to bring home the old listings which had been primitively photocopied on one side but were blank on the other side. I used the white side for my drawings and would go through reams and reams of these old listings. For the longest time I could never understand why they put all that other garbage on the 'back' of my paper. Because of this, all of my childhood drawings come with air conditioning, a two-car garage, and a spacious backyard.

"My first recorded children's book, 'The Fishing Trip' starring my dad, was dictated to my mother, who carefully printed the text underneath each of my drawings. I was not writing at this point. When the judge puts him in jail because he's caught fish over the legal limit, my dad is forced to eat all the fish and ends up as 'one fat fisherman.' Readers who didn't like the story could always turn the book over and possibly find some choice real estate.

"As a kid, I was an avid fan of comic books and cartooning in general. I'd copy the characters from the newspaper strips and write and draw original comic books with my friends. During high school I set out to get a job in comics, and through many critiques and talking to many professionals I slowly began to learn about drawing. This in turn led to learning about painting, and then illustration, during a brief year at San Jose State University.

"Later, at Art Center College of Design, I was fortunate to have David Shannon as an instructor for a children's book illustration class. Over the years he's been an invaluable resource for information about the industry. While I didn't plan on pursuing children's books full time at that time, being able to call Dave when I had a question has been a tremendous help.

"After graduating from Art Center College of Design, I began illustrating book jackets, several of which were for the Young Adult genre. The art directors for those books, as well as others in the industry, saw those jackets and began to offer me my first manuscripts.

"When illustrating a book, my first concern is to communicate the story in a compelling way, while keeping myself entertained and challenged. Ultimately of course, I have to pay my bills, so I hope I do a good job, and people like the books, buy the books, and keep me from having to get a real job!

"My books tend to take a while to complete. Thumbnailing out the manuscript or story is probably the part I enjoy the most. That's where the 'flashes of inspiration' and such occur for me. The actual production of the finished artwork is more of a mechanical process and can be frustrating at times because you want sixteen perfect paintings at the end of it all, which is never going to happen. In your head, the pictures are always perfect, but you do the best you can and resolve to make your *next* book absolutely perfect. It's a useful and marvelous self-deception.

"I like to 'putter' through my books, letting the ideas come to the surface in their own time, letting the book 'grow' very naturally. I'm convinced that my brain works on the book subconsciously all the time, and passes good ideas along when it has one ready.

"With *Right Here on this Spot,* I was trying to create a book where the visuals echoed the feeling I get from archaeology. Layers and layers of information, some of it barely discernable or only partially visible. Clues, juxtapositions, the context of the information, all communicate and clarify your understanding, but in a very subtle way. I wanted my book to convey the narrative in a similarly indirect way.

"For *The Stone Fey,* a storybook, I felt the illustrations functioned more to illuminate the text rather than explain it. The information was already there, my illustrations were more of a 'soundtrack' to accompany the story. It was still enjoyable, but because it didn't need to be sequential, it wasn't as interesting a challenge as a picture book."

The Stone Fey, by Robin McKinley, is the story of Maddy, a shepherdess, who falls in love with a stone fey—a fairy with skin the color of stone, while her betrothed is away. She forgets all about her husband-to-be, her family, and her sheep. Maddy eventually breaks the spell the stone fey has cast over her when she has a dream in which her betrothed calls out to her in distress. A *Publishers Weekly* critic praised the illustrations by saying: "Newcomer Clapp's incidental illustrations, dreamy watercolor and graphite paintings reminiscent of the work of Barry Moser, heighten the quiet drama of [Robin] McKinley's prose. The best of his landscapes evoke the serene stillness of McKinley's writing; one portrait of Maddy, with its masterful play of light and shadow, particularly showcases his craft, as it glows with the power of burgeoning love." Carolyn Phelan, writing in *Booklist,* commented: "Every few pages, a large watercolor-and-pencil illustration appears, sometimes portraying the characters rather realistically and at other times offering quite beautiful, impressionistic interpretations of the characters and the land. A haunting story in a handsome book." According to *School Library Journal* contributor Virginia Golodetz, "the luminescent graphite-and-watercolor illustrations convey the sense of another world in dreamlike landscapes, effectively contrasting with the bold, striking portraits of Maddy."

Clapp describes his newest book by saying, "In *On Christmas Eve,* the challenge was to accurately reflect the mood of the story, visually, as the boy's hopes ride the emotional roller coaster that is his Christmas Eve.

"My major influences are hard to pin down. My early training was very traditional, which provided technical skills, and my later training was very contemporary, which had a major influence on my thinking process. I don't feel that I've been very influenced at all by one artist. I can't point to any artist and say: 'He was the one!' Where I can spot major influences are in less obvious areas. I've always been inspired, and tried to emulate the behavior of artists I respect: Michelangelo, Rodin, Rembrandt, Mucha, and several others, even contemporary musicians like Lyle Lovett and Peter Gabriel. I'm impressed by how they think, how they work with metaphors, their discipline, and their honest pursuit of their respective crafts. That's how I've been influenced the most. One of my favorite things to do is to hear artists or scientists or creative individuals of any kind talk about their work. It never fails to fascinate and inspire me.

"The contemporaries whose work I love to look at are Shel Silverstein, Kevin Henkes, and Crockett Johnson. Despite the appearance of my work, the children's books I like the best are the simpler, humorous ones. Again, it's how the author thinks that gets me—how a phrase will have a double meaning or how the simplest addition to the illustration will foreshadow another event on the next page. I think too often people are 'seduced' by complicated illustrations and ignore or overlook the clumsy way they work in a given story. That's not to say that I believe complicated or realistic illustrations are inappropriate for children's books, not at all. But illustrations need to *serve* the story they depict. A pretty picture isn't good enough by itself.

"I believe the most influential factor on a person's career is their education. Nothing else even comes close. I don't necessarily mean formal education, I mean looking at people who are doing something at a very high level, and studying what they do. As important as Art Center was to my education, I still believe my earlier self-directed studies were what made Art Center as worthwhile as it was for me, and laid the groundwork for my career. I would tell a prospective artist/author to find people whose work they believe is truly amazing and then learn all they can about studying it."

Works Cited

Golodetz, Virginia, review of *The Stone Fey, School Library Journal,* January, 1999, p. 130.

Phelan, Carolyn, review of *The Stone Fey, Booklist,* November 1, 1998, p. 484.

Review of *The Stone Fey, Publishers Weekly,* August 31, 1998, p. 77.

*   *   *

COVINGTON, Dennis

Personal

Raised in Birmingham, AL; married Vicki Covington (a novelist); children: two daughters. *Education:* Iowa Writers Workshop, University of Iowa, M.F.A. *Religion:* Methodist.

Addresses

Home—Birmingham, AL. *Office*—English Department, University of Alabama, University Station, Birmingham, AL 35294.

Career

New York Times, New York City, journalist; University of Alabama-Birmingham, Birmingham, AL, currently professor and director of creative-writing program; writer and freelance journalist.

Awards, Honors

Delacorte Prize for young-adult first novel, Delacorte Press, 1991, for *Lizard;* Barrie Stavis Playwriting Award for Best New Play of the Year, National Theater Conference, 1995, for adaptation of *Lizard;* National Book Award finalist, 1995, for *Salvation on Sand Mountain: Snake Handling and Redemption in Southern Appalachia;* Rea Non-Fiction Prize, *Boston Book Review,* 1996, for *Salvation on Sand Mountain: Snake Handling and Redemption in Southern Appalachia.*

Dennis Covington received the Delacorte Prize for this sensitive novel about a facially deformed teenage boy who is rescued from a state institution by a traveling salesman claiming to be his father.

Writings

FOR YOUNG ADULTS

Lizard, Delacorte, 1991.
Lasso the Moon, Delacorte, 1995.

OTHER

Salvation on Sand Mountain: Snake Handling and Redemption in Southern Appalachia, Addison-Wesley (Reading, MA), 1995.

Also co-author with Vicki Covington of *Cleaving: The Story of a Marriage,* 1999.

Adaptations

Lizard was adapted into a play by Covington, for production at the Alabama Shakespeare Festival as part of the Southern Writers' Project, 1994, and was selected to be performed at the Olympic Arts Festival in Atlanta, GA, 1996.

Sidelights

Dennis Covington has written works of both young-adult fiction and journalistic exposition. Director of the creative-writing program at the University of Alabama-Birmingham, Covington also works as a freelance journalist. His first two published books, *Lizard* and *Lasso the Moon,* are young-adult novels, while the third, *Salvation on Sand Mountain,* is a nonfiction account of Covington's ventures into the unusual world of snake-handlers. While all three have been praised by critics, *Lizard* and *Salvation on Sand Mountain* have both been selected for literary awards.

The manuscript for *Lizard* languished for nine years until Covington submitted it to the Delacorte competition for a young-adult first novel. The story won the prize, was published in 1991, and attracted enthusiastic reviews. *Lizard* is the tale of a physically deformed boy who is wrongfully sent to a state institution for retarded children. An actor appears to claim Lucius—nicknamed "Lizard"—as his son, and although the boy knows this man is not his father, he goes with him to escape the hardships of the institution. His new life with an acting troupe is still cruel, but Lizard finds some semblance of happiness.

Lizard was praised as remarkable among young-adult literature. A *Publishers Weekly* reviewer commented on the book's "bold originality," adding that *Lizard* is an "intriguing combination of Mark Twain's *Huckleberry Finn* and *Candide.*" A *Kirkus Reviews* contributor called *Lizard* a book with "a fresh, memorably sweet picture of its offbeat characters and singular, compelling events." *Booklist* reviewer Hazel Rochman remarked that "Covington's story ... makes art out of affliction and transforms the ordinary into something rich and strange."

The author's second novel, *Lasso the Moon,* was published in 1995. The story's protagonist is April Hunter, a young high-school student who is living with her father, a recovering alcoholic who has salvaged his career as a cardiologist but not his marriage or finances. April meets and becomes emotionally attached to Fernando, an illegal immigrant who is seriously ill. The young man faces the prospect of deportation back to San Salvador, where he was once tortured and will likely be executed by the army if he returns. Susan R. Farber commented in *Voice of Youth Advocates* that the author's second book showed "an even greater depth and versatility. It is a credit to Covington's skill that the numerous, multi-layered subplots enhance the central theme." A *Publishers Weekly* reviewer remarked that "a well-observed setting and the thoughtfully probed relationships ... add complexity to this moving story."

With *Salvation on Sand Mountain: Snake Handling and Redemption in Southern Appalachia,* Covington departed from the writing of fiction to pen a personal account about his experiences in a snake-handling church—the Church of Jesus with Signs Following—in which members of the congregation demonstrate their faith by handling poisonous snakes. The project was inspired by Covington's coverage of a murder trial in which the defendant, a church member, was charged with attempting to kill his wife by forcing her hand into a box of venomous snakes. Covington became intrigued. "I found myself so interested in the people and in their religious beliefs that I ceased asking questions about the crime and started asking questions about what they did and why they did it," Covington told Don Noble in an interview for Alabama Public Television's "Writing Today" series at Birmingham-Southern. At the urging of an editor, Covington immersed himself in the Appalachian religion, eventually handling venomous snakes himself and uncovering his own family's rural, southern roots. In a larger context, Covington described the project in *Publishers Weekly* as a "book about the South that would use snake-handling as a lens." The story drew the attention of the national media and was featured on National Public Radio's (NPR) *All Things Considered,* as well as *National Geographic Explorer* and *Dateline NBC.*

The result of Covington's adventures in the Church of Jesus with Signs Following was not a conversion—he was unable to justify the dangers of snake-handling despite his fascination for the subject—but an exciting tale of personal and cultural revelations. Norman Oder wrote in *Publishers Weekly* that *Salvation on Sand Mountain* is a "mix of spiritual quest and memoir, a book that not only garnered rave reviews but also letters from New Agers to rural outcasts." In a *Los Angeles Times* review, Charles Solomon described Covington as "talented" but quipped that with the zeal the author showed for snake-handling, "he'd better not write about heroin addiction or carjacking."

Works Cited

Farber, Susan R., review of *Lasso the Moon, Voice of Youth Advocates,* April, 1995, p. 20.

Review of *Lasso the Moon, Publishers Weekly,* January 9, 1995, p. 64.

Review of *Lizard, Kirkus Reviews,* June 15, 1991, p. 787.

Review of *Lizard, Publishers Weekly,* May 24, 1991, p. 59.

Noble, Don, "The Writer's Eye: An Interview with Dennis Covington," Alabama Public Television's "Writing Today" series at Birmingham-Southern, April, 1995, published by *First Draft* at http://www.auburn.edu/~cahawf/firstdr/dennis2.html.

Oder, Norman, "The Covingtons: Taking Up Snakes Real & Symbolic," *Publishers Weekly,* January 8, 1996, p. 26.

Rochman, Hazel, review of *Lizard, Booklist,* May 1, 1991, p. 1706.

Solomon, Charles, review of *Salvation on Sand Mountain: Snake Handling and Redemption in Southern Appalachia, Los Angeles Times Book Review,* March 17, 1996, p. 11.

For More Information See

PERIODICALS

Bloomsbury Review, July-August, 1995, p. 22.

Booklist, January 15, 1995, p. 912.

Publishers Weekly, July 5, 1991, p. 38.*

D–E

DAVIS, Karen (Elizabeth) 1944-

Personal

Born February 4, 1944, in Altoona, PA; daughter of Amos (an attorney) and Mary (Orr) Davis; married George Allan Cate (a professor of English), July 9, 1983. *Education:* Shippensburg State College, M.A., 1980; University of Maryland at College Park, Ph.D., 1987.

Karen Davis with "Violetta."

Addresses

Home—Machipongo, VA. *E-mail*—karend@capaccess. org.

Career

University of Maryland at College Park, teacher of English for twelve years, and founder of Animal Rights Coalition; United Poultry Concerns, Inc. (nonprofit public-education organization), Machipongo, VA, founder and president, 1990—; Summit for the Animals, member of executive committee, 1993-94, 1999-2000.

Awards, Honors

Named "outstanding new leader of the animal rights movement," Decade of the Animals Conference, 1991; honored by Delaware Action for Animals, 1995.

Writings

FOR CHILDREN

A Home for Henny, United Poultry Concerns (Machipongo, VA), 1996.

OTHER

Instead of Chicken, Instead of Turkey: A Poultryless "Poultry" Potpourri, Featuring Homestyle, Ethnic, and Exotic Alternatives to Traditional Poultry and Egg Recipes, Book Publishing Co. (Summertown, TN), 1993.

(Contributor) *Animals and Women: Feminist Theoretical Explorations*, Duke University Press, 1995.

Prisoned Chickens, Poisoned Eggs: An Inside Look at the Modern Poultry Industry, Book Publishing Co., 1996.

Contributor to periodicals, including *Journal of English and Germanic Philology, Animals' Agenda, Between the Species: Journal of Ethics, Humane Innovations and Alternatives*, and *Guide to Healthy Eating*.

Work in Progress

More Powerful Than Eagles: The Thanksgiving Turkey in America (working title).

Sidelights

Karen Davis told *SATA:* "At the University of Maryland, I founded the Animal Rights Coalition in 1989, and I pioneered a course on the role of animals in the Western philosophic and literary tradition for the University Honors Program. In 1990 I founded United Poultry Concerns, a nonprofit public-education organization and chicken sanctuary that addresses the treatment of domestic fowl in food production, science, education, entertainment, and human-companionship situations. United Poultry Concerns promotes the compassionate and respectful treatment of domestic fowl through its chicken sanctuary, which is open to the public; its quarterly newsletter, *PoultryPress;* and many other publications,

including *Replacing School Hatching Projects: Alternative Resources and How to Order Them.*"

For More Information See

PERIODICALS

Animals' Agenda, May-June, 1997, p. 39.
AVAR Directions, spring, 1997, p. 2.
Booklist, April 1, 1997, p. 1272.
Choice, October, 1997, p. 320.
E Magazine, May, 1997, p. 50.
Library Journal, July, 1997, p. 113.
Publishers Weekly, March 17, 1997, p. 74.
Vegetarian Times, November, 1992, p. 102; May, 1995, p. 108.

*   *   *

DEWEY, Ariane 1937-
(Ariane Aruego)

Personal

Born August 17, 1937, in Chicago, IL; daughter of Charles S., Jr. and Marjorie S. (maiden name, Goodman) Dewey; married Jose E. Aruego, Jr. (an author and illustrator), 1961 (divorced, 1973); married Claus Dan-

Ariane Dewey

nasch, 1976; children: Juan Aruego. *Education:* Sarah Lawrence College, B.A., 1959; studied art (woodcuts) with Antonio Frasconi. *Hobbies and other interests:* Kayaking, bird watching.

Addresses

Home—505 East 79th St., New York, NY 10021.

Career

Harcourt, Brace & World, Inc., New York City, researcher and art editor for children's textbooks, 1964-65; freelance author and illustrator of children's books, 1969—. Member of board, Experiments in Interactive Arts, New York, 1973, and Franklin Furnace Archive, Inc., New York, 1987—; performer, "Artists in Process Improvisational Dance Group," 1973-74; participating artist, Sequential Art for Kids, New York, 1991-97.

Awards, Honors

Notable Books, American Library Association (ALA), 1971, for Robert Kraus's *Whose Mouse Are You?*, 1972, for Kraus's *Milton the Early Riser*, 1974, for Mirra Ginsburg's *Mushroom in the Rain*, and 1979, for *We Hide, You Seek;* Children's Book Show, American Institute of Graphic Art, 1972-73, and Children's Book Showcase, 1973, both for *A Crocodile's Tale;* Children's Book Showcase, 1973, for Vladimir Suteyev's *The Chick and the Duckling;* Children's Book Show, 1973-74, for Mirra Ginsburg's *Mushroom in the Rain* and Natalie Savage Carlson's *Marie Louise and Christophe;* *Boston Globe-Horn Book* Honor Book, 1974, for Kraus's *Herman the Helper;* Citation of Merit, Society of Illustrators, 1974, Brooklyn Arts Book for Children citation and inclusion in the Biennale of Illustration in Bratislava, both 1975, and all for Kraus's *Milton the Early Riser;* Notable Book, ALA, 1974, Citation of Merit, Society of Illustrators, and Children's Book Showcase, 1975, all for Kraus's *Owliver;* goldmedaille, der Internationalen Buchkunst-Ausstellung, 1977, for *Mushroom in the Rain.* Several of Dewey's illustrated books have been selected for book clubs.

Writings

AUTHOR AND ILLUSTRATOR, WITH JOSE ARUEGO; AS ARIANE ARUEGO

The King and His Friends, Scribner's, 1969.
Juan and the Asuangs, Scribner's, 1970.
Symbiosis: A Book of Unusual Friendships, Scribner's, 1970.
Pilyo the Piranha, Macmillan, 1971.
Look What I Can Do, Scribner's, 1971, Aladdin, 1988.
A Crocodile's Tale, Scribner's, 1972, Scholastic, 1975.

AUTHOR AND ILLUSTRATOR, WITH JOSE ARUEGO; AS ARIANE DEWEY

We Hide, You Seek, Greenwillow Books, 1979, Mulberry Books, 1988.
Rockabye Crocodile, Greenwillow Books, 1988, Mulberry Books, 1993.

AUTHOR AND ILLUSTRATOR; AS ARIANE DEWEY

The Fish Peri, Macmillan, 1979.
The Thunder God's Son, Greenwillow Books, 1981.
Dorin and the Dragon, Greenwillow Books, 1982.
Pecos Bill, Greenwillow Books, 1983, Mulberry Books, 1994.
Febold Feboldson, Greenwillow Books, 1984.
Laffite, the Pirate, Greenwillow Books, 1985, Mulberry Books, 1993.
Gib Morgan, Oilman, Greenwillow Books, 1987, Mulberry Books, 1993.
The Tea Squall, Greenwillow Books, 1988, Mulberry Books, 1994.
The Narrow Escapes of Davy Crockett: From a Bear, a Boa Constrictor, a Hoop Snake, an Elk, an Owl, Eagles, Rattlesnakes, Wildcats, Trees, Tornadoes, a Sinking Ship, and Niagara Falls, Greenwillow Books, 1990, Mulberry Books, 1993.
The Sky, Green Tiger Press, 1993.
Naming Colors, HarperCollins, 1995.

ILLUSTRATOR, WITH JOSE ARUEGO; AS ARIANE ARUEGO

Kay Smith, *Parakeets and Peach Pies,* Parents' Magazine Press, 1970.
Jack Prelutsky, *Toucans and Two Other Poems,* Macmillan, 1970.
Robert Kraus, *Whose Mouse Are You?*, Macmillan, 1970.
Kraus, *Leo the Late Bloomer,* Windmill Books, 1971.
Christina Rosetti, *What Is Pink?*, Macmillan, 1971.
Elizabeth Coatsworth, *Good Night,* Macmillan, 1972.
Robert Kraus, *Milton the Early Riser,* Windmill Books, 1972.
Vladimir Suteyev, *The Chick and the Duckling,* translated and adapted by Mirra Ginsburg, Macmillan, 1972.

ILLUSTRATOR, WITH JOSE ARUEGO; AS ARIANE DEWEY

Vladimir Suteyev, *Mushroom in the Rain,* translated and adapted by Mirra Ginsburg, Macmillan, 1974.
Robert Kraus, *Herman the Helper,* Windmill Books, 1974.
Kraus, *Owliver,* Windmill Books, 1974.
Natalie Savage Carlson, *Marie Louise and Christophe,* Scribner's, 1974.
Carlson, *Marie Louise's Heyday,* Scribner's, 1975.
Mirra Ginsburg, *How the Sun Was Brought Back to the Sky,* Macmillan, 1975.
Robert Kraus, *Three Friends,* Windmill Books, 1975.
Dorothy Van Woerkom, *Sea Frog, City Frog,* Macmillan, 1975.
Robert Kraus, *Boris Bad Enough,* Windmill Books, 1976.
Mirra Ginsburg, *Two Greedy Bears,* Macmillan, 1976.
Ginsburg, *The Strongest One of All,* Macmillan, 1977.
Robert Kraus, *Noel the Coward,* Windmill Books, 1977.
David Kherdian, collector, *If Dragon Flies Made Honey: Poems,* Greenwillow Books, 1977.
Natalie Savage Carlson, *Runaway Marie Louise,* Scribner's, 1977.
Maggie Duff, *Rum Pum Pum: A Folk Tale from India,* Macmillan, 1978.
Marjorie Weinman Sharmat, *Mitchell Is Moving,* Macmillan, 1978.
Robert Kraus, *Another Mouse to Feed,* Windmill Books, 1980.

Milton woke up early...

Ariane Dewey and Jose Aruego provide the appealing illustrations for Robert Kraus's **Milton the Early Riser,** *about a young panda who tries to wake up his animal friends.*

Kraus, *Musical Max,* Windmill Books, 1980.

Kraus, *Mert the Blurt,* Windmill Books, 1980.

Kraus, *Mouse Work,* Windmill Books, 1980.

Kraus, *Animal Families,* Windmill Books, 1980.

Mitchell Sharmat, *Gregory, the Terrible Eater,* Four Winds Press, 1980.

Natalie Savage Carlson, *Marie Louise and Christophe at the Carnival,* Scribner's, 1981.

Mirra Ginsburg, *Where Does the Sun Go at Night?,* Greenwillow Books, 1981.

George Shannon, *Lizard's Song,* Greenwillow Books, 1981.

Shannon, *Dance Away,* Greenwillow Books, 1982.

Shannon, *The Surprise,* Greenwillow Books, 1983.

Charlotte Pomerantz, *One Duck, Another Duck,* Greenwillow Books, 1984.

Robert Kraus, *Where Are You Going, Little Mouse?,* Greenwillow Books, 1986.

Kraus, *Come Out and Play, Little Mouse,* Greenwillow Books, 1987.

Crescent Dragonwagon, *Alligator Arrived with Apples: A Potluck Alphabet Feast,* Macmillan, 1987.

Raffi, *Five Little Ducks,* Crown, 1989.

Jovial Bob Stine, *Pork and Beans: Play Date,* Scholastic, 1989.

Mirra Ginsburg, *Merry-Go-Round: Four Stories,* Greenwillow Books, 1992.

Crescent Dragonwagon, *Alligators and Others All Year Long!: A Book of Months,* Macmillan, 1993.

Bobbye S. Goldstein, *Birthday Rhymes, Special Times,* Delacorte Press, 1993.

George Shannon, *April Showers,* Greenwillow Books, 1995.

Craig Strete, *They Thought They Saw Him,* Greenwillow Books, 1996.

Michael R. and Mary Beth Sampson, *Star of the Circus,* Holt, 1997.

Judy Sierra, *Antarctic Antics: A Book of Penguin Poems,* Harcourt Brace, 1998.

Robert Kraus, *Little Louie the Baby Bloomer,* HarperCollins, 1998.

Stephen R. Swinburne, *Safe, Warm, and Snug,* Harcourt Brace, 1999.

George Shannon, *Lizard's Home,* Greenwillow Books, 1999.

ILLUSTRATOR; AS ARIANE DEWEY

Caron Lee Cohen, *Sally Ann Thunder and Whirlwind Crockett,* Greenwillow Books, 1985, Mulberry Books, 1993.

Contributor to anthologies, including *Standing at the Feet of the Past: Retelling North American Folktale for Children.*

Several of Dewey's books have been anthologized in classroom texts; others have been translated in Spanish. Dewey's books have been published in Canada, England, France, Sweden, Denmark, Netherlands, Germany, Spain, Japan, Taiwan, Australia, New Zealand, South Africa, and Israel.

Adaptations

Several of Dewey's illustrated books have been adapted for filmstrip; *The Sky* was adapted for a UNICEF Christmas card, 1996; *Five Little Ducks* was adapted for interactive software on CD-ROM, 1997.

Work in Progress

Illustrations for *Mouse in Love,* written by Robert Kraus, for Orchard Books.

Sidelights

Ariane Dewey is an author and illustrator of children's books noted for her bright, primary colors or rich earthen tones, simple and almost primitive lines, and stories that tweak history or myth with a nudge of humor. She writes tall tales of farmers, explorers, oilmen, and pirates in her chapter books and picture books. Davy Crockett gets the Dewey treatment as does Laffite the pirate. She tackles larger-than-life subjects as well, as in *The Sky* and *Naming Colors.*

Working with her author/illustrator ex-husband, Jose Aruego, Dewey has also contributed award-winning pictures to over 65 books by other authors. Aruego draws the lines and Dewey paints the colors, which, as Dewey recently told *SATA,* "is what we each like doing best." Dewey noted in *Fourth Book of Junior Authors and Illustrators* that she relates "just about everything—objects, events, people—to color, reacting to color much more than to sound or shape. I suppose I really think in color." She also recently told *SATA* that "color is what I'm about. When I see a brilliant sunrise or pale butterfly, I memorize them to paint later."

Born in Chicago, Illinois on August 17, 1937, Dewey formed an early love for painting. One of her early pieces of "art" was a fourth-grade class project in which she painted and repainted the same scene—bright pink children swimming in a blue-green lake—so many times that the paper began to tear and the paint fleck off. Later, with more success, she designed stage sets for school plays and illustrated, wrote, and hand-bound books as class assignments. "Starting then, I was determined to always paint," Dewey noted in *Fourth Book of Junior Authors and Illustrators.*

Attending Sarah Lawrence College, she studied painting with Ezio Martinelli and also took a course in woodcuts with Antonio Frasconi, working weekends at an art gallery in nearby New York. Graduating from college, Dewey worked for a time in an industrial design firm and then as an art editor for children's textbooks. Folklore and myth also captured her imagination, and she took graduate anthropology courses at Columbia University. In 1961 she married Jose Aruego, whom she had met while he was painting a mural at New York's International House. A year later, they quit their jobs and traveled around the world for a year. Dewey once told *SATA* that this was "the most influential and memorable year of [my] life."

Starting in 1969, the two began publishing collaborative works, under the names Jose and Ariane Aruego. One of their most popular titles as well as winner of several awards is *A Crocodile's Tale,* adapted from a Philippine folk story. When the couple divorced in 1973, Dewey reverted to her maiden name, but continued to work with Aruego. Their collaboration has lasted three decades, during which time the two have illustrated the works of authors such as Robert Kraus, Mirra Ginsburg, George Shannon, and Natalie Savage Carlson. Their efforts with Kraus have been particularly fruitful, producing almost 20 titles, including award-winners such as *Owliver* and *Milton the Early Riser.* The companion pieces about a youthful tiger eager to mature, *Leo the Late Bloomer* and *Little Louie the Baby Bloomer,* are separated by 27 years, and according to Lisa S. Murphy, reviewing the latter title in *School Library Journal,* Dewey has only gotten better. Her colors are "even more brilliant than

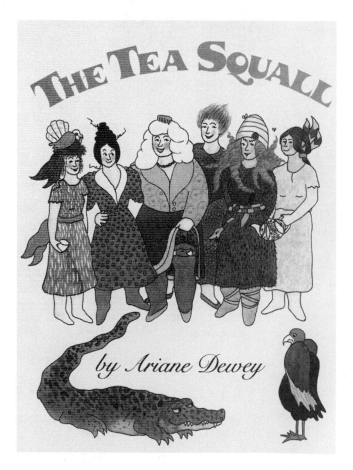

Dewey demonstrates her penchant for folkloric exaggeration in her self-illustrated tea party tall-tale. (Cover illustration by Dewey.)

Every day Leo played with his friends.
Every day he tried to play with Little Louie, too.
"What's the matter with Little Louie?" asked Plover.
"Why can't he throw a ball?" asked Elephant.
"Why can't he pull a wagon?" asked Crocodile.
"Why can't he rattle his rattle?" asked Snake.
"And he can't talk, either," said Leo.

Leo teaches his younger brother Louie such skills as how to throw a ball and pull a wagon in this story about "blooming"
late and brotherly love. (From Little Louie the Baby Bloomer, *written by Robert Kraus and illustrated by Dewey and Aruego.)*

before," according to Murphy. "The lush jungle plants and animals are even more inviting to young eyes."

Other long-term Dewey-Aruego illustrative collaborations have been with George Shannon on his "Lizard" books, and on *April Showers,* which *Horn Book*'s Mary M. Burns dubbed "bright, splashy, and fun." Lauren Peterson, writing in *Booklist,* noted the "bright, cheerful watercolors" that "splash across the page," while Laura-lyn Persson commented in *School Library Journal* that Aruego and Dewey use their "characteristic playful style to good effect, with clear, attractive colors and simple, graceful lines." *Booklist*'s Ellen Mandel captured the essence of the Dewey-Aruego collaborative effort in her review of their illustrations for *They Thought They Saw Him* by Craig Strete. Mandel called their depictions of the chameleon in the story "perky" and "cartoon art," and most importantly, "ever-popular."

Dewey's solo efforts as author/illustrator got underway in 1979 with *The Fish Peri,* and by her fourth title, *Pecos Bill,* she had found her niche, writing and illustrating easy chapter books about tall-tale characters. *Febold Feboldson,* her fifth book, employs short sentences and abbreviated chapters, as well as entertaining

illustrations, to recount the trials and tribulations of the legendary first farmer to settle in what is now Nebraska. The snow doesn't melt? No problem for Febold. He hauls in desert sand. The sun's too hot in the summer? No problem. Febold gathers the resulting popcorn. "Illustrations spill over the entire page in earthy tones of clay, grass green, and sun gold," noted Susan Roman in a *Booklist* review, adding that the humorous text is likely to cause "giggles among listeners." Liza Bliss commented in *School Library Journal* that some of Dewey's "silly exaggerations" in the seven episodes of this tall tale "will have great appeal." Bliss also praised Dewey's illustrations as "literal and pleasant" and "prominent enough to be seen when the book is used as a read-aloud."

More legends and tall tales are served up in *Laffite, the Pirate,* which recounts, in a "brief, readable chapter story," the adventures of this "dashing and romantic pirate," according to Hayden E. Atwood in *School Library Journal.* Atwood went on to praise Dewey's "characteristically simple, almost primitive" illustrations which "enhance the text," and concluded that *Laffite, the Pirate* was an "enjoyable and worthwhile book that will read well aloud." Linda Callaghan, writing in *Booklist,* commented that the legendary Laffite "is captured with humor and bravado in Dewey's words and pictures." Dewey's five short chapters detail Laffite's exploits, from capturing ships to burying stolen treasure to locking horns with the governor of Louisiana. "An appealing treatment ... sure to be popular with the read-alone crowd," concluded Callaghan.

The exploits of a legendary oilman are recounted in *Gib Morgan, Oilman,* another beginning chapter-book with plenty of illustrations "in colors as vivid as the tales being told," according to Cathy Woodward writing in *School Library Journal.* Dewey blended fact—Morgan was an actual historical figure—with tall-tale fiction in these stories to create "an irresistible tale," according to Woodward, while her use of brief, simple sentences allows primary age readers "to enjoy at their own pace." Ethel R. Twichell commented in *Horn Book* that "exaggeration and deadpan humor" are the hallmark of these tall tales that come from the early days of the oil industry. Twichell went on to observe that the stories have "a good-natured boastfulness and gift for the ridiculous" that even small children will enjoy. The ever resourceful Gib Morgan turns to a giant boa for help in extracting a stuck oil-drill bit; he uses, a la Paul Bunyon, slabs of bacon strapped to men's feet to grease a giant griddle. Roger Sutton concluded in *Bulletin of the Center for Children's Books* that "tales don't come much taller than these, and Dewey's colorful, naive paintings take all the nonsense literally."

A tall-tale tea party is presented in *The Tea Squall* with tall-tale heroines, including Florinda Fury, Katy Goodrit, and Sally Ann Thunder Ann Whirlwind Crockett. Weather is the topic of conversation at the tea party, and one guest vies with the other to outdo the severity of winter storms: words froze as the Crocketts spoke to one another, for example. The feast includes five kinds of tea, forty kinds of corn bread, blackberry grunt and blueberry slump, snickerdoodles, kinkawoodles, and more. "This is a gem," concluded *Publishers Weekly* in its review of *The Tea Squall.* "Folkloric exaggeration, eccentric tall tales and delightful peculiarities run on...." Susan Scheps, writing in *School Library Journal,* called the book "engaging entertainment," while *Booklist*'s Ilene Cooper commented that readers "will enjoy the feminist high jinks."

The famed, legendary frontiersman Davy Crockett also makes an appearance in Dewey's books, in *The Narrow Escapes of Davy Crockett.* "Dewey has had great success interpreting tall tales," noted *Booklist*'s Cooper, "and this may be her best effort yet." Davy confronts snakes, bears, eagles, an owl, and even an elk in these stories loosely based on escapades from *The Crockett Almanacs,* and Davy is also shown courting Sally Ann Thunder Ann Whirlwind and running for Congress. Cooper concluded that the book was the "essence" of what tall tales are about: "witty and wild."

Taking the sky as inspiration, Dewey created a picture book detailing sometimes with awe, sometimes with trepidation, all the wonders to be seen above our heads.

The sky contains, in Dewey's illustrations, a vast assortment of wonderful and sometimes dread objects, from droplets of moisture, birds and butterflies, rockets and UFOs, superheroes and Santa Claus, to smog, tornadoes, vampires, and ghosts. Linda Greengrass wrote in *School Library Journal* that the book was a "wonderful collaboration of words and pictures," with images suggested in the text "realized by the fanciful yet realistic pictures."

The etymology of colors is the subject of Dewey's *Naming Colors,* a look at the history of English words for colors. Starting with the words used to describe black and white, Dewey moves on to more varied hues, including sepia, puce, and even electric pink. A rich palette accompanies the descriptions. As Martha Rosen noted in *School Library Journal,* "The illustrations are lively, interesting, and well integrated with the text." Rosen noted particularly one double-page spread of a garden full of fruits and vegetables that "beg to be tasted." Sutton commented in *Bulletin of the Center for Children's Books* that each page of Dewey's book is "splashed with lively watercolor depictions of the color sources under discussion," and that it was "fun to look at."

Fun is something that all of Dewey's books emphasize, both in illustration and text. For her illustrations, Dewey does both online research and library searches. Observing nature is another favorite source of inspiration for this prolific author/illustrator. Dewey recently told *SATA:* "Doing research on the fascinatingly odd habits of animals is always fun. There are not too many jobs that require phone calls to the zoo to find out the color of a python's tongue."

Works Cited

Atwood, Hayden E., review of *Laffite, the Pirate, School Library Journal,* November, 1985, p. 68.

Bliss, Liza, review of *Febold Feboldson, School Library Journal,* August, 1984, p. 58.

Burns, Mary M., review of *April Showers, Horn Book,* May-June, 1995, p. 329.

Callaghan, Linda, review of *Laffite, the Pirate, Booklist,* September 15, 1985, pp. 130-31.

Cooper, Ilene, review of *The Tea Squall, Booklist,* April 1, 1988, p. 1342.

Cooper, review of *The Narrow Escapes of Davy Crockett: From a Bear, a Boa Constrictor, a Hoop Snake, an Elk, an Owl, Eagles, Rattlesnakes, Wildcats, Trees, Tornadoes, a Sinking Ship, and Niagara Falls, Booklist,* March 1, 1990, p. 1339.

Entry on Dewey in *Fourth Book of Junior Authors and Illustrators,* edited by Doris de Montreville and Elizabeth D. Crawford, H. W. Wilson, 1978, pp. 115-16.

Greengrass, Linda, review of *The Sky, School Library Journal,* March, 1994, p. 197.

Mandel, Ellen, review of *They Thought They Saw Him, Booklist,* April 15, 1996, p. 1447.

Murphy, Lisa S., review of *Little Louie the Baby Bloomer, School Library Journal,* July, 1998, pp. 77-78.

Persson, Lauralyn, review of *April Showers, School Library Journal,* May, 1995, p. 95.

Peterson, Lauren, review of *April Showers, Booklist,* April 1, 1995, p. 1428.

Roman, Susan, review of *Febold Feboldson, Booklist,* June 1, 1984, p. 1397.

Rosen, Martha, review of *Naming Colors, School Library Journal,* April, 1995, p. 141.

Scheps, Susan, review of *The Tea Squall, School Library Journal,* May, 1988, p. 82.

Sutton, Roger, review of *Gib Morgan, Oilman, Bulletin of the Center for Children's Books,* May, 1987, pp. 165-66.

Sutton, review of *Naming Colors, Bulletin of the Center for Children's Books,* February, 1995, p. 196.

Review of *The Tea Squall, Publishers Weekly,* May 13, 1988, p. 273.

Twichell, Ethel R., review of *Gib Morgan, Oilman, Horn Book,* May-June, 1987, pp. 349-50.

Woodward, Cathy, review of *Gib Morgan, Oilman, School Library Journal,* June-July, 1987, p. 81.

For More Information See

PERIODICALS

Horn Book, March-April, 1994, p. 189; July-August, 1996, p. 458.

Publishers Weekly, January 19, 1990, p. 109.

School Library Journal, May, 1996, p. 100; May, 1998, p. 137.

ON-LINE

Author's website at http://ariane-dewey.com.

—*Sketch by J. Sydney Jones*

*   *   *

DIXON, Franklin W.
See LANTZ, Francess (Lin)

*   *   *

ELLIOT(T), Bruce
See FIELD, Edward

F

FIELD, Edward 1924-
(Bruce Elliot(t), a joint pseudonym)

Personal

Born June 7, 1924, in Brooklyn, NY; son of Louis (a commercial artist) and Hilda (Taubman) Field; companion of Neil Derrick (a novelist), since 1959. *Education:* Attended New York University. *Politics:* Left Liberal. *Religion:* Jewish (secular). *Hobbies and other interests:* Travel abroad; spending summers in Berlin, Amsterdam, London, Paris, and Tangiers.

Addresses

Home—463 West St., No. A323, New York, NY 10014. *Agent*—Andrew Pope, Curtis Brown Ltd., 10 Astor Place, New York, NY 10003. *E-mail*—Fieldinski@Yahoo.com.

Career

Novelist and poet. Participant in poetry workshops at colleges, including Eckerd College, Sarah Lawrence College, and Hofstra University, and at YMHA Poetry Center, New York City. *Military service:* U.S. Army Air Force, 1942-46, first lieutenant. *Member:* Poetry Society of America.

Awards, Honors

Lamont Award, Academy of American Poets, 1962; Guggenheim Fellowship, 1963; Academy Award for documentary, 1965, for narration for *To Be Alive;* Shelley Memorial Award, Poetry Society of America, 1974; Prix de Rome, American Academy of Arts & Letters, 1981; Lambda Literary Award, 1993.

Writings

POETRY

Stand up, Friend, with Me, Grove Press, 1963.
Variety Photoplays, Grove Press, 1967.
(Selector and translator) *Eskimo Songs and Stories,* illustrated by Kiakshuk and Pudlo, Delacorte, 1973.
A Full Heart, Sheep Meadow Press (Riverdale-on-Hudson, New York), 1977.
Stars in My Eyes, Sheep Meadow Press, 1978.
The Lost, Dancing, Watershed Tapes, 1984.
New and Selected Poems from the Book of My Life, Sheep Meadow Press, 1987.
Counting Myself Lucky: Selected Poems, 1963-1992, Black Sparrow Press (Santa Rosa, CA), 1992.
A Frieze for a Temple of Love, Black Sparrow Press, 1998.
Magic Words: Poems, illustrated by Stefano Vitale, Harcourt Brace, 1998.

ADULT FICTION; WITH NEIL DERRICK UNDER PSEUDONYM BRUCE ELLIOT

The Potency Clinic, Bleecker Street Press, 1978.

Edward Field

Village, Avon, 1982.
The Office, Ballantine, 1987.

OTHER

(Compiler and editor) *A Geography of Poets: An Anthology of the New Poetry,* Bantam, 1979.

(Editor) Alfred Chester, *Head of a Sad Angel: Stories, 1953-1966,* foreword by Gore Vidal, Black Sparrow Press, 1990.

(Editor) Chester, *Looking for Genet: Literary Essays & Reviews,* Black Sparrow Press, 1992.

(Editor, with Charles Stetler and Gerald Locklin) *A New Geography of Poets,* University of Arkansas Press, 1992.

Poetry and essays have appeared in periodicals, including *New Yorker, New York Review of Books, New York Times Book Review, Kenyon Review, Partisan Review, Nation,* and *Evergreen.* Some of Field's work was translated into German.

Adaptations

Selections of Field's poetry, read by the author, have been recorded on audiocassette.

Work in Progress

Memoirs; research on the poet Dunstan Thompson.

Sidelights

Poet Edward Field has remained dedicated to his craft for nearly half a century. As he told SATA, "I look back with amazement at my choice of poetry, and the fidelity with which I have stuck with it . . . . There were so many other things I could have done, but without poetry, as an old man in Washington Square once said to me about mathematics, 'life isn't worth a sandwich.'" The author of several volumes of poems for adult readers, Field has also created works like *Magic Words* and the anthology *Eskimo Songs and Stories* that transmit his own enthusiasm for language to younger readers.

"My poetry speaks to ordinary people, aims for common ground," Field explained in an essay for *Contemporary Authors Autobiography Series* (*CAAS*), noting the difference between his approach to his craft and that of other, more literary writers. "It has grown directly out of what I come from, and though I've developed and changed in many ways, I've seen little reason to 'rise above it.'" Born in Brooklyn, New York, in 1924, Field was raised in neighboring Long Island, one of six children born to a Jewish couple of Eastern-European descent. Encouraged in the study of classical music and literature, he became the first person in his family to go to college. However, after spending one year studying business at New York University, Field opted out of the program, which he found boring, and enlisted in the U.S. Air Force. It was 1942, and the United States had just entered World War II; Field found himself in England by 1944, flying bombing missions over Germany. It was during his tenure with the Air Force that he was first introduced to

Field based his collection of poems on songs and stories gathered by Knud Rasmussen, who recorded Inuit legends about the universe and its creation. (Cover illustration by Stefano Vitale.)

poetry by friends who recommended the work of writers like T. S. Eliot, George Barker, and Dylan Thomas.

"Poets are often academics, but I never saw poetry as having much to do with school," Field recalled to SATA. Although he re-enrolled at New York University after returning to the United States, Field found himself restricted by the provisions of the GI Bill to a limited course selection, and gained little in the way of inspiration from his studies. However, he managed to get into classes at the nearby Washington Square College of Arts & Sciences, where he quickly discovered the "literary set." Finding topics like existentialism and socialism much more exciting than his business courses, he began spending more time with his new friends and less time in class at NYU. In 1948, he withdrew from NYU and sailed to Paris, from there traveling around Europe and living on his savings for several years. "Rarely are poets professional writers, which would have earned me the money to live on," he explained of his choice for self-expression over wealth. "Novelists sometimes, yes, and reviewers, but writing for the movies or television or periodicals, if I could have cracked those fields, would have surely usurped the place of poetry." Instead, Field grew increasingly convinced that it was as a poet that he wanted to become known.

Returning to the United States in 1950, Field realized that he had to do something to earn a living. "Making a living was a major problem, for I never cared about doing anything else enough to put much energy into it," he explained of his youthful penchant for remaining footloose. "And being gay, I didn't have to support a family, which would have forced me into commercial work whether I liked it or not." Jobs in warehouses or apprenticing to the trades did little to inspire the poetic muse; instead they were exhausting. Field then was convinced by friends to employ another strategy—study acting and perform. While he tried to keep up with his writing during the few years he spent as an actor, as he later recalled, "the acting life is quite consuming, with classes, rehearsals, making the rounds, plus relaxing with fellow actors."

Field's time as an actor ended in 1963 with the publication of his first book, *Stand up, Friend, with Me.* The volume garnered enough positive reviews to propel it into a second edition, and Field was able to earn enough money through poetry readings and book sales to support himself. "I did learn some useful things as an actor which helped me in front of audiences," Field recalled, "so it was not a waste. But first, poems must be unassailable on the page, and I've never been interested in using my actor's craft to make a poem sound better than it is." Other than stints teaching—"hated it"—, book reviewing—"it brought out a vicious streak in me I didn't like"—, and translating—"more congenial"—, writing poetry has continued to be Field's vocation. One sideline was his collection of the best of modern poetry, 1979's *A Geography of Poets,* which was hailed in *Publishers Weekly* as containing "a powerful excitement . . . that comes out of the ongoing democratization of poetry." Containing the works of over two-hundred modern poets hailing from all parts of the United States, the book presents verse that is "always interesting, sometimes striking," according to *New York Times Book Review* contributor Ray Walters.

In the mid-1960s Field was hired to write the narration for the documentary film *To Be Alive,* but quickly realized that the kind of high-pressure group participation required for such an endeavor was not his cup of tea. "The director actually expected me to write the script in his film studio!" Field recalled. "But after insisting, I was allowed to do the writing at home during my accustomed morning hours. When I brought in the daily draft of the narration, it was read against the rough cut of the film, and everyone would criticize it. I am open to criticism, for every word of a poem must stand up to every possible question, but I found that I was expected to please anyone who had anything to say about the script, even someone who had dropped in casually. In my poems I am the final arbiter, no matter what anyone says, I hold the power—and this wasn't my film, but the director's. Although my exposure to the movie world was brief and our movie won an Academy Award, I rejected future offers of work in the field."

A translation project done for a group of educators in Boston, Massachusetts was eventually published in 1973 as *Eskimo Songs and Stories.* As with all his translation projects, Fields dubbed the work an "adaptation" because, as he said, "I allow myself every liberty to make the poem work in English, however it veers from the original." Based on the works collected by Danish explorer Knud Rasmussen in the early 1920s, the volume shows the Eskimo or Inuit people to be "fully and realistically aware of the gamut of cruelty and hardship touching human life," with each woman and man "struggl[ing] against his world, recognizing all too well the sadness and painfulness of his position," according to a *Horn Book* contributor. Illustrated with the works of native Inuit artists, *Eskimo Songs and Stories* contains over thirty brief works that a *Booklist* contributor praised collectively as an "authentic folk collection" told with "utter purity and directness of expression." Field would return to Rasmussen again in 1998's *Magic Words,* which adapts these Inuit songs and creation myths into a picture-book format. Called "stunning" by a *Publishers Weekly* contributor, *Magic Words* contains language that *School Library Journal* contributor Nina Lindsay characterized as "simple, yet [with] a rhythm to it that makes for both good poetry and good storytelling."

In addition to writing poetry, translating poetry, and writing about poetry, Field has also dabbled a little in fiction, much of it in collaboration with his partner, Neil Derrick, a novelist who lost his sight several years into their relationship. Writing fiction is for Field "more in the nature of helping [Neil]" than a desire to expand into another genre, and "it does take up distressingly large amounts of time. And prose," noted Field, "is almost harder than poetry—there's so much more of it to deal with!"

When Field first became committed to his life as a poet, he felt that his verse could change the world. "Later," he recalled in *CAAS,* "I desperately believed, against the world, that poetry could save me. In spite of the evident truth that poetry can change nothing, I trust the instincts of the young and why they are attracted to poetry, as if it actually could overcome injustice. It has to do with an idealism that gets lost as you get older . . . . It has to do with poetry as magic, the magic of words." Still actively involved in his art, and "living simply but well," as he told *SATA,* on the limited income he and his partner earn through their work, Field looks at his life with satisfaction: "I am full of gratitude to Poetry for shaping my life."

Works Cited

Review of *Eskimo Songs and Stories, Booklist,* January 15, 1974, p. 541.

Review of *Eskimo Songs and Stories, Horn Book,* February, 1974, p. 45.

Field, Edward, essay in *Contemporary Authors Autobiography Series,* Volume 27, Gale, 1993, pp. 115-34.

Review of *A Geography of Poets: An Anthology of the New Poetry, Publishers Weekly,* November 27, 1978, p. 58.

Lindsay, Nina, review of *Magic Words: Poems, School Library Journal,* December, 1998, p. 135.

Review of *Magic Words: Poems, Publishers Weekly,* September 7, 1998, p. 95.

Walters, Ray, review of *A Geography of Poets: An Anthology of the New Poetry, New York Times Book Review,* January 21, 1979, p. 37.

For More Information See

BOOKS

Dictionary of Literary Biography, Volume 105: *American Poets since World War II, Second Series,* edited by R. S. Gwynn, Gale, 1988, pp. 95-103.

PERIODICALS

Booklist, September 1, 1992, p. 26.
Kirkus Reviews, December 1, 1973, p. 1311.
Kliatt, spring, 1979, p. 23.

*   *   *

FINNEY, Jack 1911-1995

Personal

Born Walter Braden Finney, October 2, 1911, in Milwaukee, WI; died of pneumonia, November 14, 1995, in Greenbrae, CA; married G. Marguerite Guest; children: Margie, Kenneth. *Education:* Attended Knox College, Galesburg, IL.

Career

Writer.

Awards, Honors

Special Prize, *Ellery Queen's Mystery Magazine* contest, c. 1946, for "The Widow's Walk"; best short story collection, *Infinity Science Fiction,* 1958, for *The Third Level;* World Fantasy life achievement award, 1987.

Writings

Five Against the House (novel), Doubleday, 1954.
The Body Snatchers (novel), Dell, 1955, reprinted as *Invasion of the Body Snatchers,* Dell, 1961, revised edition published as *The Invasion of the Body Snatchers,* Award, 1973.
Telephone Roulette (play), Dramatic Publishing, 1956.
The Third Level (short stories; includes "The Third Level," "Such Interesting Neighbors," and "Second Chance"), Rinehart, 1957 (published in England as *The Clock of Time,* Eyre & Spottiswoode, 1958).
The House of Numbers (novel), Dell, 1957.
Assault on a Queen (novel), Simon & Schuster, 1959.
I Love Galesburg in the Springtime (short stories), Simon & Schuster, 1963.
Good Neighbor Sam (novel), Simon & Schuster, 1963.
This Winter's Hobby (play), first produced in New Haven, CT, 1966.

Jack Finney

The Woodrow Wilson Dime (novel), Simon & Schuster, 1968.
Time and Again (novel), Simon & Schuster, 1970, Scribner Paperback Editions, 1995.
Marion's Wall (novel), Simon & Schuster, 1973.
The Night People (novel), Doubleday, 1977.
Forgotten News: The Crime of the Century, and Other Lost Stories (nonfiction), Doubleday, 1983.
About Time (short stories), Simon & Schuster, 1986.
Three by Finney (contains *The Woodrow Wilson Dime, The Night People,* and *Marion's Wall*), Simon & Schuster, 1987.
From Time to Time: A Novel, Simon and Schuster, 1995.

Contributor to periodicals, including *Collier's, Cosmopolitan, Good Housekeeping, Ladies' Home Journal, McCall's,* and *Saturday Evening Post.*

Adaptations

Five against the House was adapted for a movie of the same name in 1955; *The Body Snatchers* was filmed as *Invasion of the Body Snatchers* in 1956, again in 1979, and as *Body Snatchers* in 1993 by Warner Bros.; *House of Numbers* was filmed in 1957; *Good Neighbor Sam* was filmed in 1964, starring Jack Lemmon; *Assault on a Queen* was filmed in 1966; *Marion's Wall* was filmed as *Maxie,* 1985; the short story, "The Love Letter," was filmed for a television movie, 1998.

Sidelights

American author Jack Finney announced his major thematic material early in his career, in the short story "I'm Scared": "Haven't you noticed," the narrator comments, "... on the part of nearly everyone you know, a growing rebellion against the *present?*"

Indeed, Finney carried out something of a one-man crusade against the present in many of his novels and numerous short stories and in their movie adaptations, and won a cult following for his novels *The Body Snatchers* and *Time and Again*. Finney's narrator in "I'm Scared" goes on to remark: "Man is disturbing the clock of time, and I am afraid it will break. When it does, I leave to your imagination the last few hours of madness that will be left to us all; all the countless moments that now make up our lives suddenly ripped apart and chaotically tangled in time." For Finney, however, the breaking apart of time was usually an experience to be treasured, sipped like fine old wine. The past was, for him, another country that afforded a more casual pace of life, a time when faces carried less anxiety, more cheerful optimism.

Michael Beard noted in *Dictionary of Literary Biography* that "the portrait of an entire society straining semiconsciously to escape the present is a compact argument for the sensibility behind most of [Finney's] writings." But Beard also pointed out that Finney was not a writer to be categorized simply as someone working in science fiction because of the tendency on the part of many of his protagonists toward time travel. "The premise that time is malleable and subject to change through human emotions is not a common science-fiction theme," Beard wrote. "The science that underlies Finney's time-travel is often, properly speaking, not science, but sympathetic magic." Far from being a science fiction writer, or thriller writer as other critics have labeled him, or a mystery writer as still others have written, Finney was, at heart, a romantic. "Finney creates ingenious, suspenseful narratives, treats regretfully, though sometimes humorously, the tensions and conflicts in mid-20th-century America," Seymour Rudin noted in *St. James Guide to Crime and Mystery Writers,* "and contrasts the latter, though not always explicitly, with a romantic imagined pre-modern age."

In his best known works, such as *The Body Snatchers, Time and Again,* and the latter's sequel, *From Time to Time,* Finney casts a critical eye on the present. Time travel—a literal escape from the present—informs those last two works while the power of love and a rootedness in the past empowers us to transcend the soulless, all-conforming present as in *The Body Snatchers*. Over and again this theme of alienation from current time and a return to the past or an alternate time is announced in Finney's short stories, especially those collected in *The Third Level;* it is also a recurrent motif in his lesser novel-length fiction, including *The Woodrow Wilson Dime* and in *Marion's Wall,* in which reincarnation is the engine of time travel. Even in his crime and suspense fiction such as *Assault on a Queen* and *The Night People,* there is a touch of the sentimentalized past or a jaundiced view of the present that helps to fuel the engine of the plot.

For a man like Finney, who could so lovingly recreate the New York of the 1880s or the early twentieth century, it is a curiosity that so little is known of his own past. As Beard noted, "Finney is a writer who values his privacy." Born in Milwaukee, Wisconsin, in 1911, he was brought up in Chicago. He attended Knox College and worked for a time in New York City as an advertising copywriter, the profession of his best-loved protagonist, Simon Morley, from the novels *Time and Again* and *From Time to Time*. By the 1950s, he had settled in California, in Mill Valley, north of San Francisco. Here, Finney would continue to make his home with his family until his death in 1995.

Finney began publishing short stories in 1946, winning an award from *Ellery Queen's Mystery Magazine* for such early efforts as "The Widow's Walk." These first stories were mostly suspense, published in the pages of *Collier's*. Finney continued to write for such slick magazines rather than the pulps that were the home of mystery and science fiction writers. In 1954 he published his first novel, *Five Against the House,* a tale of college students who are out for excitement to enhance their dull academic lives. They create an elaborate plan to rob a nightclub in Reno in this story which, according to Beard, "sets the pattern for [Finney's] suspense stories," such as *Assault on a Queen,* in which thieves target the *Queen Mary* steamship. In *Assault on a Queen,* the thieves, older and more professional adventurers, plan to re-float a sunken World War I U-Boat as part of their scheme to rob the passenger liner. Both of these mystery-suspense novels were turned into films.

In late 1954, Finney published a serialized story in *Collier's* that changed everything for the forty-three-year-old writer and that allowed him to support his family solely on his writing.

The story in question dealt with an alien invasion of Earth and showed similarities to earlier science fiction works, such as *The Puppet Masters* by Robert Heinlein, and the short story, "The Father Thing," by Philip K. Dick. Finney's story presented non-specific aliens: there were no green-skinned creatures with antennae-eyes. Instead, Finney, in his story and in the subsequent novel, *The Body Snatchers,* deals with these aliens only in the human forms that they inhabit. It is the aliens' plan to take over Earth by physically duplicating actual earthly, who are then destroyed. These mindless, zombie-like replicas of humans are born out of giant seed pods that the aliens produce in a large nursery. Though most of the inhabitants of the small town of Santa Mira (called Mill Valley in later editions of the book) do not see anything bizarre happening, one earthling does. Dr. Miles Bennell is pitted against this invasion, a man who is "a representative of specific values," according to Beard in *Dictionary of Literary Biography*. Bennell is loyal to the past—to the home he still lives in which once belonged to his parents, and to the medical practice that he has inherited from his father. The aliens, in this context, can be read as symbolic of the present and future: the world of boring conformity and mindless obedience.

Bennell slowly comes to discover that several people in his community are complaining of loved ones and close relations who do not seem to be themselves—quite literally. There is an uncle who "looks, sounds, acts and remembers exactly" like the real uncle. "On the outside," wails his suspicious niece. "But *inside* he's different. His responses ... aren't *emotionally* right ... that look, way in back of the eyes is gone." A young son fears his mother; mysterious green pods turn up in people's houses and begin to grow human replications. Bennell comes to learn that these life forms have come from another planet and are intent on becoming an opportunistic parasite here on Earth; to take over the human inhabitants and turn them all into willing, emotionless, slaves.

In the novel, the conflict between Bennell and the aliens is countered by the love story between the doctor and Becky Driscoll, a subplot that at times overshadows the suspenseful plot. So intrusive was the romantic element, that when the book was filmed, Bennell's love interest was destroyed by the aliens. "Finney's emphasis on the love relationship suggests that romantic love of the naïve, traditional kind lines up most effectively against the forces of conformity and eroded individuality which the pods represent," concluded Beard. Eventually, with the help of Becky, Bennell is able to defeat the aliens in the book: burning the main nursery of the seed pods sends these creatures hurtling off into space, in search of some other planet to populate.

The issue of modern-day conformity raised by the novel has led many critics to view Finney's book and subsequent film adaptations (there have been three movies made thus far, though most viewers agree the first is still the best) as an allegory on life in the 1950s. Whether this allegory stands for the follow-the-leader anti-communism and McCarthyism rampant at the time, or is representative of mindless post-industrial material culture, is a debating point among critics and readers alike. In the end, Finney was not interested in presenting moral lessons, but in giving readers a good yarn to sink their mental teeth into. When Bennell finally succeeds in driving the aliens away by burning their pod nursery, this is not part of some message; rather it is the denouement of the action. Movie versions have been less kind to the human victims, but Finney, as in most of his fiction, enjoyed the traditional happy ending. E. Barbara Boatner, reviewing in *Kliatt* an expanded, 1973 version of the novel entitled *The Invasion of the Body Snatchers,* declared that "high suspense and low-profile aliens are the key to the success of the book."

Finney returned to the short story for his next publication, *The Third Level,* stories that deal almost exclusively with time travel. Though Finney was still operating only marginally in the bounds of science fiction with such stories, P. Schuyler Miller, writing in *Astounding Science-Fiction,* noted that "if you want to know the kind of SF the general public wants, this [volume of short stories] is as good a sample as you're likely to get." Collected here are stories such as "I'm Scared," "Such Interesting Neighbors," "Of Missing Persons," "Second Chance," and the title story of the volume, "The Third Level." Here are all manner of time travel adventures, both forward and backward in time, as well as space travel. All of these stories provide escapist reading in the most literal of its meanings: Finney's characters are escaping from their present predicaments. A commuter discovers a third level in Grand Central station from which trains run back in time to America of the 1890s; neighbors in California turn out to be refugees from the future, seeking a world free of the fear of the hydrogen bomb; a vintage car is the vehicle of time travel back to the 1920s in yet another story. More nostalgia for the past is found in a further short story collection, *I Love Galesburg in the Springtime,* with its title story and "The Love Letter" both providing fond glimpses of an earlier, more pristine America.

Two more novels followed these short stories; both the humorous *Good Neighbor Sam,* turned into a movie starring Jack Lemmon, and the alternate-time book, *The Woodrow Wilson Dime,* in which the eponymous coin serves as the catalyst for time travel. But by far Finney's most popular novel, *Time and Again,* was published in 1970 when the author had honed his time-travel devices over decades of writing. Beard noted in *Dictionary of Literary Biography* that this book "is the most solid and consequential of Finney's novels and the one in which his characteristic stratagems and complex turns of plot work out in the most satisfying manner."

Simon Morley, called Si by his friends, is busy at his drawing board at a New York ad agency when he is offered a seductive proposition by one Rube Prien—he has been chosen to take part in a top-secret government project that could make an enormous change in the history of mankind. Morley, suitably skeptical yet also full of curiosity and good will, accepts the challenge and discovers that the project is one of time travel. But in this project, directed by Dr. E. E. Danziger, there are no science fiction contraptions to take one into the past; instead one wills oneself backward in time, prompted by appropriate atmosphere. Morley takes up residence in New York's famous Dakota building overlooking Central Park, in a room which was uninhabited during the time to which Morley has chosen to return: New York City of the 1880s. Morley steeps himself in the period, studying dress, daily events, and moments of historical import. The past slowly becomes alive for him, and aided by hypnosis, he is able to make trial runs back in time, initially to sort out an old family problem for his twentieth-century girlfriend, Katie. Soon, however, the past has Morley in its grip; he takes a room at a boarding house on Gramercy Park, and there meets the daughter of the house, Julia, a woman who is actually some eighty years his senior. The real intentions of Danziger and Prien soon become clear to Morley: they hope that he will help to change government policy of the time making Cuba an American possession, thereby diverting twentieth-century difficulties with that island.

Kevin McCarthy and Dana Wynter star in **The Invasion of the Body Snatchers,** *a 1956 film adaptation of Finney's novel.*

However, such plot twists are secondary to this novel in which "the real fascination ... lies in Morley's discovery of the New York" of the 1880s, according to a reviewer in *Publishers Weekly.* Finney included actual photos and engravings from the time as illustrations to his book to give it an added touch of reality. Finney's talent for "making his time travel perfectly believable," concluded the *Publishers Weekly* reviewer, is achieved by "the smooth use of authentic details." Morley falls in love not only with the past, but also with Julia, and soon he must choose both between worlds and between loves. He ultimately opts for the past and for Julia, but only after contriving to thwart Danziger's attempts at controlling history. Morley destroys the future possibility of the time-travel project by diverting—in the past—a meeting between the young woman and man who would be Danziger's father and mother. Morley is left in the past with his beloved Julia. He looks around at his nineteenth-century world: "At the gaslighted brownstones beside me. At the nighttime winter sky. This too was an imperfect world, but—I drew a deep breath, sharply chill in my lungs—the air was still clean. The rivers flowed fresh as they had since time began." He goes to his new home, at Gramercy Park 19. According to Beard, it is just such a fascination with the New York of the past that has made Finney's novel "a minor cult book among New York enthusiasts."

Writing in the *New York Times Book Review,* W. G. Rogers called Finney's novel "a most ingenious confection of time now and time then," and concluded that in the pages of this book "you go back to a wonderful world and have a wonderful time doing it." A writer for *Booklist* called the novel "a scrupulously controlled, painstakingly researched entertainment," while *Horn Book's* Mary Silva Cosgrave called *Time and Again* "cleverly conceived" and concluded that the results of Morley's time travel "are as comical and thrilling as an old Keystone Cops silent movie, with an old-fashioned romance thrown in for good measure." So popular has the book been, that it has stayed in print since its publication in 1970, has been twice optioned for movies, and has had a Broadway musical treatment.

Devoted fans had to wait a quarter of a century for a sequel to the book. In 1995 Finney published *From Time to Time,* in which Morley makes a return to the present only to be recruited for yet another mission in time. On this occasion Morley's job is to stop World War I from happening, and he is dispatched to 1912 for said mission. Part of his small task is to keep the fated passenger liner *Titanic* from sinking. After all the action, Morley once again returns to his wife and child in nineteenth-century New York. Finney was undaunted by the rigors of such a plot device. As Frank Rich noted in the *New York Times Book Review,* "Mr. Finney barely

In what has been called Finney's most popular novel, Simon Morley embarks upon a journey back in time which ends up having some very serious historical consequences. (Cover photograph by Lawrence Ratzkin.)

pretends to meet the obligations of fiction, science or otherwise, as he takes us on an ebulliently guided tour of old New York." Rich noted that "the glories of 'From Time to Time' are set pieces that could be pulled out of its story entirely and read in any sequence," and that lovers of New York would "exult once more in [Finney's] sweet articulation of a fine romance." Most reviewers felt that this sequel lacked the plot coherence of the original, but that Finney's evocation of a past time, especially his description of theatrical New York of the day, provided offsetting pleasure for the reader. A *Publishers Weekly* critic concluded that "this mind-stretching escapist adventure is studded with period photos and news clippings that function as an integral part of the story," while Linda Vretos, writing in *School Library Journal,* called the novel "a real page-turner, loaded with nostalgia, detail, suspense, and a mind-boggling ending...." And writing in the *Magazine of Fantasy and Science Fiction,* Robert K. J. Killheffer provided a fine summation of Finney's final work, noting that "he offers a smart, snappy yarn, enlivened by the inherent thrill of time travel and the particular

excitement of old New York—not serious literature, perhaps, but serious fun."

Finney wrote two other novels, *Marion's Wall* and *The Night People,* as well as a collection of essays and one of stories between these two time-travel novels featuring Si Morley, but his lasting popularity lies with *Time and Again.* Talking with Vickie Sheff-Cahan of *People* magazine shortly after publication of his last book, Finney told her that as a child, he "would read about people who would get in a box that a mad professor invented.... Bells would ring, sparks would fly, and they would step out at the Battle of Waterloo." He also told Maria Ricapito of *Entertainment Weekly* that "There's no past time I'd like to stay in. I want to stay here permanently." But in the event, Finney died not long after publication of *From Time to Time,* succumbing to pneumonia on November 14, 1995 at age eighty-four.

Works Cited

Beard, Michael, "Jack Finney," *Dictionary of Literary Biography,* Volume 8: *Twentieth-Century American Science Fiction Writers,* Gale, 1981, pp. 182-85.

Boatner, E. Barbara, review of *The Invasion of the Body Snatchers, Kliatt,* spring, 1979, p. 17.

Cosgrave, Mary Silva, review of *Time and Again, Horn Book,* October, 1970, p. 502.

Finney, Jack, "I'm Scared," in *The Third Level,* Rinehart, 1957.

Finney, Jack, *Time and Again,* Simon and Schuster, 1970, p. 398.

Finney, Jack, *Invasion of the Body Snatchers,* Simon and Schuster, 1998, p. 21.

Review of *From Time to Time, Publishers Weekly,* November 28, 1994, p. 42.

Killheffer, Robert K. J., review of *From Time to Time, Magazine of Fantasy and Science Fiction,* September, 1995, pp. 19-25.

Miller, P. Schuyler, review of *The Third Level, Astounding Science-Fiction,* May, 1958.

Ricapito, Maria, "Time Passages," *Entertainment Weekly,* February 24, 1995, p. 109.

Rich, Frank, "The 20th Century Should Have Been the Best," *New York Times Book Review,* February 19, 1995, p. 10.

Rogers, W. G., review of *Time and Again, New York Times Book Review,* August 2, 1970, p. 24.

Rudin, Seymour, "Finney, Jack," *St. James Guide to Crime and Mystery Writers,* St. James Press, 1996, pp. 361-62.

Sheff-Cahan, Vickie, "Talking With Jack Finney," *People,* April 10, 1995, p. 30.

Review of *Time and Again, Publishers Weekly,* March 9, 1970, p. 81.

Review of *Time and Again, Booklist,* September 1, 1970, p. 36.

Vretos, Linda, review of *From Time to Time, School Library Journal,* August, 1995, p. 171.

For More Information See

PERIODICALS

Kliatt, May, 1995, p. 52; September, 1996, p. 53.
Los Angeles Times Book Review, March 26, 1995, p. 11.
New York Times, May 25, 1990.
New York Times Book Review, April 28, 1996, p. 36.
School Library Journal, September, 1992, p. 158.
Voice of Youth Advocates, April, 1990, p. 19.
Wilson Library Bulletin, December, 1994, p. 29.

Obituaries

PERIODICALS

Los Angeles Times, November 17, 1995, p. A32.
New York Times, November 17, 1995, p. B15.
Times (London), November 27, 1995, p. 21.
Washington Post, November 17, 1995, p. B4.*

—*Sketch by J. Sydney Jones*

*   *   *

FLYNN, Rachel 1953-

Personal

Born June 13, 1953, in Bacchus Marsh, Victoria, Australia; daughter of Keith (a vegetable grower) and Rita (a bookkeeper; maiden name, Hastie) Smith; married Gordon Flynn (a teacher), January 9, 1976; children: Alastair, Jean. *Education:* Ballarat University, Diploma of Primary Teaching, 1973; La Tribe University, B.A., 1986, M.Ed., 1998.

Addresses

Home—18 Sutton Pole, Mont Albert North, Victoria 3129, Australia.

Career

Primary-school teacher in Melbourne, Australia, 1974-90; writer, 1979—. Council of Adult Education, Melbourne, creative-writing teacher for adults, 1995—. *Member:* Australian Society of Authors.

Awards, Honors

Notable Book, Children's Book Council of Australia, 1992, for *I Hate Fridays,* and 1995, for *I Can't Wait;* grant from Literature Board, Australia Council, 1993.

Writings

I Hate Fridays, illustrated by Craig Smith, Puffin (Penguin Books, Ringwood, Australia), 1990.
It's Not Fair, illustrated by Smith, Puffin, 1992.
I Can't Wait, illustrated by Smith, Puffin, 1994.
Worried Sick, illustrated by Smith, Puffin, 1995.
Messing Around, illustrated by Smith, Puffin, 1997.
My Mummy and Me (picture book), illustrated by Smith, Puffin, 1998.

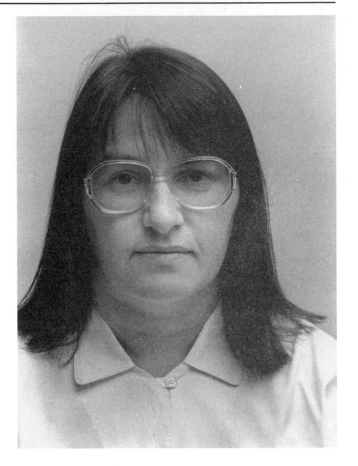

Rachel Flynn

My Daddy and Me (picture book), illustrated by Smith, Puffin, 1998.

Contributor of articles to periodicals, including *Viewpoint* and *LUPSA Journal: Professional Development and Primary Education.*

Work in Progress

Sacked, illustrated by Craig Smith, and *Whisper Wild, Freedom Child,* illustrated by Anna Pignataro, both for Penguin.

Sidelights

Rachel Flynn told *SATA:* "I was born on my parents' eleventh wedding anniversary. My mother always told me that I was the best present she had ever received. At three years old, I was one of the first students at the new kindergarten, then I attended Bacchus Marsh Primary School and High School. At seventeen I went to Ballarat to train as a teacher, and I taught in primary schools in Melbourne before having two children.

"I began writing children's books while caring for my young family. My published work is defined by themes related to ordinary suburban life and children's culture. I am best known for the 'Koala Hills' series of five school-based novels, beginning with *I Hate Fridays.* Current projects include several junior novels focusing on relationships between children and parents, and two picture books."

For More Information See

PERIODICALS

Magpies, May, 1993, p. 29; July, 1995, p. 24; September, 1995, p. 24.

*　　*　　*

FORTEY, Richard 1946-

Personal

Born February 15, 1946, in London, England; son of Frank (a fisherman) and Margaret (Wilshin) Fortey; married Bridget Thomas, October 3, 1969 (divorced, 1974); married Jacqueline Francis (an editor), June 21, 1978; children: Dominic, Rebecca, Julia, Leo. *Citizenship:* British. *Education:* University of Cambridge, B.A., 1968, M.A., 1970, Ph.D., 1971. *Politics:* "Leftish Liberal." *Hobbies and other interests:* Mycology, poetry, beer.

Addresses

Home—18 Cromwell Rd., Henley on Thames, Oxon RG9 1J4, United Kingdom. *Office*—The Natural History Museum, London SW7 5BDF, United Kingdom. *Agent*—David Godwin Associates, Goodwin's Court, St. Martin's Lane, London W1, United Kingdom. *E-mail*—raf@nhm.ac.uk.

Career

Paleontologist and author. Natural History Museum, London, England, research fellow, 1970-77, became principal scientific officer and then merit researcher, 1978—. *Member:* Palaeontological Association (London; past president), Geological Society of London (vice president).

Awards, Honors

Received an honorary D.Sc., University of Cambridge, 1986; Natural World Book of the Year citation, 1993, for *The Hidden Landscape;* Lyell Medal, Geological Society of London, 1995; fellow of the Royal Society of London, 1997; *Life* was named a Book-of-the-Month Club main selection and was named among the Books of the Year by the *New York Times* in 1998.

Writings

Fossils: The Key to the Past, Van Nostrand (New York City), 1982, Harvard University Press (Cambridge, MA), 1991.

The Dinosaurs' Alphabet, illustrated by John Rogan, Barron's (New York City), 1990.

The Hidden Landscape: A Journey into the Geological Past, J. Cape (London), 1993.

Life: An Unauthorized Biography, HarperCollins (London), 1997, published as *Life: A Natural History of the First Four Billion Years of Life on Earth,* Knopf (New York City), 1998.

Work in Progress

Trilobite!, for Knopf, was completed in 1999.

Sidelights

A paleontologist with London's Natural History Museum, Richard Fortey has written books for general readers on fossils, geological history, and the origins of life on earth. In these works, Fortey has so successfully conveyed the excitement of scientific discovery that Chet Raymo, in the *Boston Globe,* called him "a worthy successor to such Victorian masters of natural-history writing as Thomas Huxley and John Tyndall."

Fortey's first book, *Fossils: The Key to the Past,* was hailed as an excellent introduction to the subject for both adult and juvenile audiences. A *Booklist* reviewer noted that Fortey neither oversimplified his material nor relied on jargon in this book, making it a "complete, approachable introduction." *Library Journal* contributor Walter P. Coombs Jr. also deemed the book an outstanding overview for a popular audience. Fortey's 1990 children's book, *The Dinosaurs' Alphabet,* is a collection of short poems linking dinosaurs to letters of the alphabet.

In *The Hidden Landscape: A Journey into the Geological Past,* Fortey combines his expertise in paleontology with an understanding of the development of human societies. Focusing on the British Isles, Fortey explains millions of years of geological history and shows how facts of earth science contributed to the growth of flora and fauna and to the development of such human endeavors as agriculture, mining, and even manufacturing. Fortey argues, for example, that Permian and Triassic rock corridors in the vales are natural traffic routes that humans exploited with canals, and that English wool towns sprang up near natural deposits of montmorillonite, a mineral that can be used to remove natural grease from wool. The book contains several other examples of such fascinating connections.

The Hidden Landscape earned enthusiastic reviews. Laura Garwin, in *Nature,* observed that, although the book focuses on Britain, it is more generally "about how an appreciation of geology and its hidden connections can enrich one's experience of life in exactly the same way as can an understanding of art or music." A contributor to *New Scientist* appreciated the book's "sense of the joy in discovery," a quality also applauded by *Observer* reviewer Jonathan Keates. Keates, commenting favorably on the fact that Fortey "avoids anything like misty-eyed environmental piety or 'Let's-Discover-Fossils' gung-ho," concluded that "this is a colossally romantic book, imbued with its author's deep sensitivity to shifting atmospheres, his overwhelming passion for England, Wales and Scotland as living bodies ... and his contagiously personal view of his subject." *The Hidden Landscape* was named Natural World Book of the Year in 1993.

Life: An Unauthorized Biography, Fortey's 1997 exploration of evolutionary history (published in the United States as *Life: A Natural History of the First Four Billion Years of Life on Earth*), has also been well-received. Andrew H. Knoll, in *Nature,* deemed it "the best account of life's history that I know, an engaging narrative that succeeds as literature as well as science." Knoll especially lauded the way Fortey combined his scientific expertise with his sense of "paleontology as a way of knowing, illustrated honestly, and sometimes hilariously, by scenes from the life of [the author himself]." *New Scientist* reviewer Ted Nield, who ventured that the book would surpass the acclaim of *The Hidden Landscape,* also praised Fortey's blending of science with personal narrative and his allusions to literature and music. Nield noted that Fortey's position on the role of accidents in evolutionary development differs from theories put forth by biologist Stephen Jay Gould, but in degree rather than fundamentals. Fortey offers "no amazing revolutionary interpretations," Nield concluded, but "meat-and-potatoes palaeo ... the way only Fortey, it seems, can write it." And Jerry A. Coyne, in the *New York Times Book Review,* assessed Fortey's argument as "a much-needed correction to Stephen Jay Gould's famous conclusions about the creatures of the Burgess Shale." Coyne labeled "dubious" Fortey's claims that humankind's consciousness and ability to deceive fellow members of our species are what distinguishes us from other animals. While Coyne pointed out that the book lacked some of the intellectual rigor of similar books by the likes of Gould or Richard Dawkins, and was sometimes marred by "overheated prose," he concluded that *Life* was worth reading by anyone with even a slight interest in the subject. An *Economist* contributor considered *Life: An Unauthorized Biography* an "impressive synthesis of evolution" that had some omissions—in particular, on Gould's disputed theory of "punctuated equilibrium" and on the evolution of the role of sex in behavior. But the reviewer acknowledged that the author was "good at showing that the failures of the great scientists he colourfully portrays are much the same as the failures of anybody else," and admired Fortey's refusal to mock outdated scientific thinking.

Fortey comments: "My intentions are possibly rather different from science writers like Gould and Dawkins. I wish to charm and cajole readers into sharing the same delight with natural history—and particularly palaeontology—that has sustained me for a lifetime. Naturally, I have opinions, but my books are not written primarily to advance those opinions."

Works Cited

Coombs, Walter P., review of *Fossils, Library Journal,* November 15, 1982, p. 2182.
Coyne, Jerry A., review of *Life, New York Times Book Review,* April 12, 1998, p. 11.
Review of *Fossils, Booklist,* February 1, 1983, p. 704.

Richard Fortey's guide for amateur fossil collectors explains the origin of fossils, how to find and identify them, and their economic and practical importance.

Garwin, Laura, review of *The Hidden Landscape, Nature,* March 24, 1994, pp. 366-67.
Review of *The Hidden Landscape, New Scientist,* February 19, 1994, p. 42.
Keates, Jonathan, review of *The Hidden Landscape, Observer,* January, 1994.
Knoll, Andrew H., review of *Life, Nature,* August 21, 1997, pp. 731-32.
Review of *Life, Economist,* September 6, 1997, p. S13.
Nield, Ted, review of *Life, New Scientist,* August 2, 1997, pp. 42-43.
Raymo, Chet, "Pursuing Life Over 4 Billion Years," *The Boston Globe,* April 12, 1998, p. M3.

For More Information See

PERIODICALS

Junior Bookshelf, August, 1980, p. 175.
Publishers Weekly, March 2, 1998, p. 52.
School Library Journal, April, 1991, p. 110.

*   *   *

FRANKLIN, Lance
See LANTZ, Francess (Lin)

In Gayle Friesen's novel, a visit with her mother to the family farm across the country enables fourteen-year-old Claire to uncover secrets about her father and grandfather that have been eluding her for years.

debut .... The main characters are real—interesting and imperfect .... The dialogue, especially between Claire and Jane and between Claire and Jack, is full of humour and brutal honesty." In a review for *Books in Canada,* critic Alison Sutherland stated: "The writing of Friesen, a first-timer, stands up to the best of the standard works." She went on to comment that: "The book shimmers with delights. Characters ... pulse with reality." Lauding the book for its well-presented characters and dialogue that effectively combines humor and emotion, Darleen Golke, in a review for *Canadian Materials,* enthused: "[Friesen] presents a well-written, emotionally satisfying portrait of forgiveness, reconciliation and acceptance." ·

Friesen was a reader throughout her schooling. She read books, such as *Little Women* and *Anne of Green Gables* over and over again. "L. M. Montgomery influenced me in many ways, but especially with regard to her obvious respect for the imagination and spirit of children. I love the way she honored the dreams and ambitions of young people while at the same time presenting very real and flawed characters. As far as contemporary writers are concerned, Julie Johnston and Sarah Ellis have inspired me with their wonderful books."

Friesen used to write during her children's nap times, and now she writes when they are at school. Friesen told *SATA,* "I try to reserve my mornings for writing. Sometimes I work at home. Other times (when the kitchen is too messy to be endured) I go to a coffee shop. The first draft is always written long hand and after that, I take it to the computer. With re-writes I'll often go on a retreat and write for twelve hours straight. I love those getaways.

"Writing is such a personal endeavor that is makes the question of why I write difficult to answer. For myself, I love the process of writing so much that I would say that if you love what you're doing, then pursue it faithfully. Don't wait for the whole story to appear in your mind before you sit down to write. Pick up that pen (or poise those fingers above a keyboard) with the belief that the story will unfold. Learn to appreciate the fact that patience is a quality you may need to become very comfortable with. I hope to achieve the sense that a story has been well-served. I try not to inflict too much of myself on a story. I want to learn from my characters and I love not knowing (initially) exactly where they will end up."

Works Cited

Golke, Darleen, review of *Janey's Girl, Canadian Materials,* October 30, 1998.

Jenkinson, Dave, online profile of Gayle Friesen, *Canadian Materials,* http://www.umanitoba.ca/cm/profiles/friesen.html.

Mahoney, Anne Louise, review of *Janey's Girl, Quill and Quire,* September, 1998, p. 64.

Sutherland, Alison, review of *Janey's Girl, Books in Canada,* September, 1998, p. 31.

For More Information See

PERIODICALS

School Library Journal, November 1, 1998, p. 121.*

FRIESEN, Gayle 1960-

Personal

Born September 18, 1960; daughter of Peter (a principal) and Martha (Penner) Neumann; married Brian Friesen, July 11, 1981; children: Bradey, Alexandra. *Education:* University of British Columbia, B.A., 1986.

Addresses

Home—10538 Dunlop Rd., Delta, British Columbia, V4C 8B5, Canada. *Electronic mail*—Pfriesen@axionet.com.

Career

Writer. Worked at a bank and a courthouse.

Awards, Honors

Short-listed for Governor General's Literary Award, The Canada Council, 1998, for *Janey's Girl.* The Red Maple Award, the Ontario Library Association; The Young Canadian Book Award, the Canadian Library Association; and the Violet Downey Award, the National Chapter of Canada IODE, all 1999, all for *Janey's Girl. Janey's Girl* was also short listed for the Mr. Christie Award.

Writings

Janey's Girl, Kids Can Press, 1998.
Men of Stone, Kids Can Press, 2000.

Sidelights

Gayle Friesen told *SATA:* "I began my writing career in an unofficial capacity when I was old enough to pass notes around in school. Even then, I recognized that expressing myself through the written word was extremely satisfying. From there, I progressed to diary entries, creative writing assignments, a bleak poetry writing period ('Pollution, pollution, pollution, oh the shame and sorrow . . . I wonder what pollution will be like tomorrow,'), and many lengthy letters to friends and family. I always dreamed of becoming a writer but at the same time, I never thought it would really happen. Deep down, I think I felt the dream was too big."

After completing high school, Friesen traveled around Europe and attended a Bible school in Sweden. When she returned to Canada she worked in a bank, went to school for a year, then worked at a courthouse for two years before returning to school full time to study English literature. Friesen went to college believing that she would be inspired about a career, and while she enjoyed English literature, she knew she did not want to teach it.

"I graduated from the University of British Columbia in 1986 with a degree in English literature," Friesen said. "Shortly afterward I had my children, Bradey and then Alexandra. Besides adding joy and meaning to my life, having children literally made me a braver person. I remember thinking to myself, 'Well, if I can do that . . . I can do anything.'" Friesen decided to start her writing career by writing for children because she and her own kids were reading and thoroughly enjoying so many children's books. Her first efforts included picture books and short stories.

Friesen enrolled in a writing course at the University of British Columbia, where one of her instructors asked her to try writing the first chapter of a novel. Friesen continued writing the novel, and told *SATA,* "When I completed it, I knew I'd found my place. Finding a publisher proved to be a little more difficult. However, a couple of manuscripts later, I wrote *Janey's Girl,* and I felt that this was the one. I sent it off and it was accepted immediately. I'll always remember the way I felt when I received the phone call from Kids Can saying that they would like to publish *Janey's Girl.* I was delighted, of course, but mostly I was relieved because this meant I truly was doing the right thing with my life."

Janey's Girl tells the story of Jane Harrison and her fourteen-year-old daughter, Claire, who return to the town where Jane grew up. While Claire looks forward to getting to know her maternal grandmother and finding out about her mother's mysterious past, Jane has a bad feeling about the return because she now must struggle between being an independent city dweller and a family-focused woman living on a farm. Claire, meanwhile, meets Jamie, a seven-year-old boy who suffers from leukemia, and Jamie's father, Mac. It is later revealed that Mac is also Claire's father, and that Claire may be able to donate bone marrow to save Jamie's life. Jane, however, refuses to let Claire be tested. Claire learns of the situation and agrees to be tested, causing a strain in her relationship with her mother.

The idea for *Janey's Girl* came to her while she was driving to her parents' home with her daughter, Alex, Friesen reveals in an online author profile written by Dave Jenkinson for *Canadian Materials.* Friesen began to wonder what it would be like to move back to the town where she grew up and also wondered what it would be like for her daughter. She then wondered what it would be like returning especially if she had left because of a family secret, and how this secret would impact her daughter. From this point, the story just fell into place for Friesen; to her, the ease of the story's creation was like a gift. Friesen felt that as she was writing the novel, she didn't know what was going to happen next; she felt as if characters would appear and circumstances would come up, unfolding on their own. As a new circumstance arose, Friesen asked herself questions about it, which led to different scenarios that Friesen sorted through. Some of the characters in the book, such as Jamie, were surprises to Friesen, who did not at first realize what connection the boy would have to Claire.

Anne Louise Mahoney, a critic for *Quill and Quire,* praised the novel, saying, "*Janey's Girl* is a stunning

G

GODDEN, (Margaret) Rumer 1907-1998

OBITUARY NOTICE—See index for *SATA* sketch: Born December 10, 1907, in Sussex, England; died November 8, 1998, in Thornhill, Scotland. Author. Margaret Rumer Godden wrote more than sixty books, which were characterized by a light and happy outlook. Some of the most outstanding pieces of her writing uniquely captured India, a country she was fascinated with. She also wrote popular children's stories such as *The Dolls House, The Mousewife,* and *Miss Happiness and Miss Flower,* that effectively captured the thought processes and the questions of that age group. In 1972, Godden won the Whitbread Award for *The Diddakoi.* Godden spent time living in India as a child, where she acquired a love for the country. After the First World War she returned to England and studied the basics of writing at Moira House. But Godden started a career as a dancer and eventually returned to India to open a dance school—upsetting all the racial norms of the times. She began writing stories with India as the backdrop, including *Black Narcissus* (1938) which became a bestseller and made her temporarily rich. As did *Black Narcissus,* many of Godden's novels dealt with women and religion and explored the roles of mysticism and spiritual discipline in religion. Godden was appointed Officer of the Order of the British Empire (OBE) in 1993. Godden continued to write into the early 1990s; her work included verse, plays, and children's doll stories. Her later works for children included: *The Little Chair, Premulata and the Festival of Lights,* and *A Day Full of Poetry from Cockcrow to Starlight.*

OBITUARIES AND OTHER SOURCES:

BOOKS

Who's Who in America, 1999, Marquis Who's Who (New Providence, NJ), 1998.

PERIODICALS

Carousel, spring, 1999, p. 37.
London Times, November 11, 1998.
Los Angeles Times, November 11, 1998, p. A22.
New York Times, November 10, 1998, p. B12.

* * *

GRAMBO, Rebecca L(ynn) 1963-

Personal

Born February 2, 1963, in Sioux Falls, SD; daughter of Leonard C. and Delores (Misterek) Yost; married Glen Grambo (a photographer), April 8, 1989. *Education:* South Dakota School of Mines and Technology, B.Sc., 1985.

Addresses

Office—P.O. Box 910, Warman, Saskatchewan, Canada S0K 4S0.

Career

Grambo Photography and Design, Inc., Warman, Saskatchewan, president, 1995—.

Writings

FOR CHILDREN

Weird Science, Kidsbooks (Chicago, IL), 1998.
Dinosaurs, Kidsbooks, 1999.
Birds of Prey, Kidsbooks, in press.
The Kids' Nature Question and Answer Book, Kidsbooks, in press.

"AMAZING ANIMALS" SERIES

Amazing Animals: Eyes, Kidsbooks, 1997.
Amazing Animals: Colors, Kidsbooks, 1997.
Amazing Animals: Hunters, Kidsbooks, 1997.
Amazing Animals: Defenses, Kidsbooks, 1997.
Amazing Animals: Families, Kidsbooks, 1998.
Amazing Animals: Claws and Jaws, Kidsbooks, 1998.
Amazing Animals: Friends and Enemies, Kidsbooks, in press.

Rebecca L. Grambo

Amazing Animals: Homes and Hangouts, Kidsbooks, in press.

OTHER

The World of the Fox, Sierra Books (San Francisco, CA), 1995, published as *The Nature of Foxes,* Greystone Books (Vancouver, British Columbia), 1995.
Eagles: Masters of the Sky, Voyageur Press (Stillwater, MN), 1997.
Mountain Lion, Raincoast Books (Vancouver), 1998, Chronicle Books (San Francisco), 1999.

Work in Progress

Bear: A Celebration of Power and Beauty, for Sierra Club; *Mammals,* for Kidsbooks.

Sidelights

Rebecca L. Grambo comments: "I have always had a love for animals and a curiosity about their habits and behavior. While I was growing up in Beresford, South Dakota, my mother encouraged this curiosity by exempting me from some household chores if I was reading a natural history book. Eventually my continuing interest in animals pulled me away from my training as a geological engineer and into a new career as a writer and nature photographer. I now live in Warman, Saskatchewan, with my photographer husband, Glen, our rabbits Teddy and Benjamin, our fat guinea pigs Agatha and Dorothy, and our mouse Matilda. In my free time, I design realistic wildlife needlework patterns marketed internationally under the name 'Wild Threads.'

"When I begin work on a writing project, the motivation is often financial—we all have bills to pay! However, once the research begins, I become driven to share all the wonderful things I am uncovering. With the children's books especially, I want to communicate my sense of awe regarding the natural world.

"My love for animals is a definite influence on my choice of projects. As a professional photographer, I can evaluate images for inclusion in books, choosing photographs that are technically excellent, as well as artistically satisfying. I think of books in terms of complete packages, text *and* photographs, right from the beginning.

"I love the research stages of any project. The actual writing requires more discipline and isn't as enjoyable. The first draft is the most tedious but, once it's completed, then I can polish and refine. Many of the issues I write about are extremely important to me, so I want to be certain that the words I choose say precisely what I mean. I love my job! I get to work with animals, read about animals, then share all that I've learned with lots of people."

For More Information See

PERIODICALS

Booklist, September 15, 1997, p. 189.

H

HAMILTON, Peter F. 1960-

Personal

Born 1960, in Oakham, Rutland, England. *Education:* Attended Worksop College. *Hobbies and other interests:* Sports.

Addresses

Agent—Macmillan, 25 Eccleston Pl., London SW1W 9NF, England.

Career

Writer.

Writings

FOR CHILDREN

Lightstorm (part five of the "Web" series), Orion Children's Books (London, England), 1998.

NOVELS

Mindstar Rising (first volume in the "Greg Mandel" trilogy), Pan (London, England), 1993, Tor (New York City), 1996.
A Quantum Murder (second volume in the "Greg Mandel" trilogy), Pan, 1994, Tor, 1997.
The Nano Flower (third volume in the "Greg Mandel" trilogy), Pan, 1995, Tor, 1998.
The Reality Dysfunction (first volume in the "Night's Dawn" trilogy), Macmillan (London, England), 1996.
The Neutronium Alchemist (second volume in the "Night's Dawn" trilogy), Macmillan, 1997.

SHORT STORIES

A Second Chance at Eden, Macmillan, 1998.

Contributor to anthologies, including *Dreams, New Worlds 2, New Worlds 3, New Worlds 4,* and (with G. Joyce) *New Worlds 5;* contributor to science-fiction magazines, including *Far Point, Fear, Interzone,* and *New Moon.*

Work in Progress

Will-o'-the-Wisp and *The Naked God,* both novels, both for Macmillan; *Cybermetal,* a children's book (part of the Web2 series), for Orion Children's Books.

Sidelights

Successful science-fiction novelist Peter F. Hamilton started writing during a period of unemployment in 1987. By the following year, he had begun selling short stories to small magazines, and one year later he sold his first story to a mass-market science fiction magazine. His short stories led directly to his novel-writing career; a book editor at Britain's Pan publishing house read one of the stories in *Fear* magazine in 1991 and asked to see Hamilton's novel-in-progress. Two months later, Hamilton had signed a contract for a first novel, which was published as *Mindstar Rising.*

A cyberthriller set in England after global warming has wreaked havoc with that country's climate, economy, and politics, *Mindstar Rising* focuses on Greg Mandel, a freelance action hero who, as a former member of the Mindstar Battalion, has been enhanced by the surgical implantation of a gland for empathy and truth-detection. Mandel is hired to help save a cybertech company from the evil machinations of its rivals; he becomes allied with the cybernetically enhanced granddaughter of the company's dying owner and calls in another enhanced colleague to pursue an online and offline battle. A reviewer for *Publishers Weekly* asserted that *Mindstar Rising* reads "like a collaboration between William Gibson and Ian Fleming," and pointed to an action-filled plot, "exotic hardware," and compelling characters as elements that enhance the "fast-moving" novel. A critic for *Kirkus Reviews* lauded the "believable characters and a solid plot set against a carefully worked-out background," and called *Mindstar Rising* "an assured, effective debut from a writer to watch."

Mindstar Rising was the first volume in a trilogy centered on Greg Mandel; the second, *A Quantum Murder,* was published in 1994. Julia Evans, a cybernetically enhanced billionaire introduced in Hamilton's first novel, once again figures strongly in the second, as she hires Mandel to investigate the murder of a Nobel laureate who was doing research for her firm. Russell Letson, reviewing the novel for *Locus,* praised the "nifty" murder plot and its "tidy double-bluff" solution, and added: "solid mystery plotting and a science-fictional sensibility that promises a few surprises to come will keep me reading and recommending Hamilton."

The Mandel trilogy concludes with 1995's *The Nano Flower.* In this complex story, Greg Mandel has retired and taken up orange farming in a sub-tropical 21st-century England. Julia Evans shows up again, however, after receiving a mysterious extraterrestrial flower from her missing husband. "Gratifyingly complex and challenging—indeed, impossible to summarize adequately," maintained a *Kirkus Reviews* commentator, "what with battles, love stories, vendettas, imponderable aliens, and robust characters: a fine trilogy, sure, but this one's in a class by itself."

Hamilton initiated a new trilogy, the "Night's Dawn" series, with his highly regarded novel *The Reality Dysfunction.* The novel delineates events that occur in a putative golden age in the year 2600, when a criminal has a traumatic encounter with an alien entity. The book was placed on the SFX list of the ten best science-fiction novels of the year in 1996. Hamilton has also published a collection of short stories, *A Second Chance at Eden,* as well as other novels and books for young people.

Works Cited

Letson, Russell, review of *A Quantum Murder, Locus,* July, 1994, p. 65.

Review of *Mindstar Rising, Kirkus Reviews,* June 1, 1996, p. 791.

Review of *Mindstar Rising, Publishers Weekly,* July 22, 1996, p. 232.

Review of *The Nano Flower, Kirkus Reviews,* December 1, 1997, p. 1743-44.

*   *   *

HARSHMAN, Marc 1950-

Personal

Born October 1, 1950, in Randolph County, IN; son of William L. Harshman and Janice Maloon Wells; married Cheryl Ryan (a librarian and writer), August 25, 1976; children: Sarah Jayne. *Education:* Bethany College, B.A., 1973; Yale University Divinity School, M.A.R., 1975; University of Pittsburgh, M.A., 1978. *Religion:* Protestant.

Addresses

Home—Moundsville, WV. *Office*—c/o Rosanne Lauer, Cobblehill Books, 375 Hudson St., New York, NY 10014.

Career

Writer. Professional storyteller, 1978—; elementary teacher in West Virginia, 1985—.

Writings

FOR CHILDREN

A Little Excitement, illustrated by Ted Rand, Dodd, Mead, 1989.

Snow Company, illustrated by Leslie W. Bowman, Cobblehill, 1990.

(With Bonnie Collins) *Rocks in My Pockets,* illustrated by Toni Goffe, Cobblehill, 1991.

Only One, illustrated by Barbara Garrison, Cobblehill, 1993.

Uncle James, illustrated by Michael Dooling, Cobblehill, 1993.

Moving Days, illustrated by Wendy Popp, Cobblehill, 1994.

The Storm, illustrated by Mark Mohr, Cobblehill, 1995.

When the End of Summer Is Near, illustrated by Leslie Bowman, Cobblehill, 1999.

All the Way to Morning, illustrated by Felipe Davalos, Marshall Cavendish, 1999.

A Little Excitement was translated into Swedish and Danish.

POETRY

Turning out the Stones, State Street Press (Pittsford, NY), 1983.

Also contributor of poems to periodicals.

Sidelights

Picture-book author Marc Harshman fills each of his stories for young listeners with the flavor of rural America, particularly areas such as West Virginia and Indiana, where Harshman himself has lived. In books such as *The Storm* and *Rocks in My Pocket,* Harshman portrays everyday people in folktale-like circumstances, giving his works an air of timelessness. In the wryly humorous *Rocks in My Pocket,* for instance, the members of a poor farm family fill their pockets with weighty stones to keep them from blowing off the top of the mountain where they make their home; their fortunes improve drastically when their rocks find favor with rich city-dwellers looking for unique collectibles.

The Storm finds wheelchair-bound Jonathan frustrated by people's assumption that just because he would be unable to seek cover quickly, he is fearful of tornados. Jonathan's actual fears go much deeper—he is afraid of cars like the one that caused him to lose the use of his legs, and of being treated differently than the other kids

A county fair is the setting for Marc Harshman's picture book about number relationships, which shows how single objects can combine to make a unique and wonderful whole. (Cover illustration by Barbara Garrison.)

at his Midwestern school. *The Storm* is more than a story about a young person with disabilities, however; as *Booklist* contributor Stephanie Zvirin maintained in her review of Harshman's 1995 offering: "It's a knowing book that will speak to all children about self-image and hard-won success."

The winter season has been the backdrop for several of Harshman's picture books. In *A Little Excitement,* published in 1989, young Willie longs for anything that will break up the monotony of endless chores, long nights, and nagging sisters in another seemingly endless winter on the farm. When he finally gets his wish after the farmhouse stove overheats, the double dose of excitement that follows proves to be more than he really wants, in a story that a *Kirkus Reviews* contributor called "a genuine, attractively produced piece of Americana." "Harshman's narrative has a personal note that's appealing," added Denise Wilms in *Booklist;* "his message is clear but not overbearing." Of course, even young

children know that winter does bring certain rewards— snow days off from school! In *Snow Company,* a blizzard strands students and motorists alike, and people come together to find shelter and make the best of things. Teddy and his family take in several strangers, and when the power goes out, candles are lit and tales of other storms begin, in a story that contains "a sense of extraordinary events and of sharing history with friends," in the opinion of *School Library Journal* contributor Karen James.

The picture-book format is useful for building the foundation for children's understanding of mathematical concepts, and Harshman's *Only One* is up to the task. Designed to illustrate the concept of grouping, the author posits such examples as: "There may be 9 players,/ But there is only one team," and "There may be 12 eggs,/ But there is only one dozen." Although a *Publishers Weekly* reviewer opined that the book's "subject matter may be a bit sophisticated" for beginning mathematicians, the critic concluded that *Only One* "serves as a snappy-to-look-at introduction to math." Commenting on the folk-style artwork and the technique of setting the math/vocabulary book in a county fair, *Booklist* contributor Carolyn Phelan called *Only One* "unique" among books of its kind.

Harshman enjoys the time he spends meeting young readers, and encourages children to use writing as a way to express themselves. "I love being able to tell them stories and to talk with them about writing and books," he once told *SATA*. " I enjoy seeing them discover that writers are real people who use the same language that they do. I want them to see that they have at their fingertips possibilities for creating new visions of themselves and their world, visions that will not only help them be better writers, but be better people as well."

In addition to his picture books for young readers, Harshman is also the author of several poems, some of which have been anthologized in 1983's *Turning out the Stones.* "My poems are frequently narrations springing from specific and local geographies," the writer explained, "be they the rural Indiana where I was raised, the West Virginia where I have lived my adult life, or the towns and farms of Canada and England where I have traveled. I believe the poems reveal perceptions of value gleaned from the bleaker aspects of lives lived either alone or in communal isolation from the mainstream. The free verse in which I compose is intended to be voiced, to be heard, and is informed by the harmonies and rhythms of traditional verse and pushed toward new hearing by the emotional pressures of the breath itself.

"I believe our language holds the power to challenge and persuade, comfort, inform, and ultimately to reveal truths about who we are," Harshman once explained to *SATA*. "Through our language, the best of who we are is preserved. An artist's manipulation of words through rhythms, images, and countless other figures is a high calling. It is my duty to remind others that the language is their language, a living thing renewed by what they— its speakers and writers—bring to it. As a children's writer, I also see an opportunity to promote a vision of writing and storytelling that is natural to everyday living, giving children a means of responding to the world."

Works Cited

Review of *A Little Excitement, Kirkus Reviews,* August 15, 1989, p. 1245.
James, Karen, review of *Snow Company, School Library Journal,* December, 1990, p. 77.
Review of *Only One, Publishers Weekly,* May 17, 1993, p. 78.
Phelan, Carolyn, review of *Only One, Booklist,* May 15, 1993, p. 1693.
Wilms, Denise, review of *A Little Excitement, Booklist,* September 15, 1989, pp. 182-83.
Zvirin, Stephanie, review of *The Storm, Booklist,* May 1, 1995, p. 1579.

For More Information See

PERIODICALS

Booklist, December 15, 1991, p. 769; September 15, 1993, p. 157.
Kirkus Reviews, August 1, 1993, p. 1002.
Publishers Weekly, October 4, 1993, p. 80.
School Library Journal, March, 1994, pp. 215-16; July, 1995, p. 62.*

*　　　*　　　*

HAYES, Daniel 1952-

Personal

Born April 17, 1952, in Troy, NY; son of Thomas Robert (a dairy farmer) and Mary (Welch) Hayes. *Education:* State University of New York at Plattsburgh, B.S., 1973; State University of New York at Albany, M.S., 1982.

Addresses

Home—11044 State Route 40, Schaghticoke, NY 12154. *Agent*—Hy Cohen Literary Agency, P.O. Box 43770, Upper Montclair, NJ 07043. *E-mail*—hayesdm@ aol.com.

Daniel Hayes

Career

Waterford Central Catholic School, Waterford, NY, English teacher, 1975-84; Troy High School, Troy, NY, English teacher, 1984—; freelance writer.

Awards, Honors

Best Books for Young Adults, American Library Association, 1992, for *The Trouble with Lemons,* 1995, for *No Effect,* and 1998, for *Flyers;* Young Adults' Choice, International Reading Association, 1993, for *The Trouble with Lemons;* Edgar Award nomination for Best Young Adult Novel, 1997, for *Flyers.*

Writings

The Trouble with Lemons, David Godine, 1991.
Eye of the Beholder, David Godine, 1992.
No Effect, David Godine, 1994.
Flyers, Simon and Schuster, 1996.

Sidelights

Inspiration comes to writers from the most unlikely places. For Daniel Hayes, author of popular young adult fiction such as *The Trouble with Lemons, The Eye of the Beholder,* and *No Effect,* the muse took the form of slapstick comedy. "When I was a kid, I discovered the Three Stooges on television," Hayes told J. Sydney Jones in an interview for *Authors and Artists for Young Adults.* "Looking back now, I really think they've had an influence on my work, especially in the way many of my characters relate to each other. I mean, the Stooges call each other names and hit each other over the head, but no matter what happens they're still loyal to each other. My characters Tyler and Lymie from my first three books have this kind of Stooge-like friendship. They are always bantering and insulting one another, but there is no question they are friends. It's how lots of adolescent males act with each other."

Adolescent male behavior is the territory that Hayes has set out to chart. In his series novels about Tyler and Lymie, and in his novel *Flyers,* featuring an older protagonist, fifteen-year-old Gabe Riley, Hayes examines the complexity of loyalties, friendships, and dreams that fuel the engine of adolescence. His novels, more picaresque adventures than linear plot-driven works, employ comedy in large doses and hit close to the bone on issues such as adult hypocrisy, single-parenting, male virtues, and even alcoholism—though Hayes rejects the idea of problem novels. "My books start with characters," he told Jones, "and of course if you have real characters you're going to have problems. But I don't write books, like some TV movies, that 'feature' a problem or disease or whatever. For me that's putting the cart before the horse." Hayes has managed to make a success out of not following the rules in his fiction, just as many of his protagonists do in their lives. Loosely formed and organic in structure, Hayes's novels are held together more by the energy of characterization and dialogue than by a tightly woven plot.

Mystery and adventure abound in Hayes's novel about two teenage boys, Tyler and Lymie, who discover a dead body while swimming in an old quarry.

Hayes grew up outside Troy, New York, on a dairy farm. With three brothers who were very close in age and two much younger sisters, Hayes was never at a loss for things to do on the farm. "We were thirteen miles from school and town," Hayes told Jones, "and so we brothers and some neighbor kids had to make our own fun. We played baseball and basketball, built tree houses, and explored the countryside. We also helped our father and uncle with the chores. But in a way I used to envy the kids from the nearby town. It was like they were the city kids. When I went to school in the village of Greenwich, I thought that was where things were really happening—*that* was living." But Hayes was not completely seduced by the allure of Greenwich; he still chose to raise calves and show them at the county fair—an experience that he touches upon in his novel *Flyers.*

At school he was "a good under-achieving student," who focused more on sports and social activities than he did on homework. "I liked sports and outdoor things, but I also loved books. When I had nothing else to do, I would pick up a book. I remember riding the bus home from school one day in the second grade and borrowing the reader of this older girl on the bus with me. Suddenly I discovered how books can work: how they can transport you to another world. It was amazing to me how I could lose myself in that storybook world. Those stories were so real to me. So I came to look at books as a great way to escape from my own boundaries. They were a great way to travel and experience different lives." A favorite genre for Hayes was mysteries, and the influence of that reading can be seen in his own work, especially in his first novel, *The Trouble with Lemons.*

In high school, Hayes went through the usual agonies of what to be when he grew up—none of these included writing. As a freshman, he dreamed of being a star basketball player, though his height worked against such dreams. Then came a period of wanting to be a rock star. "I got an electric guitar," Hayes recalled in his interview with Jones, "but had no talent." It was not until he went to college at SUNY Plattsburgh in upstate New York

Eye of the Beholder

"Once again Hayes portrays young teens honestly and realistically, with all their bravado and doubts."
—Booklist

Daniel Hayes
Author of *The Trouble with Lemons*

The madcap adventures of Tyler and Lymie continue when the two teens play a prank that goes awry in Hayes's 1992 novel.

that he even considered writing as a possible career. He was attracted to English literature as a major "because I kind of liked to read and thought, hey, here's a way I can get a degree just by reading books. I remember specifically re-reading *Huckleberry Finn* in college, but at nineteen it was an entirely different thing—a brilliant satire and I loved the way Twain captured the dialects." The same was true for his new reading of Charles Dickens. "I'd read *Great Expectations* in high school, but upon re-reading I suddenly saw the enormous humor in it. I laughed all the way through. Dickens creates these incredibly funny minor characters and gives them all sorts of peculiar ticks and idiosyncracies." Hayes took several writing classes in college and was so eager to get out into the world that he finished his studies in three years.

Upon graduation, Hayes headed west, hoping eventually to try his luck in Hollywood as a screenwriter. He wrote some articles for *Black Belt* magazine, but the closest he got to the movie industry was working as an extra in a film that was being shot in the Los Angeles Coliseum. "We liked to refer to ourselves as 'background players'," Hayes said, laughing. After running low in money, Hayes headed back to New York state and began substitute teaching around Troy. This ultimately led to a full-time position in a Catholic school, teaching English. "I went into teaching for all the wrong reasons," Hayes commented. "I wanted to be a writer, but knew it wasn't that easy. I needed to earn a living and thought with teaching I would be able to work with literature and have time (summers) for writing. Luckily, I enjoyed teaching when I started."

Hayes taught junior high school students for his first eight years. "It's a neat age. The kids all want to tell you stuff they did last night and a lot of it was pretty funny. But at first it was difficult for me. I mean I would take it personally if the super lesson I had planned half the night bored the students. You really take that personally when you're just starting in." Earning his master's degree in 1982, Hayes moved on to teaching high school two years later. "One good thing about teaching English is that you get to talk about books all day long and get paid for it. But some of the kids—actually a lot of them—have trouble with the pace of books, especially older novels. They have grown up with the fifteen-second news clip and with MTV and computers. Novels, on the other hand, take time to get into. Kids can be resistant to that slower pace."

Another fringe benefit to Hayes's teaching job was a built-in cast of characters for the stories that he was creating in his spare time. "The books I have liked the most are coming-of-age stories, so when it came time for me to write my own, it was natural that I turned to young adult novels, although I still feel as though I'm writing for myself and my friends as well as for kids," Hayes explained in his interview with Jones. Slowly such stories began to coalesce into a novel about an adolescent boy named Tyler and his buddy Lymie. The episodic nature of that book began to hold together when Hayes read a news article. "I was in the faculty room one

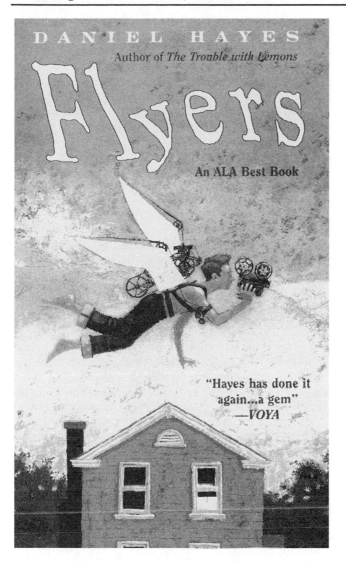

Fifteen-year-old Gabe Riley uses his filmmaking skills to solve a mystery at Blood Red Pond in Hayes's young-adult novel. (Cover illustration by Joe Cepeda.)

day and picked up a copy of the *National Enquirer* somebody had left there. I read the story of some kids partying at an old rock quarry and how they had discovered a body in the water, and I suddenly realized this was what I needed for my book."

Despite his sudden inspiration, Hayes still took six years to sell this first novel, *The Trouble with Lemons.* "I was told by editors that kids would never follow a book that meandered as much as mine. They urged me to keep the mystery aspect front and center; I often left it on the back burner while I had fun with my characters. I wanted to explore characterization, but I didn't want to write a problem novel. I guess my goal was to take young readers away and introduce them to new people and places, like books did for me when I was a kid and like they still do for me."

Persistence paid off for Hayes; ultimately he sold his novel to the publisher David Godine, and that house brought it out as their first YA novel. *The Trouble with*

Lemons is the first of what has thus far been three titles following the misadventures of two adolescent boys: asthmatic, insecure Tyler and his best friend, chubby Lymie. *The Trouble with Lemons* is, according to Cathi Dunn MacRae in *Wilson Library Bulletin,* a "mystery imbued with the thoroughly original spirit of its narrator, Tyler." This narrator lets the reader know the score right off: "I'm not even thirteen, and I've already experienced more humiliation than most adults."

Tyler's poor self-image—he sees himself as the family "lemon" of the title—is the result of childhood asthma that has kept him a steady customer of local doctors and in delicate health, of his inability to navigate the troubled waters of school society and one bully in particular, and of guilt feelings that he is somehow responsible for his parents' separation. Tyler's troubles are compounded by the death of his father in an accident. It doesn't help either that his mother and older brother are movie stars, leaving Tyler's scant achievements far behind in the dust. It is no surprise then when a late-night swim in the local quarry with Lymie ends up badly for Tyler. The pair quite literally bump into a dead body on this forbidden swim and then also witness a car leaving the scene. An anonymous call to the police from them does not solve their problem: is the culprit on to them? Are they in danger of becoming the next victims? As Nancy Vasilakis wrote in a *Horn Book* review of the novel, "Self-acceptance, the vagaries of human nature, finding one's niche ... make up the elements of this fine first novel by a promising author."

Tyler is forced to come to grips with his own insecurities and—with the aid of kindly Mrs. Saunders, the house-keeper, and Chuckie, a martial arts expert and family gardener—to trust his own instincts. Soon he becomes convinced that the principal's son is involved in the crime and he must force the real culprits to confess before they try to silence him. As Jody McCoy noted in *Voice of Youth Advocates,* Tyler "may not be a talented movie star like his mother and older brother but he can run and can face the truth when justice demands it." McCoy concluded that *The Trouble with Lemons* is a "satisfying mystery with an engaging central character in a tale that bubbles right along." Vasilakis added in *Horn Book* that Hayes's characterizations are good and the protagonist makes readers sympathize with him. She added that the novel is a "believable and appealing story." Other reviewers also commended the novel. A reviewer for *Five Owls* complimented Hayes on the "best opening chapter in recent memory," and went on to call this debut novel "a first-rate mystery .... Instead of solely creating a thriller according to formula, Hayes has taken the time to write a novel with texture and nuance." A *Publishers Weekly* critic also had high praise for this first novel: "Tyler's unique, deftly drawn character highlights this carefully crafted, powerful story. As a mystery it is intriguing, but as a novel about introspection and self-acceptance, it is irresistible." This first novel became an ALA Best Book and earned Hayes a large readership eager for more adventures featuring Tyler and Lymie.

Hayes proved his own instincts were right about the possibilities of a free-form novel. "I'm perfectly content to have kids banter and react to one another. I have to consciously remind myself to lay in plot. But I figure if you get wrapped up in character, you'll feel that my books are fast-paced. They are, however, definitely not plot-oriented."

Hayes had already started his second novel while he was trying to sell *The Trouble with Lemons,* and again this novel was in part inspired by a magazine article. This time the article spoke not of dead bodies but of phony Modigliani heads in Italy; about how young architecture students decided to play a trick on the art world by fabricating a work by the famous sculptor that was subsequently "found" and ultimately—to the horror of the pranksters—authenticated by art experts around the world. In *Eye of the Beholder,* Hayes transplanted this story to upstate New York and into the hands of Tyler and Lymie. Wakefield, where they live, is celebrating the work of a famous local sculptor, Badoglio, and the duo decide to have some fun with the serious adults.

As a Halloween prank, they carve stone heads a la Badoglio and casually throw their handiwork away in the river where the sculptor was reputed to have thrown two of his unrecovered creations. But when the heads are discovered and dubbed genuine by art critics, the boys are faced with a dilemma. "By the time the truth is discovered," noted *Horn Book*'s Nancy Vasilakis, "the boys have had a few nervous moments and learned a valuable lesson or two about adult pretensions and weaknesses." Lucinda Snyder Whitehurst commented in *School Library Journal* on Hayes's "episodic and quick pace," noting also Tyler's "fresh, natural voice," and Lymie, Tyler's "comic foil" who has "more heart than brains." A reviewer for *Publishers Weekly* concluded that "readers will delight in these protagonists' sundry predicaments, all of which are resolved with ingenuity and imagination," while a *Booklist* contributor dubbed this second Tyler/Lymie novel "downright hilarious." A *Voice Literary Supplement* reviewer described *Eye of the Beholder* as a "laugh-out-loud sequel to [Hayes's] excellent first novel."

Hayes decided that with his third Tyler/Lymie creation, *No Effect,* he wanted "nothing unusual happening," as he explained to Jones. "I wanted this one to be simply a book about school life with some unrequited love thrown in." Tyler is determined to become a man; in pursuit of this goal he joins the high school wrestling team, though he is only in the eighth grade. He has dreams of grandeur: "I'm being led off the mat. Women are going crazy. Not even girls now. Real women. And not disturbed ones either. Nice, normal women who are beautiful." Tyler falls in love with one such normal woman, but in typical Tyler fashion she is unreachable. She's the new science teacher, Miss Williams. Complications arise when Tyler finally discovers that the object of Miss Williams's affections is Chuckie, the gardener, who has become something of an older brother figure for Tyler. "The result," noted a reviewer for the *Voice Literary Supplement,* "is excruciating. But funny . . . . In

fact, Hayes has such a sure touch that he can make 13-year-old-boy humor hit your funny bone, even if you're not a 13-year-old boy."

Other reviewers also complimented the novel. Susan R. Farber wrote in *Voice of Youth Advocates* that the events of *No Effect,* told by a "less talented writer" could have been simply "slapstick" or "trite." Farber noted, however, that "Hayes is a master at imitating teenage dialogue and he smoothly integrates more serious themes without disrupting the flow or appearing didactic." A reviewer in *Publishers Weekly* applauded the novel, noting that "Hayes masterfully blends humor and heartache." *Booklist*'s Ilene Cooper concluded: "Certainly young people—and yes, especially boys—will identify with both longing for the unattainable and getting into something physical to work off all that excess energy. This one's a page-turner, but readers may also have some things to think about after they close the book."

With the 1996 novel *Flyers,* Hayes departs from the world of junior high for the more troubled waters of high school in a book featuring fifteen-year-old protagonist Gabe Riley. "After doing three Tyler books, I felt I was ready to try something different," Hayes explained. Vanessa Elder, writing in *School Library Journal,* noted that a "mysterious, supernatural element is always lurking around the corners of this story," and indeed Gabe is a grab-bag of vagaries. He is an ardent filmmaker with a good sense of humor—a must for any Hayes protagonist. He is also the son of a single-father lawyer with a drinking problem. Gabe and his friends are making a movie about ghosts and swamp monsters, but things go awry when the townspeople see these youngsters dressed in costume and take them for the real thing.

Candace Deisley had high praise for *Flyers* in the pages of *Voice of Youth Advocates,* calling it a "gem of a young adult novel" that not only deals with issues such as "dating, drinking, driving and peer pressures," but that also blends Hayes's "marvelous humor" to create a "terrific" combination. A reviewer in *Publishers Weekly* commented that this tale "goes straight from the funnybone to the heart," and that throughout, "this spry work blends wisecracks with insightful reflections on life, death and relationships."

"I want to write more about Gabe," Hayes revealed in his interview with Jones. "He's a likeable kid, and I also grew to appreciate his father. He's got some problems, but I like him a lot, too." This liking of his protagonists is an essential element in Hayes's writing method. "I write when I really have something to say," Hayes noted. "I don't force myself to write to a schedule because then it gets dry, the results aren't good and I throw most of it away. But inspiration is all around. Many of my ideas come from my own childhood, and being around kids all day teaching reminds you that there is really a generic kind of kid-dom that cuts across culture and generations. Fashions may change and language may change, but the elemental kid does not. Kids, especially younger ones, just blurt things out. They don't have the kinds of filters adults have. And in the end, kids are amazingly resilient. It's my job as a writer to show this resiliency and to poke some fun at the world in general. I hope my books have both an over-riding and underlying optimism—the sort of optimism we see at the end of a Chaplin film when Charlie gives that little click of the heels and we know he's ready for his next adventure. That's the sort of optimism I'm aiming for at the end of my books; no matter how hard life gets, hope will always find a way to bubble up."

Works Cited

Cooper, Ilene, review of *No Effect, Booklist,* May 1, 1994, p. 1595.

Deisley, Candace, review of *Flyers, Voice of Youth Advocates,* February, 1997, p. 327.

Elder, Vanessa, review of *Flyers, School Library Journal,* November, 1996, p. 120.

Review of *Eye of the Beholder, Booklist,* February 1, 1993, p. 984.

Review of *Eye of the Beholder, Publishers Weekly,* November 30, 1992, p. 56.

Review of *Eye of the Beholder, Voice Literary Supplement,* December, 1992, p. 21.

Farber, Susan R., review of *No Effect, Voice of Youth Advocates,* February, 1994, p. 368.

Review of *Flyers, Publishers Weekly,* November 4, 1996, p. 177.

Hayes, Daniel, *The Trouble with Lemons,* David Godine, 1991.

Hayes, Daniel, *No Effect,* David Godine, 1993.

Hayes, Daniel, interview with J. Sydney Jones for *Authors and Artists for Young Adults,* Volume 29, Gale, 1999.

MacRae, Cathi Dunn, "The Young Adult Perplex," *Wilson Library Bulletin,* December, 1991, pp. 102-3.

McCoy, Jody, review of *The Trouble with Lemons, Voice of Youth Advocates,* August, 1991, p. 171.

Review of *No Effect, Publishers Weekly,* November 22, 1993, p. 64.

Review of *No Effect, Voice Literary Supplement,* December, 1993, pp. 26-27.

Review of *The Trouble with Lemons, Five Owls,* January, 1992, p. 64.

Review of *The Trouble with Lemons, Publishers Weekly,* March 22, 1991, p. 80.

Vasilakis, Nancy, review of *The Trouble with Lemons, Horn Book,* July-August, 1991, pp. 462-63.

Vasilakis, Nancy, review of *Eye of the Beholder, Horn Book,* January-February, 1993, p. 91.

Whitehurst, Lucinda Snyder, review of *Eye of the Beholder, School Library Journal,* December, 1992, p. 112.

For More Information See

PERIODICALS

Booklist, March 15, 1992, p. 1364; March 15, 1998, p. 1214.

Bulletin of the Center for Children's Books, June, 1991, p. 237.

Horn Book, March, 1994, p. 205; January, 1997, p. 56.

Kirkus Reviews, March 15, 1991, p. 393; November 15, 1992, p. 1443; September 1, 1996, pp. 1322-23.

Kliatt, March, 1995, p. 6.

School Library Journal, June, 1991, p. 125; January, 1994, p. 132.

Voice of Youth Advocates, April, 1998, p. 42.

ON-LINE

Hayes's internet home page, at http://www.danielhayes.com.

—*Sketch by J. Sydney Jones*

*   *   *

HOOBLER, Dorothy

Personal

Born in Philadelphia, PA; daughter of Frederick and Eleanor (maiden name, Bystrom) Law; married Thomas Hoobler (a writer and editor), December 18, 1971; children: Ellen Marie. *Education:* Wells College, A.B., 1963; New York University, M.A., 1971. *Hobbies and other interests:* Oriental, American, and European medieval history, music, photography, gardening, travel.

Addresses

Home—New York, NY. *Agent*—Albert Zuckerman, A Writer's House.

Career

Freelance writer, 1973—. Has also worked as an editor and genealogist.

Writings

ALL WITH HUSBAND, THOMAS HOOBLER

Frontier Diary, Macmillan, 1974.

Margaret Mead: A Life in Science, Macmillan, 1974.

House Plants, Macmillan, 1975.

Vegetable Gardening and Cooking, Grosset and Dunlap, 1975.

Pruning, Grosset and Dunlap, 1975.

An Album of World War I, Watts, 1976.

Indoor Gardening, Grosset and Dunlap, 1976.

Photographing History: The Career of Mathew Brady, Putnam, 1977.

An Album of World War II, Watts, 1977.

The Trenches: Fighting on the Western Front in World War I, Putnam, 1978.

Photographing the Frontier, Putnam, 1980.

U.S.-China Relations Since World War II, Watts, 1981.

An Album of the Seventies, Watts, 1981.

The Social Security System, Watts, 1982.

The Voyages of Captain Cook, Putnam, 1983.

Joseph Stalin, with an introductory essay by Arthur M. Schlesinger, Chelsea House, 1985.

Cleopatra, Chelsea House, 1986.

Zhou Enlai, with an introductory essay by Schlesinger, Chelsea House, 1986.

(Richard B. Morris, consulting editor) *Your Right to Privacy,* Watts, 1987.

Nelson and Winnie Mandela, Watts, 1987.

Drugs and Crime, Chelsea House, 1988.

Toussaint L'Ouverture, Chelsea House, 1990.

George Washington and President's Day, pictures by Ronald Miller, Silver Burdett Press, 1990.

Vietnam, Why We Fought: An Illustrated History, Knopf, 1990.

Showa: The Age of Hirohito, Walker, 1990.

(With Hyung Woong Pak) *The Pacific Rim,* Scholastic, 1990.

Vanished!, Walker, 1991.

(With Carey-Greenberg Associates) *Aloha Means Come Back: The Story of a World War II Girl,* Silver Burdett Press, 1991.

(With Carey-Greenberg Associates) *The Sign Painter's Secret: The Story of a Revolutionary Girl,* pictures by Donna Ayers, Silver Burdett Press, 1991.

(With Carey-Greenberg Associates) *Next Stop, Freedom: The Story of a Slave Girl,* pictures by Cheryl Hanna, Silver Burdett Press, 1991.

(With Carey-Greenberg Associates) *Treasure in the Stream: The Story of a Gold Rush Girl,* pictures by Nancy Carpenter, Silver Burdett Press, 1991.

(With Carey-Greenberg Associates) *And Now, a Word from Our Sponsor: The Story of a Roaring 20's Girl,* pictures by Rebecca Leer, Silver Burdett Press, 1992.

(With Carey-Greenberg Associates) *A Promise at the Alamo: The Story of a Texas Girl,* pictures by Jennifer Hewitson, Silver Burdett Press, 1992.

(With Carey-Greenberg Associates) *The Trail on Which They Wept: The Story of a Cherokee Girl,* pictures by S. S. Burrus, Silver Burdett Press, 1992.

Lost Civilizations, Walker, 1992.

Mandela: The Man, the Struggle, the Triumph, Watts, 1992.

(With Carey-Greenberg Associates) *The Summer of Dreams: The Story of a World's Fair Girl,* pictures by Renee Graef, Silver Burdett Press, 1993.

Chinese Portraits, illustrated by Victoria Bruck, Raintree Steck-Vaughn, 1993.

Italian Portraits, illustrated by Kim Fujawara, Raintree Steck-Vaughn, 1993.

Mexican Portraits, illustrated by Robert Kuester, Raintree Steck-Vaughn, 1993.

African Portraits, Raintree Steck-Vaughn, 1993.

Confucianism, Facts on File, 1993.

The Chinese American Family Album, introduction by Bette Bao Lord, Oxford University Press, 1994.

South American Portraits, illustrated by Stephen Marchesi, Raintree Steck-Vaughn, 1994.

Russian Portraits, illustrated by John Edens, Raintree Steck-Vaughn, 1994.

French Portraits, illustrated by Bill Farnsworth, Raintree Steck-Vaughn, 1994.

Japanese Portraits, illustrated by V. Bruck, Raintree Steck-Vaughn, 1994.

The Italian American Family Album, introduction by Governor Mario M. Cuomo, Oxford University Press, 1994.

The Mexican American Family Album, introduction Henry G. Cisneros, Oxford University Press, 1994.

The Irish American Family Album, introduction by Joseph P. Kennedy II, Oxford University Press, 1995.

The African American Family Album, introduction by Phylicia Rashad, Oxford University Press, 1995.

The Jewish American Family Album, introduction by Mandy Patinkin, Oxford University Press, 1995.

The German American Family Album, introduction by Werner Klemperer, Oxford University Press, 1995.

The Japanese American Family Album, introduction by George Takei, Oxford University Press, 1996.

The Cuban American Family Album, introduction by Oscar Hijuelos, Oxford University Press, 1996.

The Scandinavian American Family Album, introduction by Hubert H. Humphrey III, Oxford University Press, 1997.

(With Casey-Greenberg Associates) *Sally Bradford: The Story of a Rebel Girl,* illustrated by Robert Gantt Steele, Silver Burdett Press, 1997.

(With Carey-Greenberg Associates) *Julie Meyer: The Story of a Wagon Train Girl,* illustrations by R. G. Steele, Silver Burdett Press, 1997.

(With Casey-Greenberg Associates) *Priscilla Foster: The Story of a Salem Girl,* illustrations by R. G. Steele, Silver Burdett, 1997.

(With Carey-Greenberg Associates) *Florence Robinson: The Story of a Jazz Age Girl,* illustrations by Robert Sauber, Silver Burdett Press, 1997.

Real American Girls Tell Their Own Stories, Atheneum, 1999.

The Ghost in the Tokaido Inn, Philomel, 1999.

Vanity Rules: A History of American Fashion and Beauty, Millbrook Press, 1999.

Sidelights

Working with her writer husband, Thomas, Dorothy Hoobler has compiled an impressive list of publications, some sixty titles of history, biography, and social issues. In two series alone, Silver Burdett's "Her Story" and a multi-cultural collection from Oxford University Press, "Family Album," the Hooblers have logged more than two dozen works detailing the fictional lives of girls in America through the ages and presenting a look at various ethnic American groups. The Hooblers' work is characterized by thorough research and clear, jargon-free text. Hoobler once told *SATA:* "In writing history, we try to learn enough about a person or event so that we can describe what it was like to live at a certain time, to experience as something new an event that is now 'history.'"

The curious minds of this husband-wife collaborative team have taken them on the voyages of Captain Cook, into the trenches of the First World War, and back to the stone ruins of lost civilizations. Their 1976 *An Album of World War I* provides an overview of that conflict, charting the progress of hostilities through major battles and important military maneuvers year by year. As a mark of their objective, journalistic approach to history, the *Booklist* reviewer of *An Album of World War I* noted that "there is no overt editorializing; statistics are left to speak for themselves." The same reviewer also noted that the book was a "perfectly functional overview" of the Great War. The Hooblers' interest in military history has also led them to write *An Album of World War II* as well as a history of the Western Front in World War I called *The Trenches.* They have also co-written a retrospective of a later conflict, *Vietnam: Why We Fought. Booklist's* Stephanie Zvirin called the volume on Vietnam "abundantly illustrated" with a "lucid and well-organized text" that is "never dry." The Hooblers begin with the political background that led to the war, then follow the progress of the war as well as events in the postwar era to look at the legacies of Vietnam. They also include comments and quotes from military leaders and politicians alike, creating "an accessible, panoramic view that will garner a wide readership," according to Zvirin. Writing in *Voice of Youth Advocates (VOYA),* Paula J. Lacey concluded that "this fairly short book is very clear and provides insight into most of the confusing aspects of the war."

Other popular general titles from the Hooblers include works on the history of photography, on drugs, the seventies, and even archaeology. In *Photographing the Frontier,* they extended an earlier work on Mathew Brady to photographers of the American frontier in the second half of the nineteenth century. A *Publishers Weekly* critic commented in a review of the book that the Hooblers effect "a neat blend of history and photography" as they had in earlier texts, and that the book detailed "in rich text and pictures the saga of adventurous photographers." One decade fell under their lens for *An Album of the Seventies,* which provides "solid, concise information in clear, easy-to-understand language that never talks down to readers," according to David A. Lindsey in *School Library Journal.* Drugs and crime are investigated in a 1988 Hoobler title of the same name. Reviewing *Drugs and Crime,* Hazel Rochman of *Booklist* observed that this "hard-hitting discussion shows how the extensive manufacture, distribution, and consumption of drugs are connected to 'rampant' violence . . . ."

The world of archaeology is examined in *Lost Civilizations,* a look at the facts and fiction surrounding such ancient cultures as Minoan Crete, the Easter Islanders, and the Olmecs, among others. Lola H. Teubert, writing in *VOYA,* felt that the separation of fact from fiction in the descriptions of these lost civilizations "will make for lively discussions in history classes," while *School Library Journal* contributor David N. Pauli felt that this approach would also help young students "understand the value of painstaking archeological research compared to unsubstantiated theories that often downplay human achievements."

Much of the Hooblers' work has been done in biography form, series that look at multi-cultural America, and as the histories of fictional young females in America. One of their earliest in-depth biographies was of Captain James Cook. *The Voyages of Captain Cook* is "an attractive biography for young adults," according to R. Scott Grabinger writing in *VOYA.* Grabinger went on to explain that the biography was "not overburdened with details, yet gives a good picture of the man and era."

Dennis Ford, writing in *School Library Journal,* noted that "Captain James Cook is realistically depicted in this excellent biography" which is comprehensive enough "to appeal even to adult readers." *Booklist's* Sally Estes concluded that *The Voyages of Captain Cook* was "a straightforward, informative, and obviously well researched account . . . ."

The Hooblers have also written biographies of such other internationally known figures as the one-time slave Toussaint L'Ouverture and the South African leader Nelson Mandela. In *Toussaint L'Ouverture,* the Hooblers tell the story of the courageous leader of a slave rebellion in Haiti against the French that was ultimately successful in winning freedom for Haiti. Dona Weisman observed in *School Library Journal* that students who need to expand their knowledge of black history or the history of the Western hemisphere "will welcome this interesting, easy-to-follow biography." Weisman concluded that the Hooblers' biography was a "clear and readable addition to history collections."

In *Mandela: The Man, the Struggle, the Triumph,* the Hooblers profile this century's most famous political prisoner, Nelson Mandela, who spent almost three decades in a South African prison for treason before

Using material culled from letters, journals, and oral histories, this book by Dorothy and Thomas Hoobler covers such topics as life in China prior to emigration, problems and prejudices encountered in the United States and clashes between old and new cultures.

In addition to explaining Confucianism as a system of ethical behavior and social responsibility that originated in China 2,500 years ago, Dorothy and Thomas Hoobler's account also details the historical development of the philosophy and its expansive influence on other Asian cultures.

becoming the first elected president of a newly democratic South Africa. Hazel Rochman noted in *Booklist* that while much of the information offered in the Hooblers' book was available in other biographies as well, theirs was "fair and readable" with "meticulously documented" sources. Janet G. Polachek commented in *VOYA* that the "narrative is clean and objective." Loretta Kreider Andrews concluded in *School Library Journal* that "the Hooblers' book provides a better overall picture of the man and his role in South Africa" than other recent biographies of Mandela.

The Hooblers have also compiled mini-biographies of notable world and historical figures in the Steck-Vaughn "Images Across the Ages" series. In *Chinese Portraits,* for example, they document the lives of a dozen men and women from artists to philosophers whose achievements affected not only their own country but also the greater world. Among others profiled in this title are Confucius, the poets Li Bo and Du Fu, and the politician Lin Xezu who fought the British opium traders. In *Italian Portraits,* they feature Caesar, Dante, Galileo, Verdi, and Montessori, among others. Their *French Portraits* include Charlemagne, Joan of Arc, Robespierre, Renoir, and Charles de Gaulle, while *Russian*

Portraits profile, among others, Peter and Catherine the Great, Pushkin, Tolstoy, Tchaikovsky, and the filmmaker Eisentstein. Of *Chinese Portraits* and *Italian Portraits,* Diane S. Marton remarked in *School Library Journal* that the short biographies were "interesting" and "anecdotal," and that the chronological organization of the books with brief introductions "provide[s] fascinating glimpses into the long social history of these countries as well." Reviewing those same books, *Booklist's* Carolyn Phelan concluded that the "lively, informative writing makes each volume more readable than most collective biographies."

Multi-ethnic America receives the Hoobler approach in Oxford University Press's "Family Album" series. Diaries, oral histories, and letters are all used to paint domestic pictures of various ethnic groups, from Italian American to Cuban American. Reviewing *The Italian American Family Album,* Marton noted in *School Library Journal* that the volume had "an enticing open format and is lavishly illustrated with interesting black-and-white photographs." Six chapters detail life in the country of origin, the waves of immigration, and adaptation to life in America, and also provide a wealth of detail on recipes, notable Italian Americans, and bits and pieces of history in sidebar format. Much the same organization is employed in other books in the series, including *The Cuban American Family Album,* a book dubbed "a good summation of the successful assimilation of Cubans into ... American culture," by a *Kirkus Reviews* critic.

A further series the Hooblers have written extensively for is "Her Story" from Silver Burdett, fictional biographies of young women from various historical epochs of America. Reviewing *Julie Meyer: The Story of a Wagon Train Girl* and *Sally Bradford: The Story of a Rebel Girl,* Kay Weisman noted in *Booklist* that the Hooblers "pay close attention to the details of local color," and that "these books will be welcomed by classrooms looking for historical novels."

"Increasing our understanding of other people is one of the reasons why we enjoy reading, and writing, history," Hoobler once told *SATA.* "It is also one reason why history is so important for young people growing up today, preparing for the twenty-first century. It is clear that all the people of the world have to come to a greater understanding of each other and learn to live with one another in a crowded dangerous world in which *mis*understanding could result in a nuclear war that could destroy the world." The Hooblers have dedicated their professional lives to writing history and biography so that such lack of understanding between cultures may become a thing of the past.

Works Cited

Review of *An Album of World War I, Booklist,* May 15, 1976, pp. 1336-37.

Andrews, Loretta Kreider, review of *Mandela, School Library Journal,* December, 1992, p. 139.

Review of *The Cuban American Family Album, Kirkus Reviews,* November 15, 1996, p. 1670.

Estes, Sally, review of *The Voyages of Captain Cook, Booklist,* April 15, 1984, p. 1159.

Ford, Dennis, review of *The Voyages of Captain Cook, School Library Journal,* April, 1984, p. 124.

Grabinger, T. Scott, review of *The Voyages of Captain Cook, Voice of Youth Advocates,* June, 1984, p. 109.

Lacey, Paula J., review of *Vietnam: Why We Fought, Voice of Youth Advocates,* October, 1990, pp. 243-44.

Lindsey, David A., review of *An Album of the Seventies, School Library Journal,* March, 1982, p. 158.

Marton, Diane S., review of *Chinese Portraits* and *Italian Portraits, School Library Journal,* August, 1993, p. 174.

Marton, Diane S., review of *The Italian American Family Album, School Library Journal,* July, 1994, p. 110.

Pauli, David N., review of *Lost Civilizations, School Library Journal,* September, 1992, p. 267.

Phelan, Carolyn, review of *Chinese Portraits* and *Italian American Portraits, Booklist,* July, 1993, p. 1954.

Review of *Photographing the Frontier, Publishers Weekly,* April 25, 1980, p. 80.

Polachek, Janet G., review of *Mandela, Voice of Youth Advocates,* June, 1992, p. 126.

Rochman, Hazel, review of *Drugs and Crime, Booklist,* March 15, 1988, p. 1240.

Rochman, Hazel, review of *Mandela, Booklist,* May 14, 1992, p. 1672.

Teubert, Lola H., review of *Lost Civilizations, Voice of Youth Advocates,* February, 1993, p. 370.

Weisman, Dona, review of *Toussaint L'Ouverture, School Library Journal,* August, 1990, p. 170.

Weisman, Kay, review of *Julie Meyer* and *Sally Bradford, Booklist,* June 1 & 15, 1997, p. 1703.

Zvirin, Stephanie, review of *Vietnam: Why We Fought, Booklist,* December 1, 1990, p. 731.

For More Information See

PERIODICALS

Booklist, January 1, 1997, p. 836; August, 1997, p. 1900.

Bulletin of the Center for Children's Books, June, 1980, p. 192.

Horn Book, April, 1984, p. 209.

Kirkus Reviews, March 15, 1992, p. 394; June 1, 1999, p. 883.

New York Times Book Review, May 8, 1994, p. 20; December 17, 1995, p. 28.

School Library Journal, May, 1988, p. 117; December, 1990, p. 130; June, 1993, p. 138; December, 1993, p. 112; August, 1997, p. 136.

Voice of Youth Advocates, August, 1990, p. 175; December, 1990, p. 314; February, 1995, p. 361.*

—Sketch by J. Sydney Jones

HOOBLER, Thomas

Personal

Born in Cincinnati, OH; son of John T. (a printer) and Jane Frances (maiden name, Pachoud) Hoobler; married Dorothy (a writer), December 18, 1971; children: Ellen Marie. *Education:* University of Notre Dame, A. B., 1964; attended University of Iowa, Writer's Workshop, 1965. *Hobbies and other interests:* Music, photography, gardening, and travel.

Addresses

Home—New York, NY. *Agent*—Phyllis Jackson, International Creative Management, 40 West 57th St., New York, NY 10019.

Career

Freelance writer and editor, 1977—. Worked in various positions at private schools in Cincinnati, OH, including teacher of English and photography, audio-visual coordinator, and basketball coach, 1965-70; trade-magazine editor, 1971-77.

Writings

WITH WIFE, DOROTHY HOOBLER

Frontier Diary, Macmillan, 1974.
Margaret Mead: A Life in Science, Macmillan, 1974.
House Plants, Macmillan, 1975.
Vegetable Gardening and Cooking, Grosset and Dunlap, 1975.
Pruning, Grosset and Dunlap, 1975.
An Album of World War I, Watts, 1976.
Indoor Gardening, Grosset and Dunlap, 1976.
Photographing History: The Career of Mathew Brady, Putnam, 1977.
An Album of World War II, Watts, 1977.
The Trenches: Fighting on the Western Front in World War I, Putnam, 1978.
Photographing the Frontier, Putnam, 1980.
U.S.-China Relations Since World War II, Watts, 1981.
An Album of the Seventies, Watts, 1981.
The Social Security System, Watts, 1982.
The Voyages of Captain Cook, Putnam, 1983.
Joseph Stalin, with an introductory essay by Arthur M. Schlesinger, Chelsea House, 1985.
Zhou Enlai, with an introductory essay by Schlesinger, Chelsea House, 1986.
Cleopatra, Chelsea House, 1986.
Your Right to Privacy, Watts, 1987.
Nelson and Winnie Mandela, Watts, 1987.
Drugs and Crime, Chelsea House, 1988.
Toussaint L'Ouverture, Chelsea House, 1990.
George Washington and President's Day, illustrated by Ronald Miller, Silver Burdett Press, 1990.
Vietnam, Why We Fought: An Illustrated History, Knopf, 1990.
Showa: The Age of Hirohito, Walker, 1990.

(With Hyung Woong Pak) *The Pacific Rim,* Scholastic, 1990.

Vanished!, Walker, 1991.

(With Carey-Greenberg Associates) *Aloha Means Come Back: The Story of a World War II Girl,* Silver Burdett Press, 1991.

(With Carey-Greenberg Associates) *The Sign Painter's Secret: The Story of a Revolutionary Girl,* illustrated by Donna Ayers, Silver Burdett Press, 1991.

(With Carey-Greenberg Associates) *Next Stop, Freedom: The Story of a Slave Girl,* illustrated by Cheryl Hanna, Silver Burdett Press, 1991.

(With Carey-Greenberg Associates) *Treasure in the Stream: The Story of a Gold Rush Girl,* illustrated by Nancy Carpenter, Silver Burdett Press, 1991.

(With Carey-Greenberg Associates) *And Now, a Word from Our Sponsor: The Story of a Roaring 20's Girl,* illustrated by Rebecca Leer, Silver Burdett Press, 1992.

(With Carey-Greenberg Associates) *A Promise at the Alamo: The Story of a Texas Girl,* illustrated by Jennifer Hewitson, Silver Burdett Press, 1992.

(With Carey-Greenberg Associates) *The Trail on Which They Wept: The Story of a Cherokee Girl,* illustrated by S. S. Burrus, Silver Burdett Press, 1992.

Lost Civilizations, Walker, 1992.

Mandela: The Man, the Struggle, the Triumph, Watts, 1992.

(With Carey-Greenberg Associates) *The Summer of Dreams: The Story of a World's Fair Girl,* illustrated by Renee Graef, Silver Burdett Press, 1993.

Chinese Portraits, illustrated by Victoria Bruck, Raintree Steck-Vaughn, 1993.

Italian Portraits, illustrated by Kim Fujawara, Raintree Steck-Vaughn, 1993.

Mexican Portraits, illustrated by Robert Kuester, Raintree Steck-Vaughn, 1993.

African Portraits, Raintree Steck-Vaughn, 1993.

Confucianism, Facts on File, 1993.

The Chinese American Family Album, introduction by Bette Bao Lord, Oxford University Press, 1994.

South American Portraits, illustrated by Stephen Marchesi, Raintree Steck-Vaughn, 1994.

Russian Portraits, illustrated by John Edens, Raintree Steck-Vaughn, 1994.

French Portraits, illustrated by Bill Farnsworth, Raintree Steck-Vaughn, 1994.

Japanese Portraits, illustrated by V. Bruck, Raintree Steck-Vaughn, 1994.

The Italian American Family Album, introduction by Governor Mario M. Cuomo, Oxford University Press, 1994.

The Mexican American Family Album, Oxford University Press, 1994.

The Irish American Family Album, introduction by Joseph P. Kennedy II, Oxford University Press, 1995.

The African American Family Album, introduction by Phylicia Rashad, Oxford Univesity Press, 1995.

The Jewish American Family Album, Oxford University Press, 1995.

The German American Family Album, introduction by Werner Klemperer, Oxford University Press, 1995.

The Japanese American Family Album, introduction by George Takei, Oxford University Press, 1996.

The Cuban American Family Album, introduction by Oscar Hijuelos, Oxford University Press, 1996.

The Scandinavian American Family Album, introduction by Hubert H. Humphrey III, Oxford University Press, 1997.

(With Casey-Greenberg Associates) *Sally Bradford: The Story of a Rebel Girl,* illustrated by Robert Gantt Steele, Silver Burdett Press, 1997.

(With Carey-Greenberg Associates) *Julie Meyer: The Story of a Wagon Train Girl,* illustrated by R. G. Steele, Silver Burdett Press, 1997.

(With Casey-Greenberg Associates) *Priscilla Foster: The Story of a Salem Girl,* illustrated by R. G. Steele, Silver Burdett, 1997.

(With Carey-Greenberg Associates) *Florence Robinson: The Story of a Jazz Age Girl,* illustrated by Robert Sauber, Silver Burdett Press, 1997.

Real American Girls Tell Their Own Stories, Atheneum, 1999.

The Ghost in the Tokaido Inn, Philomel, 1999.

Vanity Rules: A History of American Fashion and Beauty, Millbrook Press, 1999.

NOVELS

(With Burt Wetanson) *The Hunters* (for adults), Doubleday, 1978.

(With Wetanson) *The Treasure Hunters* (for adults) Playboy Paperbacks, 1983.

Dr. Chill's Project (for young adults), Putnam, 1987, published in the UK as *Dr, Chill,* Piper, 1989.

The Revenge of Ho-Tai (for young adults), Walker, 1989.

Sidelights

Thomas Hoobler forms one half of a prolific husband-wife writing team with over sixty books to their credit. Writing primarily nonfiction, the Hooblers have become well known for their biographical writings, tackling subjects from Joseph Stalin to Cleopatra. They have contributed to series ranging from Oxford University Press's portrayal of multicultural America in the "Family Album" books, to fictional accounts of young women throughout the American centuries, "Her Story" from Silver Burdett.

Born in Cincinnati, Ohio, Hoobler attended Notre Dame and spent a year at the prestigious Writer's Workshop of the University of Iowa before returning to his hometown to work as an all-purpose educator at a local private school. There he not only taught English and photography—two of his passions—but also ran the audiovisual department and even coached basketball. By 1971 he had moved on to an editorial position at a trade magazine, marrying his wife that same year. Their collaboration began in 1974 with a biography of the anthropologist Margaret Meade, followed by several adult gardening titles. Their first juvenile title together was the 1976 *An Album of World War I,* and this initial title spurred a prolific, long-standing cooperative effort, primarily in nonfiction.

Hoobler once described the collaborative process to *SATA:* "Because we have written ... books together..., one of the questions we are most often asked is: How do you work together? We think that sometimes people imagine us sitting side-by-side at twin typewriters, turning out sheets of copy (or perhaps a specially-built typewriter with two keyboards and only one sheet of paper). The truth is, that for the kind of books we write—mostly about people and events in history—a great deal of research is required. More of our time is spent in libraries looking for information or archives searching for interesting photographs or prints, than is actually spent at the typewriter."

Once the research is completed, the Hooblers discuss the current project to determine exactly how they plan to write about it. "We are fortunate in that we always have been able to write books about subjects that were interesting to us, rather than about topics that some publisher thought would sell well," Hoobler told *SATA.* "Writing a book, even a short one, is so much *work* that it would be sheer torture for us to write one about something that we weren't interested in."

Hoobler's personal interests have led him to write his own novels, as well. For a more thorough discussion of the Hooblers' joint ventures, see the *SATA* entry on Dorothy Hoobler. The present article deals with Thomas Hoobler's solo efforts, two of which have been aimed at the young-adult audience, *Dr. Chill's Project* and *The Revenge of Ho-Tai.*

In the first title, published in 1987, a group of adolescents with special talents is gathered for a secret project run by the amiable Dr. Chill, a psychologist. Dr. Chill's vocation is so-called "specials"—young people with paranormal powers such as telepathy, precognition, and telekinesis. Dr. Chill not only treats his young clients, but also encourages the development of their rare talents. Allie, who has spent many of her 15 years in a mental institution, is amazed at the sudden freedom she experiences when she arrives at Dr. Chill's halfway house. Allie's specialty is telekinesis; other kids at Dr. Chill's halfway house are Rose, who is able to read minds and predict the future; Jay, who is able to manipulate machines; Lew, who is able to make people like him and do his bidding; and Timmy, a young autistic child with extraordinary telepathic powers.

When Rose is kidnapped by a quasi-governmental group eager to use her powers for their own purposes, the others rush to her aid, using their own special gifts to fight the kidnappers. Zena Sutherland, writing in *Bulletin of the Center for Children's Books,* noted that Hoobler "creates a believable setting" and develops a "successful" Psi novel "with good momentum and style, with interesting characters and an element of suspense...." John Peters observed in *School Library Journal* that "the ESP elements are well developed" and that Hoobler's characters "show room for complexity that will make readers think." And a *Booklist* contributor concluded that despite a thin plot, "the characters, their interactions, and talents are intriguing."

In *The Revenge of Ho-Tai,* Hoobler revisits some of his own experiences as a basketball coach in Cincinnati. The new science teacher/basketball coach at Edwards Academy, Mr. Kapur, makes it seem possible *not* to have a losing year. With victory in the first game of the season, the team is excited and optimistic. Kapur uses a statue of the fat, smiling Ho-Tai as the team mascot; the seventh- and eighth-grade boys rub its belly before each game as a good-luck symbol and imagine themselves to be playing well. But when parents and administrators get wind of this ceremony, they fear the makings of a cult.

Narrated in the first person by Roger Barstow, the novel relates the events of this bizarre basketball season at Edwards Academy. The previous year's star, Dennis, is miffed at Kapur and his Ho-Tai statue, for they have brought a sense of team play to the boys. No longer is he the lone hotshot on the court. Dennis is largely responsible for getting the parents stirred up, for having Kapur fired, and for the destruction of the smiling Ho-Tai. When the roof of the school gym collapses during a snowstorm, Roger believes that Ho-Tai has gotten his revenge on the school.

"This is more complex than the average sports novel," noted Todd Morning in a *School Library Journal*

This installment in the American Family Album series uses such primary sources as diaries, letters, and interviews to document the experiences of Scandinavians who left their country for a better life in America.

review. "The story is fast moving, features characters that come to life, and is effectively told in a casual first-person style." Morning concluded that Hoobler's book was that "rare thing: a thought-provoking sports novel." Deborah Bennett, writing in *Voice of Youth Advocates,* commented that "Hoobler is adept at creating convincing adolescent characters, situations, and dialogue," and that his book "should appeal to both sports fans and readers who want 'coming-of-age' stories."

Works Cited

Bennett, Deborah, review of *The Revenge of Ho-Tai, Voice of Youth Advocates,* August, 1989, pp. 158-59.

Review of *Dr. Chill's Project, Booklist,* November 1, 1987, p. 466.

Morning, Todd, review of *The Revenge of Ho-Tai, School Library Journal,* June, 1989, p. 124.

Peters, John, review of *Dr. Chill's Project, School Library Journal,* January, 1988. P. 85.

Sutherland, Zena, review of *Dr. Chill's Project, Bulletin of the Center for Children's Books,* February, 1988, p. 118.

For More Information See

PERIODICALS

Booklist, June 15, 1989, p, 1822.
Kirkus Reviews, June 1, 1999, p. 883.
Voice of Youth Advocates, October, 1987, p. 201.
Wilson Library Bulletin, February, 1989, p. 87.

—Sketch by J. Sydney Jones

I

INGPEN, Robert Roger 1936-

Personal

Born October 13, 1936, in Melbourne, Australia; son of Thomas Roger (a manufacturer's agent) and Vida Ingpen; married Angela Mary Salmon, May 8, 1959; children: Katrina Arch, Susan, Sophie, Tom. *Education:* Geelong College, Royal Melbourne Institute of Technology, Diploma of Graphic Art, 1957.

Robert Roger Ingpen

Addresses

Home and office—29 Parker Street, Anglesea, Victoria, Australia 3230.

Career

Commonwealth Scientific and Industrial Research Organization, Australia, senior artist, 1959-68. Freelance author, illustrator, and designer, 1968—. Deakin University, Geelong, foundation councillor; Dromkeen Children's Literature Foundation, governor.

Awards, Honors

Award for illustration, Children's Book Council of Australia, 1975, for *Storm-Boy;* award for illustration, International Board on Books for Young People, 1978, for *The Runaway Punt;* Hans Christian Andersen Medal, 1986; Dromkeen Medal, 1989.

Writings

AUTHOR AND ILLUSTRATOR

Pioneers of Wool, Rigby (Adelaide, Australia), 1972.

Pioneer Settlement in Australia, Rigby, 1972, Hale (London), 1973.

Robe: A Portrait of the Past, Rigby, 1975.

Marking Time: Australia's Abandoned Buildings, Rigby, 1979.

Australian Gnomes, Rigby, 1979.

The Voyage of the Poppykettle, Rigby, 1980.

Australia's Heritage Watch: An Overview of Australian Conservation, Rigby, 1981.

The Unchosen Land, Rigby, 1981.

(With Sally Carruthers and others) *Australian Inventions and Innovations,* Rigby, 1982.

(With Graham Pizzey) *Churchill Island,* Victoria Conservation Trust (East Melbourne, Australia), 1982.

(With Mellonie Bryan) *Beginnings and Endings with Lifetimes in Between,* Hill of Content (Melbourne, Australia), 1983, published in the U.S. as *Lifetimes: A*

Beautiful Way to Explain Death to Children, Bantam, 1983.

Click Go the Shears, Collins (Sydney, Australia), 1984.

The Idle Bear, Lothian (Melbourne, Australia), 1986, Blackie (London, England), 1987, revised as *The Miniature Idle Bear,* NTC, 1989.

(With Margaret Dunkle) *Conservation,* Hill of Content, 1987, Paper Tiger (Limpsfield, England), 1987.

The Age of Acorns, Lothian, 1988, Blackie, 1990, Bedrick/Blackie (New York), 1990.

The Dreamkeeper: A Letter from Robert Ingpen to His Granddaughter Alice Elizabeth, Lothian, 1995, Dragon's World, 1995.

The Afternoon Treehouse, Lothian, 1996, Pavilion (London), 1997.

(With Ted Egan) *The Drover's Boy,* Lothian, 1997.

Once upon a Place, Lothian, 1999.

AUTHOR AND ILLUSTRATOR; WITH MICHAEL F. PAGE

Aussie Battlers, Rigby, 1982.

The Great Bullocky Race, Hill of Content, 1984, Dodd, Mead, 1988.

Encyclopedia of Things That Never Were: Creatures, Places, and People, Paper Tiger, 1985, Viking, 1987.

Out of This World: The Complete Book of Fantasy, Landsdowne Press (Sydney, Australia), 1986.

Worldly Dogs, Lothian, 1988.

The Making of Australians, Dent (Knoxfield, Australia), 1987, Houghton, 1990.

AUTHOR AND ILLUSTRATOR; WITH PHILIP WILKINSON

The Encyclopedia of Mysterious Places: The Life and Legends of Ancient Sites around the World, Mallard (Sydney, Australia), 1990, Viking, 1990.

Encyclopedia of World Events: Eighty Turning Points in History, Dragon's World (Limpsfield, England), 1991, Viking, 1991.

Encyclopedia of Ideas That Changed the World: The Greatest Discoveries and Inventions of Human History, Dragon's World, 1993, Viking, 1993.

A Celebration of Customs & Rituals of the World, Dragon's World, 1994, Facts on File, 1996.

AUTHOR AND ILLUSTRATOR; WITH BARBARA HAYES

Folk Tales & Fables of Asia & Australia, Dragon's World, 1992, Chelsea House, 1994.

Folk Tales & Fables of Europe, Dragon's World, 1992, Chelsea House, 1994.

Folk Tales & Fables of the Americas & the Pacific, Dragon's World, 1992, Chelsea House, 1994.

Folk Tales & Fables of the Middle East & Africa, Dragon's World, 1992, Chelsea House, 1994.

AUTHOR AND ILLUSTRATOR; WITH MOLLY PERHAM

Ghouls and Monsters, Dragon's World, 1995, Chelsea House, 1996.

Gods and Goddesses, Dragon's World, 1995, Chelsea House, 1996.

Heroes and Heroines, Dragon's World, 1995, Chelsea House, 1996.

Magicians and Fairies, Dragon's World, 1995, Chelsea House, 1996.

ILLUSTRATOR

Colin Thiele, *Storm-Boy,* Rigby, 1974.

Michael F. Page, *The Runaway Punt,* Rigby, 1976.

Don Dunstan, *Don Dunstan's Cookbook,* Rigby, 1976.

Andrew McKay, *Surprise and Enterprise: Fifty Years of Science for Australia,* edited by Frederick White and David Krimpton, Commonwealth Scientific Industrial Research Organization, 1976.

The Australian Countrywoman's Cookbook, photographs by Peter Gower, Rigby, 1976.

Colin Thiele, *Lincoln's Place,* Rigby, 1978.

Nick Evers, *Paradise and Beyond: Tasmania,* Rigby, 1978.

Colin Thiele, *Chadwick's Chimney,* Ashton Scholastic (Sydney, Australia), 1979.

Thiele, *River Murray Mary,* Rigby, 1979.

Colin Stone, *Running the Brumbies: True Adventures of a Modern Bushman,* Rigby, 1979.

Michael F. Page, *Turning Points in the Making of Australia,* Rigby, 1980.

Page, *Robert Ingpen,* compiled by Angela Ingpen, Macmillan (South Melbourne, Australia), 1980.

Ronald Rose, *This Peculiar Colony,* Rigby, 1981.

Mary Small, *Night of the Muttonbirds,* Methuen (Sydney, Australia), 1981.

A. B. Paterson, *Clancy of the Overflow,* Rigby, 1982.

Max Charlesworth, *Religious Worlds,* Hill of Content, 1985.

Michael F. Page, *Colonial South Australia: Its People and Buildings,* J. M. Dent (South Melbourne, Australia), 1985.

Barbara Hayes, reteller, *Folk Tales and Fables of the World,* Paper Tiger, 1987.

Mark Twain, *The Stolen White Elephant,* Ashton Scholastic, 1987.

Twain, *A Strange Expedition,* Ashton Scholastic, 1988.

Charles Dickens, *A Christmas Tree,* Ashton Scholastic, 1988.

Dickens, *The Child's Story,* Ashton Scholastic, 1988.

Patricia Wrightson, *The Nargun and the Stars,* Hutchinson (Hawthorn, Australia), 1988.

Maurice Saxby, reteller, *The Great Deeds of Superheroes,* Millennium (Newtown, Australia), 1989, Dragon's World, 1989, P. Bedrick (New York), 1990.

Saxby, reteller, *The Great Deeds of Heroic Women,* Dragon's World, 1989, Millennium, 1990.

Katherine Scholes, *Peacetimes,* Hill of Content, 1989, Dragon's World, 1989, published in the U.S. as *Peace Begins with You,* Little, Brown, 1990.

Robert Louis Stevenson, *Treasure Island,* Viking, 1992.

Philip Steele, *River through the Ages,* Eagle, 1993, Troll, 1994.

Jacqueline Dineen, *Hunting, Harvesting, and Home,* Chelsea House, 1998.

Dineen, *Feasts and Festivals,* Chelsea House, 1998.

Michael Cave, *Fabulous Places of Myth: A Journey with Robert Ingpen to Camelot, Atlantis, Valhalla, and the Tower of Babel,* Lothian, 1998.

Ejnar Agertoft, *Jacob, the Boy from Nuremberg,* Lothian, 1998.

Jacqueline Dineen, *Rites of Passage,* Chelsea House, 1999.

Dineen, *Living with the Gods,* Chelsea House, 1999.

ILLUSTRATOR; BY PHILIP WILKINSON AND JACQUELINE DINEEN

The Lands of the Bible, Dragon's World, 1992, Chelsea House, 1994.
The Mediterranean, Angus & Robertson (Pymble, Australia), 1992, Chelsea House, 1994.
People Who Changed the World, Chelsea House, 1994.
Statesmen Who Changed the World, Chelsea House, 1994.
Scrolls to Computers, Dragon's World, 1994.
Caves to Cathedrals, Dragon's World, 1994.
The Early Inventions, Chelsea House, 1995.
Art and Technology through the Ages, Chelsea House, 1995.

ILLUSTRATOR; BY PHILIP WILKINSON AND MICHAEL POLLARD

The Magical East, Angus & Robertson, 1992, Dragon's World, 1992, Chelsea House, 1994.
The Master Builders, Angus & Robertson, 1992, Dragon's World, 1992, Chelsea House, 1994.
Science and Power, Dragon's World, 1994.
Scientists Who Changed the World, Chelsea House, 1994.
Wheels to Rockets: Innovations in Transport, Dragon's World, 1994.
Generals Who Changed the World, Chelsea House, 1994.
Transportation, Chelsea House, 1995.
The Industrial Revolution, Chelsea House, 1995.

Also illustrator of maps, brochures, and other visual materials. Also author of a series of Chinese-language books for Grimm Press, Taiwan.

Storm-Boy was translated into German and French; *The Idle Bear* was translated into Japanese and Swedish.

Work in Progress

A Bear Tale, for Lothian; illustrations for *Who Is the World For?,* written by Tom Pow, for Walker.

Sidelights

Robert Ingpen is an Australian author and illustrator who has captured the natural beauty and cultural quirks of his native country within his books. Elements of the supernatural weave through the pages of many of his titles, including *Australian Gnomes* and *The Voyage of the Poppykettle,* as well as a series of books, written with Molly Perham, that includes such titles as *Ghouls and Monsters* and *Magicians and Fairies.* Ingpen's interest in not only the supernatural but in folklore, technology, and the history of ideas and politics is worldwide in scope, and evident in several titles coauthored with others that include his award-winning artwork.

Born in Melbourne, Australia, in 1936, Ingpen was raised in Geelong, Victoria. Trained in art at the Royal Melbourne Institute of Technology, he began his publishing career by writing and illustrating several books recording the history of Australia's lesser-known places. His first illustration project for young people was the book *Storm-Boy,* written by Colin Thiele and published

in 1974. Awarded several prestigious honors, including the 1986 Hans Christian Andersen medal, Ingpen's work has been compared to the illustrations of U.S. artist N. C. Wyeth in his realistic approach. Although Ingpen uses a variety of mediums, including watercolor, pencil, and pastel, his work is distinctive in its detail and its adherence to historical accuracy. Ingpen has been praised for his style, his choice of earthen hues, and his unique approach to light and shadow.

Among the fictional works penned and illustrated by Ingpen are *The Idle Bear* and *The Age of Acorns.* Teddy bears figure prominently in both works; in *The Idle Bear,* two worn teddies who have watched their owners grow up and leave them try to make sense of their place in the world, while in *The Age of Acorns,* a younger bear is accidentally left outdoors by the child he belongs to. Called both humorous and poignant, *The Idle Bear* drew praise from reviewers, including a *Publishers Weekly* commentator who concluded that "such wide-eyed bears, in dire need of family, should find a home in any reader's heart." Although a *Kirkus Reviews* contributor praised the dialogue in *The Idle Bear* as "deceptively aimless yet cadenced and philosophical," Zena Sutherland of *Bulletin of the Center for Children's Books* questioned its appropriateness for a young audience.

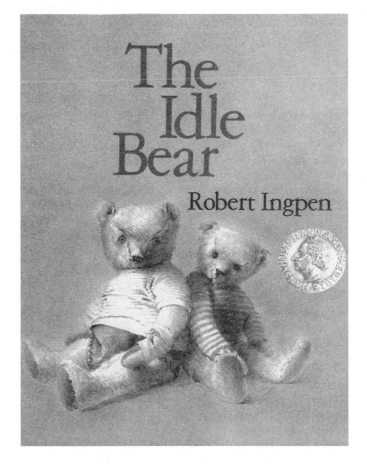

Ingpen received the 1986 Hans Christian Andersen Medal for his self-illustrated picture book about the inner thoughts and private worlds of two endearing teddy bears. (Cover illustration by Ingpen.)

This rich collection of folklore includes tales from Germany, France, England, Italy, and Greece, among other countries. (From Folk Tales & Fables of Europe, *written by Ingpen and Barbara Hayes and illustrated by Ingpen.)*

However, Sutherland went on to praise Ingpen's illustrations as "remarkable for their textural quality and their deftness in depiction of light and shade." Sutherland also praised *The Age of Acorns* in a *Bulletin of the Center for Children's Books* review, noting that "the colors are quiet, reflecting the poignant wistfulness of the story."

The Dreamkeeper, which was published in Australia in 1995, was created by Ingpen for his granddaughter, Alice. Interweaving elements of reality and fantasy, he explains how the beings conjured up by human imaginations during dreams are kept from invading reality by a Dreamkeeper, who with the use of imaginative and intricately engineered traps and other tools, returns all dream beings to their proper home in the Dreamtree. Storybook characters, as well as scarier creatures, live within the dreams of imaginative young people, and characters from Aladdin to Long John Silver to the entire cast of *Alice in Wonderland* are among those caught by the ever-vigilant Dreamkeeper. "Myth and lore collide to create a promising fantasy" in Ingpen's unique work, according to a *Publishers Weekly* contribu-

tor, who noted that the book, hand-lettered by the illustrator to resemble a letter to Alice, is by turns "mystical, dreamlike and occasionally nightmarish."

In keeping with his penchant for myth and fantasy, Ingpen collaborated with Barbara Hayes to create a series of collections of folk tales and fables from around the world, including *Folk Tales & Fables of Asia and Australia* and *Folk Tales & Fables of the Middle East & Africa.* Of the latter title, *Booklist* reviewer Julie Corsaro noted, "[Ingpen's] full-page paintings are meticulously detailed, warmly colored and strikingly composed."

While many of Ingpen's subjects come not from the world of dreams and the imagination but from the factual, real world of history, technology, and science, he is able to transform the commonplace and everyday into the marvelous, sparking the curiosity of his young fans. Describing Ingpen's work in *Children's Books and Their Creators,* essayist Suzy Schmidt cited the author/illustrator's ultimate goal as "to engage young people's imaginations both with his art and with the stories he chooses to illustrate."

Works Cited

Corsaro, Julie, review of *Folk Tales & Fables of the Middle East & Africa, Booklist,* November 15, 1994, p. 596.

Review of *The Dreamkeeper, Publishers Weekly,* June 3, 1996, p. 84.

Review of *The Idle Bear, Kirkus Reviews,* October 15, 1987, p. 1516.

Review of *The Idle Bear, Publishers Weekly,* October 9, 1987, p. 84.

Schmidt, Suzy, essay on Ingpen in *Children's Books and Their Creators,* edited by Anita Silvey, Houghton, 1995, p. 344.

Sutherland, Zena, review of *The Age of Acorns, Bulletin of the Center for Children's Books,* December, 1990, p. 88.

Sutherland, review of *The Idle Bear, Bulletin of the Center for Children's Books,* December, 1987, pp. 66-67.

For More Information See

PERIODICALS

School Librarian, February, 1996, p. 20.
School Library Journal, March, 1988, p. 167.
Voice of Youth Advocates, February, 1996, p. 403.

*   *   *

ISHMAEL, Woodi 1914-1995

OBITUARY NOTICE—See index for *SATA* sketch: Born February 1, 1914, in Lewis County, KY; died January 29, 1995, at his home in Palm Beach Gardens, Florida. Illustrator and engraver. Ishmael attended the Cleveland School of Art and began his career as a freelance illustrator of books and art director for an advertising agency in New York in 1939. He was an assistant professor at Troy State University in Troy, AL, from

1971 until his retirement in 1984. His work appeared in newspapers and magazines, including *Cosmopolitan, National Geographic,* and *The Saturday Evening Post.* Ishmael also served as art director of a small farm magazine. He illustrated dozens of books for children throughout his career, beginning with *A Boy Named John,* by John Cournos (1941). His last illustrations appeared in *Trail-Blazers in the Sky Chart* (1983) and *Tales from the Plum Grove Hills,* by Jesse Stuart (1997). Ishmael's paintings also grace federal buildings such as the White House and the Pentagon. He married Gwen Williams in 1939 and had one daughter, Candace.

OBITUARIES AND OTHER SOURCES:

BOOKS

Illustrators of Children's Books: 1744-1945, by Bertha E. Mahony, and others, Horn Book, 1958.
Illustrators of Children's Books: 1946-1956, by Bertha E. Mahony, and others, Horn Book, 1958.

PERIODICALS

The Baltimore Sun, February 2, 1995, p. 5B.
The Orlando Sentinel, February 2, 1995, p. A10.
The St. Petersburg Times, February 2, 1995, p. 5B.

—Obituary by Robert Reginald and Mary A. Burgess

J

JEWEL
See KILCHER, Jewel

* * *

JEWELL, Nancy 1940-

Personal

Born August 12, 1940, in Washington, DC. *Education:* Goucher College, B.A., 1962.

Addresses

Office—Harper & Row Publishers, Inc., 10 East 53rd St., New York, NY 10022.

Career

Author of picture books for children. Harper & Row Publishers, New York City, reader, 1966—.

Writings

The Snuggle Bunny, illustrated by Mary Chalmers, Harper, 1972.
Try and Catch Me, illustrated by Leonard Weisgard, Harper, 1972.
Calf, Goodnight, illustrated by Weisgard, Harper, 1973.
Cheer up, Pig!, illustrated by Ben Shecter, Harper, 1975.
The Family under the Moon, illustrated by Leonard Kessler, Harper, 1976.
Bus Ride, illustrated by Ronald Himler, Harper, 1978.
Time for Uncle Joe, illustrated by Joan Sandin, Harper, 1981.
ABC Cat, illustrated by Ann Schweninger, Harper, 1983.
Two Silly Trolls, illustrated by Lisa Thiesing, Harper, 1992.
Christmas Lullaby, illustrated by Stefano Vitale, Clarion, 1994.
Silly Times with Two Silly Trolls, illustrated by Lisa Thiesing, HarperCollins, 1996.
Sailor's Song, illustrated by Stefano Vitale, Clarion, 1999.

Five Little Kittens, illustrated by Elizabeth Sayles, Clarion, 1999.

Sidelights

Beginning her career in publishing as a manuscript reader for the New York publishing firm Harper & Row, Nancy Jewell has gone on to create a number of picture books that appeal to the preschool set. Among her works are the endearing *The Snuggle Bunny* and *Christmas Lullaby,* as well as more rambunctious stories featuring troll brothers Nip and Tuck, whose humorous adventures are chronicled in *Two Silly Trolls* and its sequel, *Silly Times with Two Silly Trolls.*

Born in 1940 in Washington, DC, Jewell graduated from Goucher College in 1962. She arrived in New York City four years later and began a long career with Harper, which has published most of her own books. Beginning with *The Snuggle Bunny* in 1972, Jewell has specialized in depicting small children and animals engaging in acts of friendship and affection. In *Try and Catch Me,* Jewell's text, called "simple [and] spirited" by a *Booklist* reviewer, tells the story of a young girl who dances through a country meadow before meeting up with a young boy who soon becomes her friend. *Bus Ride* finds six-year-old Janie on her way to visit her grandfather. Making the trip alone might be scary, but Janie is befriended by an elderly female passenger named Mrs. Rivers, and over the course of the trip the two become fast friends. Calling *Bus Ride* "a journey worth sharing," *Booklist* contributor Denise M. Wilms noted that Jewell's tale contains "emotional undercurrents [that] are readily apparent."

In addition to books that tell stories of young people in everyday situations, Jewell has called on her imagination in creating book such as *ABC Cat* and *Two Silly Trolls.* Her obvious affection for furry felines is apparent in the former title, her first alphabet book, as the activities of a typically curious kitty are organized by letter and told in verses augmented by affectionate pen-and-watercolor portraits by Ann Schweninger. Good-natured but bum-

In Nancy Jewell's poetic story, a mother sings to her child at bedtime about a fisherman returning home after a long trip at sea. (From Sailor Song, *illustrated by Stefano Vitale.)*

bling troll brothers Nip and Tuck find that life is a series of adventures in *Two Silly Trolls.* Containing five short stories, the book finds the pair overcoming small squabbles and "blunder[ing] their way to a happy ending" in each tale, according to a *Publishers Weekly* contributor. The reviewer also had praise for the book's "predictable, repetitive language," which "will promote fluency in beginning readers." Reviewing the stories in *Booklist,* Stephanie Zvirin agreed that they are good material for beginning readers, but also had praise for "Jewell's gentle wit and her message." Nip and Tuck continue their adventures in *Silly Times with Two Silly Trolls,* published in 1996. In this collection of three easy-reading tales, the trolls' continued good-natured antics "are almost certain to engage beginning readers," according to *School Library Journal* contributor Barbara McGinn.

In a special picture book designed to reflect the gentleness of the Christmas season, Jewell's *Christmas Lullaby* presents a rhymed version of the events surrounding the birth of Jesus. Animals come to the infant lying in the manger and bestow simple gifts that reflect the giver. A wooly lamb offers the gift of soft fleece, a cat and kittens lull the infant to sleep with their purr, while a gentle cow provides the Christ child with nourishing milk, in a book that *Horn Book* reviewer Mary M. Burns praised as a "lovely variant on seasonal offerings." Lauding the illustrations by Stefano Vitale in her *New York Times Book Review* appraisal of *Christmas*

Lullaby, Cynthia Zarin deemed the work "most successful," and noted that Jewell's "simple verse tells the parts of the tale that ... make the most sense to the very young: a baby is born; he is loved; gifts magically appear; and happy, swaddled and warm, he falls asleep."

Works Cited

Burns, Mary M., review of *Christmas Lullaby, Horn Book,* November-December, 1994, p. 712.

McGinn, Barbara, review of *Silly Times with Two Silly Trolls, School Library Journal,* July, 1996, p. 66.

Review of *Try and Catch Me, Booklist,* May 1, 1973, p. 856.

Review of *Two Silly Trolls, Publishers Weekly,* July 27, 1992, pp. 62-63.

Wilms, Denise M., review of *Bus Ride, Booklist,* March 15, 1978, p. 1180.

Zarin, Cynthia, review of *Christmas Lullaby, New York Times Book Review,* December 18, 1994, p. 26.

Zvirin, Stephanie, review of *Two Silly Trolls, Booklist,* June 15, 1992, pp. 1854-55.

For More Information See

PERIODICALS

Booklist, October 1, 1994, p. 333; April 1, 1996, p. 1375.

Bulletin of the Center for Children's Books, April, 1977, p. 127; May, 1978, p. 143; May, 1981, p. 172.

Kirkus Reviews, April 15, 1975, p. 445; September 15, 1976, p. 1035; March 1, 1978, p. 238.
New York Times Book Review, October 9, 1983, p. 38.
Publishers Weekly, January 31, 1972, p. 247; March 24, 1975, p. 48; July 29, 1983, p. 70.
School Library Journal, April, 1973, p. 56; September, 1975, p. 85; November, 1976, p. 48; May, 1978, p. 56; April, 1981, p. 114; December, 1983, p. 56.*

* * *

JIANG, Cheng An 1943- (Zheng An Jiang; Shan Cheng)

Personal

Born December 16, 1943; son of Wen Xuan Jiang (a teacher) and Shu Lan Wang (a homemaker); married Qu Zhong Yan (a teacher), March 2, 1969; children: Hong Gen (a writer under pseudonym Wei Jiang). *Education:* Lu Xun Art College, B.A., 1965.

Addresses

Home—Building 13, Unit 1, No. 501, 35 Che Gong Zhuang, West Rd., Beijing 100044, China. *Office*—Morning Glory Publishing, 35 Che Gong Zhuang, Xi Lu, Beijing 100044, China. *Agent*-Qu Zhong Yan, Morning Glory Publishing, 35 Che Gong Zhuang, Xi Lu, Beijing 100044, China.

Career

Dolphin Publishing (division of Foreign Language Press), Beijing, China, editor-in-chief, 1985-95; Morning Glory Publishing, Beijing, editor-in-chief, 1995—. *Member:* Association of Chinese Artists, Association of Chinese Creators, Association of Chinese Motion Pictures.

Awards, Honors

UNESCO Award, children's book illustration category, United Nations, 1988, for *The Little Panda Goes Home;* Seal of Approval, multicultural classic, Multicultural Publishers and Education Council of the United States, 1998, for *The Legend of Mu Lan: A Heroine of Ancient China;* Japan's Noma Award; thirty Chinese national awards for children's book illustrations.

Writings

Chinese Word Book, Bess Press (Honolulu), 1990.
Chinese Idioms, Sesame Publications (Hong Kong), 1992.
(Translator and illustrator, with daughter Wei Jiang) *The Legend of Mu Lan: A Heroine of Ancient China* (bilingual edition), Victory Press (Monterey, CA), 1992.
Chinese Historical Stories, Hsian Fu Publishing (Taiwan), 1994.
Chinese Inventors, Morning Glory Publishing (Beijing, China), 1995.

Empress of China: Wu Ze Tian (bilingual edition), illustrated by De Yuan Xu, Victory Press, 1998.

Illustrator of *The Little Panda Goes Home.*

Work in Progress

China's Most Famous Mother, a bilingual book, for Victory Press; *Water Margin; Romance of the Three Kingdoms; Dream of the Red Chamber;* and *Adventures of the Monkey King.*

Sidelights

Cheng An Jiang's United States publisher, Eileen Hu, told *SATA:* "Cheng An Jiang of Beijing, China, is a prolific writer and illustrator of Chinese children's picture books. His traditional Chinese art techniques were introduced in America with the bilingual title *The Legend of Mu Lan: A Heroine of Ancient China,* a classic story of filial piety and bravery. Mr. Jiang worked on this book with his daughter, Wei Jiang, who was at the time a recent art graduate of the Universidad Complutense de Madrid, Spain.

因她有胆有识，惯战，屡立战功，又懂演阵兵法，很快就提升为扫北上将军。

Because of her courage, intelligence and ability, she was successful in many battles. Since she was also well versed in military strategy, soon she was promoted to the rank of commanding general.

Cheng An Jiang collaborated with daughter Wei Jiang on the text and illustrations for this Chinese folk-tale about a young woman who disguises herself as a male soldier and leads her country to victory. (From The Legend of Mu Lan: A Heroine of Ancient China.)

"A humble and hard-working gentleman, Mr. Jiang can illustrate a full-color children's picture book in two months. His current position as editor-in-chief of Morning Glory Publishing leaves him less time for writing and illustration, but Mr. Jiang is continuing to work on a series of bilingual Chinese/English picture books for the Victory Press 'Heroines in History' series. *The Legend of Mu Lan* was the first book, representing a female warrior. *Empress of China: Wu Ze Tian* depicts a female ruler. The third book in the series, *China's Most Famous Mother,* portrays a single mother who raises one of the world's greatest philosophers."*

*　*　*

JONELL (Kingsriter Kratoska), Lynne 1956-

Personal

Born November 1, 1956, in Little Falls, MN; daughter of Arvid (a pastor) and Marian (an organist and music teacher; maiden name, Menzie) Kingsriter; married Bill Kratoska (a mechanical engineer), July 22, 1978; children: Chris, Rob. *Education:* Attended University of Minnesota; University of Colorado, B.S., 1979. *Politics:* Independent. *Religion:* Lutheran. *Hobbies and other interests:* Music, sailing, travel, and volunteering.

Addresses

Home—615 Narcissus Lane, Plymouth, MN, 55447.

Career

City of Lakewood, Lakewood, Colorado, graphic designer, 1980-81; Boulder Public Library, Boulder, Colorado, director of graphics, 1981-82; City of Boulder, Boulder, Colorado, director of graphics, 1982-83; freelance artist and writer, 1983—. *Member:* Society of Children's Book Writers and Illustrators.

Writings

Mommy Go Away!, illustrated by Petra Mathers, G. P. Putnam's Sons, 1997.
I Need a Snake, illustrated by Petra Mathers, G. P. Putnam's Sons, 1998.
It's My Birthday, Too!, illustrated by Petra Mathers, G. P. Putnam's Sons, 1999.
Let's Play Rough!, illustrated by Ted Rand, G. P. Putnam's Sons, 2000.
Mom Pie, illustrated by Petra Mathers, G. P. Putnam's Sons, 2001.
I Can Too Help!, illustrated by Petra Mathers, G. P. Putnam's Sons, in press.

Work in Progress

Picture books *Wake Up!, Dad's Day,* and *When Mommy Got Lost;* fantasy adventure novels for middle graders, *Door to Dyaden,* and *Return to Dyaden.*

Lynne Jonell

Sidelights

Lynne Jonell told *SATA:* "I have fond memories of a little corner in my childhood bedroom. If I opened my closet door very wide, a small triangular space was enclosed behind it; just the right size for me, my crayons, and a piece of paper. There, in a place all my own, I made my first drawings. The busy household washed like a thundering surf all around me, but I had a small island all my own where I had what every writer and artist needs—privacy.

"Later on, I found another space—behind the overstuffed chair in my big sister's room. She had on her shelf an old, tattered copy of Beatrix Potter's *Peter Rabbit;* what a find! I couldn't read all the words yet, but I understood the pictures. I shall never forget the picture of Benjamin Bunny's father walking on top of the garden wall with a switch, looking for his son. My sister Kathy, tolerant as long as I was quiet, would do her homework at the desk, or put up her hair . . . it was nice to have her companionable but silent presence. Now and then she would tell me it was time to get out, but I always found my way back again.

"By the time I was school age, I had outgrown these two corners, and needed a new one. I found it in a little storage area beneath the stairs. There was a clothes-bar across the front where long coats and dresses were hung, and they made a sort of curtain, hiding the recess behind.

But if you had been invited, you could have pushed past the coats to find yourself in a small and cozy hideaway, carpeted with thick rugs, lit by my old nursery lamp, with a large floor cushion, a tiny table, and an orange-crate bookshelf filled with old copies of *Highlights* and *Boy's Life*.

"I felt loved and accepted in my family, but there was something very appealing about having a world of my own. And so I would go there often, taking a favorite book, and plunge into piracy with Captain Hook, or stumble upon magic with the Bastable children, or find myself drawn into the enchantment that was Narnia. I loved all kinds of books, but fantasy was my meat and drink, and my golden ticket to wonders.

"When I was in grade school, I shared a bed with my little sister, Boni. Boni was lighter than I, with the result that when we shared one mattress, she would roll right down next to me and stay there, a little bundle of a toddler with a habit of elbowing me in her sleep. To get her to stay on her side of the bed (always a difficult task, because she *liked* cuddling right up next to me), I would tell her stories. If she rolled down next to me, the story would stop. She was my first and most appreciative audience, and later I would write down little tales that I had made up, illustrate them, and give them to her. She liked every story I ever thought of, and asked me for more . . . . I did not appreciate this enough at the time, of course, and no one has been so uncritical since.

"I had a third grade teacher, Marlene Glaus, of whom I was very fond. Miss Glaus encouraged me in my writing and drawing, even when little pictures began showing up on all my school papers . . . and once showed me a special drawer in which she said she would keep any story or poem or piece of art that I wanted to do just for fun. In later years, I would visit her now and then, and one time mentioned that I was planning to be an artist. She said, 'Really? I always thought you would be a writer.' And I think it was from that time on that I seriously thought of myself as someone who would one day write books. What is more, I didn't want to write just any books—I wanted to write for children. Books had been such a wonderful gift to me as a child, and had filled my life with such riches, that I thought it would be the most delightful thing in the world to give that gift back to other children someday.

"I knew that writing was a chancy occupation, and not one I could count on to pay the bills. So I studied advertising and journalism in college, thinking that I could use my skills as an artist in the advertising business and write on the side, hoping to be published someday. I wrote three middle grade novels in my twenties—long ones—which garnered the usual number of rejection slips from every publisher in New York. My husband, Bill, read them faithfully, and never once told me I was wasting my time. But it wasn't until I had my first child that I set aside the fantasy novels that I loved so much and turned my attention to picture books.

"When I was thirty, I took a writing class from Jane Resh Thomas, an established children's author living in Minneapolis. And when I read one of my very simple picture books in class—I think it was *Let's Play Rough!*—she said what I thought was an interesting thing. 'Lynne,' she said, 'you have an unusual gift. You can think like a toddler.'

"I wasn't sure this was a compliment! After all, I thought I had grown up a long time before. But I *was* truly fascinated with watching my two small sons. I saw with amusement, and great sympathy, that what Christopher and Robbie wanted more than anything was total world domination. Quite simply, each of my children was born with an instinctive desire to rule the world—or at least the little part of it that they could see—and it was my sad but necessary task to let them know that they couldn't. Worse than that, they couldn't rule me or their father.

"Poor Chris. Poor Rob. Those little boys wanted *everything*—they wanted to cross the street without holding my hand, and wear shorts in the winter, and eat spaghetti upside down. They wanted to sing Batman songs in church, and get a new toy every day, and they did *not* want me telling them what to do. I kept having to say 'No,' but secretly I wished I didn't have to because I understood so completely what it was to want my own way, every day, every minute, all the time. Maybe I really *am* a toddler at heart . . . even if I don't have screaming tantrums, I know what it is to want something passionately, and know I can't have it, and wonder if I will ever get it.

"So I decided to give my children, in fantasy, what I could not give them in reality. In *Mommy Go Away!*, I let Christopher be big, while I got small. In *I Need a Snake,* I had Robbie's pretend snakes turn into the real ones he so desperately wanted."

In *Mommy Go Away!*, Jonell's first book, Christopher's mommy shrinks and is set afloat on a toy boat in the bathtub. As Mommy expresses her fears about being so small, Christopher reassures her and tells her to have a good time with the other small mommies. Mommy is returned to full size after she admits that it is hard to be small. A *Kirkus Reviews* critic described *Mommy Go Away!* as, "a highly original book that will strike a chord in every child's experience, and one that parents will enjoy immensely." *School Library Journal* critic Lucy Rafael commented, "this story will draw a smile from independent preschoolers who hope the adults in their lives can remember what it means to be small," and *Booklist* critic Hazel Rochman stated, "toddlers and their caregivers will enjoy the gleeful role reversal in this picture book."

I Need a Snake details young Robbie's desire to own a pet snake. Robbie's mother does not want a snake, so to satisfy the boy's "need" she reads him books about snakes, takes him to a museum, a pet store, and the zoo. Robbie still wants a snake, but Mommy says he must wait until he has a house of his own. Robbie then creates his own snakes out of a shoelace, a belt, and a jump rope; when Mommy is scared of these snakes, Robbie tells her that's why she needs him. Angela J. Reynolds, writing for *School Library Journal*, remarked that, "this book is a true commentary on a loving parent-child relationship.... The boy's creative spirit will win the applause of the many children who have unsuccessfully begged for a pet," and a *Publishers Weekly* critic wrote, "Jonell understands the passions of boyhood, and her observations harbor a dry wit that parents will recognize." *Booklist* critic Hazel Rochman described *I Need a Snake* by saying "the simple, immediate text ... express[es] the push and pull in a loving family and the child's natural attraction for what makes grown-ups shudder."

"As my children got older," Jonell told *SATA*, "they began to use fantasy in the same way. Of course, each wanted to be the favorite son, shining and glorious in his parents' eyes, while the other was cast into the dungeon, humiliated by the realization that he was really not much of a son, and no great shakes as a brother either, and that everything that went wrong was probably his fault. Realizing that they could never quite accomplish this, the boys instead played a game they called 'Master and Slave,' which later changed to 'Puppy and Master.' One boy had complete control (as master), and the other was the puppy, who had to follow the master's every command. Only, strangely enough, it never quite worked out that way—because the puppy would invariably get into some kind of trouble, or whine and scratch at the door to be taken for a walk, or bite at the master's pant leg, and generally make a miserable nuisance of itself. This game turned up in *It's My Birthday, Too!*, where Christopher had a birthday, and Robbie wanted one, too, and had to turn into a puppy to get invited to the party.

"I guess I am still writing fantasy, when I think about it. And in the other books I am currently working on, there is always an element of fantasy—some wonderful surprise that is exciting and fun, but doesn't always work out the way it is supposed to. Come to think of it, maybe that's how I see life. It seems to meander along in its old boring way, when suddenly, around the corner, is something wonderful or terrifying or tender and joyous or incredibly gut-wrenching—but you never know. You can't predict it!

"You can't predict writing, either. You can think you know what you are going to write, and have an outline and a plan, but it seldom works out the way you think it will. Once I put pen to paper, it's like leaping around the corner into the unknown. I never know what is going to happen. Just last week I sat down to write, in my nice, safe office—and before I was done, I was lost in the ancient city of Ur, making friends with a prince, climbing a ziggurat and running for my life!

"Now *that's* a fun way to spend a morning."

Works Cited

Rafael, Lucy, review of *Mommy Go Away!*, School Library Journal, December, 1997, p. 94.

Review of *Mommy Go Away!*, Kirkus Reviews, August 15, 1997, p. 1036.

Review of *I Need a Snake*, Publishers Weekly, May 11, 1998, p. 66.

Reynolds, Angela J., review of *I Need a Snake*, School Library Journal, June, 1998, p. 111.

Rochman, Hazel, review of *I Need a Snake*, Booklist, May 15, 1998, p. 1632.

Rochman, Hazel, review of *Mommy Go Away!*, Booklist, October 15, 1997, p. 415.

For More Information See

PERIODICALS

Horn Book, May-June, 1999, pp. 316-17.
New York Times Book Review, April 1, 1999, p. 33.
Publishers Weekly, March 1, 1999, p. 68.*

K

KILCHER, Jewel 1974-
(Jewel)

Personal

Born May 23, 1974, in Payson, UT; daughter of Atz (a singer) and Nedra (a glass artist; maiden name, Carroll) Kilcher. *Education:* Attended Interlochen Fine Arts Academy.

Addresses

Home—San Diego, CA. *Office*—c/o HarperCollins, 10 East 53rd St., New York, NY 10022. *E-mail*—jeweljk@aol.com.

Career

Singer, songwriter, and poet. Began playing in San Diego coffeehouses, 1993; signed to Atlantic Records, 1994; released debut LP, *Pieces of You,* 1995; released second album, *Spirit,* 1998.

Writings

A Night without Armor (poetry), HarperCollins (New York City), 1998.

Work in Progress

An autobiography.

Sidelights

Folk singer Jewel was offered a $2-million contract by a major publishing house to write her memoir and book of poetry. Twenty-three years old when the latter, *A Night without Armor,* was published in 1998, Jewel had already attracted a cult-like following for her debut album, *Pieces of You.* She wrote nearly all of the songs on the album—including the hits "Who Will Save Your Soul?" and "Foolish Games"—between the ages of 17 and 19, and the album went on to sell several million copies in the years following its release.

Although she was born in Utah, Jewel and her family moved to an 80-acre farm in Homer, Alaska, when she was a very young child. Her childhood home had neither electricity nor indoor plumbing; heat came from a coal stove. Her parents, Atz and Nedra, were both folk singers, and released two albums in the late 1970s. Thus Jewel learned how to play guitar at an early age, and her mother encouraged her and her two brothers to sit at the kitchen table and write poetry. When she was eight, her parents divorced, and Jewel stayed with her father. She also began performing with him in bars and local halls, and the coarser side of human nature she witnessed there inspired her to write poetry, and later, her own songs. After attending Interlochen Fine Arts Academy in Michigan for a time, she wound up in San Diego living in her Volkswagen van. In 1993, she started playing in a local coffeehouse, and from there was discovered by an entertainment-industry executive. Atlantic Records signed her in 1994, released *Pieces of You* in 1995, and put her on tour for the next two years. Jancee Dunn, writing in *Rolling Stone,* described Jewel's million-selling debut album as "a folky collection of 14 spare, unpolished songs," and because of Jewel's relative youthfulness when she wrote them, "the album has a hopeful, tentative feel to it." Dunn, who interviewed the singer for the article, added that "Jewel will tell you herself that some of the songs are 'dorky.' . . . Part of her appeal, however, is that she is a kind of Everygirl. The downside of this is that many of Jewel's lyrics sound like . . . well, like the journal scribblings of a teenage girl," Dunn wrote.

Jewel's first book, a collection of poetry entitled *A Night without Armor,* was mined from her journal entries dating back to her fifteenth year. The title comes from her sentiment that cynical behavior and attitudes can be shed after dark, when the business of the day is done. Some of the poems reflect her early memories of growing up in rustic surroundings—the birth of a calf in the middle of the night, wolves nearby—and later ones

reflect the difficult and sometimes desperate lives she encountered as a kid playing in bars. "Grimshaw," for instance, is about a Vietnam veteran she knew who eventually killed himself. Jewel's father was also a veteran of the same war, and she writes of his experiences in her verse as well. In lighter moments, she waxes lyrical on subjects more accessible to her readership, such as first love and the heartache of a breakup. *A Night without Armor* immediately landed on the bestseller lists at its debut, but received little critical attention. Tim Appelo, a reviewer for the online retailer Amazon.com, remarked: "Jewel Kilcher was the first to admit that [*A Night without Armor*] would not have been published if her dazzling debut album ... hadn't sold 10 million copies.... But—shockingly!—Jewel's book of poetry is sold by celeb-poet standards, and a fair bit of it is actually sort of readable in its own right."

Works Cited

Appelo, Tim, review of *A Night without Armor,* http://www.amazon.com., August, 1998.

Dunn, Jancee, "Cosmic Girl," *Rolling Stone,* May 15, 1997, p. 36-41, 121, 124.

For More Information See

PERIODICALS

Entertainment Weekly, May 29, 1998, p. 70.
Time, July 21, 1997, pp. 66-67.

*   *   *

KOLLER, Jackie French 1948-

Personal

Born March 8, 1948, in Derby, CT; daughter of Ernest James (an electrical engineer) and Margaret (Hayes) French; married George J. Koller (president of a hospital), July 11, 1970; children: Kerri Mercier, Ryan, Devin. *Education:* University of Connecticut, B.A., 1970.

Addresses

Home—Westfield, MA. *Agent*—Ginger Knowlton, Curtis Brown Ltd., 10 Astor Place, New York, NY. *E-mail*—jackiek@aol.com.

Career

Writer. *Member:* Society of Children's Book Writers and Illustrators.

Awards, Honors

Best Books for Young Adults, American Library Association (ALA), for *The Primrose Way* and *The Falcon;* Notable Book, ALA, Pick of the Lists, American Booksellers Association, and Teachers' Choice, International Reading Association (IRA), all for *A Place to Call*

Jackie French Koller

Home; Books for the Teen Age, New York Public Library, for *Nothing to Fear, If I Had One Wish...,* *The Last Voyage of the Misty Day,* and *The Primrose Way;* Teachers' Choice, IRA, and Young Adults' Choice, IRA, both for *Nothing to Fear;* Recommended Books for Reluctant Readers, Young Adult Library Services Association (YALSA), ALA, for *If I Had One Wish...* and *The Last Voyage of the Misty Day;* International Honor Book, Association of School Librarians, Honor Book, Bank Street College Children's Book Committee, and Blue Ribbon designation, *Bulletin of the Center for Children's Books,* all for *No Such Thing;* Junior Library Guild selections, for *The Last Voyage of the Misty Day, No Such Thing,* and *One Monkey Too Many.*

Writings

FOR CHILDREN

Impy for Always, illustrated by Carol Newsom, Little, Brown, 1989.

Mole and Shrew, illustrated by Stella Ormai, Atheneum, 1991.

Fish Fry Tonight!, illustrated by Catharine O'Neill, Crown, 1992.

Mole and Shrew Step Out, illustrated by Stella Ormai, Atheneum, 1992.

The Dragonling, illustrated by Judith Mitchell, Archway Minstrel, 1996.

A Dragon in the Family, illustrated by Judith Mitchell, Archway Minstrel, 1996.

No Such Thing, illustrated by Betsy Lewin, Boyds Mills Press, 1997.

Dragon Quest, Archway Minstrel, 1997.

Mole and Shrew, All Year Through, illustrated by John Beder, Random House, 1997.

Dragons of Krad, Archway Minstrel, 1997.

Dragon Trouble, Archway Minstrel, 1997.

Dragons and Kings, illustrated by Judith Mitchell, Archway Minstrel, 1998.

One Monkey Too Many, illustrated by Lynn Munsinger, Harcourt, 1999.

Bouncing on the Bed, illustrated by Anna Grossnickle Hines, Orchard, 1999.

Nickommoh! A Narragansett Thanksgiving Celebration, illustrated by Marcia Sewall, Atheneum, 1999.

The Promise, Knopf, 1999.

FOR YOUNG ADULTS

Nothing to Fear, Harcourt, 1991.

If I Had One Wish..., Little, Brown, 1991.

The Last Voyage of the Misty Day, Atheneum, 1992.

The Primrose Way, Harcourt, 1992.

A Place to Call Home, Atheneum, 1995.

The Falcon, Atheneum, 1998.

OTHER

Also contributor of the long poem *What If?,* to *Cobblestone;* "Home Early," published in *Spider,* 1994; "'Oink!' Said the Cat," published in *Ladybug,* 1996; and the short story "Brother Can You Spare a Dream?" in *Time Capsule,* an anthology edited by Don Gallo, Bantam, 1999.

Work in Progress

Someday, a historical novel set in 1930s Massachusetts, for middle graders and young adults; picture and chapter books.

Sidelights

Jackie French Koller has spent her life immersed in stories: listening as her mother read to her when she was a child; conjuring up make-believe adventures to entertain herself as a schoolgirl; and developing a lifetime habit of avid reading. As a young mother, Koller found herself steeped in books again, this time for the benefit of her infant daughter, Kerri. Like giving birth many times over, the stories that Koller had inside her began emerging. "At first I wrote them for Kerri and the two little brothers who followed her, but gradually I began to share them with others, and people began to encourage me to try publication," Koller said in an interview with Diane Andreassi for *Authors and Artists for Young Adults.* After her youngest child was out of diapers, Koller began attending writers' conferences where she learned her trade. Six years and numerous rejection slips later, she sold *Impy for Always,* a chapter book, and also her first novel, *Nothing to Fear.*

Koller's determination and perseverance is an inheritance from her parents, who met at the end of World War II, married soon after, and moved to Connecticut. Koller's mother, Margaret, was one of a family of nine children who grew up in poverty in New York City during the Great Depression. Margaret's father was an abusive alcoholic who rarely worked, and her mother supported their family by working as a janitor. Margaret's family was often hungry and poorly clothed, so as a sophomore in high school Koller's mother dropped out of school to work full-time so she could help support her siblings. Koller's father, Ernest, also endured hard times as a child. Ernest was a teen when his father, an alcoholic, was sent to prison for killing a woman in a hit-and-run accident.

After Koller's grandfather was released from jail, her paternal grandparents went through a number of separations and reconciliations until they finally divorced. Determined to make a better life for himself, Ernest graduated from high school and put himself through engineering school by working four jobs. During World War II, Koller's father joined the Navy as an officer. "Needless to say, my parents didn't have the best role models in the marriage or parenting department, and they hit many snags along the way, but they tried hard to give us children the best life they possibly could, and my memories of early childhood are good ones," Koller told Andreassi.

As a youngster, Koller developed the ability to entertain and amuse herself. "I didn't have any imaginary friends per se, but I developed a vivid imagination and was forever pretending," she recalled. "I would dream up great adventures for my siblings and friends to act out, and I, of course, was always the star, the hero, or, one might say, the main character, for as I look back now I can see that those early games of pretend were my first attempts at creating stories." A tomboy who was quite bossy around children her age, Koller described herself as "the one who came up with the ideas for what we should do and how we should do it." Koller was very quiet, however, around adults because she was raised with the philosophy that children should be seen and not heard: "I was a great listener, though, and loved to creep to the top of the stairs and eavesdrop when my parents were having guests or parties."

As soon as Koller could read, books became a constant and favorite pastime. She loved to curl up in a cozy corner or in the crook of a tree and read for hours. Among her favorites were books that her mother loved: *Black Beauty, Heidi, Little Women* and fairy tales. "I could never get enough fairy tales," Koller recalled. As a youngster, school work came easily to her, and she was a straight A student. Later, however, she became somewhat bored and disenchanted with her school work, and her grades dropped—although rarely below a B. "These days I would have been put in accelerated classes and challenged, and I would probably have had a much better school experience, but in the post-war years there were thirty-five kids in a class and little time or money for special programs," Koller noted.

As an adolescent Koller was tall, bright, and tomboyish; this did not put her on the "most popular list" in school. By the time she entered sixth grade, she had sprouted to five foot eight inches tall, which made her the tallest student in the class. "To make matters worse, I got 103 on my first science test and word spread that not only was I a giant, I was a brain, too—the kiss of death for a girl back then," Koller told Andreassi. She had a hard time making friends and finally connected with other

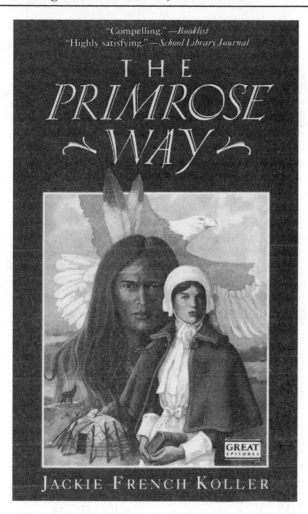

"Compelling."—*Booklist*
"Highly satisfying."—*School Library Journal*

THE PRIMROSE WAY

JACKIE FRENCH KOLLER

After sixteen-year-old Rebekah Hall befriends members of the Pawtucket tribe, she begins to question her Puritan heritage in Koller's 1992 historical novel. (Cover illustration by John Edens.)

misfits who were also struggling. In high school, Koller remembers, she was often the last to be chosen by team captains, sat out dance after dance at school events, and never was asked for a date. Koller took solace in books and nature. Living near woods, beautiful ponds, and streams, she went hiking alone after school and found herself daydreaming at length, making up stories in which she was beautiful, popular, glamorous, famous, mysterious—whatever she felt like at the time. She would return home, dive into a book, and lose herself in the story and characters, leaving all the pain of the real world behind.

During this time, Koller never dreamed of being a writer. "I didn't think it was something an ordinary person could do, and no one ever told me otherwise," Koller related in her interview with Andreassi. The author wrote well, but no teacher ever encouraged her to pursue writing as a career. In fact, it was her art work that drew the most attention, prompting Koller to contemplate a career as an animator. She considered art school, until her father convinced her that pursuing a career as an artist was a risky venture. Instead, Koller

enrolled at the University of Connecticut and studied interior design. While her coursework never really excited her, Koller began enjoying an active social life. She was no longer the tallest woman in class, and she finally fit in because being smart was admired in college. "I had friends and dates and was courted by the most prestigious sororities on campus, and had to pinch myself sometimes to see if I was still really me underneath," Koller recalled. She met George J. Koller her junior year, and the two were married in 1970. Her husband went on to graduate school, and Koller supported him by working in the insurance industry. The birth of the couple's first child, Kerri, prompted the beginnings of Koller's new career as a writer. As the author read to her infant child, her own imagination became rekindled and she began to write. At first she penned her stories solely for Kerri (and later Kerri's two younger brothers), but gradually Koller began to share them with others who encouraged her to get them published.

Koller's first novel, *Nothing to Fear,* is about an Irish immigrant family living in poverty in New York City during the Depression. The only family income is what Danny can make shining shoes and what his mother earns doing laundry. His father leaves town to seek work and Danny becomes the man of the house. Pregnant and weary, his mother loses her laundry work and Danny begins begging for food. The family finally gains relief, ironically, by helping a sick and hungry stranger who appears at their doorstep. *Voice of Youth Advocates* contributor Rosemary Moran described the story as "in turn depressing and enriching." Writing in *School Library Journal,* Ann Welton commended the novel's storyline and added that "numerous interesting supporting characters will hold readers' attention." A critic in *Kirkus Reviews* concluded that *Nothing to Fear* is an "involving account of the Great Depression ... conjuring an entire era from the heartaches and troubles of one struggling family."

Another of Koller's novels for young adults, *The Last Voyage of the Misty Day,* was inspired by her father's lifelong love of the sea and fascination with boats of all kinds. The story centers on Denny, who moves with her mother from New York City to the coast of Maine after her father's death. Struggling with a new climate and a sense of isolation, Denny meets her odd neighbor, Mr. Jones, who works endlessly repairing the wrecked boat that he has made his home. Zena Sutherland of the *Bulletin of the Center for Children's Books* commended the book's "dramatic ending," while other commentators offered a favorable assessment of the book's well-crafted characters.

By this time, Koller had begun to hone her own writing style and was building a tunnel to the publishing world. Her 1992 novel *The Primrose Way* tells of a sixteen-year-old girl, Rebekah Hall, who comes to live with her Puritan father in seventeenth-century Massachusetts. Pretending that she is converting the local Native Americans, Rebekah befriends Qunnequawese, the chief's niece. Their friendship awakens a cultural understanding between the two, and Rebekah's interest in the Native American way of life makes her question the Puritan salvation. Her problems worsen as she falls in love with the tribe's holy man, Mishannock. For Koller, getting inside the psyche of her characters meant learning the history and cultural mores of the time. "I try to find as much original source material as possible—diaries, journals, letters—and then I also read extensively, including ethno-historical studies on the people and times," Koller noted. Many commentators offered a favorable assessment of *The Primrose Way*. Esther Sinofsky wrote in *Voice of Youth Advocates* that Koller has written a "beautiful story" of Rebekah searching for her identity, with "carefully researched" scenes depicting early Massachusetts. A *Kirkus Reviews* critic proclaimed that Koller creates a vivid landscape that "successfully de-romanticizes the early settlers' struggles and avoids the absolutes (us-good, them bad)." *School Library Journal* contributor Barbara Chatton was equally impressed, remarking: "Koller's carefully researched book incorporates authentic language in a readable text."

Koller explored the foster care system, interviewing a social worker, before introducing her readers to Anna O'Dell in *A Place to Call Home*. In this novel, fifteen-year-old Anna returns home from school and finds her infant brother, Casey, screaming. Anna realizes that her alcoholic mother has left the family once again; this time, however, her mother is found drowned in a lake, having committed suicide. Anna is determined to keep her five-year-old sister, Mandy, and Casey together with her. Anna, who is biracial, shows her intelligence, strength, and determination to fight for "the greater good for her family," according to Hazel Moore in a review for *Voice of Youth Advocates*. Carolyn Noah, writing in *School Library Journal*, called *A Place to Call Home* an "eloquent depiction of impoverishment and courage," adding that the novel is "fast paced" and "compelling," with "satisfying social values." Merri Monks of *Booklist* praised the novel as a "finely written" exploration of the tragic results of sexual abuse and family rejection. In fact, these issues are Koller's main concern with society today. "We pay a lot of lip service to the importance of family values and education, but very little ever changes," Koller told Andreassi. "Children should be our number one national priority—their health, their well being, their education. Children's caregivers should be among the most highly respected and highly paid professions we have."

In *The Falcon,* published in 1998, Koller employs the format of a journal to reveal a secret about Luke, the novel's principal protagonist. Luke's self-destructive behavior lands him in a psychiatric hospital, where he must overcome a deep emotional scar on his way to recovery. "Koller's portrayal of a foolhardy teen who feels invincible is incredibly well drawn," asserted *School Library Journal* contributor Alison Follos, who added: "[Luke's] past seeps out surreptitiously, adding powerful impact to an already interesting life." Writing in *Booklist,* reviewer Roger Leslie maintained that "Luke's strong voice comes through quite believably

Fifteen-year-old Anna struggles alone to care for her two younger siblings after their alcoholic mother commits suicide. (Cover illustration by Elizabeth Sayles.)

throughout." *Kliatt* contributor Paula Rohrlick called *The Falcon* an "involving and often suspenseful tale."

Koller has also penned a number of well-received picture books for children, including *No Such Thing* and *One Monkey Too Many*. The former offers a unique twist on a familiar childhood fear: in *No Such Thing,* Howard has just moved with his family into a new home, but he cannot get to sleep because he is certain that there is a monster under his bed, and he summons his mother over and over in a futile attempt to convince her. Meanwhile, a little monster under Howard's bed cannot get to sleep because he is certain there is a boy on top of his bed, and he is also unable to convince his reassuring mother. Taking matters into their own hands, the little boy and monster meet and conspire to teach their mothers a lesson. "Any child who has been convinced of the presence of a monster at bedtime will feel vindicated by [this] satisfying story from Koller," maintained a *Kirkus Reviews* critic. The same commentator added: "This tautly told tale of two stern mothers who get their comeuppances is irresistible." *One Monkey Too Many* is a lively counting book centering on the adventures of vacationing monkeys. "Seven mischievous monkeys wreak havoc as 'one monkey too many' climbs first onto a bike made for one, then into a golf cart for two, then into a canoe for three, and so on," noted *Horn Book* reviewer Marilyn Bousquin, who praised the book's "infectious, rollercoaster rhythm." *School Library Journal* contributor Lauralyn Persson similarly asserted: "The infectious rhythm of the text never falters.... Spilling, breaking, dropping, and crashing have never been this much fun." A *Publishers Weekly* critic dubbed *One Monkey Too Many* a "mischievous rhyming and counting book" that "revels in excess," and commended Koller for "turn[ing] the childhood impulse to join in the fun into a tale that will appeal to the imp in everyone."

Koller, whose hobbies include making gingerbread houses, lives and writes at home, on ten acres of mountaintop land in Western Massachusetts with her husband, her youngest son, and two Labrador retrievers. She writes at least seven hours a day, four times a week. "I talk to myself a lot," Koller revealed in her interview with Andreassi. "That's the only way I can describe it. I get an idea for a story and I decide on the main character and then I walk around having conversations with that character until I know him or her well enough to start putting his/her story down on paper." Koller noted that she always keeps her audience in mind while she is writing, and that she often stops and asks herself if the story is going to hold the interest of a reader, and whether or not it is a subject to which a young audience can relate. "Sometimes I start out thinking I'm writing a picture book and then realize that it's getting too involved and sophisticated, so I'll start over with an older audience in mind and write the story as a chapter book or novel," Koller explained. "I hope young readers will see themselves or others that they know in my books and that my books will encourage a love of reading."

Works Cited

Bousquin, Marilyn, review of *One Monkey Too Many, Horn Book,* March-April, 1999, p. 194.

Chatton, Barbara, review of *The Primrose Way, School Library Journal,* September, 1992, p. 278.

Follos, Alison, review of *The Falcon, School Library Journal*, May, 1998, p. 142.

Koller, Jackie French, interview with Diane Andreassi for *Authors and Artists for Young Adults,* Volume 28, Gale, 1999.

Leslie, Roger, review of *The Falcon, Booklist,* April 15, 1998, p. 1436.

Monks, Merri, review of *A Place to Call Home, Booklist,* October 15, 1995, p. 396.

Moore, Hazel, review of *A Place to Call Home, Voice of Youth Advocates,* February, 1996, p. 373.

Moran, Rosemary, review of *Nothing to Fear, Voice of Youth Advocates,* October, 1991, p. 228.

Noah, Carolyn, review of *A Place to Call Home, School Library Journal,* October, 1995, p. 155.

Review of *No Such Thing, Kirkus Reviews,* January 1, 1997, p. 60.

Review of *Nothing to Fear, Kirkus Reviews,* March 1, 1991.

Review of *One Monkey Too Many, Publishers Weekly,* April 19, 1999, p. 72.

Persson, Lauralyn, review of *One Monkey Too Many, School Library Journal,* May, 1999, p. 92.

Review of *The Primrose Way, Kirkus Reviews,* September 15, 1992, p. 1189.

Rohrlick, Paula, review of *The Falcon, Kliatt,* July, 1998.

Sinofsky, Esther, review of *The Primrose Way, Voice of Youth Advocates,* December, 1992, p. 280.

Sutherland, Zena, review of *The Last Voyage of the Misty Day, Bulletin of the Center for Children's Books,* April, 1992, p. 211.

Welton, Ann, review of *Nothing to Fear, School Library Journal,* May, 1991, p. 93.

For More Information See

PERIODICALS

Bulletin of the Center for Children's Books, March, 1991, p. 168; March, 1997, p. 237.

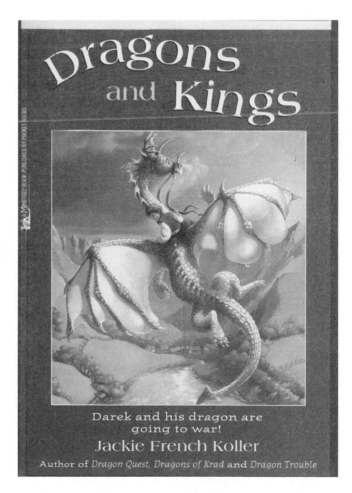

Darek, his friends, and their fathers return from the mountains to discover that their village has been taken over by a tyrant in the sixth book in Koller's "Dragonling" series. (Cover illustration by Judith Mitchell.)

Publishers Weekly, December 30, 1996, p. 67.
School Library Journal, June, 1992, p. 116; June, 1997, p. 95.

L

LANIER, Sterling E(dmund) 1927-

Personal

Born December 18, 1927, in New York, NY; married Martha Hanna Pelton, 1961 (divorced, 1978); married Ann Miller McGregor, 1979; children: (first marriage) a son and daughter. *Education:* Harvard University, A.B., 1951; attended University of Pennsylvania, 1953-58.

Addresses

Home—Sarasota, FL. *Agent*—Curtis Brown Ltd., 575 Madison Avenue, New York, NY 10022.

Career

Winterthur Museum, Switzerland, research historian, 1958-60; John C. Winston Company, editor, 1961; Chilton Books, editor, 1961-62, 1965-67; Macrae-Smith Company, editor, 1963-64; writer and sculptor, 1967—. *Military service:* Served in World War II and the Korean War.

Awards, Honors

Charles W. Follett award, 1970, for *The War for the Lot.*

Writings

The War for the Lot (for children), Follett (Chicago, IL), 1969.
The Peculiar Exploits of Brigadier Ffellowes (short stories), Walker, 1972.
Hiero's Journey, Chilton (Radnor, PA), 1973.
Science Fiction Special (34): Hiero's Journey; The War for the Lot, Sidgwick and Jackson (London), 1981.
The Unforsaken Hero, Ballantine, 1983.
Menace under Marswood, Ballantine, 1983.
Hiero Desteen (omnibus), Doubleday, 1984.
The Curious Quests of Brigadier Ffellowes (short stories), D. M. Grant (West Kingston, RI), 1986.

Sidelights

The author of works that are most often a blend of fantasy and science fiction, Sterling E. Lanier has been praised by critics for his storytelling abilities. Lanier's novels frequently center on themes of war, nuclear holocaust, nature, the environment, and the eternal quest for knowledge, while occasionally employing elements characteristic of medieval romances. In other genres, Lanier has written a highly regarded children's book and two collections of short stories that parody Victorian tall-tales.

One of Lanier's best-known works is *Hiero's Journey,* a post-nuclear holocaust tale set in the Metz Republic of Kanda (Canada). Subtitled "A Romance of the Future," the story follows the exploits of Per Hiero Desteen, who works against the "Unclean"—a group of evil, radiation-scarred scientists who caused the nuclear holocaust and who are trying to rule the world. Hiero hopes to find the long-lost "computers" that can give him knowledge of the past. Other key figures in the book are the maiden Luchare; Brother Aldo, a priest from the Brotherhood of the Eleventh Commandment (which is "Thou shalt not despoil the earth and the life thereon"); and Hiero's talking animal friends, the bear Gorm and moose Klootz.

A *Publishers Weekly* critic found much to commend in *Hiero's Journey,* asserting that Lanier "has created his unique milieu with loving care .... and drives his anti-technology message home without preaching." Lawrence R. Ries, in an entry on Lanier in *St. James Guide to Science Fiction Writers,* noted that Lanier "is at his best when weaving a suspenseful tale," adding: "the world he creates, filled with radiation-induced mutants, ancient, knowing wizards, and fur-covered dwarves, lives fully in the imagination and allows the reader to partake fully in the suspenseful quest."

A sequel, *The Unforsaken Hero,* was anticipated by Lanier's readers to reveal Hiero's fate. In the sequel, Hiero, now married to Luchare, is kidnapped by the Unclean, who neutralize his telepathic powers. His escape and resulting travels conclude with a battle between the good forces of the Metz and the evil Unclean. A *Kirkus Reviews* writer described the battle: "Good (with their talking cats, bears, moose, etc.) mop up the Bad (with their nasty talking rats, dogs, and other beasts)." Despite a Metz triumph, Roland Green of *Booklist* concluded that "the ending of this book hints that Lanier is now resolved on a saga...." A reviewer for *Publishers Weekly* similarly asserted that "readers of this rousing adventure will eagerly await" the next novel. Another installment in the Hiero series is yet to be written.

In *The War for the Lot* Lanier explores the theme of ecological warfare on a smaller scale in a story for middle graders. Alec March, a boy visiting a Connecticut farm, becomes involved in a struggle between woodland animals that live on a wooded piece of land, known as "The Lot," and an invading group of evil rats who come from the town dump. Alec discovers that he can understand the woodland animals because he has special telepathic powers to communicate with them. Although the various creatures—including skunks, foxes, owls, mice, and a cat—are natural enemies, they join to fight a greater, mutual opponent. Aileen Pippett praised *The War for the Lot* in the *New York Times Book Review,* citing Lanier's "beautiful writing" and "sound observation of animal habits," as well as the book's "plain moral and a happy peace at the end." Readers will "relax and enjoy the depiction of the individual animals," wrote Jean C. Thomson in *Library Journal.* *Booklist* reviewer Ruth P. Bull asserted that *The War for the Lot* is "marked by fine writing, authentically and convincingly drawn animal characters, and a satisfying conclusion." In addition to such favorable critical attention, *The War for the Lot* received the Charles W. Follett award in 1970.

Lanier's two short-story collections chronicle the adventures of a retired English soldier, Brigadier Ffellowes. As narrated by Ffellowes in the comfort of his men's club, the stories parody Victorian tall-tales that use the device of a story within a story within a story. Lanier fills these sketches with fanciful monsters and supernatural powers. The collection *The Peculiar Exploits of Brigadier Ffellowes,* with the exception of one previously unpublished story, is made up of stories originally published in *The Magazine of Fantasy and Science Fiction.* The collection was deemed "charmingly old-fashioned" by Charles de Lint in *Fantasy Review,* who continued, "but there's nothing old-fashioned about his prose.... Lanier's contemporary voice, rather than any stilted attempt at turn-of-the-century prose, brings a fresh breath of air into this old form of storytelling." A *Publishers Weekly* commentator maintained that Lanier gives evidence of "a straight-faced sense of humor" as he "gently parodies" the Victorian form. In 1986, Lanier expanded on this series of stories with *The Curious Quests of Brigadier Ffellowes.*

Before he became a full-time writer and sculptor in 1967, Lanier worked as a research historian at the Winterthur Museum and as an editor at various publishing companies, including Chilton Books and the Ma-crae-Smith Company. Some of his miniature sculptures are included in the permanent collection of the Smithsonian Institution. Lanier has said that he is often inspired to write while sculpting.

Works Cited

Bull, Ruth P., review of *The War for the Lot, Booklist,* March 15, 1970, p. 928.

de Lint, Charles, review of *The Curious Quests of Brigadier Ffellowes, Fantasy Review,* January, 1987, p. 39.

Green, Roland, review of *The Unforsaken Hiero, Booklist,* July, 1983, p. 1389.

Review of *Hiero's Journey, Publishers Weekly,* April 30, 1973, p. 54.

Review of *The Peculiar Exploits of Brigadier Ffellowes, Publishers Weekly,* March 6, 1972, p. 57.

Pippett, Aileen, review of *The War for the Lot, New York Times Book Review,* November 9, 1969, Part 2, p. 30.

Ries, Lawrence R., entry on Lanier in *St. James Guide to Science Fiction Writers,* St. James Press, 1996, pp. 547-48.

Thomson, Jean C., review of *The War for the Lot, Library Journal,* May 15, 1970, p. 1945.

Review of *The Unforsaken Hiero, Kirkus Reviews,* March 15, 1983, p. 340.

Review of *The Unforsaken Hiero, Publishers Weekly,* April 15, 1983, p. 44.*

*   *   *

LANTZ, Fran
See LANTZ, Francess (Lin)

*   *   *

LANTZ, Francess (Lin) 1952-
(Fran Lantz; Lance Franklin, a pseudonym; Franklin W. Dixon, Jamie Suzanne, house pseudonyms)

Personal

Born August 27, 1952, in Trenton, NJ; daughter of Frederick W. (an architect) and Dorthea (a secretary/treasurer; maiden name, Lingrell) Lantz; married John M. Landsberg (a physician/filmmaker), 1983; children: Preston. *Education:* Dickinson College, B.A., 1974; Simmons College, M.L.S., 1975. *Hobbies and other interests:* "I like to ride horses, kayak, hike, boogie board, and visit schools to talk to kids about my books."

Addresses

Office—P.O. Box 23234, Santa Barbara, CA 93121. *Agent*—Ashley Grayson, 1342 18th St., San Pedro, CA 90732. *E-mail*—writer@silcom.com.

Francess Lantz

Career

Children's book writer. Dedham Public Library, Dedham, MA, children's librarian, 1976-79. Speaker at schools and conferences; teacher of writing courses for adults and children at Santa Barbara City College and Montecito Union School, 1989—. *Member:* Society of Children's Book Writers and Illustrators, California School Librarian Association, California Reading Association.

Awards, Honors

Best Books for Reluctant Readers, American Library Association (ALA), for *Double Play;* Pick of the List, *Booklist,* for *Dear Celeste, My Life Is a Mess;* Best Books for Young Adults, ALA, Books for the Teen Age, New York Public Library, and Young Adult Choice, International Reading Association, all for *Someone to Love;* recommended books, *Children's Book Insider,* 1998, for *Fade Far Away* and *Stepsister from the Planet Weird.*

Writings

YOUNG-ADULT NOVELS

(As Francess Lin Lantz) *Good Rockin' Tonight,* Addison-Wesley, 1982.
A Love Song for Becky, Berkley, 1983.
Surfer Girl, Berkley, 1983.
Rock 'n' Roll Romance, Berkley, 1984.
Senior Blues, Berkley, 1984.
(As Fran Lantz) *Making It on Our Own,* Dell, 1986.
(As Fran Lantz) *Can't Stop Us Now,* Dell, 1986.
Someone to Love, Avon, 1997.
Fade Far Away, Avon, 1998.

MIDDLE-GRADE NOVELS

Woodstock Magic, Avon, 1986.
Star Struck, Avon, 1986.
All Shook Up, Avon, 1987.
The Truth about Making Out, Bantam, 1990.
Mom, There's a Pig in My Bed!, Avon, 1991.
Dear Celeste, My Life Is a Mess (sequel to *The Truth about Making Out*), Bantam, 1991.
Randy's Raiders, Troll, 1994.
Neighbors from Outer Space, Troll, 1996.
Spinach with Chocolate Sauce, Troll, 1997.
Stepsister from the Planet Weird, Random House, 1997.
The Case of the Missing Mummy ("New Adventures of Mary-Kate and Ashley" series), Scholastic, 1998.

"VARSITY COACH" SERIES; UNDER PSEUDONYM LANCE FRANKLIN

Take Down, Bantam, 1987.
Double Play, Bantam, 1987.

"SWEET VALLEY TWINS" SERIES; UNDER HOUSE PSEUDONYM JAMIE SUZANNE

Center of Attention, Bantam, 1988.
Jessica's Bad Idea, Bantam, 1989.

"HARDY BOYS" SERIES; UNDER HOUSE PSEUDONYM FRANKLIN W. DIXON

Danger Unlimited, Pocket Books, 1993.
Mystery with a Dangerous Beat, Pocket Books, 1994.

OTHER

(With husband, John Landsberg, and April Rhodes) *The One and Only, No-Holds-Barred, Tell-It-Like-It-Is Santa Barbara Restaurant Guide,* Elan Press, 1988.
Rock, Rap, and Rad: How to Be a Rock or Rap Star, photographs by John Landsberg, Avon, 1992.
Be a Star!, photographs by John Landsberg, Rainbow Bridge, 1996.

Contributor to books, including *Children's Writer's & Illustrator's Market,* edited by Alice Pope, Writers Digest Books, 1999, and *The Graceful Lie: A Method for Making Fiction,* edited by Michael Petracca, Prentice Hall, 1999. Contributor to periodicals, including *Kliatt;* contributor of film and restaurant reviews to *Santa Barbara Independent.*

When a spoiled child star is kidnaped from his parents' restaurant, prime suspect Puck sets out to solve the mystery and finds himself in more danger than he ever imagined. *(Cover illustration by Paul Casale.)*

Work in Progress

You're the One, for Aladdin Paperbacks; a young-adult novel; a middle-grade series.

Sidelights

After working as a children's librarian for several years, Francess Lantz decided that she too wanted to contribute to the wealth of literature for young people that made its way to her library's shelves. Beginning her writing efforts in the early 1980s, Lantz has developed a reputation as a respected author of fiction for both preteen and young-adult readers. Among her most highly praised works are the novels *Fade Far Away, Someone to Love,* and *Dear Celeste, My Life Is a Mess.* Lantz has also contributed to the "Sweet Valley Twins," "Hardy Boys," "Varsity Coach," and "Adventures of Mary-Kate and Ashley" series under a variety of pseudonyms.

Born in 1952 in Trenton, New Jersey, Lantz displayed a passion for writing at a young age. "I loved to write

stories and illustrate them," she once told *SATA.* "My father was an architect, and we spent long hours drawing together, including creating 'tattoos' on each other's hands and arms with ballpoint pens."

Lantz grew up in Bucks County, Pennsylvania, where she gained a reputation as a tomboy among her friends. "My stories were usually about war, or spies, and they were always violent," she recalled. "Despite this, my fifth-grade teacher encouraged my talent and allowed me to stay inside during recess to tape record my stories with my friends."

While her early dreams involved growing up to become a famous writer, the Beatles' coming to the United States in 1964 changed everything for the twelve-year-old budding author. "I chucked literature in favor of rock 'n' roll," Lantz remembered. "I took guitar lessons, wrote songs, and soon began performing. After college, I moved to Boston to become a rock star. It never happened, but I had fun trying," and, as Lantz explained on her website, "starvation sent me back to school to become a children's librarian."

After completing her graduate degree in 1975, Lantz got a job as a children's librarian in Dedham, Massachusetts. "I used to put on a graveyard story-hour every year (yes, I took the kids to a nearby graveyard and scared the pants off them)," the author told *SATA.* "After a couple of years I was having trouble finding new stories that were short, easy to read aloud, and really scary. In desperation, I wrote some myself. They were a big hit with the kids and that was when I first thought, 'hey, maybe I could write children's books.'"

Lantz's first manuscripts were picture-book texts, followed by a scary fantasy novel, and then two mysteries. Although none of those sold, she remained determined. That determination paid off: Lantz's next effort, a young adult-novel she titled *Good Rockin' Tonight,* was picked up by a publisher, and Lantz's childhood dream of one day becoming a published author was realized.

While Lantz began her career by writing young-adult novels loosely based on her own life, she eventually switched to middle-grade books, where she could add more humorous elements to her stories. In 1991's *Mom, There's a Pig in My Bed!,* Lantz captures readers with her title and doesn't let go. The story finds Dwight Ewing hoping that the earth will swallow him up, so he wouldn't have to endure his embarrassing family. After moving them to a small town, Dwight's father draws all sorts of attention to the family through his determination to raise seeing-eye pigs for blind people who have allergies to the dogs traditionally assigned to this sort of task. As a way of saving face, Dwight convinces everyone that his father is really wealthy and is engaged in his present porcine pursuits in an attempt to educate his children as to the ways of regular folks. Along with the predicted backfire to Dwight's misrepresentation, *Mom, There's a Pig in My Bed!* contains "some very funny scenes" involving swine, as well as insight into the problems that can spring from even an innocent lie, according to *School Library Journal* contributor Nancy P. Reeder. In another book with a title sure to draw preteen readers, *Stepsister from the Planet Weird* introduces readers to Megan, who is in despair over her mother's upcoming marriage because it will mean having a "perfect" stepsister. Lantz tells her tale in the form of diary entries, and the book's "zany humor" combines with the author's "wit ... [and] character development" to result in a novel that appeals to even reluctant readers, in the opinion of *School Library Journal* reviewer Cheryl Cufari.

Perhaps one of the reasons Lantz's books have proven so popular with preteen readers is that she can remember the details of her own adolescence. "I can vividly recall my feelings when I first heard the [Beatles'] *Sergeant Pepper* album, when the cute older boy I had a crush on turned to me in the hall and patted me on the head, when I learned that my father had died. At the same time," she added, "I can now view the events from an adult perspective. Both views, I feel, are required to write young children's novels. If the author can see the world through a child's eyes and nothing more, the book will be one-dimensional and claustrophobic. If the author can only view children from an adult perspective, the story will be manipulative and didactic. So far I think I've been able to integrate both perspectives. If I ever lose that ability, it will be time to stop writing children's novels and move on to something else."

While Lantz concentrated on writing for preteens during the 1980s and much of the 1990s, she has returned to her focus on young adults with her more recent novels, including *Someone to Love* and *Fade Far Away*. In *Someone to Love,* published in 1997, fifteen-year-old Sara finds that her liberal ideals conflict with her parent's self-serving, materialistic lifestyle. When her parents decide to adopt the soon-to-be-born child of the free-spirited Iris, Sara is drawn to Iris, who represents the independence, romance, and adulthood Sara dreams of. As a result, Sara finds herself withdrawing emotionally from both her father and mother during what should have been an exciting time. Again focusing on a fifteen-year-old protagonist, *Fade Far Away* is narrated by Sienna, the artistic daughter of a famous sculptor and his wife, a woman obsessed with her husband's advancement in the arts community to the exclusion of all else, including Sienna. In a novel that *Kliatt* reviewer Claire Rosser called "intense and challenging," Sienna must contradict her mother and support her father's efforts to reevaluate his priorities after he is diagnosed with a brain tumor. "This emotionally charged coming-of-age story borrows the glamorous trappings of the art world," while showing Sienna coming to terms with not only her father's failings but her own growing sense of self, according to a *Publishers Weekly* critic.

In writing for older teens, Lantz enjoys what she sees as "more challenging stories that stretch my abilities as a writer and, I hope, stretch my readers' abilities too. In the future," she told *SATA*, "I want to write more and better YA novels, and maybe some middle-grade books that are both funny and poignant." In addition to continuing to write fiction, Lantz contributes articles to magazines and newspapers, and has dabbled in nonfiction with *Rock, Rap, and Rad: How to Be a Rock or Rap Star,* which *Voice of Youth Advocates* contributor Patrick Jones praised as "an interesting book aimed at all the teens who ever wanted to see their faces on MTV." She and her family live in Santa Barbara, California, where she enjoys visiting local schools to talk to budding authors.

Works Cited

Cufari, Cheryl, review of *Stepsister from the Planet Weird,* *School Library Journal,* February, 1998, p. 109.

Review of *Fade Far Away, Publishers Weekly,* June 29, 1998, p. 60.

Jones, Patrick, review of *Rock, Rap, and Rad: How to Be a Rock or Rap Star, Voice of Youth Advocates,* April, 1993, p. 55.

"Planet Fran," http://silcom.com/~writer (February 18, 1999).

Reeder, Nancy P., review of *Mom, There's a Pig in My Bed!, School Library Journal,* January, 1993, pp. 100-01.

Rosser, Claire, review of *Fade Far Away, Kliatt,* May, 1998, p. 7.

For More Information See

PERIODICALS

Booklist, July, 1993, p. 1955; March 15, 1998, p. 1216.
Kirkus Reviews, February 1, 1997, p. 224.

ON-LINE

Author's website at http://www.silcom.com/~writer.

* * *

LAWHEAD, Stephen R. 1950- (Steve Lawhead)

Personal

Born July 2, 1950, in Kearney, NE; son of Robert and Lois Lawhead; married Alice Slaikeu, 1972; children: Ross, Drake. *Education:* Kearney State College, B.A.; attended Northern Baptist Theological Seminary. *Hobbies and other interests:* Playing guitar, travel, walking, painting.

Career

Writer. Associated with *Campus Life* magazine for five years; managed the Christian rock band DeGarmo & Key; managed Ariel Records.

Writings

FANTASY NOVELS; "DRAGON KING" SERIES

In the Hall of the Dragon King, Crossway (Westchester, IL), 1982.
The Warlords of Nin, Crossway, 1983.

Stephen R. Lawhead

The Sword and the Flame, Crossway, 1984.

"EMPYRION SAGA" SERIES

The Search for Fierra, Crossway, 1985.
The Siege of Dome, Crossway, 1986.
Empyrion (contains *The Search for Fierra* and *The Siege of Dome*), Lion (Oxford), 1990.

"PENDRAGON CYCLE" SERIES

Taliesin, Crossway, 1987.
Merlin, Crossway, 1988.
Arthur, Crossway, 1989.
Pendragon, Avon, 1994.
Grail, Avon, 1997.

"SONG OF ALBION" SERIES

The Paradise War, Lion (Batavia, IL), 1991.
The Silver Hand, Lion, 1992.
The Endless Knot, Lion, 1993.

"CELTIC CRUSADES" SERIES

The Iron Lance, HarperPrism/Zondervan, 1998.

OTHER FICTION

Dream Thief, Crossway, 1983.
Byzantium, HarperCollins, 1996.
Avalon, Avon, 1999.

FOR CHILDREN; AS STEVE LAWHEAD

Howard Had a Spaceship, Lion, 1986.
Howard Had a Submarine, Lion, 1987.
Howard Had a Shrinking Machine, Lion, 1988.
Howard Had a Hot Air Balloon, Lion, 1988.

FOR CHILDREN; AS STEPHEN LAWHEAD

Brown Ears, Multnomah Press, 1988.
Brown Ears at Sea, Multnomah Press, 1990.

FOR CHILDREN; "RIVERBANK STORIES"; AS STEPHEN LAWHEAD

The Tale of Timothy Mallard, Lion, 1990.
The Tale of Jeremy Vole, Lion, 1990.
The Tale of Anabelle Hedgehog, Lion, 1990.

NONFICTION; AS STEVE LAWHEAD

(Editor) *After You Graduate: A Guide to Life after High School,* Zondervan, 1978, revised edition published as *After You Graduate: Answers to Twenty-Seven Most Frequently Asked Questions,* Zondervan, 1985.
Rock Reconsidered: A Christian Looks at Contemporary Music, InterVarsity Press, 1981.
(Editor) *Welcome to the Family,* Zondervan, 1982.
(With Alice Slaikeu Lawhead) *The Ultimate Student Handbook,* Crossway, 1983, revised edition published as *The Ultimate College Student Handbook,* Harold Shaw (Wheaton, IL), 1989, revised and updated as *The Total Guide to College Life,* Harold Shaw, 1997.
Decisions! Decisions! Decisions!, Victor Books, 1984.
(With Karl Slaikeu) *The Phoenix Factor: Surviving and Growing through Personal Crisis,* Houghton, 1985.
(With Alice Slaikeu Lawhead) *Judge for Yourself,* Victor Books, 1985.
Rock of This Age: The Real & Imagined Dangers of Rock Music, InterVarsity Press, 1987.

Work in Progress

The Black Rood and *The Mystic Rose,* both for the "Celtic Crusades" series.

Sidelights

Stephen R. Lawhead has parlayed his long-time interest in history and mythology into a successful career writing historical fantasy novels. His most successful series, "The Pendragon Cycle," is based on the legends of King Arthur and Merlin. Lawhead's imaginative reworking of the Arthur story appealed to many readers, earning him a loyal following and brisk book sales. A versatile writer, Lawhead has also penned other groupings of fantasy novels as well as a number of books for children. In addition, he has edited, compiled, and written a number of nonfiction studies for young adults.

Lawhead grew up in Kearney, Nebraska, during the 1950s. Always interested in music and the arts, he financed his way through Kearney State College by playing in the rock band Mother Rush. While in college, he pursued a fine arts curriculum. The multi-talented Lawhead was also a good writer—several of his poems were published in the college journal and he also wrote a humor column for the school newspaper.

After graduation, Lawhead decided to attend Northern Baptist Theological Seminary in Chicago, Illinois. But he was not totally convinced that he would enter a religious career. "As a Christian," he told Bob Summer of *Publishers Weekly,* "I thought a dose of theology might not be a bad idea. But I enrolled also in some classes in a nearby graduate school in the Chicago area. One of them was on editing and writing taught by the publisher of *Campus Life*. One night—it was an evening class—he asked me if I would like a job on the magazine, and I said 'Yes, please.' So I jumped ship, and spent the next five years there."

Lawhead's work acquainted him with many musicians, and he became manager of the Christian rock group DeGarmo & Key. He eventually left *Campus Life* to form his own record company—Ariel Records. Unfortunately, the company failed, leaving Lawhead, who had moved to Memphis, Tennessee, struggling to find a way to support his family—a wife and a child, with another child on the way. The week after Lawhead closed his business, he began to write his first novel, *In the Hall of the Dragon King*.

In the Hall of the Dragon King was picked up by Crossway, a Christian publisher, but Lawhead explains that he didn't insist that a religious publisher take his works. "I don't write for a particular market," he told Summer. "It just happens that my novels are published by . . . a Christian publisher, because that was where I started out, and they have been good enough to stay with me."

In the Hall of the Dragon King features fifteen-year-old Quentin, an acolyte in the temple of Ariel. Quentin undertakes to deliver a message to the Queen. Her husband, King Eskevar, has been kidnapped by the evil magician Nimrood who is in alliance with the King's younger brother, Jaspin. Jaspin wants the throne for himself. The Queen takes Quentin and a few brave knights to try to rescue the king and foil Jaspin's plan. Kathy Piehl, writing in *School Library Journal*, asserted that *In the Hall of the Dragon King* "is well constructed and engrossing." Piehl added: "The book should please most fantasy and adventure fans."

Lawhead continued Quentin's tale in *The Warlords of Nin*. Quentin has been named Prince of Dekra, and he has gone on a quest to find an ore, lanthanil, from which to forge a special sword, Zhaligkeer. Meanwhile, Quentin's love, Bria, and the people of her kingdom are threatened by the hordes of Nin, a fearsome and evil invader. Although King Eskevar falls victim to the barbarians, Quentin arrives and uses his new sword to bring peace—and a new sovereignty—to the land. *School Library Journal* contributor Lyle Blake Smythers praised *The Warlords of Nin* as "a fresh and spellbinding approach to heroic fantasy with Christian overtones."

The concluding volume to the "Dragon King" trilogy, *The Sword and the Flame*, takes place ten years after the crucial battle with Nin. Quentin and Bria have married and now have a family with three young children. All seems to be well within the kingdom until the magician Nimrood, who was thought to be dead, returns—more deceptive than ever. Things go quickly from bad to worse when Quentin's son is kidnapped, his good friend is killed, and his sword loses its power. With the strength of the sword gone, his kingdom soon rebels against him.

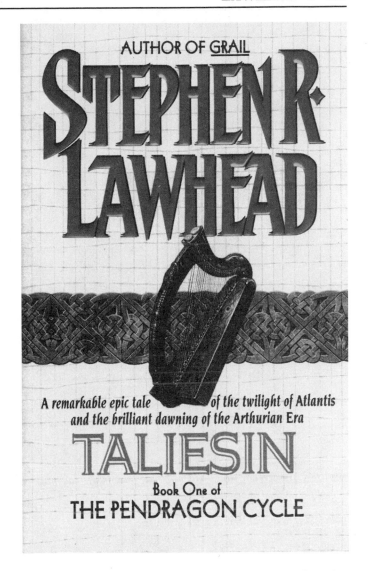

Years after Prince Elphin adopts him, the orphaned Taliesin meets and marries Charis, a princess from Atlantis, who eventually bears a son named Merlin. (Cover illustration by Eric Peterson.)

Lawhead spent a year in England researching for his most famous series, "The Pendragon Cycle." After a brief return to Nebraska, the author decided to make Oxford, England, his permanent home, cementing his commitment to produce historical mythology. "The Pendragon Cycle" was inspired by a book he had in his home. "I have very eclectic interests and keep a lot of old things around," he told Summer. In his *Reader's Encyclopedia* he was reading about King Arthur when he discovered a tidbit about how Arthur had been connected with the mythological lost realm of Atlantis. "That one sentence put a new slant on things," he told Summer. From this tiny bit of information, he began to create a new mythology of Arthur. Instead of setting his books in the medieval age, as most writers had done, he centered his work in the fifth century. In order to create his works, Lawhead explained that he "had to master the archeology of the time, besides church history, Roman history and cultural anthropology."

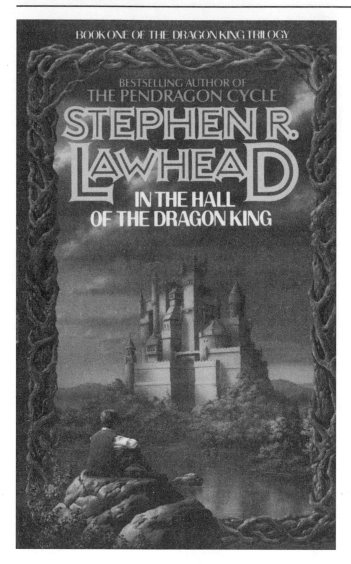

When Quentin, a young priest in training, rescues King Eskevar from evil forces, he saves an entire kingdom and become spiritually reborn. (Cover illustration by Tim Jacobus.)

His research gave him a different perspective on the old legends. In an interview in *Books,* Lawhead commented that "Mallory, Tennyson and Walt Disney have made us think of Arthurian legend as courtly medieval romances. That's far from the truth. As I read the old Welsh and Irish legends I found myself face to face with a fiercer, darker world, the world of Arthur the Celtic warlord, battling for Britain's survival in the power vacuum left by the withdrawal of the Roman legions." *Taliesin* is the first book in the series. The work follows Taliesin, who is found sewn into a sealskin sack as a child and adopted by Prince Elphin, and Charis, a princess living on Atlantis. Beautiful and graceful, she studies to become a bull-dancer on her island. When Atlantis is destroyed by a powerful earthquake, the refugees find their way to Britain, where Charis and Taliesin meet, fall in love, and eventually marry.

Merlin follows the young prince in Britain during the end of Rome's rule of the country. Merlin must prove himself as a warrior before he assumes his role as protector of the future King Arthur. Along the way, however, he gains and loses a kingdom, as well as a young wife. Despite his personal pain, he remains faithful to the prophesy that he will be a prophet for the future king. Reviewer Anne Frost of *Voice of Youth Advocates* admitted that the book is "beautifully written" and commented that "*Merlin* is as engrossing and spellbinding as the character himself."

Arthur chronicles Uther's nephew—the son of Aurelius, his dead brother—and his rise to rule Britain. Arthur begins as a savage brute; only with the help of Merlin does he become worthy of getting the Sword in the Stone that signifies that he is the Summer King. To accomplish this feat, Merlin takes Arthur away from his family. The story of his life is told by people in the court, giving the text a multi-layered quality. Jerome V. Reel, writing in *Kliatt,* praised the book, asserting that "the story is so good and so well paced that I suspect most readers will love it."

The tales of King Arthur's early years at court are told in *Pendragon.* In this work, Arthur is crowned in Londonium and the Irish warrior princess Gwenhwyvar comes to the coronation to become his wife. Soon thereafter, the King must travel to Ireland, where the Vandals have invaded. The Vandals are turned back, but they then decide to rampage through Britain, a campaign that pits Arthur against his fiercest enemies ever. A reviewer in *Publishers Weekly* claimed that in *Pendragon* Lawhead "brilliantly creates an authentic and vivid Arthurian Britain."

Lawhead's "Pendragon Cycle" continues with *Grail,* in which Arthur makes peace with the Vandals but finds himself confronting another evil power—Morgian, the Queen of Air and Darkness. Irish knight Llenlleawg unites with Morgian in order to defeat Arthur and steal the Holy Grail. Arthur must fight off monsters and magic in order to remain King. A *Kirkus Reviews* critic praised the work, indicating that "Lawhead's interpretation is different and distinctive."

Lawhead's "Song of Albion" series has also been well-received. The series chronicles the lives of two friends, Lewis Gillies and Simon Rawnson, who gain entrance to a mysterious Celtic Otherworld known as Albion. In the first book of the trilogy, *The Paradise War,* the two travel to Scotland to check on the sighting of an aurochs, an ox thought to have been extinct. Other equally unusual events start taking place because of turbulence between the manifest world and the Otherworld. Simon then disappears into Albion, and Lewis follows him. The two become fierce Celtic warriors and are drawn into battle when the powerful Lord Nudd, with whom Simon has aligned himself, threatens both worlds. "Lawhead treats his Celtic lore with respect; the upshot is well handled and pleasingly restrained, a solid and readable opener for the series," asserted a *Kirkus Reviews* commentator. Judith H. Silverman, writing in *Kliatt,* called *The Paradise War* "fast-moving," adding that the

"Song of Albion" series "may be a successor to Tolkien."

In *The Silver Hand,* Lewis, now named Llew, is chosen successor to the throne after Meldryn Mawr, King of the Llwyddi, is slain. Meldron, the King's son, is not happy with the choice, and he cuts off Llew's hand, preventing him from taking power, since a man with a disability is not allowed to rule. As Meldron assumes power, Llew and his friend, the bard Tegid Tathal, escape to found Dinas Dwr, a city they hope will act as a safe haven for those who are who are oppressed by the new king. "Lawhead invests his often poetic vision of a Celtic land living by ancient laws with charm and dignity," noted a *Publishers Weekly* commentator in a review of *The Silver Hand.*

The Endless Knot finishes the story of Simon and Llew. Since Llew has restored hope to the kingdom of Albion, his friend in the manifest world, Professor Nettleton, urges him to come back to his previous life. Llew, however, believes in the prophesy that would make him king in Albion, and he stays to marry Goewyn. Soon, Goewyn is kidnapped and Llew must journey to Tir Aflan, the Foul Land, and there do battle with magical creatures to reclaim her. A critic in *Kirkus Reviews* called the "Song of Albion" series an "admirably restrained and above-average Celtic trilogy."

Despite Lawhead's commitment to solid research and well-developed works, he also knows that his tales should be centered in solid storytelling. "I do try to give my readers a good story. The way I look at it, my license as a writer of popular fiction says 'license to entertain,'" he told Summer. Apparently, he has succeeded. His many fans and his well-traveled Internet Web site are a testament to his popularity. As for his future, readers should keep an eye on his homepage, where the author recently stated: "I am putting the finishing touches on *The Black Rood,* and after that will begin *The Mystic Rose,* finishing the 'Celtic Crusades' series. And then . . . perhaps something completely different."

Works Cited

Review of *The Endless Knot, Kirkus Reviews,* May 1, 1993, p. 561.

Frost, Anne, review of *Merlin, Voice of Youth Advocates,* April, 1989, pp. 43-44.

Review of *Grail, Kirkus Reviews,* May 1, 1997, p. 686.

Interview with Stephen Lawhead, *Books,* November-December, 1994, p. 25.

Review of *The Paradise War, Kirkus Reviews,* May 1, 1991, p. 571.

Review of *Pendragon, Publishers Weekly,* October 3, 1994, p. 54.

Piehl, Kathy, review of *In the Hall of the Dragon King, School Library Journal,* November, 1982, p. 101.

Reel, Jerome V., review of "The Pendragon Cycle," *Kliatt,* January, 1991, p. 24.

Review of *The Silver Hand, Publishers Weekly,* May 4, 1992, p. 45.

While investigating the sightings of a supposedly extinct beast in Scotland, two students, Lewis and Simon, stumble upon a mysterious otherworld. (Cover illustration by Daniel Horne.)

Silverman, Judith H., review of *The Paradise War, Kliatt,* September, 1992, p. 22.

Smythers, Lyle Blake, review of *The Warlords of Nin, School Library Journal,* October, 1983, p. 170.

Stephen R. Lawhead's Internet homepage: http:// www.stephenlawhead.com, May 15, 1999.

Summer, Bob, "Crossway's Crossover Novelist," *Publishers Weekly,* October 6, 1989, pp. 28, 32.

For More Information See

PERIODICALS

Booklist, September 1, 1987, p. 31; October 1, 1988, p. 220; August, 1989, p. 1949; June 1, 1992, p. 1749; October 1, 1994, p. 245; September 1, 1996, p. 62.

Kirkus Reviews, July 1, 1987, p. 965; May 1, 1991, p. 571; October 1, 1998, p. 1422.

Library Journal, May 15, 1991, p. 111.

Locus, August, 1989, p. 15.

Publishers Weekly, August 14, 1987, p. 99; April 19, 1991, p. 61; September 13, 1993, p. 124; June 16, 1997, p. 50; November 30, 1998, pp. 54-55.
Voice of Youth Advocates, February, 1990, p. 371; December, 1993, p. 311; February, 1997, p. 336.

*　　*　　*

LEWIS, Shannon
See LLYWELYN, Morgan

*　　*　　*

LLYWELYN, Morgan 1937-
(Shannon Lewis)

Personal

Born December 3, 1937, in New York, NY; surname legally changed to Llywelyn, August, 1981; daughter of Joseph John (an attorney) and Henri Llywelyn (a university professor; maiden name, Price) Snyder (changed from the original Shannon); married Charles Winter (a professional pilot), January 1, 1957 (died March 25, 1985); children: John Joseph. *Education:* Attended high school in Dallas, TX.

Addresses

Agent—Richard Curtis Associates, 171 East 74th St., New York, NY, 10021; Abner Stein, 10 Roland Gardens, London SW7 3PH, England. *E-mail*—Boru@ celt.net.

Career

Fashion model and dance instructor in Dallas, TX, 1954-56; secretary in Denver, CO, 1956-59; riding instructor in Denver, 1959-61; amateur equestrian, training and showing her own horses, 1961-76; writer, 1974—. *Member:* National League of American Penwomen, Authors League of America, Authors Guild, Fantasy and Science Fiction Writers Association, Gaelic Arts League, St. Brendan Society, Irish Society of Pittsburgh, National Geographic Society.

Awards, Honors

Women's U.S. equestrian high jump record, 1953; Cultural Heritage Award, and Award of Merit, Texas Booksellers Association, both for *Lion of Ireland: The Legend of Brian Boru;* Best Novel, National League of American Penwomen, 1983, Best Books for Young Adults citation, American Library Association, and Historical Novel of the Year, RT Times Awards, all for *The Horse Goddess;* Poetry in Prose award, Galician Society, University of Santiago de Compostela, and Award of Merit, Celtic League, both for *Bard: The Odyssey of the Irish;* Bisto Award for Excellence in Children's Literature, for *Brian Boru;* Bisto Award for Excellence in Children's Literature, and winner of

Morgan Llywelyn

Reading Association of Ireland Biennial Award for Best Book for Children, both for *Strongbow;* Nebula Award nomination, for short story "Fletcher Found"; Stafford Prize, for short story "The Man Who Killed the Last Great Auk."

Writings

The Wind from Hastings, Houghton, 1978.
Lion of Ireland: The Legend of Brian Boru, Houghton, 1979.
The Horse Goddess, Houghton, 1982.
(Under the pseudonym Shannon Lewis) *Personal Habits,* Doubleday, 1982.
Bard: The Odyssey of the Irish, Houghton, 1984.
Grania: She-King of the Irish Seas, Houghton, 1986.
Xerxes, Chelsea House, 1988.
Isles of the Blest, Ace Books, 1989.
Red Branch, Morrow, 1989, published as *On Raven's Wing,* Heinemann (England), 1990.
Brian Boru, Tor, 1990, O'Brien Press (Ireland), 1990.
Druids, Morrow, 1991, Heinemann, 1991.
The Last Prince of Ireland, Morrow, 1992, published as *O'Sullivan's March,* Heinemann, 1992.
Strongbow, Tor, 1992, O'Brien Press, 1992.
The Elementals, Tor, 1993.
Star Dancer, O'Brien Press, 1993.
Finn MacCool, Tor, 1994, Heinemann, 1994.
(With Michael Scott) *Silverhand: Volume I of The Arcana,* Baen, 1995.
(With Michael Scott) *Ireland: A Graphic History,* Element (United Kingdom), 1995.
Cold Places, Poolberg Press (Ireland), 1995.

Pride of Lions, Tor, 1996, Poolberg Press, 1997.

(With Michael Scott) *Silverlight: Volume II of The Arcana,* Baen, 1996.

(With Michael Scott) *19 Railway Street,* Poolberg Press, 1996.

Vikings in Ireland, O'Brien Press, 1996.

1916: A Novel of the Irish Rebellion, Forge, 1998.

The Essential Library for Irish Americans, Forge/St. Martin's Press, 1999.

Author of novella *Galway Bay,* included in *Irish Magic,* Kensington Press, 1995. Also author of numerous nonfiction articles for various publications, and of short stories, which have been published in anthologies.

Llywelyn has a manuscript collection at the University of Maryland, College Park.

Work in Progress

Whom the Gods Love, a historical fantasy co-authored with Michael Scott; *1921,* a sequel to *1916: A Novel of the Irish Rebellion.*

Sidelights

Having sold more than forty million copies of her books, New York-born author Morgan Llywelyn is one of the world's leading popular chroniclers of Celtic culture and history. A prolific storyteller, she has written more than twenty books over the past two decades. In the words of *Twentieth Century Romance and Historical Writers* contributor Judith A. Gifford: "Drawing on the history and lore that are part of her own heritage, the works of Morgan Llywelyn concern themselves with Celtic heroes and heroines, both real and mythical, bringing them and the times they inhabited to life with stunning clarity." Pauline Morgan, writing in the *St. James Guide to Fantasy Writers,* asserted: "The majority of Morgan Llywelyn's books may be regarded as fictional biographies. Each book takes a person, often historical or legendary, and relates the story of their life. Most of the novels with a fantasy connection rely heavily on Celtic mythology, particularly that of the Irish. Each book is complete in itself."

Morgan Llywelyn was born December 3, 1937, in New York City. While neither of her parents was a writer, words and storytelling were certainly in their blood. Llywelyn recalled in a 1999 interview with Ken Cuthbertson for *Authors and Artists for Young Adults* that "a lot of related influences were brought to bear" on her during her childhood. Her father Joe Snyder, an attorney by profession, was by inclination "an Irish *seanchai* (storyteller) in the classic sense"; her mother Henri was a university professor, whose own father was a newspaper publisher and printing company owner. Young Morgan grew up in a house that was filled with books, and being extremely bright (she is a lapsed member of Mensa) and precocious, she read "voraciously and omnivorously." As she told Cuthbertson, "I began with adult books because my family had an immense library—the only so-called 'children's books' I remember reading were *Wind in the Willows, Winnie the Pooh,* and *Black Beauty.* I always loved animal stories. My early favorite authors were Enid Bagnold, Ray Bradbury, Joseph Conrad, and John Steinbeck. Come to think of it, I would still classify them among my favorites."

Blessed with striking good looks and exceptional athletic ability, Llywelyn was employed as a fashion model and a dance instructor from 1954 to 1956 in Dallas, Texas, where she had attended high school. In late 1956, she moved to Denver, Colorado, where she worked as a secretary and riding instructor. There she married and got seriously involved in equestrian training and the showing of horses. To this point in her life, Llywelyn recalls she had never even thought of becoming a writer, although in a way she already was one. "I was the sort of person who always wrote thirty-five page letters to her friends," she recalled in an interview with Jean W. Ross for *Contemporary Authors.*

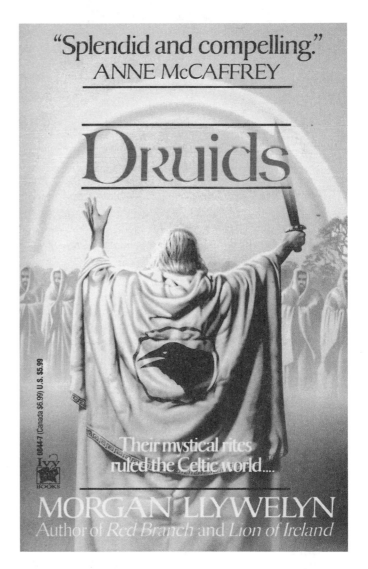

In Llywelyn's 1991 novel, a young orphan named Ainvar is taken in by the chief druid of the Carnutes and learns the secrets of the druids' magical powers.

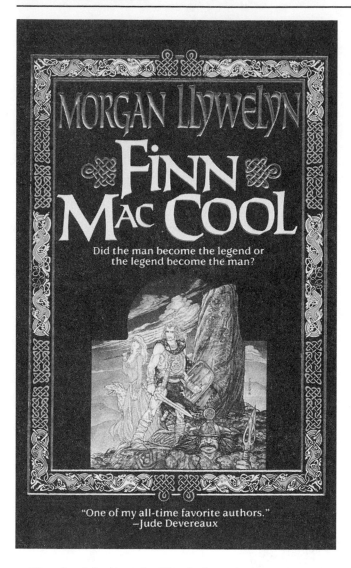

Llywelyn delves into the life of a legendary Irish hero in her 1994 fictional biography. (Cover illustration by Jim Fitzpatrick.)

Her involvement with horses spurred Llywelyn to take the next step toward becoming a writer. To help pay the costs of trying to make the U.S. Olympic equestrian team, she began writing articles about horse training, selling them to such publications as *Classic, Western Horseman,* and *Horse Lover.* Llywelyn failed to earn a spot on the Olympic team, but two good things came of her journalistic efforts. For one, as Llywelyn told Ross, she found that she "enjoyed the sculpting of the words, putting them together, the assimilation of facts and then transmitting those facts." For another, Llywelyn began working on her first novel in an attempt to ease the frustrations that she was feeling and to "distract ... [and] entertain myself."

Llywelyn began delving into her own family's history, and while doing so she came across a story that intrigued her. When she related the details to her husband, her enthusiasm proved infectious. "Before I knew what I had done, he had insisted I write it down," Llywelyn told Ross. "I had about two hundred pages written, and good

heavens, it was almost a book." Llywelyn also found that the genealogical research she had done piqued her curiosity. "I became interested in the family of man, in everybody's family and where we all came from. So I moved out of that earlier, narrow focus into all of Western Europe," she added.

Although she knew nothing about how to write a novel, Llywelyn forged ahead. "I operated from a position of ignorance, in that I did not know it couldn't be done—which I think is always an advantage," she recalled in her interview with Ross. From the beginning, Llywelyn (she adopted her mother's middle name) relied heavily on the meticulous historical research that has become her trademark. She thinks and reads extensively about whatever period she is writing about. The early fruit of Llywelyn's labors was her first novel, which appeared in 1978. *The Wind from Hastings* is a historical romance set in England around the time of the Battle of Hastings, the 1066 encounter in which the invading Normans conquered England by defeating the Saxons. The book is a fictionalized account of the story of Aldith of Mercia, the real-life wife of the vanquished King Harold. "[Aldith] was an interesting person," Llywelyn told Ross. "Her life was very vivid. The thing that made her difficult to write about in some ways was that she was not a catalyst in any sense of the word. She was just an observer. But what she observed was historic and important." Reviewing *The Wind from Hastings,* Ellen Kaye Stoppel of *Library Journal* wrote that Llywelyn "describes [this period of British history] as seen by a woman participating in it, an unusual and interesting approach."

Llywelyn had little time to ponder her first reviews; she was too busy to do so, already being hard at work on her next novel. That book, *Lion of Ireland: The Legend of Brian Boru,* is a fictional portrait of one of Ireland's greatest heroes, a legendary tenth-century king and warrior who laid the foundations for Irish nationhood by defeating the invading Vikings. The book received nearly unanimous praise. *Library Journal* contributor W. Keith McCoy lauded Llywelyn for her "vivid portrait" of Brian Boru and for "battle scenes and court life as colorful as the central character." A reviewer from *Booklist* agreed, praising *Lion of Ireland* as a "spellbinding tale ... with style and passion."

Llywelyn continued to win legions of fans (among them the then-president Ronald Reagan) as she mined the rich mother lode of Celtic folklore history with her next three novels: *The Horse Goddess, Bard: The Odyssey of the Irish,* and *Grania: She-King of the Irish Seas. The Horse Goddess* is another ambitious effort set not in medieval England or Ireland, but rather in central Europe, prior to the Celts' emigration from the British Isles. The central character in the work is a young woman named Epona, who falls in love with Kazhak, a Scythian warrior from the Russian steppes, and runs off with him in order to escape a lecherous and evil Druid priest. Llywelyn tells the story of Epona's adventures and of how she eventually returns to her people to become a high priestess among them. Calling *The Horse Goddess* "Epic in character and vivid in its descriptions," Nancy Chapin of *School Library Journal* declared that "the novel does for Celtic mythology something of what Mary Renault's [1958 novel] *The King Must Die* did for that of the Greeks."

Bard: The Odyssey of the Irish is similarly steeped in history. The story centers on Amergin, a real-life fourth-century Celtic bard who is said to have inspired his warrior clan, the Gaels, to cross the sea from the Iberian Peninsula to conquer Irene—the present-day Ireland. "I studied the ancient Celtic poets, trying to pick up the alliterations, to get the appropriate style for that book," Llywelyn told Ross. A *Booklist* critic called *Bard* a "full-bodied historical novel" that is "rich in color and a sense of druidic mystery," with "characters [who] ... come to life as individuals."

Llywelyn has continued to win fans and enjoy enormous popular success in recent years, with more novels rooted in Celtic history, and with works of historical nonfiction such as *Xerxes,* a commissioned biography of the ancient Persian king, and *Vikings in Ireland,* which is—as the title indicates—a history of the Viking experience in Ireland. Included in Llywelyn's literary output have been novels that present unadulterated historical facts, as well as others that venture into the realm of mythology, melding fantasy with reality. "Novels such as *Grania* and *The Last Prince of Ireland* are straight and very gritty history," Llywelyn explains in an interview that appears on her Web page. Other novels such as *Druids,* which examines the druidic culture of ancient Gaul, and *Strongbow,* a fictionalized biography of two twelfth-century historical figures, feature the strong spiritual—or "fantasy"—element that lies at the root of much of Llywelyn's fiction. "Since the Otherworld was very real to the Celts, actually an alternate reality, it is impossible to attempt an accurate recreation of the Celtic past without including their view of that Otherworld," Llywelyn adds. "Magical realism and elevated reality, those current literary catch-phrases, had serious meaning for the Celts. The same holds true for the Celtic Irish." Llywelyn novels that reflect this theme include *Red Branch* and *Finn MacCool.* "[They] are retellings of two of the great mythic hero-tales of Ireland. In each case, I have attempted to depict the protagonists as real men living in a real time," she notes.

While much of what Llywelyn writes is what she terms "speculative history," her books have found favor and been widely praised by academics and other experts, who admire the realism and attention to detail that she pours into them. Llywelyn reads Gaelic and some Welsh, has accumulated an extensive library on Celtic history, and whenever possible she spends time in the areas she is writing about; according to her Web page, she is "the only woman to have walked the breadth and length of Ireland"—all 427 miles of it. "I try to nail everything down concretely first that can be nailed down. I deal with anthropologists and archaeologists, with all the tangible artifacts that we know, and the current level ... of scientific knowledge about an era," Llywelyn told Ross.

Set in tenth-century Ireland, Llywelyn's novel details the life of Irish hero Brian Boru.

Llywelyn has tried her hand at writing pure fantasy with *The Elementals,* a series of four linked novellas, each of which focuses on a story about one of the classical elements—earth, air, water, and fire. Llywelyn told Cuthbertson in her *Authors and Artists for Young Adults* interview that the book "explores man's troubled relationship with the planet, beginning with the ancient Irish post-Deluge story, going from there to Thera and the explosion which may have been the destruction of Atlantis, thence to modern America, a story set in the State of New Hampshire, and finally to a conclusion somewhere in the American southwest, a century or so in the future."

Llywelyn has also collaborated with Michael Scott, an author whom the *Irish Times* newspaper has hailed as "the king of fantasy in these Isles." One project the pair have teamed to write is a two-book series called "The Arcana." The first volume in the series, *Silverhand,* appeared in 1995. This epic, action-filled saga is about a teenage superhero named Caeled who battles a pair of evil magician twins. Caeled loses an arm in an attack by a savage creature known as a weredog, but friendly monks use long-dormant technologies to build him a powerful prosthetic silver replacement limb. Thus "rearmed," Caeled sets out in search of the magical implements of the Arcana. "This rich tale shows how good fantasy can be when its authors neither denigrate their audience's intelligence nor obscure their ideas with overwrought language and overblown symbologies," a *Publishers Weekly* reviewer wrote. A second volume in the "Arcana" series appeared in 1996. In addition, Llywelyn and Scott have co-authored *19 Railway Street,* a ghost novel for young adults, an adult work entitled *Ireland: A Graphic History,* and an historical fantasy about Etruscan culture, *Whom the Gods Love.*

In a completely different vein, Llywelyn has written *1916: A Novel of the Irish Rebellion.* A *Publishers Weekly* reviewer described the novel as having an "easy, gripping style [that] will enthrall casual readers with what is Llywelyn's best work yet." A. J. Anderson of *Library Journal* also had high praise for the novel, writing that Llywelyn "has succeeded in capturing and vivifying one of the most critical moments in Ireland's troubled history."

Llywelyn was particularly pleased to receive such positive reviews, for she says she regards *1916* as the first step in a fresh direction for her career. She notes that it is the first book she has done in which the subject matter is not rooted in ancient history or mythology, but rather on contemporary events with powerful political undertones. "[It] is the book I have been 'working up to' writing for many years," Llywelyn told Cuthbertson. "It is a departure in several ways. Firstly, it is set in this century. Secondly, it explores an Ireland which no longer has any recognizable elements of the ancient Druid culture, but is desperately struggling to carve a new identity for itself. Thirdly, my own grandfather, Henry Mooney Price, is one of the major characters. It is straight history in the purest sense, with no event altered in any degree to produce a more dramatic structure. The story itself is so dramatic it didn't need any help from me! All my previous historical novels about Ireland have been laying a background for *1916* and the ... books which will follow it."

Works Cited

Anderson, A. J., review of *1916: A Novel of the Irish Rebellion, Library Journal,* February 15, 1998, pp. 170-71.

Review of *Bard: The Odyssey of the Irish, Booklist,* September 1, 1984, p. 3.

Review of *Bard: The Odyssey of the Irish, Publishers Weekly,* August 17, 1984, p. 45.

Chapin, Nancy, review of *The Horse Goddess, School Library Journal,* December, 1982, p. 87.

Gifford, Judith A., "Morgan Llywelyn," *Twentieth-Century Romance and Historical Writers,* St. James Press, 1990, pp. 400-01.

Review of *Lion of Ireland, Booklist,* February 1, 1980, p. 757.

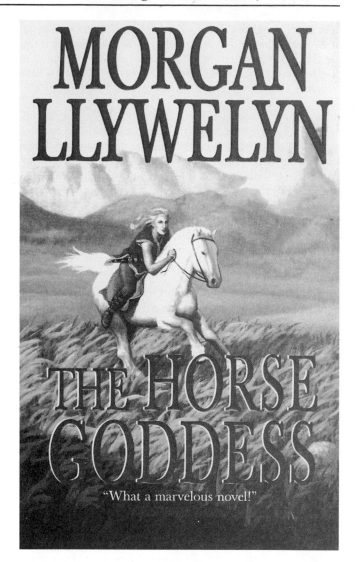

Epona and her Scythian warrior and lover Prince Kazhak travel across Europe to escape the druid priest Kernunnos in Llywelyn's historical novel set in the eighth century. (Cover illustration by David Kramer.)

Llywelyn, Morgan, interview with Jean Ross for *Contemporary Authors New Revision Series,* Volume 16, Gale, 1986, pp. 226-30.

Llywelyn, Morgan, interview with Ken Cuthbertson for *Authors and Artists for Young Adults,* Volume 29, Gale, 1999.

Llywelyn, Morgan, comments on author's Web site located at http://celt.net/Boru.

McCoy, W. Keith, review of *Lion of Ireland: The Legend of Brian Boru, Library Journal,* January 15, 1980, p. 225.

Morgan, Pauline, "Morgan Llywelyn," *St. James Guide to Fantasy Writers,* St. James Press, 1996, pp. 370-71.

Review of *1916: A Novel of the Irish Rebellion, Publishers Weekly,* February 16, 1998, p. 204.

Review of *Silverhand: The Arcana, Book I, Publishers Weekly,* March 13, 1995, p. 64.

Stoppel, Ellen Kaye, review of *The Wind from Hastings, Library Journal,* June 1, 1978, pp. 1196-97.

For More Information See

PERIODICALS

Analog, December 15, 1993, p. 162.
Booklist, December 1, 1990, p. 692; August, 1992, pp. 1995-96; May 15, 1993, pp. 1678, 1682; February 1, 1994, p. 979; February 15, 1995, pp. 1059, 1067; March 15, 1995, p. 1315; March 1, 1996, p. 1227.
Kirkus Reviews, June 1, 1995, p. 782; January 1, 1996, p. 16; April 1, 1996, p. 533; February 15, 1998, p. 216.
Library Journal, September 15, 1982, p. 1770.
Locus, March, 1990, p. 64; January, 1991, p. 25; July, 1993, p. 44; April, 1994, p. 31.
New York Times Book Review, July 16, 1989, p. 24.
Publishers Weekly, December 10, 1979, pp. 58-59; March 9, 1992, p. 48; February 28, 1994, p. 74; February 6, 1996, p. 77.
School Library Journal, July, 1991, p. 97; December, 1994, p. 144.
Washington Post Book World, October 7, 1984, p. 10; June 21, 1992, p. 12.
Voice of Youth Advocates, December, 1993, p. 311; August, 1996, p. 157.

LOCKER, Thomas 1937-

Thomas Locker

Personal

Born June 26, 1937, in New York, NY; son of Bernard (a lobbyist) and Nan (a book dealer; maiden name, Alpern) Locker; married Marea Panares Teske, 1964 (divorced, 1971); married Maria Adelman (in the dress business); children: (first marriage) Anthony; (second marriage) Aaron, Josh, Jonathan, Gregory. *Education:* University of Chicago, B.A., 1960; American University, Washington, DC, M.A., 1963. *Politics:* Democrat. *Religion:* Jewish.

Addresses

Home—Stuyvesant, NY. *Office*—8700 Riverview St., Stuyvesant, NY 12173.

Career

Author and illustrator. Franklin College, Franklin, IN, professor of art, 1963-68; Shimer College, Mt. Carroll, IL, professor of humanities, 1968-73; full-time landscape painter, 1973-84. *Exhibitions:* Work has been shown in over fifty one-man exhibitions in Chicago, London, Los Angeles, Atlanta, and New York City, including two exhibitions at the Hammer Gallery in New York City. Work featured in several museum exhibitions, including three one-man exhibitions at the Albany Institute of History and Art, Albany, NY, and two at the Columbia County Museum, Kinderhook, NY. *Military service:* U.S. Army, 1955-56. *Member:* Authors League.

Awards, Honors

Ten Best Illustrated Books of the Year, *New York Times,* Notable Book, *New York Times,* and Parents' Choice Award, all 1984, Outstanding Science Trade Book for Children, National Science Teacher's Foundation, Children's Reviewer's Choice, *Booklist,* Pick of the List, American Booksellers Association, Children's Book of the Year, Child Study Association (CSA), all 1985, all for *Where the River Begins;* Children's Books of the Year, CSA, 1985, and Colorado Children's Book Award (runner-up), University of Colorado, 1986, both for *The Mare on the Hill;* Book Award, American Institute of Graphic Arts, Ten Outstanding Picture Books, *New York Times,* Editor's Choice, *Booklist,* all 1987, all for *Sailing with the Wind;* award from New Jersey Institute of Technology, 1988; Christopher Award, 1989, for *Family Farm;* John Burroughs medal, and award from the Council of Christian Schools, both 1998, both for *Sky Tree.*

Writings

AUTHOR AND ILLUSTRATOR

Where the River Begins, Dial, 1984.
The Mare on the Hill, Dial, 1985.
Sailing with the Wind, Dial, 1986.
Family Farm, Dial, 1988.
(Adapter) Washington Irving, *Rip Van Winkle,* Dial, 1988.

Locker provided both text and illustrations for this picture book about a previously abused mare who comes to trust the children who take care of it for the winter.

The Young Artist, Dial, 1989.

The Land of Gray Wolf, Dial, 1991.

Anna and the Bagpiper, Philomel, 1994.

Miranda's Smile, Dial, 1994.

(With Candace Christiansen) *Sky Tree: Seeing Science through Art,* HarperCollins, 1995.

Water Dance, Harcourt, 1997.

(Compiler) *Home: A Journey through America,* Harcourt, 1998.

The Man Who Paints Nature, photographs by Tim Holmstrom, Richard C. Owen (Katonah, NY), 1999.

ILLUSTRATOR

Hans Christian Andersen, *The Ugly Duckling,* retold by Marianna Mayer, Macmillan (New York), 1987, Collier Macmillan (London), 1987.

Lenny Hort, reteller, *The Boy Who Held Back the Sea,* Dial, 1987.

Josette Frank, editor, *Snow toward Evening: A Year in a River Valley: Nature Poems,* Dial, 1990.

Herman Melville, *Catskill Eagle,* Philomel, 1991.

Candace Christiansen, *Calico and Tin Horns,* Dial, 1992.

Joseph Bruchac and Jonathan London, *Thirteen Moons on Turtle's Back: A Native American Year of Moons,* Philomel, 1992.

Jean Craighead George, *The First Thanksgiving,* Philomel, 1993.

Candace Christiansen, *The Ice Horse,* Dial, 1993.

Jean Craighead George, *To Climb a Waterfall,* Philomel, 1995.

Joseph Bruchac, *The Earth under Sky Bear's Feet: Native American Poems of the Land,* Philomel, 1995.

Joseph Bruchac, *Between Earth & Sky: Legends of Native American Sacred Places,* Harcourt, 1996.

Keith Strand, *Grandfather's Christmas Tree,* Harcourt, 1999.

Adaptations

Where the River Begins was adapted as a filmstrip with cassette and released by Random House, 1986; *The Mare on the Hill* was adapted as a filmstrip with cassette and released by Random House, 1987; *Family Farm* was adapted as a filmstrip and released by Dial, 1988.

Work in Progress

In Blue Mountains, for Bell Pond Books; *Cloud Dance,* for Harcourt.

Sidelights

Illustrator and author Thomas Locker began his career as a landscape painter before focusing his attention on book illustration. Reminiscent of the detailed work of nineteenth-century artists, particularly those who traveled the then-undeveloped portions of North America to capture the beauty of nature, Locker's oil paintings focus on the natural tableau created by rolling hills, rocky outcroppings, cool, quiet forests, and sparkling rivers, avoiding the paved roads, telephone lines, sprawling suburbs, and other signposts of modern civilization. Praised for his skill as an author/illustrator, Locker has also received positive critical response to his stories for young readers that show children exploring the natural world. Praising Locker's skill in upholding "the great American [fine-art] tradition of people in the landscape, a territory empty of modern features," *New York Times Book Review* contributor John Seelye called Locker's approach to his craft "a kind of time travel that thrusts us backward. Sophisticated in technique, it is primitivistic in spirit . . . a kind of portable window into a landscape long since disappeared."

Locker was born in New York City in 1937, and his urban surroundings gave him an appreciation for the more rural parts of the region where he was raised. Attending the University of Chicago and the American University in Washington, DC, Locker then started an academic career that found him teaching at Franklin College in Indiana and Shimer College in Illinois. But in 1973, after exhibiting his growing portfolio of oil paintings at galleries around the country, he made the decision to leave the academic life and devote himself to art.

Locker worked hard at his craft throughout the 1970s and early 1980s, and saw his work shown at galleries across the United States; from Los Angeles to New York City, and even as far away as London. But while busy raising a family, he discovered another outlet for his creative talent. "After a long career in gallery painting, I discovered the art form of the picture book while reading to my five sons," Locker once told *SATA.* "I gave it a try as a lark and now I devote most of my time to books."

Locker's first self-illustrated book was *Where the River Begins,* which was published in 1984. The story follows two boys and their grandfather as they decide to find the source of the river that runs past their home. *The Mare on the Hill,* Locker's second self-illustrated project, again joins the characters from *Where the River Begins* as they watch as a horse's world expands as it leaves the confines of the stable to canter through grassy pastures and meet a host of new animals and people. In *Sailing with the Wind,* published in 1986, a young girl ventures out on her first sailing trip, while a brother and sister find a way to save their family from losing their farm in *Family Farm,* which *Booklist* reviewer Denise M. Wilms called "a lovely offering whose optimism is a pleasure."

Despite the fact that Locker's storylines and text are simple, his stories often have complex emotions and situations embedded within them. Arguments arise and feelings are hurt; grandparents feel old and abandoned; the vastness of the natural world can sometimes be scary; parents sometimes die. But in Locker's stories, life's complexities are ultimately resolved, and tranquility is once again restored in the lives of his young characters. In *The Land of Gray Wolf,* for example, his paintings show the disruption caused when European colonists settled Indian lands, cutting down forests, scarring the land with roads and towns, and ultimately killing many of the Native Americans who once lived in harmony with nature. However, the book ends as those same lands are abandoned for the growing cities of the white man, and, in the words of *School Library Journal* contributor Shirley Wilton, "beaver and raccoons, in the end, return to the old Indian hunting grounds." And in *Miranda's Smile,* a young girl is thrilled to sit while her artist father paints her portrait until the loss of a front tooth threatens to derail the project. Fortunately, the pair soon realize that Miranda's happy spirit comes through as well in her bright eyes as in her smile. Calling *Miranda's Smile* a "quiet story," reviewer Wendy Lukehart made much of Locker's illustrations in *School Library Journal:* "the figures . . . have a pearl-like glow; enhanced by soft, shadowy backgrounds, they invite lingering looks that synchronize perfectly with the pace of the text."

Like *Miranda's Smile,* many of Locker's books have to do with artists. Principal among them is his 1989 work *The Young Artist,* which finds twelve-year-old Adrian Van der Weld apprenticed to an experienced painter, who passes on his own love of landscapes to the young man. However, painters in the courts of old earned a living by painting portraits, not landscapes, and Adrian must learn to show the nobles who commission him in their best light. This task is problematic for the young painter, "who can only paint the truth as he sees it," according to *School Librarian* contributor Jennifer Taylor. When he is assigned by the king to paint a group portrait of the royal family and their twenty-seven attendant courtiers, Adrian finds himself in a fix; knowing that the truth will never please the pompous bunch, he stalls for time by doing numerous portraits of the king's young daughter, who is truly beautiful. While noting that the story's sophisticated presentation of a moral dilemma makes it more appropriate for older readers, *Booklist* reviewer Ilene Cooper praised the illustrations as "breathtaking; like Adrian, Locker does his best work when painting the scenic vistas and compelling sunsets that grace the pages here."

In several of his books for children, Locker has combined his love of art with his love of nature to create books that are both beautiful to look at and educational as well. In *Sky Tree,* which he co-authored with Candace Christiansen, he outlines the relationship between art and science through the artistic depiction of a tree at various times of day and through various seasons of the year. "If only classroom texts were as compelling as this ... picture book, learning might be the adventure that it should be, the joy that it could be," declared Mary Bahr Fritts in *The Five Owls,* commending the book showing the contrasting ways in which scientists and artists view the same thing. *Booklist* reviewer Stephanie Zvirin echoed Fritts's praise, writing that "it's rare that a book so obviously meant to serve more than one purpose manages the task with such polish." Another book that combines science and art is 1997's *Water Dance,* a description of the water cycle told in free verse and illustrated by land- and seascapes. Following the path of water as it transforms into rain, mist, snow, river, and clouds, Locker's thirteen paintings were highly praised by *Bulletin of the Center for Children's Books* critic Elizabeth Bush. Describing the "dank green-grays of the storm front" as "eerily threatening and oppressive," Bush adds that the book's final two-page spread, a sunset, "blazes like technicolor hellfire."

For Locker, bringing together children, nature, and painting is one of the main goals of his work. "I rejoice in the expressive potential of joining words with images and painting in narrative order," he once told *SATA.* "I see my books as a kind of bridge between generations and a way to bring fine art to the young mind."

Works Cited

Bush, Elizabeth, review of *Water Dance, Bulletin of the Center for Children's Books,* May, 1997, p. 328.

Cooper, Ilene, review of *The Young Artist, Booklist,* October 15, 1989, p. 460.

Fritts, Mary Bahr, review of *Sky Tree: Seeing Science through Art, The Five Owls,* September-October, 1995, pp. 12-13.

Lukehart, Wendy, review of *Miranda's Smile, School Library Journal,* September, 1994, p. 189.

Seelye, John, "Time Travel by Water," *New York Times Book Review,* November 11, 1984, p. 49.

Taylor, Jennifer, review of *The Young Artist, School Librarian,* August, 1990, p. 102.

Wilms, Denise M., review of *Family Farm, Booklist,* April 15, 1988, p. 1435.

Wilton, Shirley, review of *The Land of Gray Wolf, School Library Journal,* July, 1991, p. 60.

Zvirin, Stephanie, review of *Sky Tree: Seeing Science through Art, Booklist,* June 1, 1995, p. 1756.

For More Information See

BOOKS

Children's Literature Review, Volume 14, Gale, 1988, pp. 157-61.

PERIODICALS

Booklist, May 15, 1991, pp. 1804-05; September 1, 1994, pp. 52-53; March 1, 1997, p. 1164.

The Five Owls, May-June, 1991, p. 90.

Kirkus Reviews, March 1, 1997, p. 384.

Publishers Weekly, March 17, 1997, p. 83; September 7, 1998, p. 95.

School Library Journal, December, 1989, p. 85; October, 1995, p. 128; October, 1998, p. 125.

M

MacDONALD, Suse 1940-

Personal

Given name rhymes with "news"; born March 3, 1940, in Evanston, IL; married Stuart G. MacDonald (an architect) July 14, 1962; children: Alison Heath, Ripley Graeme. *Education:* Attended Chatham College, 1958-60; University of Iowa, B.A., 1962; also attended Radcliffe College, Art Institute, and New England School of Design.

Addresses

Home—P.O. Box 25, South Londonderry, VT 05155. *Agent*—Phyllis Wender, 3 East 48th St., New York, NY 10017.

Career

Caru Studios, New York City, textbook illustrator, 1964-69; MacDonald & Swan Construction, South Londonderry, VT, architectural designer, 1969-76; author and illustrator, 1976—. *Member:* Society of Children's Book Writers and Illustrators, Authors Guild.

Awards, Honors

In 1986, *Alphabatics* was a *Booklist*'s Editor's Choice, a *School Library Journal*'s Best Book of the Year, a Child Study Association of America's Children's Books of the Year, and an American Booksellers Association Pick of the List. In 1987 it received a Caldecott Honor from the American Library Association and the Golden Kite Award from the Society of Children's Book Writers and Illustrators. In 1995, *Nanta's Lion* was selected for a Gold Medal in the preschool category of the National Parenting Publication Awards (NAPPA). In 1998 it was nominated for the Missouri Building Block Award.

Writings

SELF-ILLUSTRATED

Alphabatics, Bradbury, 1986.
Space Spinners, Dial, 1991.
Sea Shapes, Harcourt, 1994.
Nanta's Lion: A Search-and-Find Adventure, Morrow, 1995.
Peck, Slither, and Slide, Harcourt, 1997.
Elephants on Board, Harcourt, 1999.

Suse MacDonald

Twelve basic shapes are transformed into vibrant and beautiful sea creatures in MacDonald's Sea Shapes *for the picture-book audience.*

SELF-ILLUSTRATED; WITH BILL OAKES

Numblers, Dial, 1988.
Puzzlers, Dial, 1989.
Once upon Another, Dial, 1990.

ILLUSTRATOR

Hank de Zutter, *Who Says a Dog Goes Bow-wow?,* Doubleday, 1993.
Jean Marzollo, *I Love You: A Rebus Poem,* Scholastic, Inc., 2000.

Sidelights

Children's book author and illustrator Suse MacDonald has a unique graphic style. Familiar shapes—whether they be letters, numbers, or other symbols—limber up and transform into new objects, stretching young imaginations in the process. Among her works for children are the Caldecott Honor award-winning *Alphabatics,* as well as *Sea Shapes, Elephants on Board,* and *Peck, Slither,*

and Slide, a guessing game about animals and their habitats. Seeking to expand her audience's visual sense, MacDonald finds the process of illustrating children's fiction to be full of opportunities and challenges for expanding her audience's creativity.

Born in 1940, MacDonald grew up in Glencoe, Illinois, a suburb of Chicago. Her father, a professor at Northwestern University, took his family during the summer months to an old farm in Weston, Vermont, where MacDonald enjoyed swimming and collecting specimens in the pond, horseback riding, and investigating the mysteries of an old barn in which she kept a playhouse, several forts, and numerous catwalks and perches. She worked at the local summer theater handling the box office, pounding nails, and painting sets.

By the time MacDonald had graduated from high school and enrolled at Chatham College in Pittsburgh, Pennsylvania, she was certain she wanted to be an artist. During her junior year in college she transferred to the art school at the State University of Iowa, where she received her B.A. in 1962. During MacDonald's college years her classes were limited to fine-art techniques and art appreciation, because the concept of studying "commercial" art was not deemed appropriate for an academic institution. So the building blocks of her degree consisted of a traditional art curriculum: life drawing, printmaking, sculpture, and painting. While each of these areas of study intrigued her, MacDonald was a pragmatic young woman and had difficulty envisioning where such expertise would fit into a future career.

Married to Stuart MacDonald shortly after completing her bachelor's degree, Suse and her husband settled in New York City, where she hoped to get a job using her artistic talents. However, competition for art-oriented jobs was fierce, and it would be several years before she landed a position. In 1964, she accepted a job illustrating textbooks at Manhattan-based Caru Studios.

In 1969 the MacDonalds decided they needed a change from fast-paced city life. They moved to the MacDonald family farm in Vermont and ran a construction company for ten years, during which time they raised their two children. When their second child entered first grade, MacDonald decided to return to school and study illustration. She drove between Vermont and Boston for four years and attended classes at Radcliffe, the Art Institute, and the New England School of Art and Design. "It's hard to pinpoint the time when I decided that children's book illustration was the field in which I wanted to concentrate my energies," she later recalled. "My interests always seemed to lean in that direction."

While enrolled in a class in children's book writing and illustration at Radcliffe College, Macdonald became serious about children's books. By writing and illustrating several stories, she learned how to make sketched and colored "dummies," which are the first stage of life for a picture book. After completing her studies, she and two other artists bought an old house in South Londonderry, Vermont, renovated it, and created five artists' studios: one for each of the women and two for rental. MacDonald assembled a portfolio of her illustrations and began to look for work, in both advertising and the children's book field. Her first assignments were paper sculpture for advertising. These jobs kept her going financially as she began to make the rounds of the publishers.

The idea for MacDonald's first book, *Alphabatics,* emerged while she was enrolled in a typography course during her art training. Working with letter forms, she discovered a technique for manipulating their shapes in various ways. Intrigued by the process, she felt there were possibilities for a book. Bradbury Press saw the possibilities as well, and *Alphabatics* was published in 1986, to positive reviews and many awards.

"*Alphabatics* relates the shape of each letter in the alphabet to an object whose name starts with that letter,"

MacDonald once explained. "By changing the letter's shape, it evolves into something which is familiar but exciting to a child. This removes the alphabet from the adult world of letters on pages and brings it into the child's world of action and visual image." Margaret Hunt, in a review in *School Librarian,* noted: "Very few alphabet books ... can be said to be as versatile and imaginative as this ... one."

Encouraged by the success of her first book, MacDonald followed *Alphabatics* with several other books in which familiar shapes transform into something else. In *Numblers,* one of several books MacDonald would create with fellow artist/author Bill Oakes, the numbers one to ten evolve into familiar objects. *School Library Journal* contributor Judith Gloyer deemed *Numblers* "a stretch for the imagination and an enjoyable way to introduce children to numbers."

Also created with Oakes, *Puzzlers* uses such transformations to demonstrate concepts such as back-to-back, upside down, and tallest. A *Kirkus* reviewer called the work "Handsome and clever," while Deborah Abbott noted in *Booklist* that *Puzzlers* "will keep grade-school youngsters happily entertained."

In *Sea Shapes* ocean-dwelling creatures are distilled into geometric shapes: triangle, diamond, heart, circle, and oval. Each creature is described in a section of "sea facts" which provides information about each animal's behavior and physical characteristics. *Horn Book* reviewer Margaret A. Bush praised MacDonald's use of "shades of blue, green, and tan [that] illuminate the watery terrain and complement warm, unconventional tones of pink, orange, and purple."

MacDonald has used her cut-paper artistry to illustrate several narrative tales for young listeners. In her picture book *Space Spinners,* spider sisters Kate and Arabelle become the first arachnids to survive space travel, spinning a beautiful web during a NASA space voyage. Calling MacDonald's collages "a wonder," *Booklist* contributor Abbott maintained that *Space Spinners* "blasts off with a lively story line and first-rate artwork."

Nanta's Lion takes young listeners to Africa, where a Masai girl goes in search of a lion that has stolen cattle from her small village. A "search and find" story, *Nanta's Lion* allows readers to participate in Nanta's search by hiding the lion figure amid the African landscape; Nanta never finds her lion but readers certainly do.

Equally challenging is *Peck, Slither, and Slide,* which provides clues about ten different animals, each characterized by a different action verb. The word "Build" pairs with a depiction of beavers in a stream, while "Wade" finds the long legs of the initial picture attached to pink flamingoes on the next page. Comparing MacDonald's cut-tissue-paper work to that of popular illustrator Eric Carle, a *Kirkus* reviewer praised the "simple, uncluttered wildlife scenes" in *Peck, Slither, and Slide,* while *School Library Journal* contributor

Kate McClelland praised the "engaging art and inventive format" of a work that *Bulletin of the Center for Children's Books* critic Elizabeth Bush hailed as "an enticing gallery of animals on the move."

One of MacDonald's greatest joys as an author/illustrator has been "encouraging my readers to go beyond their usual stopping points and make their own artistic discoveries," as she explains on her website: www.susemacdonald.com. "Children are inventors. They just need situations that bring out that quality of inventiveness. In my books I create those opportunities."

Works Cited

Abbott, Deborah, review of *Puzzlers, Booklist,* September 15, 1989, p. 186.

Abbott, Deborah, review of *Space Spinners, Booklist,* December 15, 1991, p. 770.

Bush, Elizabeth, review of *Peck, Slither, and Slide, Bulletin of the Center for Children's Books,* June, 1997, pp. 366-67.

Bush, Margaret A., review of *Sea Shapes, Horn Book,* November-December, 1994, p. 722.

Gloyer, Judith, review of *Numblers, School Library Journal,* November, 1988, p. 92.

Hunt, Margaret, review of *Alphabatics, School Librarian,* August, 1989, p. 100.

MacDonald, Suse, commentary on website: http://www.susemacdonald.com/about.html (February 19, 1999).

McClelland, Kate, review of *Peck, Slither, and Slide, School Library Journal,* April, 1997, p. 128.

Review of *Peck, Slither, and Slide, Kirkus Reviews,* April 15, 1997, pp. 643-44.

Review of *Puzzlers, Kirkus Reviews,* August 15, 1989, p. 1247.

For More Information See

PERIODICALS

Booklist, September 1, 1994, p. 46; April 15, 1995, p. 1506.

Publishers Weekly, July 29, 1988, p. 230; August 25, 1989, p. 63; August 10, 1990, p. 444; April 24, 1995, p. 71.

School Library Journal, November, 1990, p. 96; November, 1994, p. 84; May, 1995, p. 86.

*   *   *

MAPPIN, Strephyn 1956-
(S. R. Martin)

Personal

Born January 11, 1956, in Perth, West Australia; son of Alf (a teacher) and Francis (a clerk; maiden name, Green) Mappin; married Tina Krantis (a masseuse), April 21, 1991; children: Georgia, Caiden, Zacariah. *Education:* Curtin University, B.A., 1977; attended Australian Film and Television School, 1984. *Hobbies and other interests:* Diving, filmmaking.

Strephyn Mappin

Addresses

Home and office—111 The Esplanade, Semaphore, South Australia 5019. *Agent*—Tony Williams, William Morris Agency, P.O. Box 1379, Darlinghurst, New South Wales 2010, Australia.

Career

Worked as writer and creative director for advertising agencies in Australia, Hong Kong, Scotland, Taiwan, and the United States, including Ogilvy & Mather, Saatchi & Saatchi, and Young & Rubicam; writer, 1997—. *Member:* Australian Society of Authors.

Awards, Honors

Billy Blue Literary Award; West Australian Sesquicentennial Award; Mattoid Award; Maryborough Golden Wattle Award; and Lyndall Hadow Award for Short Fiction.

Writings

Chiaroscuro (stories), illustrated by Alan Muller, Fremantle Arts Centre Press (Fremantle, Australia), 1984.

Heart Murmurs (stories), Fremantle Arts Centre Press, 1989.

In the Absence Of... (short film), Great Southern Films, 1998.

The Book Keeper (short film), Anifex, 1999.

"INSOMNIACS" HORROR MYSTERY SERIES; UNDER PSEUDONYM S. R. MARTIN

Roadkill Breakfast, Scholastic Australia (Gosford, Australia), 1997, published as *Road Kill,* Scholastic (New York City), 1999.

Cold, Scholastic Australia, 1997.

The Tunnel, the Dark, Scholastic Australia, 1997, published as *Tunnel,* Scholastic (New York City), 1999.

Overmantel, Scholastic Australia, 1997.

The Thumper, Scholastic Australia, 1997.

Talk to Me, Scholastic Australia, 1997, Scholastic, 1999.

Chair, Scholastic Australia, 1997.

Slice 'n' Dice, Scholastic Australia, 1997.

The Figment, Scholastic Australia, 1998.

Strange Station, Scholastic Australia, 1998.

Fungus, Scholastic Australia, 1998.

Stench, Scholastic Australia, 1998.

Frozen, Scholastic, 1999.

OTHER WRITINGS UNDER PSEUDONYM S. R. MARTIN

Swampland (first volume of a science fiction mystery trilogy), Scholastic Australia, 1997.

Tankworld (second volume of "Swampland" trilogy), Scholastic Australia, 1998.

Floating Ida Round the Moon, Scholastic Australia, 1998.

Endsville (third volume of "Swampland" trilogy), Scholastic Australia, 1999.

The Odour of Garlic (horror novel), Fremantle Arts Centre Press, 1999.

OTHER

Work represented in Australian anthologies. Contributor of short stories to magazines. Coeditor, *Compass,* 1982-85.

Work in Progress

Reservoir Hogs and *Grey Matter,* crime novels under the pseudonym S. R. Martin; research on Norse and Viking myths and legends for the novel *Loki's Legion; Leftovers,* a screenplay, for Notorious Films; *The Sandman,* a screenplay based on the novel by Miles Gibson, for Great Southern Films; *Swampland,* a screenplay based on the "Swampland" trilogy, with John Lyons, for Great Southern Films.

Sidelights

Strephyn Mappin told *SATA:* "In many ways, my fascination with stories and storytelling is directly related to being brought up in the country. Television was only introduced into Australia in 1956, the year I was born, and I didn't get to see any until I was eight or so years old. Instead, I read or listened to the radio, which instilled in me an enormous love of creating images and situations in my mind. I was also addicted to reading myths and legends. It didn't matter which country or culture they came from—Greek, Irish, Norse, American, Roman, Aborigine—I'd consume them like popcorn. From there I graduated to authors like Poe or Saki, short story writers who created fantastically macabre tales which led young readers like myself along untrodden paths, teasing and terrifying as they went. Then I went on to more modern practitioners of the art of storytelling, like Peter Carey, Jorge Luis Borges, Ian McEwan, and Tobias Wolff.

"Mark Twain once talked about 'the most beautiful lies ... full of surprises, and adventures, and incongruities, and contradictions, and incredibilities,' and it is this which best defines my attitude to creating fiction, no matter what age group I happen to be writing for. Writing should be alive with possibilities. It should take readers outside of themselves, creating worlds which are both believable and impossible. At the same time, it should also bring readers to a moment of illumination, a different way of looking at either the world or themselves. More than anything, writing should involve, delight, and stimulate. It should leave readers wanting to read more, rather than feeling they've completed a task."

For More Information See

PERIODICALS

Australian Book Review, June, 1991, p. 31; May, 1997, p. 61.

Magpies, July, 1997, p. 38.

*   *   *

MARTIN, S. R.
See MAPPIN, Strephyn

*   *   *

MATOTT, Justin 1961-
(Gabriel Peters)

Personal

Born August 14, 1961, in Fort Collins, CO; son of Glenn E. (a professor) and Julia M. (a professor; maiden name, Nickel) Matott; married, wife's name Andrea M. (a doctor), June 22, 1985; children: J. J., Ethan. *Education:* Earned B.A. *Religion:* Christian. *Hobbies and other interests:* Skiing, jogging, water sports, reading, gardening, brewing.

Addresses

Home and office—Littleton, CO. *E-mail*—randomwrtr@aol.com. *Agent*—Jacques de Spoelberch, J de S Associates, Inc., 9 Shagbark Rd., South Norwalk, CT 06854.

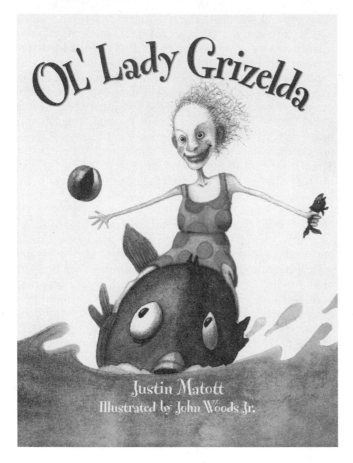

A little boy teaches a lesson about tolerance when he befriends a strange and reclusive woman named Grizelda in Justin Matott's 1998 book for young readers. (Cover illustration by John Woods Jr.)

Career

Writer. Clove Publications, Inc. (publisher of children's books), owner. Sales and marketing consultant in business re-engineering.

Writings

FOR CHILDREN

Ol' Lady Grizelda, Clove Publications, 1998.

OTHER

My Garden Visits (nonfiction), Ballantine, 1997.
A Harvest of Reflections (nonfiction), Ballantine, 1998.

Contributor to periodicals, including *Rocky Mountain News.* Some writings appear under the pseudonym Gabriel Peters.

Work in Progress

Wallflowers and *A Case for Cigars,* both novels; *The Pathway of the Wind,* nonficiton; children's books.

Sidelights

Justin Matott commented: "I began to write as a cathartic release from an occupation that was not creatively challenging. As daily writing became my practice, I depended on it as any other sustenance. Writing is simply something I must do. Writing allows one to dabble in the darker, lighter, funny, serious side of one's mind. It allows expression in many genres, whether for publication or private practice. Few other activities offer the same.

"An early influence was Truman Capote. His ability to cross over from nonfiction to fiction was intriguing. Dickens was another influence. One of my most relevant influences was my father, an unpublished novelist who created worlds and characters from experience and imagination. As a child, I hoped to do the same someday.

"I do not outline much. I allow the work to flow freely with no editorial interruption during the process. Then I go back to tighten and improve upon what I've written. I write every day with few exceptions. I bounce from nonfiction to fiction to children's work, depending on what is most creative. At most times I have ten projects going.

"Inspiration often comes from thin air. Sometimes I follow it to little end; sometimes an inkling of an idea while jogging will consume me until completion. I have a four-foot stack of these printed inspirations. Whether they are ever published or not, they've improved my writing."

*   *   *

McCRUMB, Sharyn 1948-

Personal

Born in North Carolina in 1948; married, husband's name David (a corporate environmental director); children: Spencer, Laura. *Education:* Graduated from University of North Carolina; Virginia Tech, M.A. in English.

Career

Full-time novelist and lecturer, 1988—. Teacher of journalism and Appalachian Studies at Virginia Tech. Has worked as a reporter.

Awards, Honors

Best Appalachian Novel Award, 1985, for *Lovely in Her Bones,* and 1992, for *The Hangman's Beautiful Daughter;* Edgar Award, Mystery Writers of America, 1988, for *Bimbos of the Death Sun;* New York Times Notable Book citations, 1990, for *If Ever I Return, Pretty Peggy-O,* and 1992, for *The Hangman's Beautiful Daughter;* Los Angeles Times Notable Book citations, 1992, for *The Hangman's Beautiful Daughter,* and 1994, for *She*

Sharyn McCrumb

Walks These Hills; Macavity Award for best novel, for *If Ever I Return, Pretty Peggy-O; She Walks These Hills* received the Nero Award, Agatha Award, Anthony Award, and Macavity Award for best novel; Outstanding contribution to Appalachian Literature, 1997.

Writings

"BALLAD" SERIES

If Ever I Return, Pretty Peggy-O, Scribner, 1990.
The Hangman's Beautiful Daughter, Scribner, 1992.
She Walks These Hills, Scribner, 1994.
The Rosewood Casket, Dutton, 1996.
The Ballad of Frankie Silver, Dutton, 1998.

"ELIZABETH MacPHERSON" SERIES

The Windsor Knot, Ballantine, 1990.
Lovely in Her Bones, Ballantine, 1990.
Missing Susan, Ballantine, 1991.
MacPherson's Lament, Ballantine, 1992.
Sick of Shadows, Ballantine, 1992.
Highland Laddie Gone, Ballantine, 1992.
If I'd Killed Him When I Met Him..., Ballantine, 1995.
Paying the Piper, Ballantine, 1996.

"JAY OMEGA" SERIES

Bimbos of the Death Sun, TSR Books, 1987.
Zombies of the Gene Pool, Simon and Schuster, 1992.

SHORT STORIES

Foggy Mountain Breakdown and Other Stories, Ballantine, 1997.

Sidelights

Sharyn McCrumb, who has won several major literary awards for her southern crime fiction, likens her bestselling books to Appalachian quilts. "I take brightly colored scraps of legends, ballads, fragments of rural life, and local tragedy, and I piece them together into a complex whole that tells not only a story, but also a deeper truth about the culture of the mountain South," McCrumb said in an interview in *Armchair Detective.* Her signature style traces the connection between the culture of the British Isles and the Appalachian Mountains of east Tennessee, incorporating elements from such distinct genres as historical fiction, mystery, and fantasy.

A voracious reader even as a child, McCrumb was seven when she knew that she wanted to be a writer. Reading a book a day nurtured an early love for storytelling, a trait that ran in her family. McCrumb's great-grandfathers were circuit preachers in North Carolina's Smoky Mountains, riding horseback from community to community. She attributes her own talent to these ancestors. Her father's family lived in the Smoky Mountains that divide North Carolina and Tennessee in the late 1700s. McCrumb's books also delve into other branches of her family, tracing back to her Scottish ancestor, Malcolm McCourry, who, as legend had it, was kidnapped when he was a boy living on Islay in the Hebrides in 1750 and was forced to work as a ship cabin boy. He grew up to become an attorney in New Jersey, fought in the American Revolution, and settled in Mitchell County, North Carolina, in 1794.

McCrumb grew up in North Carolina close to Chapel Hill and graduated with a bachelor's degree from the University of North Carolina at Chapel Hill. "I wanted to be an English major, but my father said that there was no future in that," McCrumb said in the *Armchair Detective* interview. "So I majored in Communications and Spanish and therefore could have been a Cuban disk jockey, but as it was I did journalism for a while and all those sorts of things that liberal arts majors do while they're trying to figure out what they want to be. Finally, after about ten years of that sort of thing I went back and got my master's in English [from Virginia Tech], damn it. And then I became a writer."

During that discovery period, McCrumb taught journalism and Appalachian Studies at Virginia Tech. She also worked as a newspaper reporter at a small newspaper in Bryson City in the North Carolina mountains (and in fact her popular "Ballad" series features a small-town newspaper). Since 1988, she has worked full-time writing books and lecturing at halls around the world, including the University of Bonn, the American Library in Berlin, Oxford University, the Smithsonian Institution, and at literary festivals and universities throughout the United States.

McCrumb's first book, *Sick of Shadows,* introduces the southern-born heroine, Elizabeth MacPherson, a forensic anthropologist who "finds death all over the place but

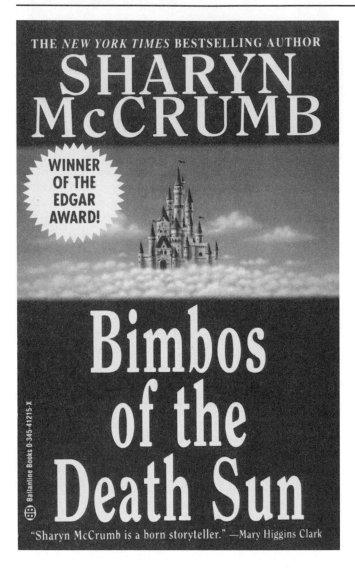

THE *NEW YORK TIMES* BESTSELLING AUTHOR

SHARYN McCRUMB

WINNER OF THE EDGAR AWARD!

Bimbos of the Death Sun

"Sharyn McCrumb is a born storyteller." —Mary Higgins Clark

A science-fiction and fantasy convention provides a colorful setting for the mystery of a murdered best-selling author.

more often than not in Scotland," explained Peter Robertson in *Booklist*. MacPherson attends the wedding of her cousin, Eileen Chandler, to a man nobody much likes because they suspect he's after her $200,000 inheritance. A murder occurs before the wedding, and everyone in the wedding party becomes a suspect.

Highland Laddie Gone and *Paying the Piper* are also part of the "MacPherson" series. *Highland Laddie Gone* centers around Elizabeth's adventures at the Scottish-American Highland Games. There is no shortage of suspects when the head of the Campbell Clan is murdered; it seems *everyone* wanted him dead. *Paying the Piper* is about a crew of American and British archaeologists—amateurs and experts alike—who meet during an archaeological dig into prehistoric burial rites on a small Scottish island. Suspense builds when an American is found dead in his tent, and then another crew member dies mysteriously. MacPherson looks for the reason behind the deaths.

In *The Windsor Knot,* MacPherson rushes to marry her Scottish fiancee; he has been invited to the Queen's garden party and only immediate relatives of the guest share such an invitation. When Elizabeth arrives in Georgia for the wedding preparations, she encounters a mystery about a local woman's husband who has apparently died twice—several years apart. "McCrumb writes with a sharp-pointed pen," according to Charles Champlin in *Los Angeles Times Book Review*. In *Missing Susan* MacPherson takes a busman's holiday of England's most notorious murder sites. Unknown to her, the tour guide, catty Rowan Rover, plans to murder one of the other tourists. According to Ira Hale Blackman in *Armchair Detective, Missing Susan* is "a strong, but humorous, cozy-thriller." Marilyn Stasio of the *New York Times Book Review* stated: "Whenever Sharyn McCrumb suits up her amateur detective, Elizabeth MacPherson, it's pretty certain that a trip is in the offing and that something deadly funny will happen on the road."

In another novel, *MacPherson's Lament,* Elizabeth travels to Virginia to save her brother, Bill, a lawyer, from a charge that could land him in prison. Bill also makes an appearance in *If I'd Killed Him When I Met Him....* The book tells of a jilted wife who kills her former husband and his new bride; a middle-aged woman whose husband has brought home a sixteen-year-old girl to serve as his second wife and a female sculptor who wants Bill to challenge laws that prohibit her from marrying a dolphin. McCrumb manages "not only to make a reader laugh out loud but also to shed a tear or two," according to Pat Dowell in the *Washington Post Book World.*

McCrumb won a 1988 Edgar Award for *Bimbos of the Death Sun,* a "send-up of science fiction fandom," according to Edward Bryant in *Locus.* That work introduced Dr. James Owen Mega, a university professor who, under the pseudonym "Jay Omega," has published some science fiction novels, and fellow professor Marion Farley. In the sequel, *Zombies of the Gene Pool,* James and Marion attend a reunion of science fiction writers and fans. The weekend includes the opening of a time capsule buried beneath a lake and, of course, a murder. A critic in *Kirkus Reviews* applauded the work, saying that McCrumb's "deadpan humor and bull's-eye accuracy skewers the science fiction genre, its eccentric authors, outlandish fans, and their nitpicking fanzines." Blackman, in *Armchair Detective,* found *Zombies of the Gene Pool* "sensitive, funny, and clever."

Some of McCrumb's most widely read and acclaimed books are part of the "Ballad" series that includes *If Ever I Return, Pretty Peggy-O* and *The Hangman's Beautiful Daughter.* McCrumb told Robertson in *Booklist* that these stories are important to her because they are set in Appalachia, where her ancestors from Scotland first settled. *If Ever I Return, Pretty Peggy-O* takes place in Hamelin, Tennessee, where a series of gruesome crimes occur while preparations are underway for the twentieth reunion of Hamelin High's class of 1966. The class-mates' internal struggles are also represented; this is the

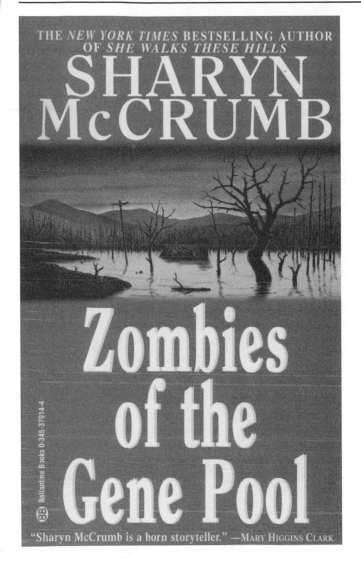

THE *NEW YORK TIMES* BESTSELLING AUTHOR
OF *SHE WALKS THESE HILLS*

SHARYN McCRUMB

Zombies of the Gene Pool

"Sharyn McCrumb is a born storyteller." —MARY HIGGINS CLARK

When murder occurs at the reunion of eight science-fiction writers, it is up to detective Jay Omega to uncover secrets that have been buried for over forty years.

stories. In the introduction to the work, McCrumb tells readers that spending her childhood in the mountains gave her a colorful outlook on life. It was, she said, "a wild, exciting place," adding that, "the quiet tales of suburban angst so popular in modern fiction are Martian to me." McCrumb explained in the *Armchair Detective* interview that she hoped to change how people feel about Appalachia, which is often stereotyped as culturally backward, with the "Ballad" series: "I think if people know more about the culture of the mountains, perhaps, I could do something to change that stereotype," adding, "I want to show them how much history we have and what real connections there are within the culture."

Works Cited

Blackman, Ira Hale, review of *Missing Susan, Armchair Detective,* Spring, 1992, p. 234.

Blackman, Ira Hale, review of *Zombies of the Gene Pool, Armchair Detective,* Fall, 1992, p. 500.

Bryant, Edward, review of *Zombies of the Gene Pool, Locus,* June, 1992, p. 21.

Carroll, Mary, review of *She Walks These Hills, Booklist,* August, 1994, p. 1989.

Champlin, Charles, review of *The Windsor Knot, Los Angeles Times Book Review,* September 9, 1990, p. 10.

Champlin, Charles, review of *The Hangman's Beautiful Daughter, Los Angeles Times Book Review,* April 12, 1992, p. 12.

Corrigan, Maureen, review of *The Rosewood Casket, Washington Post Book World,* April 21, 1996, p. 7.

Dowell, Pat, review of *If I'd Killed Him When I Met Him . . .* , *Washington Post Book World,* June 18, 1995, p. 11.

Edgerton, Clyde, review of *She Walks These Hills, New York Times,* January 8, 1995.

Maio, Kathleen, review of *If Ever I Return, Pretty Peggy-O, Wilson Library Bulletin,* September 1990, p. 106-07.

McCrumb, Sharyn, interview in *Armchair Detective,* Fall, 1995.

Melton, Emily, review of *The Rosewood Casket, Booklist,* March 15, 1996, p. 1219.

Robertson, Peter, "The *Booklist* Interview: Sharyn McCrumb," *Booklist,* March 15, 1992, p. 1340.

Review of *She Walks These Hills, Publishers Weekly,* August 29, 1994, p. 63.

Stasio, Marilyn, review of *If Ever I Return, Pretty Peggy-O, New York Times Book Review,* May 20, 1990.

Stasio, Marilyn, review of *Missing Susan, New York Times Book Review,* September 15, 1991.

Stasio, Marilyn, review of *The Hangman's Beautiful Daughter, New York Times Book Review,* April 19, 1992.

Review of *Zombies of the Gene Pool, Kirkus Reviews,* January 1, 1992, p. 22.

For More Information See

PERIODICALS

Booklist, September 1, 1991, p. 34.

Library Journal, September 1, 1997, p. 222.

Los Angeles Times, June 11, 1995, p. 7.

New York Times Book Review, May 20, 1990, p. 53; January 18, 1998.

Publishers Weekly, March 27, 1995, p. 78.

Tribune Books (Chicago), May 5, 1996.

* * *

McGOWEN, Thomas E. 1927-
(Tom McGowen)

Personal

Born May 6, 1927, in Evanston, IL; son of William Robert (a salesperson) and Helene (maiden name, Nelson) McGowen; married Loretta Swok; children: Alan, Gayle, Maureen, Kathleen. *Education:* Attended Roosevelt College of Chicago (now Roosevelt University), 1947-48, and American Academy of Art, 1948-49.

generation that lost its innocence to the Vietnam War. Kathleen Maio, writing in the *Wilson Library Bulletin,* thought McCrumb tried to include too many issues: "Because McCrumb is trying to say so much about an entire generation, her narrative remains frustratingly unfocused." However, Maio concluded that the book is a "worthwhile read by a talented writer." *New York Times Book Review* contributor Marilyn Stasio remarked that "the author threads the theme of self-awareness through-out her suspenseful narrative."

The Hangman's Beautiful Daughter concerns Nora Bonestell, an elderly Tennessee mountain woman who is said to have "the Sight," a gift of clairvoyance which allows her to foretell tragic events. The story focuses on the slaughter of a new family in the area during a teenager's murderous rampage; a fire that kills a mother leaving her young child orphaned; and incidents of cancer and stillbirths attributed to a polluted river. Marilyn Stasio in the *New York Times Book Review* stated that McCrumb "writes with quiet fire and maybe a little mountain magic about these events and the final, cleansing disaster that resolves them.... Like every true storyteller, she has the Sight." Champlin, in the *Los Angeles Times Book Review,* noted that McCrumb is one of "the funniest crime writers.... But she can also be movingly serious, a side of her versatility wonderfully displayed in *The Hangman's Beautiful Daughter.*" He went on to say that McCrumb makes readers care about the characters and leaves them believing "that what has gone on has been not invention but experience recap-tured."

A *Publishers Weekly* reviewer noted that in *She Walks These Hills,* the third novel in the "Ballad" series, McCrumb "weaves ... colorful elements into her satisfying conclusion as she continues to reward her readers' high expectations." The novel takes place in the hills and hollows of present day Appalachia, and McCrumb strings together an intriguing cast of charac-ters: the ghost of Katie Wyler, a teenager kidnapped by Shawnees in 1779; Hiram Sorley, an elderly escaped convict who cannot recall recent events because of a rare mental illness; Sorley's former wife and daughter; a radio talk show host interested in Sorley's past; and a frightened girl with an abusive husband and a demand-ing baby. *Booklist* reviewer Mary Carroll maintained that McCrumb revels in her homeland, "probes the multilayered puzzles of past and present, and meditates on human suffering and the survival instinct with sensitivity and compassion." Clyde Edgerton of the *New York Times* noted that in *She Walks These Hills* McCrumb "handles several scenes deftly by not overex-plaining. In these, the economy allows the reader to visualize action that is not intrusively described." Edgerton goes on to say, however, that overwriting in other scenes bogs the story down, as does inappropriate-ly placed literary references. He concluded that the novel is "an interesting story, but distractions limit its effect."

The Ballad of Frankie Silver and *The Rosewood Casket* continue the "Ballad" series. *The Ballad of Frankie Silver* is an examination of capital punishment. Sheriff

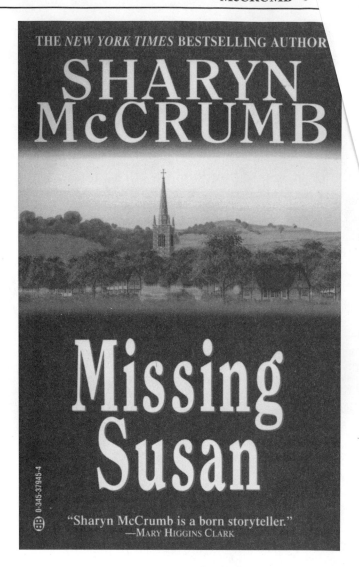

Sleuth and heroine Elizabeth MacPherson sets out to solve the mystery of a woman who is murdered during a tour of England's famous crime scenes.

Spencer Arrowood, haunted by his role in the case of death row inmate "Fate" Harkryder, delves once more into the case, as well as the 1833 hanging of Frankie Silver, the first woman hanged for murder in North Carolina. In a review of *The Rosewood Casket, Booklist* commentator Emily Melton wrote that what is most notable about this story is "the aptness of McCrumb's observations about people and life." The novel focuses on Old Man Stargill, who is dying, and his four sons who are called to his bedside to fulfill his wish that they build him a rosewood casket. As the sons come together, long-simmering family tensions and long-forgotten trag-edies surface. "In an earlier life, McCrumb must have been a balladeer, singing of restless spirits, star-crossed loves, and the consoling beauty of nature," Maureen Corrigan noted in the *Washington Post Book World.*

McCrumb, who lives in a Virginia Blue Ridge farm-house with her husband, David, and their children, Spencer and Laura, also wrote *Foggy Mountain Break-down and Other Stories,* her first collection of short

Thomas E. McGowen

Hobbies and other interests: War-gaming, gourmet cooking, classical music, historical research, travel.

Addresses

Home—4449 North Oriole Blvd., Norridge, IL 60656.

Career

Writer, 1966—. Sidney Clayton & Associates (advertising firm), Chicago, IL, production manager, 1949-53; Justrite Manufacturing Co., Chicago, advertising manager, 1953-54; National Safety Council, Chicago, sales promotion director, 1954-59; Hensley Co., (advertising firm), Chicago, creative director, 1959-69; World Book, Inc. (publishers), Chicago, senior editor, 1969-88. *Military Service:* U.S. Navy, member of hospital corps during World War II. *Member:* Children's Reading Round Table.

Awards, Honors

Notable Children's Book in the Field of Social Studies citation, Association of Social Science Teachers, 1976, for *Album of Prehistoric Man;* Outstanding Science Book for Children citations, National Science Teachers Association-Children's Book Council, 1980, for *Album of Whales,* and 1986, for *Radioactivity: From the Curies to the Atomic Age;* Children's Editors Choice Award, *Booklist,* and nominations for Rebecca Caudill Young Readers Book Award, Sequoyah Young Readers Award, and Young Hoosier Book Award, all 1987, and all for *The Magician's Apprentice;* Children's Reading Round

Table Annual Award for Outstanding Contributions to the Field of Children's Literature, 1990; Book for the Teen Age citation, New York Public Library, 1991, for *The Great Monkey Trial: Science versus Fundamentalism in America;* Children's Book of the Year Citation, Child Study Children's Book Committee, 1992, for *A Trial of Magic.*

Writings

FOR CHILDREN; AS TOM McGOWEN

The Only Glupmaker in the U.S. Navy, self-illustrated, Albert Whitman, 1966.

The Apple Strudel Soldier, illustrated by John E. Johnson, Follett, 1968.

Dragon Stew, illustrated by Trina Schart Hyman, Follett, 1969.

Last Voyage of the Unlucky Katie Marie, illustrated by Dev Appleyard, Whitman, 1969.

The Biggest Toot in Toozelburg, illustrated by Appleyard, Reilly & Lee, 1970.

Hammett and the Highlanders, illustrated by David K. Stone, Follett, 1970.

Sir MacHinery, illustrated by Hyman, Follett, 1970.

The Fearless Fossil Hunters, illustrated by Frances Gruse Scott, Whitman, 1971.

Album of Dinosaurs, illustrated by Rod Ruth, Rand McNally, 1972.

Album of Prehistoric Animals, illustrated by Rod Ruth, Rand McNally, 1974.

Odyssey from River Bend, Little, Brown, 1975.

Album of Prehistoric Man, illustrated by Rod Ruth, Rand McNally, 1975.

The Spirit of the Wild, Little, Brown, 1976.

Album of Sharks, illustrated by Rod Ruth, Rand McNally, 1977.

Album of Reptiles, illustrated by Rod Ruth, Rand McNally, 1978.

Album of Astronomy, illustrated by Rod Ruth, Rand McNally, 1979.

Album of Whales, illustrated by Rod Ruth, Rand McNally, 1980.

Album of Rocks and Minerals, illustrated by Rod Ruth, Rand McNally, 1981.

Encyclopedia of Legendary Creatures, illustrated by Victor G. Ambrus, Rand McNally, 1981.

Album of Birds, illustrated by Rod Ruth, Rand McNally, 1982.

Album of Space Flight, illustrated by Lee Brubaker, Rand McNally, 1983.

Midway and Guadalcanal, F. Watts, 1984.

King's Quest, TSR, 1984.

War Gaming, F. Watts, 1985.

George Washington, F. Watts, 1986.

Radioactivity: From the Curies to the Atomic Age, F. Watts, 1986.

The Magician's Apprentice, Lodestar, 1987.

The Circulatory System: From Harvey to the Artificial Heart, F. Watts, 1987.

Chemistry: The Birth of a Science, F. Watts, 1988.

The Time of the Forest, Houghton, 1988.

The Magician's Company, Lodestar, 1988.

The Magicians' Challenge, Lodestar, 1989.

Epilepsy, F. Watts, 1989.

The Great Monkey Trial: Science versus Fundamentalism in America, F. Watts, 1990.

The Shadow of Fomor, Lodestar, 1990.

The Magical Fellowship, Lodestar, 1991.

A Trial of Magic, Lodestar, 1992.

The Korean War, F. Watts, 1992.

A Question of Magic, Lodestar, 1993.

World War I, F. Watts, 1993.

World War II, F. Watts, 1993.

Lonely Eagles and Buffalo Soldiers: African-Americans in World War II, F. Watts, 1995.

"Go for Broke": Japanese-Americans in World War II, F. Watts, 1995.

Yearbooks in Science: 1900-1919, Twenty-First Century Books, 1995.

Yearbooks in Science: 1960-1969, Twenty-First Century Books, 1995.

The Black Death, F. Watts, 1995.

Adventures in Archaeology, Twenty-First Century Books, 1997.

African-Americans in the Old West, Children's Press, 1998.

The Beginnings of Science, Twenty-First Century Books, 1998.

The Battle for Iwo Jima, Children's Press, 1999.

Germany's Lightning War!: Panzer Divisions of World War II, Twenty-First Century Books, 1999.

Sink the Bismarck: Germany's Super-Battleship of World War II, Twenty-First Century Books, 1999.

Sidelights

Tom McGowen is the author of over fifty books for young readers, including fantasy fiction as well as nonfiction in history and science. His popular "Album" series on natural science for Rand McNally has explicated subjects from whales to space travel for juvenile readers, while his fantasy trilogies, "The Magicians," set on Earth some 3,000 years after a nuclear holocaust, and the "Age of Magic," set in 30,000 B.C. on Earth, have both attracted readers who enjoy having their imaginations stretched. As McGowen once reported in *Contemporary Authors,* he came to writing in his late thirties and continues to look at writing for children as "the most meaningful and important work I could possibly do.... My fiction, mainly fantasy, is designed to entertain; my nonfiction, mainly in the area of general science, is intended both to entertain and to help children understand the reasons for things, whether the behavior of a particular kind of wild animal or the twinkle of a star."

Born in Evanston, Illinois, on May 6, 1927, McGowen served in the Navy in World War II, then went on to college and the American Academy of Art in the late 1940s. He worked in advertising for many years until he published his first children's book in 1966, *The Only Glupmaker in the U.S. Navy,* which he also illustrated. Several of his early titles were picture books, including *The Apple Strudel Soldier,* in which Max the baker saves his town with his mouth-watering confections. *Booklist* called *The Apple Strudel Soldier* "a pleasant picture-story book with a jolly hero and an appetizing motif."

More cookery was served up in *Dragon Stew,* "a light-hearted and palatable story," according to *Bulletin of the Center for Children's Books,* with a fledgling cook, Klaus Dinkelspiel, doing a cram course to please a fussy king and earn himself a position as royal chef. "Illustrations in black and white and in color accentuate the humor of this short original tale," noted a reviewer for *Booklist.*

Longer works followed for McGowen. The first, in 1970, was the novel *Sir MacHinery,* "a fast-paced, lighthearted fantasy," according to *Booklist,* in which a robot is mistaken for a Scots knight by a brownie troop. Later came *Odyssey from River Bend* in 1975, and *The Spirit of the Wild* in 1976. In the former title, McGowen delves far into the future, to a time when the world is inhabited only by animals. Kipp, an elderly badger, hungers for knowledge and gathers a band of stalwarts around him to explore the Haunted Land of the past. The discovery of an ancient book helps Kipp in his quest. Susan Davie noted in *School Library Journal* that the fantasy was "well paced ... with intriguing detail," and that "most middle-grade readers will enjoy the trip." Zena Sutherland, writing in *Bulletin of the Center for Children's Books,* commented that there was enough "excitement and adventure en route to satisfy readers' love of action, and the animals are quite believable and well-differentiated." Fantasy is also paramount in *The Spirit of the Wild,* in which a bulldozer uncovers a magic door that has kept the wild spirit of the title, Weendigo, imprisoned in another world. The Nelson children, from whose farm the spirit has emerged, set out to save civilization from the chaotic spirit. While many reviewers complained that the ending is implausible, *Booklist* noted that "the intriguing story line and lively heroine will appeal to the 'I want a short, exciting book' crowd."

By the early 1970s, McGowen had also turned his hand to writing about natural science topics, developing a cycle of very readable and closely researched books on subjects from snakes to minerals to sharks. The "Album" works, many illustrated by Rod Ruth, are geared for middle-grade readers and all provide coherent summaries of their subjects. McGowen's award-winning *Album of Prehistoric Man,* published in England as *Collins Book of Prehistoric People,* is "a readable book for intelligent children," according to *The Junior Bookshelf,* whose reviewer went on to note that it is also "carefully authentic and not unduly simplified." Another award-winning title, *Album of Whales,* presents "a clear, well-researched overview," according to *Booklist*'s Barbara Elleman, which is "highly readable" and "informative." *Publishers Weekly* commented that the author and illustrator, "praised for previous volumes on natural subjects, will captivate readers with their big, new, informative and exciting science-history...." *Album of Astronomy* was called a "handsome entry in the 'Album of' ... series" that will "not soon become badly dated," by Margaret L. Chatham in *School Library Journal.* Denise M. Wilms noted in *Booklist* that this same title is an "efficient beginner's introduction to astronomy" which also functions as "a broad outline of the universe."

Further titles in the "Album" series include, among others, *Album of Rocks and Minerals,* which details the discovery and uses of some five dozen rocks and minerals and will be "attractive to browsers, while students needing report information will find the essays readable and fact-filled," according to *Booklist*'s Wilms; and *Album of Birds,* "a proficient, general introduction to bird life," according to Wilms in *Booklist,* and a book that functions as both "field guide and textbook," according to Kay Webb in *School Library Journal.*

Another award-winner in science is the 1986 book, *Radioactivity: From the Curies to the Atomic Age,* a book that "emphasizes the human side of scientific research," according to Jonathan R. Betz-Zall in *School Library Journal.* Betz-Zall went to note that the book is written in a "clear, engaging style," sections of which "would make good read-alouds to science classes." Looking at five scientists who delved into the mystery of radiation, including Wilhelm Roentgen and his discovery of X-rays, the Curies who isolated two radioactive elements, and Ernest Rutherford who developed the first somewhat accurate model of the atom, McGowen created a "smooth narrative," according to *Booklist*'s Wilms, "that avoids lengthy technical definitions and is easily understandable."

McGowen takes an abbreviated look at the history of chemistry in his *Chemistry: The Birth of a Science,* which provides young people with a "good introduction to the evolution of scientific thought and the dependence of scientists upon one another's work," according to Margaret M. Hagel, writing in *School Library Journal.* Carolyn Phelan of *Booklist* called McGowen's science history "clear, direct, and eminently readable." McGowen has also tackled the battle between evolution and creationism in *The Great Monkey Trial,* which describes a fight waged by Fundamentalists, represented by William Jennings Bryan, against evolutionists, defended by the eloquent Clarence Darrow. The book won a Children's Book of the Year citation from the Child Study Children's Book Committee in 1992.

Other nonfiction science titles include *Epilepsy,* as well as McGowen's contributions to the "Yearbooks in Science" series, including *1900-1919,* and *1960-1969.* McGowen has also written on the history of war, *The Korean War, World War I,* and *World War II,* as well as on battles, *Midway and Guadalcanal, The Battle for Iwo Jima,* and *Sink the Bismarck,* among others. Drawing on his own war experience, as well as on his love for research, McGowen presents "a fast-moving narrative, filled with facts, figures, and action," according to *Booklist*'s Hazel Rochman in a dual review of *World War I* and *World War II.*

Equally popular as his nonfiction books are McGowen's books of fantasy fiction, in particular the two trilogies, the "Magicians" and the "Age of Magic" cycles. The first trio includes *The Magician's Apprentice, The Magician's Company,* and *The Magicians' Challenge.* Set three millennia after a nuclear holocaust has ravaged the Earth, these books detail the adventures of young

Tigg, apprenticed to the master magician Armindor. In the first of the three-part series, Tigg is caught ransacking the magician's house and instead of a beating is enlisted on an expedition to the "wild lands." Eleanor K. MacDonald noted in *School Library Journal* that this novel "is both shorter and easier to read than many in this genre," making it a good choice for those readers who enjoy sci-fi or fantasy but do not have high reading skills. Winner of several awards and award nominations, *The Magician's Apprentice* "has the kind of action and setting that will hold youngsters' attention," as Betsy Hearne commented in *Bulletin of the Center for Children's Books.* The story of Tigg and Armindor is taken forward in *The Magician's Company,* wherein the duo rescue Jilla, a young puppeteer, in a tale that "has all the elements of good fantasy," according to *Voice of Youth Advocates* contributor Marijo Duncan. The conclusion of this initial trilogy comes with *The Magicians' Challenge,* also written for middle-grade readers, in which Armindor, Tigg, and Jilla battle to save humankind from the ratlike "reen." Ilene Cooper, writing in *Booklist,* called this third book a "dynamic conclusion to an engrossing series."

A second series, the "Age of Magic," was launched with *The Magical Fellowship,* the story of how a seer's vision of earth's destruction ultimately brings all its various races into cooperation with one another. Set in 30,000 B.C., the story focuses on the wizard Mulng and his 12-year-old son, Lithim who, along with the young female wizard Natl, travel to the land of the dragons to make an alliance and save Earth. "McGowen sets up a fine premise," observed *Kirkus Reviews,* "and though neither plot nor characters break new ground, his writing is compact and articulate, while the story flows swiftly." Candace Smith, writing in *Booklist,* commented that an "engaging set of characters, lively action, and worthy themes ... make Book One of The Age of Magic trilogy compelling." In the second volume, *A Trial of Magic,* Lithim and friends organize a defense against the prophesied attack by creatures from the sky. Steven Engelfried, in *School Library Journal,* found this second novel "Much more involving" than the first in the trilogy, "with many tense and exciting moments." Smith noted in *Booklist* that "once again, McGowen captivates with riveting action and deft characterization." The "satisfying conclusion," to the series, according to *Booklist*'s Smith, comes in *A Question of Magic,* when the long foretold invasion of the Industrious Ones from space arrives at Earth and the mages, trolls and wizards must put their defensive plan into action. In this volume, Mulng and young Lithim travel to the oracle Gurda for advice.

Whether writing no-nonsense nonfiction on history and science, or mind-stretching fantasy novels, McGowen is known for his clear presentation and articulate, economical style well suited to a middle-grade readership. As McGowen told *Contemporary Authors,* "I believe that if children can come to understand the why and how of things going on around them ... they'll be more likely to grow into comfortable, confident, *civilized* adults, unencumbered by superstition and irrationality. If one of my fiction books can turn just *one* child on to the imagination-stimulating world of fantasy; if one of my nonfiction books can make just *one* child aware of the equally stimulating world of nature and natural science, I'll have achieved my personal goal."

Works Cited

Review of *Album of the Whale, Publishers Weekly,* June 20, 1980, p. 86.

Review of *The Apple Strudel Soldier, Booklist,* October 1, 1968, pp. 188-89.

Betz-Zall, Jonathan R., review of *Radioactivity: From the Curies to the Atomic Age, School Library Journal,* August, 1986, p. 102.

Chatham, Margaret L., review of *Album of Astronomy, School Library Journal,* August, 1980, p. 66.

Review of *Collins Book of Prehistoric People, The Junior Bookshelf,* June, 1977, p. 164.

Cooper, Ilene, review of *The Magicians' Challenge, Booklist,* September 15, 1989, p. 187.

Davie, Susan, review of *Odyssey from River Bend, School Library Journal,* September, 1975, pp. 107-08.

Review of *Dragon Stew, Booklist,* June 15, 1969, p. 1177.

Review of *Dragon Stew, Bulletin of the Center for Children's Books,* March, 1970, p. 114.

Duncan, Marijo, review of *The Magician's Company, Voice of Youth Advocates,* December, 1988, p. 247.

Elleman, Barbara, review of *Album of Whales, Booklist,* January 1, 1981, p. 625.

Engelfried, Steve, review of *A Trial of Magic, School Library Journal,* June, 1992, p. 122.

Hagel, Margaret M., review of *Chemistry: The Birth of a Science, School Library Journal,* December, 1989, p. 126.

Hearne, Betsy, review of *The Magician's Apprentice, Bulletin of the Center for Children's Books,* February, 1987, p. 113.

MacDonald, Eleanor K., review of *The Magician's Apprentice, School Library Journal,* January, 1987, p. 76.

Review of *The Magical Fellowship, Kirkus Reviews,* March 15, 1991, p. 396.

McGowen, Thomas E., comments in *Contemporary Authors, New Revision Series,* Volume 50, Gale, 1996, pp. 323-24.

Phelan, Carolyn, review of *Chemistry: The Birth of a Science, Booklist,* January 15, 1990, p. 1006.

Rochman, Hazel, review of *World War I* and *World War II, Booklist,* June 1 & 15, 1993, p. 1824.

Review of *Sir MacHinery, Booklist,* December 15, 1974, p. 367.

Smith, Candace, review of *The Magical Fellowship, Booklist,* March 1, 1991, p. 1372.

Smith, Candace, review of *A Trial of Magic, Booklist,* May 15, 1992, p. 1682.

Smith, Candace, review of *A Question of Magic, Booklist,* October 15, 1993, p. 432.

Review of *The Spirit of the Wild, Booklist,* September 1, 1976, p. 40.

Sutherland, Zena, review of *Odyssey from River Bend, Bulletin of the Center for Children's Books,* January, 1976, p. 82.

Webb, Kay, review of *Album of Birds, School Library Journal,* April, 1983, p. 115.

Wilms, Denise M., review of *Album of Astronomy, Booklist,* February 15, 1980, p. 835.

Wilms, Denise M., review of *Album of Rocks and Minerals, Booklist,* March 15, 1982, p. 899.

Wilms, Denise M., review of *Album of Bird Life, Booklist,* March 15, 1983, p. 971.

Wilms, Denise M., review of *Radioactivity: From the Curies to the Atomic Age, Booklist,* July, 1986, pp. 1614-15.

For More Information See

PERIODICALS

Booklist, April 1, 1988, p. 1352; September 1, 1988, p. 82; December 1, 1995, p. 628.

Bulletin of the Center for Children's Books, March, 1982, p. 134; March, 1983, pp. 129-30; April, 1985, p. 153; May, 1988, pp. 184-85.

Kirkus Reviews, May 1, 1976, p. 535; November 1, 1986, p. 1649; January 15, 1988, p. 125; July 1, 1993, p. 863.

School Library Journal, October, 1985, p. 184; March, 1985, p. 175; December, 1988, p. 109; November, 1989, p. 112; August, 1993, p. 164; January, 1996, p. 128; May, 1996, p. 119.

Voice of Youth Advocates, February, 1990, pp. 361, 372; April, 1990, p. 39; October, 1990, p. 247; April, 1991, p. 46; October, 1993, p. 232.*

—*Sketch by J. Sydney Jones*

* * *

McGOWEN, Tom
See McGOWEN, Thomas E.

* * *

MINOR, Wendell G. 1944-

Personal

Born March 17, 1944, in Aurora, IL; son of Gordon and Marjorie (a nursery school director; maiden name, Sebby) Minor; married Florence Friedmann (a project coordinator), October 14, 1978. *Education:* Graduated from Ringling School of Art and Design, 1966. *Hobbies and other interests:* Painting outdoors, bird watching.

Addresses

Home and office—15 Old North Rd., P.O. Box 1135, Washington, CT 06793. *E-mail*--minorart@aol.com.

Career

Artist and illustrator. School of Visual Arts, New York City, member of faculty, 1975-86; freelance author/illustrator, 1995—. Member of advisory council, Connecticut Center for the Book, Hartford, CT. Lecturer to college and universities in the United States. *Exhibi-*

Wendell G. Minor

tions: New York Art Directors Club Exhibition, NY, 1992; Mystic Maritime Gallery, Mystic, CT, 1992-95; Society of Illustrators National Exhibition, 1998; Lyman Allyn Art Museum, New London, CT, Columbus Museum of Art, Columbus, OH, Art Institute of Chicago, Boston Public Library, and Silo Gallery, New Milford, CT. Work included in permanent collections at Illinois State Museum, Mattatuck Museum, Arizona Historical Society, NASA, Library of Congress, Museum of American Illustration, U.S. Coast Guard, the Norman Rockwell Museum, and the Mazza Collection, Findlay University. *Member:* Society of Illustrators (president, 1989-91; member of Hall of Fame committee).

Awards, Honors

Notable Children's Trade Books in Social Studies, National Council for the Social Studies/Children's Book Council, 1988, for *Mojave,* 1989, for *Heartland,* 1991, for *Sierra,* 1992, for *The Seashore Book;* John and Patricia Beatty Award, California Library Association, and Teachers' Choice designation, International Reading Association, both 1992, both for *Sierra;* Outstanding Science Trade Books for Children, National Science Teachers Association/Children's Book Council, 1991, for *Sierra,* and 1991, for *The Seashore Book;* Merit award, New York Art Directors Club, 1993, for *Heartland;* Award of Excellence, *Communication Arts,* 1993, for illustrations from *Red Fox Running;* Notable Book designation, *Smithsonian,* 1995, and Silver Honor award, Parents Choice Foundation, and named Notable Children's Trade Book in the Field of Social Studies,

both 1996, all for *Everglades; Smithsonian*'s Notable Books for Children award, 1998, for *Grand Canyon;* Certificate of Merit, Bookbuilders West Book Show, 1998, for *Grassroots;* over two hundred other awards and honors.

Writings

SELF-ILLUSTRATED

Grand Canyon: Exploring a Natural Wonder, Blue Sky Press, 1998.
(With wife, Florence Minor) *Art for the Written Word: Twenty-five Years of Book Cover Art,* Harcourt, 1995.

ILLUSTRATOR

Jane Goodsell, *Eleanor Roosevelt,* Crowell, 1970.
Diane Siebert, *Mojave,* Crowell, 1988.
D. Siebert, *Heartland,* Crowell, 1989.
Siebert, *Sierra,* HarperCollins, 1991.
Charlotte Zolotow, *The Seashore Book,* HarperCollins, 1992.
Jean Craighead George, *The Moon of the Owls,* HarperCollins, 1993.
Eve Bunting, *Red Fox Running,* Clarion, 1993.
J. C. George, *Julie,* HarperCollins, 1994.
George, *Everglades,* HarperCollins, 1995.
Ann Turner, *Shaker Hearts,* HarperCollins, 1997.
George, *Arctic Son,* Hyperion, 1997.
George, *Julie's Wolf Pack,* HarperCollins, 1997.
Carl Sandburg, *Grassroots* (poetry), Browndeer Press (San Diego), 1998.
George, *Morning, Noon, and Night,* HarperCollins, 1999.
George, *Snow Bear,* Hyperion, 1999.
Pat Brisson, *Sky Memories,* Delacorte, 1999.
Alice Schertle, *A Lucky Thing* (poems), Harcourt, 1999.
Jack London, *The Call of the Wild,* Atheneum, 1999.
A. Turner, *Abe Lincoln Remembers,* HarperCollins, in press.

Illustrator of book covers; contributor of artwork to "Scenic America" postcard stamp series, U.S. Postal Service; contributor of monthly illustrations to novel section, *Good Housekeeping.* Illustrations have appeared in periodicals, including *Idea, Print, American Artist, Southwest Art, Wildlife Art,* and *Graphic Design,* as well as in anthologies.

Work in Progress

Illustrations for *When We Were There,* written by Eve Bunting, for Clarion.

Sidelights

Even people who don't read picture books or visit art galleries are likely to have encountered the work of artist and illustrator Wendell Minor. In addition to providing the illustrations to works by some of the most noted children's book authors, such as Jean Craighead George and Alice Schertle, Minor has created cover art for such bestsellers as David McCullough's Pulitzer Prize-winning *Truman,* Pat Conroy's *Beach Music,* and LaVyrle Spencer's *Small Town Girl.* Commissioned by the

National Aeronautic and Space Administration (NASA) to record the lift-off of the space shuttle *Discovery,* Minor has also created several postcard stamps for the U.S. Postal Service. His style, which has been lauded for its classic elements, graces books such as *Red Fox Running, Julie,* and a collection of poetry by Carl Sandburg titled *Grassroots,* as well as Minor's own work, *Grand Canyon.*

Born in Aurora, Illinois, in 1944, Minor knew he was going to be an artist by the time he hit the fourth grade, and translated his interest in U.S. history and nature into his drawings. The encouragement he received from parents, friends, and teachers fueled his self-esteem and made him more determined than ever to develop his natural talent enough to be able to devote his adult years to art. Although his mother was supportive of his budding talent, his father—a sportsman from whom Minor inherited a love of the outdoors—was concerned that his son would find it difficult to make a living. However, Minor also had a strong work ethic; after graduating from high school he got a job at a local slaughter house to save up for college. A class in mechanical drawing at a nearby community college satisfied his need to feel he was making strides toward his eventual career, and it also taught him some useful

Minor provides naturalistic illustrations for Eve Bunting's text about a hungry fox who hunts all day until he kills a bobcat to bring home to his mate and cubs.

technical skills. Eventually, a combination of scholarship money and savings from summer jobs brought him to Sarasota, Florida's Ringling School of Art and Design, and he graduated in 1966.

In 1968 Minor began working as an illustrator for the studio of Paul Bacon, where he got his first taste of book production by illustrating a full-color book cover. Two years later, in 1970, he began working independently, taking a studio in New York's Greenwich Village. Even with his professional training and two years of experience, Minor needed commissions of his own in order to remain an independent artist. Inspired by such professional artists as Winslow Homer, Rockwell Kent, Thomas Moran, and Norman Rockwell—the last against whose work Minor's own efforts have often been favorably compared—he developed his own style, assembled a portfolio, and went in search of paying clients. Not unexpectedly, his search took him to publishing houses, and he was able to get his first illustration job working on a biography of Eleanor Roosevelt for Crowell. Contracts to create book covers would follow, and Minor, confident that he could now be able to pay the rent on his studio, felt like a budding success.

In 1988 Minor decided to make the transition from book jacket illustration to children's book illustration, believing that children's books allow artists the greatest creative freedom. He enjoyed two aspects of the work in particular: the ability to work with the author in envisioning and refining the story, and passing along his beliefs and passions to the next generation. A move to rural Connecticut also proved beneficial, as the influences of nature began to be seen more and more within his works. Minor's obvious love for the natural world is especially noted in books like 1993's *Red Fox Running,* which was written by Eve Bunting, and the wealth of nature centers and open spaces north of New York City have proved to be invaluable in studying foxes and other animals and their habitats.

Minor's *Grand Canyon: Exploring a Natural Wonder* would find the author/illustrator taking the same path as many other artists who have explored America's wild places and recorded their visual and emotional impressions. On a twelve-day excursion in May of 1997, he recorded the National Park in both watercolor paintings and text. *Grand Canyon* "enables youngsters to see a much-photographed natural wonder through the admiring, philosophical mind and the swift, careful fingers of an artist," comments *School Library Journal* contributor Patricia Manning in praise of the work, while a *Kirkus* reviewer noted that Minor's observations on nature, sketches, and paintings "will delight young armchair travelers and naturalists."

Among all the books Minor has illustrated, one in particular harkens back to his childhood. "Jack London was my favorite," he recalled to *SATA* of the many books a special sixth-grade teacher introduced him to during his middle school years. "I will never forget *The Call of the Wild.* Mr. Gilkey's deep voice made the

Inspired by the works of other American artist-explorers, Minor set up his easel on site and produced his watercolors impressions of the Grand Canyon.

words come alive with vivid pictures of the far North. It was at that moment that my visual world and reading came together. In retrospect, it was that particular experience that forged my future as an illustrator of books!" In 1999 a new edition of London's classic novel was published by Scribners; it bears Minor's expertly detailed paintings. Dedicating this work to the memory of Mr. Gilkey, Minor adds that with this project, "Life has come full circle."

Minor credits his Midwest upbringing and his parents with being a major influence upon his career. "I was very fortunate to have grown up in the Midwest in the 1950s and experience the rural landscape near my hometown of Aurora, Illinois. My mother and father both grew up on farms, and their sensibilities were well-rooted in the Illinois soil. They taught me to appreciate the simple joys of everyday life: the sweet smell of a freshly plowed field after a rainstorm; tending the large bird house for a purple martin colony that would return

faithfully to our backyard every spring; the smell of burning leaves in autumn and the celebration of harvest time at the county fair. These images are indelibly etched in my memory forever. It has taken me a lifetime to realize how much those early experiences in nature have defined my identity as a mature artist."

In 1986 Minor was given a copy of the poem "Mojave," by author Diane Siebert. "I remember that day very well," he recalled to *SATA,* "and knew immediately that I wanted to paint pictures for Diane's visually rich and beautifully descriptive text. We clearly shared a love of nature and passion for a sense of place. From that day forward I knew that my mission as an artist was to communicate to future generations of children that love of nature and sense of place. My interest in reading, natural history, science, landscape painting, and America would be brought together in one place to create children's picture books celebrating all manner of natural environments from every corner of our great land." From his studio in Washington, Connecticut, he visits groups of students to encourage them to pursue their creative outlets. Recalling his father's concern over his own preoccupation with art as "frivolous," Minor told *New York Times* contributor Jackie Fitzpatrick, "Kids need as much encouragement in the creative arts as they can get."

When asked what he hoped young readers would gain from his work, Minor recalled his own influences—the work of the great American naturalist painters from the nineteenth century, as well as authors like Carl Sandburg, whose work made a lasting impression on him as a child. "What I would like to be remembered for is a man who wanted to bring a positive message to the next generation," Minor told an interviewer for Borders.com, "but also show in a positive light how beautiful this country is, how wonderful our history is, how wonderful . . . other creative [Americans] have been."

Works Cited

Fitzpatrick, Jackie, "Books to Delight the Child in Us All," *New York Times (Connecticut edition),* November 5, 1995.
Review of *Grand Canyon, Kirkus Reviews,* July 15, 1998, p. 1044.
Manning, Patricia, review of *Grand Canyon, School Library Journal,* August, 1998, p. 180.
Minor, Wendell, interview with Borders.com, http://www.borders.com/features/mmk98014.html (December 10, 1998).

For More Information See

PERIODICALS

Booklist, September 15, 1995, p. 42; March 15, 1998, p. 1242; July, 1999, p. 8.
Horn Book, January-February, 1998, p. 71.
Library Journal, August, 1995, p. 72.
People, September 18, 1995, p. 42.
Publishers Weekly, June 5, 1995, p. 63; February 23, 1998, p. 75; September 7, 1998, p. 93.

ON-LINE

www.minorart.com

*   *   *

MIRANDA, Anne 1954-

Personal

Born July 6, 1954, in Cleveland, OH; daughter of Allen Shields (a violist) and Mary Jane (a managing editor; maiden name, Evans) Martin; married Saturnino L. Miranda (an engineer), July 29, 1978; children: Evan Michael, Tyler Martin. *Education:* Attended University of Massachusetts. *Religion:* Christian.

Addresses

Home and office—Calle Nuria 93 Apt. 2A, 28034 Mirasierra, Madrid, Spain. *Agent*—Liza Pulitzer Voges, Kirchoff/Wohlberg, Inc., 866 U.N. Plaza, New York, NY 10017.

Career

Boston Education Research, Boston, MA, staff writer, 1974-75; freelance writer, 1978—.

Writings

Baby Talk, illustrated by Dorothy Stott, Dutton, 1987.
Baby Walk, illustrated by D. Stott, Dutton, 1988.
Baby-Sit, illustrated by Stott, Joy Street Books, 1990.
(Self-illustrated) *Night Songs,* Bradbury Press, 1993.
Does a Mouse Have a House?, Bradbury Press, 1994.
What Do You Hear?, illustrated by Jean Pidgeon, Time-Life Books, 1994.
Cownting, illustrated by Barbara Leonard Gibson, Time-Life Books, 1994.
The Elephant at the Waldorf, illustrated by Don Vanderbeek, BridgeWater, 1995.
Pignic: An Alphabet Book in Rhyme, illustrated by Rosenkrans Hoffman, Boyds Mills Press, 1996.
To Market, to Market, illustrated by Janet Stevens, Harcourt, 1997.
(With Ed Emberley) *Glad Monster, Sad Monster: A Book about Feelings,* Little, Brown, 1997.
Vroom, Chugga, Vroom-Vroom, illustrated by David Murphy, Turtle Books, 1998.
Monster Math, illustrated by Polly Powell, Harcourt, 1999.
Beep! Beep!, illustrated by D. Murphy, Turtle Books, 1999.

Sidelights

Anne Miranda is the author of a number of picture books for the preschool set. Beginning with a series of "flip" books about a baby's exploration of the world around it, Miranda has gone on to write more sophisticated books, such as the lullaby story *Night Songs,* the humorous *The Elephant at the Waldorf,* and the folksy *To Market, to Market,* all of which feature rhyme and rhythm to capture the attention of listeners.

Born in 1954, in Cleveland, Ohio, Miranda always wanted to be an artist of some type. "I remember when I was about four, my mother sat me down with a set of pastels and a glass of warm milk," she once recalled to *SATA.* "She told me to dip the pastels in the warm milk so the chalk would stick to the paper and the colors would be brighter. We drew beautiful vases of colorful flowers. It was heavenly!" When she was about nine, she went to the Cleveland Art Museum and saw an exhibit of the work of nineteenth-century artist Vincent Van Gogh. "I marveled at vases of colorful flowers, beautiful countrysides, and a dark table where a family sat down to a meal of potatoes." While the experience reminded her of the flowers she had drawn with her mother and made her dream of spending her life as a painter, reality would get in the way.

Anne Miranda

However, Miranda was able to involve herself in a career that tapped her creativity. In the early 1970s, she wrote some stories for use in a reading program her mother was involved with at Boston Educational Research. Miranda did such a good job that she was hired as a staff writer. "I found writing another way to put the pictures in my head down on paper, with words instead of colors," she later recalled to *SATA*. "It was a very satisfying alternative."

Baby Talk, the first of three "lift-the-flap" books she would create for toddlers, was published in 1987. Closely followed by *Baby Walk* and *Baby Sit,* the book follows a curious baby through its day as it attempts to involve itself in household activities, from helping Daddy shave—"No, no!"—to helping Mom sort through the laundry. Calling the text "warm and satisfying," a *Kirkus Reviews* critic praised Miranda's first effort, while in *School Library Journal* contributor Kathy Piehl noted that the book's simple text "will insure that ... toddler[s] will soon be able to 'read' the book aloud."

In 1993's *Night Songs,* Miranda creates both text and illustrations in her recreation of a mother lulling her young child to sleep. A "quiet tapestry of lyrical word pictures interwoven with visual landscapes" in the words

of *Booklist* contributor Quraysh Ali, the picture book depicts the rising of the moon that separates day from night. Equally impressed by the work, a *Publishers Weekly* reviewer maintained that Miranda's "lyrical language combines fresh imagery with lullaby rhythms that soothe and comfort," while also praising the author's artwork as "beautifully designed."

Animals make their way into high society in Miranda's 1995 picture book offering, *The Elephant at the Waldorf,* which is based on a real event the author witnessed. When a circus troupe is hired to perform at the famous Waldorf Astoria Hotel, it looks like it will be curtains for their performance when the elephant refuses to get out of his truck. After several attempts to force the animal out of the vehicle, a young boy decides that what is needed is some basic good manners, in a book that a *Kirkus Reviews* contributor called "a light, goofy tale." In Miranda's *Pignic: An Alphabet Book in Rhyme,* an extended family of swine gather for their yearly get together, each member bringing his or her favorite edible. Letter by letter, the picnic menu is revealed—"Auntie Anne made apple pie/ Ben brought beans from Boston."—resulting in a book that *School Library Journal* contributor Carolyn Angus termed "fun for all—and a special treat for pig fans." The animal antics

Energy and humor are in abundance as a woman makes multiple trips to the supermarket in Anne Miranda's recasting of a classic nursery rhyme. (From To Market, To Market, *illustrated by Janet Stevens.)*

continue in *To Market, to Market,* as a colorfully clad old woman brings a number of animals home from market, only to find they have disrupted her household in unusual ways. Hailing the book's imaginative take on traditional nursery rhyme subject, a critic in *Kirkus Reviews* called *To Market, to Market* a shopping spree that "jiggity jigs off in time-honored nursery-rhyme fashion, but almost immediately derails into well-charted chaos." Heide Piehler agreed in her *School Library Journal* appraisal of Miranda's 1998 work, calling the book "a delightful, albeit raucous, romp."

Working as a writer of children's books has allowed Miranda to collaborate with her mother, an editor, on several projects, and Miranda feels indebted for the help.

The children's book author also feels grateful to her mother for allowing her to fulfil her dream of being an artist, by encouraging Miranda to illustrate some of her own texts. "She suggested, very strongly, that I illustrate a poetry book I had written. So I did." The book was *Night Songs,* which was published in the spring of 1993.

Since 1995, Miranda has studied painting in Madrid, Spain. She is also writing and hopes to add many more works to her life list. "Sometimes dreams do come true," Miranda exclaimed.

Works Cited

Ali, Quraysh, review of *Night Songs, Booklist*, April 1, 1993, p. 1441.

Angus, Carolyn, review of *Pignic, School Library Journal*, May, 1996, p. 95.

Review of *Baby Talk, Kirkus Reviews*, October 1, 1987, p. 1466.

Review of *The Elephant at the Waldorf, Kirkus Reviews*, February 15, 1995, p. 229.

Review of *Night Songs, Publishers Weekly*, March 1, 1993, p. 55.

Piehl, Kathy, review of *Baby Talk, School Library Journal*, January, 1988, p. 67.

Piehler, Heide, review of *To Market, to Market, School Library Journal*, January, 1998, p. 90.

Review of *To Market, to Market, Kirkus Reviews*, October 15, 1997, p. 1584.

For More Information See

PERIODICALS

Booklist, March 1, 1996, p. 1186; May 1, 1998, p. 1522.

Bulletin of the Center for Children's Books, November, 1997, p 93.

Kirkus Reviews, August 15, 1990, p. 1178; August 15, 1994, p. 1135; December 15, 1995, pp. 1773-74.

Publishers Weekly, January 9, 1995, p. 63; March 2, 1998, p. 67.

School Library Journal, October, 1990, p. 97; June, 1993, p. 84; December, 1994, p. 78; April, 1995, p. 113.

*   *   *

MONTERO, Gloria 1933-

Personal

Born in 1933, in Australia; emigrated to Canada, 1955; married; children: Allegra Fulton.

Addresses

Home—Barcelona, Spain. *Agent*—c/o Ecco Press, 100 West Broad St., Hopewell, NJ 08525.

Career

Writer. Has worked in Canada as a singer, actress, broadcaster, television interviewer, and producer of radio and documentaries. Producer of film documentaries, including (with David Fulton) *The Cry of the Gull*, 1976.

Writings

FOR CHILDREN

Billy Higgins Rides the Freights, Lorimer (Toronto), 1982.
The Summer the Whales Sang, Lorimer, 1985.

OTHER

The Immigrants, Lorimer, 1977.

We Stood Together: First-Hand Accounts of Dramatic Events in Canada's Labour Past, Lorimer, 1979.
Frida K. (one-woman play), produced in Toronto, 1994.
The Villa Marini (novel), Ecco Press (Hopewell, NJ), 1997.

Sidelights

The author of fiction and nonfiction as well as works for the stage and film, Gloria Montero is inspired by her fascination with history, most often Canadian. Her first two forays into writing were historical studies: *The Immigrants*, published in 1977, and 1979's *We Stood Together: First-Hand Accounts of Dramatic Events in Canada's Labour Past*.

In the 1980s, Montero turned her hand to children's fiction, using historical subjects as the basis for her stories. *Billy Higgins Rides the Freights*, published in 1982, explores the Great Depression from the perspective of its thirteen-year-old protagonist. Based on actual accounts of the Regina Riot and the On-to-Ottawa Trek, the book "brings alive events of the '30s," according to Lucille Marr in *Quill & Quire*. "The story starts slowly," observed *Books in Canada* contributor Mary Ainslie Smith, "but once the freight cars begin to move out of Vancouver, Billy's excitement and fears, his discomfort and exhilaration carry the story along very convincingly."

With *The Summer the Whales Sang*, published in 1985, Montero once again indulges her interest in history, presenting another teen protagonist, Vivi, who learns about sixteenth-century Basque whalers. The book is more a coming-of-age tale than traditional historical fiction, maintained R. G. Moyles in *Canadian Children's Literature*. "Caught in that 'scary' space between childhood and adulthood, Vivi Aguirre speaks for a multitude of other teenagers," Moyles wrote, adding: "[The] first-person point of view is, in fact, Gloria Montero's strongest asset as a juvenile novelist."

An intense female protagonist characterizes Montero's first novel, *The Villa Marini: A Family Saga*, which helped Montero attract widespread critical attention outside Canada. Set on an Australian sugarcane plantation at the turn of the century, *The Villa Marini* follows its Cuban-born heroine, Marini, from tragedy to triumph and back again over the course of a long life beginning near the turn of the century and encompassing two world wars. Comparing the novel to a one-volume version of Lawrence Durrell's *Alexandria Quartet*, *Library Journal* contributor Jo Manning noted that *The Villa Marini* "offers spare, poetic prose; vibrant characters; and strong sense of time, place and space that combine forcefully to create a unique literary experience." A *Publishers Weekly* critic praised Montero's "vivid descriptions" of the Australian pioneer experience and plantation life that "provide insight into the social climate of the time" as well as a strong historical grounding within a complex story. "With beautiful imagery and a steady pace, Montero creates a slightly magical world."

Works Cited

Manning, Jo, review of *The Villa Marini, Library Journal,* September 1, 1997, p. 219.

Marr, Lucille, review of *Billy Higgins Rides the Freights, Quill & Quire,* September, 1982, p. 62.

Moyles, R. G., review of *The Summer the Whales Sang, Canadian Children's Literature,* No. 44, 1986, pp. 53-54.

Smith, Mary Ainslie, review of *Billy Higgins Rides the Freights, Books in Canada,* June-July, 1982, pp. 31-32.

Review of *The Villa Marini, Publishers Weekly,* August 11, 1997, p. 386.

For More Information See

PERIODICALS

Books in Canada, December, 1985, p. 12.
Calgary Sun, October 4, 1997.
Kirkus Reviews, August 1, 1997, p. 1143.
Maclean's, November 4, 1996, p. 72.
New York Times Book Review, January 25, 1998, p. 19.*

*   *   *

MOWRY, Jess 1960-

Personal

Born March 27, 1960, in Starkville, MS; son of Jessup Willys Mowry (a crane operator); partner of Markita Brown (a social worker); children: Jeremy, Weylen, Shara, Keeja. *Education:* Attended elementary and middle school in Oakland, CA. *Politics:* "Survival."

Addresses

Home—Oakland, CA.

Career

Works with inner city street children at drop-in center; cartoonist; writer, 1988—. Has also worked as a mechanic, truck driver, tugboat engineer, and scrap metal collector.

Awards, Honors

PEN-Oakland Josephine Miles Award, 1990, for *Rats in the Trees;* Best Books for Young Adults Award, American Library Association (ALA), 1993, for *Way Past Cool;* Pushcart Anthology Prize, 1993; Quick Picks for Reluctant Young Adult Readers, ALA, 1997, for *Ghost Train.*

Writings

Rats in the Trees (stories), John Daniel & Co., 1990.
Children of the Night, Holloway House, 1991.
Way Past Cool, Farrar, Straus and Giroux, 1992.
Six Out Seven, Anchor, 1993.
Ghost Train, Henry Holt, 1996.

Jess Mowry

Babylon Boyz, illustrated by Eric Dinger, Simon & Schuster, 1997.
(With Yule Caise) *Way Past Cool* (screenplay based on novel of same name), Redeemable Features, 1998.
Bones Become Flowers, Pride and Imprints, 1999.

Also author of stage play, *Skeleton Key.* Contributor to various anthologies and to periodicals, including *Writer's Digest, Alchemy, Obsidian, Sequoia, Santa Clara Review, Nation, Los Angeles Times, Might Magazine, Buzz Magazine,* and *San Francisco Examiner.*

Work in Progress

Burma Jeep, a novel "about kids exploited via the Internet for 'kiddie porn'"; *The Black Gang,* a novel about caring for the world's children versus caring for animals; a novel based on Mowry's stage play entitled *Skeleton Key;* a screenplay based on the novel *Six Out Seven.*

Sidelights

Most people who have lived the kind of life that Jess Mowry did in his youth are in jail, dead, or are fated to a life of hardship and poverty. Yet Mowry, at age thirty-nine, has defied the odds to become both an accomplished author and a role model for the young black street kids whom he works with and writes about. Mowry is such a powerful, visceral writer that the editor of one of his books has likened him to Charles Dickens. The comparison is not far-fetched, for Mowry's talent and his gift for articulating the searing rage and frustrations of the black youth is nothing short of remarkable. According to Cathi Dunn MacRae of the *Wilson Library Bulletin,* the writer's "own life is so solidly enmeshed in his work that perhaps we need a new word for it. Such social commentary is actually 'docufiction.'" In a *Nation* review of *Way Past Cool,* Mowry's novel about rival Oakland street gangs, Ishmael Reed echoed that idea, hailing Mowry as "the Homer of inner-city youth."

With seven books, two movie screenplays, a stage play, and numerous short stories to his credit, Jess Mowry has emerged during the 1990s as one of America's most original and important—yet relatively unheralded—black writers. His low profile is as much a matter of personal preference as of any lack of merit or of public interest in his writing. Mowry has declined to take "the easy way," refusing to be seduced by fame or money, or to play the role of "angry black man," which America's mainstream media seem intent on ascribing to him. Instead, Mowry remains socially committed and aware; he prefers doing things his way as he works to improve the lives and self-image of black street kids. To that end, Mowry continues to live in his old neighborhood, and to work at a youth drop-in center. He also tries to advise young writers of color and to encourage them to follow his lead in breaking down the stereotypes that he feels have become so harmful to young blacks in America's inner cities. Mowry is as frank about his own role in that process as he is realistic. "The 'powers that be'—in this case meaning the 'mainstream' publishing industry (also film, music, and American society in general) WANT to see these stereotypes," Mowry told Ken Cuthbertson in an interview for *Authors and Artists for Young Adults.* "Stereotypes are very reassuring to them (yes, these kids are not really 'human,' so we don't have to feel bad about how we're treating them), but I'm only one man. I can't 'save' the world, or all the kids in it; I can only do the best I can with what I've got."

Everything that Jess Mowry has, he's worked hard for. His early life was a hardscrabble existence, filled with the kind of pain and struggle that breaks—or hopelessly embitters—most people. Mowry was born on March 27, 1960, near the town of Starkville, Mississippi, the product of an interracial relationship; his father is black, his mother white. "One has only to read about the social mores (or lack of same) in Mississippi in that era to know that this was 'not a good thing,'" Mowry told Cuthbertson. "My mother 'disappeared,' and has not been heard of to this day, though I haven't been interested enough ... to try to find her. Nor do I care to." Mowry's father, Jessup, moved west with his infant son to Oakland, California, about three months later. Young Jess was raised there, learning the ways of the street early on. Yet Mowry recalls a childhood filled "with much love and fun," although he does point out that his upbringing was anything but conventional "by today's white middle-class American standards."

Mowry inherited his passion for words from his father. Jessup Mowry was "a voracious, eclectic reader," the author recalled. "When one grows up surrounded by

books of all sorts—even if they be mostly junk-shop paperbacks—then reading is a very natural thing." Like his dad, Mowry read anything that was at hand. While the environment made it difficult for him to succeed in school, Mowry was precocious, which sometimes put him in conflict with "the system." He angered his fourth-grade teacher, for instance, by reading ahead in assigned books. Mowry read the Herman Melville classic *Moby Dick* when his teacher had criticized him by saying that someone his age could never understand such a serious novel. Mowry didn't stop with Melville; he went on to read books by John Steinbeck (whose 1947 novel *The Wayward Bus* remains Mowry's favorite book), by black novelist Ralph Ellison, and horror and fantasy writers such as H. P. Lovecraft and J. R. R. Tolkien, among others.

Despite his love of reading, the siren call of the streets proved irresistible. Mowry dropped out of school in grade eight to become a drug dealer's bodyguard. He survived for nine years in this tough, kill-or-be-killed world. However, by the still-young age of seventeen, he had seen enough violence and death; Mowry decided to go straight. He worked by times as a mechanic, a truck driver, a tugboat engineer (in Alaska), and a scrap metal collector. In 1976, Mowry and his partner, Markita Brown, gave birth to the first of their four children. The family set up housekeeping in an abandoned Greyhound bus, and soon the vehicle also began to serve as an ersatz drop-in center for neighborhood youths. Mowry's involvement with street kids eventually moved him to become a writer.

"I began writing stories for and about the kids at a West Oakland youth center in 1988," he told Cuthbertson. "I sent one of those stories to *Zyzzyva* (a San Francisco literary magazine). They published it. The rest, as they say, is history." Using money he'd earned by collecting aluminum cans, Mowry bought an old 1923 model Underwood typewriter for eight dollars. To help dispel negative media stereotypes and to offer positive messages these same kids could relate to, he began writing down some of the stories he had been creating about street kids. The product of Mowry's efforts is *Rats in the Trees,* a collection of nine related stories about a thirteen-year-old Oakland street kid named Robby. "*Rats* reflects the inner-city conditions for kids during the late 1980s, ... when crack-cocaine was starting to flood into U.S. 'ghettoes,'" Mowry explains in an essay about his writing, which appears on his Web page. The book, which is written in the gritty lingo of the streets, was published in paperback by a small Santa Barbara publisher, and distribution was limited. However, what little critical response there was to Mowry's literary debut in the United States was highly favorable, and the book was also published overseas in the United Kingdom, Germany, and Japan. A *Publishers Weekly* reviewer wrote that *Rats in the Trees* "at once saddens, overwhelms and charms as it explores a realm unto itself—urban gangs." Cathi Dunn MacRae of the *Wilson Library Journal* observed: "Rarely has street life been so encapsulated in its own language."

ISBN 0-87067-575-3 $3.95

THEY WERE GOOD KIDS,
DIRT POOR AND THE ONLY
WAY OUT WAS TO DEAL DRUGS
TO KIDS EVEN YOUNGER.
OR WAS IT?

In Mowry's 1991 novel, thirteen-year-old Ryo must reconsider his decision to sell crack to younger children in his neighborhood after his friend is killed during a drug run.

It is with no sense of satisfaction that Mowry points out on his Web page how the grim predictions he made in 1990 in *Rats in the Trees* have come to pass. "Sadly, all [of them] have come true...," he writes, "the ever-increasing and senseless Black-on-Black crime, the 'guns, gangs, drugs, and violence' in U.S. inner cities, the kids killing kids, and the decline in the quality of public education.... It was also predicted in *Rats* that 'guns, gangs, drugs and violence' would move into 'white suburbia,' too—as Chuck (an older white teenager in *Rats*) said: 'Coming soon to a neighborhood near YOU!'—and they have."

Despite favorable reviews and positive word-of-mouth for *Rats in the Trees,* mainstream publishers failed to take note of Jess Mowry or of his writing. As a result, when his second book, a novel called *Children of the Night,* was published in 1991 by Holloway House, another small West Coast publisher, again it was as an inexpensive paperback. The book is the story of Ryo, a

thirteen-year-old West Oakland youth and his "homey" Chipmunk, who go to work for a neighborhood crack dealer named Big Bird. When Chipmunk is killed in a drug run, Ryo reevaluates the life that he has chosen and then sets out to save himself and destroy Big Bird.

Children of the Night is gritty, vivid, and uncompromising in its condemnation of the parasitic drug lords and the systemic racism which confines young black street kids to lives of poverty, crime, and hardship. As Mowry points out, speaking through one of the characters in the book, Brownie, a big problem is "[white] people not believin' what's goin' on in places like this ... as long as they can keep it in places like this." Despite Mowry's hopes, *Children of the Night* attracted little media attention. However, the few reviews there were again hailing Mowry as an important new black literary voice; for example, Cathi Dunn MacRae praised his novel as a "vibrant, mesmerizing evocation ... of an underworld that the classes above ignore." "Mowry," she added "captures that world with descriptions of ugly places and desperate people so lyrical that they force us to really see what we would rather not."

With two critically acclaimed books to his credit, in 1992 Mowry suddenly won the kind of literary success that he had never dared to dream about. The street-kid-turned-author's next book, another novel about black youth gangs—"Little Rascals with Uzis," he termed them—was published by Farrar, Straus and Giroux, a major New York-based national publisher. Farrar, Straus and Giroux made *Way Past Cool* its lead fiction title in its spring catalog. According to Bronwen Hruska writing in the *Voice Literary Supplement,* Mowry received a $30,000 advance. What's more, according to Hruska, the "Disney studios optioned the film rights to the book for another $75,000." That money, more than Mowry had ever earned before in his life, enabled him to move his family into an apartment. He spent what was left on worthwhile projects in his own neighborhood. Hruska explained, Mowry "didn't write *Cool* for profits.... He wrote it for the kids it's about—even though they won't be the ones laying down the $17 for the hardback edition." Daniel Max of the entertainment industry trade publication *Variety* later reported that Mowry turned down a request to write a screenplay based on the book. He eventually did so, however, for a company called Redeemable Features, the third company to option the rights. "The screenplay they had was such a mess I just basically said, 'Oh here, let me do the damn thing!'" Mowry told Cuthbertson.

"It seems as if many writers will have one book in their careers for which they will be remembered more than for any others they write," Mowry notes on his Web page. "It seems that for me the book I will probably be most 'remembered' (if at all) for is *Way Past Cool.*" This "has been both a blessing and a curse," he adds. "A 'blessing' in that I was able to tell the truth and to show the world a view of how the U.S. treats [black street kids] ... but a 'curse' in that I seem to be expected (by the 'mainstream' publishers) to write this kind of 'ghetto fiction' for evermore; and it has become clear to me ... that 'they' are not about to publish anything of mine outside of or beyond this type of work—and DEFINITELY not 'just stories.'"

Unlike Mowry's first two books, *Way Past Cool* grabbed the media's attention. Novelist Robert Ward, writing in the *Los Angeles Times Book Review,* praised the work as "a gut-wrenching, heart-breaking suspense novel about black gang life in Oakland." However, reviewers for many mainstream publications were not quite as enthusiastic in their assessments. Nelson George of the *New York Times* described *Way Past Cool* as "maddeningly uneven, occasionally poetic." Reviewer Nick Kimberley, writing in *New Statesman & Society,* mused that "There's tough urgency in its street ellipses, and a pulpy cheerfulness in its sudden switches of mood and scene.... But its very mobility eventually drains *Way Past Cool* of its purpose." Although Mowry concedes that he is disappointed by negative reviews, he says that he is not surprised by them. "Many are racist," he told Cuthbertson in his interview for *Authors and Artists for Young Adults.* "Often, it seems, without their (white) writers being aware of it; they really want to see the stereotypes, and it angers and/or confuses them when they don't."

Undeterred, Mowry continued to write about issues that he felt were of vital concern to the black community. His next novel, *Six Out Seven* (which was actually written before *Way Past Cool,* but published after), is "basically a 'country-mouse, city-mouse,' kind of tale," according to Mowry's Web page. The story deals with Corbitt Wainwright, a thirteen-year-old black youth from rural Mississippi, who moves to Oakland to escape some trouble back home. In the novel's early chapters, Mowry juxtaposes details of Corbitt's life in the two locales. He then goes on to describe Corbitt's enforced coming of age after he joins a street gang called The Collectors; the boy becomes a foot soldier in the deadly turf war that's being fought on the streets of Oakland and other American cities—a war where to "kick" someone is to kill him, and "dirt nap" is a euphemism for death. Mowry explained on his Web site, "Unlike *Way Past Cool,* which presented a view of Black kids trapped in the inner city—knowing there was probably a way out but too caught up in day-to-day survival to try to find it—*Six Out Seven* dug deeper in to the reasons WHY these kids have to live as they do—the 'self-cleaning oven,' the fact that 'gang-violence,' and kids killing kids is actually encouraged by certain segments of white U.S. society, and that drugs are seldom if ever brought into the U.S. and poured into the 'ghettoes' by Black people."

In the words of Bob Sipchen of the *Los Angeles Times Book Review,* in *Six Out Seven* Jess Mowry "grapple[s] angrily and honestly with the forces killing young black men; with individual and societal responsibility; with the complexities of modern racism, including drive-by shooters whom, Mowry says, roam inner cities "like the KKK's Afro-American auxiliary." Sipchen went on to praise *Six Out Seven* as a "heartfelt, beautifully written book that will make readers see that the kids (Mowry)

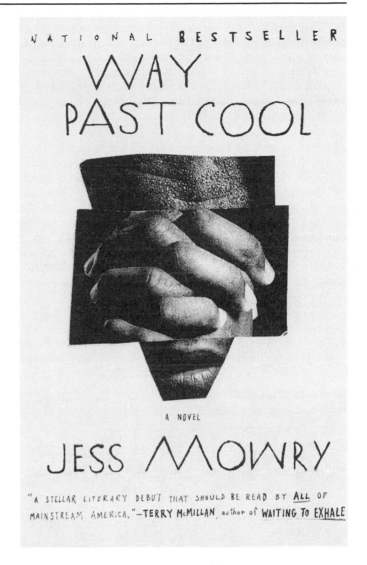

Mowry writes about black gang life in this suspenseful young-adult novel set in Oakland, California.

portrays are *everyone's* kids, and to let their dreams wither unnurtured is *everyone's* shame." Clarence Petersen, writing in the Chicago *Tribune Books,* echoed those comments when he wrote, "Mowry tells us things we need to hear with a raw eloquence that both touches and enrages."

Mowry's next book is decidedly lighter fare and a clear change of pace for him. *Ghost Train* is a supernatural mystery story aimed at young readers. The story is about Remi DuMont, a young Haitian immigrant, who with help from his new American friend Niya, sets out to solve a fifty-year-old murder mystery. Mowry spins a suspense-filled yarn about time travel, social issues, and Voodoo magic—the latter being a subject in which the author himself has a keen interest. Mowry says his main purpose in writing *Ghost Train* was to tell a good story, something he feels that not enough black male writers are doing, or being allowed to do by a white-dominated publishing industry that insists on turning out books about stereotypical black characters living in a world of guns, drugs, gangs, and killing, and by black intellectuals who feel writing—or reading—escapist fiction is not a worthwhile pastime. "Of course our young people should know their history and be aware of racism on all levels, and of social issues and concerns in the world around them," Mowry writes on his Web page, "but they MUST also be entertained in positive ways," and offered valid, realistic role models.

Mowry apparently succeeded on all counts with *Ghost Train.* Although reviewer Ann C. Sparanese of the *Voice of Youth Advocates* faulted the "dialog['s] stilted quality" that intercepts the story's flow, she asserted that "the novel's strength is in its plot." From the start of the novel, "the suspense pulls the reader along to the climactic last chapter, where danger gives way to a satisfying resolution." Susan L. Rogers of *School Library Journal* praised *Ghost Train* as a "short, easy-to-read, and very successful mystery."

Mowry returned to familiar turf with *Babylon Boyz,* a 1997 novel about three teenage friends named Dante, Pook, and Wyatt, who live in a run-down inner-city Oakland neighborhood called Babylon. Mowry tells the

Corbitt Wainwright, a thirteen-year-old from Mississippi, moves to Oakland to escape his past, but encounters more trouble after joining a local street gang. (Cover photograph by Kurt Mundahl.)

story of what happens when the youths find a suitcase full of drugs, which has been discarded by a white drug dealer on the run. Dante, Pook, and Wyatt are suddenly confronted with gut-wrenching decisions about whether or not to try to sell the drugs. *Babylon Boyz* is a tough, hard-hitting story with earthy dialogue, violence, and some graphic sex scenes. "While it's sometimes difficult to read about this subject matter, toning it down would have sadly compromised the story's realism," maintained *Voice of Youth Advocates* contributor Florence Munat. "Instead, Mowry has delivered a realistic, tenacious tale of urban hopes and dreams." Bill Ott of *Booklist* agreed, writing: "Each of the boys rises above the stereotypical aspects of his character to become, not emblems of hard life in the ghetto, but vivid reminders that we are all more than the sum of our situations." *School Library Journal* contributor Beth Wright observed that *Babylon Boyz* offers a view of "family, friendship, love, and ... kids living in poverty and victimized by drugs still trying to make the right choices in their lives."

In addition to his novels and short stories, Mowry has shown his versatility by writing a stage play called *Skeleton Key,* which was staged at a private school in Berkeley, and by collaborating on the screenplay for a film based on his novel *Way Past Cool.* Nonetheless, Mowry feels that he still faces an uphill struggle to succeed as a writer, even if he does concede that he is still learning, about writing and about life. "One radio talk-show host gave me a left-handed compliment on the air by saying how 'well I expressed myself, considering that I'd only completed seventh grade,'" Mowry said in his interview. "I replied that I'd always thought life was a learning process that never stopped, as opposed to those who had finished high school and perhaps college and so felt they had learned everything they needed to know."

Mowry's own independence of mind (he has been with four literary agents in his brief career and is now representing himself), which is one of his strengths, has also been one of the biggest obstacles he has had to overcome. However, he insists that an even greater difficulty is the racism that he—and other blacks—face on a daily basis in American society. "In the case of [black] writers, musicians, or filmmakers it's very hard because 'they' (and you should know who 'they' are) control everything," Mowry explained to Cuthbertson. "A 'black book' that does not please a white editor will not be published.... A white writer with my track record—ALL of my books still in print after almost ten years (in eight languages), a film, and a play—would have no problem finding a publisher for their next work. With me, it's a case of back to square-one every time and start all over again. It's very tiring to say the least."

Mowry feels strongly that every successful black man or woman has a duty to serve as a role model for young people in their communities. To that end, he continues to speak out against social injustice and to do all that he can to help smash the harmful black stereotypes that are perpetuated in the media. "I'd be less than human if I

In Mowry's 1997 novel three teenage friends find a discarded suitcase filled with drugs and consider whether or not to sell them. (Cover illustration by Eric Dinyer.)

didn't [get angry]. Although I try to temper my anger with the 'I used to be disgusted, now I'm just amused' philosophy," Mowry related in his interview with Cuthbertson.

Mowry's stories have been included in various anthologies, and he has also written two more novels, including *Bones Become Flowers.* "I consider [*Bones Become Flowers*] to be the BEST writing I have done to date," Mowry asserts on his Web page. The novel, which is set in Haiti, is an entertaining story about children, Voodoo, a search for God, and the exploitation of poor nations by rich nations. "*Bones Become Flowers* may turn out to be my last try at writing. It will certainly prove to me whether I am right or wrong in thinking that Black readers of all ages want more than just 'guns, gangs, drugs, and violence.'"

Works Cited

George, Nelson, "Boyz Against the Hoods," *New York Times,* May 24, 1992, p. 21.

Hruska, Bronwen, "Goodbye, Cool World," *Voice Literary Supplement,* May, 1992, p. 31.

Kimberley, Nick, "Unhappy Days," *New Statesman & Society,* July 17, 1992, pp. 46-47.

MacRae, Cathi Dunn, "The Young Adult Perplex," *Wilson Library Bulletin,* March, 1991, pp. 112-13.

MacRae, Cathi Dunn, "The Young Adult Perplex," *Wilson Library Bulletin,* September, 1992, pp. 96-97, 126-27.

Max, Daniel, "Will Hollywood get serious about black lit?" *Variety,* January 27, 1992, p. 68.

Mowry, Jess, author's Web page at http://members.tripod.com/~Timoun/index-7.htm.

Mowry, Jess, interview with Ken Cuthbertson for *Authors and Artists for Young Adults,* Vol. 29, Gale, 1999.

Munat, Florence, review of *Babylon Boyz, Voice of Youth Advocates,* June, 1997, p. 112.

Ott, Bill, review of *Babylon Boyz, Booklist,* February 15, 1997, p. 1020.

Petersen, Clarence, "Paperbacks," *Tribune Books* (Chicago), September 18, 1994, p. 8.

Review of *Rats in the Trees, Publishers Weekly,* March 2, 1990, p. 78.

Reed, Ishmael, "The Activist Library: A Symposium," *Nation,* September 21, 1992, pp. 293-94.

Rogers, Susan L., review of *Ghost Train, School Library Journal,* December, 1996, p. 139.

Sipchen, Bob, "What the Use in Dreamin?" *Los Angeles Times Book Review,* November 7, 1993, pp. 2, 9.

Sparanese, Ann C., review of *Ghost Train, Voice of Youth Advocates,* February, 1997, p. 330.

Ward, Robert, "Dispatch From the Hood," *Los Angeles Times Book Review,* April 19, 1992, pp. 2, 7.

Wright, Beth, review of *Babylon Boyz, School Library Journal,* September, 1997, p. 222.

For More Information See

BOOKS

Contemporary Black Biography, Volume 7, Gale, 1994.

PERIODICALS

Booklist, September 15, 1993, p. 128; February 15, 1997.

Kirkus Reviews, August 1, 1993, p. 960; April 15, 1997.

New York Times Book Review, October 31, 1993, p. 9.

People, June 22, 1992, p. 66.

Publishers Weekly, February 3, 1997, p. 107.

Washington Post Book World, November 2, 1993, p. E-2.

*   *   *

MYERS, Walter Dean 1937-
(Walter M. Myers)

Personal

Given name Walter Milton Myers; born August 12, 1937, in Martinsburg, WV; son of George Ambrose and Mary (Green) Myers; raised from age three by Herbert Julius (a shipping clerk) and Florence (a factory worker) Dean; first marriage dissolved; married second wife, Constance Brendel, June 19, 1973; children: (first marriage) Karen, Michael Dean; (second marriage) Christopher. *Education:* Attended City College of the

Walter Dean Myers

City University of New York; Empire State College, B.A., 1984.

Addresses

Home—2543 Kennedy Blvd., Jersey City, NJ 07304.

Career

New York State Department of Labor, New York City, employment supervisor, 1966-70; Bobbs-Merrill Co., Inc. (publisher), New York City, senior trade books editor, 1970-77; full-time writer, 1977—. Teacher of creative writing and black history on a part-time basis in New York City, 1974-75; worked variously as a post-office clerk, inter-office messenger, and an interviewer at a factory. *Military service:* U.S. Army, 1954-57. *Member:* PEN, Harlem Writers Guild.

Awards, Honors

Council on Interracial Books for Children Award, 1968, for the manuscript of *Where Does the Day Go?;* Children's Book of the Year, Child Study Association of America (CSAA), 1972, for *The Dancers;* Notable Book, American Library Association (ALA), 1975, and Woodward Park School Annual Book Award, 1976, both for *Fast Sam, Cool Clyde, and Stuff;* Best Books for Young Adults, ALA, 1978, for *It Ain't All for Nothin',* and 1979, for *The Young Landlords;* Coretta Scott King Award, 1980, for *The Young Landlords;* Best Books for Young Adults, ALA, 1981, and Notable Children's Trade Book in the Field of Social Studies,

National Council for Social Studies and the Children's Book Council, 1982, both for *The Legend of Tarik;* runner-up, Edgar Allan Poe Award, and Best Books for Young Adults, ALA, 1982, both for *Hoops;* Parents' Choice Award, Parents' Choice Foundation, 1982, for *Won't Know Till I Get There,* 1984, for *The Outside Shot,* and 1988, for *Fallen Angels;* New Jersey Institute of Technology Authors Award, 1983, for *Tales of a Dead King;* Coretta Scott King Award, 1985, for *Motown and Didi;* Children's Book of the Year, CSAA, 1987, for *Adventure in Granada;* Parents' Choice Award, 1987, for *Crystal;* New Jersey Institute of Technology Authors Award and Best Books for Young Adults, ALA, 1988, Coretta Scott King Award, 1989, and Children's Book Award, South Carolina Association of School Librarians, 1991, all for *Fallen Angels;* Notable Book, ALA, and Best Books for Young Adults, ALA, 1988, both for *Me, Mop, and the Moondance Kid;* Notable Book, ALA, 1988, and Newbery Medal Honor Book, ALA, 1989, both for *Scorpions;* Parents' Choice Award, 1990, for *The Mouse Rap;* Golden Kite Award Honor Book, 1991, Jane Addams Award Honor Book, 1991, Coretta Scott King Award, 1992, and Orbis Pictus Award Honor Book, 1992, all for *Now Is Your Time! The African-American Struggle for Freedom;* Parents' Choice Award, 1992, for *The Righteous Revenge of Artemis Bonner; Boston Globe-Horn Book Award* Honor Book, 1992, Coretta Scott King Award Honor Book, 1993, Newbery Medal Honor Book, 1993, all for *Somewhere in the Darkness;* Jeremiah Ludington Award, Educational Paperback Association, 1993, for creating "18 Pine St." series; CRABberry Award, 1993, for *Malcolm X: By Any Means Necessary;* Coretta Scott King Award, 1997, for *Slam!; Boston Globe-Horn Book Award* Honor Book, 1997, for *Harlem: A Poem.* Myers received the Margaret A. Edwards Award from the American Library Association and *School Library Journal* in 1994 for his contributions to young adult literature, and has also received several child-selected awards.

Writings

FICTION; FOR CHILDREN AND YOUNG ADULTS

Fast Sam, Cool Clyde, and Stuff, Viking, 1975.
Brainstorm, photographs by Chuck Freedman, Watts, 1977.
Mojo and the Russians, Viking, 1977.
Victory for Jamie, Scholastic, 1977.
It Ain't All for Nothin', Viking, 1978.
The Young Landlords, Viking, 1979.
The Golden Serpent, illustrated by Alice and Martin Provensen, Viking, 1980.
Hoops, Delacorte, 1981.
The Legend of Tarik, Viking, 1981.
Won't Know Till I Get There, Viking, 1982.
The Nicholas Factor, Viking, 1983.
Tales of a Dead King, Morrow, 1983.
Motown and Didi: A Love Story, Viking, 1984.
The Outside Shot, Delacorte, 1984.
Sweet Illusions, Teachers & Writers Collaborative, 1986.
Crystal, Viking, 1987.
Scorpions, Harper, 1988.

Me, Mop, and the Moondance Kid, illustrated by Rodney Pate, Delacorte, 1988.

Fallen Angels, Scholastic, 1988.

The Mouse Rap, HarperCollins, 1990.

Somewhere in the Darkness, Scholastic, 1992.

Mop, Moondance, and the Nagasaki Knights, Delacorte, 1992.

The Righteous Revenge of Artemis Bonner, HarperCollins, 1992.

The Glory Field, Scholastic, 1994.

Darnell Rock Reporting, Delacorte, 1994.

Shadow of the Red Moon, illustrated by Christopher Myers, Scholastic, 1995.

Sniffy Blue, Ace Crime Detective: The Case of the Missing Ruby and Other Stories, illustrated by David J. A. Sims, Scholastic, 1996.

Slam!, Scholastic, 1996.

The Journal of Joshua Loper: A Black Cowboy, Atheneum, 1999.

The Journal of Scott Pendleton Collins: A World War II Soldier, Normandy, France, 1944, Scholastic, 1999.

Monster, illustrated by Christopher Myers, HarperCollins, 1999.

"THE ARROW" SERIES

Adventure in Granada, Viking, 1985.

The Hidden Shrine, Viking, 1985.

Duel in the Desert, Viking, 1986.

Ambush in the Amazon, Viking, 1986.

NONFICTION; FOR YOUNG PEOPLE

The World of Work: A Guide to Choosing a Career, Bobbs-Merrill, 1975.

Social Welfare, Watts, 1976.

Now Is Your Time! The African-American Struggle for Freedom, HarperCollins, 1992.

A Place Called Heartbreak: A Story of Vietnam, illustrated by Frederick Porter, Raintree (Austin, TX), 1992.

Young Martin's Promise (picture book), illustrated by Barbara Higgins Bond, Raintree, 1992.

Malcolm X: By Any Means Necessary, Scholastic, 1993.

One More River to Cross: An African American Photograph Album, Harcourt, 1995.

Turning Points: When Everything Changes, Troll Communications, 1996.

Toussaint L'Ouverture: The Fight for Haiti's Freedom, illustrated by Jacob Lawrence, Simon & Schuster, 1996.

Amistad: A Long Road to Freedom, Dutton, 1998.

At Her Majesty's Request: An African Princess in Victorian England, Scholastic, 1999.

PICTURE BOOKS

(Under name Walter M. Myers) *Where Does the Day Go?,* illustrated by Leo Carty, Parents Magazine Press, 1969.

The Dragon Takes a Wife, illustrated by Ann Grifalconi, Bobbs-Merrill, 1972.

The Dancers, illustrated by Anne Rockwell, Parents Magazine Press, 1972.

Fly, Jimmy, Fly!, illustrated by Moneta Barnett, Putnam, 1974.

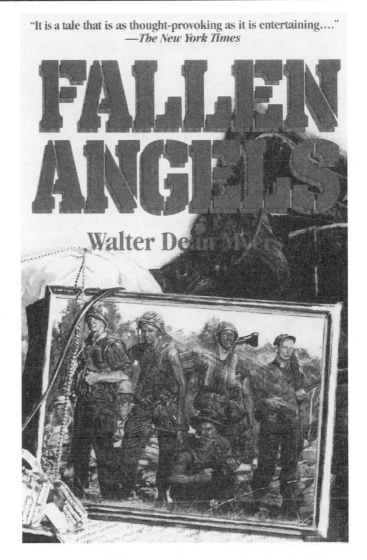

"It is a tale that is as thought-provoking as it is entertaining...."
—*The New York Times*

A compelling story about the Vietnam War, Myers's novel has been favorably compared with Stephen Crane's **The Red Badge of Courage.**

The Black Pearl and the Ghost; or, One Mystery after Another, illustrated by Robert Quackenbush, Viking, 1980.

Mr. Monkey and the Gotcha Bird, illustrated by Leslie Morrill, Delacorte, 1984.

The Story of the Three Kingdoms, illustrated by Ashley Bryan, HarperCollins, 1995.

How Mr. Monkey Saw the Whole World, illustrated by Synthia Saint James, Bantam, 1996.

Harlem: A Poem, illustrated by Christopher Myers, Scholastic, 1997.

POETRY; ILLUSTRATED WITH PERIOD PHOTOGRAPHS

Brown Angels: An Album of Pictures and Verse, HarperCollins, 1993.

Remember Us Well: An Album of Pictures and Verse, HarperCollins, 1993.

Glorious Angels: A Celebration of Children, HarperCollins, 1995.

Angel to Angel: A Mother's Gift of Love, HarperCollins, 1998.

OTHER

Creator and editor of the "18 Pine Street" series of young adult novels that feature African American characters and are published by Bantam, 1992—. Work represented in anthologies, including *What We Must SEE: Young Black Storytellers,* Dodd, 1971, and *We Be Word Sorcerers: Twenty-five Stories by Black Americans.* Contributor of articles and fiction to periodicals, including *Alfred Hitchcock Mystery Magazine, Argosy, Black Creation, Black World, Boy's Life, Ebony, Jr.!, Espionage, Essence, McCall's, National Enquirer, Negro Digest,* and *Scholastic;* also contributor of poetry to university reviews and quarterlies. In addition, Myers has contributed essays and reviews to a variety of books and periodicals focusing on literature for children and young adults.

Adaptations

The Young Landlords was made into a film by Topol Productions. *Mojo and the Russians* was made into a videorecording by Children's Television International and released by Great Plains National Instructional Television Library in 1980. Demco Media released videos of *Fallen Angels* and *Me, Mop, and the Moondance Kid* in 1988, *Scorpions* in 1990, and *The Righteous Revenge of Artemis Bonner* in 1996. *Darnell Rock Reporting* was released on video in 1996. *Harlem: A Poem* was released as a combination book and audio version in 1997. *Scorpions* was issued as a sound recording in 1998.

Sidelights

Called "one of today's most important authors of young adult literature" by Rudine Sims Bishop in *Presenting Walter Dean Myers* and "a giant among children's and young adult authors" by Frances Bradburn of *Wilson Library Bulletin,* Myers is regarded as one of the best contemporary American writers for children and young adults. An author of African American descent, he is credited with helping to redefine the image of blacks in juvenile literature. A group of African American writers emerged in the 1960s and 1970s who are credited with providing more realistic storylines and more well-rounded portrayals of black characters than those by previous authors. As a member of this group, which includes such writers as Alice Childress, Lucille Clifton, Eloise Greenfield, Virginia Hamilton, and Sharon Bell Mathis, Myers is distinguished by bringing both humor and poignancy to his books as well as for creating works with special appeal to boys; in addition, he is considered the only prominent male writer of the group to have consistently published books of quality. A versatile and prolific author, Myers has written realistic and historical fiction, mysteries, adventure stories, fantasies, nonfiction, poetry, and picture books for a diverse audience of young people. Although he is praised for his contributions to several genres, Myers is perhaps best known as the writer of books for readers in junior high and high school that range from farcical, lighthearted stories for younger teens to powerful, moving novels for older

adolescents. Myers is credited with stressing the more positive aspects of black urban life in his works. Often setting his books in his boyhood home of Harlem, Myers is acknowledged for depicting the strength and dignity of his characters without downplaying the harsh realities of their lives.

Although he features both young men and women as protagonists, Myers is noted for his focus on young African American males. His themes often include the relationship between fathers and sons as well as the search for identity and self-worth in an environment of poverty, drugs, gangs, and racism. Although his characters confront difficult issues, Myers stresses survival, pride, and hope in his works, which are filled with love and laughter and a strong sense of possibility for the future of their protagonists. Lauded for his understanding of the young, Myers is acclaimed as the creator of believable, sympathetic adolescent characters; he is also praised for creating realistic dialogue, some of which draws on rap music and other African American idioms. Calling him "a unique voice," Rudine Sims Bishop said that Myers has become "an important writer because he creates books that appeal to young adults from many cultural groups. They appeal because Myers knows and cares about the things that concern his readers and because he creates characters that readers are happy to spend time with." R. D. Lane of *African American Review* noted that the author "celebrates children by weaving narratives of the black juvenile experience in ways that reverse the effects of mediated messages of the black experience in public culture.... Myers's stratagem is revolutionary: the intrinsic value to black youth of his lessons stands priceless, timeless, and class-transcendent." In her entry in *Dictionary of Literary Biography,* Carmen Subryan concluded, "Myers's books demonstrate that writers can not only challenge the minds of black youths but also emphasize the black experience in a nondidactic way that benefits all readers."

Born in Martinsburg, West Virginia, Myers was originally named Walter Milton Myers. At two years old, he lost his mother, Mary Green Myers, during the birth of his younger sister Imogene. Since his father George Ambrose Myers was struggling economically, Walter and two of his sisters were informally adopted by two friends of his parents, Florence and Herbert Dean; later, Myers would write about surrogate parenting in several of his stories, including *Won't Know Till I Get There* and *Me, Mop, and the Moondance Kid.* The Deans moved their family to Harlem when Myers was about three. He wrote in *Something about the Author Autobiography Series (SAAS),* "I loved Harlem. I lived in an exciting corner of the renowned Black capital and in an exciting era. The people I met there, the things I did, have left a permanent impression on me." When he was four, Myers was taught to read by his foster mother; his foster father sat the boy on his knee and told him what Myers called "endless stories" in *SAAS.* The author wrote in *Children's Books and Their Creators,* "Somewhere along the line I discovered that books could be part of a child's world, and by the time I was nine I found myself

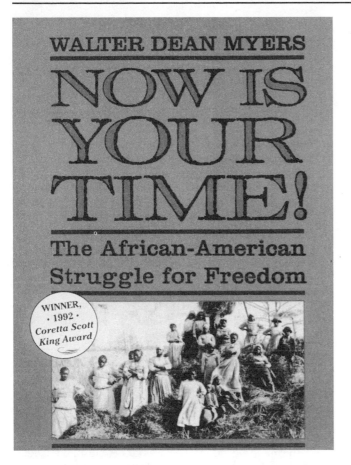

WALTER DEAN MYERS

NOW IS YOUR TIME!

The African-American Struggle for Freedom

WINNER, · 1992 · Coretta Scott King Award

Myers offers an engrossing history of the African-American struggle for freedom and equality, highlighting particular events that have had far-reaching significance.

spending long hours reading in my room. The books began to shape new bouts of imagination. Now I was one of 'The Three Musketeers' (always the one in the middle), or participating in the adventures of Jo's boys. John R. Tunis brought me back to sports, and I remember throwing a pink ball against the wall for hours as I struggled through baseball games that existed only in the rich arena of invention."

When he wasn't reading, Myers enjoyed playing sports, especially stickball, baseball, and basketball; the latter provides the background for three of the author's most popular young adult novels, *Hoops, The Outside Shot,* and *Slam!* At school, Myers enjoyed classwork but found that a speech impediment caused him some difficulty. His fellow classmates would laugh at him and, as a result, he would fight back; consequently, he was often suspended from school. When Myers was in fifth grade, he wrote in *SAAS,* "a marvelous thing happened." Made to sit at the back of the class for fighting, Myers was reading a comic book during a math lesson when the teacher, Mrs. Conway, caught him. Mrs. Conway, who was known for her meanness, surprised Walter by saying that if he was going to read he might as well read something decent. She brought him a selection of children's books; Myers remembered Asbjornsen and

Moe's *East of the Sun and West of the Moon,* a collection of Norwegian folktales, as a turning point in his appreciation of literature. Mrs. Conway also required her students to read aloud in class. In order to avoid some of the words that he had trouble speaking, she suggested that Walter write something for himself to read. The poems that he wrote for class—which deliberately skirted problematic consonants—were Myers's first literary attempts.

After completing an accelerated junior high school program that consolidated the seventh and eighth grades into one year, Myers attended the prestigious Stuyvesant High School, a school for boys that stressed academic achievement. Although he struggled somewhat with the school's focus on science, Myers met another influential teacher, Bonnie Liebow, who interviewed each of her students and made up individualized reading lists for them; Myers's list included works by such European authors as Emile Zola and Thomas Mann. Liebow also told Myers that he was a gifted writer, and he began thinking of writing as a career. He wrote every day, sometimes skipping school to sit in a tree in Central Park to read or work on his writing. However, at age sixteen Myers began to feel frustrated. Although he won a prize for an essay contest and was awarded a set of encyclopedias for one of his poems, Myers realized that writing "had no practical value for a Black child." He recalled: "These minor victories did not bolster my ego. Instead, they convinced me that even though I was bright, even though I might have some talent, I was still defined by factors other than my ability." In addition, Myers was depressed by the fact that he would not be able to attend college due to his family's financial status. Consequently, he wrote in *SAAS,* he began "writing poems about death, despair, and doom" and began "having doubts about everything in my life." When not writing or working odd jobs, Myers hung out in the streets: "I was steeped in the mystique of the semi-hoodlum," he recalled in *SAAS.* Myers acquired a stiletto and acted as a drug courier; he also became a target for one of the local gangs after intervening in a fight between three gang members and a new boy in the neighborhood. Finally, influenced by the war poems of English poet Rupert Brooke, Myers joined the army at seventeen in order to, as he wrote in *SAAS,* "hie myself off to some far-off battlefield and get killed. There, where I fell, would be a little piece of Harlem."

Myers's army experience was less than the glorious adventure promised by the poetry he had read; he went to radio-repair school and spent most of his time playing basketball. "I also learned several efficient ways of killing human beings," he wrote in *SAAS.* In *Presenting Walter Dean Myers,* the author told Rudine Sims Bishop, "I learned something about dying. I learned a lot about facilitating the process, of making it abstract." Myers developed a strong antiwar attitude that would later become part of his young adult novel *Fallen Angels,* the story of a young black soldier in Vietnam. After three years in the army, Myers returned to his parents, who had moved to Morristown, New Jersey. After a brief period, he moved back to Harlem, where he took an apartment and began to work at becoming a professional writer. Calling this his "starving artist period" in *SAAS,* Myers wrote poetry and read books about the Bohemian life by such authors as George Orwell and Andre Gide; he also lived on two dollars a week from unemployment compensation and lost fifty pounds. Finally, when a friend suggested that he take the Civil Service exam, Myers went to work for the post office, a job that lasted only a few months. He also married Joyce, a woman he called "wonderful, warm, beautiful, religious, caring" in *SAAS.* Even after becoming a father—two of his three children, Karen and Michael, are from his first marriage—Myers continued to try to live a romantic lifestyle. While working odd jobs in a factory and an office, he played bongos with a group of jazz musicians, some of whom were into heroin and cocaine, and wrote jazz-based poetry, some of which was published in Canada. He also began to be published in African American magazines such as the *Negro Digest* and the *Liberator* as well as in men's magazines such as *Argosy* and *Cavalier.* "I also," Myers recalled in *SAAS,* "drank too much and ran around too much." Eventually, his marriage collapsed.

In 1961, Myers enrolled in a writing class with the author Lajos Egri, who told him that he had a special talent. A few years later, Myers attended City College of the City University of New York as a night student, but dropped out. He then enrolled at a writer's workshop at Columbia University. The workshop was led by John Oliver Killens, a successful African American novelist who recommended Myers for a new editorial position at the publishing house Bobbs-Merrill. Myers got the job and became an acquisitions editor. In 1968, he entered a contest for African American writers sponsored by the Council on Interracial Books for Children. The manuscript that Myers submitted was selected as the first-prize winner in the picture book category; in 1969, it was published by Parents' Magazine Press as *Where Does the Day Go?* The book features Steven, a small black boy whose father takes him and a group of children of various races for an evening walk in the park. When Steven wonders where the day goes, his friends each provide imaginative opinions of their own. Finally, Steven's daddy explains that the day and night are different, just like people, and that the times of day are caused by the rotation of the Earth. "Integration, involvement, and togetherness are all deftly handled," noted Mary Eble of *School Library Journal,* while Zena Sutherland, Dianne L. Monson, and May Hill Arbuthnot claimed in *Children and Books* that the story has "other strong values in addition to its exploration of the mystery of night and day." The critics noted that *Where Does the Day Go?* "explains natural phenomena accurately, and it presents an exemplary father...."

After the publication of his first book, Myers changed his name from Walter Milton Myers to, as he wrote in *SAAS,* "one that would honor my foster parents, Walter Dean Myers." He also remarried, and he and his wife Connie had a son, Christopher, an artist who has illustrated several of his father's works. In 1972, Myers published *The Dragon Takes a Wife,* a picture book that is often considered his most controversial book. The story features Harry, a lonely dragon who cannot fight, and Mabel May, the African American fairy who helps him. In order to acquire a wife, Harry must defeat a knight in battle. When Mabel May turns into a dragon to show Harry how to fight, Harry falls in love with her, defeats the knight, and wins her hand (not to mention a good job at the post office). Myers received mixed reviews for *The Dragon Takes a Wife.* For example, a critic in *Kirkus Reviews* called it "pointless intercultural hocus-pocus," while Nancy Griffin of the *New York Times Book Review* praised it as "the funniest, most-up-to-the-minute fairy tale of 1972." Some readers were angered by the fact that Mabel May was black and spoke in hip lingo; they were also concerned that this character appeared in a fairy tale for young children. *The Dragon Takes a Wife* was banned by some libraries; Myers also received hate mail from disgruntled adult readers of the book.

In 1975, Myers published his first novel for young adults, *Fast Sam, Cool Clyde, and Stuff.* Set in a Harlem neighborhood much like the one in which its author grew up, the story describes a group of young teens who take a positive approach to living in a difficult environment. The story is narrated by eighteen-year-old Stuff, who recalls the year that he was thirteen and formed a sort of anti-gang, the Good People, with his best friends Fast Sam and Cool Clyde plus five other boys and girls from the neighborhood. The Good People have several hilarious adventures, including one where Sam and Clyde—who is dressed as a girl—win a dance contest. However, they also deal with such problems as mistaken arrest and the deaths of one of their fathers and a friend who has turned to drugs. The children survive, both through their inner strength and the fellowship of their friends, who are dependable and respectful of one another. Writing in *English Journal,* Alleen Pace Nilsen called *Fast Sam, Cool Clyde, and Stuff* "a rich, warm story about black kids in which Myers makes the reader feel so close to the characters that ethnic group identification is secondary." Paul Heins of *Horn Book* noted that "the humorous and ironic elements of the plot give the book the flavor of a Harlem *Tom Sawyer* or *Penrod.*" *Fast Sam, Cool Clyde, and Stuff* continues to be one of Myers's most popular works, especially among middle graders and junior high school students. Writing in SAAS, the author remarked, "I was writing humor in *Fast Sam* ... something that comes to me fairly easily. I was also writing about the positive side of my Harlem experience, which most of it was."

In 1977, after being fired from his job as a senior editor for Bobbs-Merrill due to a dispute with a company vice-president, Myers became a full-time writer. *It Ain't All for Nothin',* a young adult novel published the next year, is considered the first of the author's more serious, thought-provoking works. The novel features twelve-year-old Tippy, a motherless Harlem boy who has been living with his loving, principled grandmother since he was a baby. When she goes into a nursing home, Tippy moves in with his father Lonnie, an ex-con who makes his living by stealing and who beats his son viciously.

Lonely and afraid, Tippy begins drinking whiskey. When Lonnie and his pals rob a store, he coerces Tippy into participating. Bubba, a member of the group, is shot; in order to save Bubba and save himself, Tippy calls the police and turns in his father. At the end of the novel, Tippy goes to live with Mr. Roland, a kind man who has befriended him. *It Ain't All for Nothin'* was praised by Steven Matthews in *School Library Journal* as "a first-rate read, in the class of Alice Childress' *A Hero Ain't Nothin' But a Sandwich*" and by a critic in *Kirkus Reviews* as "like Tippy—a winner." Although questioning "how many children are really going to 'drop a dime' on their father?," Ashley Jane Pennington concluded in her review in *Interracial Books for Children Bulletin* that *It Ain't All for Nothin'* "is a devastating book which needed to be written...." In 1984, Myers published *Motown and Didi: A Love Story,* a highly praised spin-off novel from *It Ain't All for Nothin'* that features two of the latter's peripheral characters. A romance between two Harlem teens, *Motown and Didi* includes a strong antidrug message as well as the theme that love can conquer all.

In 1988, Myers published *Scorpions* and *Fallen Angels,* two novels for young people that are considered among his best. In *Scorpions,* twelve-year-old Jamal lives in Harlem with his mother and younger sister. He is approached to take the place of his older brother Randy, who is in jail for killing a man, as the leader of his gang, the Scorpions. At first, Jamal refuses; however, he is fascinated with the gun that Randy's friend Mack gives him and is searching for a way to help his family raise the money for Randy's appeal. Jamal and his best friend Tito, a sensitive Puerto Rican boy, join the Scorpions, who are dealing cocaine. During a confrontation, Jamal is defended by Tito, who uses the gun that Mack had given Jamal to kill to protect his friend. Marcus Crouch of the *Junior Bookshelf* wrote that Myers "writes with great power, capturing the cadences of black New York, and keeps a firm hold on his narrative and his emotions. He is a fine story-teller as well as a social critic and, I suspect, a moralist." Writing in *Bulletin of the Center for Children's Books,* Roger Sutton noted that Myers's "compassion for Tito and Jamal is deep; perhaps the book's seminal achievement is the way it makes us realize how young, in Harlem and elsewhere, twelve years old really is."

Fallen Angels describes the horrors of the Vietnam War from the perspective of Richie Perry, a seventeen-year-old African American boy who has joined the Army as a way to make life easier for his mother and younger brother in Harlem. During the course of a year, Richie experiences fear and terror as he fights in the war; he burns the bodies of American soldiers because they cannot be carried and—with a rifle at his head—shoots a North Vietnamese soldier in the face; finally, after being wounded twice, he is sent home. Underscoring the novel, which includes rough language and gallows humor, is a strong antiwar message; Myers also addresses such issues as racial discrimination within the service and the conditions faced by the Vietnamese people. Calling Myers "a writer of skill, maturity, and

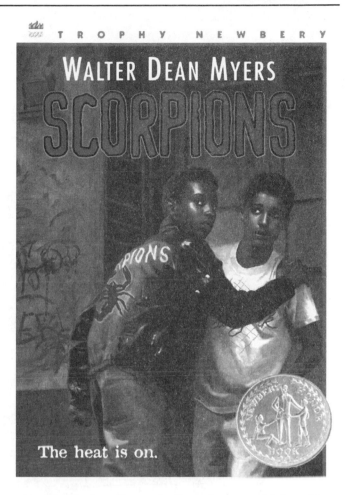

In this Newbery Honor-book, twelve-year-old Jamal is pressured to join the gang his imprisoned older brother used to lead. (Cover illustration by Andy Bacha.)

judgment," Ethel L. Heins of *Horn Book* maintained: "With its intensity and vividness in depicting a young soldier amid the chaos and the carnage of war, the novel recalls Stephen Crane's *The Red Badge of Courage.*" W. Keith McCoy, writing in *Voice of Youth Advocates,* commented, "Everything about this book rings true," while Mary Veeder of *Chicago Tribune—Books* noted that *Fallen Angels* "may be the best novel for young adults I've read this year." Writing in *School Librarian,* a British periodical, Alison Hurst claimed, "The dialogue is so convincing that American accents rang around my head as I read." Myers wrote *Fallen Angels* as a tribute to his brother Sonny, who was killed on his first day as a soldier in Vietnam; he also based much of the book on his own experience in the Army. In discussing both *Fallen Angels* and *Scorpions* with Kimberly Olson Fakih in *Publishers Weekly,* Myers called these books "a departure" and "very serious, probing work." He concluded: "Not that the others didn't address serious issues, too, but the new ones were more difficult to write." In 1993, Myers published *A Place Called Heartbreak: A Story of Vietnam,* a well-received biography of Colonel Fred V. Cherry, an Air Force pilot and African American who was held as a prisoner of the North Vietnamese for nearly eight years.

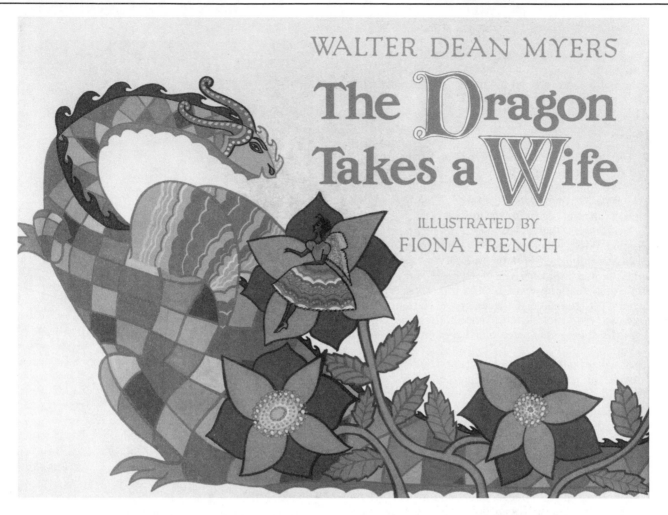

Myers's first picture book depicts the unlikely friendship between a kindhearted jive-talking fairy named Mabel Mae Jones and a dragon who wants to get married. (Cover illustration by Fiona French.)

In addition to his fiction, Myers has written several highly praised informational books for children and young people. In these works, the author characteristically outlines the fight for freedom by people of color; he has also written biographies of such figures as Toussaint L'Ouverture, Martin Luther King, and Malcolm X. *Now Is Your Time! The African-American Struggle for Freedom,* is one of Myers's most well regarded works of nonfiction. In this book, the author recounts the history of African Americans through both overviews and profiles of individuals. "What happens," wrote a critic in *Kirkus Reviews,* "when a gifted novelist chooses to write the story of his people? In this case, the result is engrossing history with a strong unifying theme, the narrative enriched with accounts of outstanding lives." Michael Dirda of *Book World* added that Myers "writes with the vividness of a novelist, the balance of a historian, and the passion of an advocate. He tells a familiar story and shocks us with it all over again." Writing in *Voice of Youth Advocates,* Kellie Flynn noted that this history "is alive and vital—with breathing biographical sketches and historic interpretations like rabbit punches." With *Amistad: A Long Road to Freedom,* a book published in 1998, Myers tells the dramatic story of the captive Africans who mutinied

against their captors on the slave ship *Amistad* in the late 1830s. The book recounts the hellish journey on the ship and the forced landing in Connecticut as well as the landmark trial and the struggle of the West Africans to return home. Writing in *Booklist,* Hazel Rochman stated, "The narrative is exciting, not only the account of the uprising but also the tension of the court arguments about whether the captives were property and what their rights were in a country that banned the slave trade but allowed slavery." Gerry Larson of *School Library Journal* added, "With characteristic scholarship, clarity, insight, and compassion, Myers presents readers with the facts and the moral and historical significance of the *Amistad* episode."

A longtime collector of historical photographs and documents depicting the lives and culture of African Americans, Myers has used his art to illustrate several of his informational books. The photos and letters from the author's collection have also inspired several of his works, including volumes of original poetry on black children and mothers and the biography *At Her Majesty's Request: An African Princess in Victorian England.* Published in 1999, this work reconstructs the life of Sarah Forbes Bonetta, a child of royal African descent who became a goddaughter of Queen Victoria as well as a British celebrity. Saved from a sacrificial rite in Dahomey by English sea captain Frederick E. Forbes, orphaned Sarah (named after her rescuer and his ship) was brought to England as a gift for Queen Victoria from the Dahomian king who slaughtered her family. Victoria provided the means for Sarah—nicknamed Sally—to be educated as a young woman of privilege in a missionary school in Sierra Leone. Sally, who often returned to England to visit her benefactor, grew up to marry a West African businessman—a marriage arranged by Buckingham Palace; she named her first-born child Victoria. Returning with her husband to Africa, Sally taught in missionary schools until she died of tuberculosis at the age of thirty-six. Working from a packet of letters he discovered in a London bookstore, Myers tells Sally's story, which he embellishes with quotes from Queen Victoria's diary, newspapers, and other memoirs of the time. A critic in *Kirkus Reviews* commented, "This vividly researched biography will enthrall readers, and ranks among Myers's best writing." Calling *At Her Majesty's Request* a "fascinating biography" and a "moving and very humane portrait of a princess," a reviewer in *Publishers Weekly* concluded that Myers "portrays a young woman who never truly belongs."

Writing in *SAAS,* Myers stated that he feels the need to show young blacks "the possibilities that exist for them that were never revealed to me as a youngster; possibilities that did not even exist for me then." He continued: "As a Black writer I want to talk about my people.... I want to tell Black children about their humanity and about their history and how to grease their legs so the ash won't show and how to braid their hair so it's easy to comb on frosty winter mornings. The books come. They pour from me at a great rate.... There is always one more story to tell, one more person whose life needs to be held up to the sun." He added, "[T]here are times when I see someone reading one of my books, or when I get a letter from some person who has read a story or book of mine, and it makes me feel so good it hurts." The author recalled when he was sitting in his parents' Harlem apartment at about thirteen or fourteen reading the *New York Times Book Review.* He wrote, "I read the reviews and had an idea that this writing, this talking about books and reading books was as much the stuff of life as anything. I think I was right." In an interview in *Teaching and Learning Literature,* Myers said, "What I do with whatever art I have is to try to communicate the human experience." He continued that he wants to communicate this experience to "my sons, my son's sons, daughters, the next generation, and that is what life is about. We are the ones that have the gift of story, the gift of passing it on." Writing in *Children's Books and Their Creators,* Myers concluded, "What I do with my books is to create windows to my world that all may peer into. I share the images, the feelings and thoughts, and, I hope, the delight."

Works Cited

Review of *At Her Majesty's Request: An African Princess in Victorian England, Kirkus Reviews,* December 15, 1998, p. 1802.

Review of *At Her Majesty's Request: An African Princess in Victorian England, Publishers Weekly,* February 8, 1999, p. 215.

Bishop, Rudine Sims, *Presenting Walter Dean Myers,* Twayne, 1991.

Bradburn, Frances, review of *The Righteous Revenge of Artemis Bonner, Wilson Library Bulletin,* January, 1993, p. 88.

Crouch, Marcus, review of *Scorpions, Junior Bookshelf,* August, 1990, pp. 190-91.

Dirda, Michael, review of *Now Is Your Time! The African-American Struggle for Freedom, Book World,* March 8, 1992, p. 11.

Review of *The Dragon Takes a Wife, Kirkus Reviews,* March 1, 1972, p. 256.

Eble, Mary, review of *Where Does the Day Go?, School Library Journal,* April 15, 1970, p. 111.

Fakih, Kimberly Olson, "Walter Dean Myers," *Publishers Weekly,* February 26, 1988, p. 117.

Flynn, Kellie, review of *Now Is Your Time! The African-American Struggle for Freedom, Voice of Youth Advocates,* February, 1992, p. 398.

Greever, Ellen A. and Patricia Austin, "Making Connections in the Life and Works of Walter Dean Myers," *TALL,* September-October, 1998, pp. 42-54.

Griffin, Nancy, review of *The Dragon Takes a Wife, New York Times Book Review,* April 19, 1972, p. 8.

Heins, Ethel L., review of *Fallen Angels, Horn Book,* July-August, 1988, pp. 503-04.

Heins, Paul, review of *Fast Sam, Cool Clyde, and Stuff, Horn Book,* August, 1975, pp. 388-89.

Hurst, Alison, review of *Fallen Angels, School Librarian,* August, 1990, pp. 118-19.

Review of *It Ain't All for Nothin', Kirkus Reviews,* October 15, 1978, p. 1143.

Lane, R. D., "'Keepin' It Real': Walter Dean Myers and the Promise of African-American Children's Literature," *African American Review,* spring, 1998, p. 125.

Larson, Gerry, review of *Amistad: A Long Road to Freedom, School Library Journal,* May, 1998, p. 158.

Matthews, Steven, review of *It Ain't All for Nothin', School Library Journal,* October, 1978, p. 158.

McCoy, W. Keith, review of *Fallen Angels, Voice of Youth Advocates,* August, 1988, p. 133.

Myers, Walter Dean, comments in *Children's Books and Their Creators,* edited by Anita Silvey, Houghton Mifflin, 1995, p. 475.

Myers, Walter Dean, essay in *Something about the Author Autobiography Series,* Volume 2, Gale, 1986, pp. 143-56.

Nilsen, Alleen Pace, "Love and the Teenage Reader," *English Journal,* March, 1976, pp. 90-92.

Review of *Now Is Your Time! The African-American Struggle for Freedom, Kirkus Reviews,* December 1, 1991, p. 1537.

Pennington, Ashley Jane, review of *It Ain't All for Nothin', Interracial Books for Children Bulletin,* Volume 10, number 4, 1979, p. 18.

Rochman, Hazel, "Some Versions of *Amistad*," *Booklist,* February 15, 1998, p. 1003.

Subryan, Carmen, "Walter Dean Myers," *Dictionary of Literary Biography,* Volume 33: *Afro-American Fiction Writers after 1955,* Gale, 1984, pp. 199-202.

Sutherland, Zena, Dianne L. Monson, and May Hill Arbuthnot, "Books for the Very Young," *Children and Books,* Scott, Foresman, 1981, p. 99.

Sutton, Roger, review of *Scorpions, Bulletin of the Center for Children's Books,* July-August, 1988, p. 235.

Veeder, Mary, review of *Fallen Angels, Chicago Tribune-Books,* November 13, 1988, p. 6.

For More Information See

BOOKS

Children's Literature Review, Gale, Volume 16, 1989, pp. 134-44, Volume 35, 1995, pp. 173-206.

Johnson, Diane, *Telling Tales: The Pedagogy and Promise of African-American Literature for Youth,* Greenwood, 1990.

Patrick-Wexler, Diane, *Walter Dean Myers,* Raintree, 1996.

Silbert, Martha F., essay on Myers in *Children's Books and Their Creators,* edited by Anita Silvey, Houghton Mifflin, 1995, p. 474.

Smith, Karen Patricia, editor, *African-American Voices in Young Adult Literature: Tradition, Transition, Transformation,* Scarecrow Press, 1994.

PERIODICALS

Bulletin of the Center for Children's Books, February, 1999, p. 211; May, 1999, p. 323.

Horn Book, January-February, 1997, p. 63; January-February, 1999, pp. 52-53.

Kirkus Reviews, June 1, 1999, p. 887.

New York Times Book Review, November 9, 1986, p. 50.

Publishers Weekly, March 23, 1999, pp. 45-46; April 5, 1999, pp. 242-43.

School Library Journal, June, 1994, pp. 24-28; July, 1999, p. 98.

Voice of Youth Advocates, February, 1997, pp. 330-31; April, 1999, p. 62; August, 1999, p. 185.

—*Sketch by Gerard J. Senick*

*   *   *

MYERS, Walter M.
See MYERS, Walter Dean

N–O

NOLAN, Han 1956-

Personal

Born August 25, 1956, in Birmingham, AL; married September 12, 1981. *Education:* University of North Carolina at Greensboro, B.S. in dance, 1979; Ohio State University, master's degree in dance, 1981. *Hobbies and other interests:* Reading, hiking, running, swimming, "I love to move and be outside."

Han Nolan

Addresses

Office—c/o Harcourt Brace & Company, 525 B St., Suite 1900, San Diego, CA 92101-4495.

Career

Writer. Teacher of dance, 1981-84. *Member:* Society of Children's Book Writers and Illustrators, PEN.

Awards, Honors

People's Choice Award and National Book Award nominee, both 1996, both for *Send Me Down a Miracle;* Books for the Teen Age, New York Public Library, 1994, for *If I Should Die Before I Wake,* 1996, for *Send Me Down a Miracle,* and 1997, for *Dancing on the Edge;* National Book Award, 1997, and Best Books for Young Adults, American Library Association, 1998, both for *Dancing on the Edge.*

Writings

If I Should Die Before I Wake, Harcourt, 1994.
Send Me Down a Miracle, Harcourt, 1996.
Dancing on the Edge, Harcourt, 1997.

Work in Progress

A Face in Every Window, a young adult novel, for Harcourt.

Sidelights

The 1997 winner of the National Book Award for her young adult novel, *Dancing on the Edge,* Han Nolan speaks directly to teenage readers in a voice at once empathic and down-home humorous. The author of three published novels, Nolan has already captured a wide and loyal readership with her themes of tolerance and understanding, and with her youthful protagonists who discover—in the course of her books—who they are and what they want. "Thoughtful is how I would describe my books," Nolan commented in an interview with J.

Sixteen-year-old Hilary Burke—a present-day neo-Nazi—learns what it's like to be hated when she time-travels to a Polish ghetto during the Holocaust as a Jewish girl in Nolan's 1994 novel. (Cover illustration by David Kahl.)

Sydney Jones for *Authors and Artists for Young Adults.* "I put a lot of thought into my novels and I hope they are also thought-provoking, but I guess that is for someone else besides me to judge."

Unlike many authors of books for young adults, with Nolan there was no serendipity in the audience for whom she chose to write. From the beginning of her career she set out to write novels for young readers. "I really love the YA readership, teens. I like how their minds work. They're just coming into their own; it's an exciting, new, and scary time for them. They are learning how the world works. It's feverish and passionate. Also, I liked my own teen years. It's a time for us to wake up. We're no longer blind children led by our parents." Nolan hopes her books provide a chance for teens "to enter a private world and stop and think about their lives. They need this chance to go somewhere private and think about things that they might not be able to talk about with their friends."

Nolan's books have dealt with neo-Nazis, religious zealotry, and the lies a family promulgates to supposedly protect its children. Her characters—Hilary, Charity, Miracle—are young women on the cusp, emerging into an uncertain adulthood from shaky adolescence. They are young women who must learn to stand up for themselves—to throw off the influences of adults and peers and find their own center in a turbulent universe. Hilary in *If I Should Die Before I Wake* becomes a time-traveler to learn a lesson of tolerance, literally trading places with the Jews whom she professes to hate. Her own experience of the dark night of the Holocaust changes her profoundly and allows her to become her own person. Likewise, Charity in *Send Me Down a Miracle* learns—in a less dramatic manner perhaps—to stand up for herself and thus be able to deal with her dominating father. And Miracle, the protagonist of *Dancing on the Edge,* must pass through the private hell of psychosis before she puts to rest the secrets that have riven her family. "Thoughtful" is indeed the word that comes to mind when reviewing Han Nolan's work.

Born in the South, Nolan was raised in the North, specifically the northeast urban sectors around New York City. As a result, she has something of a dual citizenship to regional America: roots in the Southern sensibility of languorous tales after dinner, and feet firmly planted in the go-ahead urban ethic. The next to youngest of five children, Nolan and the rest of her family "moved around a lot," as she told Jones, "something that teaches you how to make new friends quickly." Friends and neighborhoods changed, but a constant in the family was a love of books and the arts. "We were big time readers in my family. I remember my father used to bring three books home every night for my mother, and she would finish them by the next morning."

Like the rest of her family, Nolan loved books and reading from an early age. "As a young child, the book that really influenced me to become a writer was *Harriet the Spy.* After reading that, I of course wanted to be a spy not a writer, but I did begin keeping journals of my observations like Harriet. It's the journal-keeping that was so influential, that helped turn me into a writer. I still keep journals." Later favorite authors were Charles Dickens and John Steinbeck. "I also loved to write stories, and began putting them down on paper as soon as I learned how to write."

School was another matter, however. "Elementary school was very difficult for me," Nolan related. "I was a hyperactive kid as a result of food allergies that I've only recently discovered. So it was hard for me to pay attention." Junior high was a more positive experience, and when Nolan was thirteen, she began dancing, an activity that enabled her to focus: "As a result, I'd say I had very happy teen years." Added to this life in New York were summers Nolan and her family spent in the South, in Dothan, Alabama, where many of her relations lived on one street. There she got in touch with another part of her heritage, listening to a favorite aunt stretch out the evening with her long tales. "My Southern relatives loved to sit and listen to these stories. Everything is a story, a blend of wit, humor, and intelligence. They had the ability to laugh at everything, including themselves. There was seriousness in these long tales, and tragedy, too. But they were always leavened with humor. When I was a child I would sit and listen for hours."

Upon graduation from high school, Nolan decided to go south for college. "I chose the University of North Carolina at Greensboro because of the dance major they offered. The program turned out to be incredibly well-rounded, requiring courses in the sciences, physical education, and education, and in addition there were all the English courses I naturally gravitated to. So I had a full education." Graduating in 1979, she went on to a master's program in dance at Ohio State University, where she met her future husband, who was working on his doctorate in Classics. In 1981 she graduated, married, and began teaching dance. When the couple decided on adopting children several years later, Nolan also opted for a career change.

"I wanted to be home with my kids," she noted in her interview, "so I thought about work I could do at home. I always loved to write and took some creative writing classes, but it was not something you could actually do for a living. I fancied being able to write and living on Cape Cod, but those were fantasies, not reality. I just always figured I would do something more practical." Then discussing it with her husband one afternoon, he helped make the decision for her. "Suddenly he just took off, saying he'd be back in a bit. When he finally came back he had one of these writers' market guides for me, and that just started me writing."

Thus began Nolan's writing career. She studied not only markets, but every book on writing technique that she could get her hands on. She wrote stories and sent some out with no success. Then she tackled lengthier projects, writing a mystery that won some attention with a publisher but was not purchased. Nonetheless, there was encouragement in the fact that an editor had taken interest in her work. She joined or formed writers' groups where she happened to be living—in Pennsylvania and Connecticut. She began another mystery, but one of the characters was stubbornly going off on her own, dreaming about the Holocaust.

"This kept coming into the story and getting bigger and bigger," Nolan recalled. In addition to Nolan's subconscious at work, there were also contemporary events impinging. "Here I was in Connecticut, and I discovered that there was a KKK group in town. Hate crimes were being reported, and I was appalled by this whole neo-Nazi fascination. As a young teenager I came across Viktor Frankl's *Man's Search for Meaning* in my parents' bookshelves, and reading that I remember how shocked I was to read about the Holocaust. First, that this should have been allowed to happen, and second, that I had not known about it before—that it was not being taught to us as students. There was a kind of horror I internalized then that finally found a way to come out in my writing. A sense of horror that was recharged by events around me."

In her debut novel, *If I Should Die Before I Wake,* Nolan recast the character from her mystery as Hilary Burke, a young neo-Nazi who is lying in a coma in a Jewish hospital. Hilary has history: her father died years before, his death caused (so Hilary believes) by a Jew, and her Bible-thumping mother temporarily abandoned her. She has found a home with a group of neo-Nazis; her boyfriend is the leader of the group. Hilary now lies in a hospital as a result of a motorcycle accident. In her coma, she sees another patient, an elderly Jewish woman named Chana in her room. Chana is a Holocaust survivor, but to Hilary she is sarcastically labeled "Grandmaw." Suddenly Hilary spins back in time, trading places with Chana, becoming herself the persecuted young girl in Poland. She experiences firsthand the horrors of the Holocaust: her father is shot; she lives in the ghetto for a time; she escapes with her grandmother from the ghetto only to be captured, tortured, and sent to Auschwitz-Birkenau. Hilary constantly drifts back to herself in the hospital. Meanwhile, her mother, a born-again Christian, and her boyfriend visit. By the end, "Hilary has come back from her own near-death experience as well as Chana's to be a more understanding, tolerant person," Susan Levine wrote in *Voice of Youth Advocates.*

"I wanted to say to neo-Nazis 'How would you like this to happen to you?'," Nolan related. "I wanted to put them into the same situations the Jews suffered. The writing of the book was very difficult. Working on the historical parts, I felt that I was actually there. I was afraid to write the book. I didn't think that I had enough talent to tackle the subject. And I'm not Jewish. But it was a story I had to tell. I was so compelled, and I wanted to write the book not so much for Jewish readers—they know their history—but for non-Jewish teenagers. To let them know, to make sure that we can't let this happen again. Just can't. I knew I was going to take some flack for the book and I did."

The first review Nolan read—or actually had read to her by her husband over the phone while attending a writer's conference—questioned the taste of the book. This was shattering enough for Nolan to later warn off a would-be purchaser of her first novel at the conference. "I told this person, 'Oh no, you don't want to read that. It got a bad review.' What did I know? I was just starting." Most reviewers, however, responded positively to this first effort. Levine went on in her *Voice of Youth Advocates* review to note that the novel is a history and ethics lesson enveloped in a riveting plot. Levine concluded that Nolan had written "an interesting and moving story." Roger Sutton, writing in the *Bulletin of the Center for Children's Books,* commented that Nolan is forthright in dealing with her material, "and her graphic descriptions of camp life have a morbid interest that teeters on exploitation but comes down on the side of the truth." *Booklist*'s Mary Harris Veeder stated that Nolan's "first novel has great strengths and weaknesses." Among the latter, Veeder felt, were the time travel episodes and certain contemporary characterizations. "Chana's story, however, is brilliantly rendered," Veeder noted, and "carries memorable emotional impact." A *Kirkus Reviews* critic remarked that "Nolan's first novel is ambitious indeed," and concluded that "the book as a whole is deeply felt and often compelling."

Nolan was already 100 pages into her next novel by the time of publication of *If I Should Die Before I Wake.* "My next book was lighter," Nolan admitted. "It was a fun book to write, because I used material from my own summers in the South. I needed something lighter after writing about the Holocaust. We were still living in Connecticut, and I was now taking my own children down to Dothan for the summers. It brought back all those old memories for me." Soon these memories were added to by the fact that Nolan and her family moved to the South, to Birmingham, Alabama.

Nolan began to find her own writing method also. Starting with a character or situation or location rather than a plot outline, she writes long enough to get to know her characters and where they want to take things. This can take up to sixty pages of manuscript, much of which gets tossed with revisions and tightening of story. "My characters are made up as I go along," Nolan explained. "They're all parts of me, composites. It's sort of like Michelangelo's theory of sculpture. The figure is already there under the stone; it's the artist's job to release it by chipping away. The first sixty pages are me chipping away at the stone.

"And there's a vagueness to the whole process. You have something you want to say in the first place. That's why you sit down to write. But it's elusive, and I tend to write around what the thing is I really want to say. Sometimes it's difficult for me to confront it, to come face to face with what it is I truly want to say. It's like I'm looking through a tiny pinhole at first, and sometimes this broadens to a window, but mostly it's a very narrow view I'm allowed through my characters and story. Much of the time I am writing in the dark. I'm seeing it all in my mind."

With *Send Me Down a Miracle,* Nolan follows the fortunes of fourteen-year-old Charity Pittman as she battles for a sense of self in her hometown of Casper—a locale inspired by the Dothan of Nolan's childhood. Charity feels trapped at home with her younger sister Grace and preacher father now that her mother has left them. Her father's stern interpretation of Christianity has chased away Charity's mother, but soon Charity is attracted to the cosmopolitan Adrienne Dabney, who has returned from New York to her family home, where she sets about trying a deprivation experiment. For three weeks Adrienne locks herself away in her inherited home, without visitors, light, or food. Emerging from the experiment, she says that Jesus has visited her, sitting in the chair in her living room. This proclamation splits the small town asunder: Charity and many others believe in the chair and its miraculous powers; Charity's father calls it all blasphemy, warning that Adrienne is evil incarnate. Caught between the prickly father whom she

loves and Adrienne, who has taken her on as a friend and fellow artist, Charity must finally learn to make up her own mind. When her father comes to destroy the chair, Charity is there to stand up to him.

"The dichotomy of professing one's faith and actually living it is interestingly portrayed throughout this novel," commented Jana R. Fine in a *School Library Journal* review of *Send Me Down a Miracle.* Fine also noted that readers were brought into the "heart of a young girl" who learns to meld her religious background with compassion and forgiveness. A critic in *Kirkus Reviews* called *Send Me Down a Miracle* a "busy, hilarious, tragic story," and concluded that "readers will be dizzied by the multiple subplots and roller-coaster highs and lows" in this story of a small town. *Horn Book Guide* noted that this "offbeat coming-of-age novel is peopled with a host of peculiar, yet intriguing, characters," and *Booklist's* Ilene Cooper remarked that Nolan's "plot is intricate, sharp, and invigorating." Award committees agreed with the reviewers: *Send Me Down a Miracle* was nominated for the National Book Award in 1996.

Nolan's next book, *Dancing on the Edge,* three years in the writing, was inspired by her own adopted children. "I wanted to somehow deal with the theme of adoption, the difficulty such children have in finding their own identity not knowing their birth parents. This search for identity is so vital to all of us, and some children without families have to borrow an identity to be able to find their own. I once knew a person who'd been adopted. This person used to go to the drawer where her birth certificate was kept just to make sure she really existed. So in part this novel is for those kids in search of an identity, and also it's a novel about secrets, about the damage secrets can do in a family. Children can read adults; they know when we're lying. The truth may be hard, but it's better than lies. The truth can cure."

Miracle McCloy, the young protagonist of *Dancing on the Edge,* is so named because she was delivered after her mother was killed in an accident. Her spiritualist grandmother Gigi calls it "the greatest miracle to ever come down the pike," but Miracle is not convinced. She feels a misfit, hardly special at all. She is ten at the beginning of the novel, living in Alabama with her father, Dane, a one-time child prodigy who now sits around in his bathrobe in the basement all day, and with Dane's mother, Gigi, who spends her time with matters of the occult. Dane suddenly disappears one day, and Gigi tells Miracle that her father has "melted." Gigi and Miracle then go to live with Opal, Gigi's ex-husband. Here Miracle finds some stability in the form of her gruff grandfather who buys her a bicycle and starts her in dancing lessons. Dance proves to be a momentary salvation for Miracle, something that actually makes her feel as special as everyone is always saying she is. But when she starts imitating her grandmother's occult fancies, casting spells and making love potions for her classmates, troubles arise. Accused of being a phony by another student, Miracle sets herself on fire.

Fourteen at the time of this attempted suicide, Miracle is put into a mental hospital, where her Aunt Casey and a kindly doctor help her to come to terms with the secrets in her life. This second part of the novel details Miracle's therapy and recovery as she slowly uncovers the truths that have eluded her all these years. She discovers that her mother, a ballerina, was committing suicide when struck by a speeding ambulance and that she has been abandoned by her father. "Nolan skillfully discloses" the nature of her cast of offbeat characters, a *Kirkus Reviews* critic noted, calling the novel "intense" and "exceptionally well-written." Miriam Lang Budin, writing in *School Library Journal,* dubbed *Dancing on the Edge* an "extraordinary novel," and concluded that "Nolan does a masterful job of drawing readers into the girl's mind and making them care deeply about her chances for the future." Again award committees agreed. *Dancing on the Edge* was nominated for a National Book Award, the first time an author had been nominated for that prestigious award two years in a row. And 1997 proved to be Nolan's year: her novel won the award, commended by the panel of judges as "a tale of chilling reality."

Nolan was already deep into her next novel by the time of the awards ceremony, but found taking time out from her writing and going to New York to be "great, pure fun." Awards are one form of feedback for Nolan, who does not pay much attention to reviews any longer. Another form of response to her work comes in letters from fans. These letters, interestingly enough, come not just from young readers. "Adults seem to enjoy reading my books, as well as teens," Nolan explained. "I try to write on many different levels and add layers of understanding to my novels. So it is heartening to know that the books speak across the generations. But in the end I think sometimes adults underestimate teenagers. If the letters I receive from young readers is any indication, we need to write to them, not write down to them. They are out there and they are hungry for good literature. Don't underestimate them."

Works Cited

Budin, Miriam Lang, review of *Dancing on the Edge, School Library Journal,* September, 1997, p. 223.

Cooper, Ilene, review of *Send Me Down a Miracle, Booklist,* March 15, 1996, p. 1263.

Review of *Dancing on the Edge, Kirkus Reviews,* August 1, 1997, p. 1227.

Fine, Jana R., review of *Send Me Down a Miracle, School Library Journal,* April, 1996, p. 157.

Review of *If I Should Die Before I Wake, Kirkus Reviews,* March 1, 1994, p. 308.

Levine, Susan, review of *If I Should Die Before I Wake, Voice of Youth Advocates,* June, 1994, p. 88.

Nolan, Han, *Dancing on the Edge,* Harcourt, 1997.

Nolan, Han, interview with J. Sydney Jones for *Authors and Artists for Young Adults,* Gale, conducted October 13, 1998.

"Nolan Wins 1997 National Book Award," *School Library Journal,* January, 1998, p. 22.

Raised by her grandmother, a young girl searches for her true identity in Nolan's 1997 National Book Award-winning novel. (Cover illustration by Paul Lee.)

Review of *Send Me Down a Miracle, Horn Book Guide,* fall, 1996, p. 304.

Review of *Send Me Down a Miracle, Kirkus Reviews,* March 15, 1996, p. 451.

Sutton, Roger, review of *If I Should Die Before I Wake, Bulletin of the Center for Children's Books,* April, 1994, pp. 267-68.

Veeder, Mary Harris, review of *If I Should Die Before I Wake, Booklist,* April 1, 1994, p. 1436.

For More Information See

PERIODICALS

ALAN Review, winter, 1998.

Bulletin of the Center for Children's Books, July, 1996, p. 382; December, 1997, pp. 135-36.

Horn Book Guide, fall, 1994, p. 322.

Kliatt, July, 1996, p. 15.

Publishers Weekly, January 31, 1994, p. 90; August 18, 1997, p. 94; November 24, 1997, p. 14.

School Library Journal, April, 1994, pp. 152-53.

Voice of Youth Advocates, June, 1996, p. 99; June, 1997, p. 86.

OGBURN, Charlton (Jr.) 1911-1998

OBITUARY NOTICE—See index for *SATA* sketch: Born March 15, 1911, in Atlanta, GA; died of asphyxiation, October 19, 1998, in Beaufort, South Carolina. Government official, novelist, nonfiction writer. Ogburn's best known work is his contribution to Shakespeare studies: in several books on the subject he explained and defended his view that the name William Shakespeare was a pseudonym of the 17th Earl of Oxford. The son of a lawyer, Ogburn was born in Atlanta, and raised in Washington, DC, and New York. He earned his bachelor's degree from Harvard University in 1932 and worked in publishing until the onset of World War II. During the war he fought in the China-Burma-India theater as a member of Merrill's Marauders, a famous unit named after the brigadier general who formed it, Frank Merrill. Ogburn wrote about these experiences in his book *The Marauders,* published in 1959, and adapted for a 1962 film, *Merrill's Marauders,* starring Jeff Chandler. By the end of World War II, Ogburn was working for the State Department in Washington, where he served as director of research for the Near East, South Asia, and Africa until 1957, when he retired to write full time. Over the next four decades, he produced two novels, several works on nature, and in 1984, the book for which he is best known, *The Mysterious William Shakespeare: The Myth and the Reality.* This went into a second edition in 1992, and was followed in 1995 by *The Man Who Was Shakespeare.* In defense of his contention that "Shakespeare" was a pseudonym, Ogburn appeared on *Frontline* on PBS and with William F. Buckley on *Firing Line.* He contributed articles to numerous journals, and received the Writer of the Year Award from the Georgia Writers Association in 1960, 1966, and 1967.

OBITUARIES AND OTHER SOURCES:

PERIODICALS

New York Times, October 25, 1998, p. A53.
Washington Post, October 22, 1998, p. D6.

P

PAROTTI, Phillip (Elliott) 1941-

Personal

Born May 18, 1941, in Silver City, NM; son of Abramo Angelo (a college professor) and Geraldine Ann (a pianist; maiden name, Elliott) Parotti; married Shirley Brewer (a librarian), July 3, 1964; children: Lisa Marie, Angela Ann. *Education:* U.S. Naval Academy, B.S., 1963; University of New Mexico, M.A., 1969, Ph.D., 1972; summer study at Western New Mexico University, 1963, 1967. *Hobbies and other interests:* Travel, rugby, trout fishing, reading.

Addresses

Home—3719 Morgan Lane, Huntsville, TX 77340. *Office*—English Department, Sam Houston State University, Huntsville, TX 77341.

Career

Fiction writer, educator, and former naval officer. Sam Houston State University, Huntsville, TX, professor of English, 1972—. Fiction editor, *Texas Review,* 1976-84. *Military Service:* U.S. Navy, 1963-67; commissioned ensign, 1963, advanced through grades to lieutenant commander; U.S. Naval Reserve, Lieutenant Commander, 1967-72. *Member:* South Central Modern Language Association, South Central Renaissance Conference, Illinois Classical Conference.

Writings

FICTION

The Greek Generals Talk: Memoirs of the Trojan War (short stories), University of Illinois Press (Urbana, IL), 1986.
The Trojan Generals Talk: Memoirs of the Greek War (short stories), University of Illinois Press, 1988.
Fires in the Sky (novel), Ticknor & Fields (New York City), 1990.

Short stories published in literary magazines, including *Georgia Review, Southern Humanities Review, Arizona Quarterly, Sewanee Review, Bilingual Review, Kansas Quarterly,* and *New Mexico Humanities Review.*

Sidelights

Although he has led a varied life, Phillip Parotti is the author of fiction displaying a remarkable unity: all three of his published books deal with ancient Troy and its military conflicts. Parotti himself is a former military man, having served with the United States Navy as a commissioned officer after graduating from the Naval Academy at Annapolis in 1963. As reviewers often point out, Parotti's background has helped to inform his writings with a tone of authority when these address the lives of soldiers and comment on military strategy and tactics.

The seeds of Parotti's literary aspirations were sown, according to the author, at about the same time as those of his military career. He once commented: "At seventeen, after first being introduced to the work of Hemingway and Steinbeck, I conceived the notion of becoming a writer, rejecting it almost immediately as an unrealistic pipe dream. Ever since, I have written as though driven by compulsion."

After serving four years with the Navy, Parotti went back to the university to earn a doctorate, and became a professor at Sam Houston State University in 1972. Parotti's first book of short stories, *The Greek Generals Talk,* was published in 1986, and followed a distinctive pattern: each of the twelve stories in the book was a monologue narrated by one of the victorious Greek leaders in the Trojan War. Critics offered a favorable estimation of Parotti's debut work: a *Publishers Weekly* reviewer declared that the concept was "a charming (if slightly mad) idea" and that despite some artificiality in the narrators' styles, the book was "on the whole a notable achievement." *Chicago Tribune* contributor Blair T. Birmelin called the collection an "insightful historical recreation," praising it for its "sober imaginativeness." Nicholas Goodhue, writing in the *Los Angeles Times Book Review,* declared the twelve monologues "highly affecting" and recommended the book "to anyone interested in ancient classical civilization."

Parotti followed his first story collection with a second volume of linked monologues, *The Trojan Generals Talk.* This successful sequel consisted of stories narrated by ten generals from the losing side of the Trojan War. *Chicago Tribune* contributor Liz Rosenberg praised the work as being of keen interest to anyone with a fondness for the subject, and added, "One feels that a great deal of scholarship and heart went into *The Trojan Generals Talk.*" *Atlantic Monthly* reviewer Phoebe-Lou Adams also offered a favorable assessment of the work, maintaining that Parotti "has succeeded in making his Trojans as interesting as the Greek generals of his previous novel."

Adams was also enthusiastic about Parotti's next effort, *Fires in the Sky,* which was the author's first novel. *Fires in the Sky,* related from the perspective of a single narrator, explores the little-remembered wars which Troy fought with its Mysian neighbors before their much more famous conflict against the Achaean Greeks. The novel emphasizes the precise details of training and battle, and Adams commented that "Parotti's distinction lies in his ability to weave into his recreation ... oblique hints of far more recent wars." *School Library Journal* contributor Joan Lewis Reynolds appreciated the novel (and its informative appendices) as "an involving prelude to the Trojan War." A *Publishers Weekly* commentator, praising *Fires in the Sky* as "a quietly majestic historical novel," maintained: "Parotti provides strong characterizations and captures the rough-and-tumble collision of cultures in this timely morality tale about the fall of empire."

Works Cited

Adams, Phoebe-Lou, review of *The Trojan Generals Talk, Atlantic Monthly,* November, 1988, p. 99.

Adams, Phoebe-Lou, review of *Fires in the Sky, Atlantic Monthly,* October, 1990, p. 136.

Review of *The Greek Generals Talk, Publishers Weekly,* June 13, 1986, p. 68.

Birmelin, Blair T., review of *The Greek Generals Talk, Chicago Tribune,* August 17, 1986, p. 43.

Goodhue, Nicholas, review of *The Greek Generals Talk, Los Angeles Times Book Review,* September 21, 1986.

Review of *Fires in the Sky, Publishers Weekly,* July 6, 1990, p. 59.

Reynolds, Joan Lewis, review of *Fires in the Sky, School Library Journal,* March, 1991, p. 228.

Rosenberg, Liz, review of *The Trojan Generals Talk, Tribune Books* (Chicago), January 15, 1989, p. 3.

For More Information See

PERIODICALS

Hudson Review, spring, 1987, pp. 138-39.

Kirkus Reviews, June 1, 1986, p. 815.

PATON WALSH, Gillian 1937- (Jill Paton Walsh)

Personal

Born April 29, 1937, in London, England; daughter of John Llewellyn (an engineer) and Patricia (Dubern) Bliss; married Antony Edmund Paton Walsh (a chartered secretary), August 12, 1961 (marriage dissolved); children: Edmund Alexander, Margaret Ann, Helen Clare. *Education:* St. Anne's College, Oxford, Dip. Ed., 1959, M.A. (honours) in English. *Politics:* None. *Religion:* "Skepticism." *Hobbies and other interests:* Reading, photography, gardening, cooking, carpentry, travel.

Addresses

Home—72 Water Lane, Histon, Cambridge CB4 4LR, England; also has a home near St. Ives, Cornwall, England.

Career

Enfield Girls Grammar School, Middlesex, English teacher, 1959-62; writer, 1962—. Whittall Lecturer, Library of Congress, Washington, DC, 1978. Visiting Faculty Member, Center for the Study of Children's Literature, Simmons College, Boston, 1978-86. Founder, with John Rowe Townsend, of Green Bay Publishers,

Gillian Paton Walsh

Hemingford Grey, England, 1986. *Member:* Society of Authors (member of Management Committee), Children's Writers Group.

Awards, Honors

Book World Festival Award, 1970, for *Fireweed;* Notable Books designation, *New York Times,* 1972, for *Goldengrove;* Whitbread Prize (shared with Russell Hoban), 1974, for *The Emperor's Winding Sheet; Boston Globe-Horn Book* Award, 1976, for *Unleaving;* Smarties Award (runner-up), 1983, and Universe Prize, 1984, for *A Parcel of Patterns;* Smarties Award Grand Prix, 1984, for *Gaffer Samson's Luck.* Best Book, *School Library Journal,* 1992, for *Grace.* Mother Goose Award (runner-up), 1992, for *How Grandma Came. Fireweed* and *A Chance Child* were named American Library Association Notable Books while *A Parcel of Patterns* was named an ALA Best Book for Young Adults. *Knowledge of Angels* was shortlisted for the Booker Prize. Paton Walsh received Arts Council Creative Writing Fellowships in 1976 and 1977. She was awarded a CBE for her body of work and was also named a fellow of the Royal Society of Literature.

Writings

FOR CHILDREN AND YOUNG ADULTS; FICTION AND PICTURE BOOKS, EXCEPT AS NOTED; UNDER NAME JILL PATON WALSH

Hengest's Tale, illustrated by Janet Margrie, St. Martin's Press (New York), 1966, Macmillan (London), 1966.

The Dolphin Crossing, St. Martin's Press, 1967, Macmillan, 1967.

Fireweed, Macmillan, 1969, Farrar, Straus (New York), 1970, Peter Smith, 1998.

(With Kevin Crossley-Holland) *Wordhoard: Anglo-Saxon Stories,* Farrar, Straus, 1969, Macmillan, 1969.

Goldengrove, Farrar, Straus, 1972, Macmillan, 1972, Peter Smith, 1993.

The Dawnstone, illustrated by Mary Dinsdale, Hamish Hamilton (London), 1973.

Toolmaker, illustrated by Jeroo Roy, Heinemann (London), 1973, Seabury Press (New York), 1974.

The Emperor's Winding Sheet, Farrar, Straus, 1974, Macmillan, 1974.

The Butty Boy, illustrated by Juliette Palmer, Macmillan,1975, published in the United States as *The Huffler,* Farrar, Straus, 1975.

The Island Sunrise: Prehistoric Britain (nonfiction), Deutsch (London), 1975, published as *The Island Sunrise: Prehistoric Culture in the British Isles,* Seabury Press, 1976.

Unleaving, Farrar, Straus, 1976, Macmillan, 1976, Peter Smith, 1998.

Crossing to Salamis (first novel in trilogy; also see below), illustrated by David Smee, Heinemann, 1977.

The Walls of Athens (second novel in trilogy; also see below), illustrated by Smee, Heinemann, 1977.

Persian Gold (third novel in trilogy; also see below), illustrated by Smee, Heinemann, 1978.

Children of the Fox (contains *Crossing to Salamis, The Walls of Athens,* and *Persian Gold*), illustrated by Robin Eaton, Farrar, Straus, 1978.

A Chance Child, Farrar, Straus, 1978, Macmillan, 1978.

Babylon, illustrated by Jenny Northway, Deutsch, 1982.

The Green Book, illustrated by Joanna Stubbs, Macmillan, 1981, illustrated by Lloyd Bloom, Farrar, Straus, 1982, published as *Shine,* Macdonald, 1988.

A Parcel of Patterns, Farrar, Straus, 1983, Kestrel (London), 1983, Peter Smith, 1995.

Gaffer Samson's Luck, illustrated by Brock Cole, Farrar, Straus, 1984, Viking (London), 1985.

Lost and Found, illustrated by Mary Rayner, Deutsch, 1984, Dutton, 1985.

Torch, Viking Kestrel, 1987, Farrar, Straus, 1988.

Birdy and the Ghosties, illustrated by Alan Marks, Farrar, Straus, 1988, Macdonald, 1989.

Can I Play Farmer, Farmer (picture book), illustrated by Jolyne Knox, Bodley Head (Oxford, England), 1990.

Can I Play Jenny Jones (picture book), illustrated by Jolyne Knox, Bodley Head, 1990.

Can I Play Queenie (picture book), illustrated by Jolyne Knox, Bodley Head, 1990.

Can I Play Wolf (picture book), illustrated by Jolyne Knox, Bodley Head, 1990.

Grace, Viking, 1991, Farrar, Straus, 1992.

Matthew and the Sea Singer, illustrated by Alan Marks, Simon & Schuster (Hemel Hempstead, England), 1992, Farrar, Straus, 1993.

When Grandma Came (picture book), illustrated by Sophie Williams, Viking, 1992.

Thomas and the Tinners, illustrated by Alan Marks, Macdonald Young Books, 1995, Hove, Farrar Straus & Giroux.

Connie Came to Play (picture book), illustrated by Stephen Lambert, Viking (London), 1995, Viking (New York), 1996.

Pepi and the Secret Names (picture book), illustrated by Fiona French, Lothrop, 1995, F. Lincoln (London), 1996.

When I Was Little Like You (picture book), illustrated by Stephen Lambert, Viking, 1997.

FOR ADULTS; FICTION, EXCEPT AS NOTED; UNDER NAME JILL PATON WALSH

Farewell, Great King, Coward McCann, 1972, Macmillan, 1972.

(Editor) *Beowulf* (structural reader), Longman, 1975.

Five Tides (short stories), Green Bay (Hemingford Grey, England), 1986.

Lapsing (autobiographical fiction), Weidenfeld & Nicolson, 1986, St. Martin's, 1987.

A School for Lovers, Weidenfeld & Nicolson, 1989.

The Wyndham Case: An Imogen Quy Mystery, St. Martin's Press, 1993, Hodder & Stoughton (London), 1993.

Knowledge of Angels, Houghton, 1994, Green Bay, 1994.

A Piece of Justice: The Second Imogen Quy Mystery, St. Martin's Press, 1995, Hodder & Stoughton (London), 1995.

The Serpentine Cave, Doubleday (London), 1997, St. Martin's Press, 1997.

(With Dorothy L. Sayers) *Thrones, Dominations,* St. Martin's Press, 1998, Hodder & Stoughton, 1998.

OTHER

Contributor to children's literature reviewing sources and to newspapers and magazines for children and adults, including the *Times Literary Supplement* and the *Writer,* as well as to reference books on juvenile literature such as *Twentieth-Century Children's Writers.* Paton Walsh's manuscripts and papers are housed in the Kerlan Collection, University of Minnesota, Minneapolis.

Adaptations

The Green Book was released on video cassette by PBS Video in 1988. *A Parcel of Patterns* was released on audio cassette by Listening Library, *Knowledge of Angels* was released on audio cassette by Dual Dolphin Publishing, and *A Piece of Justice* was released on audio cassette by Chivers North America, all in 1996. *Thrones, Dominations* was released on audio cassette by Chivers North America in 1998. *Torch* was adapted for television by the British Broadcasting Corporation.

Sidelights

A writer of "singular gifts [who creates] books of surpassing loveliness" according to a critic in *Publishers Weekly,* Paton Walsh is considered one of England's most brilliant and perceptive authors for children and young people. Acknowledged for her range and versatility, she writes historical fiction, contemporary realistic fiction, science fiction, nonfiction, and picture books as well as original folktales; she is also the author of well-received mysteries, realistic fiction, and short stories for adults. Paton Walsh is perhaps best known as the writer of realistic and historical fiction for older primary graders and young adults. Her books, which utilize settings from prehistory through the future, characteristically portray England throughout time; she places her works in such eras as the Anglo-Saxon period, the seventeenth century, the Victorian Age, and most frequently, the period surrounding World War II. Several of Paton Walsh's books are set on the Cornish seacoast, an area where she spent five years of her childhood and where she currently keeps a residence.

Paton Walsh has contributed most consistently to the genre of historical fiction. She stresses character and event in these works, examining history through the reactions of her young male and female protagonists; the author is often praised for creating exciting stories that are both immediate and historically accurate. In all of her books, Paton Walsh explores profound questions about life and human nature. Her themes include, for example, courage and the nature of heroism; war and its effects; the power of love and generosity; the importance of relationships; the value of community; and the need for culture and literacy. Caught up in war or other dangerous situations, her protagonists take desperate measures, often at the risk of their lives, to survive. Through their experiences, her characters learn about the complexity of life while becoming stronger and more mature. Paton Walsh writes frequently about the transition from childhood to adulthood, and she is often

Drawing on selkie folklore, Walsh tells the story of a young boy who is rescued from an orphanage and, under the auspices of a local parson, uses his beautiful singing voice to enchant churchgoers.(Cover illustration by Alan Marks.)

celebrated for her understanding of and respect for the young. Although her books include death, child abuse, tragedy, and other horrors as well as war, they usually end with positive conclusions that underscore the author's belief in humanity. A literary stylist, Paton Walsh is lauded as a storyteller and also for the beauty of her spare but resonant prose. Considered a writer with a particularly visual style, she employs literary techniques such as multiple viewpoints and interior monologues and is often acknowledged for her evocation of atmosphere and place. Although some reviewers find her books too disturbing and demanding, most observers revere Paton Walsh as a writer of exceptional talent and depth whose rich, powerful books introduce children to the sophistication of adult literature. Writing in her *Thursday's Child,* Sheila Egoff commented, "Of [the many] skilled and sensitive writers [for young people], Walsh is the most formally literary. Her writing is studded with allusions to poetry, art, and philosophy that give it an intellectual framework unmatched in children's literature." Writing in *Twentieth-Century Children's Writers,* Marcus Crouch called Paton Walsh a "writer of the highest quality . . . . Her dominant characteristic is integrity." Crouch concluded, "This is a writer who never wastes her rare talents, but who brings to each book the same professionalism, wisdom, and regard for her craft and her public."

The eldest of four children, Paton Walsh was born in North Finchley, a suburb of London. A breech baby, she was born with a condition called Erb's Palsy that is caused when a person's arm is stretched during delivery; consequently, Paton Walsh had limited movement in her right arm. Since the condition was not completely understood at the time of their daughter's birth, Paton Walsh's parents were told that the disability was a result of brain damage. In her essay in *Something about the Author Autobiography Series (SAAS)*, Paton Walsh remarked that she considers her disability "of great importance, not in any physical way, but psychologically. In the first place, all my life the people around me have supposed I would not be able to do things—like carrying trays, or standing on my hands—which I found, as soon as I tried them, to be perfectly possible for me. And this has left me with a life-long disposition to have a shot at things. Confronted with a difficult task, ... I am still inclined to tackle it, reflecting that if someone else can do it, I probably can." In addition to her physical condition, Paton Walsh, who came from a verbal family, did not talk until she was almost three years old. Finally, when a neighbor leaned over her playpen and said, "What do you do all day, little girl?" Paton Walsh replied, "Normally, I play with bricks." She noted in *SAAS*, "When every utterance I delivered from cot or playpen was greeted with rapture by my parents and family, I was quickly convinced that I was good with words...."

Paton Walsh and her siblings two brothers and a sister—were raised in a loving, empowering environment. She wrote in *SAAS*, "I might not be able to carry a tray, but I, or any of us, could win scholarships, get to university, become professors, politicians, inventors, captains of industry ... anything we liked. And, to an unusual degree, everyone was without prejudices against, or limited ambitions for, girls. As much was expected of me as of my brothers. And therefore, of course, more, in a way." In contrast to the warmth of her home life, there were economic difficulties and hardships caused by World War II. When Paton Walsh's hometown was bombed during the Blitz, her grandfather took her mother, brothers, and sister to live with him in St. Ives, a picturesque town on the coast of Cornwall; Paton Walsh's father, an engineer who was the world's first television cameraman and who pioneered public broadcast television, was sent to another town to help with radar research. When her mother and siblings returned to London, Paton Walsh, who was in nursery school, stayed with her grandparents until she was eight. "A part of me," she wrote in *SAAS*, "is still rooted in that rocky shore, and it appears again and again in what I write."

When her beloved grandmother died suddenly in 1944, Paton Walsh was sent home to London, where she found her house occupied by her mother's relatives. Exiled from Burma due to its occupation by the Japanese, the Dubern family had lived a pampered upper-class life, including being waited on by servants, before arriving in war-torn London. The "home-from-Burma brigade," Paton Walsh recalled in *SAAS*, "treated me with pointed dislike." They saw reading as priggish and thought it inappropriate for children—especially girls—to disagree with adults. Paton Walsh said, "I found myself slapped down sixty times a day for being what my father and grandfather encouraged me to be." However, Paton Walsh discovered a new appreciation for her mother, who encouraged her daughter to keep on reading and talking. Paton Walsh followed her mother's advice, devouring the rows of classic novels on her grandfather's bookshelves and developing a thick skin regarding her visiting relatives. She remembered in *SAAS*, "I learned not to care what other people think. I would say what I liked, read what I was interested in, go on my own way, and ignore what the invading hoards of aunts and uncles thought, about me, or about anything else." Now, Paton Walsh wrote, it "is not what others expect of me, but what I expect of myself that governs me."

At St. Michael's Convent, a Catholic grammar school in North Finchley, Paton Walsh discovered that her teachers, a group of nuns, were suspicious of her because she found her schoolwork easy. "They found it odd, and dangerous, to want a university degree," she wrote in *SAAS*. When Paton Walsh was accepted by St. Anne's College at Oxford University, the nuns offered a mass for her soul. Paton Walsh found life at Oxford stimulating both academically and socially. Deciding to major in English with a concentration on medieval literature and philology, she was taught by C. S. Lewis, the author of the "Narnia" series, and J. R. R. Tolkien, the author of "The Lord of the Rings" trilogy, who lectured on these subjects. Paton Walsh noted in *SAAS* that "the example they set by being both great and serious scholars, and writers of fantasy and books for children was not lost on me." She also became conversant in languages such as French, Latin, Italian, Icelandic, and Old English. While an undergraduate, she met fellow student Antony Paton Walsh; the couple became engaged while still in school. After graduating with honors, Paton Walsh received a degree in education from Oxford, and taught English for three years in a grammar school for girls in Middlesex. In 1961, her second year as a teacher, she married Antony Paton Walsh. The author recalled in *SAAS*, "I liked teaching; I hated being a teacher. That is, I liked the company of young people. I liked discussing books with them, reading what they wrote for me, trying to get them through exams.... I hated it when they all felt they had to duck out of sight of me on the bus home because they weren't wearing school hats, or when they were embarrassed at meeting me in the shops with their boyfriends." Eighteen months after her marriage, Paton Walsh became pregnant with her first child, Edmund, and left teaching shortly before he was born; Jill and Antony Paton Walsh also had two other children, Margaret and Clare, before the demise of their marriage. After Edmund's birth, Paton Walsh remembered in *SAAS*, "I was bored frantic. I went nearly crazy, locked up alone with a howling baby all day and all night." Edmund had a stomach problem that kept both him and

After helping her father rescue the survivors of a shipwreck on the English coast in 1838, Grace Darling becomes an unwilling national hero. (Cover illustration by Viqui Maggio.)

his mother awake for months. Since her husband worked during the day and studied for professional exams at night, Paton Walsh was left without anyone with whom to talk. "Finally," she wrote in *SAAS,* "a moment came when I realised that I would soon—before the day was out—crack up and be taken to a mental hospital .... As plants need water and light, as the baby needed milk, I needed something intellectual, cheap, and quiet." After finding a way to feed Edmund that left her more independent, Paton Walsh began writing a book on an old portable typewriter given to her by one of her brothers. "It was," she noted in *SAAS,* "a children's book. It never occurred to me to write any other kind." She added that when she "started on that battered typewriter, muffled as far as possible by being put on a folded blanket on the desk—I didn't want to wake the baby—I suddenly came clear to myself."

Paton Walsh's first attempt at writing a book for children, a historical novel set in England at the time of King Alfred, remains unpublished; in her essay in *SAAS,* the author called it "a dreadfully bad book." However, the story led to her association with Kevin Crossley-

Holland, a noted author who at the time was working as the children's books editor for Macmillan in London. Crossley-Holland offered Paton Walsh an option on her next book, *Hengest's Tale,* a retelling from *Beowulf* that became her first published work. Told as he lay dying by the title character, a fifth-century warrior who was one of the earliest Saxon invaders of Britain, the story describes a man in conflict, caught between love and duty. A reviewer in the *Times Literary Supplement* stated, "The greatest triumph in so remote and fate-haunted a tale is that the characters all live." A critic in *Kirkus Reviews,* comparing Paton Walsh to Henry Treece, stated "Seldom has the gloom and fear of the Dark Ages been induced with such immediacy, nor the shifting demands of primitive loyalty and honor been so effectively juxtaposed; and seldom, indeed, does historical fiction sustain such knife-edge suspense throughout." In *A Sounding of Storytellers,* John Rowe Townsend called *Hengest's Tale* "undeniably impressive. The author who, writing for children, could piece together this fierce and testing tale was alarmingly talented, and she was not yet thirty years old." Paton Walsh wrote of *Hengest's Tale* in *SAAS,* "I have never forgotten the difference it made to be able to say, to others, certainly, but above all, to myself, 'I am a writer.'" In 1969, Paton Walsh and Kevin Crossley-Holland collaborated on *Wordhoard: Anglo-Saxon Stories,* a collection of tales—four by each author—based on real and imaginary figures of the period. Called the "first successful attempt to present a sensitive vision of Anglo-Saxon life to teens" by Bruce L. MacDuffie in *School Library Journal, Wordhoard* shows "a loving absorption by both authors of the historical texts," according to a reviewer in the *Times Literary Supplement.*

The Dolphin Crossing, a historical novel published in 1967, remains one of Paton Walsh's most popular works. The story, which has as its theme the rescue of the British Army from the Battle of Dunkirk in World War II, is set in 1940 and describes how two teenage boys from a small coastal town aid in the evacuation of three thousand retreating troops. John, a sensitive teen from a wealthy family, and Pat, a resourceful Cockney evacuee, take John's boat, the *Dolphin,* across the English Channel to France. For two days, they remove groups of stranded soldiers and, in the process, learn about the realities of war as well as about themselves. At the end of the novel, Pat—struggling with the idea that some soldiers have yet to be rescued—sneaks back to Dunkirk; he does not return. "More than anything else," wrote Ethel L. Heins in *Horn Book,* "the story emphasizes, as any good war story must, that transcending patriotism, courage, and idealism, is the realization of the uselessness and the ultimate waste of war." John Rowe Townsend, writing in *A Sounding of Storytellers,* noted that the theme "is brilliantly handled, with the unsparing realism that the author has already displayed." Although he called *The Dolphin Crossing* "deficient in the creation of people who live and breathe," Townsend concluded that John and Pat are "representatives of all of us, struggling to survive and win through."

Like *The Dolphin Crossing,* Paton Walsh's next novel, *Fireweed,* is set in England during the Second World War. The story features two young teenagers, Bill and Julie, who meet in a bomb shelter—a tube (subway) station—during the London Blitz. The children, who have escaped evacuation, make a home in the cellar of a bombed building. They become responsible for each other, establishing a tender relationship while trying to evade meddling adults and take care of Dickie, a small boy whom they have found. At the end of the novel, Julie, injured when the cellar collapses, is rescued and returned to her upper-class family. Bill, who comes from the lower class, realizes after a visit that he will not be accepted by her parents and feels that Julie herself is rejecting him. After their visit, Bill does not see Julie again. The title of the novel refers to a plant that, according to Marie Peel in *Books and Bookmen,* grows "only out of the scars of ruin and pain, whether caused by bombs or people." Writing in *Punch,* John Rowe Townsend called *Fireweed* "a book to be read, remembered, and reread: a book worth buying." Zena Sutherland of *Saturday Review* called the ending of *Fireweed* "as poignant, as bitter, and as inevitable as a classic tragedy," while a critic in *Children's Literature in Education* concluded, "as a historical recreation at children's level of London in the Blitz the book is unsurpassed." Writing in *SAAS,* Paton Walsh noted that *Fireweed* "really made my name as a writer."

Goldengrove and its sequel *Unleaving* are considered among Paton Walsh's best works. The author called these books, published in 1972 and 1976 respectively, "those I think of with the most affection...." Set in St. Ives, the Cornwall town in which Paton Walsh spent five happy years of her childhood, the novels take their titles and the name of their main character—sensitive teenager Margaret Fielding, called Madge—from the poem "Spring and Fall: To a young child" by the English poet Gerard Manley Hopkins. In the first book, Madge travels to Goldengrove, her grandmother's home in Cornwall, to spend the last part of her holidays with Gran and her younger cousin Paul. Kept apart for most of the year by the antagonism between her mother and his father, the girl and boy have been brought together as a healing measure by Gran. In the past, they have revelled in each other's company as well as in the beauty of the Cornish coast during the summer. However, circumstances have delayed this year's visit until September, and things are different. When Madge arrives, she is not allowed to share a room with Paul and begins to do things without him. She also meets Ralph Ashton, a blind, middle-aged professor who has become bitter after losing his sight and being deserted by his wife. Madge begins reading to him, and falls in love. Finally, Gran tells Madge and Paul that they are not cousins, but brother and sister, kept apart by the antagonism of their parents. Paul is thrilled, but Madge feels betrayed by her father. She offers her heart to Professor Ashton, who rejects her. At the end of the novel, Madge goes to the beach and heads by boat to the lighthouse offshore. In the process, she almost drowns, but is rescued. Finally, Madge realizes that some wounds cannot be healed; knowing that her childhood is over, she prepares to keep on living.

Writing in *A Sounding of Storytellers,* John Rowe Townsend stated, "[A]lthough the title and the main theme come from Hopkins, the true literary correspondences are with Virginia Woolf. A fixed mark in Jill Paton Walsh's seascape is Godrevy lighthouse, the same one as in *To the Lighthouse* ... Goldengrove is a book full of light, of endlessly changing sea and sky; and, as with Virginia Woolf, there is an acute—one might say exquisite—perception of the living moment, which can only be joyful." Calling *Goldengrove* "an intensely lyrical, subtle, and wise novel," Michele Landsberg of *Entertainment Weekly* concluded that it is "a perfect bridge to the challenges and rewards of adult literature," while C. S. Hannabuss of *Children's Book Review* noted that *Goldengrove* "is one of the few books to take [the subject of how children become adolescents] and at the same time remain a children's book." Writing in the *New York Times Book Review,* Barbara Wersba called *Goldengrove* "a brilliant novel" and noted that Paton Walsh "has not forgotten [childhood]—and I am rather in awe of her. She writes as though she were still 12 years old, choking back angry tears and incapable of dissembling."

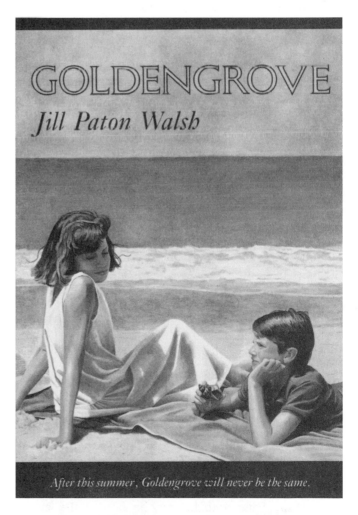

Vacations at Goldengrove, her grandmother's seaside home, will never be the same again for Madge after a family secret is revealed to her during one life-changing summer. (Cover illustration by Diana McKee.)

Unleaving, according to Virginia Haviland of *Horn Book,* "shows a deeper portrayal of human relationships and raises profound questions about life, death, and love." Set a few years after the end of its predecessor, the novel describes how Madge, who has inherited Goldengrove after her grandmother's death, becomes involved with Patrick Tregeagle, the teenage son of an Oxford professor who has rented the house with another professor, their families, and a group of students engaged in a summer "reading party." As she becomes friends with Patrick, Madge realizes that he is suffering because of the teasing inflicted on his little sister Molly, a Mongoloid, for whom he foresees a bleak future. On a picnic with the students, Madge thinks she sees Patrick push Molly off a seaside cliff; both the little girl and the man who try to rescue her are drowned. Keeping Patrick's action a secret, Madge becomes his comforter. As he works out his guilt, Patrick and Madge express their feelings for each other, at the end of the story, the two teens realize that their lives are joined together. Throughout the novel, Paton Walsh includes scenes that appear to be flashbacks: an old woman talks to her children, watches her grandchildren play, and recalls the past. When the narratives come together, Paton Walsh discloses that the speaker in these scenes is Madge herself, sixty years hence, and that she and Patrick married, had a daughter, and live at Goldengrove.

Virginia Haviland of *Horn Book* commented that Paton Walsh "has dealt with the whole book brilliantly, deftly raising issues without overburdening her story." Writing in the *New York Times Book Review,* Alice Bach called Paton Walsh "too wise to attempt answers about growing, living, dying, ethical choices. She exalts the mystery, the unknowing itself. This is a beautiful novel, and an enduring one." John Rowe Townsend, writing in *A Sounding of Storytellers,* called *Unleaving* "a profoundly beautiful book" and concluded that the "working together of the two themes is achieved with great formal beauty; and even more than *Goldengrove* the story is full of sea, superb in all its moods; of light and landscape; the celebration of the passing but immortal moment." Writing in *Twentieth-Century Children's Writers* about both *Goldengrove* and *Unleaving,* Marcus Crouch called them "beyond question books of the highest excellence in which the process of growing up is explored with fine sensitivity and in which, to a degree rare in this writer's work, the reader becomes deeply involved." Crouch completed his assessment by stating, "[I]n these books Paton Walsh's highest achievement is to be found."

In *A Sounding of Storytellers,* John Rowe Townsend called *The Emperor's Winding Sheet,* a book published in 1974, "possibly the best historical novel to be published on any British list, adult's or children's, in its decade." The story describes how Piers Barber, an English boy, is shipwrecked in Greece on his way to the Holy Land. Faint with hunger, he falls at the feet of Constantine Dragases, the last Roman Emperor of Constantinople. Piers is greeted as the fulfillment of a prophecy, a talisman who, as long as he stays with the Emperor, will ensure that both he and the Byzantine Empire will survive. Renamed Vrethiki—Greek for "lucky find"—Piers is held in Constantinople for two years. During this time, the Holy War begins. Turkish forces, outnumbering the Greeks by tens of thousands, besiege the city. Over a period of sixty days, Piers learns about patriotism, endurance, dignity, and commitment as well as the horrors of war; he also develops a great respect for Constantine and a loyalty to his empire. When the city is sacked, Constantine is killed in battle; his body is discovered and hidden by Piers. At the end of the novel, the boy decides to return to England, filled with sadness but also with new courage and self-knowledge. Favorably comparing *The Emperor's Winding Sheet* to the richness of Herodotus and the discipline of the *Annals* of Tacitus, C. S. Hannabuss of *Children's Book Review* stated, "A period has been brought to life in this book . . . ." Writing in *Horn Book,* Paul Heins claimed that Paton Walsh "conveys a powerful sense of the interplay between tragic history and private experience."

Three of Paton Walsh's stories—*A Chance Child, A Parcel of Patterns,* and *Gaffer Samson's Luck*—are considered among her most affecting. *A Chance Child,* a novel published in 1978, incorporates both time travel fantasy and the harsh realities surrounding the practice of child labor in nineteenth-century England. Paton Walsh shows clearly the horrendous conditions and violence that faced the child laborers of more than a hundred years ago. In this work, an abused, unwanted young boy from the twentieth century called Creep—the only name he has ever known—runs away from home and finds a boat that takes him back in time to the Industrial Revolution. The boat, which seems to have a mind of its own, carries Creep to a mine, where he takes one of the child employees, Tom Moorhouse, with him after he sees the boy thrown against a wall by an overseer. The boys are then taken to an iron factory, where they meet Lucy, a little girl nicknamed Blackie because half of her face is scarred from the burns she received after falling into a fire at the factory. As the children go from job to job, Creep becomes more at one with the past: at first, only the young can see him, but he finally crosses over completely and becomes visible to everyone. Creep's half-brother Christopher, the only person who loved him, searches for the boy in the twentieth century. Finally, after Christopher realizes that Creep now belongs to the past, he finds a reference in the Parliamentary Papers that states that Creep became a printer, married Lucy, and had children. Writing in the *New York Times Book Review,* Jane Langton called *A Chance Child* "a brilliant novel," asserting: "Most stunning of all are the pictures of mine and foundry, forge and mill. Walsh's splendid descriptive power seems to blow the hot sparks of the forge in our faces and the choking lint of the mill into our lungs. Our ears ring with the massive hammer in the ironworks . . . and at last they hear even the inaudible cries of the beaten children in the mill." John Rowe Townsend, writing in *A Sounding of Storytellers,* stated, "*A Chance Child* is both clear-eyed and compassionate. And Jill Paton Walsh's descriptive powers have never been put to more impressive use than here." A reviewer in *Publishers Weekly* noted that Paton Walsh "has never written with such impact" and concluded, "Not even Dickens portrayed abused children (of yesterday and today) as Walsh does here."

Set during the Great Plague of 1665, *A Parcel of Patterns* addresses the themes of faith, courage, and the meaning of community. When Parson William Momphesson is sent by the Restoration Church to the village of Eyam in Derbyshire to replace Parson Thomas Stanley, the Puritan minister, he lets Stanley—who is supposed to be sent away—live in the village. Momphensson's wife, Catherine, wants some pretty clothes; when the village tailor orders a package of patterns from London, they bring the Black Death to Eyam. The villagers, who decide to quarantine themselves in order to keep the disease from spreading, join together as a community, although not without difficulty. They are held together by the previously opposed philosophies of parsons Mompheson and Stanley. The story is told by Mall Percival, a young woman who goes through a crisis of faith. Mall loves Thomas, a man from a neighboring village. In order to protect him from the plague, Mall refuses to see Thomas; when he continues to contact her, she pretends to have died. Thinking that he has nothing left to live for, Thomas comes to Eyam and perishes in the plague. At the end of the novel, Mall, who questions why God has allowed these deaths, plans to leave Eyam to begin a new life. Calling *A Parcel of Patterns* "an extraordinary and compelling tour de force," Neil Philip of the *Times Educational Supplement* said, "This is a most dreadful, moving story, and it is related by Jill Paton Walsh with a quiet, unerring restraint which will disturb and possess the reader long after the frenzy aroused by a sensational approach would have died away." A reviewer in *Bulletin of the Center for Children's Books* called *A Parcel of Patterns* "[a] strong, strong story" that is "moving as a personal document" and "impressive because it serves to illustrate dramatically the complexity and interdependence of community life." Writing in the *Observer,* Christopher Wordsworth concluded that Paton Walsh is "a fine storyteller who knows that the tragic essence of love and death can't be diluted to appease any notion of suitability."

Inspired by her move to a little cottage near Cambridge in the English Fens that she shares with author and critic John Rowe Townsend, Paton Walsh published *Gaffer Samson's Luck* in 1984. A story for primary graders, the book outlines how James, a young boy who has moved to a new village, becomes accepted through his relationship with Gaffer Samson, an elderly man who is terminally ill. Seventy years before, Gaffer had buried his good-luck charm, a stone given to him by a gypsy, in the marshes. After Gaffer is hospitalized, James attempts to find the stone for him. Through his search, James becomes familiar with his new landscape and learns to appreciate it. He also confronts Terry, the leader of the village gang, so that he can borrow Terry's boat. In order to use the boat, Terry tells James that he must submit to a dare—to make it across the Rymers, a dangerous weir. James crosses the Rymers successfully, but Terry is critically injured. After James finds the

stone, Gaffer gives it to him; James goes to the hospital and slips it into Terry's hand before his operation. Writing in the *Dictionary of Literary Biography,* Rosanne Fraine Donahue called *Gaffer Samson's Luck* a "deceptively simple story about belonging, change, courage, and generosity," while Marcus Crouch in *Twentieth-Century Children's Writers* commented that the "simple story is told with rare beauty of style and with deep understanding." Claiming that the book reflects "a dependably fine writer at her best," a reviewer in *Bulletin of the Center for Children's Books* called *Gaffer Samson's Luck* "a trenchant story about a child's courage and adaptability...."

In the 1990s, Paton Walsh moved in a new direction as a writer: picture books and original folktales for young children. She began focusing on works for a younger audience because, as she told Barbara James in *Magpies,* "my own children have grown up. I feel quite detached from the teenage audience because I am not living with them ... and not living their exact kind of life. On the other hand, my partner now has grandchildren, and there are very young children in my life again so I still find it quite easy to write picture books and retell folktales. The teenage line has, so to speak, dried up, but I'm expecting it to resume when the grandchildren grow up!" Paton Walsh has written two literary folktales about Birdy, a generous young girl: *Birdy and the Ghosties* and *Matthew and the Sea Singer.* In *Birdy and the Ghosties,* the title character, the daughter of a ferryman who takes travelers across a river, learns that she has second sight. On a ride with her father, Birdy sees three horrible ghosts—a man, woman, and child. However, she describes the ghosts to her father as royals dressed in finery. The ghosts reward Birdy with a toy belonging to the boy ghost—a net full of mussel shells, each of which contains a pearl. In *Matthew and the Sea Singer,* Birdy uses her birthday shilling to buy an orphan boy, Matthew, from a cruel orphan master. Matthew, who sings beautifully, is kidnapped by the seal-folk for his golden voice. When Matthew disappears, Birdy calls upon the seal-queen, a selkie, and makes a deal with her: if Matthew is returned, the village parson—who has been teaching the boy to sing church songs—will teach one of the seal-queen's pups to sing. When Matthew comes back, the seal-pup, Pagan, is instructed by the parson. Pagan's singing, dark and haunting, blends perfectly with Matthew's bright tones. At the end of the story, Paton Walsh intimates that Birdy and Matthew marry and that he is still heard joined in song with Pagan. Writing in *Bulletin of the Center for Children's Books,* Betsy Hearne claimed that Paton Walsh is "as effective in layering short stories with depth and style as she is in elaborating complex novels." Emily Melton of *Booklist* added that the author "tells a wonderfully imaginative, humorous, and thoroughly enchanting story, which sounds as if it were part legend, part myth, and part nonsense made up by white-whiskered old men sitting in front of blazing fires."

Paton Walsh has often described satisfying intergenerational relationships in her books for older children and young people; two of her picture books, *When Grandma*

Came and *When I Was Little Like You,* also share this theme. In *When Grandma Came,* Paton Walsh portrays an adventurous grandmother, a traveler to such exotic places as the Arctic and the desert, who greets her growing granddaughter with compliments that compare her favorably to the wondrous places she has visited and the amazing things she has seen. Finally, the little girl has grown enough to be able to tell her grandmother that she loves her, too. Roger Sutton of *Bulletin of the Center for Children's Books* said that "this soothing litany ... would make a perfect bedtime story ... for Grandma. Kids, though, may find the story repetitive and the mood a little too cozy." However, Stephanie Zvirin of *Booklist* called *When Grandma Came* "an affectionate intergenerational picture book about growing up with someone you love and who loves you back." In *When I Was Little Like You,* a book that is set in Paton Walsh's childhood home of St. Ives in Cornwall, little Rosie and her Gran stroll through the seaside village. As Rosie points out the things she sees—for example, a train, a candy store, and a fish shop—Gran recalls how each of these things were different when she was young. When Rosie asks Gran if she preferred the world then, she concludes by telling her granddaughter how much more fun the world is now that she is in it. A reviewer in *Publishers Weekly* commented, "While Walsh has some lyrical descriptions, ... her prosaic subject matter lacks the drama and drive to hold the target audience's interest—and the two characters' refrains quickly wear thin." However, *School Library Journal* contributor Beth Tegart called *When I Was Little Like You* a "delightful story about times past, grandparents, and change" and concluded that the book "deserves a space in picture-book collections, not for how it can be used but for what it is—a warm 'read it again' story."

In *Twentieth-Century Children's Writers,* Paton Walsh commented on herself as a writer: "My governing principle has always been to make whatever I am writing as plain and accessible as possible, not only to appeal to young readers, but to make my work as far as I can the sort of thing I like. My preferred subjects lie predominantly in the large area of experience that children and adults have in common...." In an essay in *A Sounding of Storytellers,* she wrote, "I write now for children out of wild ambition, having understood that they are the best audience for many things, but also the hardest. To reach their possibilities without stumbling over their limitations, one pares one's subject to the bones of its simplicity; one must find the ultimate structure of what truth one is dealing in, one must have the world clear and bright in view.... [O]nce it is not clogged up by hesitation and pretension almost anything can be told to [children] as a story. Now that I *have* understood how difficult a task I set myself when I began to write for children, it seems to me, though daunting, endlessly fascinating: technically far more challenging than the adult novel, and unambiguously worth doing. I shall keep trying as long as I have my wits about me, and energy to try anything." In her essay in *SAAS,* Paton Walsh concluded, "I don't know where I'll go next. That's part of the endless fun. For being a writer *is* fun.... A writer is what I shall be as long as there is a daydream in my head, and I have strength to sit up and type."

Works Cited

Bach, Alice, review of *Unleaving, New York Times Book Review,* August 8, 1976, p. 18.

Review of *A Chance Child, Publishers Weekly,* December 11, 1978, p. 69.

Crouch, Marcus, essay on Paton Walsh in *Twentieth-Century Children's Writers,* 3rd edition, St. James Press, 1989, pp. 760-62.

Donahue, Rosanne Fraine, "Jill Paton Walsh," *Dictionary of Literary Biography,* Volume 161: *British Children's Writers Since 1960,* Gale, 1996, pp. 245-57.

Egoff, Sheila A., "Realistic Fiction," *Thursday's Child: Trends and Patterns in Contemporary Children's Literature,* American Library Association, 1981, pp. 31-65.

Review of *Fireweed, Children's Literature in Education,* summer, 1977.

Review of *Gaffer Samson's Luck, Bulletin of the Center for Children's Books,* January, 1985, p. 97.

Review of *Hengest's Tale, Times Literary Supplement,* November 24, 1986, p. 1079.

Hannabuss, C. S., review of *The Emperor's Winding Sheet, Children's Book Review,* summer, 1974, p. 71.

Hannabuss, C. S., review of *Goldengrove, Children's Book Review,* February, 1973, p. 15.

Haviland, Virginia, review of *Unleaving, Horn Book,* August, 1976, p. 408.

Hearne, Betsy, review of *Matthew and the Sea Singer, Bulletin of the Center for Children's Books,* May, 1993, pp. 298-99.

Heins, Ethel L., review of *The Dolphin Crossing, Horn Book,* February, 1968, p. 72.

Heins, Paul, review of *The Emperor's Winding Sheet, Horn Book,* June, 1974, p. 289.

Landsberg, Michele, review of *Goldengrove, Entertainment Weekly,* June 8, 1990, p. 75.

Langton, Jane, review of *A Chance Child, New York Times Book Review,* June 17, 1979, pp. 24-25.

MacDuffie, Bruce L., review of *Wordhoard: Anglo-Saxon Stories, School Library Journal,* February, 1970, pp. 91-92.

Melton, Emily, review of *Matthew and the Sea Singer, Booklist,* April 15, 1993, p. 1518.

Review of *A Parcel of Patterns, Bulletin of the Center for Children's Books,* March, 1984, p. 136.

Paton Walsh, Jill, interview with Barbara James, *Magpies,* September, 1998, pp. 14-16.

Paton Walsh, Jill, "My Life So Far," *Something about the Author Autobiography Series,* Volume 3, Gale, 1987, pp. 189-203.

Paton Walsh, Jill, commentary in *A Sounding of Storytellers* by John Rowe Townsend, Lippincott, 1979, p. 365.

Paton Walsh, Jill, commentary in *Twentieth-Century Children's Writers,* 3rd edition, St. James Press, 1989, pp. 760-61.

Peel, Marie, review of *Fireweed, Books and Bookmen,* February, 1970, p. 36.

Philip, Neil, "A Terrible Beauty," *Times Educational Supplement,* January 13, 1984, p. 42.

Sutherland, Zena, review of *Fireweed, Saturday Review,* May 9, 1970, p. 69.

Sutton, Roger, review of *When Grandma Came, Bulletin of the Center for Children's Books,* February, 1993, p. 196.

Tegart, Beth, review of *When I Was Little Like You, School Library Journal,* December, 1997, pp. 102-03.

Townsend, John Rowe, "Growing Up," *Punch,* December 17, 1969, p. 1016.

Townsend, John Rowe, "Jill Paton Walsh," *A Sounding of Storytellers,* Lippincott, 1979, pp. 153-64.

Wersba, Barbara, review of *Goldengrove, New York Times Book Review,* Part 2, November 5, 1972, p. 6.

Review of *When I Was Little Like You, Publishers Weekly,* November 17, 1997, p. 60.

Review of *Wordhoard: Anglo-Saxon Stories, Times Literary Supplement,* October 16, 1969, p. 1196.

Wordsworth, Christopher, "Fires in the Heather," *Observer,* December 4, 1983, p. 32.

Zvirin, Stephanie, review of *When Grandma Came, Booklist,* November 1, 1992, p. 523.

For More Information See

BOOKS

Contemporary Literary Criticism, Volume 35, Gale, 1985, pp. 429-34.

Riley, Patricia, essay on Paton Walsh in *Children's Books and Their Creators,* edited by Anita Silvey, Houghton Mifflin, 1995, pp. 509-10.

Twentieth-Century Young Adult Writers, St. James Press, 1994.

PERIODICALS

Booklist, April 15, 1995, p. 1501.
Magpies, March, 1996, p. 26.
New Advocate, fall, 1996, p. 327.
School Library Journal, August, 1993, pp. 50-51.
Writer, February, 1987, pp. 19-21.

—Sketch by Gerard J. Senick

*   *   *

PATON WALSH, Jill
See PATON WALSH, Gillian

*   *   *

PETERS, Gabriel
See MATOTT, Justin

*   *   *

PETERSEN, David 1946-

Personal

Born May 18, 1946, in Oklahoma City, OK; son of Archie L. and Frances (Harper) Petersen; married Gwendolyn Odom, February 14, 1965 (divorced, 1978); married Carolyn Sturges (a homemaker), October 30, 1981; children: (first marriage) Christine Anne. *Education:* Chapman College, B.A., 1976; Fort Lewis College, B.A., 1982. *Politics:* Independent. *Religion:* "Deep Ecology." *Hobbies and other interests:* Whitewater boating, nature observation, bow hunting, fly fishing, camping.

Career

Road Rider, Laguna Beach, CA, editor, 1976-80; freelance writer, 1980-83; *Mother Earth News,* Hendersonville, NC, editor, 1983-90. Part-time English and writing instructor at Fort Lewis College, Durango, CO. *Military service:* U.S. Marine Corps, achieved rank of captain, 1968-74. *Member:* Outdoor Writers Association of America.

Writings

NONFICTION FOR CHILDREN

Airports, Childrens Press, 1981.
Airplanes, Childrens Press, 1981.
Helicopters, Childrens Press, 1982.
Newspapers, Childrens Press, 1983.
Submarines, Childrens Press, 1984.
Solar Energy at Work, Childrens Press, 1985.
(With Mark Coburn) *Meriwether Lewis and William Clark: Soldiers, Explorers, and Partners in History,* Childrens Press, 1988.
Apatosaurus, Childrens Press, 1989.
Tyrannosaurus Rex, Childrens Press, 1989.
Racks: The Natural History of Antlers and the Animals That Wear Them, illustrated by Michael McCurdy, Northland, 1989.
Ishi: The Last of His People, Childrens Press, 1991.
The Anasazi, Childrens Press, 1991.
Sequoyah, Father of the Cherokee Alphabet, Childrens Press, 1991.
Canyonlands National Park, Childrens Press, 1992.
Mesa Verde National Park, Childrens Press, 1992.
Yellowstone National Park, Childrens Press, 1992.
Waterton-Glacier International Peace Park, Childrens Press, 1992.
Grand Teton National Park, Childrens Press, 1992.
Grand Canyon National Park, Childrens Press, 1992.
Zion National Park, Childrens Press, 1993.
Great Smoky Mountains National Park, Childrens Press, 1993.
Yosemite National Park, Childrens Press, 1993.
Rocky Mountain National Park, Childrens Press, 1993.
Carlsbad Caverns National Park, Childrens Press, 1994.
Moose, Childrens Press, 1994.
Death Valley National Monument, Childrens Press, 1994.
Dinosaur National Monument, Childrens Press, 1995.
Mountain Lions, Childrens Press, 1995.
Death Valley National Park, Childrens Press, 1996.
Petrified Forest National Park, Childrens Press, 1996.
Bryce Canyon National Park, Childrens Press, 1996.
Denali National Park and Preserve, Childrens Press, 1996.
Africa, Childrens Press, 1998.
Europe, Childrens Press, 1998.
Australia, Childrens Press, 1998.

Asia, Childrens Press, 1998.
North America, Childrens Press, 1998.
South America, Childrens Press, 1998.
Antarctica, Childrens Press, 1998.
Saguaro National Park, Childrens Press, 1999.
Arches National Park, Childrens Press, 1999.
Great Sand Dunes National Monument, Childrens Press, 1999.
Chaco Culture National Historic Park, Childrens Press, 1999.

OTHER

(Editor) *Big Sky, Fair Land: The Environmental Essays of A. B. Guthrie Jr.,* Northland, 1988.
Among the Elk: Wilderness Images, photographs by Alan Carey, Northland, 1988.
Wind, Water, and Sand: The Natural Bridges Story, Canyonlands Natural History Association, 1990.
Among the Aspen: Life in an Aspen Grove, photographs by Branson Reynolds, Northland, 1991.
Ghost Grizzlies, Holt, 1995, as *Ghost Grizzlies: Does the Great Bear Still Haunt Colorado?,* Johnson Books, 1998.
(Editor) *A Hunter's Heart: Honest Essays on Blood Sport,* Holt, 1996.
The Nearby Faraway: A Personal Journey through the Heart of the West, Johnson Books, 1997.
Elkheart: A Personal Tribute to Wapiti and Their World, Johnson Books, 1998.

Contributor of hundreds of articles to magazines.

Sidelights

Nonfiction author David Petersen cites his primary interests as natural history and environmentalism, and his many books for children reflect those interests. Working with New York City's Childrens Press, Petersen has produced a number of books introducing the U.S. National Park system, as well as books on animal species and Native American tribes. Peterson refers to himself as an "outdoor writer," citing Edward Abbey and A. B. Guthrie Jr., as major inspirations. Petersen's books for adults include editorship of Guthrie's essays in *Big Sky, Fair Land: The Environmental Essays of A. B. Guthrie Jr.,* and *The Nearby Faraway: A Personal Journey through the Heart of the West,* published in 1997.

Several of Petersen's books focus on the North American terra firma. In books such as *Yellowstone National Park* and *Grand Canyon National Park,* he focuses on the geological marvels that make each of these federally protected areas unique. His *North America,* published in 1999, features satellite photographs of the continent's topography in addition to pictures, maps, and art reproductions that introduce young readers to what *Booklist* contributor Ellen Mandel lists as the varied "land formations, climates, indigenous plants and animals, and native peoples" of North America. Other books in the series include *Australia, Europe,* and *South America.*

In Earth's evolution, when land was formed, animals soon moved across its surface, and Petersen engages young readers with some of the earliest species in a series of books focusing on dinosaurs. In *Apatosaurus,* young dino fans learn the meaning of such terms as *gastrolith* and *ichnology,* and the book "makes excellent use of comparison," as *School Library Journal* contributor Denia Lewis Hester remarked upon learning that a single leaf-eating apatosaurus might weigh as much as twenty cars would today. In *Booklist,* Denise Wilms praises *Apatosaurus* for clarifying "the dinosaur species that was commonly called brontosaurus." In *Tyrannosaurus Rex* the granddaddy of all dinosaurs is discussed, and Petersen introduces readers to a new theory about the way the giant lizard walked, sparking budding scientists to realize that lives of the dinosaurs are still shrouded in the unknown. The process by which dinosaur fossils have been uncovered is also discussed in relation to tyrannosaurus rex.

After the dinosaurs died out but before the arrival of pale-skinned Europeans, North America was populated by many diverse tribes of people who are now referred to collectively as Native Americans. Such a classification does little to distinguish the wealth of differences that existed between tribes, and in such books as *Sequoyah: Father of the Cherokee Alphabet* and *Ishi: The Last of His People,* Petersen attempts to address such differences. Ishi was the sole survivor of California's Yahi tribe and was discovered, half-starved, in 1911. While Petersen provides readers with an understanding of Ishi's last years, his "straightforward" approach is unable to "convey the tragedy ... of being the last of an entire nation to survive," according to *School Library Journal* contributor Lisa Mitten. *Sequoyah,* published in 1991, was deemed more successful by reviewers. Eunice Weech noted that Petersen's biography is "filled with anecdotal stories that make [this scholarly son of a white father and a Cherokee mother] come to life" in her appraisal of the book in *School Library Journal.* Other books detailing the lives of precolonial Americans include *Meriwether Lewis and William Clark: Soldiers, Explorers, and Partners in History,* which includes in-depth coverage of the explorers' guide and interpreter, Sacagawea, and "plausible theories about [the young mother's] life after the expedition," according to *Booklist* contributor Beth Herbert.

Works Cited

Herbert, Beth, review of *Meriwether Lewis and William Clark: Soldiers, Explorers, and Partners in History, Booklist,* March 1, 1989, p. 1132.
Hester, Denia Lewis, review of *Apatosaurus, School Library Journal,* December, 1989, pp. 114-15.
Mandel, Ellen, review of *North America, Booklist,* January 1, 1999, p. 869.
Mitten, Lisa, review of *Ishi: The Last of His People, School Library Journal,* January, 1992, p. 106.
Weech, Eunice, review of *Sequoyah: Father of the Cherokee Alphabet, School Library Journal,* March 19, 1992, p. 232.

Wilms, Denise, review of *Apatosaurus, Booklist,* September 1, 1989, p. 70.

For More Information See

PERIODICALS

Booklist, January 1, 1999, p. 869.
Magpies, March, 1991, p. 33.
School Library Journal, August, 1995, p. 137; May, 1997, p. 123.*

*   *   *

PRIMAVERA, Elise 1954-

Personal

Born May 19, 1954, in West Long Branch, NJ; daughter of Jerry (a builder) and Corrine (a housewife; maiden name, Miller) Primavera. *Education:* Moore College of Art, B.F.A., 1976; attended Arts Students League, 1980-84.

Addresses

Home—343 East 74th St., 14M, New York, NY 10021.

Career

Freelance fashion illustrator, 1976-79; freelance children's book illustrator, 1979—.

Awards, Honors

New Jersey Institute of Technology Award, 1983, for *The Bollo Caper: A Furry Tale for All Ages,* by Art Buchwald, and 1988, for *Christina Katerina and the Time She Quit the Family* by Patricia Lee Gauch; *New York Times* Notable Books selection, 1986, for *Make Way for Sam Houston,* by Jean Fritz.

Writings

ALL SELF-ILLUSTRATED

Basil and Maggie, Lippincott, 1983.
Ralph's Frozen Tale, Putnam, 1991.
The Three Dots, Putnam, 1993.
Plantpet, Putnam, 1994.
Auntie Claus, Harcourt, 1999.

ILLUSTRATOR

Joyce St. Peter, *Always Abigail,* Lippincott, 1981.
Dorothy Crayder, *The Joker and the Swan,* Harper, 1981.
Margaret K. Wetterer, *The Mermaid's Cape,* Atheneum, 1981.
Eila Moorhouse Lewis, *The Snug Little House,* Atheneum, 1981.
Margaret K. Wetterer, *The Giant's Apprentice,* Atheneum, 1982.
Art Buchwald, *The Bollo Caper: A Furry Tale for All Ages,* Putnam, 1983.
Natalie Savage Carlson, *The Surprise in the Mountains,* Harper, 1983.

Delia Ephron, *Santa and Alex,* Little, Brown, 1983.
Miriam Anne Bourne, *Uncle George Washington and Harriot's Guitar,* Putnam, 1983.
Elaine Moore, *Grandma's House,* Lothrop, 1985.
Margaret Poynter, *What's One More?,* Atheneum, 1985.
Jean Fritz, *Make Way for Sam Houston,* Putnam, 1986.
Jamie Gilson, *Hobie Hanson, You're Weird,* Lothrop, 1987.
Patricia Lee Gauch, *Christina Katerina and the Time She Quit the Family,* Putnam, 1987.
Jamie Gilson, *Double Dog Dare,* Lothrop, 1988.
Elaine Moore, *Grandma's Promise,* Lothrop, 1988.
Jane Yolen, *Best Witches: Poems for Halloween,* Putnam, 1989.
Patricia Lee Gauch, *Christina Katerina and the Great Bear Train,* Putnam, 1990.
Diane Stanley, *Moe the Dog in Tropical Paradise,* Putnam, 1992.
Diane Stanley, *Woe Is Moe,* Putnam, 1995.
Mary-Claire Helldorfer, *Jack, Skinny Bones, and the Golden Pancakes,* Viking, 1996.
Helen Elizabeth Buckley, *Moonlight Kite,* Lothrop, 1997.
Jerdine Nolen, *Raising Dragons,* Silver Whistle, 1998.
Jerdine Nolen, *Hewitt Anderson's Big Life,* Silver Whistle, 2000.

Sidelights

Elise Primavera has contributed her imaginative and endearing artwork to numerous picture books, some self-penned and a host of others written by noted authors such as Jane Yolen, Natalie Savage Carlson, and Jerdine Nolen. Combining the soft edges of brightly colored pastels or subtle charcoal drawings with the more opaque mediums of gouache and acrylic, Primavera's illustrations have been praised for their liveliness and imagination, and compared to the work of fellow illustrator Lane Smith. "Primavera's ... illustrations ... fairly burst forth from the pages, adding to the exaggerated humor" of Mary-Claire Helldorfer's *Jack, Skinny Bones, and the Golden Pancakes,* in the opinion of *Booklist* contributor Kay Weisman, while a *Publishers Weekly* reviewer noted that her "dynamic spreads heighten the suspense" of the story and deemed her illustrations, on the whole, "rip-roaring."

Born in West Long Branch, New Jersey, in 1954, Primavera attended Moore College of Art, where she earned her B.F.A. in 1976. She began her illustration career by producing fashion illustrations, but after several years began to feel that her creativity was not being challenged. In 1979, she decided to make a change and delve into children's book illustration. As part of her career transition she attended an illustrator's workshop, which gave her the confidence she needed. "I felt very encouraged after three weeks," Primavera told Jim Roginski in an interview. "I spent the summer of 1979 putting a portfolio together to show publishers." While she had an agent to market her fashion illustration skills, Primavera decided to represent herself as a children's illustrator; she hit the streets of New York City. "I saw everybody and anybody who would give me an appointment," the author/illustrator recalled of her first year, "and once I got in the door I'd always ask if there was anyone else that could see me while I was there."

Primavera's first break came when she was hired to create a book jacket for Harper & Row, and a picture book assignment followed only a few months later. By 1981, Primavera had two illustrated picture books to her credit: Dorothy Crayder's *The Joker and the Swan,* and Joyce St. Peter's *Always Abigail.* Two years later, she could add "author" to her credits with the publication of *Basil and Maggie,* the story of a young girl who receives an unusual gift of a pony named Basil. Visions of walking away with a blue ribbon at the local horse show vanish into smoke after Basil proves himself less than surefooted next to his sleek thoroughbred competitors, but Maggie falls in love with him anyway in a story that a *Publishers Weekly* contributor called "just the antidote to have on hand when everything goes wrong." Primavera's illustrations were the target of praise as well; *School Library Journal* contributor Roberta Magid commented that the book's "charcoal drawings accentuate the humorous situation."

Other books by Primavera include *The Three Dots,* a story of a trio of animals—Sal the moose, Henry the frog, and Margaret the duck—whose odd polka-dotted markings inspire them to form a musical group and take Manhattan by storm. Praising Primavera's "off-the-wall volume" for its "kicky watercolors" and "hilarious scenes," a *Publishers Weekly* contributor concluded that *The Three Dots* "should get lots of play." While less enthusiastic about the text, Dot Minzer raved over the book's "colorful, oversized" pictures. In her *School Library Journal* appraisal of *The Three Dots,* she maintained that Primavera's "spirited and amusing ... pictures will grab a young audience and bring smiles to their faces." An animal protagonist is also featured in *Ralph's Frozen Tale,* a 1991 picture book that finds Arctic explorer Ralph stuck without a dogsled until he is helped by a polar bear that can speak. "Primavera's swirling blues, greens, purples and whites give depth and beauty to the trackless, snowy wastes traversed by her heros," noted *School Library Journal* contributor Lisa Dennis in praise of the volume's humorous and highly detailed illustrations. And in 1994's intriguingly titled *Plantpet,* a lonely junk collector discovers a caged plant which under suitable care and watering grows into a leaf-covered gardener in what a *Publishers Weekly* critic characterized as "another quirky tale that celebrates buddydom."

A disciplined artist, Primavera's work day begins at 7:00 A.M. "I work straight through until three o'clock or so," she told Roginski. "As far as my work time goes I spend much of it working out the sketches and dummy and the 'look' of the book. I try to capture its mood through an appropriate style. This takes a good deal of time because I'm not always comfortable or facile in a particular style. So I spend a lot of time not only on sketches, composition, and characterization (and the dummy in general), but also on the finishes because I'm working in an unfamiliar medium."

In all her illustration projects, whether for her own books or the text of other authors, Primavera makes it a point to "make the most bizarre thing seem possible and real to the reader. It's sort of like watching a good magician perform: you know he really can't be pulling that rabbit out of the hat, but it all looks so real that for a moment something magical really is happening. This is the response that I try to work for through my illustrations."

Primavera counts among her inspirations the artist-illustrators associated with Howard Pyle and the Brandywine School that developed in and around Chadd's Ford, Pennsylvania, in the early 1900s. "I especially like N. C. Wyeth, Jessie Willcox Smith, and Charlotte Harding," she told *SATA.* Of her own artwork, one of the most memorable projects was creating the illustrations for Jane Yolen's poetry collection *Best Witches.* "For research, I spent a lot of time in the local costume store," Primavera recalled. "When I actually finished *Witches* (nine months later), my studio was crammed with witches' hats, rubber skeletons, fright wigs, plastic frogs, and black hairy spiders. At the time I was selling my house, and I used to love to watch my real estate agent show prospective buyers the studio—I don't think they knew whether to laugh or report me to the local authorities!"

Works Cited

Review of *Basil and Maggie, Publishers Weekly,* April 29, 1983, p. 52.

Dennis, Lisa, review of *Ralph's Frozen Tale, School Library Journal,* February, 1992, pp. 76-77.

Review of *Jack, Skinny Bones, and the Golden Pancakes, Publishers Weekly,* November 11, 1996, p. 73.

Magid, Roberta, review of *Basil and Maggie, School Library Journal,* May, 1983, p. 65.

Minzer, Dot, review of *The Three Dots, School Library Journal,* January, 1994, p. 97.

Review of *Plantpet, Publishers Weekly,* August 8, 1994, p. 434.

Roginski, Jim, "Primavera," *Behind the Covers: Interviews with Authors and Illustrators of Books for Children and Young Adults,* Libraries Unlimited, 1985, pp. 161-66.

Review of *The Three Dots, Publishers Weekly,* October 4, 1993, p. 78.

Weisman, Kay, review of *Jack, Skinny Bones, and the Golden Pancakes, Booklist,* October 15, 1996, p. 426.

R

REVENA
  See WRIGHT, Betty Ren

*   *   *

ROBINSON, Kim Stanley 1952-

Personal

Born March 23, 1952, in Waukegan, IL; married Lisa Howland Nowell, 1982; two children. *Education:* University of California, San Diego, B.A. (literature), 1974, Ph.D. (literature), 1982; Boston University, M.A. (English), 1975.

Addresses

Agent—Ralph Vicinanza, 111 Eighth Ave., New York, NY 10011.

Career

Writer; visiting lecturer at University of California, San Diego, 1982 and 1985, and University of California, Davis, 1982-84 and 1985.

Awards, Honors

Nebula Award nomination, Science Fiction Writers of America, 1981, for "Venice Drowned," 1983, for "Black Air," 1984, for *The Wild Shore* and "Lucky Strike," 1986, for "Escape from Kathmandu," 1990, for "Before I Wake," 1992, for "Vinland the Dream," and 1994, for *Green Mars;* Hugo Award nomination, World Science Fiction Society, 1983, for "To Leave a Mark," 1984, for "Black Air," 1985, for "Lucky Strike" and "Ridge Running," 1986, for "Green Mars," 1987, for "Escape from Kathmandu," 1988, for "The Blind Geometer" and "Mother Goddess of the World," 1991, for "A Short, Sharp Shock," and 1993, for *Red Mars;* World Fantasy Award for best novella, World Fantasy Convention, 1983, for "Black Air"; Locus Award for best first novel,

Kim Stanley Robinson

Locus magazine, 1985, for *The Wild Shore;* Nebula Award for best novella, 1987, for "The Blind Geometer," and for best novel, 1993, for *Red Mars;* John W. Campbell Award, 1991; British Science Fiction Award, 1992; Hugo Award for best novel, 1994, for *Green Mars,* and 1997, for *Blue Mars;* National Science Foundation grant for study in Antarctica, 1995.

Writings

NOVELS

The Wild Shore, Ace, 1984.
Icehenge, Ace, 1984.

The Memory of Whiteness: A Scientific Romance, Tor, 1985.

The Gold Coast, Tor, 1988.

Pacific Edge, Tor, 1990.

A Short, Sharp Shock, illustrations by Arnie Fenner, M. V. Ziesing, 1990.

Red Mars, Bantam, 1993.

Green Mars, Bantam, 1994.

Blue Mars, Bantam, 1996.

Antarctica, Bantam, 1998.

The Martians, Bantam, 1999.

SHORT STORIES

The Blind Geometer, illustrated by Judy King-Rieniets, Cheap Street, 1986.

The Planet on the Table, Tor, 1986.

Black Air, Pulphouse, 1991.

Remaking History, Tor, 1991.

A Sensitive Dependence on Initial Conditions, Pulphouse, 1991.

Escape from Kathmandu, Orb, 1994.

Remaking History and Other Stories, Orb, 1994.

Stories represented in anthologies, including *Orbit 18* and *Orbit 19,* both edited by Damon Knight, Harper, 1975 and 1977; *Clarion SF,* edited by Kate Wilhelm, Berkeley, 1977; *Universe 11, Universe 12, Universe 13, Universe 14,* and *Universe 15,* all edited by Terry Carr, Doubleday, 1981-85; and *The Year's Best Science Fiction 1,* edited by Gardner Dozois and Jim Frenkel, Bluejay Books, 1984. Contributor of stories to science fiction magazines, including *Isaac Asimov's Science Fiction Magazine.*

OTHER

The Novels of Philip K. Dick, UMI Research Press, 1984.

Editor, *Future Primitive: The New Ectopias,* Tor, 1994.

Sidelights

There are no little green men on the Mars of science fiction writer Kim Stanley Robinson. His is the Mars of the satellite photos and geologic surveys of NASA's Mariner and Viking missions. It is the Mars of hard science brought to life through human endeavors and pulsed by human history, culture, politics, and ethics, all of which Robinson explores in his epic trilogy about the twenty-first-century colonization of Mars.

That trilogy, according to Edward James in the *Times Literary Supplement,* has established Robinson "as the pre-eminent contemporary practitioner of science fiction. He has earned that position by taking the central tenet of science fiction—the extrapolation of current trends and beliefs into the construction of a future history—to greater lengths than any of his predecessors, and the Mars books are likely to be the touchstone of what is possible in the genre for a long time to come."

Before setting out for the red planet, Robinson had already blazed his own trail into science fiction with consistently well-received short stories, novellas, and novels, including a trilogy depicting three near-future

versions of southern California. Notable throughout his work is a narrative style informed by history and literature, one which relies heavily on setting and which bypasses science fiction's typical action-plotting devices in favor of telling stories through thematic extrapolation, character study, and multiple, often conflicting, points of view. The scientific and technical detail, interdisciplinary themes, and adult relationships depicted in Robinson's work both require and reward reader maturity. "The novels and short stories of Kim Stanley Robinson constitute one of the most impressive bodies of work in modern science fiction," hailed Gerald Jonas in the *New York Times Book Review.* Jonas added in a later critique: "If I had to choose one writer whose work will set the standard for science fiction in the future, it would be Kim Stanley Robinson."

Given the rigorous scientific detail that characterizes his best known work, it may be surprising to learn that Robinson is not a scientist. Instead, his credentials are decidedly literary. Born in Waukegan, Illinois, in 1952, Robinson grew up in Orange County, California, and graduated from the University of California, San Diego in 1974 with a degree in literature. He went on to earn a master's degree in English from Boston University the following year, and then returned to the University of California, San Diego to earn a doctorate in literature in 1982, writing his dissertation on the novels of Philip K. Dick. (Dick, who died in 1982, is best known for his 1968 novel *Do Androids Dream of Electric Sheep?,* on which the 1982 movie *Bladerunner* was based, and for his 1962 Hugo Award-winner, *The Man in the High Castle.* Dick's science fiction is characterized by metaphysical concerns and psychological intensity; the changing points of view in Robinson's narrative hearken those used by Dick.)

Many of Robinson's short stories were first published in the 1970s and early 1980s in the science fiction journals *Orbit* and *Universe,* garnering him major award nominations. Some of Robinson's best short stories have been incorporated into longer works, notably *Icehenge* (based on his stories "On the North Pole of Pluto" and "To Leave a Mark") and *The Memory of Whiteness: A Scientific Romance* (based on the story "In Pierson's Orchestra"). Other well-known shorter works by Robinson are *Escape from Kathmandu,* four novella-length stories which tell of the Himalayan adventures of two American expatriates, and *A Short, Sharp Shock,* a fantasy novella in which a man wakes up in a strange world surrounded by water and can remember nothing but a vanished woman with whom he washed up on the beach. His becomes a dream-like quest through a society of peaceful tree people and brutal "spine kings" as he seeks out answers, identity, and his unknown companion. Robinson's first novel, *The Wild Shore,* was published in 1984, and the following year, he left his university teaching job in order to devote himself to world travel and a full-time writing career.

The Wild Shore was chosen to relaunch the discontinued Ace Specials, a line of cutting-edge science fiction novels first published in the 1960s by Ace Books. It and

Robinson's subsequent *The Gold Coast* and *Pacific Edge* comprise the "Orange County" trilogy, which, according to David P. Snider in *Voice of Youth Advocates,* is in its entirety "an excellent exercise in what speculative fiction is all about: 'What if?'"

What if there were a nuclear disaster? Described by numerous reviewers as a Huckleberry Finn-like frontier novel, *The Wild Shore* features a seventeen-year-old narrator named Henry who is making his way into adulthood in an America destroyed decades ago by a nuclear holocaust. Since the country is under a United Nations quarantine and barred from redeveloping its technology, Henry and his friend Steve know little more about America than what they can see from their isolated coastal village and what they hear in the past-glorifying stories of old-timers. As Henry strikes out to pursue his own adventures and discoveries in a dangerous new world, a novel that appears on the surface to be yet another post-nuclear disaster tale becomes a character-rich coming-of-age story. "By the novel's end, Henry's family and friends have been brought to life with a vivid depth rarely encountered in science fiction," remarked Stephen P. Brown in the *Washington Post Book World.* "Robinson's approach to storytelling is the traditional literary one, in its best sense, rather than the unique tone science fiction has developed in years of trying to translate commercial values into literature," wrote Algis Budrys in the *Magazine of Fantasy and Science Fiction.* Budrys called *The Wild Shore* "a remarkably powerful piece of work."

Its follow-up, *The Gold Coast,* also depicts a dystopian Orange County, but one that tries to answer a different question: What might America be like in the next century if current trends continue? Robinson's answer is a freeway-tracked, polluted, overdeveloped, overpopulated, defense-industry-dependent society. Wandering through it is a disconnected young poet named Jim McPherson, who, with his zoned-out friends, seeks to dull his idealistic pangs with designer drugs and casual sex. At last trying to take meaningful action in his life, he rebels against the establishment beliefs of his parents—his father is an aerospace engineer and his mother a devout Christian—by joining a revolutionary group that targets weapons manufacturers, including his father's employer. "*The Gold Coast* is ambitious, angry, eccentric," asserted *Los Angeles Times Book Review* contributor T. Jefferson Parker. Though Parker called Robinson's dialogue writing weak, he concluded that "Robinson has succeeded at a novelist's toughest challenge: He's made us look at the world around us. This isn't escapist stuff—it sends you straight into a confrontation with yourself."

In the trilogy's concluding book, *Pacific Edge,* Robinson creates his version of utopia, a place that is not yet perfect but moving in that direction. This novel's El Modena, California, is part of a new society brought about by peaceful revolution, where multinational corporations no longer rule and technology serves people's simpler, ecology-friendly lifestyles. Newly elected town councilman Kevin finds himself in the midst of conflict,

In the first installment in Robinson's "Three Californias" trilogy, a young man struggles to survive life near the Pacific coast following a nuclear war. (Cover illustration by Tony Roberts.)

however, when water-rights issues and the potential commercial development of a pristine hillside threaten to split the community. The political troubles are further complicated by personal relationships between allies and opponents. *New York Times Book Review* contributor Jonas maintained: "Through a blend of dirt-under-the-fingernails naturalism and lyrical magical realism, [Robinson] invites us to share his characters' intensely personal, intensely local attachment to what they have. The result is a bittersweet utopia that may shame you into entertaining new hope for the future."

Robinson is an avid mountain trekker who loves wilderness landscapes, and much in his fiction seeks to shed light on the disconnection he sees between urban life and nature. "I spend as much time as I can in the wilderness," he told Sebastian Cooke in an *Eidolon* interview. "It's got me thinking about the environmental catastrophe we're sitting on the edge of and solutions to that. It doesn't make any sense just to throw up your hands in despair and say, 'The world is doomed!'" Robinson does not see environmental movements like those suggested in *Pacific Edge* as utopian. "There will always be competing interests that will be viciously fought over ... to pretend otherwise is what makes people uninterested," Robinson told Cooke.

Just such conflicting human interests drive Robinson's award-winning and best-selling "Mars" trilogy, described by a critic in *Science Fiction Weekly* as "what might be one of the grandest literary science fiction epics to date." Totaling some 1,600 pages and taking six years to write, *Red Mars, Green Mars,* and *Blue Mars* chronicle human efforts over a period of several hundred years to colonize and "terraform" Mars.

The term terraforming was coined in 1938 by science fiction writer Jack Williamson, and refers to the process of creating an Earth-like biosphere on a dead planet, so that life can be introduced and sustained there. "I got interested in the whole idea because Mars is one of the best candidates for terraformation that you can possibly imagine: its conditions are close to those of Earth in terms of gravity, it's got water and it also contains all the various volatile chemicals to create an atmosphere," Robinson explained in an on-line interview for Harper-Collins, adding that "It has now become clear that this isn't just science fiction, or pie in the sky, it's something that could be done with the science and technology that we have now."

The colors in the books' titles represent the stages of Martian transformation: red for its original state, green for the successful introduction of plant life there, and blue for eventual creation of oceans and an oxygen-enriched atmosphere. "Having decided to write a novel about the terraforming of Mars, I was committed to a long novel. The long novel, or the Really Long Novel, is another sub-genre slightly different from the novel, like the novella in the other direction," Robinson explained in an on-line question and answer session for *Science Fiction Weekly.*

Robinson began the "Mars" trilogy with just twenty or so pages of notes—ideas and dialogue out of which he hoped to create a book. "Then, as I went along, the story as written began to require that other things happen later in it. This is the great interest of novel writing; 20 pages of image fragments have to be worked out into 1,600 pages of narrative. A lot of it necessarily gets worked out en route, and some of what appears late in the game is very surprising to me," he said in *Science Fiction Weekly.* Once you've mastered the science, colonizing Mars sounds straightforward enough, until you delve, as Robinson so thoroughly does, into another of its key components: humanity. As Faren Miller wrote in *Locus* magazine, the central question behind Robinson's "Mars" trilogy is as social and cultural as it is scientific: "As planets are transformed, human societies change as well—but are the social transformations entirely controlled, rational, and to the good?"

"December 21st, 2026: they were moving faster than anyone in history. They were on their way. It was the beginning of a nine-month voyage—or of a voyage that would last the rest of their lives. They were on their

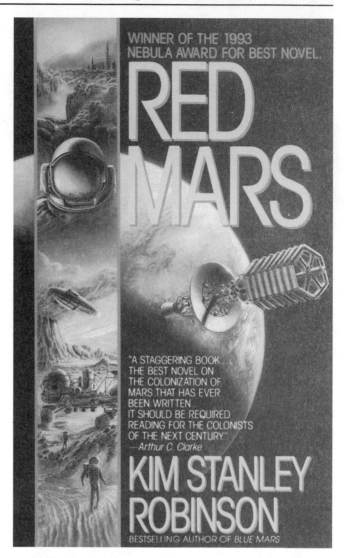

One hundred settlers are sent to Mars to give the planet an Earth-like atmosphere in Robinson's Nebula Award-winning story. (Cover illustration by Don Dixon.)

own." Thus, in *Red Mars,* the first colonists—100 carefully selected scientists who hold a diversity of views about the political and ethical aspects of their mission—journey to Earth's frigid, lifeless neighbor to create settlements and begin a terraforming process that will take hundreds of years to complete. "The science of *Red Mars* is impeccably researched, convincing, and often thrilling in its moments of peril and grand implications," observed Miller in *Locus.* Liaisons and clashes soon emerge between strong personalities like those of team leaders Frank Chalmers and Maya Toitova, early Mars pioneer John Boone, political renegade Arkady Bogdanov, and subversive ecologist Hiroko Ao, among others.

Perhaps most fierce and divisive is the argument that persists throughout the trilogy: whether Mars should be terraformed as quickly and fully as possible, a position advocated by the "Green" character Sax Russell and strongly supported by Earth governments, or whether its natural environment and evolution should be studied and preserved, a less popular position held by geologist Ann Clayborne and her "Red" followers. By the end, initial visions for Mars's future are nearly subsumed by the multicultural complexities and mixed motives of an influx of new settlers, which lead to acts of sabotage and ultimately, a violent revolt. "In the debate over terraforming and its consequences, Mr. Robinson has all the makings of a philosophical novel of suspense. The stakes are high, the sides are shrewdly drawn, the players on both sides range from politically naive idealists to ambitious manipulators without discernible scruples," wrote Jonas in the *New York Times Book Review*.

Robinson's own views on the terraforming issue "are almost perfectly split down the middle, which I think is one of the driving emotional forces in me for writing" the "Mars" trilogy, he told Cooke in *Eidolon*. "There's a part of me that thinks that terraforming is a beautiful spiritual, almost religious project and that to be able to walk around on Mars in the open air ... is absolutely one of the great human projects and ought to be done." He added, however, that he also thought this was a desecration of a unique, beautiful landscape. The different views give energy to the characters and the argument.

Red Mars begins with a murder in an established Martian settlement, then backtracks to the beginning of the colonization story so that readers may trace the motive, a plot device that some reviewers found faulty. Many note, however, that plot is less important to Robinson than point of view: Each chapter is told from the perspective of a different character, allowing Robinson to put forth a society of views that is in keeping with the scale of the terraforming effort. "His point is the reshaping of a world; people are hardly more than footnotes, and if their motives ultimately seem a little thin and their actions futile, never mind," concluded Tom Easton in *Analog*.

The colonists are ultimately upstaged, many conclude, by Mars itself, through Robinson's descriptive landscaping and the science and technology he uses to bring Mars to life. "On one level, the planet itself becomes a major character," observed Jonas in the *New York Times Book Review*. The reader feels the changes in the atmosphere and the "beauty of this fundamentally inhuman setting and its effect on its all-too-human inhabitants," Jonas continued.

Green Mars begins about twenty years later and it chronicles the next forty years of life on Mars. Due to anti-aging treatments, many of the "first 100" characters are still around, though driven underground by the failed rebellion that closes *Red Mars*. Focusing on the coming-of-age journey of a new young character, Nirgal, who has grown up in a southern colony established by rebel Hiroko Ao, the plot recalls some of the pioneering spirit of *Red Mars*. For the most part, however, *Green Mars* is devoted to the process of creating a central Martian government out of its numerous colonies. It concludes with revolutionary war and an environmental disaster on Earth.

Some critics found that *Green Mars* suffers from "the middle book problem," meaning the way in which second books in trilogies often struggle to keep up the established pace while at the same time trying to become more than just a bridge between the first and final books. "There are enough kidnappings, murders, rescues, disasters, and acts of sabotage to keep it all exciting, but the tale is driven by the problems of gaining independence from both earthly governments and the giant corporations who continually seek ways of exploiting the Martian colony. This leads to long passages of political and economic debate that slow down Robinson's momentum," remarked Gary K. Wolfe in *Locus*. Another *Locus* contributor, Russell Letson, asserted: "The breadth of Robinson's interests makes for a dense and intellectually ambitious book: psychology, political-economic theory, history, the planetary sciences and ecology, and the interactions of all these. Robinson often shows a reluctance to depend on plot as the driving force of a narrative." With most of the action taking place off stage, so to speak, Letson noted that "it's as if Robinson were avoiding as much of the vulgarity of action as he could and still have a narrative in which crucial events occur. What we get instead is a book tied together by thematics and character."

Having successfully gained independence from Earth, Martian society's biggest threat in *Blue Mars* is the ongoing battling between the Reds, who want to sever ties with Earth and protect what's left of untouched Mars, and the Greens who want to continue altering the planet for human use. At the risk of setting an ice age in motion, Green leader Sax Russell attempts to make peace with Red leader Ann Clayborne by removing from orbit the mirrors that create the atmospheric heat necessary for terraforming. As a result, the rival factions must together begin hammering out an appropriate government for themselves. Meanwhile, Earth faces a population crisis and impending planetary flooding, as its polar cap melts and ocean levels rise due to global warming. The crisis puts pressure on Mars to allow for the immigration of Terran refugees and leads to further Martian conflict. Describing *Blue Mars* in a Bantam Double Day on-line feature, Robinson said, "Events branch out as in a genealogical chart, and the problem is to keep a handle on them all.... And on a personal level, the characters we began with in *Red Mars* are getting very, very old, with interesting results."

"Robinson is as meticulous with his details as ever," noted *Science Fiction Weekly* contributor Clinton Lawrence, "whether he's describing the mechanisms of memory, the political and economic theories behind the new Martian constitution, or his characters' internal emotional and mental struggles." Lawrence added: "In *Blue Mars* it becomes clear that Robinson is writing about humanity's next great cultural leap as much as he is writing about the colonization of Mars."

As vivid a reality as Robinson makes Martian colonization seem, he does not in the end believe Mars is a means of escaping Earth's current and impending environmental and population problems. "The only solutions are going to be right here on Earth," Robinson stated in *Science Fiction Weekly.* "Mars can help as experiment in planetary engineering—what we learn there will be applicable here—but it cannot help us as a new physical space, because the problems will be severe in the next hundred years, and Mars cannot be made inhabitable in less than 300 years; probably more like 3,000.... Mars is a mirror, not a bolt hole."

Among the most recent of Robinson's efforts, the novel *Antarctica* presents new territory that is closer to home but no less harsh or complex. In 1995, Robinson won a National Science Foundation grant—the first science fiction writer to do so—and spent six weeks in Antarctica, accompanying a glacier research team on field work and visiting the McMurdo American base camp there. With Antarctica's oil riches at stake, the potential environmental, political, and territorial conflicts of the twenty-first century set the stage for his *Antarctica,* a novel depicting a time in the near future when overpopulation, global warming, and deforestation have escalated to life-threatening proportions. "Robinson bring to this novel a passionate concern for landscape, ecology and the effects of the 'Gotterdammerung capitalism' that he sees as the most serious threat to the survival of our species," maintained a *Publishers Weekly* critic. The same commentator added: "Moving back and forth between breathtaking descriptions of the alien, out-of-scale beauty of Antarctica, gripping tales of adventure on the ice and astute analyses of the ecopolitics of the southernmost continent, Robinson has created another superb addition to what is rapidly becoming one of the most impressive bodies of work in [science fiction]."

"The issues that Robinson explores in his fiction reflect a world view that is initially dark but ultimately hopeful," Elisabeth Sherwin wrote in a *Davis Enterprise* column, in which Robinson told her, "I'm not cheerful about the future. Historically, the world has not responded well to crises but I want to remain hopeful. We have the spiritual and technical abilities to pull through ... we could get in balance with the environment and manage the population."

Science fiction, Robinson believes, has a role to play in political discourse, by using the future as a way to view the present. "It's some kind of funhouse mirror where you exaggerate some parts and minimize others depending on what you're talking about at the time," Robinson explained in the HarperCollins interview. "Future fictions are not truly about the future which will always be different to what any science fiction novel talks about. So these novels are not predictions, but ways of talking about the situation now and what it might become. Novels about the future deal with what we might work towards and what we might try to guard against."

Works Cited

Review of *Antarctica, Publishers Weekly,* May 11, 1998, p. 54.

Brown, Stephen P., review of *The Wild Shore, Washington Post Book World,* April 22, 1984, p. 11.

Budrys, Algis, review of *The Wild Shore, Magazine of Fantasy and Science Fiction,* May, 1984, pp. 38, 40.

Cooke, Sebastian, "An Earth-Man With a Mission," *Eidolon,* July, 1993.

Easton, Tom, review of *Red Mars, Analog: Science Fiction/Science Fact,* August, 1993, p. 249.

James, Edward, "The Landscape of Mars," *Times Literary Supplement,* May 3, 1996, p. 23.

Jonas, Gerald, review of *Pacific Edge, New York Times Book Review,* December 9, 1990, p. 32.

Jonas, Gerald, review of *Red Mars, New York Times Book Review,* January 31, 1993, p. 25.

Jonas, Gerald, review of *Blue Mars, New York Times Book Review,* June 30, 1996, p. 28.

"Kim Stanley Robinson: The Man from Mars," from HarperCollins on-line feature at http://www.harper collins.co.uk/voyager/intervws.

Lawrence, Clinton, review of *Blue Mars, Science Fiction Weekly,* June 17, 1996.

Letson, Russell, review of *Green Mars, Locus,* November, 1993, p. 19.

Miller, Faren, review of *Red Mars, Locus,* October, 1992, pp. 19, 21.

Parker, T. Jefferson, "Orange County, Thus Will You Live," *Los Angeles Times Book Review,* March 13, 1988, p. 6.

Robinson, Kim Stanley, interview from Bantam Doubleday Dell Online at http://www.bdd.com.

Robinson, Kim Stanley, *Red Mars,* Bantam, 1993.

Robinson, Kim Stanley, interview in *Science Fiction Weekly,* June 17, 1996.

Sherwin, Elisabeth, "Robinson Completes Mars Trilogy, Turns to Antarctica," *Davis Enterprise,* January 21, 1996.

Sherwin, Elisabeth, "Next Stop for Mars Junkies? How About 'Antarctica'," *Davis Enterprise,* November 2, 1997.

Snider, David P., review of *Pacific Edge, Voice of Youth Advocates,* June, 1991, p. 113.

Wolfe, Gary K., review of *Green Mars, Locus,* November, 1993, p. 55.

For More Information See

BOOKS

Contemporary Literary Criticism, Volume 34, Gale, 1985.
St. James Guide to Science Fiction Writers, Fourth Edition, St. James Press, 1996.

PERIODICALS

Analog, September, 1988; April, 1990; August, 1990.
Kirkus Reviews, May 15, 1998.
Los Angeles Times Book Review, February 3, 1991.
New York Times Book Review, October 20, 1985; September 21, 1986; May 8, 1994.
Publishers Weekly, December 14, 1992; February 21, 1994; May 13, 1996.

School Library Journal, May, 1994; February, 1995.
Voice of Youth Advocates, October, 1994; April 1, 1997.
Washington Post Book World, August 25, 1985; February 28, 1988.
Wilson Library Bulletin, February, 1993.*

* * *

ROWLING, J(oanne) K. 1965(?)-

Personal

Born c. 1965, in Chipping Sodbury, England; children: Jessica. *Education:* Attended Exeter University.

Addresses

Home—Edinburgh, Scotland. *Agent*—c/o Scholastic, Inc., 555 Broadway, New York, NY 10012.

Career

Amnesty International, secretary; teacher of English as a Foreign Language, Portugal. Writer, 1996—.

Awards, Honors

Scottish Arts Council Grant, 1996; Children's Book of the Year, British Book Awards, and Gold Winner, Smarties Book Prize, both 1997, Birmingham Cable Children's Book Award, the Young Telegraph Paperback of the Year, Sheffield Children's Book Award, and short-listed for The Guardian Fiction Award and the Carnegie Medal, all for *Harry Potter and the Philosopher's Stone;* Gold Winner, Smarties Book Prize, 1998, and shortlist, Whitbread Children's Book of the Year Award, both for *Harry Potter and the Chamber of Secrets;* Anne Spencer Lindbergh Prize in Children's Literature, 1997-98, and ABBY Award, American Booksellers Association, 1999, both for *Harry Potter and the Sorcerer's Stone.*

Writings

Harry Potter and the Philosopher's Stone, Bloomsbury, 1997, published in the U.S. as *Harry Potter and the Sorcerer's Stone,* Scholastic, 1998.
Harry Potter and the Chamber of Secrets, Bloomsbury, 1998, Scholastic, 1999.
Harry Potter and the Prisoner of Azkaban, Bloomsbury, 1999.

Adaptations

Harry Potter and the Sorcerer's Stone and *Harry Potter and the Chamber of Secrets* have been optioned for motion pictures by Warner Bros.

Rowling's "Harry Potter" books have been translated into French, German, Italian, Dutch, Greek, Finnish, Danish, Spanish, and Swedish.

A twist of fate transports Harry Potter from the mundane world in which his adoptive family treats him poorly to a magical realm of witches and wizards in J. K. Rowling's debut novel.(Cover illustration by Mary Grand Pre.)

Work in Progress

More novels about the school career of Harry Potter (to a total of seven).

Sidelights

J. K. Rowling is a British author of novels for young people who caused an overnight sensation with her first book, *Harry Potter and the Philosopher's Stone,* which sold out of its first edition quickly and has been reprinted many times. Even before publication, publishers in the United States were vying for rights to the book, with top bidding going to Scholastic, which paid $100,000, the most ever for a first novel by a children's book author. *Harry Potter and the Philosopher's Stone* rose to the top of the children's best-seller lists in 1998, and was optioned by Warner Brothers for a movie. Its sequel, *Harry Potter and the Chamber of Secrets,* went to the top of the adult best-seller lists in England shortly after its 1998 release, and consumer demand in the U.S. for the book brokered a new era in Internet sales of books internationally, fueling concern over publishing rights.

Rowling plans to continue her Harry Potter saga for seven books, spinning a magical blend of wit and fantasy—a surreal melange of "the dark juvenile novels of Roald Dahl and C. S. Lewis," according to Carla Power, writing on the "Harry Potter" phenomenon in *Newsweek.* Rowling is good copy: a busy mom who wrote much of her first "Harry Potter" adventure while sitting in coffeehouses as her little daughter napped beside her, she presents a Cinderella story every bit as fanciful as the one she concocted in her book. But Rowling herself, winner of numerous awards and now employed full-time in her life's ambition as a writer, has taken her success in stride, changing her old one-bedroom flat in Edinburgh for a comfortable house, but still continuing her habit of writing in cafes.

Born near Bristol, England, Rowling grew up with a younger sister and a distinct inclination toward story-telling. Rabbits played a large part in her early tales, for Rowling and her sister badly wanted a rabbit. Her first story, at age five or six, involved a rabbit dubbed, quite logically, Rabbit, who got the measles and visited his friend, a giant bee named Miss Bee. As Rowling commented, "Ever since Rabbit and Miss Bee, I have wanted to be a writer, though I rarely told anyone so. I was afraid they'd tell me I didn't have a hope."

Two moves took the Rowling family eventually to the town of Tutshill near Chepstow in the Forest of Dean along the border of England and Wales. This brought a long-time country-living dream to fruition for Rowling's parents, both Londoners, and the nine-year-old Rowling learned to love the countryside in this new abode. She and her sister could wander unsupervised amid the fields and play along the River Wye. "The only fly in the ointment was the fact that I hated my new school," Rowling once noted. It was an old-fashioned school with roll-top desks and a teacher who frightened Rowling.

From Tutshill Primary, Rowling went to Wyedean Comprehensive School. "I was quiet, freckly, short-sighted and rubbish at sports," she commented of these years. Rowling confided to Roxanne Feldman in an interview in *School Library Journal* that the character of Harry's friend Hermione is loosely based on herself at age eleven. English was her favorite subject and she created serial stories for her friends at lunchtime, tales involving heroic deeds. Contact lenses soon sorted out any feelings of inferiority in the young Rowling; writing became more a compulsion and less of a hobby in her teenage years. Attending Exeter University, Rowling studied French, something she later found to be a big mistake. Her parents had advised her that bilingualism would lead to a successful career as a secretary. "Unfortunately I am one of the most disorganised people in the world," she related, which obviously posed a significant problem to a budding secretary.

Working at Amnesty International, Rowling discovered one thing to like about life as a secretary: she could use the computer to type up her own stories during quiet times. At age twenty-six, Rowling gave up her office job to teach English in Portugal. It was there that she began yet another story that might become a book, about a boy who is sent off to wizard school. All during the time she spent in Portugal, Rowling took notes on this story and added bits and pieces to the life of her protagonist, Harry Potter. In Portugal she also met the man who became her husband, had a daughter, and got divorced. She does not believe in doing things by half measures.

Back in England, she decided to settle in Edinburgh and set about raising her daughter as a single mother. Accepting a job as a French teacher, she set herself a goal: to finish her novel before her teaching job began. This was no easy task with an active toddler in hand. Rowling confined her writing to her daughter's nap time, much of it spent in coffeehouses where the understanding management allowed her space for her papers. In her interview with Feldman, Rowling commented that she had no idea what sort of reception the book would get, if she was even able to get it published. "I knew how difficult it would be just to get a book published. I was a completely unknown writer. I certainly could never have expected what's happened. It's been a real shock." She was able to send off her typed manuscript to two publishers before beginning her teaching post, but it was not until several months later that the happy news arrived that her long-time intimate, Harry Potter, would appear between the covers of a book in England. And then a few months later, the American rights were bought for a stupendous price and Rowling said good-bye to teaching.

"Think Luke Skywalker," opined an Associated Press writer in a profile of the suddenly successful author which appeared in *Hoosier Times.* "Then add a broom, a bunch of oddball buddies like the Goonies, and an athletic contest where wizards great and small desperately try to fix the outcome." This is only a rough approximation of the world to which Rowling's first novel, *Harry Potter and the Sorcerer's Stone* (published as *Harry Potter and the Philosopher's Stone* in England) introduces the reader.

Harry Potter, an orphan, has led a miserable life with the Dursley family, his maternal aunt and uncle. Ever since Harry arrived unannounced at their doorstep the Dursleys have been put out, as has their vile son, Dudley. Harry has taken up residence in a broom closet under the stairs, bullied at school and mistreated by the Dursleys. Small, skinny, and bespectacled, Harry is an unlikely hero. The only thing physically interesting about Harry is the lightning-shaped scar on his forehead.

"Harry had a thin face, knobbly knees, black hair and bright green eyes," Rowling wrote in the novel. "He wore round glasses held together with a lot of Scotch tape because of all the times Dudley had punched him in the nose." That quote goes a long way to demonstrating not only Rowling's tongue-in-cheek humor, but also her sensitivity in portraying the difficulties of being a child.

When Harry turns eleven, he receives a letter. Of course the Dursleys keep it from him, but finally another letter gets through to Harry telling him that he has been admitted to Hogwarts School of Witchcraft and Wizardry. This is the first that Harry has known about his parents being wizards, or that they were killed by the evil sorcerer, Voldemort, or that he himself is something of a legend in wizard circles for having survived Voldemort's attack, which, by the way, left the scar on his forehead. Before he knows what is happening, he is swept off by the giant Hagrid, keeper of the keys at the school, on a flying motorcycle. Thus begins what Rayma Turton in *Magpies* called "a ripping yarn," and a "school story with a twist." Instead of boring math and geography, Harry takes lessons in the History of Magic and in Charms, or Defenses against the Dark Arts. He becomes something of a star at the school athletic contest, quidditch, an aerial sort of soccer match played on broomsticks. He forms friendships with Ron and Hermione and encounters students not quite so pleasant, such as the sly Draco Malfoy. He investigates the secrets of the forbidden third floor at Hogwarts, battles evil in the form of professor Snape whom Harry fears means to steal the sorcerer's stone which promises eternal life, and discovers the secret behind his scar. In short, Harry learns to be his own person.

"The language is witty, the plotting tight, the imagination soars," Turton commented. "It's fun." A writer for the Associated Press observed that "Rowling has an unerring sense of what it means to be 11, and her arresting, brick-by-brick construction of Harry's world has turned a rather traditional plot into a delight." Hogwarts is a composite of the typical English public school (which is actually private in America), yet turned on its head. Harry is lodged in Gryffindor house, rivals of another house, Slytherin; his school supplies include a message-bearing owl and a magic wand. "The light-hearted caper travels through the territory owned by the late Roald Dahl," observed a reviewer for *Horn Book,* who concluded that *Harry Potter and the Sorcerer's Stone* is a "charming and readable romp with a most sympathetic hero and filled with delightful magic details." A *Booklist* commentator called the book "brilliantly imagined and written," while a critic for *Publishers Weekly* noted that there "is enchantment, suspense and danger galore . . . . " A classic tale of good versus evil, as well as a coming-of-age novel with a unique flavor, *Harry Potter and the Sorcerer's Stone* is not simply a novel about magic and wizardry. As Michael Winerip commented in the *New York Times Book Review,* "the magic in the book is not the real magic of the book." For Winerip, and countless other readers, it is the "human scale" of the novel that makes it work. "Throughout most of the book, the characters are impressively three-dimensional," Winerip noted, concluding that Rowling "had wizardry inside," achieving "something quite special" with her first novel.

Even as enthusiastic reviews were pouring in from America, Rowling's second installment of the "Harry Potter" saga was published in England. *Harry Potter and the Chamber of Secrets* takes up where the first novel

stopped. Harry returns to second term at Hogwarts in a flying car, and deals with old and new characters alike. One of these newcomers is Nearly Headless Nick, a poor creature upon whom an executioner made a messy cut; another is a ghost who inhabits the girls' bathrooms, Moaning Myrtle. Valerie Bierman, writing in *Carousel,* noted that "this plot is brilliantly scary with horrible happenings, mysterious petrifyings and a terrifying conclusion." A reviewer in *Publishers Weekly* asserted that, if possible, the story is even more inventive than *Harry Potter and the Sorcerer's Stone* and Rowling's "ability to create such an engaging, imaginative, funny and, above all, heartpoundingly suspenseful yarn is nothing short of magical."

The third installment in the "Potter" series, *Harry Potter and the Prisoner of Azkaban,* begins when Harry is thirteen and starting his third year at Hogwarts School for Witchcraft and Wizardry. A notorious mass murderer who is a henchman of the evil Lord Voldemort has escaped from Azkaban Prison and comes looking for Harry. Despite the danger, Harry is quite preoccupied with an upcoming match of quidditch where he plays the most important position, that of the Seeker. Perhaps therein lies part of the secret to the success of the Potter books opined Gregory Maguire in *New York Times Book Review:* "J. K. Rowling's fantasies celebrate a boy's relish in physical prowess as well as the more bookish values of moral and intellectual accomplishment." And even while the adventures are thrilling, a reviewer in *Publishers Weekly* felt that they appear to be laying the groundwork for even more breathless excitement. "The beauty here lies in the genius of Rowling's plotting. Seemingly minor details established in books one and two unfold to take on unforeseen significance, and the finale, while not airtight in its internal logic, is utterly thrilling."

Harry Potter and the Chamber of Secrets and *Harry Potter and the Prisoner of Azkaban* leapt to number one on the adult best-seller lists in England, prompting a feeding frenzy for them in America. But eager readers have reason for solace as well. Rowling has sketched out plots for seven "Harry Potter" novels in all, taking him through his years at Hogwarts, to age seventeen and graduation. Maguire conjectured: "Maybe by then J. K. Rowling will have achieved what people who love the best children's books have labored after: breaking the spell of adult condescension that brands as merely cute, insignificant, second rate the heartiest and best of children's literature."

Works Cited

Bierman, Valerie, "Working from Home," *Carousel,* summer, 1998, p. 23.

"British Author Rides up Charts on a Wizard's Tale," *Hoosier Times,* http://www.hoosiertimes.com/stories/ 1998/11/29/lifestyle.981129_ D7_ JJP10151. sto, November 29, 1998.

Feldman, Roxanne, "The Truth about Harry," School Library Journal, September, 1999, pp. 137-39.

Review of *Harry Potter and the Chamber of Secrets, Publishers Weekly,* May 31, 1999, p. 94.

Review of *Harry Potter and the Prisoner of Azkaban, Publishers Weekly,* July 19, 1999, p. 195.

Review of *Harry Potter and the Sorcerer's Stone, Booklist,* January 1, 1999, p. 783.

Review of *Harry Potter and the Sorcerer's Stone, Horn Book,* January, 1999, p. 71.

Review of *Harry Potter and the Sorcerer's Stone, Publishers Weekly,* July 20, 1998, p. 220.

Maguire, Gregory, "Lord of the Golden Snitch," *New York Times Book Review,* September 5, 1999, p. 12

Power, Carla, "A Literary Sorceress," *Newsweek,* December 7, 1998, p. 79.

Rowling, J. K., *Harry Potter and the Sorcerer's Stone,* Levine/Scholastic, 1998.

Rowling, J. K., http://www.okukbooks.com/harry/rowling.htm.

Turton, Rayma, review of *Harry Potter and the Philosopher's Stone, Magpies,* March, 1999.

Winerip, Michael, review of *Harry Potter and the Sorcerer's Stone, New York Times Book Review,* February 14, 1999, p. 26.

For More Information See

PERIODICALS

Books for Keeps, September, 1997, p. 27; July, 1999, pp. 6-7.

Kirkus Reviews, June 1, 1999, p. 888.

Publishers Weekly, February 15, 1999, pp. 33-34.

Reading Time, February, 1999, p. 43.

School Librarian, August, 1997, p. 147; spring, 1999, p. 35.

School Library Journal, October, 1998, pp. 145-46; July, 1999, pp. 99-100.*

—Sketch by J. Sydney Jones

S

SANDERS, Scott R(ussell) 1945-

Personal

Born October 26, 1945, in Memphis, TN; son of Greeley Ray (in farming and industrial relations) and Eva (an artist and homemaker; maiden name, Solomon) Sanders; married Ruth Ann McClure (a biochemist), August 27, 1967 ; children: Eva Rachel, Jesse Solomon. *Education:* Brown University, B.A. (summa cum laude), 1967;

Scott R. Sanders

Cambridge University, Ph.D., 1971. *Politics:* Liberal. *Religion:* Christian. *Hobbies and other interests:* Carpentry, gardening, hiking, bicycling, wild flowers, voyaging.

Addresses

Home—1113 East Wylie St., Bloomington, IN 47401. *Office*—Department of English, Indiana University, Bloomington, IN 47405.

Career

Indiana University-Bloomington, assistant professor, 1971-74, associate professor, 1975-80, professor, 1980, distinguished professor of English, 1996—. *Member:* Orion Society, Audubon Society, Wilderness Society, Sierra Club, Association for the Study of Literature and the Environment, Phi Beta Kappa.

Awards, Honors

Woodrow Wilson fellow, 1967-68; Danforth fellow, 1967-71; Marshall scholar, 1967-71; Bennett fellow in creative writing, 1974-75; National Endowment for the Arts fellow, 1983-84; *Bad Man Ballad* selected one of *School Library Journal*'s Best Books for Young Adults, 1986; Lilly Fellowship, 1986-87; award in creative nonfiction, Associated Writing Programs, 1987, for *The Paradise of Bombs;* Guggenheim Fellowship, 1992-93; Ohioana Book Award, 1994; Lannan Literary Award, 1995; Great Lakes Book Award, 1996.

Writings

FOR YOUNG READERS

Hear the Wind Blow: American Folksongs Retold, illustrated by Ponder Goembel, Bradbury Press, 1985.
Aurora Means Dawn, illustrated by Jill Kastner, Bradbury Press, 1989.
Warm as Wool, illustrated by Helen Cogancherry, Bradbury Press, 1992.

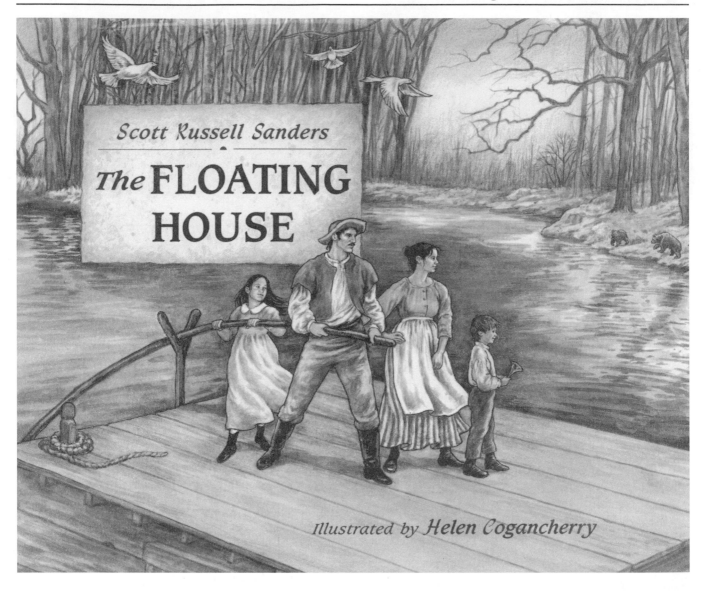

The McClure family travels down the Ohio River in a flatboat, carrying all their worldly belongings, in hopes of making a new life in Indiana in Sanders's historical novel. (Cover illustration by Helen Cogancherry.)

Here Comes the Mystery Man, illustrated by Helen Cogancherry, Bradbury Press, 1993.

The Floating House, illustrated by Helen Cogancherry, Macmillan, 1995.

Meeting Trees, illustrated by Robert Hynes, National Geographic Society, 1996.

A Place Called Freedom, illustrated by Thomas B. Allen, Atheneum, 1997.

Crawdad Creek, illustrated by Robert Hynes, National Geographic Society, 1999.

FICTION; FOR ADULTS

Wilderness Plots: Tales about the Settlement of the American Land, illustrated by Dennis B. Meehan, Morrow, 1983, new edition, Ohio State University Press, 1988.

Fetching the Dead: Stories, University of Illinois Press, 1984.

Wonders Hidden: Audubon's Early Years, Capra, 1984.

Terrarium, Tor, 1985.

Bad Man Ballad, Bradbury Press, 1986.

The Engineer of Beasts, Orchard Books, 1988.

The Invisible Company, Tor, 1989.

OTHER

D. H. Lawrence: The World of the Five Major Novels (criticism), Viking, 1974.

Stone Country, photographs by Jeffrey A. Wolin, Indiana University Press, 1985, as *In Limestone Country,* Beacon Press, 1991.

(Editor) John James Audubon, *Audubon Reader,* Indiana University Press, 1986.

The Paradise of Bombs, University of Georgia Press, 1987.

Secrets of the Universe, Beacon Press, 1991.

Staying Put: Making a Home in a Restless World, Beacon Press, 1993.

Writing from the Center, Indiana University Press, 1995.

Hunting for Hope: A Father's Journey, Beacon Press, 1998.

The Country of Language, Milkweed Editions, 1999.

Contributor to anthologies. Author of column, "One Man's Fiction," *Chicago Sun-Times,* 1977-83. Fiction editor, *Cambridge Review,* 1969-71, and *Minnesota Review,* 1976-80.

Contributor to literary journals and popular magazines, including *Audubon, Orion, Harper's, North American Review, Georgia Review, Utne Reader,* and *Wild Earth.*

Sidelights

Scott Russell Sanders is equally as captivated by language and the history of the United States as he is by environmental science and technology. His works reflect that diversity, for Sanders has contributed fictional works to genres from historical fiction to folktales to speculative science fiction, while his nonfiction ranges from literary criticism to personal essays. Included among his books for younger readers are picture books that illustrate the bravery and strength of character of the early pioneers making their way across the vast interior of North America: *The Floating House, Aurora Means Dawn,* and *A Place Called Freedom* each feature American families attempting to start new lives in an environment that they must learn to understand.

"I have long been divided, in my life and my work, between science and the arts," Sanders once told *SATA.* Born in Memphis, Tennessee, in 1945, he quickly gained a love of history and an appreciation for the beauty of nature. The conflict between his two passions came to a head while planning his course of graduate study at Cambridge University in the late 1960s, and Sanders chose literary studies rather than theoretical physics. However, science continued to provide the framework for Sanders's approach to literature. "When I began writing fiction in my late twenties," he explained to *SATA,* "I wanted to ask, through literature, many of the fundamental questions that scientists ask. In particular, I wanted to understand our place in nature, trace the sources of our violence, and speculate about the future evolution of our species. My writing might seem diverse in form—realistic fiction, science fiction, folktales, stories for children, personal essays, historical novels— yet it is bound together by this web of questions. In all of my work, regardless of period or style, I am concerned with the ways in which human beings come to terms with the practical problems of living on a small planet, in nature and communities. I am concerned with the life people make together, in marriages and families and towns, more than with the life of isolated individuals."

Sanders' stories for young readers focus on the lives of rural families: parents raising their children or perhaps dealing with elderly family members. In picture books such as *The Floating House,* he follows one such family, the McClures. After the spring thaw of 1815, Jonathan and Mary McClure and their parents put all their belongings—including cattle, tools, and furniture—on a flatboat docked in Pittsburgh and make the trip down the Ohio River to Indiana. Their attempts to begin a new life in the still-unsettled Midwest comes to life in a story that was praised by *School Library Journal* contributor Rita

Soltan for its ability to convey "the children's sense of wonder, anticipation, and excitement." The westward trek from Connecticut to Ohio is the subject of *Aurora Means Dawn,* as the Sheldons and their seven children reach the town of Aurora and realize that what they were led to believe was a town is actually only a wilderness area marked by a signpost. "Although Sanders's text is spare and unadorned, readers cannot help but be touched by the story's events," noted Ilene Cooper in a *Booklist* appraisal of the 1989 picture book, which is supplemented with historical notes and maps. *School Library Journal* contributor Eleanor K. MacDonald deemed Sanders's work a "low-key portrayal" of the pioneering experience, and noted that "this brief fragment of history, quietly portrayed," could provide a suitable introduction to such works as Laura Ingalls Wilder's "Little House" books.

In *Warm as Wool,* which takes place in 1803, the Ward family has survived their first winter and search for ways to make the second more comfortable. Fortunately, the purchase of several sheep, and the shearing, carding, and spinning required to produce knitting wool allows Betsy Ward to make warm garments for her children, in a book that Sanders "narrates with energy, in a colorful style spiced with concrete words," according to a *Kirkus Reviews* contributor. Noting that the story is based on an actual family's experiences, *Booklist* contributor Kathryn Broderick called *Warm as Wool* a "warm book" that portrays "a strong heroine ... in both story and pictures." As characteristic of pioneer life as battling the elements was the arrival of traveling peddlers, the focus of Sanders's *Here Comes the Mystery Man.* Taking place in Indiana, the picture book portrays the children's awe at a flute-playing peddler who possesses all manner of exotic goods. The author successfully "communicates the excitement that members of such an isolated community must have felt at the sight of a visitor," in the opinion of a *Publishers Weekly* critic.

A different kind of journey is the subject of Sanders's 1997 picture book, *A Place Called Freedom.* Released from slavery in the early 1830s, seven-year-old James Starman and his family travel by foot from Tennessee to Indiana, where they build a home and plant crops on the banks of the Wabash River. As other former slaves make the trip to join the Starmans, a town is created and called Freedom. Sanders's story, which has its roots in the history of the town of Lyles Station, Indiana, is framed as a series of James's recollections, and the book's "memorable images," as well as its unique "focus and fine writing," make it "a breath of fresh air," according to *School Library Journal* contributor Wendy Lukehart.

In addition to picture books, Sanders has authored several works for older readers. In the novel *Bad Man Ballad,* seventeen-year-old Ely travels in search of his missing older brother in the wilderness of the early 1800s. Stumbling upon a murder, he joins forces with a Philadelphia lawyer named Owen to bring the murderer—a mute giant who has lived alone in the wilderness—to justice, only to realize that he has made a terrible mistake. Praising *Bad Man Ballad* as "more than just an adventure story," a *Kirkus Reviews* critic called the work "a forceful rendering of the notions of justice in an outsize land," while *Booklist* contributor Hazel Rochman remarked that Sanders "raises wider issues of the law that is not justice, the violence done to the natural order in the name of civilization." Sanders has also produced novel-length works of science fiction, such as *The Engineer of Beasts,* which finds a rough-and-tumble orphan named Mooch longing to escape the domed city of New Boston for the wilderness beyond. She finds solace in the city's mechanical zoo, which she tries to remake to resemble the fields and forests she reads about in books. Praising *The Engineer of Beasts* in a *Bulletin of the Center for Children's Books* review, Robert Strang concluded that "there is strong storytelling at work here," and praised Sanders for both the heroism and the satire personified in the quirky Mooch.

Sanders's stories and novels tend to follow the traditional rules of form and style; as he noted to *SATA,* "I do not much value experimentation ... if it is not engendered by new insights into human experience. I do value clarity of language and vision." A contributor and participant in a number of literary magazines, he believes their health to be "a good gauge of the health of literature at any given time." Active in protests against the Vietnam war, in support of a ban on nuclear weapons, and against increasing military funding, he actively supports efforts to protect and preserve the environment, particularly North America's few remaining wilderness areas. "Marriage and child-rearing are important influences on the shaping of my imagination," Sanders added.

Works Cited

Review of *Bad Man Ballad, Kirkus Reviews,* August 1, 1986, p. 1205.

Broderick, Kathryn, review of *Warm as Wool, Booklist,* November 15, 1992, p. 611.

Cooper, Ilene, review of *Aurora Means Dawn, Booklist,* September 15, 1989, p. 190.

Review of *Here Comes the Mystery Man, Publishers Weekly,* July 26, 1993, p. 72.

Lukehart, Wendy, review of *A Place Called Freedom, School Library Journal,* August, 1997, p. 141.

MacDonald, Eleanor K., review of *Aurora Means Dawn, School Library Journal,* November, 1989, p. 93.

Rochman, Hazel, review of *Bad Man Ballad, Booklist,* October 1, 1986, p. 220.

Soltan, Rita, review of *The Floating House, School Library Journal,* June, 1995, p. 95.

Strang, Robert, review of *The Engineer of Beasts, Bulletin of the Center for Children's Books,* September, 1988, p. 20.

Review of *Warm as Wool, Kirkus Reviews,* September 15, 1992, p. 1193.

For More Information See

BOOKS

American Nature Writers, Volume II, Scribner's, 1996, pp. 793-804.

Contemporary Authors, New Revision Series, Volume 15, Gale, 1985, p. 390.

Who's Who in Writers, Editors, and Poets: United States and Canada, third edition, December Press, 1989-1990.

World Authors 1990-1995, H. W. Wilson, 1999.

PERIODICALS

Booklist, November 15, 1993, p. 634; June 1, 1995, p. 1789; June 1 & 15, 1997, pp. 1721-22.

Bulletin of the Center for Children's Books, July-August, 1997, p. 412.

Publishers Weekly, January 3, 1986, p. 52.

School Library Journal, December, 1992, p. 90; October, 1993, pp. 111-12.

*   *   *

SANDERSON, Ruth (L.) 1951-

Personal

Born November 24, 1951, in Ware, MA; daughter of C. Kenneth and Victoria (Sasur) Sanderson; married Kenneth Robinson; children: Morgan. *Education:* Attended Paier School of Art, 1970-74. *Hobbies and other interests:* Horseback riding.

Addresses

Home—P.O. Box 638, Ware, MA 01082.

Career

Illustrator of books for children. *Member:* Western Massachusetts Illustrators Group, Society of Children's Book Writers and Illustrators.

Ruth Sanderson

Sanderson provides both text and illustrations for her original fairy-tale about the youngest son of a king who attempts to save the kingdom after his brothers have failed. (From The Enchanted Wood.*)*

Lovely Sophia is too caught up in herself to be a good minder of Papa Gatto's kittens. (*From* Papa Gatto: An Italian Fairy Tale, *written and illustrated by Sanderson.*)

Awards, Honors

Outstanding Science Book Award, National Association of Science Teachers, for *Five Nests;* Notable Children's Trade Book in the Field of Social Studies, National Council for Social Studies and Children's Book Council, 1982, for *A Different Kind of Gold; The Animal, the Vegetable, and John D. Jones* was chosen one of *School Library Journal*'s Best Books of 1982; Irma S. Black Award, Bank Street College of Education, 1991, and Young Hoosier Award, Association for Indiana Media Educators, 1992, both for *The Enchanted Wood.*

Writings

AUTHOR AND ILLUSTRATOR

(Reteller) *The Twelve Dancing Princesses,* Little, Brown, 1990.

The Enchanted Wood, Little, Brown, 1991.

The Nativity: From the Gospels of Matthew and Luke, Little, Brown, 1993.

(Reteller) *Papa Gatto: An Italian Fairy Tale,* Little, Brown, 1995.

(Reteller) *Rose Red and Snow White: A Grimms Fairy Tale,* Little, Brown, 1996.

(Reteller) *Tapestries: Stories of Women in the Bible,* Little, Brown, 1998.

(Reteller) *The Crystal Mountain,* Little, Brown, 1999.

ILLUSTRATOR; FOR CHILDREN

Ilka List, *Grandma's Beach Surprise,* Putnam, 1975.

Glenn Balch, *Buck, Wild,* Crowell, 1976.

Watty Piper (pseudonym of Mabel Caroline Bragg), reteller, *The Little Engine That Could,* Platt & Munk, 1976.

Mary Francis Shura, *The Season of Silence,* Atheneum, 1976.

Mary Towne, *First Serve,* Atheneum, 1976.

Clyde Robert Bulla, *The Beast of Lor,* Crowell, 1977.

Charles E. Mercer, *Jimmy Carter* (biography), Putnam, 1977.

Willo Davis Roberts, *Don't Hurt Laurie!,* Atheneum, 1977.

Robert Louis Stevenson, *A Child's Garden of Verses,* Platt & Munk, 1977.

Charlene Joy Talbot, *The Great Rat Island Adventure,* Atheneum, 1977.

Greta Walker, *Walt Disney* (biography), Putnam, 1977.

Lynn Hall, *The Mystery of Pony Hollow,* Garrard, 1978.

Beverly Hollett Renner, *The Hideaway Summer,* Harper, 1978.

Papa Gatto, a cat who serves as advisor to the prince, learns not to judge by appearances when he hires the beautiful but neglectful Sophia to care for his kittens. (Cover illustration by Sanderson.)

Miriam Schlein, *On the Track of the Mystery Animal: The Story of the Discovery of the Okapi* (nonfiction), Four Winds, 1978.

William Cole, compiler, *The Poetry of Horses,* Scribner, 1979.

Susan Clement Farrar, *Samantha on Stage,* Dial, 1979.

Norma Simon, *We Remember Philip,* A. Whitman, 1979.

William Sleator, *Into the Dream,* Dutton, 1979.

Caroline Arnold, *Five Nests* (nonfiction), Dutton, 1980.

Margaret Chittenden, *The Mystery of the Missing Pony,* Garrard, 1980.

Nikki Amdur, *One of Us,* Dial, 1981.

W. Cole, compiler, *Good Dog Poems,* Scribner, 1981.

L. Hall, *The Mysterious Moortown Bridge,* Follett, 1981.

L. Hall, *The Mystery of the Caramel Cat,* Garrard, 1981.

Cecily Stern, *A Different Kind of Gold,* Harper, 1981.

Betsy Byars, *The Animal, the Vegetable, and John D. Jones,* Delacorte, 1982.

Linda Hayward, *When You Were a Baby,* Golden Press, 1982.

Edward Lear, *The Owl and the Pussycat,* Golden Press, 1982.

Peggy Archer, *One of the Family,* Golden Press, 1983.

Judith Gorog, *Caught in the Turtle,* Philomel, 1983.

Lois Meyer, *The Store-bought Doll,* Golden Press, 1983.

Joan Webb, *Poochie and the Four Seasons Fair,* Western, 1983.

Johanna Spyri, *Heidi,* Knopf, 1984.

The Pudgy Bunny Book, Grosset, 1984.

Linda Hayward, *Five Little Bunnies,* Golden Press, 1984.

Jane Yolen, reteller, *The Sleeping Beauty,* Knopf, 1986.

Phyllis Krasilovsky, *The Happy Times Storybook,* Western, 1987.

Frances Hodgson Burnett, *The Secret Garden,* Knopf, 1988.

Fran Manushkin, *Puppies and Kittens,* Western, 1989.

Samantha Easton, reteller, *Beauty and the Beast,* Andrews & McMeel, 1992.

Bruce Coville, reteller, *William Shakespeare's "The Tempest,"* Delacorte, 1994.

Sanderson illustrated her own retelling of the Grimm Brothers' **The Twelve Dancing Princesses.**

Clement Clarke Moore, *The Night before Christmas,* Turner, 1994.

The Story of the First Christmas: A Carousel Book, Turner, 1994.

Shirley Climo, *A Treasury of Princesses: Princess Tales from around the World,* HarperCollins, 1996.

Cats, Andrews & McMeel, 1997.

Jane Yolen, *Where Have the Unicorns Gone?,* Simon and Schuster, in press.

Also illustrator of revised editions of "Black Stallion" books by Walter Farley.

"NANCY DREW" SERIES; BY CAROLYN KEENE (COLLECTIVE PSEUDONYM)

The Triple Hoax, Wanderer Books, 1979.
The Flying Saucer Mystery, Wanderer Books, 1980.
The Secret in the Old Lace, Wanderer Books, 1980.
The Greek Symbol Mystery, Wanderer Books, 1981.

"THE BOBBSEY TWINS" SERIES; BY LAURA LEE HOPE (COLLECTIVE PSEUDONYM)

Secret in the Pirate's Cave, Wanderer Books, 1980.
The Dune Buggy Mystery, Wanderer Books, 1981.
The Missing Pony Mystery, Wanderer Books, 1981.
The Rose Parade Mystery, Wanderer Books, 1981.

Adaptations

The Little Engine That Could (filmstrip with cassette or book), 1976.

Sidelights

Ruth Sanderson's sumptuous illustrations of such classic fairy stories as *The Twelve Dancing Princesses* and *Rose Red and Snow White* have been applauded by critics and readers alike for their attention to detail and what *Booklist* contributor Phyllis Wilson characterized as a "sun-dappled, old-master-landscape feeling." In addition to bringing to life the works of a host of popular picture book authors, including William Sleator, Jane Yolen, and Clyde Robert Bulla, Sanderson has also written an original fairy story, *The Enchanted Wood,* which she illustrated and published in 1991.

Born in 1951, Sanderson was raised in the small town of Monson, Massachusetts, which she recalled to *SATA* as "a magical place." She began drawing during childhood and shared her enthusiasm for her hobby with her friends. "I held an art class for my second-grade friends and taught them all how to draw horses. When my mother bought me *How to Draw Horses* by Walter

Foster, I spent hours copying horses, trying to get them right." In addition to drawing horses, she also spent many years riding and caring for them; in fact, Sanderson credits her love of horses with fueling her desire to become an illustrator.

Sanderson attended Paier School of Art in Hamden, Connecticut, where she studied anatomy, figure drawing, and painting, and majored in illustration. "I gravitated towards illustration because I liked having problems to solve," she later explained to *SATA*. "I preferred developing concepts and pictorial impressions of a manuscript to initiating my own ideas. As an exercise, we were asked to find a book in the library, read the story and come up with new ideas for the cover illustration. During my senior year, I studied with illustrator Michael Eagle. He made us think in new and different ways, stretching our imagination. Every teacher at Paier contributed something to our training. Thus our development was a group effort."

During her senior year, Sanderson accepted an apprenticeship with a corporate editorial illustrator for six months. Her mentor passed her portfolio to a children's book agent who was looking for new artists, and "within six months she had given me so much freelance work that I had to decide whether to follow in [my mentor's] footsteps and work in commercial adult magazine illustration or strike out on my own and try children's books. I opted for children's books. I started doing textbook illustration and then slowly worked my way up to trade books and then jacket illustration." During the years she has worked as an illustrator, Sanderson has worked in every medium: watercolor, oils, acrylic, air brush, colored pencil, and alkyd.

Beginning with book covers, Sanderson soon graduated to her first picture book illustration project: Ilka List's *Grandma's Beach Surprise,* published in 1975. Since then, she has amassed countless illustration credits. Most notable of her books have been those in the fairy tale genre, as the medieval overtones of the stories complement Sanderson's own style. In the Grimm Brothers' *The Twelve Dancing Princesses,* which she both retold and illustrated, her oil paintings, painted "in a realistic yet romantic style ... have the dark, rich texture of old velvet," in the opinion of *School Library Journal* contributor Linda Boyles, who went on to praise Sanderson's text as "coherent and fully fleshed out," and reads "with a straightforward formality that is complemented by the classic nature of the illustrations." Similar accolades were bestowed upon *Rose Red and Snow White,* as a *Publishers Weekly* contributor lauded Sanderson for her use of "rusty tones" to create "heroines whose warm coloring blends perfectly with the woods they roam in and with the firelit domesticity of their mother's neat cottage."

Parting company with the Brothers Grimm, Sanderson has also given new life to the Italian folk tale *Papa Gatto,* about a father cat in service to the king who hires two stepsisters—one beautiful but selfish and the other plain but giving—to care for his bewhiskered and motherless offspring. Sanderson's "elegant, richly descriptive language" enhances the charming story, according to *Booklist* reviewer Janice Del Negro, and her oil paintings "are as beautifully handled as the narrative." "Familiar elements in combination with new twists, the perennial appeal of intelligent animals interacting with people on equal terms, and the drama of treachery and romance" combine to make *Papa Gatto* "an especially good story," added a contributor to *Quill and Quire.* Other works both written and illustrated by Sanderson include *Tapestries: Stories of Women in the Bible,* which includes tales from both the Old and New Testaments that profile ten biblical heroines. Each of the ten stories, "enlivened with dialogue" and accompanied by a detailed oil portrait done in a style resembling a woven tapestry, "allow ... readers to visualize the choices these women made and for which they will long be remembered," according to a *Publishers Weekly* contributor.

"Finding the mental image is a different experience for every book," Sanderson explained to *SATA* in describing how she approaches such diverse projects as biblical stories and humorous modern tales. "I study the manuscript very closely, carefully reading and re-reading the book until I find the essence of what the author is saying. Then I try to pick the moments that are important and dramatic that really tell the story. What inspires me in a text is the descriptive ability of the author. Descriptions are so helpful. Some books are situational and contain a lot more dialogue than environment. It's hard to get a good mental image out of a book of this type. It's not easy to create a pleasing pictorial image for the 'troubled child' stories, for example, stories where the characters are either home or at school. This type of illustration involves drawing a convincing portrait of an emotional child when all the author has given you is the character's inner turmoil."

"I've always used models but I work with a camera. It would be outrageous to expect people to pose for hours. I'm not making portraits; I'm working on scenes and actions. I take a roll of film for each scene and then pick the moment that looks right. Many times I will have to take shots of one model one day and another the next. I make sure my lighting is consistent and I splice the photographs together."

Sanderson spends a complete forty-hour week in her studio working at her craft. When she works on book covers, she has five or six covers in process at the same time, but bigger projects, like her picture books, require a concentrated effort. "Someday I hope to have time to paint *and* do illustration," she added. Among Sanderson's more intensive projects was a new edition of the novel *Heidi,* which required one hundred full-color oil paintings. While she loves working with oils, she had not dappled in the medium since art school, "mainly because of the time constraint—oils take a long time to dry. After the first coat you must wait two or three days until you can go over it again and then it's another two or three days before the second coat dries. Oils are not conducive to tight deadlines. Because I had a year to do the *Heidi* project, I could wait for some of the paintings to dry, work on others, and then go back."

And what artists does Sanderson turn to for inspiration? "My favorite illustrators are N. C. Wyeth and Maxfield Parrish. I'm drawn to the fine arts of the pre-Raphaelite period whose work is illustrative and tells a story, as well as to the impressionist painters. Though my own style is fairly representational, I love symbolic art, particularly the work of Magritte." Still, as she once told *SATA,* "Everything at one time or another inspires me."

In addition to illustrating and writing, Sanderson devotes much of her time to speaking at school assemblies, "so that kids will have an opportunity to see that it is a real person creating art and not a machine." Her advice to aspiring young artists: "Practice a lot, on your own. I'm still improving as an artist, as an illustrator; I am better now than when I started ten years ago. Every year you improve, hopefully. You never want to stay in one place."

Works Cited

Boyles, Linda, review of *The Twelve Dancing Princesses, School Library Journal,* June, 1990, p. 116.

Del Negro, Janice, review of *Papa Gatto, Booklist,* December 1, 1995, p. 624.

Review of *Papa Gatto, Quill and Quire,* September, 1995, p. 76.

Review of *Rose Red and Snow White, Publishers Weekly,* April 14, 1997, p. 74.

Review of *Tapestries: Stories of Women in the Bible, Publishers Weekly,* July 27, 1998, p. 70.

Wilson, Phyllis, review of *The Twelve Dancing Princesses, Booklist,* March 1, 1990, pp. 1348-49.

For More Information See

BOOKS

Kingman, Lee, and others, compilers, *Illustrators of Children's Books: 1967-1976,* Horn Book, 1978.

PERIODICALS

Booklist, April 15, 1997, p. 1433; September 15, 1997, p. 238.

Bulletin of the Center for Children's Books, December, 1995, p. 139.

Publishers Weekly, October 6, 1997, p. 56.

School Library Journal, October, 1995, p. 129; May, 1997, pp. 124-25.

ON-LINE

Author's website at http://www.RuthSanderson.com

*   *   *

SCOTT, Melissa 1960-

Personal

Born August 7, 1960, in Little Rock, AR; partner of Lisa A. Barnett (a writer) since 1979. *Education:* Harvard/

Radcliffe College, B.A. (magna cum laude), 1981; Brandeis University, Ph.D., 1992.

Addresses

Agent—Richard Curtis, Richard Curtis Agency, 171 East 74th St., New York, NY 10021.

Career

Writer. Has worked as an usher, teller, answering service operator, teaching assistant, stock person, secretary, and receptionist. Founder and contributing editor of *Wavelengths,* a review of science fiction of interest to a gay/lesbian/bisexual readership.

Awards, Honors

John W. Campbell Memorial Award, World Science Fiction Society, 1986, for the best new science fiction writer of the year; Lambda awards for Best Science Fiction/Fantasy Novel, Lambda Book Report, 1994, for *Trouble and Her Friends,* and 1995, for *Shadow Man.*

Writings

NOVELS

The Game Beyond, Baen (New York City), 1984.

Five-Twelfths of Heaven (part of the "Silence Leigh" trilogy), Baen, 1985.

A Choice of Destinies, Baen, 1986.

Silence in Solitude (part of the "Silence Leigh" trilogy), Baen, 1986.

The Empress of Earth (part of the "Silence Leigh" trilogy), Baen, 1987.

The Kindly Ones, Baen, 1987.

(With Lisa A. Barnett) *The Armor of Light,* Baen, 1988.

The Roads of Heaven (the "Silence Leigh" trilogy; contains *Five-Twelfths of Heaven, Silence in Solitude,* and *The Empress of Earth*), Doubleday, 1988.

Mighty Good Road, Baen, 1990.

Dreamships, Tor, 1992.

Burning Bright, Tor, 1993.

Trouble and Her Friends, Tor, 1994.

(With Barnett) *Point of Hopes,* Tor, 1995.

Proud Helios (part of the "Star Trek: Deep Space Nine" series), Pocket Books, 1995.

Shadow Man, Tor, 1995.

Night Sky Mine, Tor, 1996.

Dreaming Metal, Tor, 1997.

The Shapes of Their Hearts, Tor, 1998.

The Jazz, Tor, in press.

(With Barnett) *Point of Dreams,* Tor, in press.

OTHER

Conceiving the Heavens: Creating the Science-Fiction Novel (nonfiction), Heinemann (Portsmouth, NH), 1997.

Sidelights

Melissa Scott writes science fiction and fantasy that is informed by her educational background in history and

Melissa Scott

by her identity as a lesbian. She uses her stories to contemplate such issues as the impact of technology on society, the role of gender in the formation of identity, and the consequences of creating boundaries among societies with different ideologies. Reviewers have consistently praised Scott's ability to create comprehensive, believable worlds.

After her initial foray into the genre with *The Game Beyond,* in which people compete in a gaming tournament to decide who will rule a planetary community, Scott wrote *Five-Twelfths of Heaven.* The story became the first in a trilogy featuring spaceship pilot Silence Leigh, a woman who struggles against the male-dominated society of which she is a part. In the first story, financial hardship causes her to lose ownership of a spaceship left to her by her grandfather. Denis Balthasar, her guardian on her home planet, asks her to be a pilot on a voyage to Earth in his craft Sun-Treader. The novel focuses on the relationships among Leigh, Balthasar, and spaceship engineer Chase Mago as they try to reach their destination.

Silence in Solitude, the second book of the trilogy, focuses on Leigh's struggle to facilitate communication between the Earth and the rest of the interstellar

community in order to prove herself as a pilot. *The Empress of Earth* concludes the trilogy as Silence and two husbands endeavor to save the Earth from rule by the villainous Rose Worlders. The novel details an entire technology inspired by the sciences of the Middle Ages and the beliefs of Aristotle. When Silence displays her magical abilities, the people of Earth regard her as a savior. Complimenting the use of the invented science, Don Sakers noted in the *Wilson Library Bulletin,* "The mystical technology is so well conceived and exhaustively thought-out that by the end one finds oneself convinced that it is real."

In 1987's *The Kindly Ones* Scott depicts lunar communities on the moons Orestes and Electra. In the novel, survivors of a space disaster form a society in which the inhabitants are expected to follow a code of honor. People who disobey are relegated to the community of "ghosts" and are forbidden to speak to the "living." The plot revolves around the development of the Necropolis, a den of hedonism formed by the outcasts; on attempts by the living and the ghosts to communicate through Trey Maturin, a medium with the ability to convey messages between the two groups; and on the weakening of the society when the rulers of the communities begin to quarrel.

In 1988, Scott collaborated with partner Lisa A. Barnett on *The Armor of Light,* which is set in England in the 1590s. *The Armor of Light* was not the first of Scott's novels to benefit from her background in history. *A Choice of Destinies,* published in 1986, reveals how history could have been altered if Alexander the Great had chosen to conquer the Roman Empire instead of India. In *The Armor of Light,* Scott and Barnett employ such historical figures as playwright Christopher Marlowe and explorer Sir Walter Raleigh as they tell the story of England at a critical time in its history. In the novel, a royal astronomer predicts the ruin of England unless King James of Scotland inherits the throne. Sir Philip Sidney is dispatched by Queen Elizabeth to ensure that evil forces do not preclude James from ruling England. Don Sakers in *Wilson Library Bulletin* called *The Armor of Light* "a beautifully written, artfully crafted fantasy."

"This is the stuff of which sense of wonder is made" —*Locus*

MELISSA SCOTT
DREAMSHIPS

"Intellectually neat, emotionally satisfying."
—*The New York Times*

In Melissa Scott's science-fiction novel, a wealthy corporation-owner hires a space pilot to find her brother—an insane man who may have created the first artificial intelligence. (Cover illustration by Tony Roberts.)

In *Mighty Good Road,* Scott develops a planetary system connected by a transportation system that allows for rapid travel from one station stop to another. The novel focuses on a mission to salvage some important cargo from an airwreck over one of the planets. When the leader of the effort to retrieve the equipment begins to ponder the circumstances of the crash, the company that commissioned the rescue mission turns against the contractors.

Dreamships, published in 1992, also focuses on a rescue mission. In this novel, pilot Reverdy Jian and partner Imre Vaughn are charged with the task of tracking down their employer's brother. They are guided by Manfred, an on-board set of systems nearly capable of displaying artificial intelligence. The programmed overseer, in fact, is so able to approximate humanity that it raises the possibility of whether it deserves rights to the same degree that humans do. Although Tom Easton of *Analog* felt that Scott occasionally provided too many details of the subterranean community from which the protagonists hail, he called *Dreamships* "thoughtful and ingenious."

Burning Bright features Quinn Lioe, a pilot who lands on a planet where virtual-reality gaming is a serious preoccupation of the inhabitants and visitors. When Quinn involves herself in directing the Game with her own imagined scenarios, she alters the political climate of the Burning Bright community by making participants of people involved in power struggles outside of the gaming environment. As the novel progresses, Lioe threatens the fabric of Burning Bright by daring to construct a scenario that will conclude the Game. In *Voice of Youth Advocates,* Katharine L. "Kat" Kan encouraged young adult readers to make an effort to read the novel, stating that "readers will have to pay close attention to what they read, but they will be rewarded with a highly satisfying adventure with lots to think about after."

In *Trouble and Her Friends* lesbian lovers Cerise and Trouble are expert computer hackers who use their abilities to steal corporate secrets and sell them. Both Cerise and Trouble are equipped with the "brainworm," a technological enhancement that allows them to receive sensations when connected to computer networks. When Congress threatens to put a stop to the use of the brainworm, Trouble ends her life as a criminal. But she is pulled back into the criminal underworld when another hacker begins using "Trouble" as an alias. Because the new Trouble has invaded the company for which Cerise now works, both of the stable lives that the former hackers have created for themselves are threatened. The two join forces to undermine the scheme of the imposter.

Scott collaborated again with Barnett on *Point of Hopes,* a novel that is set in a fantastic city at the time of an annual celebration. The inhabitants of the city are anticipating a major astronomical event that will mark the ascendancy of a new monarch to the throne. Coincidentally, the children of the city are vanishing.

The protagonist, Nico Rathe, is called upon to solve the mystery.

After writing *Proud Helios,* a novel for the "Star Trek: Deep Six Nine" series, Scott explored issues concerning gender in science fiction with *Shadow Man.* In the novel, Scott develops a galaxy that identifies five distinct genders. The use of drugs to ease the effects of faster-than-light travel has contributed to the development of the new genders. A planet in the system whose inhabitants are conservative and self-righteous, has outlawed all but two genders—male and female. When Warreven Stiller is identified as androgynous, however, the ideologies held by the people of the planet are threatened.

In *Night Sky Mine,* published in 1996, galactic cops are called upon to investigate the mysterious abandonment of an asteroid owned by the Night Sky Mine company. Central to the plot are the contributions of an orphan found in a separate mining shaft years before the incident under investigation. Scott's fictional universe is also populated with computer-programs that compete with one another, reproduce, and mutate, just like organisms.

Throughout her career Scott has featured strong female protagonists in stories that explore—among other issues—situations brought about by the introduction of technology to communities. Her stories have earned recognition for the attention that Scott pays to developing intricate and believable universes. In addition to earning the praise of reviewers, Scott has proven herself a favorite to readers; in 1986, she received a John W. Campbell Award, which is a reader's choice award given to the best new science fiction writer of the year.

Scott commented: "I have always been most interested in the intersection of technology and society—of the hard and soft sciences—and I think that is reflected in my science fiction. I am fascinated by technology and its developments—and I enjoy the challenge of playing by the rules of the genre, getting the science as 'right' as possible—but I'm more interested in the effects of that technology on characters and imagined societies than in the development of some new machine or program. In other words, I tend to set my novels fifty years after a great breakthrough, and consider its aftereffects, rather than write the story of the discovery itself. My academic training (as a historian specializing in early modern Europe) meant that I was exposed to the work of social and cultural historians, from Michel Foucault to Natalie Zemon-Davis and Simon Schama, and the tools I learned for analyzing past cultures have proved invaluable for creating future ones. (In fact, my dissertation ended up being oddly similar to my science fiction, in that it was concerned with the effects of a technological change—the development of gunpowder weapons—and the unintended consequences of the model created to make use of it.)

"Of course, since I'm a novelist rather than a futurist, all of this has to be expressed through plot and character.

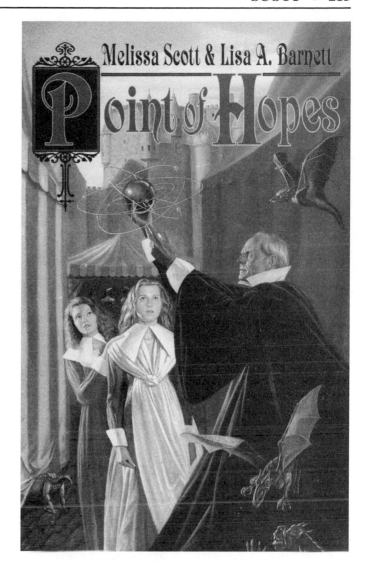

Scott collaborated with Lisa A. Barnett on this fantasy, set in an alternative Middle Ages, about the kidnapping of children from a summer street fair. (Cover illustration by Kevin Eugene Johnson.)

It's very hard to talk about the creative process without making it sound either stilted ('this developed from my interest in . . .') or mystical ('this character/place appeared . . .'), especially when both statements are always at least partially true. I tend to spend a great deal of time on the settings of my novels, cultural and social as well as physical, and to let both the plot and the characters grow organically from that process. I find that as I work out the details, particularly the ways that technology influences or upsets social norms (and vice versa), the inevitable contradictions that emerge are the most fruitful sources for the characters and their stories. I enjoy the complexity and messiness of the real world, and believe that one of the real challenges of any fiction is to model that complexity without losing sight of the structure that makes a good novel.

"It's also fairly obvious that I'm one of the few lesbians writing about queer characters whose science fiction is published by the so-called mainstream science fiction

"William Gibson meets Samuel R. Delany! Melissa Scott's *Night Sky Mine* is her best book yet, with first-rate world-building and first-rate storytelling."

—Robert J. Sawyer

Scott invents a complex futuristic society in which Ista Kelly, the only survivor of a pirate raid on an asteroid mine, searches for her true identity.

houses. I began writing about queer women first out of the usual impulse: I wanted to read about people who were 'like me,' and almost no one else was doing it. As I've gotten older, however, I've begun to realize that behind that superficially naive statement is something actually quite useful. Even in science fiction, there is a limited budget for novelty, both for the writer and for the reader; if one is creating something new in one part of the novel, other parts must of necessity be drawn from that which is familiar. In most of my novels, the technological and social changes are the new things, and, as a result, I draw on the people and culture in which I live to make up the balance. It's that culture, my own culture, people like me, that provides the emotional background of my novels. Certainly my fascination with masks, identity, and roles, comes from living in a culture that is deeply concerned, seriously and in play, with just these issues.

"I was drawn to science fiction largely because of the radical (in a nonpolitical sense) nature of the genre: here is a form of writing that starts from the premise that change is inevitable. Good or bad, it will happen, and the writer's job is to imagine plausible change and depict its possible consequences for people and their worlds. I've been lucky in being able to blend my own various interests into stories that catch readers' imaginations. Because, of course, science fiction, like any other fiction, is ultimately about the story, about the communication between writer and reader, the moment in which the reader is, fully, deeply, and willingly, part of the writer's world. Without the story, characters, plot, and setting, the writer has no right to ask for that participation; with it, the writer can take the reader into worlds s/he would never otherwise have considered."

Works Cited

Easton, Tom, review of *Dreamships, Analog,* October, 1992, pp. 164-65.
Kan, Katharine L., review of *Burning Bright, Voice of Youth Advocates,* October, 1993, p. 234.
Sakers, Don, review of *The Empress of Earth, Wilson Library Bulletin,* May, 1988, pp. 86-87.
Sakers, Don, review of *The Armor of Light, Wilson Library Bulletin,* February, 1989, p. 94.

For More Information See

PERIODICALS

Analog Science Fiction and Fact, October, 1993, pp. 162-63.
Booklist, June 1, 1985, pp. 1373-74; October 15, 1986, p. 327; November 1, 1987, p. 437; September 1, 1987, p. 31; October 15, 1988, p. 368; November 1, 1995, p. 458; June 1, 1995, p. 1737; May 15, 1998, p. 1607.
Kirkus Reviews, May 1, 1992, p. 577; March 1, 1993, p. 266; March 15, 1994, p. 350; October 1, 1995, pp. 1387-88; June 15, 1996, p. 865; May 15, 1998, p. 701.
Library Journal, March 15, 1985, pp. 74-75; October 15, 1995, p. 91; June 15, 1995, pp. 97-98; August, 1996, p. 119; June 15, 1998, p. 111.
Publishers Weekly, May 9, 1986, p. 250; July 31, 1987, p. 73; May 4, 1992, p. 45; April 4, 1994, p. 61; June 26, 1995, p. 91; July 22, 1996, p. 230; April 27, 1998, p. 50.
Voice of Youth Advocates, June, 1985, p. 140; October, 1985, pp. 269-70; April, 1988, p. 42; April, 1989, p. 46; December, 1990, p. 302.
Wilson Library Bulletin, November, 1994, p. 103.

*   *   *

SEGUIN-FONTES, Marthe 1924-

Personal

Born December 2, 1924, in Marseille, France; daughter of Jules (an engineer) Fontes; married Robert Seguin (an art professor); children: Jean-Philippe. *Education:* Lycee Longchamp, received degree, 1944; Ecole Normal Superieure, Paris, teacher's certificate, 1949, 1951.

Addresses

Home—8 rue du Bosquet, Marseille, 13004, France.

Career

School of Art and Advertising, Marseille, teacher, 1958-82; full-time author and illustrator, 1982—.

Writings

FOR CHILDREN; SELF ILLUSTRATED; "I WENT INTO MY GARDEN" SERIES

Les fruits (title means "Fruits"), Gautier-Languereau (Paris), 1979.

Les legumes (title means "Vegetables"), Gautier-Languereau, 1979.

Les fleurs (title means "Flowers"), Gautier-Languereau, 1979.

Les oiseaux (title means "Birds"), Gautier-Languereau, 1979.

Les arbres (title means "Trees"), Gautier-Languereau, 1979.

Le bouquet de la cuisiniere (title means "Herbs"), Gautier-Languereau, 1979.

Le bouquet de sante (title means "Medicinal Plants"), Gautier-Languereau, 1979.

FOR CHILDREN; "STRING OF IMAGES" SERIES

Cherchez-moi, Larousse (Paris), 1982, translation by Sandra Beris published as *Find Me,* Larousse (New York City), 1984.

A cause d'une goutte d'eau, Larousse (Paris), 1982, translation by Sandra Beris published as *All Because of a Drop of Water,* Larousse (New York City), 1985.

Le long voyage d'une lettre, Larousse (Paris), 1982.

De deux choses l'une, Larousse (Paris), translation by Sandra Beris published as *The Cat's Surprise,* Larousse (New York City), 1983.

Ensemble a la noce, Larousse (Paris), translation by Sandra Beris published as *A Wedding Book,* Larousse (New York City), 1983.

La bouilloire a un secret, Larousse (Paris), 1983, translation by Sandra Beris published as *Secret Sounds Around the House,* Larousse (New York City), 1984.

Par quatre chemins, Larousse (Paris), 1984.

Suppose que la mer soit sucree, Larousse (Paris), 1984, translation by Sandra Beris published as *If the Sea Were Sweet,* Larousse (New York City), 1985.

OTHER BOOKS FOR CHILDREN

Poin, poin, points! (a counting book), Gautier-Languereau, 1982.

Mon herbier, (title means "My Herb Garden"), Gautier-Languereau, 1984.

Le livre de poupees, (title means "A Book of Dolls"), Gautier-Languereau, 1985.

Le grenier aux jouets, (title means "The Toy Attic"), Gautier-Languereau, 1987.

Quel temps fait-il? (title means "What Time Is It?"), Gautier-Languereau, 1988.

Le grand album de bebe, Phidal (Montreal), 1992.

FOR ADULTS

Joies de la couleur, (title means "The Joys of Color"), Editions Fleurs (Paris), 1970.

(With Robert Seguin) *757 Idees pour tout decorer,* translation by Marion Hunter published as *Ideas for Decoration,* Evans Brothers (London), 1977.

Le Second souffle de la creativite, (title means "On Creativity"), Dessain et Tolra (Paris), 1977.

For More Information See

PERIODICALS

Instructor, September, 1986, p. 122.
Publishers Weekly, July 22, 1983, p. 132.
School Library Journal, February, 1984, p. 64.
Science Books and Films, November, 1985, p. 98.*

* * *

SHADER, Rachel
See SOFER, Barbara

* * *

SHEFFIELD, Charles 1935-

Personal

Born June 25, 1935, in Hull, England; immigrated to the United States, 1971. *Education:* St. John's College, Cambridge, B.A., 1957, M.A., 1961, Ph.D., 1965.

Charles Sheffield

Addresses

Home—2833 Gunarette Way, Silver Springs, MD 20906. *Agent*—Eleanor Wood, Spectrum Literary Agency, 111 Eighth Ave., Room 1501, New York, NY 10011.

Career

Earth Satellite Corp., chief scientist and board member, 1971—; freelance writer, c. 1978—. *Member:* American Astronomical Society (former president), Science Fiction Writers of America (former president).

Awards, Honors

Sei-un Award, 1991, for *The McAndrew Chronicles;* John W. Campbell Award, 1992, for *Brother to Dragons;* Hugo Award, and Nebula Award, both 1994, both for *Georgia on My Mind and Other Places.*

Writings

YOUNG ADULT NOVELS

(With Jerry Pournelle) *Higher Education: A Jupiter Novel,* Tor, 1996.
The Billion Dollar Boy: A Jupiter Novel, Tor, 1997.
Putting Up Roots: A Jupiter Novel, Tor, 1997.
The Cyborg From Earth: A Jupiter Novel, Tor, 1998.

NOVELS

Sight of Proteus, Ace (New York City), 1978.
The Web Between the Worlds, Ace, 1979.
(With David F. Bischoff) *The Selkie,* Macmillan (New York City), 1982.
Erasmus Magister, Ace, 1982.
My Brother's Keeper, Ace, 1982.
Between the Strokes of Night, Baen (New York City), 1985.
The Nimrod Hunt, Baen, 1986, expanded version published as *The Mind Pool,* 1993.
Trader's World, Ballantine (New York City), 1988.
Proteus Unbound, Ballantine, 1989.
Proteus Manifest, Guild America (New York City), 1989.
Summertide, Ballantine, 1990.
Divergence, Easton Press (Norwalk, CT), 1991.
Transcendence, Ballantine, 1992.
Brother to Dragons, Easton Press, 1992.
Cold as Ice, Tor (New York City), 1992.
The Heritage Universe, Guild America, 1992.
Godspeed, Tor, 1993.
(With David F. Bischoff) *The Judas Cross,* Blue Moon (Eugene, OR), 1994.
Proteus Combined, Baen, 1994.
Proteus in the Underworld, Baen, 1995.
The Ganymede Club, Tor, 1995.
Convergence, Baen, 1997.
Tomorrow and Tomorrow, Bantam Books (New York City), c. 1997.
Aftermath, Bantam Spectra, 1998.
Starfire, Bantam Spectra, 1999.

SHORT STORY COLLECTIONS

Vectors, Ace, 1979.
Hidden Variables, Ace, 1981.

The McAndrew Chronicles, Tor, 1983, expanded version published as *One Man's Universe: The Continuing Chronicles of Arthur Morton McAndrew,* Tor, 1993.
Dancing With Myself, Baen, 1993.
Georgia on My Mind and Other Places, Tor, 1995.
(Editor) *How to Save the World,* Tor, 1995.

NONFICTION

Earthwatch: A Survey of the World From Space, Macmillan, 1981.
(Editor with John L. McLucas) *Commercial Operations in Space 1980-2000,* American Astronautical Society (San Diego, CA), 1981.
Man on Earth: How Civilization and Technology Changed the Face of the World, Macmillan, 1983.
(With Carol Rosin) *Space Careers,* Morrow (New York City), 1984.
(Editor with Marcello Alonso and Morton A. Kaplan) *The World of 2044: Technological Development and the Future of Society,* Paragon House (St. Paul, MN), 1994.
The Borderlands of Science, Baen, 1999.

OTHER

Also author of more than one hundred technical papers since 1965; contributor of stories and articles to periodicals, including *Analog.*

Sidelights

Charles Sheffield is one of the premiere voices in contemporary hard science fiction. A native of Great Britain, he earned his doctorate in physics from Cambridge University before coming to the United States to work in the space industry. He has worked on projects connected with the National Aeronautics and Space Administration (NASA), and is the chief scientist and board member of the Earth Satellite Corporation. Sheffield has also served in the past as president of the American Astronautical Society.

Sheffield took up writing science fiction somewhat late in his career, with his first novel in the genre, *Sight of Proteus,* seeing print in 1978. He has since become prolific in the field, and continues to produce stories and novels as well as nonfiction books and articles about space. Many critics agree that the scientific ideas explored in Sheffield's fiction are often spectacular, and his works have garnered him science fiction's most prestigious honors, including the Hugo and Nebula Awards. His novels often revolve around interplanetary or interspecies conflict. Sheffield has often been compared to fellow science fiction great Arthur C. Clarke.

Examining the morality of science, the novel *Sight of Proteus* introduces a future Earth where mankind has perfected the ability to change their shape through the trials of genetic research and plastic surgery. Most people utilize the technique solely for cosmetic reasons, but some abuse it. It is the task of Behrooz Wolf of the Biological Equipment Corporation to track down this abuse and put an end to it. In addition, Wolf must match wits with a man who is using the new technology to adapt the human body for life on other planets. Dan Miller in *Booklist* called *Sight of Proteus* an "intelligent and sophisticated" effort, and Carolanne Isola in the *Library Journal* hailed the book as "a compelling story and fascinating reading." *Publishers Weekly* contributor Barbara A. Bannon discussed Sheffield's debut, asserting that it proved him "one of the most imaginative, exciting talents" to break into science fiction during the 1970s.

In 1979's *The Web Between the Worlds,* Sheffield explores the idea of a "space elevator"—a huge, strong cable that is grounded at the earth's equator and extends into space—a creation that Sheffield labels a "beanstalk." As Tom Easton of *Analog* reported, Clarke proposed a similar creation in his science fiction. "What is surprising," announced Easton, "is that someone should do a job that is in ways better than Clarke's, and that he should correct Clarke's physics in a way that makes the story's accomplishment even more spectacular." A reviewer for *Publishers Weekly* remarked that "the author manages to invoke ... the sense of wonder."

Sheffield worked in the genre of historical fantasy for 1982's *Erasmus Magister.* The book's hero is the grandfather of famed evolutionary theorist Charles, and who was also a well-respected scientist in his time. The novel shows the elder Darwin solving mysteries using scientific principles and deductive reasoning, in much the same way as Sir Arthur Conan Doyle's Sherlock Holmes. Don Strachan in the *Los Angeles Times Book Review* recommended *Erasmus Magister* for adolescent readers, while Roland Green in *Booklist* praised the novel as having been "researched thoroughly" and "written well."

With David F. Bischoff, Sheffield collaborated on the 1982 horror novel *The Selkie.* Based on the Scottish legend of wereseals who must mate with human females in order to reproduce, *The Selkie* follows the troubled marriage of Don and Mary Willis. While on an expedition at the Scottish coast, Mary is seduced by a man named Jamie McPherson, who is not exactly what he seems. A *Kirkus Reviews* contributor asserted that: "Steady writing and rich backgrounds give a touch of class" to *The Selkie.* James McPeak, writing in *Voice of Youth Advocates* (*VOYA*), proclaimed it "one of the better supernatural novels to come down the pike." A *Publishers Weekly* reviewer found *The Selkie* "very readable." Sheffield teamed with Bischoff again for 1994's *The Judas Cross,* a tale which concerns an artifact supposedly containing the trapped soul of Judas Iscariot, betrayer of Jesus Christ.

Between the Strokes of Night, published in 1985, portrays a future in which the only humans to survive a worldwide nuclear holocaust were those traveling in space when it occurred. They have colonized other planets, and have developed over time into two separate races—one that lives almost forever but has trouble reproducing, and one which is fertile, but has a relatively brief lifespan. Critics varied in their opinion of *Between*

the Strokes of Night. Publishers Weekly contributor Sally A. Lodge called it a "tantalizing but less than satisfying novel." Gene Deweese in the *Science Fiction Review,* however, declared that *Between the Strokes of Night* "has more than enough sense of wonder" and is "one of the best of its kind for 1985."

In 1986, Sheffield published a novel entitled *The Nimrod Hunt,* which he later revised as *The Mind Pool.* This tale features a universe where there are four known races of sentient beings, of which humans are the only ones who are able to kill. Thus a human is needed for each team in search of rogue intelligent machines originally intended to patrol the far reaches of the universe, but which are now turning upon their creators. The second version of the story drew a positive response from critics. Thomas Pearson in *VOYA* affirmed that "the aliens [in *The Mind Pool*] are as well-realized and seem as interesting as the human characters," and summed up the book as "an

Sheffield and Jerry Pournelle create a memorable protagonist in Rick Luban, who embarks on a career in asteroid mining only to find out that life in space presents more challenges than he expected. (Cover illustration by Vincent di Fate.)

entertaining and thought-provoking novel." Howard G. Zaharoff announced in *Kliatt* that "Sheffield speculates about the future with the best of them," then concluded that *The Mind Pool* "is hard SF at its best."

Sheffield again used a post-nuclear setting for *Trader's World.* In this novel, however, people have survived on Earth, but they exist in many splintered nations that are suspicious of one another. One society, the Traders, attempts to restore the world to what it once was. In the course of the novel, they recruit an orphan named Mike and utilize a master computer named Daddy O. Penny Kaganoff, a contributor reviewing *Trader's World* for *Publishers Weekly* conceded that "each segment of the book is clever and colorful in itself," and Peter L. Robertson in *Booklist* asserted that Sheffield "has a pleasing way with his characters."

Sheffield returned to the world of Behrooz Wolf with 1989's *Proteus Unbound.* In this sequel to *Sight of Proteus,* Wolf's investigative work sends him on travels to the Outer System, which is a rival to his own Earth and its allies. War threatens the two systems, but the odd phenomena Wolf is tracking turns out to be the work of a space pirate named Black Ransome. A *Publishers Weekly* contributor praised *Proteus Unbound* as "a fine sequel." Sheffield penned another book about Wolf, 1995's *Proteus in the Underworld.* The latter title sees Wolf drawn from retirement by a young woman named Sondra Dearborn employed by the Office of Form Control. Dearborn enlists Wolf's aid to solve yet another form-change mystery. Mary K. Chelton in *VOYA* hailed *Proteus in the Underworld* as "interesting, accessible hard science fiction."

In 1990, Sheffield began another fiction trilogy, set in the Heritage Universe. In *Summertide,* the known universe is thought to be populated by only two races of sentient beings—humans and Cecropians, a race of large, bug-like creatures. A third race, the deadly and vicious Zardalu, is known to have existed, but is believed to be extinct until the heroes and heroines of *Summertide* encounter them in *Divergence,* the second novel in the series. In all of the books of the "Heritage Universe" trilogy, including the third, *Transcendence,* the characters find huge artifacts strewn about the universe—the products of what turns out to be a fourth race, the unknown Builders.

Critical reaction to *Summertide, Divergence,* and *Transcendence* has been varied. "I found myself gripped," reported Gerald Jonas in the *New York Times Book Review,* speaking of his experience reading *Summertide.* He also observed that Sheffield was obviously "concerned with the inner life of his characters." *Publishers Weekly* reviewer Sybil Steinberg hailed *Summertide* as a "promising first installment." *Divergence,* according to Jackie Cassada in the *Library Journal,* proved a "fast-paced sequel," though a *Kirkus Reviews* contributor judged that it contained "no real surprises, but no disappointments either." Roland Green in *Booklist* labeled *Divergence* "the liveliest sort of hard-science sf." Of *Transcendence,* the third installment of the

In the second book of the "Jupiter" series, Sheffield writes about a wealthy kid who he finds himself stranded on a mining ship twenty-seven light years from Earth. (Cover illustration by Vincent di Fate.)

series, *Publishers Weekly* critic Sybil Steinberg concluded that the "narrative is smooth, and the joys, pitfalls and dangers of exploration are conveyed well."

In 1992, fans of Sheffield's work were treated to *Cold as Ice.* This novel is set after a bloody interplanetary war in which characters hunt for a lost secret weapon. The weapon turns out to be a new species scientifically created by humans. *Booklist's* Roland Green felt it was quite possibly "Sheffield's best book yet." David E. Jones in the Chicago *Tribune Books* was similarly complimentary, putting forth the opinion that the characters' struggle against each other "is ... unlike any conflict that has invaded your imagination in novels past."

Brother to Dragons, which also saw print in 1992, drew comparisons of Sheffield with famed nineteenth-century British novelist Charles Dickens. Dickens's heroes were often poor, handicapped, or otherwise disadvantaged. In

Brother to Dragons Sheffield's story hinges upon Job, born with birth defects to a crack-addicted mother, abandoned, and not expected to live beyond infancy. Job not only survives, but after being virtually drafted into the underworld of crime, leads a revolution against the privileged classes. *Brother to Dragons* prompted Dennis A. Hinrichs in *Kliatt* to remark that "Sheffield is a witty and clever writer," while Green predicted in another *Booklist* review that this novel "will ... attract the broader range of readers that Sheffield is coming to deserve." Penny Kaganoff summed up the book for *Publishers Weekly* as "a highly readable, entertaining novel by one of science fiction's brightest lights."

Godspeed features another young protagonist, Jay Hara. He is stuck on the isolated planet Erin, which, like many other colonized outposts, is suffering a slow decline because of the mysterious malfunction of the Godspeed drive that in the past had allowed faster-than-light space travel. But Hara and his family take in a fugitive, who, before he dies, presents Hara with what might be the key to another Godspeed drive. *Godspeed* prompted Cassada in *Library Journal* to state that "Sheffield never slights his characters or his science," while Karen Jay Fowler, critiquing the novel in the *Washington Post Book World,* assured readers that its "pace never flags, until we reach a satisfyingly smart and exciting climax."

Sheffield, in collaboration with fellow famed science-fiction author Jerry Pournelle, began his "Jupiter" series—books aimed at more adolescent fans of science fiction—with 1996's *Higher Education.* This novel has the premise that the public school systems have deteriorated to such a degree that students are unable to receive a suitable education—until they are taken under the wing of private corporations and strictly trained for their jobs. Such is the case with protagonist Rick Luban, who is sent to work mining asteroids. A *Kirkus Reviews* contributor announced that "the novel opens as a dead-on satire on public education," and *Publishers Weekly* reviewer Steinberg lauded it as a "high-spirited exemplar" of the "SF coming-of-age novel." Sheffield continued the "Jupiter" series without Pournelle, producing titles such as *The Billion Dollar Boy, Putting Up Roots,* and *The Cyborg From Earth.*

The Billon Dollar Boy takes place one-and-a-half centuries later than *Higher Education,* and much farther from Earth. Spoiled rich kid Shelby Cheever starts out on a space cruise and ends up being hurtled twenty-seven light years out where he is rescued by a family that mines interstellar dust clouds. Shelby learns to adapt and become a useful member of the crew. Susan Hamburger of *Library Journal* called the book "well-written," and *Booklist's* Green asserted that Sheffield puts his own brand on the familiar coming-of-age theme, "providing first-rate scientific and technical extrapolation, brisk pacing and a more plausible depiction of his young hero's maturation."

Putting Up Roots, the third novel in the "Jupiter" series, finds Josh Kerrigen and other abandoned teenagers shipped off to a distant farming planet. Instead of a benign agrarian paradise unpopulated by intelligent life, the ragtag teens meet a native species called ruperts and end up in the middle of a war between two giant corporations over the rights to mine hidden mineral wealth. A *Publishers Weekly* reviewer praised the novel's characterization, calling it "the richest of the Jupiter series so far," and *Booklist's* Green echoed that sentiment, saying "Josh and his autistic cousin, Dawn, are the best drawn of any in the series so far."

Throughout the years he was penning novels, Sheffield was also crafting short stories, and he has put out several collections of shorter fiction. The first of these is 1979's *Vectors,* which Spider Robinson, another well-known science fiction author, reviewed in *Analog.* He remarked that "Sheffield's scientific speculations are fascinating indeed, informed and plausible and imaginative." *Hidden Variables,* another Sheffield collection, was printed in 1981. Its stories, according to Valentin R. Zivada in *Kliatt,* are "all stimulating and worth reading at any level." *Dancing With Myself,* which also included scientific articles along with the stories, became available in 1993; this collection brought rave reviews from Easton in *Analog.* "Sheffield," Easton stated, "is one of the few who can do it all—both the science and the fiction—himself." Sheffield also penned the *McAndrew Chronicles, Georgia on My Mind and Other Places,* and edited a collection of short fiction by other authors entitled *How to Save the World.*

Sheffield has also made his mark with nonfiction books about space. *Earthwatch: A Survey of the World From Space* and *Man on Earth: How Civilization and Technology Changed the Face of the World* both feature photographs taken from space and computer-processed by Sheffield's Earth Satellite Corporation. When *Earthwatch* first saw print in 1981, a *Choice* reviewer pointed out that its photographs are "far superior to those in any previous book of its kind." Laurie Tynan in *Library Journal* hailed *Earthwatch* as a "very attractive collection of previously unpublished pictures." William Bradley Hooper in *Booklist* appreciated *Man on Earth* as a "fascinating, large-format book."

Sheffield teamed with Carol Rosin to create 1984's *Space Careers,* a volume aimed at helping adolescents find the proper educational facilities and opportunities to prepare them for careers related to all aspects of the space program. Denise P. Donovin in *Booklist* applauded it as "a valuable resource," while Pat Royal praised it in *School Library Journal* as "a clear, concise, readable, well thought-out book." Ten years later, he helped to edit *The World of 2044: Technological Development and the Future of Society,* which includes speculative ideas such as nasal spray birth control and underwater amusement parks. According to a critic for the *Futurist,* the volume "portrays futures worth getting excited about—and working for."

Works Cited

Bannon, Barbara A., review of *The Selkies, Publishers Weekly,* March 12, 1982, p. 77.

Bannon, Barbara A., review of *Sight of Proteus, Publishers Weekly,* July 31, 1978, p. 95.

Bannon, Barbara A., review of *The Web Between the Worlds, Publishers Weekly,* June 25, 1979, pp. 114, 116.

Cassada, Jackie, review of *Divergence, Library Journal,* February 15, 1991, p. 224.

Cassada, Jackie, review of *Godspeed, Library Journal,* November 15, 1993, p. 102.

Chelton, Mary K., review of *Proteus in the Underworld, Voice of Youth Advocates,* December, 1995, p. 317.

Deweese, Gene, review of *Between the Strokes of Night, Science Fiction Review,* November, 1985, p. 22.

Review of *Divergence, Kirkus Reviews,* January 1, 1991, p. 24.

Donovin, Denise P., review of *Space Careers, Booklist,* May 1, 1984, p. 1215.

Review of *Earthwatch: A Survey of the World From Space, Choice,* February, 1982, pp. 785-86.

Easton, Tom, review of *Dancing with Myself, Analog,* May, 1994, p. 166.

Easton, Tom, review of *The Web Between the Worlds, Analog,* January, 1980, pp. 167-68.

Fowler, Karen Jay, review of *Godspeed, Washington Post Book World,* January 30, 1994, p. 15.

Green, Roland, review of *The Billion Dollar Boy, Booklist,* April 1, 1997, p. 1283.

Green, Roland, review of *Brother to Dragons, Booklist,* October 15, 1992, p. 407.

Green, Roland, review of *Cold as Ice, Booklist,* June 15, 1992, p. 1811.

Green, Roland, review of *Divergence, Booklist,* February 1, 1991, p. 1115.

Green, Roland, review of *Erasmus Magister, Booklist,* September 15, 1982, p. 95.

Green, Roland, review of *Putting Up Roots, Booklist,* August, 1997, p. 1887.

Hamburger, Susan, review of *The Billion Dollar Boy, Library Journal,* December, 1996, p. 152.

Review of *Higher Education, Kirkus Reviews,* April 15, 1996, p. 607.

Hinrichs, Dennis A., review of *Brother to Dragons, Kliatt,* March, 1993, p. 20.

Hooper, William Bradley, review of *Man on Earth: How Civilization and Technology Changed the Face of the World—A Survey From Space, Booklist,* September 15, 1983, p. 122.

Isola, Carolanne, review of *Sight of Proteus, Library Journal,* January 1, 1979, p. 130.

Jonas, Gerald, review of *Summertide, New York Times Book Review,* March 25, 1990, p. 30.

Jones, David E., "Williamson, Bova and Pohl Are Turning Their Lights on Mars," *Tribune Books* (Chicago), August 30, 1992, p. 7.

Kaganoff, Penny, review of *Brother to Dragons, Publishers Weekly,* October 19, 1992, p. 74.

Kaganoff, Penny, review of *Proteus Unbound, Publishers Weekly,* February 10, 1989, p. 65.

Kaganoff, Penny, review of *Trader's World, Publishers Weekly,* October 14, 1988, p. 69.

Lodge, Sally A., review of *Between the Strokes of Night, Publishers Weekly,* June 14, 1985, p. 70.

McPeak, James, review of *The Selkies, Voice of Youth Advocates,* October, 1982, p. 46.

Miller, Dan, review of *Sight of Proteus, Booklist,* January 1, 1979, p. 740.

Pearson, Thomas, review of *The Mind Pool, Voice of Youth Advocates,* October, 1993, p. 234.

Review of *Putting Up Roots, Publishers Weekly,* August 11, 1997, p. 391.

Robertson, Peter L., review of *Trader's World, Booklist,* November 15, 1988, p. 544.

Robinson, Spider, review of *Vectors, Analog,* May, 1980, pp. 165, 173.

Royal, Pat, review of *Space Careers, School Library Journal,* April, 1985, pp. 108-09.

Review of *The Selkie, Kirkus Reviews,* February 15, 1982, pp. 229-30.

Steinberg, Sybil, review of *Higher Education, Publishers Weekly,* May 27, 1996, p. 70.

Steinberg, Sybil, review of *Summertide, Publishers Weekly,* December 15, 1989, p. 60.

Steinberg, Sybil, review of *Transcendence, Publishers Weekly,* May 4, 1992, p. 45.

Strachan, Don, review of *Erasmus Magister, Los Angeles Times Book Review,* August 1, 1982, p. 8.

Tynan, Laurie, review of *Earthwatch: A Survey of the World From Space, Library Journal,* October 1, 1981, p. 1936.

Review of *The World of 2044: Technological Development and the Future of Society, Futurist,* January-February, 1995, p. 62.

Zaharoff, Howard G., review of *The Mind Pool, Kliatt,* July, 1993, p. 20.

Zivada, Valentin R., review of *Hidden Variables, Kliatt,* winter, 1982, p. 23.

For More Information See

PERIODICALS

Booklist, September 1, 1995, p. 48; January 1, 1997, p. 826.

Kirkus Reviews, January 1, 1991, p. 24; May 1, 1992, p. 578; November 1, 1996.

Library Journal, December, 1996, p. 152; August, 1997, p. 141; January, 1998, p. 149.

New York Times Book Review, March 25, 1990, p. 30.

Publishers Weekly, January 16, 1995, pp. 442-43; November 4, 1996, p. 78; February 9, 1998, p. 80.

Voice of Youth Advocates, December, 1992, p. 295.

—Sketch by Elizabeth Wenning

*　　*　　*

SOFER, Barbara 1949- (Rachel Shader, Rachel Sofer, pseudonyms)

Personal

Born April 13, 1949, in New London, CT; daughter of Abraham (a teacher and salesperson) and Adelaide (a teacher; maiden name, Lubchansky; present surname, Kahn) Slopak; married Gerald Schroeder (a scientist and

Barbara Sofer

writer), June 20, 1975; children: Avi, Josh, Hadas, Yael, Hannah. *Education:* University of Pennsylvania, B.A., 1971; Hebrew University of Jerusalem, M.A., 1975. *Religion:* Jewish. *Hobbies and other interests:* Hiking, travel, squash, swimming.

Addresses

Home—5 Hahish Dr., Jerusalem, Israel 93223. *E-mail*—BSofer@compuserve.com. *Agent*—Jean V. Naggar, Jean V. Naggar Literary Agency, 216 East 75th St., New York, NY 10021.

Career

English teacher at university high school in Jerusalem, Israel, 1971-76; Kibbutz Experimental School, Maagen Michael, Israel, English teacher, beginning in 1977; Director of Public Relations, Hadassah Network in Israel, 1999—. *Member:* American Society of Journalists and Authors, Hadassah, Keren Klitah, Israel Women's Network, Forum for Religious Women, Religious Women for the Sanctity of Life.

Awards, Honors

Sydney Taylor Award, best Jewish children's book of the year, Association of Jewish Libraries, 1996, for *Shalom Haver, Goodbye Friend;* five Simon Rockower Awards for outstanding Jewish journalism.

Writings

The Holiday Adventures of Achbar (juvenile fiction), Kar-Ben (Rockville, MD), 1983.
Kids Love Israel, Israel Loves Kids (travel guide), Kar-Ben, 1988, revised edition, 1996.
Shalom Haver, Goodbye Friend (memorial album), Kar-Ben, 1996.
The Thirteenth Hour (novel), Dutton (Bergenfield, NJ), 1997.

Contributor to books, including *Fodor's Israel, 1993* and *The Hadassah Magazine Jewish Parenting Book.* Contributor to magazines and newspapers, including *Popular Mechanics, Parents, Woman's Day,* and *Reader's Digest.* Contributing editor, *Hadassah* and *Inside.* Also uses the pseudonyms Rachel Shader and Rachel Sofer.

Work in Progress

A novel.

Sidelights

An American emigre to Israel since the 1970s, Barbara Sofer is the author of four books in a variety of genres, all concerning Israel and/or Jewish themes. She has also written hundreds of magazine articles on many topics, including education, family life, and spirituality, and lectures widely on Israel, Judaism and women's spirituality.

Sofer's first published work is a collection of children's stories, *The Holiday Adventures of Achbar,* released in 1983. The stories focus on Achbar, a mouse living in a religiously observant household of the Schuster family. With the help of Achbar, Detective Schuster solves mysteries which revolve around each Jewish holiday. "Sofer skillfully handles a dual viewpoint" of human and mouse, according to *School Library Journal* contributor Gerda Haas, and "in each case, the plot is logical and characters are well developed."

Kids Love Israel, Israel Loves Kids, Sofer's family guidebook to Israel, has been fully revised since its first appearance in 1988. The volume was widely praised by critics: *Booklist* reviewer Denise P. Donavin noted approvingly that *Kids Love Israel* is "packed with facts and advice," and Donald Wismer, writing for *Small Press,* offered another favorable assessment, concluding: "Altogether a fine work; the prospective traveler would be well served with this book, with or without kids." Both reviewers expressed appreciation for what Wismer termed the book's "nice touches," such as a mileage chart, information on climate, a good index, and a calendar of Jewish holidays. A contributor to the *Jerusalem Report* commented that "Sofer's guide offers hundreds of ideas and tips you're unlikely to find elsewhere."

In 1995, after the assassination of Prime Minister Yitzhak Rabin, Sofer wrote the memorial tribute *Shalom Haver, Goodbye Friend,* with the help of Rabin's only sibling, his sister Rachel. The book, geared toward children ages four to eight, includes a brief text in English and Hebrew accompanying forty-six photos of Rabin from his family album as a child through all stages of his life. Marcia W. Posner, reviewing the book for *School Library Journal,* called it a "beautiful tribute and memento." *Shalom Haver* received the Sydney Taylor Award from the Association of Jewish Libraries as the best Jewish children's book of 1996.

Sofer's first novel, *The Thirteenth Hour,* is a thriller set in modern Israel with women protagonists, one Jewish, one Palestinian. Deborah Stern, an American biologist living in Israel, is frightened by a local terrorist attack in which four women are murdered. She signs up for a self-defense class and is recruited by the teacher, a university professor who has a double life in Israel's security establishment, to help foil a terrorist plot by working for the famed General Security Service. Raba Alhassan, a Palestinian psychologist born in Gaza but educated in Detroit, is settling into her happy marriage to an aristocratic Palestinian surgeon in Jericho, when she learns to her horror that her brother is the terrorist who killed the four women. She is coerced into working for the Moslem fundamentalist terrorist organization which Deborah is trying to help uncover. The women are ultimately squared off against each other in the town of Bethlehem.

A *Kirkus Reviews* contributor praised *The Thirteenth Hour* as a "vivid and all-too-believable thriller," with a climax that is "deftly choreographed." Equally enthusiastic was *Booklist* contributor Melanie Duncan, who called *The Thirteenth Hour* a "thought-provoking, intense read." A reviewer for *Publishers Weekly* found the book "gripping." The latter review called attention to the novel's complex portrayal of the two central women, and concluded that Sofer "succeeds in conveying the psychological climate of a troubled land through a timely and resonant story." In the *New York Times Book Review,* Marilyn Stasio commented that Sofer "paces her story at a tense clip, jump-cutting scenes and otherwise turning screws to set us up for the big-bang climax."

Offering insight on the influences that have shaped her work, Sofer comments: "I grew up in Colchester, Connecticut, a small, New England town with a green and white church in the center. My father was a leather goods/arts and crafts salesman, working with the blind. Later he became a math teacher. My mother taught third grade and later became a reading specialist in the high school. I was involved in high school in student council and served as editor of the newspaper for two years. Most of my free time was absorbed by Young Judaea, a Zionist youth movement. When I was eighteen, I decided that I should live in Israel to fulfill my responsibility as a Jew. I spent my junior year abroad in Israel, and then moved there after graduation.

"I have been writing since I was a little girl. I remember having my father type out my stories so I could read them to classmates at recess. In high school I sold articles to regional newspapers instead of babysitting. I write because it is what I like most to do. I have been able to earn a living at it.

"Although I had written one collection of juvenile short stories, I was primarily a nonfiction writer until I took a fiction course in 1989. I met fiction teacher Pam Painter on a project in Israel and managed to get my family to Boston for a year so that I could study with her. The course helped me to develop my fiction skills and to break some of my journalist's habits. I began writing short stories but knew that I really wanted to write a novel.

"I began *The Thirteenth Hour* after four women were killed in a park near my home in Jerusalem. Like other parents, I asked myself what I would have done if I'd been in that park. I took a self-defense course, and as I learned the steps—poking eyes and breaking toes—I began to imagine the plot of the novel. As a journalist covering stories in the Palestinian sector, I have had opportunities for espionage. What if I were asked to plant a listening device in a Palestinian office while on assignment? How far would I go on a nationalist quest? Would I betray my role as writer or mother? These are among the moral questions on which the novel turns. I am more interested in moral decisions than the mechanics of plot. I also wanted the dominant voices in the novel to be those of women, who are nearly always silent in the Middle East. Terrorism takes place in a woman's world—the corner grocery, the city bus, the school yard.

"The heroines of *The Thirteenth Hour* are two women, one Jewish and one Palestinian. They are recruited against their will to work for Israel's General Security Services and for a Moslem fundamentalist terror squad. They're faced off against each other in the little town of Bethlehem. The novel tells a compelling story, but in many ways it represents my worst fears and greatest hopes.

"I had just finished the revision of the family travel guide, *Kids Love Israel, Israel Loves Kids,* when Prime Minister Yitzhak Rabin was assassinated. My publisher asked for my help in producing a memorial album. I wrote the text and searched for photographs, but I wasn't satisfied. In the end I contacted his sister Rachel Rabin on a kibbutz in the north. She graciously shared childhood memories and photographs with me.

"Israel is a land of manifold stories—historical and modern. I continue to live and write Israel's history and stories outside the Middle East. I have been sent on assignment to Europe and the United States. In general, I am interested in stories where the average person does something larger than life. There is a hero in all of us."

Works Cited

Donavin, Denise P., review of *Kids Love Israel, Israel Loves Kids: A Travel Guide for Families, Booklist,* June 15, 1988, p. 1705.

Duncan, Melanie, review of *The Thirteenth Hour, Booklist,* October 1, 1996, p. 323.

Haas, Gerda, review of *The Holiday Adventures of Achbar, School Library Journal,* March, 1984, p. 165.

Review of *Kids Love Israel, Israel Loves Kids, Jerusalem Report,* February 8, 1996.

Posner, Marcia, review of *Shalom Haver, Goodbye Friend, School Library Journal,* July, 1996, p. 96.

Stasio, Marilyn, review of *The Thirteenth Hour, New York Times Book Review,* February 2, 1997, p. 22.

Review of *The Thirteenth Hour, Kirkus Reviews,* September 1, 1996, p. 1264.

Review of *The Thirteenth Hour, Publishers Weekly,* October 7, 1996, p. 62.

Wismer, Donald, review of *Kids Love Israel, Israel Loves Kids: A Travel Guide for Families, Small Press,* October, 1988, p. 85.

For More Information See

PERIODICALS

Armchair Detective, winter, 1997, p. 116.
Kirkus Reviews, May 15, 1996, p. 751.

*   *   *

SOFER, Rachel
See SOFER, Barbara

*   *   *

SPIEGELMAN, Art 1948-

Personal

Born February 15, 1948, in Stockholm, Sweden; immigrated to United States, 1951; naturalized citizen; son of Vladek (a salesperson and businessman) and Anja (Zylberberg) Spiegelman; married Francoise Mouly (a publisher), July 12, 1977; children: Nadja Rachel, Dashiell Alan. *Education:* Attended Harpur College (now State University of New York at Binghamton), 1965-68.

Addresses

Agent—Deborah Karl, 52 West Clinton Ave., Irvington, NY 10533.

Career

Free-lance artist and writer, 1965—; Topps Chewing Gum, Inc., Brooklyn, NY, creative consultant, artist, designer, editor, and writer for novelty packaging and bubble gum cards and stickers, including "Wacky Packages" and "Garbage Pail Kids," 1966-89; artist and contributing editor, *New Yorker* Magazine, 1991—. Instructor in studio class on comics, San Francisco Academy of Art, 1974-75; instructor in history and aesthetics of comics at New York School of Visual Arts, 1979-87. Advisory board member of the Swann Founda-

tion. *Exhibitions:* Artwork exhibited in numerous gallery and museum shows in the United States and abroad, including the Museum of Modern Art, New York City, 1991; "The Road to Maus," at Galerie St. Etienne, New York City, 1992; and shows at the New York Cultural Center, the Institute of Contemporary Art in London, England, and the Seibu Gallery in Tokyo, Japan. *Member:* PEN.

Awards, Honors

Annual *Playboy* Editorial Award for best comic strip and Yellow Kid Award (Italy) for best comic strip author, both 1982; Regional Design Award, *Print* magazine, 1983, 1984, and 1985; Joel M. Cavior Award for Jewish Writing, and National Book Critics Circle nomination, both 1986, both for *Maus: A Survivor's Tale, My Father Bleeds History;* Inkpot Award, San Diego Comics Convention, and Stripschappenning Award (Netherlands) for best foreign comics album, both 1987; Special Pulitzer Prize, National Book Critics Circle award, *Los Angeles Times* book prize, and Before Columbus Foundation Award, all 1992, all for *Maus: A Survivor's Tale II, and Here My Troubles Began;* Spiegelman also received a Guggenheim fellowship for his work on *Maus.*

Writings

COMICS

The Complete Mr. Infinity, S. F. Book Co., 1970.
The Viper Vicar of Vice, Villainy, and Vickedness, privately printed, 1972.

Art Spiegelman

Zip-a-Tune and More Melodies, S. F. Book Co., 1972.

(Compiling editor with Bob Schneider) *Whole Grains: A Book of Quotations,* D. Links, 1972.

Ace Hole, Midget Detective, Apex Novelties, 1974.

Language of Comics, State University of New York at Binghamton, 1974.

(Contributor) Don Donahue and Susan Goodrich, editors, *The Apex Treasury of Underground Comics,* D. Links, 1974.

Breakdowns: From Maus to Now, an Anthology of Strips, Belier Press, 1977.

Work and Turn, Raw Books, 1979.

Every Day Has Its Dog, Raw Books, 1979.

Two-Fisted Painters Action Adventure, Raw Books, 1980.

(Contributor) Nicole Hollander, Skip Morrow, and Ron Wolin, editors, *Drawn Together: Relationships Lampooned, Harpooned, and Cartooned,* Crown, 1983.

Maus: A Survivor's Tale, My Father Bleeds History, Pantheon, 1986.

(Editor with wife, Francoise Mouly, and contributor) *Read Yourself Raw: Comix Anthology for Damned Intellectuals,* Pantheon, 1987.

(With Francoise Mouly) *Jimbo: Adventures in Paradise,* Pantheon, 1988.

Maus: A Survivor's Tale II, and Here My Troubles Began, Pantheon, 1991.

Contributor to numerous underground comics. Editor of *Douglas Comix,* 1972; editor, with Bill Griffith, and contributor, *Arcade, the Comics Revue,* 1975-76; founding editor, with Mouly, and contributor, *Raw,* 1980—.

Maus has been translated into eighteen languages, including Japanese, Korean, and Hungarian.

FOR CHILDREN

Open Me ... I'm a Dog, HarperCollins, 1996.

OTHER

(Editor, with Francoise Mouly and R. Sikoryak) *Warts and All / Drew Friedman and Josh Alan Friedman,* Penguin, 1990.

(Illustrator) Joseph Moncura March, *The Wild Party: The Lost Classic,* Pantheon, 1994.

Sidelights

"Art Spiegelman's *Maus* is among the remarkable achievements in comics," wrote Dale Luciano in *The Comics Journal.* The comic, an epic parable of the Holocaust that substitutes mice and cats for human Jews and Nazis, marks a zenith in Spiegelman's artistic career. Prior to the *Maus* books, Spiegelman made a name for himself on the underground comics scene. He has been a significant presence in graphic art since his teen years, when he wrote, printed, and distributed his own comics magazine. By the end of his first year in college Spiegelman was employed by Topps Chewing Gum as a creative consultant, artist, and writer. His affiliation with the company has wrought such pop culture artifacts as "Wacky-Packs" and the "Garbage Pail Kids." In the early 1980s Spiegelman and his wife, Francoise Mouly, produced the first issue of *Raw,* an

underground comics (or as Spiegelman and Mouly refer to them, "comix") anthology that grew into a highly respected alternative press by the middle of the decade. It was not until the publication of the first *Maus* collection in 1986, however, that a wide range of readers became aware of Spiegelman's visionary talent and his considerable impact on the realm of comics.

Spiegelman was born in Stockholm, Sweden, to Vladek and Anja, two survivors of the Holocaust, Nazi Germany's massacre of six million Jews during World War II. As a young child, his family moved to the United States, where he grew up in Rego Park, New York. Spiegelman recalls an early affinity for cartoons and comics. "I think ... that I learned to read from looking at comics," he told Joey Cavalieri in *Comics Journal,* citing early exposure to the likes of *Mad* magazine and various superhero books. By the age of twelve, Spiegelman was emulating the artists whose creations had captured his imagination and funnybone. As a hobby he began to draw his own cartoons, but as he told Cavalieri, "it was a pastime only for a brief period. It became an obsession very quickly." At the age of thirteen, Spiegelman was illustrating for his school newspaper, and by his fourteenth year he had already made his first professional sale, a cover for the *Long Island Post*—for which he was paid fifteen dollars.

Spiegelman continued his interest in drawing when he entered the High School of Art and Design in New York, where, as part of a cartoon course assignment, he wrote and illustrated a comic strip. The strip attracted the interest of a New York publishing syndicate. The experience made Spiegelman aware that the parameters for conventional comics were too narrowly defined for his ideas. He sought and found a creative outlet with the burgeoning underground comics scene, including printing and distributing his own magazine, *Blase* (the title is French for 'apathetic' or 'world-weary'). Spiegelman was still unclear as to what kind of career he would forge out of his artistic activity, as he told Cavalieri, "I just knew I wanted to do lines on paper and write at the same time."

Spiegelman was influenced by a number of artists working in the comics field, among them *Mad* magazine creator Harvey Kurtzman, *Mad* artist John Severin, and Jack Davis, who drew baseball cards for Topps Chewing Gum. Eager to get his hands on cards with original Davis art on them, Spiegelman sent a copy of *Blase* to Topps, hoping that they would send him some cards in return. The company responded by complimenting his work and inviting him out to Topps headquarters for lunch. Spiegelman visited the production studios and returned home with a handful of Jack Davis originals. A few years later, during his first year at Harpur College, Spiegelman received a phone call from Topps asking him if he would like a summer job with the company. He accepted their offer, assuming the duties of "resident tinkerer" at Topps, creating various novelty items. He also streamlined Topps's production process from an inefficient circuit between conception and realization to a smooth idea-to-artist procedure. "I sort of created a job that hadn't been there before because I was able to both write a bit and draw a bit," Spiegelman told Cavalieri. By the summer's end Spiegelman was an integral part of Topps's production, and the company asked him to continue working with them. He maintained his affiliation with the company for twenty-five years.

Spiegelman's employment with Topps included writing and drawing various card series and humorous other items. His biggest contribution, however, came about in response to another product that the company was planning. An executive at Topps was interested in issuing a series of cards featuring the miniaturized labels of supermarket products. Spiegelman, seeing little curiosity value in commercial artwork that was not antiquated enough to be charming, decided to poke fun at the project. He drew up a parody version of a company's package art. Spiegelman's loopy version of the product label was a hit with Topps, and "Wacky Packages" were born. Marketed with a stick of gum like baseball cards, "Wacky Packages" soon became a fixture of the 1970s alongside such items as the lava lamp, the hula-hoop, and black light posters. "Wacky Packages" offered a humorous alternative to the ever increasing onslaught of advertised products. The small sticker-cards depicted such skewed and vaguely familiar products as "Fright Guard" deodorant, "Bustedfinger" candy bars, and "Koduck" film—"for ducks." Some adults found "Wacky Packages" crude and remotely offensive. Children, however, were delighted with a product that appealed to their sense of humor, and they gleefully displayed the stickers on their bedroom doors, lunchboxes, and school books. In the 1980s Spiegelman mounted a second wave of humorous stickers with the creation of the "Garbage Pail Kids," which featured drawings of slovenly children accompanied by information that cited the children's more unsavory attributes.

While Spiegelman was devoting time to Topps, he never lost touch with the comics scene. By the mid-1970s the influx of new underground products was staggering. With so many new titles being produced, many readers, fearing low quality, would only purchase their tried and true favorites. This was distressing news to Spiegelman, who was a proponent of new material. So along with fellow artist Bill Griffith, author of the popular *Zippy the Pinhead* strip, Spiegelman formed *Arcade,* a comics anthology that would highlight the new work of some of the best underground artists and writers. *Arcade* debuted in 1975 and featured work by such esteemed artists as Kim Deitch, Robert Crumb, and Spiegelman himself.

Spiegelman's work with *Arcade* lasted a short time, owing in large part to his desire to work at a more deliberate pace rather than worry about making deadlines for the magazine's frequent publication. Following his departure from *Arcade,* Spiegelman began to publish books that compiled his own comics. One such book, 1977's *Breakdowns,* featured numerous short works that he had written over the years. Among the stories is a "comics noir" piece titled "Ace Hole, Midget Detective," which recounts the exploits of a diminutive detective on the case of an art theft ring. Among the

Both an autobiographical and historical commentary, Spiegelman's unique and powerful tale is based on the experiences of his father, a Holocaust survivor. (Cover illustration by Spiegelman.)

characters Ace encounters is a young woman drawn in mock-Picasso style whose profile lines become darker and more defined as Ace follows her, until she proclaims, "I'm being shadowed!" The humor is the double play on the word "shadow," which is both an artistic technique and a detective's term for trailing a suspect. Inside jokes regarding art and outright references to artistic technique such as this are a trademark of Spiegelman's, and many of his strips offer glimpses into his creative procedure. *Two-Fisted Painters Action Adventure,* a 1980 work, uses artistic process as a centerpiece. The book is essentially a satire, with Spiegelman mixing and comparing comics and fine art. As Michael Dooley wrote in *Comics Journal:* "'Painters' is an elaborate study of contrasts and conflicts: fine art vs. commercial art; originality vs. cliche; color vs. black and white; even creativity vs. impotence, and life vs. death." Not only is *Painters* considered intelligent and funny—Dooley called the book a *"tour de force"*— it also displays Spiegelman's extensive and esoteric knowledge of both classic and comics art.

When he was editing the *Arcade* anthologies, Spiegelman found that, due to the magazine's publication schedule, he was spending more time as an editor than as a contributor. Considering himself an artist by vocation and an editor by necessity, Spiegelman reasoned that his next venture into publishing would have to allow for his creativity. Thus in 1980 he and his wife and partner, Francoise Mouly, published the first issue of *Raw,* an anthology magazine that would come out once or twice a year and feature adult comics work from around the world. From the start Spiegelman and Mouly sought to differentiate *Raw* from other comics anthologies. The magazine is printed on high quality paper and cut a size larger than conventional magazines, giving it a distinct visual appeal. For the content Spiegelman and Mouly made their own contributions and solicited work from some of the world's finest comics purveyors, including France's Jacques Tardi and Holland's Joost Swarte. The first issue of *Raw* debuted under the subtitle *"The Graphix Magazine of Postponed Suicides."* Explaining the reason for the title, Spiegelman told Cavalieri, "Every moment that you don't commit suicide is an affirmation. It's deciding to live some more." He continued that a postponed suicide "implies an act of faith has been committed. Which is, to create a work of art, a book, a painting, a poem, a magazine, a comic strip, whatever, and that the work is in itself a justification for remaining alive."

Spiegelman and Mouly's ambitions for *Raw* were modest: they expected to print three thousand copies of the first issue. As Spiegelman described *Raw* to Aron Hirt-Manheimer in *Reform Judaism,* "When we began we weren't thinking of it as an ongoing magazine. We just wanted to do the ultimate prototype and hoped some other publisher would get the idea." Contrary to their expectations, *Raw* sold out the entire print run for its first two issues, and by the third issue Spiegelman and Mouly were printing ten thousand copies. The magazine took hold among mature comics readers, providing a graphics haven for those whose tastes had outgrown superheroes and pulp fiction. The material in *Raw* often centers on the confusion and pathos of modern life and reflects these emotions in its structural style. Conventions such as linear narrative and simplistic imagery are often eschewed in favor of elliptical jumps and oblique text that challenge the reader to search for deeper meanings. Whereas underground comics were once perceived as a wellspring of scatological and graphic sexual humor, *Raw* demonstrated a different facet of graphic art. *Raw*'s willingness to make its readers think earned it a devoted following of educated readers.

Raw's popularity increased with each new issue. Public demand for the original magazines prompted Spiegelman and Mouly to compile the first three issues into a book titled *Read Yourself Raw.* The magazine's success not only vindicated Spiegelman's comics ethic but reflected a flowering of his own artistic output. Beginning with the second issue of *Raw,* Spiegelman began serializing *Maus,* the work that would change both his and the comics world's perception of graphic art.

Spiegelman has described *Maus* as "the point where my work starts." As he told Cavalieri: "Up to that point, I feel like I'd been floundering.... All of a sudden, I found my own voice, my own needs, things that I wanted to do in comics." Although his work on *Maus* began in earnest in the 1980s, the comic actually had its genesis as a three page strip back in 1972. In that year Spiegelman was approached to contribute to a compilation titled *Funny Aminals* (sic), whose only dictum required the strips to feature animals exhibiting human characteristics. Spiegelman contemplated several ideas and finally hit upon his theme while watching old cartoons. Viewing cartoons that featured cats and mice, Spiegelman related to Cavalieri that he was struck with the epiphany that "this cat and mouse thing was just a metaphor for some kind of oppression." Initially he thought of using cats and mice for a strip dealing with slavery, but being a white Jewish man, he reasoned that he could not be true to what was, regardless the form, a black man's story. He decided to explore a theme that was much closer to him, his mother and father's experience in, and survival of, a Nazi concentration camp.

Maus starts with Spiegelman, representing himself as a humanoid mouse, going to his father, Vladek, for information about the Holocaust. As Vladek's tale begins, he and his wife, Anja, are living in Poland with their young child, Richieu, at the outset of World War II. The Nazis, as cats, have overrun much of Eastern Europe, and their oppression is felt by everyone, especially the Jews/mice. The story recalls Vladek's service in the Polish army and subsequent incarceration in a German war prison. As he returns to Anja and his home, the Nazi "Final Solution"—to exterminate the entire Jewish race—is well under way. There is much talk of Jews being rounded up and shipped off to the camps, where they are either put to strenuous work or put to death. Vladek and Anja's attempt to flee is thwarted and they are sent to Auschwitz, Poland, site of one of the most notorious camps. As the first book of *Maus* concludes, Richieu has been taken from his parents by the Nazis—never to be seen again—and Vladek and Anja are separated and put in crowded train cars for shipment to Auschwitz.

As the second volume, *And Here My Troubles Began,* opens, Art and his wife, Francoise, are visiting Vladek at his summer home in the Catskills. During the visit Art and his father resume their discussion. Vladek recounts how he and Anja were put in separate camps, he in the Auschwitz facility, she in the neighboring Birkenau. The horrors and inhumanity of concentration camp life are related in graphic detail. Vladek recalls the discomfort of cramming three or four men into a bunk that is only a few feet wide and the ignominy of scrounging for any scrap of food to sate his unending hunger. His existence at Auschwitz is marked by agonizing physical labor, severe abuse from the Nazis, and the ever present fear that he—or Anja—may be among the next Jews sent to the gas chambers. Despite these overwhelming incentives to abandon hope, Vladek is bolstered by his clandestine meetings with Anja and the discovery of supportive allies among his fellow prisoners. In an encounter with a former priest, Vladek is told that the numerals in his serial identification, which the Nazis tattooed upon their victims, add up to eighteen, a number signifying life.

Vladek manages to hold on through several harrowing incidents, including a bout with typhus. As the war ends and the Allied troops make their way toward Auschwitz, Vladek and some fellow prisoners flee the camp and eventually make their way to safety. In the haste of his escape, however, Vladek loses contact with Anja and does not know if she is alive. Their reunion marks a happy point in Vladek's tale. As the book continues Vladek and Anja desperately search orphanages in Europe for Richieu, to no avail. They eventually emigrate to Sweden where Art is born, and from there the family moves to America. The horrors of the war have scarred Anja permanently however, and in 1968 she commits suicide. The book concludes with Art visiting Vladek just before his death in 1982.

Although *Maus* is essentially the story of Vladek and Anja's ordeal, the two books also serve in an autobiographical sense for Spiegelman, who appears at intervals throughout the narrative. He has stated that *Maus* is, in part, a meditation on "my own awareness of myself as a Jew." There are deeply personal passages depicting conversations between Art and his psychiatrist, Pavel, who, like Vladek, survived the Nazi's attempted purge. Their conversation ranges from Anja's suicide to the guilt that Art feels for being successful in light of his father's tribulation. As much as *Maus* serves as a piece of edifying literature, it also provided its creator with an opportunity to confront his personal demons. As Spiegelman wrote in an article in *Voice, Maus* was motivated "by an impulse to look dead-on at the root cause of my own deepest fears and nightmares."

A good deal of discussion has arisen since the publication of the *Maus* books, much of it regarding Spiegelman's use of animals in the place of humans. When the story originated in *Funny Aminals,* Spiegelman made no mention of Jews or Nazis. The protagonists were mice, persecuted because they were "Maus." Likewise, the antagonists were cats, or "Die Katzen," and they chased the mice, although "chasing" the mice meant rounding them up in camps for work, torture, and extermination. The closest the strip comes to an outright identification with the Holocaust is in the name of the concentration camp, "Mauschwitz." As Spiegelman began the expanded version however, he found that he had to write in terms of "Jews" and "Nazis" when going into detail. As he told Cavalieri: "One can't keep changing it to metaphor. It would come out like some clumsy version of *Animal Farm* or something. It wouldn't ring true." Spiegelman decided to maintain his characters as animals however, citing a fear that using human characters would turn the work into a "corny" plea for sympathy. As he explained to Cavalieri, "To use these ciphers, the cats and mice, is actually a way to allow you past the cipher at the people who are experiencing it. So it's really a much more direct way of dealing with the material." As Lawrence Weschler described *Maus* in *Rolling Stone:* "Spiegelman's draftsmanship is clean and direct, his characterizations are charming and disarm-ing—the imagery leads us on, invitingly, reassuringly, until suddenly the horrible story has us gripped and pinioned. Midway through, we hardly notice how strange it is for us to be having such strong reactions to these animal doings." Dale Luciano also agreed with Spiegelman's reasoning, as he described *Maus* in *The Comics Journal:* "By making the characters cats and mice, the result is that the characters' *human* qualities are highlighted all the more, to an inexplicably poignant effect." Luciano continued, "The situations recalled and acted-out in *Maus* place the characters in a variety of delicate situations: they express themselves with a simplicity and candor that is unsettling because it is so accurately *human.*"

Spiegelman's exploration of social issues in his work has led him to realizations about the modern world. *Maus* raised his comprehension of humanity's dark capabilities. In an article he wrote for the *Voice,* Spiegelman stated that while there is a certain level of awareness and moral outrage toward the events of the Holocaust, society at large still operates on a level of denial. As he wrote: "It's like the old Looney Tunes cartoons where the character runs past the edge of a cliff and keeps running through midair. It takes a while to notice there's no ground left to run on. Finally he notices and plummets earthward with a crash. So, Western Civilization ended at Auschwitz. And we still haven't noticed."

Summarizing the importance of *Maus* for young people, *School Library Journal* contributor Rita G. Keeler, reviewing the first *Maus* work, *A Survivor's Tale,* asserted: "This is a complex book. It relates events which young adults, as the future architects of society, must confront, and their interest is sure to be caught by the skillful graphics and suspenseful unfolding of the story." Patty Campbell, writing in the *Wilson Library Bulletin,* similarly maintained: "*Maus* has been analyzed and praised by some of the best critics in the business.... [This] is a book that is supremely important and appropriate for young adults. Not only because teenagers have always found the comic strip congenial, not only because it is a story of the pain of parent-child conflict, not only because it is a superbly original piece of literature, but also because it is a stunning evocation of the terror of the Holocaust—and we dare not let the new generation forget."

In a lighter vein, Spiegelman has also written and illustrated a picture book for primary graders that showcases his trademark humor. *Open Me ... I'm a Dog!* is a puppy-sized book with an attached leash that proclaims itself a dog under the spell of a wizard's curse. "It's a winning conceit, with ingenuous tongue-in-cheek illustrations," noted a *Kirkus Reviews* commentator. Deborah Stevenson of the *Bulletin of the Center for Children's Books,* reviewing *Open Me ... I'm a Dog!,* asserted that Spiegelman's "original approach and dorky humor will make many kids eager to get their paws on" the book.

Works Cited

Campbell, Patty, "The Young Adult Perplex," *Wilson Library Bulletin,* February, 1987, pp. 50-51, 80.

Cavalier, April, 1969.

Cavalieri, Joey, "An Interview with Art Spiegelman and Francoise Mouly," *Comics Journal,* August, 1981, pp. 98-125.

Dooley, Michael, "Art for Art's Sake," *Comics Journal,* April, 1989, pp. 110-17.

Hirt-Manheimer, Aron, "The Art of Art Spiegelman," *Reform Judaism,* spring, 1987, pp. 22-23, 32.

Keeler, Rita G., review of *Maus: A Survivor's Tale, School Library Journal,* May, 1987, p. 124.

Luciano, Dale, "Trapped by Life," *Comics Journal,* December, 1986, pp. 43-45.

Review of *Open Me ... I'm a Dog!, Kirkus Reviews,* June 1, 1997, p. 880.

Spiegelman, Art, "Maus and Man," *Voice,* June 6, 1989, pp. 21-22.

Stevenson, Deborah, review of *Open Me ... I'm a Dog!, Bulletin of the Center for Children's Books,* September, 1997, p. 28.

Weschler, Lawrence, "Mighty 'Maus,'" *Rolling Stone,* November 20, 1986, pp. 103-06, 146-48.

For More Information See

PERIODICALS

Five Owls, March-April, 1988, p. 61.

New York Times Book Review, November 3, 1991, pp. 1, 35-36; December 21, 1997, p. 18.

Publishers Weekly, April 26, 1991.

Voice of Youth Advocates, June, 1992, p. 133.

*   *   *

SUZANNE, Jamie
See LANTZ, Francess (Lin)

T–U

THEROUX, Paul 1941-

Personal

Born April 10, 1941, in Medford, MA; son of Albert Eugene (a salesman) and Anne (Dittami) Theroux; married Ann Castle (a radio producer), December 4, 1967 (divorced, 1993); married Sheila Donnely, November 18, 1995; children: (first marriage) Marcel Raymond, Louis Sebastian. *Education:* Attended University of Maine, 1959-60; University of Massachusetts, B.A., 1963; Syracuse University, further study, 1963. *Hobbies and other interests:* Rowing.

Paul Theroux

Addresses

Home—35 Elsynge Rd., London SW18 2HR, England.

Career

Soche Hill College, Limbe, Malawi, lecturer in English, 1963-65; Makerere University, Kampala, Uganda, lecturer in English, 1965-68; University of Singapore, Singapore, lecturer in English, 1968-71; professional writer, 1971—. Visiting lecturer, University of Virginia, 1972-73. *Member:* American Academy of Arts and Letters, Royal Geography Society, Royal Society of Literature.

Awards, Honors

Robert Hamlet one-act play award, 1960; *Playboy* Editorial Award, 1971, 1976; Editors' Choice citation, *New York Times Book Review*, 1975, for *The Great Railway Bazaar;* American Academy of Arts and Letters award for literature, 1977; American Book Award nominations, 1981, for *The Old Patagonian Express,* and 1983, for *The Mosquito Coast;* Thomas Cook Travel Book Prize, 1989; honorary degrees from Trinity College and Tufts University, both 1980, and University of Massachusetts—Amherst, 1988.

Writings

FOR CHILDREN

A Christmas Card, illustrated by John Lawrence, Houghton, 1978.

London Snow: A Christmas Story, illustrated with wood engravings by J. Lawrence, Houghton, 1979.

The Mosquito Coast (young adult novel), illustrated by David Frampton, Houghton, 1982.

Millroy the Magician (young adult novel), Random House, 1994.

FICTION; FOR ADULTS

Waldo, Houghton, 1967.

Fong and the Indians, Houghton, 1968.

Girls at Play, Houghton, 1969.

Murder in Mount Holly, Alan Ross, 1969.

Jungle Lovers, Houghton, 1971.

Sinning with Annie and Other Stories (short stories), Houghton, 1972.

Saint Jack, Houghton, 1973, adapted as a screenplay with Peter Bogdanovich and Howard Sackler, New World, 1979.

The Black House, Houghton, 1974.

The Family Arsenal, Houghton, 1976.

The Consul's File (short stories), Houghton, 1977.

Picture Palace, Houghton, 1978.

World's End and Other Stories (short stories), Houghton, 1981.

The London Embassy (short stories), Houghton, 1983.

Doctor Slaughter, Hamish Hamilton, 1984.

Half Moon Street: Two Short Novels (includes *Doctor Slaughter* and *Doctor DeMarr;* also see below), Houghton, 1984.

O-Zone, Putnam, 1986.

The White Man's Burden (two-act play), Hamish Hamilton, 1987.

My Secret History, Putnam, 1989.

Doctor DeMarr, illustrated by Marshall Arisman, Hutchinson, 1990.

Chicago Loop, Random House, 1991.

My Other Life, Houghton, 1996.

Kowloon Tong, Houghton, 1997.

The Collected Stories (short stories), Viking, 1997.

NONFICTION; FOR ADULTS

V. S. Naipaul: An Introduction to His Works, Africana Publishing Corp., 1972.

The Great Railway Bazaar: By Train through Asia (travel) Houghton, 1975.

The Old Patagonian Express: By Train through the Americas, Houghton, 1979.

The Kingdom by the Sea: A Journey around Great Britain, Houghton, 1983.

Sailing through China, illustrated by Patrick Procktor, Houghton, 1984.

(With Steve McCurry) *The Imperial Way,* Houghton, 1985.

Sunrise with Seamonsters: Travels and Discoveries, 1964-1984, Houghton, 1985.

(With Bruce Chatwin) *Patagonia Revisited,* Houghton, 1986.

Riding the Iron Rooster: By Train through China, Ivy, 1989.

Travelling the World: The Illustrated Travels of Paul Theroux, Random House, 1990.

To the Ends of the Earth: The Selected Travels of Paul Theroux, Random House, 1990.

The Happy Isles of Oceana: Paddling the Pacific, Fawcett, 1992.

(With others) *Islands: A Treasury of Contemporary Travel Writing,* Capra, 1992.

The Pillars of Hercules: A Grand Tour of the Mediterranean, Putnam, 1995.

On the Edge of the Great Rift, Viking Penguin, 1996.

Sir Vidia's Shadow: A Friendship across Five Continents, Houghton, 1998.

Foreign Affairs, Viking Penguin, 1999.

OTHER:

Education by Radio: An Experiment in Rural Group Listening for Adults in Uganda, Makerere University, Kampala, Uganda, 1966.

Contributor of fiction to periodicals, including *Encounter, Atlantic Monthly,* and *Playboy;* contributor of reviews to *New York Times,* London *Times,* and other periodicals in the United States and England.

Adaptations

Mosquito Coast was adapted as a motion picture directed by Peter Weir and starring Harrison Ford, 1985; *Doctor Slaughter* was adapted as the motion picture *Half Moon Street,* starring Michael Caine and Sigourney Weaver, 1986. *London Snow* was recorded as an audiobook narrated by Stephen Thorne, G.K. Hall, 1979.

Sidelights

Paul Theroux is considered by many critics to be among the most noted travel writers of the twentieth century, as well as an expert chronicler of the attitudes and feelings of men and women living in a culture that was not theirs at birth. Many of his novels take place in such areas as Singapore, Malawi, and Honduras, where British and American citizens attempt to refashion a life in the image of the culture they left behind while remaining open to the changes that exposure to their new home will bring. Included among his works are such travel books as *The Old Patagonian Express: By Train through the Americas* and *The Pillars of Hercules: A Grand Tour of the Mediterranean,* as well as a number of novels for adults. Among his works for children are *A Christmas Card* and its companion volume, *London Snow: A Christmas Story,* published between 1978 and 1979. "Reading ought to be a pleasure. It ought to take you away," Theroux explained to Joseph Barbato in *Express,* in discussing the purpose behind his writing.

Theroux was born in the Boston suburb of Medford, Massachusetts, in 1941, the third of seven children born to a shoe-leather salesman and a former school teacher. From the age of fourteen he held aspirations of becoming a writer. "You can't hide very easily in a large family, but there was always privacy in reading," he once recalled to *SATA.* His favorite books involved exotic jungle adventures and safari hunting in Africa, choices that reflected his growing desire to explore new places.

Graduating from the University of Massachusetts in 1963, Theroux joined the Peace Corps and spent some time in Africa teaching English. He also started to try his hand at fiction writing, and published his first novel, *Waldo,* in 1967. By the early 1970s, with five published novels under his belt, Theroux quit his teaching job and decided to make a commitment to his writing. He moved to England, which was his wife's home. While he didn't plan on staying long, Theroux discovered England to be an ideal place to set up shop as a writer. Not only was it within easy access of the entire European continent, but, as he explained to *SATA,* "Here [in England] writing is seen as a profession—unmagical—and no one here associates a writer with someone who is going to break the bank. In the States, it's very difficult to describe yourself as a writer without explaining how you make ends meet."

In 1975 Theroux boarded a train at London's Victoria Station and began a four-month trip that took him through Asia and resulted in *The Great Railway Bazaar,* one of the few travel books to become a best-seller. "Ever since childhood, when I lived within earshot of the Boston and Maine, I have seldom heard a train go by and not wished I was on it," Theroux wrote in *The Great Railway Bazaar.* "Those whistles sing bewitchment: railways are irresistible bazaars, snaking along perfectly level no matter what the landscape, improving your mood with speed, and never upsetting your drink .... If a train is large and comfortable you don't even need a destination; a corner seat is enough, and you can be one of those travelers who stay in motion, straddling the tracks, and never arrive or feel they ought to."

Theroux would follow the success of his first book about train travel with several others, including *Riding the Iron Rooster: By Train through China* and *The Old Patagonian Express,* which described his trip from Boston to the tip of South America. Although Theroux has also written several books of fiction, his name remains synonymous with the literature of travel, particularly travel via the rails.

Theroux's fictional output includes novels, books for children, short stories, and poetry. His first book for children, published near the beginning of his writing career in 1978, was *A Christmas Card.* Combining the spirit of the holiday season with the supernatural, Theroux introduces readers to nine-year-old Marcel, who is stranded, along with his family, in a strange, rickety New England town during a snowstorm. Fortunately for them, it happens to be the one night during the year when a portrait hanging in a local museum comes to life, and the museum throws open its doors to Marcel and his family, as well as other lost travelers. Barbara Elleman, reviewing the work for *Booklist,* praised *A Christmas Card* as "a thought-provoking, sensitive story" that reflects "the wondrous quality of Christmas." Calling it "a small enchantment," a *Kirkus* reviewer likewise found praise for Theroux's first book for young readers, and noted that the magical elements are interjected with "delicacy and finesse" in a tale "elegantly and expertly crafted, which all ages can share." In a similar vein is *London Snow,* a holiday tale reminiscent of Charles Dickens's classic work, that finds a scrooge of a landlord threatening to evict a woman and her two foster children during the Christmas season. When the landlord becomes lost in a terrible blizzard, the woman convinces the reluctant police to track him down, causing the landlord to turn over a more generous leaf and let the family remain. A *Kirkus* reviewer, enthused over the old-fashioned warmth of the tale, called *London Snow* "a well-made trifle, smacking of fond dalliance with Christmas-story conventions."

Fourteen-year-old Jilly Farina disguises herself as a boy to become Millroy the Magician's assistant in this 1994 novel. (Cover illustration by Ruth Ross.)

In addition to his novels for adults, Theroux has authored several works of longer fiction considered appropriate for young adult readers. In his 1982 novel, *The Mosquito Coast,* a New England farmer moves with his family to the jungles of Honduras to escape the ravages of modern society. Unfortunately, the puritan work ethic and independent attitude of old New England is no match for the jungle, in a novel that *Booklist* reviewer James Brosnahan praised for its insights and called "a gripping yarn and a provocative critique of [American] character." By contrast, 1994's *Millroy the Magician* serves up a large helping of magic, as the wizard of the title gains his magical powers through a healthy diet. When he spies a horribly undernourished young girl at a fair where he preaches the good news about whole grains and fiber, he "takes her under his wing, disguises her as his son ... and ... transforms himself into a national celebrity," according to *Booklist* contributor Donna Seaman. Seaman's overview of the work as "often hilarious, and strangely romantic" was echoed by *Voice of Youth Advocates* contributor Janet

Harrison Ford plays the eccentric Allie Fox in this 1986 film adaptation of Theroux's **The Mosquito Coast.**

Polacheck, who dubbed *Millroy the Magician* "just as intriguing as ... *Mosquito Coast*," a "rare gem" that should have a prominent place in a young adult library collection.

When asked about his goal as a writer, Theroux responded that he hopes readers will have an emotional reaction to his books. "I want people to burst into tears, I suppose, or be thrilled. Or to give the book to someone else and say, 'Read this book, I hope you like it as much as I do.' Because offering a person a book is like offering him a destination. You say, 'Take this and you'll be happy.' We're all trying to find something that will give the world a sense of order. And that's what fiction does. In the case of my travel books, if a person says to me, 'Your book made me want to go there,' that always makes me feel I've failed. He should say, 'I'm glad I read your book, now I don't have to go there.' That's an important distinction. In a sense the travel writer is traveling for the reader. The book should be an intense experience of the place, and the reader should receive the experience as freshly and directly as I have."

Regarding his literary career, Theroux maintains that writing "made me a free man. No other profession could have done that. When you think that writing is something you do by yourself, that you're making something out of nothing, it's like a conjuring trick in one sense—

there is nothing like it. Except, I suppose, painting, composing music, the other creative professions. All of those make you free. They free you from dogma, they free you from every sort of earth constraint, they give you a tremendously vivid dream life, and they add to your sense of joy and liberation. And that's the only point of going on living, being able to feel that as your time on earth progresses you're becoming steadily more free. You can't feel as if you're subject to someone else's will. I suppose that's why rich people buy an island or a jet plane. In a material sense they want to be free, and they're trying to do it with money. But it is possible with the imagination."

Works Cited

Barbato, Joseph, "Books Should Take You Away," *Express*, June, 1982.

Brosnahan, James, review of *The Mosquito Coast, Booklist*, December 15, 1981, p. 522.

Review of *A Christmas Card, Kirkus Reviews*, December 15, 1978, pp. 1358-59.

Elleman, Barbara, review of *A Christmas Card, Booklist*, September 15, 1978, p. 227.

Review of *London Snow, Kirkus Reviews*, October 15, 1980, p. 1357.

Polacheck, Janet, review of *Millroy the Magician, Voice of Youth Advocates*, August, 1994, p. 150.

Seaman, Donna, review of *Millroy the Magician*, *Booklist*, October 15, 1993, p. 395.
Theroux, Paul, *The Great Railway Bazaar: By Train through Asia*, Houghton, 1975.

For More Information See

BOOKS

Contemporary Literary Criticism, Gale, Volume 5, 1976; Volume 8, 1978.
Samuel Coale, *Paul Theroux*, Twayne, 1987.

PERIODICALS

Booklist, February 15, 1991, p. 1185.
Book Report, September, 1994, p. 47.
Bulletin of the Center for Children's Books, December, 1980, p. 81.
Christian Science Monitor, December 4, 1978, p. B20; March 12, 1982, p. B2; April 8, 1983, p. B7.
English Journal, January 1991, p. 87.
Growing Point, November, 1981, p. 3989.
Junior Bookshelf, February, 1979, p. 62, February, 1981, p. 31.
Kirkus Reviews, October 1, 1993, p. 1225.
New Republic, December 16, 1978, p 28.
New Statesman, November 3, 1978, p. 591; December 20, 1985, p. 61.
New York Times Book Review, June 26, 1978, p. 117; December 14, 1980, p. 37; February 14, 1982, p. 1; February 27, 1983, p. 43; November 1, 1993, p. 66. March 6, 1994, p. 9+.
School Librarian, November, 1989, p. 135.
School Library Journal, October, 1978, p. 113.
Spectator, October 12, 1974; December 16, 1978, p. 24.
Times Educational Supplement, November 17, 1978, p. 26; December 14, 1979, p. 21; November 21, 1980, p. 36; December 20, 1982, p. 34.
Times Literary Supplement, November 21, 1980, p. 1326; October 8, 1993, p. 26; December 3, 1993, p. 12.*

*　　*　　*

TUNG, Angela 1972-

Personal

Born April 18, 1972, in Oakland, CA; daughter of Jwu-sheng (a pharmaceutical researcher) and Alice (Lee) Tung. *Education:* Columbia University, B.A. (magna cum laude), 1994; Boston University, M.A., 1996. *Hobbies and other interests:* Reading, watching films, running, attending cultural events such as readings, concerts, and art exhibitions.

Addresses

Home—1 Pollak Court, Cranbury, NJ 08512.

Career

Writer.

Awards, Honors

First place award, Raymond Carver Short Story Contest, 1997, for "Paper Horses."

Writings

Song of the Stranger (young adult novel), Roxbury Park Books/Lowell House (Los Angeles, CA), 1999.

Contributor of stories and poetry to magazines, including *New Digressions*, *Toyon*, and *Asian Pacific American Journal*.

Work in Progress

Novels about coming of age in the late 1980s and about the author's parents; a book of stories about family members and growing up.

Sidelights

Angela Tung told *SATA:* "I have wanted to be a writer since I was twelve years old, and, over the years since then, I have never once loosened my grip on that dream. Finally all the hard work and determination paid off with my first book, *Song of the Stranger*. This young adult novel started out as just a way to pay the bills while I pursued my own, more 'serious' projects. This attitude was evident in a horribly mediocre first draft, to which—luckily for me and my publisher—I decided I could not attach my name. I proceeded to rewrite the entire manuscript, this time with more heart and soul."

For More Information See

PERIODICALS

Children's BookWatch, February, 1996, p. 7.

*　　*　　*

UPITIS, Alvis

Personal

Education: Rochester Institute of Technology, B.S.; Utah State University, M.F.A.

Addresses

Home—620 Morgan Ave. S., Minneapolis, MN 55405-2034. *Electronic mail*—AUPhoto@aol.com.

Career

Professional photographer, specializing in advertising and corporate photography. Associated with The Image Bank, 1977—; work represented in collections and shows, including Cardiff College, Atlanta College of Art, Keikrug Gallery, New York Photo Show, and Utah Fine Arts Gallery. Minneapolis College of Art and Design, senior photography instructor and associate professor, 1972-81; guest lecturer at Ohio Institute of

Alvis Upitis's informative photographs complement Cris Peterson's book about the processes of milking, pasteurization, and cheese production. (Cover photograph by Upitis.)

Photography, Film in the Cities, Commercial Photographers of St. Louis, and University of Minnesota-Twin Cities; Minnesota State Fair, fine art photography judge. Worked with Eastman Kodak to develop experimental color films; aerial color photography consultant to U.S. Air Force. *Member:* American Society of Magazine Photographers (founding president of Minneapolis chapter).

Awards, Honors

Grants from Ford Foundation.

Illustrator

Cris Peterson, *Extra Cheese, Please! Mozzarella's Journey from Cow to Pizza,* Boyds Mills Press (Honesdale, PA), 1994.
Peterson, *Harvest Year,* Boyds Mills Press, 1996.
Peterson, *Horsepower: The Wonder of Draft Horses,* Boyds Mills Press, 1997.
Peterson, *Century Farm: One Hundred Years on a Family Farm,* Boyds Mills Press, 1999.

Contributor to periodicals, including *Newsweek, Time, Forbes, Money,* and *National Geographic.*

Work in Progress

Illustrating *Wild Horses* (tentative title), a photographic essay on wild mustangs in the Black Hills, for Boyds Mills Press.

For More Information See

PERIODICALS

Booklist, March 15, 1994, p. 1368.
Publishers Weekly, February 1, 1999, p. 85.
School Library Journal, April, 1994, p. 121.

W–X

WALSH, Jill Paton
See PATON WALSH, Gillian

* * *

WEAVER, Will 1950-

Personal

Born January 19, 1950, in Park Rapids, MN; son of Harold Howard (a farmer) and Arlys A. (Swenson) Weaver; married Rosalie Mary Nonnemacher (a teacher), March 2, 1975; children: Caitlin Rose, Owen Harte. *Education:* Attended Saint Cloud State University, 1968-69; University of Minnesota, B.A., 1972; Stanford University, M.A., 1979 *Politics:* Progressive. *Hobbies and other interests:* Mountain hiking, hunting and fishing, studying short story form, rock and roll.

Addresses

Home—Bemidji, MN. *Office*—Bemidji State University, 1500 Birchmont Drive, Bemidji, MN 56601. *Agent*—Lazear Agency, 326 South Broadway, Suite 214, Wayzata, MN 55391. *E-mail*—weaverww@vax1. bemidji.msus.edu.

Will Weaver

Career

Writer and educator. Farmer, Park Rapids, MN, 1977-81; Bemidji State University, Bemidji, MN, part-time writing instructor, 1979-81, associate professor, 1981-90, professor of English, 1990—.

Awards, Honors

Minnesota State Arts Board Fellowship for Fiction, 1979, 1983; "Grandfather, Heart of the Fields" was named one of the "Top Ten Stories of 1984," PEN and the Library of Congress; "Dispersal" was named one of the "Top Ten Stories of 1985," PEN and the Library of Congress; Bush Foundation fiction fellow, 1987-88; Friends of American Writers Award, 1989; Minnesota Book Award for Fiction, 1989; Pick of the Lists, American Booksellers Association, 1993, and Best Books for Young Adults, American Library Association (ALA), 1994, both for *Striking Out;* Best Books for Young Adults, ALA, and Distinguished Book Award, International Reading Association, both 1996, and Best Books for Teens lists in Texas and Iowa, all for *Farm Team;* South Carolina "Best Books," Texas Lone Star List, and Minnesota Book Award Finalist, 1999, all for *Hard Ball.*

He needs a hit for the home team

In the first of Weaver's three novels featuring protagonist Billy Baggs, Billy discovers baseball as a way to help channel his frustrations over the gruesome death of his older brother five years earlier.

Writings

Red Earth, White Earth (adult novel), Simon & Schuster, 1986.

A Gravestone Made of Wheat (short stories; includes title story, "Going Home," "Gabriel's Feathers," "Cowman," "From the Landing," "The Bread-Truck Driver," "Dispersal," "You Are What You Drive," "Blood Pressure," and "Grandfather, Heart of the Fields"), Simon & Schuster, 1989.

Striking Out (young adult novel), HarperCollins, 1993.

Farm Team (young adult novel), HarperCollins, 1995.

Hard Ball (young adult novel), HarperCollins, 1998.

Contributor to periodicals, including *Loonfeather, Prairie Schooner, Hartford Courant, San Francisco Chronicle, Kansas City Star, Chicago Tribune, Minneapolis Tribune, Newsday, Northern Literary Quarterly, Milkweed Chronicles, Library Journal, Chapel Hill Advocate,* and *Minnesota Monthly.* Weaver's short stories for

young adults have been collected in several anthologies: "Stealing for Girls," in *Ultimate Sports,* edited by Don Gallo, Delacorte, 1995; "The Photograph," in *No Easy Answers,* edited by Gallo, Delacorte, 1997; and "Bootleg Summer," in *Time Capsule,* edited by Gallo, Delacorte, 1999.

Adaptations

Red Earth, White Earth was adapted as a television film, airing on the Columbia Broadcasting System (CBS-TV) in 1989.

Work in Progress

Memory Boy, a natural disaster novel for young readers, set in the future; a young adult short story collection.

Sidelights

Will Weaver's country is the upper Midwest, the heartland. It's his home and his material; he occupies the terrain in his fiction as naturally as he does in life. Here is Weaver on a prairie thunderstorm witnessed by the protagonist of his adult novel, *Red Earth, White Earth:* "Outside [Guy] stood among the flax and watched the oncoming weather. Now waist-high and blooming blue on the higher swells of the field, the flax's uncertain colors matched the sky. Southwest were the high, shining cumulus cloud towers.... From the Northwest came the lower, darker, faster-moving clouds of the cold front. Guy for a half-hour watched the two fronts collide. Their clouds in slow motion churned and tumbled and rolled upward dark and bulbous. Supported now by yellow spider legs of lightning, the two fronts were no longer clouds but great spiders struggling for control of the reservation sky."

It is this sort of textured writing that has earned Weaver praise as "a writer of uncommon natural talent," according to Frank Levering in *Los Angeles Times Book Review,* and as a writer who views "America's heartland with a charitable but candid eye," in the words of Andy Solomon in the *New York Times Book Review.* Weaver turned his ample talents to young adult fiction after a highly successful adult novel and story collection, and the result is a trio of books built around the central character of Billy Baggs; books containing the same nuance of detail and depth of characterization as his adult fiction. Billy is a farm boy for whom baseball becomes a release, a passion, a metaphor for life's potentials. But Weaver's are not simply baseball books. "They are not play-by-play sports novels," Weaver told *Authors and Artists for Young Adults* in an interview. "The score of the game is not what is important. It is the *human* game that is important."

Raised on a dairy farm near Park Rapids, Minnesota, Weaver knows intimately whereof he writes. "I grew up in the upper Midwest," Weaver revealed, "on a traditional dairy farm—a red barn with a white house on one-hundred and sixty acres." One of three children, Weaver attended the local country school. "It was the old-fashioned sort with two classes per room, and the teacher would divide her time between the classes. The younger kids started out school in the basement, and then you would work your way up the floors of the building through the various grades." At home, life was simple, but close. "We had what you might call a very plain style of living. A Scandinavian household that focussed on the scriptures and where silence was not a bad thing. My parents did not believe that everything modern was necessarily good. We grew up without a television, and I still credit the growth of my imagination to that."

Farm life could be hard, but it had its advantages. "There was so much independence on the farm. Sure there was work every day of the year, but there was also the kind of freedom for a young kid there that you could not find in town. You could drive at a young age and go fishing and hunting." Without the interruption of television, there was plenty of time for the imagination and for getting outside and doing things. Books came in the form of condensed novels initially. "I remember with real clarity the *Readers Digest* condensed books we used to get. They got me started with reading; they introduced me to the feel of story and march of words."

Part of the legacy of his farm youth, however, was also the feeling of being an outsider. "When I went to school in Park Rapids, I felt as though I was miles behind these other kids in ways. I felt that the town kids were more sophisticated, and they were. Also, the absence of television made me feel even more out of it. But this feeling of being outside is not a bad thing for a writer to have. Of course I had no intention of being a writer back then." A steady 'B' student, Weaver enjoyed being out in nature more than stuck at a desk earning higher grades. In high school one English teacher took an interest in Weaver, encouraging his writing and appreciation of literature. "This altered my direction," Weaver recalled. "Here was a teacher showing interest in my abilities and it gave me great confidence."

Weaver attended college at both Saint Cloud State University and at the University of Minnesota to earn his bachelor's degree. His was the first generation in his family to attend college, and for Weaver it was a time to process changes, to take a long look at the world and see where he fit.

It was not until after college that Weaver began writing. "I didn't even take a creative writing course in Minnesota," Weaver noted. "It was just not in my mind. I studied literature, not writing." Upon graduation, Weaver left for California. Like his grandfather before him, Weaver had applied for and been granted a conscientious objector status. Separated by generations, and reacting to different wars, the two Weavers nonetheless responded to the same sort of inner voice. In California Weaver believed he would find more possibilities for alternate service to fulfill his CO status, but in fact there were few to be found. Soon the draft ended as the Vietnam War wound down and Weaver was spared alternate service.

In the third novel in Weaver's series, Billy and longtime rival King Kenwood learn valuable lessons about life when they are forced to spend a week with each other. (Cover illustration by Michael Koelsch.)

Staying on in California, in and around the Bay Area, Weaver began writing. "I was lonely for the Midwest and started to write about it. The early sketches led to short stories." Soon he was joined in California by his girlfriend from college days and the two were married. On the strength of a couple of short stories, Weaver was admitted to Stanford's prestigious writing program, where once again he felt the consummate outsider. "Here I was, this rube from the Midwest, with a few pages of short stories in my notebooks while other students had stories published in major magazines or were sons or daughters of famous writers. It was a somewhat traumatic experience at first, but then later I discovered the value of the experience." Weaver and his wife also began careers in California's Silicon Valley. Starting as a technical writer, Weaver soon became manager of a high-tech company. "We were on our way, but neither I nor my wife really wanted that life. We both missed the Midwest and finally decided to move back to Minnesota."

At first settling in Minneapolis-St. Paul, the couple soon migrated farther north. In 1976, Weaver took over the running of his father's dairy farm, but quickly learned that such a routine could be more draining than expected. "There's an old joke about two farmers," Weaver told *Authors and Artists for Young Adults.* "One says to the other, 'What would you do if you had a million dollars?', and the other one answers,' 'Farm until it's all gone.' That was sort of our experience on the farm, plus there was very little time or energy to continue with my writing." The Weavers spent two years on the farm, and during this time Weaver also began teaching at a nearby college, Bemidji State University. Eventually the teaching and writing won out over farming, and Weaver began fashioning his short stories into a much larger work, the novel *Red Earth, White Earth.*

Weaver spent two years on his first novel, a tale of the return of a prodigal son to the Minnesota of his youth. Like Weaver, this fictional protagonist also returns from Silicon Valley, and once back in the Midwest must confront unrest between Native Americans and local farmers. *Red Earth, White Earth* earned critical praise and became a television movie three years after its publication. Suddenly Weaver was a literary figure, a Midwestern voice. His collection of short stories, *A Gravestone Made of Wheat,* confirmed the promise of his first novel. "I began to see that I wanted to capture with my writing some of the small-farm texture that is so rapidly disappearing," Weaver explained. "I want to record that in a texture of aesthetic realism."

Weaver set to work on another long realistic novel about the Midwest but part way through suddenly made a discovery. "My children were in middle school at the time," he continued. "They were full of stories from school and about their friends, and there I was hiding out in my study, struggling with my novel. I was trying to balance a tenure faculty position, writing, and being a good father. Listening to my kids talking about middle school, I was reminded of my own youth. I suddenly thought that I would write books my kids might enjoy reading. I'd go with the grain of my family life. Besides, there are certainly affinities for YA in my adult work, large parts of them that younger readers could enjoy as well."

Such a decision coincided with his son starting out in Little League. "This was like a bridge between me and my son," Weaver explained. "As a kid I loved playing baseball, and watching my son learn the game, I felt a connection across the generations. The irony was that he was one of those town kids; that made me flashback to those days when I felt an outsider around the kids from town."

Weaver took this assorted inspiration, melding it together in a tale of a thirteen-year-old farm boy who uses baseball to transcend his feelings of being an outsider. In Billy Baggs, a name inspired by the author's friend Mike Crocker, Weaver developed a character at once enigmatic and sympathetic. "His last name is evocative for me," Weaver maintained. "Billy has a lot of baggage to carry through life." The first title in the series, *Striking Out,*

finds Billy trying to deal with the gruesome death of his older brother in 1965, five years earlier. Billy still feels responsible for the accidental death, and the austere life of do's and don't's imposed by his stern father, Abner, make Billy's life that much more difficult. Abner, a victim of childhood polio (like Weaver's own father), expects the worst from life and often gets it. Billy's mother, on the other hand, is still hopeful about life: with saved egg money, she buys a typewriter and teaches herself enough typing skills to get a job in town at the medical clinic. But Abner proposes no such escape for his son—he will work on the farm.

Visiting town one day, Billy sees some kids playing baseball and feels an outsider to them in their sport. Retrieving a ball hit over the fence, he throws it back to the players with the force of an arm built strong through heavy farm work. The coach sees the potential to make a pitcher of the young boy, and eventually talks Abner into letting Billy play baseball. Billy, however, must overcome his own self-consciousness as well as hostility from some of the teammates to find his place on the team and lead them to victory in the final game of the season. "If this plot suggests a throwback to the ... sports-oriented series from the 1940s and '50s," noted a reviewer for *Publishers Weekly,* "the subplots, involving teenage sex and the mother's decision to take an office job in town, are clearly the stuff of contemporary YA fiction." This same reviewer concluded that a "wealth of lovingly recounted details evokes the difficult daily life on a small dairy farm, while flashes of humor serve as relief." Dolores J. Sarafinski commented in *Voice of Youth Advocates* that "Weaver prevents the plot from becoming too cloying by the realistic representation of life on the farm and Billy's sexual interest in a young neighbor.... Weaver writes well and students ten years old and up will enjoy Billy's struggle, the baseball experience, and the vivid description of life on the farm." Betsy Hearne, writing in *Bulletin of the Center for Children's Books,* pointed out the "clearly focussed plot" and the "fine-tuned psychological and physical pacing" that would "hold junior high school and high school readers," while Mary Harris Veeder declared in the *Chicago Tribune Books* that Weaver's name should be added to the list of the "few talented authors for this age group who manage to catch the significance of sports as the language in which much growing up expresses itself." Veeder concluded that "Many boys stop reading for fun in middle school; this book is good enough to change that."

Weaver continued the saga of Billy Baggs in *Farm Team* and *Hard Ball,* following Billy's progress at ages fourteen and fifteen respectively. In the former novel, the action picks up where it left off in *Striking Out,* with Billy's father taking revenge on a used car salesman who sold his wife a clunker. Running amok in the car lot with a tractor, Abner is carted off to jail and Billy must spend the summer working the farm with no time for pitching fast balls. Billy's mom comes to the rescue, helping to set up a playing field on their property and initiating Friday night games for some relaxation. Billy leads a makeshift group of country kids on the farm team and they ultimately defeat the pompous town kids in a game ending on a fly ball hit by Billy's rival, King Kenwood, and caught by Billy's dog.

While some reviewers found *Farm Team* less substantive than *Striking Out,* Todd Morning in *School Library Journal* thought that the novel was "a successful sequel," and that the final game was "wonderfully evoked." Morning concluded that "Most readers will come away from this book looking forward to the next installment in the life of Billy Baggs." A reviewer for *Publishers Weekly* commented that "Weaver combines wickedly sharp wit with a love of baseball and intimate knowledge of farm life to yield an emotionally satisfying tale." The same reviewer summed up the optimistic ending: "In a good old-fashioned ending, our hero bests his nemesis, ... earns Abner's grudging respect and wins the admiration of the girl who makes his heart sing."

The third novel in the series, *Hard Ball,* continues the competition between Billy and King Kenwood, but in this story the two must learn to deal with each other as well as the expectations of their respective fathers. King is from the better side of town, a child of privilege. The boys compete on the baseball field and for the heart of Suzy—a rivalry that adds piquancy to their feud. It does not help that their fathers are as much at odds with one another as the sons are. As a result of a physical fight between Billy and King, the coach suggests that the boys spend a week together, splitting the time between each household. In the process, King discovers a grudging admiration for the harsh farm life Billy leads and also begins to see how difficult Billy's father can be. Billy in turn learns that a softer life does not necessarily mean an easier one.

Claire Rosser, reviewing *Hard Ball* in *Kliatt,* noted that "There's a welcome earthiness here, in the language and in the farm situations, which add humor and realism." Rosser concluded that "Weaver gets this world exactly right, with the haves and have nots living separate lives, even in sparsely populated Minnesota farmland." Mary McCarthy commented in *Voice of Youth Advocates* that "Billy is an engaging, realistic character who leaves the reader rooting for more.... An excellent read for a hot summer night, baseball fan or not." *Kirkus Reviews* dubbed the book an "offbeat, exciting narrative," while *Bulletin of the Center for Children's Books* concluded that "Weaver will have readers in the palm of his glove."

"I don't want to be pigeon-holed as a sports writer," Weaver told *Authors and Artists for Young Adults.* "Partly for that reason I am letting Billy Baggs go his own way for a time. My current projects do not deal with him at all. Also, I feel my characters were getting a little tired of my intrusions—they needed some breathing room. Billy needs to decide whether or not he wants to go ahead and finish high school. But I am sure I'll get back to Billy soon. I know from the letters I get from young readers that they are anxious to know how life turns out for him. That is one of the enjoyable fringe benefits of writing for younger readers—that they take

stories seriously and are eager to give feedback. Writing for this audience is a bit like a dialogue."

Weaver brings the same demanding rules of craft to his YA novels that he did to his adult work. "I generally work without an outline; I only like to know a chapter or two ahead—like writing only as far as I can see by headlights. But the trouble is, sometimes you take the wrong turn with this method. You have to be flexible; you need to be able to start all over again, to throw away what does not work." Much of Weaver's writing is confined to the summer months when he is free of his teaching load. "I work about half a day," he noted. "I get between three and ten pages a day and I do my writing in a study off the garage."

Weaver is a firm believer in revision. "I always tell aspiring writers that they must be ready to revise. Only Mozart got it right the first time. Some of my short stories have been through twenty revisions; my novels through six to ten rewrites. I am very concerned with quality. If there is anything that will cement a writer's reputation, it's the sense that each book is as good as or better than the last one. That's a real goal of mine."

Weaver's gritty Midwestern realism sets the tone for each of his books, whether adult or YA. He speaks of "stealth literary value," of a "textured readability," and these are the qualities that both reviewers and readers alike have responded to. "If I have a message with all my books, it is that we can do things if we really put our minds to it. But we can't do it alone. We have to trust in humanity, in our family and friends."

Works Cited

Review of *Farm Team, Publishers Weekly,* June 26, 1995, p. 108.

Review of *Hard Ball, Bulletin of the Center for Children's Books,* May, 1998, p. 343.

Review of *Hard Ball, Kirkus Reviews,* December 1, 1997, p. 1781.

Hearne, Betsy, review of *Striking Out, Bulletin of the Center for Children's Books,* February, 1994, p. 204.

Levering, Frank, review of *Red Earth, White Earth, Los Angeles Times Book Review,* October 19, 1986, p. 9.

McCarthy, Mary, review of *Hard Ball, Voice of Youth Advocates,* June, 1998, p. 126.

Morning, Todd, review of *Farm Team, School Library Journal,* July, 1995, p. 96.

Rosser, Claire, review of *Hard Ball, Kliatt,* July, 1998, p. 9.

Sarafinski, Dolores J., review of *Striking Out, Voice of Youth Advocates,* December, 1993, p. 304.

Solomon, Andy, review of *A Gravestone Made of Wheat, New York Times Book Review,* March 12, 1989, p. 22.

Review of *Striking Out, Publishers Weekly,* August 30, 1993, p. 97.

Veeder, Mary Harris, review of *Striking Out, Chicago Tribune Books,* June 19, 1994, p. 6.

Weaver, Will, *Red Earth, White Earth,* Simon and Schuster, 1986.

Weaver, Will, interview with J. Sydney Jones for *Authors and Artists for Young Adults,* conducted January 28, 1999.

For More Information See

PERIODICALS

Booklist, November 15, 1993, p. 515; March 15, 1994, p. 1359; September 1, 1995, p. 66; March 15, 1996, p. 1284.

Bulletin of the Center for Children's Books, September, 1995, pp. 32-33.

Kliatt, September, 1996, p. 5.

Los Angeles Times Book Review, March 12, 1989, pp. 1, 13.

Minneapolis Tribune, September 3, 1995.

New York Times Book Review, November 9, 1986, p. 33.

School Library Journal, October, 1993, p. 156.

Voice of Youth Advocates, October, 1995, p. 226.

Washington Post Book World, November 2, 1986, p. 8; March 26, 1989, p. 11.

—Sketch by J. Sydney Jones

*   *   *

WIELER, Diana (Jean) 1961-

Personal

Surname is pronounced "wheeler"; born October 14, 1961, in Winnipeg, Manitoba, Canada; daughter of Heinz Egon (a chef) and Jean Florence (an accounts receivable manager; maiden name, Zebrasky) Petrich; married Larry John Wieler (a trucking parts national sales manager), May 2, 1981; children: Benjamin. *Education:* Attended Southern Alberta Institute of Technology (Calgary, Alberta, Canada), 1979-80. *Hobbies and other interests:* Painting, doll making, portraiture.

Addresses

Home—133 Spruce Thicket Walk, Winnipeg, Manitoba, Canada R2V 3Z1.

Career

Writer, 1980—. CKXL Radio, Calgary, Alberta, Canada, advertising copywriter, 1980-82; CJWW Radio, Saskatoon, Saskatchewan, Canada, advertising copywriter, 1982-89; *Star Phoenix,* Saskatoon, creative features writer, late 1980s-early 1990s; full-time writer, 1989—. Writers-in-Electronic-Residence (WIER) Program, York University Faculty of Education and the Writers' Development Trust, writer-in-electronic-residence, 1995-96. *Member:* Manitoba Writers' Guild.

Awards, Honors

H. Gordon Love Award, Alberta Advertising Association, 1982, for excellence in advertising; CBC Radio Literary Competition, Children's Story category, first prize, 1985, for "To the Mountains by Morning"; Major

Diana Wieler

Award, Saskatchewan Writers' Guild, 1985, for "The Lucky Charm"; Vicky Metcalf Short Story Award, Canadian Authors' Association, 1986, for "The Boy Who Walked Backwards"; Max and Greta Ebel Memorial Award for Children's Writing, Canadian Society of Authors, Illustrators and Performers, 1987, for *Last Chance Summer;* Governor General's Literary Award for Children's Literature (English text), Canada Council, 1989, for *Bad Boy;* International Honor List selection, International Board on Books for Young People, 1990, for *Bad Boy;* Ruth Schwartz Children's Book Award, Ontario Arts Council, 1990, for *Bad Boy;* Young Adult Book of the Year Award, Young Adult Services Interest Group of the Canadian Library Association, 1990, for *Bad Boy;* Mr. Christie's Book Award (Best English Book for Twelve Years and Up), Christie Brown & Company, 1993, for *Ran Van the Defender;* Ruth Schwartz Children's Book Award finalist, Ontario Arts Council, 1994, for *Ran Van the Defender;* Governor General's Literary Award for Children's Literature (English text) finalist, Canada Council, 1995, for *Ran Van: A Worthy Opponent;* McNally Robinson Young Adult Book of the Year, 1997, for *Ran Van: Magic Nation,* and 1998, for *Drive;* finalist, Ruth Schwartz Children's Book Award, Ontario Arts Council, 1998, for *Drive.* Several of Wieler's books have been Canadian Children's Book Centre *Our Choice* selections, including *Last Chance Summer,* 1986-87, *Ran Van the*

Defender, 1993-94, and *To the Mountains by Morning* and *Ran Van: A Worthy Opponent,* both 1995-96.

Writings

FOR CHILDREN

A Dog on His Own, illustrated by Diana Wieler, Prairie Publishing Company, 1983.

To the Mountains by Morning, Nelson Canada, 1987, reissued as a picture book, illustrated by Ange Zhang, Groundwood/Douglas & McIntyre, 1995.

FOR YOUNG ADULTS

Last Chance Summer, Western Producer Prairie Books, 1986, Delacorte, 1991.

Bad Boy, Groundwood/Douglas & McIntyre, 1989.

Ran Van the Defender, Groundwood/Douglas & McIntyre, 1993.

Ran Van: A Worthy Opponent, Groundwood/Douglas & McIntyre, 1995.

Ran Van: Magic Nation, Groundwood/Douglas & McIntyre, 1997.

Drive, Groundwood/Douglas & McIntyre, 1998.

OTHER

Short stories are represented in *Prairie Jungle: Songs, Poems and Stories for Children,* edited by Wenda McArthur and Geoffrey Ursell, Coteau Books, 1985; and *Canadian Children's Annual: Number Twelve,* edited by Brian Cross, Potlatch Publications, 1987.

Wieler's works have been translated into French, German and Danish.

Work in Progress

Another young adult novel.

Sidelights

Diana Wieler, author of short stories, picture books, and novels, is considered one of Canada's finest writers for young adults. Many of her works have won prestigious Canadian awards and honors, including the Governor General's Literary Award. Wieler's fiction is respected for both its style and its content, as the author writes openly, respectfully, creatively and with insight about themes and issues relevant to contemporary teens. Wieler also has the reputation of being a risk-taker; in the *Globe and Mail,* Elizabeth MacCallum called her "a good writer with more than a small dose of courage." Bridget Donald, in her *Quill & Quire* review of Wieler's novel *Ran Van: Magic Nation,* commented: "Wieler has not shied away from difficult subjects in any of her novels for young adults, but she brings them out ... in full force and treats them with intelligence and grace."

Like the boy in Wieler's award-winning short story "The Boy Who Walked Backwards," who claims he's walking not the *wrong* way but the *other* way, Wieler's main characters are rebels and loners. A loner herself as a child, Wieler grew up without a father in the 1960s when single-parent families were the exception to the normal.

She remembers feeling very "different" from her friends. At first, she dealt with the difference by becoming introspective; then she became a rebel. During high school, where she ran with the "bad" crowd, one teacher told her she was like a pinball arcade, always busy but never going anywhere.

Born in Winnipeg, Manitoba, Wieler lived in Calgary, Alberta, during her teen years. After high school, she enrolled at the Southern Alberta Institute of Technology in Calgary, where she completed the first year of a two-year program in television, stage and radio arts. She left school to take a writing job. At nineteen, she was working as an advertising copy writer at CKXL, a Calgary radio station. Eighteen months later, she married and moved to Saskatoon, Saskatchewan, where she wrote advertising copy for another radio station by day and worked on her creative writing on evenings and weekends. In 1983, her first volume, the picture book *A*

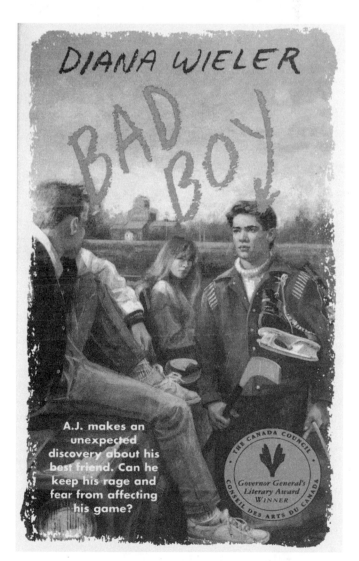

After learning that his best friend is gay, A. J. Brandiosa, a star hockey player, vents his fear and rage on the ice as he tries to cope with his own and his friend's sexuality. (Cover illustration by Laurie McGaw.)

Dog on His Own, was published. The following year, Wieler left radio for a position as a creative features writer with the Saskatoon *Star Phoenix.*

Newspaper writing occupied Wieler's working hours for the next five years. Meanwhile, she continued to pursue her own writing interests in her spare time. Prestigious short story awards from CBC Radio, the Canadian Authors' Association and the Saskatchewan Writers' Guild provided a steady stream of encouragement. *To the Mountains by Morning,* one of Wieler's award-winning short stories, was published as a school reader in 1987. It was reissued as a picture book in 1995.

Wieler's day job, requiring the discipline to write to the newspaper's strict word limits and tight deadlines, helped fine tune a writing style that has characterized and distinguished her work as a novelist. Her first novel, *Last Chance Summer,* was published in 1986. In *Canadian Children's Literature,* book reviewer Douglas Thorpe described its prose as "refreshingly spare." The story, about a twelve-year-old, foster-home misfit, drew on Wieler's experience as a volunteer crisis worker with the Saskatoon Sexual Assault Centre. Tim Wynne-Jones, writing for the *Globe and Mail,* commented that Wieler "writes with imagination" and "exhibits insight and great compassion." The Canadian Society of Children's Authors, Illustrators, and Performers agreed and awarded *Last Chance Summer* the 1987 Max and Greta Ebel Memorial Award for Children's Writing.

Wieler's impressive debut as a writer of fiction for young people created much anticipation for the author's second novel. As Wieler wrote *Bad Boy,* she realized it was controversial. Nevertheless, she was devastated when Western Producer Prairie Books declined to accept it for publication. Fortunately, there was an eager publisher waiting in the wings. Douglas & McIntyre's Groundwood Books snapped up the story of A. J., a sixteen-year-old severely shaken by the discovery that his best friend and hockey teammate is gay. Feeling betrayed, angry and confused, A. J. takes his emotional turmoil out onto the ice, becoming a hockey goon and earning a "bad boy" reputation.

While its sports orientation guaranteed that *Bad Boy* would be a hot potato in some circles, others were more interested in how Wieler handled the delicate subject of homosexuality in writing for teen readers. *Globe and Mail* book reviewer Elizabeth MacCallum maintained: "[Wieler] deftly integrates a difficult issue into the plot with tact and wisdom. Neither judgmental nor sanctimonious, Wieler still takes a stand. Homosexuality is treated as reality." *Bad Boy* won the 1989 Governor General's Literary Award for Children's Literature, the 1990 Canadian Library Association Young Adult Book of the Year Award, and the 1990 Ruth Schwartz Children's Book Award. In *The New Republic of Childhood,* Sheila Egoff and Judith Saltman compared Wieler's *Bad Boy* to works by Kevin Major. "Like Major," they summarized, "Wieler writes prose that is brash and staccato, charged with youthful profanity, but sprinkles her narrative with tender moments."

In the last volume in Wieler's "RanVan" trilogy, protagonist Ran, who has moved away from home, encounters his old nemesis, the Iceman, and falls in love for the first time. (Cover illustration by Ludmilla Temertey, photograph by Ralph Mercer.)

By 1990, Wieler determined to make a full-time commitment to writing books; her target audience would be young people. "It's a tough audience who would just as soon flip on a TV as read a book," she told Kevin Prokosh of the *Winnipeg Free Press.* "They're cynical, sophisticated and not very tolerant. That's what makes it exciting."

Since then, Wieler has completed her Ran Van trilogy about a teenage loner whose video game alter ego transforms him into a super hero. In a *Quill & Quire* review of *Ran Van the Defender,* the series' first title, Patty Lawlor asserted: "Diana Wieler has her fingers firmly on the pulse of the mainstream teen reader. That she's confident enough in herself and in her readers to give conventional setting and staging a bit of a push is, in large part, what makes her the very distinguished author she is becoming." *Ran Van the Defender* won a Mr. Christie's Book Award. It's sequel, *Ran Van: A*

Worthy Opponent, was a finalist for the 1995 Governor General's Literary Award for Children's Literature.

When it comes to writing, Wieler has always felt the pull to create. She recalls the journals she kept as a girl. "They were full of real literary stuff, all about the boys I had crushes on and the girls I was mad at," she commented. "It was a really good experience, though, putting my thoughts down. And then in junior high they started us writing journals in school and I found that to be a really positive experience as well." The experience was so positive that Wieler continues the practice today. "I write a minimum of three pages every morning, come hell or high water, to clear the gunk out of my system," she commented. "You put down all of the trivial stuff and the emotions and it clears the slate for writing."

When Wieler was thirteen, she read Ayn Rand's *We the Living.* "That book was really meat and drink to me," she commented. "The sheer drama and beautifully subtle prose carved itself on me, I know it did. Sometimes when I write, I can feel the cadence of those words, like an echo."

From the time her son Ben leaves for school in the morning until the time he comes home at night, Wieler thinks and rethinks her stories, often returning to her desk in the evening for a final three-hour stint before bed. In an interview in *Children's Book News,* she told the Canadian Children's Book Centre, "I think if I have anything, it's empathy. I don't think of myself as an exceptional writer or wonderful wordsmith. But ever since I was a little kid I was able to put myself in the other guy's shoes and think what it would be like or imagine how that person would feel."

When she's not writing, Wieler prefers to spend time with family and friends, and is involved in artistic pursuits. She belongs to a local art group, paints, collects and makes dolls. Why the disparate interests? "I need that balance between hands and brain," she related. "It's a really absorbing way to relax."

Wieler commented that her interest in dolls prompted an interesting remark from her son. "He said, 'Mom, I can't believe you can write such good boy stories when you're such a *girl.*'" His remark is a variation on a question many people ask Wieler about her writing. How can a woman who grew up in an all-female household know so much about the hearts and minds of teenage boys?

Wieler believes that it was precisely because she grew up in an all-female household that she has such an intense curiosity about men and has undertaken such a careful study of the male gender. "We are always told to 'write what you know,'" Wieler noted in comments to *St. James Guide to Young Adult Writers,* "but for me, I hunger to go places I've never been, look into experiences I probably will never have. As a woman, the most foreign and exciting landscape is the male perspective.

"'But how can you do this?' young writers ask. For me, research is about watching and listening and asking questions. I find that almost everyone is interesting: my doctor, my mechanic, the person who sits beside me in art class. The world is full of fascinating people who will share their stories if you are a good listener. I also draw on the experiences of my husband and son. Just living with them is an adventure of discovery."

While lacking a male role model at home may have strengthened Wieler's observation skills, her parents' divorce weakened her self-esteem. "It was in the sixties when everyone was still married," she remarked. "I just felt so different and so poor. I felt so isolated. I wanted so desperately to be liked."

Today, a more confident Wieler reflects on her writing and her life. She believes good has come from the adversity she experienced as a child and appreciates the blessings that have come along the way. "I have to admit there have always been moments of magic in my life— corners I've turned that felt like the push of the universe," she commented. "I really believe that writing is an emotional and a spiritual process. It's not just what I do, it's who I am. My neighbors read my books and they say, 'Where are you? I can't see you in here.' I tell them it's all me."

Explaining why she has chosen to write for young adults readers, Wieler told *St. James Guide to Young Adult Writers:* "I write about the teen years because that was a vivid, terrible, exhilarating time of my life. So much happens in a short space, and lives change forever. As a writer, that's the promise I make to my reader: someone's life is going to change forever. I can't think of any work more exciting than that."

Works Cited

Canadian Children's Book Centre, "Meet the Author: Diana Wieler," *Children's Book News,* fall, 1990, p. 12.

Donald, Bridget, review of *Ran Van: Magic Nation, Quill & Quire,* October 1997, p. 36.

Egoff, Sheila, and Judith Saltman, *The New Republic of Childhood: A Critical Guide to Canadian Children's Literature in English,* Oxford University Press, 1990, pp. 75-76.

Lawlor, Patty, review of *Ran Van the Defender, Quill & Quire,* August, 1993, p. 38.

MacCallum, Elizabeth, review of *Bad Boy,* "Difficult Issues and Complex Sexuality," *Globe and Mail,* August 26, 1989, p. C19.

Prokosh, Kevin, "Bad Boy Vies for Top Prize," *Winnipeg Free Press,* February 25, 1990, p. 18.

Thorpe, Douglas, review of *Last Chance Summer,* "What Troubles Troubled Kids," *Canadian Children's Literature,* Number 46, 1987, pp. 86-87.

Wieler, Diana, comments in *St. James Guide to Young Adult Writers,* St. James Press, 1999, pp. 890-91.

Wynne-Jones, Tim, review of *Last Chance Summer, Globe and Mail,* February 21, 1987, p. E19.

For More Information See

BOOKS

Canadian Children's Book Centre, *Writing Stories, Making Pictures: Biographies of 150 Canadian Children's Authors and Illustrators,* Canadian Children's Book Centre, 1994, pp. 321-23.

PERIODICALS

Books in Canada, December 1986, pp. 15-17.
Canadian Book Review Annual, 1986, pp. 156-157; 1989, p. 328; 1993, p. 6195; 1995, pp. 490, 521.
Canadian Children's Literature, Number 76, 1994, pp. 22-30; spring, 1999, pp. 100-01.
Globe and Mail, October 30, 1993, p. C25; November 11, 1995, p. C21.
Quill & Quire, August 1986, p.35; August 1995, pp. 32-33.
School Library Journal, April, 1999, p. 142.
Voice of Youth Advocates, August, 1999, pp. 186-87.

*   *   *

WILLIAMSON, Gwyneth 1965-

Personal

Born July 20, 1965, in Warrington, England; daughter of Arnold (a civil servant) and Jean (Griffiths) Williamson; married Antony Sean Downham (a trading standards officer), March 31, 1990; children: Alice Rebecca, Carrie Rose. *Education:* Humberside College of Higher Education, B.A. (with first class honors), 1987; Leeds Polytechnic, Postgraduate Certificate in Education.

Addresses

Home—17 Stainburn Ave., Moortown, Leeds LS17 6PQ, England.

Career

Freelance illustrator, 1987—. Britannia Products, Bradford, England, humor art designer for greeting cards, 1988-91; primary teacher, Leeds, England, 1992-93.

Awards, Honors

Shortlist, Sheffield Children's Book Award, 1997, for *Ridiculous;* shortlist, Stockport Children's Book Award, 1999, for *Beware of the Bears!*

Illustrator

Kaye Umansky, *The Fwog Pwince the Twuth,* A. and C. Black, 1989, Chivers North America, 1998.
Anne Mangan, *The Lonely Little Bear,* Magi (London, England), 1993, Little Tiger Press (Waukesha, WI), 1998.
Julia Jarman, reteller, *The Ghost Next Door,* Ginn (Aylesbury, England), 1994.
Michael Coleman, *Lazy Ozzie,* Magi, 1994, Little Tiger Press, 1996.
Coleman, *Ridiculous,* Magi, 1996, Little Tiger Press, 1996.

Gwyneth Williamson

Dee Reid, *Mr. Big Is a Big Help,* Heinemann Educational (Oxford, England), 1996.
Reid, *Mr. Big Goes on Holiday,* Heinemann Educational, 1996.
Reid, *Mr. Big Goes to the Park,* Heinemann Educational, 1996.
Reid, *Mr. Big Has a Party,* Heinemann Educational, 1996.
Michael Coleman, *One, Two, Three, Oops,* Magi, 1998, Little Tiger Press, 1998.
Coleman, *The King Who Lost His Crown,* Magi, 1998, Little Tiger Press, 1998.
Alan MacDonald, *Beware of the Bears!* Magi, 1998, Little Tiger Press, 1998.
Linda Jennings, *Catkin and Tiger,* Magi, 1998, Little Tiger Press, 1998.
Alison Hawes, *The Polite Knight,* Heinemann Educational, 1998.
Little Mouse and the Big Red Apple, Magi, 1998, Little Tiger Press, 1999.

Work in Progress

Illustrating books for educational publishers, including *Gingerbread Boy,* for Ginn, and *Stone Soup,* for Rigby; greeting card designs for Hanson White; *Titus's Troublesome Tooth,* for Magi and Little Tiger Press.

Sidelights

Gwyneth Williamson told *SATA:* "Since leaving college my work has evolved into a humorous, quirky style, using gouache and pen, although I also like to dabble with acrylics and oil pastels. My favorite illustrators are Quentin Blake and Tony Ross; I like their fluid, humorous styles.

"I am constantly inspired and influenced by those around me, so when I was at school my art teacher Robin Morris had to take a lot of the blame for me being where I am today! When I left school to start an art foundation course at Jacob Kramer College (with the likes of Damien Hirst) I was more of a painter than an illustrator. However, the course allowed for a lot of experimentation and many cups of coffee! We were encouraged to speed up, to capture a life drawing very quickly so marks were worry-free and positive.

"In the end I found myself drifting toward illustration, as I was not enjoying the endless drivel of fine artists justifying their latest 'piece.' I'm a great believer in art speaking for itself. We shouldn't have to look at everything too deeply. Too many artists were more interested in listening to their own voices than in producing anything worth talking about. I also wanted to try to make a living from my art. This was looked on as selling yourself to commercialism by fine artists, but we all have to eat!

"When I graduated from Humberside College with a First Class degree, I plunged straight into freelancing. My style, which had become quite loose, had to tighten up to become more commercial. It began to take on a 'cartoony' feel when I went to work as a humor designer at a greeting card company. My books for Magi have involved lots of animals, which I find really challenging—give me people any day! Although I still illustrate greeting cards, it is children's books I love to work on most. Now I have two young daughters and find I have my very own critics at home. In the future I hope to write as well as illustrate."

For More Information See

PERIODICALS

Booklist, January 1, 1999, p. 886.
Publishers Weekly, March 15, 1996, p. 8; February 15, 1999, p. 106.
School Library Journal, March, 1999, p. 173.

*   *   *

WRIGHT, Betty Ren 1927-
(Revena)

Personal

Born June 15, 1927, in Wakefield, MI; daughter of William (a teacher) and Revena (a teacher; maiden name, Trezise) Wright; married George Frederiksen (a

Betty Ren Wright

commercial art director), October 9, 1976; stepchildren: Judith, John, Deborah. *Education:* Milwaukee-Downer College (now Lawrence University), B.A., 1949; additional study, University of Wisconsin, and Breadloaf Writers' Conference at Middlebury College, Vermont. *Politics:* Independent. *Religion:* Methodist. *Hobbies and other interests:* Reading, travel, pets.

Addresses

Home—6223 Hilltop Drive, Racine, WI 53406. *Agent*—Sternig & Byrne Literary Agency, 3209 S. 55th St., Milwaukee, WI 53219-4433.

Career

Western Publishing, Racine, WI, editorial assistant and editor, 1949-67, managing editor of editorial department, 1967-78; full-time writer, 1978—. Lecturer and teacher at workshops. *Member:* Allied Authors, Council for Wisconsin Writers, American Association of University Women, Phi Beta Kappa.

Awards, Honors

Children's Choice Award, International Reading Association and the Children's Book Council, 1981, for *Why Do I Daydream?;* Notable Children's Trade Book in

In Wright's story for middle-graders, twelve-year-old Amy finds her great-grandparents' killer with the help of a haunted miniature dollhouse she discovers in the attic.

Social Studies, National Council for the Social Studies and Children's Book Council, 1982, for *My Sister Is Different; Booklist*'s Reviewer's Choice, 1983, Edgar Allan Poe Award Runner-up for Best Juvenile, Mystery Writers of America, 1984, Texas Bluebonnet Award, Texas Library Association, Mark Twain Award, Missouri Association of School Librarians, and Young Reader's Choice Award, Pacific Northwest Library Association, all 1986, California Young Reader Medal, California Reading Association, 1987, Iowa Children's Choice Award, and Wyoming Indian Paintbrush Award, both 1988, New Mexico Children's Choice Award, and Rebecca Caudill Young Readers Book Award, Illinois Association for Media in Education, both 1989, all for *The Dollhouse Murders;* Children's Choice Award, 1984, for *Ghosts Beneath Our Feet* and for *Christina's Ghost,* 1985; Juvenile Book Award, Council for Wisconsin Writers, 1985, Kansas City Children's Choice Award (Kansas City Three), Texas Bluebonnet Award, Sequoyah Children's Book Award, Oklahoma Library Association, South Carolina Children's Book Award, South Carolina Association of School Librarians, and Georgia Children's Book Award, College of Education, University of Georgia, all 1988, Young Hoosier Book Award, Association for Indiana Media Educators, 1989, and

Virginia Young Readers Program, State Reading Association 1990, all for *Christina's Ghost; The Summer of Mrs. MacGregor* was selected one of *Redbook*'s Ten Top Books for Teens, 1987; South Carolina Junior Book Award, 1995, and Young Hoosier Book Award, 1996, both for *A Ghost in the House;* Utah Children's Book Award, 1995, Oklahoma Sequoyah Book Award, and Missouri Mark Twain Award, both 1996, all for *The Ghosts of Mercy Manor;* Children's Book Award, *Child Magazine,* 1995, and Council for Wisconsin Writers Juvenile Book Award, 1995, both for *Out of the Dark.* Six of Wright's books have been named Junior Library Guild selections: *The Secret Window, The Dollhouse Murders, Christina's Ghost, The Summer of Mrs. MacGregor, A Ghost in the Window,* and *The Pike River Phantom.* In addition, Wright received the Alumni Service Award, Lawrence University, 1973, for her contributions to children's literature and the Lynde and Harry Bradley Major Achievement Award, 1997, for her body of work.

Writings

FOR CHILDREN

Willy Woo-oo-oo, illustrated by Florence Sarah Winship, Whitman (Racine, WI), 1951.

Snowball, illustrated by Winship, Whitman, 1952.

The Yellow Cat, illustrated by Sari, Whitman, 1952.

Jim Jump, illustrated by Sharon Banigan, Whitman, 1954.

Poppyseed, illustrated by Winship, Whitman, 1954.

(Under pseudonym Revena) *Mr. Mogg's Dogs,* illustrated by Si Frankel, Whitman, 1954.

My Big Book, illustrated by Louise Myers and Jack Myers, Whitman, 1954.

Train Coming!, illustrated by Florian, Whitman, 1954.

(Adapter) *Bear Country* (based on the Walt Disney movie), illustrated by Edward Godwin and Stephani Godwin, Whitman, 1954.

(Adapter) *Beaver Valley* (based on the Walt Disney movie), illustrated by Marjorie Hartwell, Whitman, 1954.

(Adapter with Alice Hanson) *Water Birds* (based on the Walt Disney movie), illustrated by Hartwell, Whitman, 1955.

(Reteller) *American Folklore,* illustrated by Walt Disney Studio, Whitman, 1956.

Roundabout Train, illustrated by Charles Clement, Whitman, 1958.

Good Morning, Farm, illustrated by Fred Weinman, Whitman, 1964.

I Want to Read, illustrated by Aliki, Whitman, 1965.

This Room Is Mine, illustrated by Judy Stang, Whitman, 1966.

Teddy Bear's Book of 1-2-3, illustrated with photographs by Gerry Swart, Golden Press (Racine, WI), 1969.

(With Joanne Wylie) *Elephant's Birthday Party: A Story about Shapes,* illustrated by Les Gray, Golden Press, 1971.

Bunny Button, Whitman, 1953, published under pseudonym Revena as *Histoire dun Lap in Gris,* Editions des deux coqs d'or, 1965, and *El conejo rabito,* illustrated by Bernice Myers, Organizacion Editorial Novaro, 1971.

THE SUMMER OF MRS. MacGREGOR

Betty Ren Wright

Jealous of her beautiful and well-loved older sister, twelve-year-old Caroline begins to see herself in a different light after she is befriended by the glamorous Lillina MacGregor.

The Cat Who Stamped His Feet, illustrated by Tom O'Sullivan, Golden Press, 1975.

The Rabbit's Adventure, illustrated by Maggie Swanson, Golden Press, 1977.

Roger's Upside-Down Day, illustrated by Jared D. Lee, Western, 1979.

The Day Our TV Broke Down, illustrated by Barbara Bejna and Shirlee Jensen, Raintree (Milwaukee, WI), 1980.

Why Do I Daydream?, illustrated by Tom Redman, Raintree, 1981; illustrated by Marc Glessner, Raintree, 1981.

(Adapter) H. G. Wells, *The Time Machine,* illustrated by Ivan Powell, Raintree, 1981.

(Adapter) Stephen Crane, *The Red Badge of Courage,* illustrated by Charles Shaw, Raintree, 1981.

I Like Being Alone, illustrated by Krystyna Stasiak, Raintree, 1981.

My New Mom and Me, illustrated by Betsy Day, Raintree, 1981.

My Sister Is Different, illustrated by Helen Cogancherry, Raintree, 1981.

Getting Rid of Marjorie, Holiday House (New York), 1981, reissued as *Getting Rid of Katherine,* Troll, 1996.

The Secret Window, Holiday House, 1982.

(Adapter) Emily Bronte, *Wuthering Heights,* illustrated by H. Cogancherry, Raintree, 1982.

The Dollhouse Murders, Holiday House, 1983; published in England as *The Ghosts in the Attic,* Hippo Books, 1983.

Ghosts Beneath Our Feet, Holiday House, 1984.

Christina's Ghost, Holiday House, 1985; British edition illustrated by Ann Johns.

The Summer of Mrs. MacGregor, Holiday House, 1986.

A Ghost in the Window, Holiday House, 1987.

The Pike River Phantom, Holiday House, 1988.

Rosie and the Dance of the Dinosaurs, Holiday House, 1989.

The Ghost of Ernie P., Holiday House, 1990.

A Ghost in the House, Scholastic, 1991.

The Cat Next Door, illustrated by Gail Owens, Holiday House, 1991.

The Scariest Night, Holiday House, 1991.

The Ghost of Popcorn Hill, illustrated by Karen Ritz, Holiday House, 1993.

The Ghosts of Mercy Manor, Scholastic, 1993.

The Ghost Witch, illustrated by Ellen Eagle, Holiday House, 1993.

The Ghost Comes Calling, illustrated by Ellen Eagle, Scholastic, 1994.

Out of the Dark, Scholastic, 1995.

Nothing but Trouble, illustrated by Jacqueline Rogers, Holiday House, 1995.

Haunted Summer, Scholastic, 1996.

Too Many Secrets, Scholastic, 1997.

The Ghost in Room 11, illustrated by Jacqueline Rogers, Holiday House, 1997.

A Ghost in the Family, Scholastic, 1998.

The Phantom of Five Chimneys, illustrated by Frank Morris, Troll, 1998.

Pet Detectives, illustrated by Kevin O'Malley, BridgeWater (Mahwah, NJ), 1999.

OTHER

Wright's works have been published in Swedish, Spanish, and Danish. Contributor of short stories to periodicals, including *Alfred Hitchcock's Mystery Magazine, Cosmopolitan, Ladies' Home Journal, Redbook, Saturday Evening Post, Seventeen, Woman's Day, Woman's World,* and *Young Miss.*

Sidelights

A prolific and popular author for primary and middle graders, Betty Ren Wright—who also writes as Revena—is the creator of picture books, mysteries, ghost stories, bibliotherapy, and nonfiction as well as a reteller and adapter. Although she contributes to a variety of genres, Wright is best known as the author of supernatural fiction. Her ghost stories blend the paranormal with the realistic in what is usually considered a believable and effective fashion. Writing in *Horn Book,* Elizabeth S. Watson called Wright a "master of the genre" while a critic in *Kirkus Reviews* called her a "premier author of reliable ghost stories." Wright is especially acknowledged for writing ghost stories for early primary graders, an audience to whom this type of genre fiction is rarely directed. In these works, the author is credited with using supernatural elements that are scary without being terrifying, for writing in a style that is only moderately chilling, and for investing her books with more depth than is usual in works of this type. Her books are often considered suitable alternatives to R. L. Stine's *Goosebumps* and other similar series as well as titles appropriate for older reluctant readers. Characteristically, Wright offers her audience imaginative variations on classic ghost and mystery stories. Often set in haunted houses in the author's home state of Wisconsin, her books—which range from gently spooky to genuinely frightening—combine thrills and chills with insightful explorations of family, peer, and intergenerational relationships.

Often missing one or both parents, Wright's young male and female protagonists frequently encounter ghosts from the past who engage the children in solving murder cases. By facing their fears and demonstrating courage, resilience, and initiative, the boys and girls unravel the mysteries and devise plans that allow the ghosts to be laid to rest. The children develop independence and maturity and, ultimately, a sense of belonging through their experiences, which often take place over summer vacation. Underlying the stories are subplots noted for their thought-provoking qualities. Wright often writes about relationships in families, and her characters learn to understand their parents, siblings, relatives, or foster families while learning about themselves. The author also addresses such issues as dealing with grief, peer pressure, and divorce as well as the importance of values such as honesty and trust. In addition, Wright consistently addresses the resentment that children can feel when faced with helping to take care of siblings or other relatives who are disabled; she often includes supporting characters who are mentally or physically challenged. Although she has been criticized for the incredulity of some of her plots, Wright is generally considered a writer of enjoyable, well-constructed stories that are both suspenseful and incisive. Reviewers have noted her excellent timing, skill with characterization, and understanding of children and what appeals to them.

Born in Wakefield, Michigan, the author is the daughter of two teachers, William and Revena Wright; later, Betty Ren Wright would use her mother's first name as the pseudonym for some of her early works. When she was seven, Wright began to write her first book, a collection of poems that she completed at the age of ten. She once told *SATA:* "My mother bought a black looseleaf notebook, had my name lettered on it, and there it was—a book with my name on the cover. That was a dream come true, a dream that I wanted to repeat!" She wrote in an essay for the *Sixth Book of Junior Authors and Illustrators* that this notebook "made me decide ... that I wanted to be A WRITER. The wonder has never ended." Poetry remained Wright's primary focus until she reached Milwaukee-Downer College (now Lawrence University), where she contributed to the college literary magazine and gradually shifted from poetry to short stories. Wright told *SATA,* "I was blessed with teachers in grade school, high school, and college who encouraged me a great deal, always with the

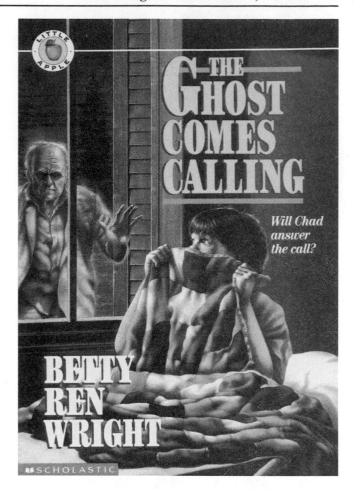

In Wright's ghost story, nine-year-old Chad and his friend Jeannie encounter a ghost who has been haunting his family's vacation home on Perch Lake.

warning that I'd better plan on another job besides writing. With that warning in mind, I went to work as an editorial assistant; it was as close as I could get to writing and still be sure of a steady income." After graduating in 1949, Wright got a job at Western Publishing in Racine, Wisconsin; she was to stay at Western for nearly thirty years, retiring as the managing editor of the editorial department. She told *SATA,* "Editing turned out to be a wonderful occupation, and I enjoyed it for many years, while continuing to write, mostly adult short fiction, in my free time." While working at Western, Wright found herself drawn to children's books. She told the *Sixth Book of Junior Authors and Illustrators,* "I found I was leading a peculiar kind of double life. Juvenile books, particularly picture books, filled my days, while adult magazine fiction took my spare time...." Her stories were published in magazines directed both to adults, such as *Alfred Hitchcock's Mystery Magazine* and *Redbook,* and young people, such as *Seventeen* and *Young Miss.*

While editing juvenile manuscripts for Western, Wright began to write original picture books, both under her own name and under her pseudonym; her first picture book was published in 1951. The author wrote in the *Sixth Book of Junior Authors and Illustrators,* "Picture books were fun; I loved sending a story to an illustrator and seeing how his imagination and talent enriched it." In the early 1950s, Wright published adaptations of three Walt Disney nature films and retold stories from American folklore in a book that was illustrated by the Walt Disney Studio. She served as the managing editor of juvenile books for Western from 1968 to 1976; during this period, she lived in an apartment in a haunted house, an experience that would influence her later works. In 1976, Wright married George Frederiksen, a Wisconsin artist and former art director; two years later, she left publishing to become a freelance writer. Wright told *SATA*, "When I left editing to free-lance in 1978, I intended to concentrate on adult fiction. First, though, I decided to try one novel for boys and girls—and since I'd recently married and become a step-grandmother that seemed like a good subject for a story. I'd married into a warm, welcoming family, but it was easy to imagine what life might have been like if there had been one grandchild who was totally hostile to the idea of a new grandmother. That was how *Getting Rid of Marjorie* was born. Writing that book was fun! I decided to try one more—and one more—and then another ... and I'm still loving it."

Wright began her freelance career by writing picture books and adaptations of classic adult novels such as H. G. Wells's *The Time Machine* and Stephen Crane's *The Red Badge of Courage* for younger readers. In 1981, she published *My Sister Is Different,* bibliotherapy for children in the early primary grades, and *Getting Rid of Marjorie,* her first story for an older audience. *My Sister Is Different* is narrated by Carlo, a boy whose older sister Terry is retarded. Carlo has to take care of Terry, a responsibility that he resents. However, when Terry gets lost, Carlo remembers her affectionate, gentle nature and realizes that he loves her. After Terry is found, Carlo gives her a beautiful birthday card. Zena Sutherland of *Bulletin of the Center for Children's Books* wrote, "This is intended to help children see that retarded children also have likable—or lovable—qualities, and it does that adequately; however, it begs the question of whether any child should be expected to assume daily responsibility for a sibling, especially since the home situation (a mother and grandmother at home) indicates no urgent need." Writing in *Interracial Books for Children Bulletin,* Judith J. Trotta noted, "This appealing book can be read to younger children, and even adults will warm to its gentle understanding and respect for those who are labeled mentally retarded." *Getting Rid of Marjorie* features eleven-year-old Emily, who worships her widowed grandfather. When he returns from Los Angeles with a new wife, Marjorie, Emily feels betrayed. In retaliation, she develops a plan to terrify Marjorie and send her back to L.A. Emily convinces Marjorie that burglars are stalking her house; however, when she learns the childhood origins of Marjorie's terror, Emily repents. Writing in *Booklist,* Ilene Cooper stated, "What most interests one here is the exploration of the darker side of a child's nature." Cooper added that it does not take long for Emily's "kernel of hate" to overwhelm her, and concluded, "It is the power of that feeling which makes Emily's quick mea culpa detract from the

strength of an otherwise well-grounded book." A reviewer in *Publishers Weekly* called *Getting Rid of Marjorie* "an affecting, funny story" and claimed, "The characters and happenings seem vibrantly alive in the author's sympathetic handling, especially venomous Emily."

In 1982, Wright published *The Secret Window,* a novel for junior high school students in which Meg Korshak, a seventh grader, learns to accept her psychic gifts. Meg has had prophetic dreams—many of which have come true—for several years; however, she is uncomfortable with her powers. Meg's grandmother, who is also a psychic, and a new friend counsel her. After one of her dreams saves the life of her best friend, Meg finally learns to appreciate her "secret windows" into the future. Ilene Cooper of *Booklist* noted that Meg's recurring dreams "have a life of their own that keeps up the pace. The whole psychic aspect is handled unsensationally, giving this a more natural tone than some stories involving parapsychology." Writing in *School Library Journal,* Will Manley commented, "The excellent relationship between Meg and her grandmother serves as a good example of the importance of the extended family, and there is a realistic portrayal of how a young person can go about successfully resisting peer pressure to make independent judgments." The Korshak family returns seven years later in *A Ghost in the Window,* a novel published in 1987. Her parents, whose marriage was breaking up in the previous book, have divorced, and fourteen-year-old Meg goes to stay with her father for three weeks. A mystery surrounds the death of the husband of Mrs. Larsen, her father's landlady and fiancee. Accused of stealing fifty thousand dollars, Mr. Larson begins appearing in Meg's dreams. She hopes to prove the man's innocence; however, his ghostly presence finally directs her to the treasure that he stole. Through the course of the novel, Meg learns some truths about her family and herself that help her to be able to accept her parents's divorce and her father's remarriage. Writing in *School Library Journal,* Elaine Fort Weischedel called Meg "a likable and believable heroine" and added that "Wright's many fans will not be disappointed with this title. It's a solid addition to any collection." Ilene Cooper of *Booklist* concluded that the author "does a credible job of interweaving mystery, psychic phenomena, and family issues, making this solid and enjoyable fare for middle graders."

In 1983, Wright published what is perhaps her most popular book, *The Dollhouse Murders.* In this story for middle graders, twelve-year-old Amy Treloar goes to stay with her Aunt Clare, in town to sort through an old Victorian house that belonged to Amy's great-grandparents; the couple had been murdered thirty years before by an unknown assailant. Amy has gone to stay with her aunt as a reprieve from taking care of her younger sister, Louann, who is brain-damaged. In the attic of the old house, Amy finds a miniature replica of the house, complete with a family of dolls. At first, she is delighted with the dollhouse; however, at night it gives off an eerie glow and the dolls move about, repositioning themselves. When her aunt sees the placement of the dolls, she is furious: they have moved themselves into the same positions that her great-grandparents had assumed on the night they were murdered. Amy realizes that the dolls are trying to get a message to her about the killer. With Louann's help, Amy solves the mystery and identifies the murderer. Writing in *Booklist,* Ilene Cooper asserted: "More than just a mystery, this offers keen insight into the relationship between handicapped and nonhandicapped siblings and glimpses into the darker adult emotions of guilt and anger." Mary M. Burns of *Horn Book* concluded, "While deftly fashioned as a mystery with elements of psychic phenomena, the book also provides insight into the conflicting emotions besetting families forced to cope with the problems of retardation." Inspired to write *The Dollhouse Murders* by a friend, Wright told *SATA,* "She shared with me the satisfaction and real pain that comes with recreating, in miniature, a beloved home remembered from childhood. She uncovered disturbing feelings when she began looking backward so intently, and it seemed to me that a dollhouse so laden with memory might well be haunted." Wright added, "In my mysteries, I like to explore relationships. Partial inspiration for *The Dollhouse Murders* arose from my interest in the problems and adjustments of life with a retarded sibling. One summer years ago, I saw two brothers in a park, the younger one retarded. Their obviously loving relationship made me marvel at all the work necessary to reach that point."

Another of Wright's most popular books is *Christina's Ghost,* a story for middle graders published in 1985. When ten-year-old Christina goes to stay for the summer with her Uncle Ralph in the Victorian mansion where he is house-sitting, she sees the ghost of a young boy. She learns that the boy, Russell Charles, and his tutor, Thomas Dixon, were murdered in the house thirty years before because of the rare stamps that the tutor had stolen. Christina and her uncle, who is drawn into the mystery when he also senses a ghostly presence, find the stamps and lay the ghosts—including the vengeful tutor—to rest. Writing in *School Library Journal,* Lisa Smith noted that Wright "conveys the wistfulness of the boy and the terrifying presence of Dixon without turning them into caricatures of human beings"; the critic concluded that although *Christina's Ghost* is not as suspenseful as *The Dollhouse Murders,* it "will nicely fill the request for 'a good scary ghost story, please.'" Ilene Cooper of *Booklist* stated, "Wright's straightforward ghost story is bolstered by the questions surrounding an unsolved mystery and is humanized by the evolving relationship between Christina and Uncle Ralph"; she added that middle graders will "delight in the several hair-raising scenes in which a malevolent ghost makes himself known."

In *The Summer of Mrs. MacGregor,* Wright describes how twelve-year-old Caroline learns to begin to appreciate herself through her friendship with the exotic, sophisticated teenager who is visiting her neighbor. Caroline's older sister Linda has a serious heart condition that absorbs much of their parents' attention; consequently, Caroline feels jealous and insecure. When she develops a relationship with the young woman who

introduces herself as Mrs. Lillina MacGregor, a New York socialite/novelist/model, Caroline starts to look beyond herself. Lillina is finally unmasked as a fraud: after Caroline catches her stealing money, she learns that Lillina is actually an unmarried high school sophomore from Michigan. Writing in *Booklist,* Denise M. Wilms commented that Wright "captures the hero-worship dynamic between Caroline and Lillina nicely. Caroline's naivete regarding Lillina is credible, as are her disillusionment and ultimate ability to take charge of herself." Karen J. Levi of *School Library Journal* noted that "the importance of self-esteem and enjoying what makes each individual special continues to be the author's strongest theme," while a reviewer in *Publishers Weekly* concluded, "Wright has created a most appealing character in Caroline, who takes small but credible steps toward growing up. Lillina, too, wins readers' sympathies, providing a contrast to Caroline's down-to-earth sensibility." Wright told *SATA,* "Mrs. MacGregor is an unlikely source—an eccentric, wildly unreliable young lady who lives in a world of her own imagining, but who is, nevertheless, just what Caroline needs during a very painful time in her life. I suspect we each have a Mrs. MacGregor at some time or other—a person who could have hurt us but instead provided strength and inspiration. The book began as a short story, 'The Afternoon of Mrs. MacGregor,' published in *Woman's Day* magazine in October, 1974. As the title suggests, the story brought Mrs. MacGregor and Caroline together for just a few hours. I always felt, however, that there was more to tell about the two girls and how they affected each other, and writing the book gave me a chance to know them much better. The book also gave me an opportunity to write about some of the problems that come with failing health and old age, as seen in Mr. Jameson. It's a subject close to my heart, since my mother was in a nursing home for six years."

In *The Pike River Phantom,* twelve-year-old Charlie Hocking deals with a malevolent ghost, an old lady who grows steadily younger. Since his father has been in prison for theft, Charlie has come to live with his grandparents and his thirteen-year-old cousin Rachel in the small Wisconsin town of Pike River. After Charlie meets the ghost in an abandoned house, he learns that she has a vendetta against the townspeople that endangers his family. Reluctantly, he begins to confide in his father, who has been released from prison. With the help of his dad and his cousin, Charlie prevents the ghost from carrying out her threat. Carolyn Phelan of *Booklist* commented that "the nice blend of character development and large dollops of suspense will involve [readers] from first page to last," while Ruth Sadasivan of *School Library Journal* added that *The Pike River Phantom* is "a fast-paced, entertaining, and mildly scary story" that is a "fine addition to Wright's other popular books for young readers." Wright told *SATA,* "Like most stories, *The Pike River Phantom* had several starting points. The ghost herself—a peculiar creature who grows younger with each sighting—has been drifting around in my brain for a long time. Charlie Hocking, the person who discovers her, came about because so many boys had asked why all my books have been about girls.

There is no good answer to that question—and so I began to think about Charlie. I've always been intrigued, too, by the special kind of problem Charlie has in getting to know and understand his father. When we are very young, our parents are simply our parents, perfect because they are who they are. As we get older, we begin to see them as individuals, and sometimes we must get to know them all over again. Since Charlie's father has spent five years in prison, they have missed a long period of getting to understand and appreciate each other, and they have a lot of catching up to do. Finally, I like to write about small towns, even though I've lived in fairly large cities most of my life. When I was a little girl, we spent summer vacations in a town much like Pike River; I remember it as a wonderful place in which to grow up. The town recently celebrated its centennial, and the parade in *The Pike River Phantom* is based on the parade that marked the climax of the centennial activities."

In the 1990s, Wright continued to write well-received novels and stories that blend the natural and the supernatural. One of her most popular works is *A Ghost in the House,* a tale for middle graders published in 1991. The story describes how twelve-year old Sarah deals with the arrival of great-aunt Margaret, an elderly invalid who returns to her childhood house from a nursing home. Required to take care of her disagreeable relative while her parents are at work, Sarah sees a ghost in her house; Aunt Margaret realizes that the ghost is the abusive father of one of her childhood friends and that it is seeking revenge for a tragedy that happened fifty years before. Sarah and Margaret form an alliance and defeat the ghost; in the process, they come to care for one another. Writing in *Booklist,* Chris Sherman commented that Wright "has created a suspenseful ghost story that has a terrific climax, so be prepared for swarms of eager readers." Jeanette Larson of *School Library Journal* concluded that readers who believe in ghosts "will enjoy Wright's spine-tingling descriptions.... Those who can't suspend disbelief will still find a good story about an intergenerational relationship that grows and a family's ability to pull together to face a problem." Another of Wright's most highly regarded works is *Out of the Dark.* In this thriller, the author relates how middle grader Jessica Belland, who has moved to her grandmother's house in rural Wisconsin, begins having dreams of an old schoolhouse and an irate woman dressed in blue. With the help of her disabled neighbor, Toni Draves, Jessie finds the schoolhouse and discovers a blue hair ribbon inside. Learning that her grandmother had attended the schoolhouse, Jessie begins to read the journal that her grandmother kept as a teen. The ghost moves out of Jessie's dreams and starts to haunt her while she is awake; finally, it traps Jessie and Toni in a vault in the schoolhouse on a stormy night. The ghost is dispatched when Jessie's grandmother returns, but Jessie realizes that its need for revenge is linked to her beloved grandma. Writing in *Bulletin of the Center for Children's Books,* Roger Sutton suggested, "Send kids sated with or scared by the lurid paperback horror series here: the spooky cover will invite them in and the storytelling won't let them down." Calling *Out of the Dark* "effective and well-crafted," Anne Connor of *School Library Journal* predicted that it "will please Wright's many fans and win her some new ones," while *Voice of Youth Advocates* contributor Laura Lent added, "Like Wright's previous ghost yarns, this imaginative tale will intrigue, entertain, and delight all who read it."

Wright is also the creator of a trilogy of spooky stories—*The Ghost Comes Calling, Too Many Secrets,* and *A Ghost in the Family*—that she directs to readers in the primary grades. In *The Ghost Comes Calling,* nine-year-old Chad Weldon has moved into the run-down log cabin that his father, a widower, has bought on a lake. He makes friends with Jeannie Nichols, a bossy older girl, who tells him that the shack is haunted by its builder, Tim Tapper. Tim was accused of causing an accident while he was driving a group of children in his truck. Chad sees Tim's ghost at his window and hears the old man's dog howling in the woods. With Jeannie's help, Chad finds a way to clear Tim's name; in the process, Chad and Jeannie become friends. Hazel Rochman of *Booklist* noted, "With a taut sense of timing and shivery suspense, Wright revitalizes the story of the mean ghost who cannot rest.... Wright picks up our fear of the rustle in the woods, the shadow on the porch, the uncertainty outside and in." Deborah Stevenson of *Bulletin of the Center for Children's Books* called *The Ghost Comes Calling* "a smooth and easy read, and there's a nice prickly relationship between Chad and Jeannie, the would-be know-it-all who's been demoted to sidekick...."

In *Too Many Secrets,* Chad gets a job dog-sitting for Benson, the Labrador retriever that belongs to his elderly neighbor, Miss Beane. While Miss Beane—who fell and broke her leg while investigating noises in her home—is in the hospital, Chad and Jeannie hear sounds in her house; convinced that the noises are caused by a burglar searching for the treasure that Miss Beane is rumored to possess, the pair decide to capture the robber on their own. Chad, Jeannie, and Cap Colby—an older neighborhood boy who is originally a prime suspect—eventually nab the real burglar, who turns out to be a total stranger, and save Miss Beane's treasure, which turns out to be a collection of antique teddy bears. A critic in *Kirkus Reviews* said, "Wright offers readers an intriguing mystery, an interesting subplot, and believable characters, but Benson steals every scene that he's in." Writing in *Booklist,* Carolyn Phelan concluded, "Although the plot strains the reader's credulity as well as the conventions of mystery fiction..., the characters are likable." In *A Ghost in the Family,* Chad and Jeannie go to Milwaukee to visit her aunt Rosebud for two weeks. Aunt Rosebud runs a boarding house filled with interesting guests, including a fortune-teller who tells Chad that he is in danger. Chad senses the presence of someone in his room; in addition, he and Jeannie are caught up in the search for a missing diamond bracelet. In the course of solving the mystery and routing the ghost, the pair encounter such creepy situations as finding a mummy in a closet. Writing in *School Library Journal,* Megan McGuire concluded, "While Wright's fans may choose this title based on her previous books, it isn't one of the author's strongest stories." However, Susan Dove Lempke of *Booklist* called *A Ghost in the Family* "a surefire hit for the middle grades" and Elizabeth S. Watson of *Horn Book* concluded, "For those ubiquitous suspense fans who insist upon a 'scary book' that's 'not too long,' here's the ticket."

Writing in the *Sixth Book of Junior Authors and Illustrators,* Wright commented, "Often my books turn out to be ghost stories, since I've always enjoyed supernatural tales myself, but I like to write other kinds of books as well. I still write an occasional short story, but I think—no, I'm sure—I've found the audience I enjoy most." She told *SATA,* "Each of my books has sizeable chunks of my own life in it—people or events or feelings, or all three. The ideas sometimes grow out of a very small incident, but making that small incident grow seems to me to be the most exciting part of writing." She concluded, "I love being scared! The question I've heard most often is, 'Have you ever seen a ghost?' I'm sorry the answer has to be no—I do keep looking, and hoping!—but since I haven't actually met one the next best thing has to be to make up my own."

Works Cited

Burns, Mary M., review of *The Dollhouse Murders, Horn Book,* December, 1983, pp. 703-04.

Connor, Anne, review of *Out of the Dark, School Library Journal,* January, 1995, p. 110.

Cooper, Ilene, review of *Christina's Ghost, Booklist,* February 1, 1986, p. 815.

Cooper, Ilene, review of *The Dollhouse Murders, Booklist,* October 1, 1983, pp. 301-02.

Cooper, Ilene, review of *Getting Rid of Marjorie, Booklist,* October 15, 1981, p. 313.

Cooper, Ilene, review of *The Ghost in the Window, Booklist,* November 15, 1987, p. 573.

Cooper, Ilene, review of *The Secret Window, Booklist,* November 15, 1982, p. 449.

Review of *Getting Rid of Marjorie, Publishers Weekly,* October 30, 1981, p. 63.

Larson, Jeanette, review of *A Ghost in the House, School Library Journal,* November, 1991, p. 125.

Lempke, Susan Dove, review of *A Ghost in the Family, Booklist,* June 1, 1998, p. 1769.

Lent, Laura, review of *Out of the Dark, Voice of Youth Advocates,* October, 1995, p. 227.

Levi, Karen J., review of *The Summer of Mrs. MacGregor, School Library Journal,* November, 1986, p. 95.

Manley, Will, review of *The Secret Window, School Library Journal,* August, 1983, p. 81.

McGuire, Megan, review of *A Ghost in the Family, School Library Journal,* September, 1998, p. 212.

Review of *Out of the Dark, Kirkus Reviews,* February 15, 1995, pp. 235-36.

Phelan, Carolyn, review of *Too Many Secrets,* October 1, 1997, p. 333.

Phelan, review of *The Pike River Phantom, Booklist,* December 15, 1988, p. 715.

Rochman, Hazel, review of *The Ghost Comes Calling, Booklist,* February 15, 1994, p. 1083.

Sadasivan, Ruth, review of *The Pike River Phantom, School Library Journal,* October, 1988, p. 149.

Sherman, Chris, review of *A Ghost in the House, Booklist,* November 1, 1993, p. 523.

Smith, Lisa, review of *Christina's Ghost, School Library Journal,* December, 1985, p. 96.

Stevenson, Deborah, review of *The Ghost Comes Calling, Bulletin of the Center for Children's Books,* March, 1994, p. 239.

Review of *The Summer of Mrs. MacGregor, Publishers Weekly,* October 11, 1986, p. 69.

Sutherland, Zena, review of *My Sister Is Different, Bulletin of the Center for Children's Books,* March, 1982, p. 140.

Sutton, Roger, review of *Out of the Dark, Bulletin of the Center for Children's Books,* February, 1995, p. 219.

Review of *Too Many Secrets, Kirkus Reviews,* June 15, 1997, p. 959.

Trotta, Judith J., review of *My Sister Is Different, Interracial Books for Children Bulletin,* Volume 13, numbers 4-5, 1982, p. 11.

Watson, Elizabeth S., review of *A Ghost in the Family, Horn Book,* July-August, 1998, p. 501.

Watson, Elizabeth S., review of *The Ghost Comes Calling, Horn Book,* September-October, 1994, p. 594.

Weischedel, Elaine Fort, review of *A Ghost in the Window, School Library Journal,* October, 1987, pp. 130-31.

Wilms, Denise M., review of *The Summer of Mrs. MacGregor, Booklist,* November 1, 1986, p. 415.

Wright, Betty Ren, essay in *Sixth Book of Junior Authors and Illustrators,* edited by Sally Holmes Holtze, Wilson, 1989, pp. 323-25.

Wright, Betty Ren, interview in *Something about the Author,* Volume 63, Gale, 1991, pp. 196-99.

For More Information See

PERIODICALS

Booklist, February 15, 1993, pp. 1061-62; March 1, 1998, p. 31.

Horn Book, July, 1993, p. 463.

School Library Journal, December, 1991, p. 197; September, 1993, p. 236; August, 1997, p. 144.

Voice of Youth Advocates, December, 1993, p. 304.

—*Sketch by Gerard J. Senick*

Cumulative Indexes

Illustrations Index

(In the following index, the number of the *volume* in which an illustrator's work appears is given *before* the colon, and the *page number* on which it appears is given *after* the colon. For example, a drawing by Adams, Adrienne appears in Volume 2 on page 6, another drawing by her appears in Volume 3 on page 80, another drawing in Volume 8 on page 1, and so on and so on . . . .)

YABC

Index references to *YABC* refer to listings appearing in the two-volume *Yesterday's Authors of Books for Children,* also published by The Gale Group. *YABC* covers prominent authors and illustrators who died prior to 1960.

Illustrations Index

Author Index

The following index gives the number of the volume in which an author's biographical sketch, Autobiography Feature, Brief Entry, or Obituary appears.

This index includes references to all entries in the following series, which are also published by The Gale Group.

YABC—*Yesterday's Authors of Books for Children: Facts and Pictures about Authors and Illustrators of Books for Young People from Early Times to 1960*
CLR—*Children's Literature Review: Excerpts from Reviews, Criticism, and Commentary on Books for Children*
SAAS—*Something about the Author Autobiography Series*

Author Index

Author Index